Spanish Central America

Spanish Central America

A SOCIOECONOMIC HISTORY, 1520–1720

Murdo J. MacLeod

UNIVERSITY OF CALIFORNIA PRESS

Berkeley   Los Angeles   London

University of California Press
Berkeley and Los Angeles, California

University of California Press, Ltd.
London, England

Copyright © 1973, by The Regents of the University of California
ISBN: 0-520 02137-1
Library of Congress Catalog Card Number: 70-174456
Printed in the United States of America

To my mother and father,
Mary and Murdo MacLeod

Contents

List of Figures

Preface

The seventeenth century was characterized some time ago as "Latin America's forgotten century." Yet with the exception of a few pioneering works, which are suggestive rather than detailed in nature, few attempts have been made to fill this vacuum in our knowledge.[1] Textbooks still emphasize the things which human curiosity finds exciting—the events and heroes of the conquest, the culture clash of the sixteenth century, the new thinking of the Enlightenment in the eighteenth century, and the bloody struggles leading to independence. Oversimplifying somewhat, the general picture we are given of colonial Spanish America is that the area went through the epic of its discovery and conquest, lay dormantly watching Spain's struggle with decline—the so-called colonial siesta—and then, tiring of it all, and encouraged by the new ideas and trade coming from other parts of Europe, discarded the old mistress in a bloody war of independence. But the colonial Spanish society of the sixteenth century was very different from the one described in the eighteenth century. What happened in the Latin American colonies between the first conquests, the seizure of long-accumulated Indian wealth, the first silver booms, and the period of modern raw material supply? How did Latin America move from one stage to the other? What were these intermediate economic stages, and what effect did they have on the peoples living in Latin America?

This general set of circumstances and questions was what first aroused my interest in the Spanish American seventeenth century. I soon found that several works, particularly those of Borah, Chaunu, and Chevalier, had suggested some general tendencies for the period, research paths and conclusions which might be worth following or testing.[2] It became apparent that a valid approach might be to test their general propositions, and other concepts which interested me, against a detailed examination of one circumscribed area of Spanish America. Circumstances and general interest allowed me to concentrate on the area known during the colonial period as the Audiencia of Guatemala. I therefore began to read as much seventeenth-century Central American printed material as I could find, and as much archival material as I could squeeze into one frantic summer.

The limitations of this naïve approach were soon apparent. It became obvious that seventeenth-century Central America was living in the aftermath of a series of interrelated disasters. To dismiss this problem quickly by stating that it was all the wake of a military conquest was too easy. After all, the main Central American conquests were over by 1545, and to suggest that the seventeenth century was still suffering principally from a military shock after half a century was not satisfactory. Besides, from taste and training I believed in the significance of gradual social processes and multi-causal change rather than phenomenological history and cataclysmic events.

Some very serious questions about the seventeenth century in Central America began to dominate my research. For example, the embattled seventeenth-century elite entrepreneurs of the area spent a great deal of time and effort protecting stagnant industries, trying to revive them, or looking for alternatives to them. Why had these industries stagnated; and why, to look at the other side of the coin, had they been relatively prosperous at some time in the preceding century? Then again, Central America in the seventeenth century suffered from a chronic shortage of labor; yet the first conquistadors had found teeming populations. Where had the Indian workers gone, and why? What effect did the demographic collapse have on Indian society?

New and uniquely seventeenth-century tendencies began to appear. Spaniards and Creoles in the early seventeenth century became much more interested than before in occupying and owning large stretches of rural land. Given the late feudal background attributed to sixteenth-century Spaniards, and the consequent seignorial ambitions which many were supposed to have, why had this rush to the land not occurred earlier, or, for that matter, why did it not take place later? In short, I realized that to explain the seventeenth century I would have to study the sixteenth century, where many of these and other problems had their origins.

At the other end of the time span which originally interested me a similar series of difficulties began to emerge. In the last few years of the seventeenth century and the early years of the eighteenth, some slow but significant changes began to intrude on the picture which I had put together of the middle years of the century. For some Spaniards and Creoles economic circumstances began to improve, and one or two previously stagnant export industries showed signs of new growth. What caused these slow changes, or, to be more deterministic for a moment, what had happened to Central Americans to revive some of their hopes? Obviously the period 1690–1720 would have to be studied and compared with the years preceding it. In short, to answer a whole series of questions about the seventeenth century it became necessary to study the sixteenth and early eighteenth centuries in Central America. There was no help for it but to return to the printed material and to the archives of Central America and Europe, especially the Archive of the Indies in Seville.

During the research process the original periodization by centuries was gradually abandoned as naïve and general. What seemed to me a typically "sixteenth century" society, with plentiful although rapidly declining Indian laboring populations, with successful and successive silver, slaving, and cacao export industries, with the encomienda rather than the hacienda, with busy mercantile Spanish cities—came to an end in the 1570s, a decade of serious epidemics in Central America; and by the 1580s the region had entered an unprecedented era of experimentation, governmental regulation, and innovation which lasted until the early 1630s. The decline of human and cattle populations and the growing difficulties in trading abroad were not yet seen as irreversible processes, and the introduction of new forms of farming and of a new and seemingly successful export crop, indigo, led entrepreneurs, agriculturalists, and officials to believe that new approaches could solve their problems.

By the late 1630s these adjustments had been tried, and most of them had failed. From this time until about 1680, Central America appears to me typically "seventeenth century." This half century was one of isolation, of economic stagnation and depression, of cities which were no longer primarily market places but rather administrative and conventual centers, of rural areas where a few Spaniards were beginning to build the first haciendas and to use sparse Indian labor in more modern ways. After 1680 until about 1720, we see the beginnings of a revival based on smuggling and other factors, and new pressures on the Indians.

The long-term process which has just been described, a time of relative prosperity, a depression, and then a recovery, is one which is familiar to historians of medieval and early modern Europe. I have therefore made comparative use of published material which describes the situation in Europe after the first epidemics of the Black Death in 1348, and, to a lesser extent, similar material about seventeenth-century Europe and its much debated mid-century crisis.

This attempt to describe and explain Central America's first great economic, demographic, and social cycle lays no claims to completeness. I have all but ignored narrative and institutional history on the grounds that it is available in general texts or is being presently undertaken by competent historians elsewhere. I have also made some perhaps arbitrary judgments about which economic and social trends contribute most to an understanding of life in a preindustrial, agrarian, post-conquest, colonial society. As a result of these judgments on my part factors such as land and export crops receive detailed attention, whereas other worthwhile themes are hardly touched.

The choice of Central America, the area between Tehuantepec and Panama, for this case study is of course idiosyncratic; it was the first area in Latin America of which I gained any firsthand knowledge, so my choice is at once justifiable and indefensible. On the other hand, I now believe that Central America suggested itself for this study for several good reasons. Its colonial experience is relatively unknown compared to that of its great neighbors, which has brought the satisfaction of breaking fairly new ground. Also, in spite of their appallingly scattered nature, archival and primary published sources are abundant and reasonably well-ordered. A more significant reason is the area's own intrinsic importance as a representative region. Colonial Central America was far from being the insignificant divided area which it appears to be today. With Yucatan, it was the home of the Maya, one of the great pre-Columbian cultures. If one ignores the fact that it is divided today into one Mexican state (Chiapas), the disputed colony of British Honduras, and five independent republics, it becomes apparent that this isthmian area, then called the Audiencia of Guatemala, lying between the two oceans, close to Jamaica, Curaçao, Veracruz, Havana, and Portobelo, the center of pirate battles and coveted by other European powers, was a large, once fairly populous, and always strategically significant stretch of land. Although it was of far less importance than Mexico or Peru, its economy and society were not "skewed" by the mining wealth and governmental attention which those great centers received. It has been called "the richest of the poor, or the poorest of the rich relations," and this may be the best summation of its demographic, cultural, economic, and political history as a Latin American colony.[3]

Work on this history was begun in 1962 and continued with one lengthy interruption until December 1970. There is at present much valuable work in progress on Central America, and no doubt the tenth and subsequent volumes of the *Handbook of Middle American Indians* will correct many of the weaknesses and errors herein; but research must stop somewhere and the end of 1970 was arbitrarily chosen.

Any scholar who attempts a project over an extended period becomes aware that he is to some extent merely the originator and coordinator of a large communal effort. Readers of this work will quickly see that it depends heavily for its theoretical foundations on a few well-known bodies of research. What Pierre Chaunu has called "l'école de Berkeley," the demographic studies in the *Ibero-Americana* series of such as Borah, Cook, and Simpson provided a methodology and a comparative basis for studying what happens in periods of drastic population decline. French economic historians such as Chaunu and Mauro, with demographers of the European Middle Ages and seventeenth century such as Carpentier, Le Roy Ladurie, and Baratier provided yet another comparative dimension. The large body of work on Mexican history by U.S. and Mexican scholars such as Gibson and Miranda, to name but two, gave me guidelines for following land and labor sequences in Central America. And finally, a few pioneer writers in Central America gave me information and suggestive ways of interpreting it. Particularly helpful were writers such as Chamberlain, West, Smith, Sherman, Rubio, Castro y Tosi, and Floyd. My debt to these scholars is obvious from the Notes.

On a more personal level, I owe thanks to the following who have aided me with information, instruction, or criticism: R. E. W. Adams, Woodrow Borah, the late Howard F. Cline, Norberto Castro y Tosi, Frederick Dunn, Douglas G. Madigan, Lyle N. McAlister, Walter Payne, Manuel Rubio, Julius Rubin, William T. Sanders, France V. Scholes, William Sherman, William Smole, Juan Adolfo Vázquez, Robert C. West, Donald Wisdom, and the directors and staffs of the Central American and European archives where I have studied. My research in Spain, France, and England was supported in part by a generous grant from the American Philosophical Society. Two of my three summers in Central America were made possible by financial help from the International Dimension Fund at the

University of Pittsburgh. Much of the bibliographic work was done at the Library of Congress, where the staff of the Hispanic Foundation was especially helpful. The forbearance of my wife and children was a critical factor in enabling me to finish this book. Of course none of my sources, critics, helpers, or benefactors is in any way responsible for errors of fact or gaucheries of interpretation.

M. J. M.

Spanish Central America

"After a hundred years the kings are peasants."
"After two hundred years the peasants are kings."
Old Spanish proverbs

Ring a-ring a-Roses
A pocketful of posies
'Tishoo, 'tishoo
We all fall down!

Nursery rhyme from the time
of the Great Plague of London

By Way of Introduction:
The War of the Worlds

By the last decades of the thirteenth century, many parts of central and western Europe had reached unprecedented heights of prosperity and population density. The number of people on the land had grown until many rural areas were veritable hives of activity. New lands had been brought into cultivation and were yielding their first harvests. The historian looking back gains an impression of growing commerce and agriculture, an expanding middle class, burgeoning cities, and a general air of well-being.[1]

In the next half century this cheerful picture began to disintegrate, earlier in some regions than in others, and by 1400 Europe had become a forbidding and gloomy place haunted by a century or more of disasters. Between 1250 and 1350, there were ominous difficulties on the land. (And this was still basically an agrarian society.) Many regions suffered an alarming series of bad summers. Rains, summer hailstorms, and a lack of sunshine produced molds and blights, rotted the crops, and brought on poor harvests, sometimes for two or more years in succession. These calamities led inevitably to famine and to a rise in the deaths caused by the ailments which more readily afflict people suffering from malnutrition.[2]

The people of the times usually attributed these calamities, and all other manifestations of hard times, to the wrath of God, provoked beyond endurance by the sinfulness of the age; disasters were thus often accompanied by processions, mass penitence, and such extremes as mass flagellation.[3] Moderns have turned to a variety of explanations. Some have simply stated that a series of fortuitous bad years hit an unprepared and insouciant general population.[4] Others, more plausibly but more deterministically, have argued that Malthusian theory is still of general validity where a population lives

1

primarily off a limited agricultural base and employs a primitive technology. This argument then continues that a Malthusian crisis or apex had been reached in many parts of Western Europe, that the equilibrium between the demands of the population for food supplies and the ability of the land to supply these needs had broken down, and that consequently the coming of any natural disaster, such as the floods, hailstorms, mudslides, and general dankness of these years, was enough to push the supply and demand pattern into disintegration.[5]

Studies in England and France have shown that in the last years of the fourteenth century extraordinary pressures were being placed on some lands. Forests were cut down; marginal clays, heathlands, and other poor soils were brought under the plough for the first time. In fact some of these lands have not been cultivated before or since the era in question.[6] (Partly this is because of the unprofitability of agriculture in such poor areas; partly it may be because of the destruction caused in such areas by this very cultivation in the Middle Ages.) Cutting the ground cover, ploughing steep slopes, and general abuse and overuse of marginal soils can lead to leaching of soil nutrients, gullying, sheet erosion, and finally the exposure of uncultivable hardpan or rock.[7]

Why would such lands be brought under cultivation? A political argument based on social class would go as follows. The feudal landowners increased their demands for taxes or tributes in kind, thus forcing the same population numbers as before to work harder in order to produce a greater yearly surplus. Another possibility is that an improved technology allowed people to use lands which previously had been too difficult for the methods at their command. Still another line of reasoning would argue that the landowners of the time began to evict their peasantry from areas of better soils, thus driving them to marginal ones, the landowners hoping perhaps to run more commercial farms to supply the cities, or to raise greater numbers of sheep and cattle. An example of this kind of behavior occurred much later and farther north during the "highland clearances" in nineteenth-century Scotland. The growing needs of the Yorkshire woolen industry for raw wool encouraged landowners to evict their tenants and to replace them with sheep, thus driving the highland peasantry to rocky marginal soils along the coasts, or abroad to Nova Scotia, the United States, Australia, and New Zealand.[8]

It is apparent that these three explanations would tend to emphasize socio-political rather than demographic and ecological factors. In fact these theories would remain logical even in times of static or falling populations. They are all coherent explanations, but to the extent that they have been tested against the known history of Western Europe in the Middle Ages they have not found great support in the evidence.

The Malthusian and ecological arguments must then take precedence, at least for the moment. We know that in England, France, Germany, Italy, and most other parts of Western and Central Europe, there was a steady growth in population during the eleventh and twelfth centuries which continued in most areas for most of the thirteenth century.[9] In the same period, with some local exceptions perhaps, there was no dramatic general change in the technologies applied to agriculture. As a result, more and more people had to be fed from the same technological and soil base. The "safety valve" adopted, at least in some parts of Europe, was the attempt to bring new lands under the plough by draining marshes, cutting down forests, and turning thin or inferior soils. Such lands often have very limited possibilities and a short life span under intensive cultivation, and if the population continues to grow while their productivity declines, a food crisis may be reached.

Another factor was the presence of sheep and cattle. Although these domesticated animals now exist for human exploitation, before the agrarian and industrial revolutions they lived with European man in constant and dramatic competition for land. As marginal grazing land was taken from cattle and put under the plough, the supply of calories expanded but the protein supply contracted. Even worse, manure supplies for maintaining the fertility of these virgin but poor soils decreased with the number of cattle, thus hastening the pace at which such soils became exhausted. Conversely, of course, as marginal agricultural land was abandoned in the fourteenth and fifteenth centuries, the return of grasses and grazing animals helped to rest and restore exhausted soils and to fixate the nitrogens which had previously been washed out. This, however, meant a decline in total caloric yields from the land, because grazing animals, although high in protein value, produce five times fewer calories per acre than do, for example, cereals.[10]

One objection to this general ecological and Malthusian explanation correctly asserts that many areas of Europe—Scotland, Sweden, Basse Provence, and Catalonia among them—were not overcrowded, and therefore that Europe as a whole was not suffering from a crisis of population density and resources.[11] But the

Europe of the fourteenth century did not enjoy the interregional
and international coordination or communications of today. Peasants could not, and perhaps would not, move far, and they had no
knowledge of where to go in search of vacant lands anyway. For the
moment, then, it seems that a population and food crisis may well
be a partial explanation of the reverses suffered in Western Europe
after 1300.

The Malthusian-ecological explanation outlined here has been
considerably strengthened by new historical research into the climatic conditions of the Northern Hemisphere. The great Viking
sagas show us that increasing pressure on the small agrarian patches
at the heads of the Norwegian fjords, coupled with political anarchy
and a search for plunder, drove Norse seafarers to the British Isles,
Normandy, Sicily, along the Russian river systems to the Ukraine,
and across the Atlantic to Iceland, Greenland, and the North American mainland (known to the Vikings as Markland, Helluland, and
Vinland).[12]

Eirik the Red, possibly the first modern real estate promoter,
named his new discovery in the far north Greenland, in the hope of
attracting settlers there.[13] In the late tenth century he himself began
to farm at Brattalid, and in a few years was able to bring Icelandic
immigrants to two settlements on the west coast. Eventually a
church was built at Gardar, a bishop installed, and several hundred
farms developed. Most of these homesteads concentrated on stockraising, but a few hardy cereals and other crops were also grown in
favorable spots, suggesting a tolerable climate and a fairly long
growing season. Greenlanders from the two settlements began to
push northwest and to spend part of the Arctic summer in the
northern reaches of the Baffin Straits, where they were able to hunt
and gather exotic Arctic products such as sealskins, walrus tusks,
furs, and eiderdown, which paid for the European goods such as
iron and meal, which they had to import. A considerable trade
developed between Greenland and Europe, sometimes via Iceland.[14]

The sailing route between Iceland and Greenland, used first by
Eirik the Red and then by the trading ships of the eleventh and
twelfth centuries, ought to surprise us. Leaving Rekjavik or Norway,
the Icelandic longships sailed approximately west to a point on the
eastern shore of Greenland near Mount Forel. They then turned
south southeast along the coast until they raised Greenland's south-
ernmost tip, Cape Farewell. After rounding the Cape, they sailed
northwest to the two small settlements. For most of the year such
a route would be unthinkable today, especially for small vessels.[15]

In the late thirteenth and fourteenth centuries, just as in Europe, serious problems began to affect these small but thriving Greenland communities. The old sailing route had to be abandoned for a much more southerly one because of the presence of increasing numbers of icebergs and ice floes off the east coast of Greenland. As a result of sailing this new route, Norse ships with their primitive navigation systems ran the risk of passing south of Cape Farewell and thus missing Greenland altogether.[16] (We may owe some of the landfalls on the American continent to such misadventures.)

The settlers found summer conditions in the Baffin Straits increasingly severe, and as a result they were unable to provide the Arctic goods which Europe demanded in exchange for its supplies. The Eskimo people of northern Greenland pushed south as the seals and walrus retreated from the growing harshness of the climate, and they began to intrude on the western settlement. (Actually the northern settlement would be a better name.) By about 1350 they had either sacked or absorbed it, and shortly thereafter they may have appeared at the "eastern" settlement near Cape Farewell.

Regular sailings from Iceland to Greenland ceased in the early fifteenth century. Norway also lost interest. When Greenland was rediscovered by Europeans in the sixteenth century, the Norse people of Greenland had vanished. Excavations have shown that the last generations suffered from extreme malnutrition. The settlements had been the victims of gradual deterioration of the climate in the northern hemisphere.[17]

The disappearance of Europeans in Greenland is the most dramatic illustration of the approach of the Arctic in the thirteenth and fourteenth centuries, but evidence provided by E. Le Roy Ladurie and others shows that the continent of Europe was also affected. The northern limit of tolerance of several plants moved south. Alpine glaciers expanded dramatically. The wet, dreary summers and severe winters which late medieval people noticed between 1270 and 1320 were not then fortuitous accidents, but signs of a worsening climate, a situation which added to the strains which a large population had already placed on the basically agrarian economy of western Europe.[18]

Indications are that the population peak was reached around 1300 in many parts of western Europe, and that by the 1340s, because of famine, disease, and psychological, physiological, or even deliberate limitation of family size, population had begun to fall. Natural disasters, however, were an ever-present threat to medieval man, and it may well be argued that given sufficient time new adjustments could have been made within the existing systems of agricultural technology and land use.[19]

In the late 1340s, however, new and terrible rumors of disaster from the Orient began to sweep the Mediterranean. Travelers told of a pestilence in Asia which had left veritable hecatombs in its wake.[20] The Great Death, or the Black Death as modern Europeans were to dub it, first came to their direct notice in the Crimea. An enclave of Genoese traders there was trapped by Tartar invaders, who laid seige to the port where the Genoese had taken shelter.

The Tartars seem to have carried the plague with them from its central Asian source, and it quickly spread within the besieging army. From the besiegers it was transferred to the besieged Genoese, some say by means of catapulting dead and infected corpses into the city, an early form of bacteriological warfare. When the Genoese finally fled by sea they carried the contagion with them. They, or other ships from the plague-stricken eastern Mediterranean, quickly infected the Sicilian ports of Catania and Messina.[21] Whatever its origins, by the spring of 1348, the pestilence which later centuries were to call the Black Death was firmly established in Sicily and had consolidated a few beachheads on the mainland.[22]

Thereafter, as might be expected, the Black Death followed the great European trade routes. Northern and Central Italian cities such as Florence, Siena, and Orvieto suffered catastrophic mortality.[23] Rural areas seem to have suffered slightly less, and some pockets of population such as Milan were inexplicably spared.[24] It seems safe to say that one third of the population of the Italian peninsula disappeared during this first pandemic.[25] From Italy the plague spread to populous France. Marseilles suffered greatly, as did Perpignan, and within a few weeks the disease had reached Paris and the north. Overall mortality in France equalled that of Italy, and may even have exceeded it in the great urban centers.[26]

Germany shows an irregular pattern. Once again the great cities, such as Hamburg and Bremen, were badly afflicted. In Bremen one scholar found that some seventy per cent of the population had disappeared. On the other hand, only one quarter of the people of Lübeck died, and Bohemia seems to have escaped unscathed.[27] Similar patterns appeared in the rest of Western Europe. Spain and Portugal, Norway and Sweden, have been less studied in this respect, but the statistics available are similar to those for Italy and France.[28]

The history of this first epidemic of plague in Britain is a microcosm of events in Europe. It first appeared in a small southern port—which one is still a matter of debate—established itself there, and then spread outward. It seems to have appeared first during the summer of 1348, but did not spread rapidly until the following year. In London the Black Death raged for almost two years (1349–50), and a third, perhaps even a half, of the populace died. Death rates just north of London in East Anglia were particularly high. In Lincolnshire whole villages vanished, and arable land reverted to fen.[29] From England the plague spread to the periphery. In Scotland and Ireland it was noticed that mortality, as could be expected, was much higher among the poor. (This differential mortality rate is mentioned sporadically throughout plague literature for various countries.)[30]

By late 1350 the Black Death had run its course. Even distant Iceland had suffered. Some areas had unaccountably escaped completely, or with comparatively low mortality rates, but the general impact had been catastrophic. We have already noted that many European populations were already in decline when the Black Death struck, and this complicates the task of arriving at a rough estimate. After assembling much of the relevant material on the matter and attempting to balance the areas which were spared, such as Bohemia, against the areas where most people died, such as Tuscany, one observer concludes that "to maintain that one European in three died during the period of the Black Death can never be proved, but, equally, cannot be wildly far from the truth."[31] Thus in a career of some two and a half years, a disease previously unknown to that population had killed one third of the people of Western Europe.

What we now know of the Black Death helps to confirm these mortality rates. There is no doubt that the pandemic which struck Europe was caused by the three related illnesses brought on by *pasteurella pestis,* the plague bacillus. This organism lives ordinarily in the bloodstream of commensal fleas and rodents, and among both it has its preferred types (*xenopsylla cheopis* in the flea family and *rattus rattus,* the small black rat, among the rodents). Under certain conditions the infected flea will abandon its infected rodent host and will bite humans. If the flea is "blocked," that is, if the multiplication of plague bacilli has so inflamed its stomach entrance that it is unable to swallow blood into the stomach, then it will disgorge ingested blood full of plague bacilli back upon the human skin and into the wound caused by its bite. The result is bubonic plague.[32] Rarely, the entrance of plague bacilli directly to the human bloodstream will cause a virulent, fulminating septicaemia, the so-called septicaemic plague, which is invariably fatal. In both these types, however, it will be noted that infection is caused by the bite of a flea. Transmission from human to human is well nigh impossible in the bubonic variety and rare in the few cases of septicaemic plague. Thus widespread bubonic plague in humans can exist only where there is a large number of infected rats, and where the human population is flea-ridden and living in close contact with a rat population. Dissemination of the disease is therefore slow and sporadic.[33]

Many of the first and later outbreaks of plague in fourteenth century Europe can be readily identified as having begun as bubonic plague. The onset is sudden and accompanied by fever and prostration. Within a few days buboes or boils appear, usually in the groin or armpit. Sometimes patches of skin become discolored. The course of the disease is about a week, with death often intervening. Death is caused by vast cellular necrosis and resultant heart failure. While morbidity rates in a human population can be quite low in some ecological circumstances, mortality rates are invariably high, seldom lower than fifty per cent. Even under modern therapeutic conditions, where streptomycin is the most recommended specific, failure to arrive at an early diagnosis often means death. Those who recover are left in extremely debilitated condition and often succumb to heart failure during convalescence. All these characteristics of the disease were described in medieval accounts. There were also a few references to sporadic occurrences of septicaemic plague.[34]

The third type of plague is the one which must concern us here. It is, in fact, very probably one of the major phenomena which would dominate Central America for the two centuries after the Spanish conquest. Only this third type of plague can explain the rapid and deadly transmission of the disease from the eastern Mediterranean, throughout Western Europe to Iceland, in a period of just over two years—and this in an age of slow-moving, unmechanized methods of transportation.

By processes not yet fully understood, perhaps the bursting of a plague abscess in the lung of a sufferer from the disease, some cases of bubonic plague attack mainly the lungs and respiratory system. (It has been suggested, but not proved, that this happens because some victims infected during the early stages of a bubonic outbreak were already suffering from bronchitis, pneumonia, or some other respiratory infection at the time of the infected flea bite.)

When plague attacks the lungs, the victim becomes ill with pneumonic or pulmonary plague. This disease runs an extremely rapid course. There is fever and prostration. Symptoms mentioned throughout plague literature are intense pains in the side ("dolores de costado" in Spain, "points aigus de côté" in France), and nosebleeds or bleeding from the mouth. Death often arrives within three days and recovery is extremely rare. Death usually intervenes before the characteristic buboes become evident, but autopsy reveals them to exist in an early, undeveloped stage.[35]

The significant difference between pulmonary plague and the other two varieties is that it is readily transmissable via human breath droplets, blood, or sputum. This kind of plague is, in fact, extremely contagious and can spread, especially in areas of concentrated population, with astonishing rapidity.

Both major types of plague, and a rare case of septicaemic plague, evidently existed in Europe in 1348. Some medieval people recognized the difference between bubonic and pulmonary plague, and understood that contact with an individual infected with pulmonary plague was extremely dangerous—thus the flights of the upper classes to the countryside, the quarantines imposed upon infected individuals, the barring up of plague-stricken houses, and the difficulties in finding reliable individuals to nurse the sick and bury the dead.[36]

The three illnesses together, therefore, comprise the Black Death epidemic of 1348–50, but the pulmonary variety was responsible for its rapid dissemination, high morbidity, and great mortality. Plague flourishes between 50 and 85 degrees Fahrenheit, with the pulmonary variety tending to flourish at the lower temperatures, and the bubonic at the upper temperatures of this range. Thus, significantly, pulmonary plague is a "winter" disease, when other chest infections are likely to be present, and often dies down or shifts to the less virulent bubonic variety when weather is warm and dry.[37] (As already noted, the climate of Europe apparently became colder and wetter in the late thirteenth and fourteenth centuries.)

Debate over the reasons for the Black Death, and over the results of it, has been as diverse as the arguments over the causes of the crisis of the half century or so which preceded it. Some point out that the other two apocalyptic horsemen, war and famine, were also present. Obviously these disasters reinforce one another, but studies show that it is disease which causes the greatest number of fatalities in such circumstances, and war the least.[38]

Those who do not admit that a Malthusian and ecological crisis existed before 1348, or who assert that the crisis was fortuitous or socio-political in origin, conclude that the pandemic was not directly related to conditions at the time. Some claim that malnutrition was not severe in the 1340s and continue that even if it were to be granted that 1270–1350 was an era of overlarge, hungry populations, then the Black Death, if this logic be followed, should have restored the population and food supply equilibrium by removing one third of the hungry mouths. Why then did the plague recur, as it did inexorably throughout the next century? There were pandemics in 1361, 1368, 1371, 1375, 1390, and numerous local outbreaks. In some regions it became endemic for centuries.[39]

In reply it has been argued that the Black Death left severely weakened populations unable to resist further onslaughts. Another argument would have it that centuries of soil abuse and overpopulation cannot be corrected in two years, and that the rapid population recoveries which took place in some parts of Europe after the first pandemic renewed the strain on resources, and that it required recurrent plague epidemics to keep the size of the population down, in fact to slowly decrease it, until soils gradually recovered and a new modus vivendi between man, soil, and technology had been evolved.[40]

Yet these explanations, while cogent, seem partial when accounting for the repeated visits of the plague and other diseases from the fourteenth to the seventeenth centuries. In short, the Malthusian and ecological arguments can bear most of the explicatory weight up to 1348, but seem inadequate to fully explain the continuous disasters of the next centuries.

In searching for further reasons for the persistence of this "age of adversity" it may well be appropriate to look at the nature and history of human diseases and epidemics. Much of the explanation which is required many reside in the nature of plague itself, a subject which has become more thoroughly understood in recent years.

The cyclical habits of the disease are now fairly well known. Its first impact on peoples who do not know it is always terrible, with very high mortality. This first epidemic, the Black Death of 1348-50 in our case, is followed by a period in which the plague becomes endemic in certain localities, and these places become foci for new large-scale outbreaks in the general population. It is noticeable, however, that the succeeding pandemics lessen in frequency and mortality, and plague finally vanishes, several hundred years in some cases, after the initial outbreak.[41]

This pattern fits fairly well with what we know of the epidemic history of Europe between 1348 and 1665. After the Black Death of 1348 the succeeding fourteenth-century epidemics, while still appalling to those experiencing them, gradually diminished in intensity. During the fifteenth century the abatement continued, and the prosperous sixteenth century was generally free of large-scale visitations of the disease. The plague flared up in one last frightful series in the seventeenth century, and then disappeared, one hopes forever, as a major force in European history.[42]

European historians have come to recognize certain demographic cycles in Europe's history between 1000 and the industrial revolution. A period of prosperity, a phase A, is followed by a crisis, perhaps Malthusian or climatic in origin, and that in turn is succeeded by a gloomy phase B, in which population is either falling or stagnant, and in which new and slow adjustments are made between men and their environments. Then a new growth begins and the cycle repeats itself until the scientific, agrarian, and industrial revolutions of the eighteenth century ended—or perhaps simply prolonged—this cyclical pattern.[43]

Regions vary enormously when this periodization is applied specifically, but a gross picture of the process in Europe would show a long phase A from before 1000 to about 1275, a calamitous phase B roughly between 1300 and 1450, a new phase A between the later years of the fifteenth century and the second decade of the seventeenth century. Next would come the much disputed seventeenth-century depression, the "general crisis" which seems to vary so greatly in impact and chronology. This depression, perhaps the first modern one in that it was global in scale, as we shall see, was waning by the last decade of the seventeenth century, and a new recovery began.[44]

Obviously, then, what we know of the seventeenth century—new strains in some areas between a growing population and its land base, wars and famine in central Europe, depopulation in Spain and elsewhere—helps to explain why there was a short and violent late recrudescence of the slowly diminishing plague epidemics which began so terribly in 1348.[45]

To sum up, it would seem from the above review of the evidence on plague in Europe between 1348 and 1665 that we are in the presence of a very complex set of relationships, in which two of the critical variables seem to be the mass socioeconomic and nutritional condition of large human groups at any given time, and the still only partly understood laws of immunology in mankind. The

general well-being of any individual human organism and its immunological readiness are thus in a complex interrelationship which
becomes of great importance when a new disease appears on the
scene.

Plague had been unknown in medieval Europe, at least since
the time of the plagues which followed the plague of Justinian (542
A.D.). The disease had been absent from Europe for over 500 years
at least.[46] When it first appeared in the eastern Mediterranean and
southern Italy in 1348 it found human populations with no physiological immunities to it, who, in addition, were experiencing a crisis
in their food supply. The result was catastrophic. Succeeding epidemics of the fourteenth and fifteenth centuries, still virulent but
gradually declining in ferocity, may well indicate a human population which, in aggregate, was gradually building up its immunity to
plague, and also its socioeconomic well-being. The brief flare-up in
the seventeenth century can be interpreted as being related to a
series of local returns to poor nutritional and socioeconomic conditions. The history of other epidemic diseases, cholera, influenza,
typhus, and perhaps even malaria and smallpox, apparently follows
somewhat similar patterns.[47]

The impact on Europe of the Black Death and the other epidemics of the fourteenth and early fifteenth centuries has been
much debated. Two factors make an assessment difficult. If, as much
evidence shows, the population in many areas was already in decline, then the outbreaks of plague may not be the main agents in
causing this demographic collapse, at least initially. The other problem is that modern scholars, noting that a third or even more than
half of the population of the European areas which they are studying
disappeared after the Black Death, and that succeeding epidemics
were only slightly less damaging, expect that such a change should
have dramatic results. Yet, with few exceptions there were no immediate peasant revolts, revolutions, or dramatic changes in class
structure. In amazement some scholars therefore conclude that
death was a familiar companion to medieval peoples, as indeed it
was, and that their recuperative powers were such that epidemics
had little impact beyond the mortality of the years when they were
present.

The true assessment would seem to lie somewhere between. It
would be foolish to write the history of the late Middle Ages with
the Black Death as the leading actor, and equally simplistic to ignore
such dramatic events. (Certainly plague was the most direct and

rapid tie between economic and demographic conditions, swiftly adjusting the population to its productive capability.)

The first consideration should be the effect on population. The recovery of numbers from an epidemic can be remarkably rapid, and there is evidence that there was such a recovery in some regions after the Black Death. The recurrence of the epidemics, however, striking like hammer blows once in every one or two generations, killed each of these recoveries and succeeded in containing or depressing population growth for about a century. In fact, much of Western Europe continued to lose population for a century after 1348.[48]

The thirteenth century, as we have seen, was one of population pressure and land hunger. Too many peasants were looking for too few tenancies and too few jobs. The landowners of feudal Europe could then approximate an employer's or a landowner's dream— two men for every job and two applicants to rent every piece of vacant land. These factors kept wages low and rents high. They depressed the poorer sectors of the peasantry, a large part of the population because Europe was still basically agricultural, and they tied these peasants to the soil. An individual who left his tenancy for another village, if he were not captured, would find it hard to obtain another plot there, and would no doubt encounter hostility from the peasants of that village who did not relish the prospect of one more competitor for the limited land available.[49]

After the first epidemics, however, this situation had radically changed. Land had become a surplus commodity and labor had become scarce. Wages went up and rents went down. High labor costs and decreasing rents meant that the profit margins enjoyed by the rich in the thirteenth century became smaller. Prices of staple cereals declined, while the price of manufactured and luxury goods, which the peasants hardly consumed at all, rose sharply.

As a result of these changes, peasants could move, when they escaped or were permitted to leave, and might then expect to find land or employment in new localities. Landowners and even monarchs were well aware of the unfavorable turn of events—the balance had shifted against them and towards the lower classes. The Ordinance of Laborers promulgated by Edward III in 1349, after half a century of population decline and the first visitation of the plague, is a typical reaction. It is a blunt attempt to depress wages, to prevent peasants and artisans from moving about the countryside looking for better wages and lands, and to coerce vagrants and vagabonds into productive employment. It was designed so that employers would not have to compete for the services of the lower classes.[50]

The delicate balance between men and domesticated grazing animals was also altered. Sheep and cattle require more extensive areas and less manpower to care for them than do agricultural crops. As the population declined and formerly tilled lands were abandoned, sheep and cattle moved into the vacuum created and grew considerably in numbers. In time, of course, this readjustment of the balance between men and cattle would have a benefit for man, for the increase of animals meant more protein for him, and the return of soils to grasses and grazing animals rehabilitated areas which had been eroded and overcultivated.[51]

While social mobility between classes does not seem to have altered, yet mobility within some classes may have accelerated in some towns. Deaths in city councils and other elite corporate bodies allowed the entry of younger, more dynamic, and less experienced men, with the result that some of these groups changed in character. There also seems to have been a blurring of class lines within the peasantry itself. Village solidarity was one result, which increased the difficulties of the landowners when negotiating with the lower classes.[52]

The changes wrought by this time of troubles upon peoples' minds, and upon the literature and art of the period, are harder to assess. Literature moved from its former unified outlook to extremes. Writing on chivalry became an unconscious parody of itself, and love literature varied between the sanctification of women and naked eroticism. Man's outlook became tinged by an obsessive preoccupation with death. The dance of death, the charnel house, and the grave became favorite subjects in art and poetry. Religion also moved from its former unity and turned to flagellation and mysticism, indulgences, and humanism.[53]

H. G. Wells, in his novel *The War of the Worlds,* tells the story of a Martian invasion of the earth. The invaders carry all before them. Death and destruction terrify the earthlings and all seems lost. Suddenly the survivors note that noise and movement have died down, and gradually they emerge from their hiding places to find that all the invaders from Mars are dead, killed by the bacteria and microbes common to earth, but to which they had no immunities.[54]

In human history similar but reversed situations have occurred. With the possible exception of syphilis, it is the invaders who have carried their bacterial allies with them, and the invaded populations which have found themselves immunologically defenseless in the face of the onslaughts.

Observers became aware of this phenomenon in the first few centuries of European expansion. Wherever they wandered from the contiguous land mass of Eurasia and Africa, they noticed that their arrival brought destructive diseases and rapid drops in native populations. War and conquest, they realized, could not nearly account for the magnitude of these disasters. The more isolated the population had been before their arrival the harsher the epidemic attacks. If the original isolated population was small, such as in some Pacific Islands or in Tierra del Fuego, it was likely to disappear entirely.[55]

The destruction in the Pacific was particularly notable. Hawaii, Tahiti, and especially Australia were devastated.[56] Fatality was so great that some simply could not believe that it could all be because of disease. Sir Basil Thomson wrote in 1894: "Apart from bacilli of foreign diseases, there is now no doubt that the different races of man are themselves uncongenial, and that their first meeting generates a mysterious poison fatal to the weaker race. In the Pacific, Tahiti, Niue [Savage Island], and Penrhyn Island in particular, were swept by a destructive epidemic immediately after the visit of the first European ship, though the visitors were not themselves suffering from any such ailment at the time."[57]

Here Thomson is hesitantly coming close to a consideration of "culture shock," the sudden onset whereby isolated cultures are dragged into the modern world and forced to forsake many former values and their entire cosmic view. Culture clash is an important variable. Early accounts often mention the disheartened native who simply pines away and dies of no apparent pathological cause. Such deaths, however, nowhere approach the number caused by disease.

To a limited extent we are able to observe the same phenomenon today. The differential morbidity and mortality rates between those naturally or artificially immunized against diseases which allow of immunization, and those who are not, needs no further comment. More analogus to the considerations here, western peoples within the last century have continued to encounter isolated tribes who have previously had little contact with the outside world. Rates of population loss of 90 and 100 per cent are not uncommon after these first contacts. The best known example is the Amazon basin of South America, where many tribal groupings have rapidly disappeared, or are still in the process of disappearing, despite energetic efforts to keep infection from them.[58]

Of all the regions in the world which Eurasians did not know in the fifteenth century, the Americas were the most significant in geographical size, in number of inhabitants, and in their isolation from Eurasia. The very name which has persisted, the New World, is indicative of the immensity and novelty of this discovery to Europeans.

One reads of Welshmen in Georgia, Phoenicians in Brazil, Kon-Tiki rafts and African reed vessels reaching Barbados. That the Norse reached North America very briefly in the eleventh century is beyond question. But the overwhelming evidence is that the Americas and the Eurasian land mass lived in ignorance of one another before Columbus, and, what more concerns us here, they did not share the same store of human diseases.

Our knowledge of the existence and pathology of diseases in pre-Columbian America is imperfect, and, given the nature of the problem and the evidence, will probably remain incomplete. Indications are strong, nevertheless, that many of the major scourges known in the Old World since ancient times were not present in the New World before the arrival of Europeans at the end of the fifteenth century. We have the testimony of the Indians of New Spain themselves that smallpox and measles had been unknown before. Plague and cholera seem to be Asiatic in origin. Archeological evidence suggests that tuberculosis was absent. Yellow fever, typhoid, and typhus seem to have been introduced from Africa, and there is both historical and modern evidence of a rather conclusive nature that malaria is not native to the Americas and was introduced from Africa. Recent coprolitic evidence suggests that there may even have been an absence in the Americas of some kinds of intestinal worms and parasites. The origin of syphilis has provoked endless argument, but for the moment, at least to this observer, those who would claim an American origin for the disease seem more convincing.[59]

In sum, present indications point to an absence of the major Old World epidemic diseases in pre-Columbian America, and we must assume that where a disease has long been absent, so also will be an acquired physiological immunity to it. Many of the major illnesses of which we have record in pre-1492 America seem to arise from food shortages or nutritional deficiencies.[60]

The demographic history of pre-Columbian populations in America is in its early stages. For Mesoamerica, a region which is of more direct concern in this study, the situation is slightly better. Two scholars have drawn a coherent evolutionary picture which presents Mesoamerica as a symbiotic cultural and economic region composed of contrasting but complementary climatic and ecological zones. The population picture which is presented is one of gradual growth as agricultural methods, trade patterns, and systems of social and political organization developed. The greatest population in Mesoamerica, for these authors, is the one which the Spaniards encountered in the second decade of the sixteenth century.[61]

Another approach has been to apply the known agricultural technology employed by the Mesoamerican Indians, and the agricultural methods which they used, to the soils and climates which they inhabited. Again, for several areas, the result has been surprising population densities in many parts of Mesoamerica.[62]

A third approach, different from the preceding two only in emphasis, has sought to study the profiles of soil use, that is, erosion morphology, in order to discover the gross trends of occupation history before the Spanish conquest. This work has been done in various parts of Central and Western Mexico, and the results show close similarities to the demographic history of medieval and early modern, pre-industrial Europe. In what had obviously been an agrarian society there is evidence of a Malthusian cycle in land use and land occupancy. During a lengthy phase A, use of the soil intensified until erosion and soil exhaustion intervened. After this crisis soil use decreased, because the population fell or moved elsewhere, and the soil was able to recover from agricultural abuse—a typical example of phase B. As soil fertility returned, the population grew again; in fact, another Malthusian and ecological crisis, the culmination of yet another phase A, had been reached when the Spanish conquest of Mexico began in 1519.[63]

The same investigator has demonstrated that there is evidence of demographic strain and crisis in the years immediately preceding the conquest. He suggests that the crisis had been reached, and was perhaps already past its peak by 1519. If this were so, the population was on the verge of contraction when the European invaders first appeared.[64] Similar conditions can be postulated for some other parts of the Americas, such as the Inca empire and the Mayan areas of Central America. These and other populations had certainly reached impressive size, possibly their greatest size up to that date, at the moment of Spanish contact.[65]

It would serve no purpose here to become involved in a debate over the exact numerical size of pre-Columbian populations. Scholars who claim that the conquistadors and those who came immediately after them were lying about the gross size of the population have a heavy burden of proof placed upon them, because if their assertions are true, then these seemingly pathological falsehoods continued for generation after generation in logical and linear order, so that it must be concluded that there was a vast conspiracy of overestimation through time, indeed through more than a century, if the thesis of small populations is to be sustained. The case for small populations has been further damaged by the work of historians who have used tribute counts, ecclesiastical records, and other evidence to arrive at gross population figures, and by the work of archeologists, anthropologists, ecologists, and soil chemists, who have demonstrated that the soil, yields, and technologies of that period could, and in fact did, support large populations.[66]

Given that crop yields in Europe varied between 3 and 15 to 1 in the fifteenth century, and that yields in the maize and mandioc areas of the Americas were many times higher, perhaps as high as 60 to 1 in some parts of Mexico, it is surprising that a population estimate of about sixty million for Europe in the sixteenth century finds fairly general acceptance, while one of eighty million or more in America, many times larger than Europe, raises so many doubts.[67]

In sum, most scholars now believe that the population of America was considerably larger than that of Europe in 1492, and the debate has moved to a more sophisticated level. How large were these large populations? To what extent did density vary from region to region, and what are the best techniques—tribute counts, house mound counts, soil analysis, or others—for arriving at the closest estimates?[68]

The picture drawn thus far of the Mesoamerican areas of high culture about 1500 bears many striking resemblances to the Europe which awaited its crisis and attack from the Black Death about 1300. Mesoamerica's Amerindians had been isolated from the diseases which were about to strike them, in fact isolated to a far greater degree than the fourteenth century populations on the Eurasian land mass had been from plague. As a consequence of this isolation they had no immunological defenses. The society was as agrarian one, depending heavily on one crop, maize. Its agricultural dependence—its servitude to maize might be a better expression—was even greater than that of fourteenth century Europe with its grains, legumes, and domesticated animals. Indian Mesoamerica had reached its greatest population size ever, and, at least in one major part of its total area, it offered signs of having reached, for at least the second time in its long history, a grave Malthusian crisis of population and food supply. There is some justification for saying that if fourteenth century Europe was ripe for disaster, then Mesoamerica was overripe.

The arrival of the first Old World epidemics in the Americas was an even more traumatic matter than the Black Death in the Europe of 1348, for it came accompanied by invading aliens of a very different culture. The Hundred Years War in Europe, destructive as it no doubt was, was fought between people of similar backgrounds who observed a tacitly accepted code of warfare. The Spanish conquest caused large-scale destruction, a dividing of the autochthonous peoples, and new and strange forms of subjection to taxation and civil and religious authorities.[69]

There can be no doubt that the impact of these factors, and above all that of the new diseases, was a severe one. The first epidemics produced veritable holocausts, killing a third or a half of the Indian populations. The first epidemic was smallpox, but by the time it had moved on to areas of Mesoamerica beyond Central Mexico it seems to have been joined by the old European scourge, plague. Certainly the descriptions of the disease found in the Guatemalan Indian annals resemble those of pulmonary plague.[70] The great pandemics of cocoliztli or matlazáhuatl which struck the highlands of Mexico and Central America in 1545–48 and in 1576–81, sweeping away vast numbers of Indians, but affecting the Spaniards with their European immunities much less, are described symptomatically in exactly the same language as plague in Spain. Anyone who has read of the nosebleeds, the deaths after three days of prostration, the "dolores de costado" in both Spain and the New World, may conclude while awaiting more evidence that cocoliztli (in Guatemala gucumatz) was none other than the old enemy, pulmonary plague.[71]

No doubt other European and African diseases were present. Measles, smallpox, and typhus caused many deaths in the highlands, and yellow fever, malaria, and other tropical diseases emptied coastal areas. In the Caribbean islands of Puerto Rico, Hispaniola, Cuba, and Jamaica the aboriginal populations had all but disappeared within half a century of the first European contact.[72] The isthmus of Panama quickly followed a similar pattern.[73]

In Mexico there was a dense population, and some Indians survived. On its tropical coasts almost all disappeared, but in the highlands more were able to withstand the onslaught. After a century of Spanish occupation some ninety per cent of the Amerindian population of Mexico had disappeared.[74] Similar histories were repeated at a later date in Central America, as we shall see, in Colombia, Peru, and Chile.[75] The invasion of a New World by another world which had been isolated from it may well have caused the greatest destruction of lives in history. One scholar has noted that a population which amounted to about twenty per cent of mankind in 1490 was reduced to three per cent within a century.[76]

We have noted that before the population decline in Europe, land was scarce and men were cheap. A similar situation obtained in pre-conquest Mesoamerica, and a similar reversal took place. After the third great epidemic series of matlazáhuatl plague in the 1570s, Indian labor became increasingly scarce, and new attempts were made to coerce Indian workers and force them to stay in one place.[77] Just as in Europe, the empty agricultural lands were filled by rapidly multiplying cattle and sheep, corporate hierarchies were destroyed in the Indian communities, and the early Renaissance optimism of the conquistadors changed to the extremes and introversion of the seventeenth-century American baroque. A century of depression followed.[78]

From these general considerations we must now pass to the specific. Central America will be subjected to a closer scrutiny to find out how the peoples who lived there responded to these dramatic times, what forms these responses took, and how some of them were able to escape from the depressed conditions in which they found themselves. Certainly such a closer case study will illuminate some of the intricate details of the larger processes described above.

PART I
The Society of Conquest and Encomienda, 1520-1576

1

The Central American Background and Conquest

Central America was not to be spared the destructive processes and the rapid changes which come in the wake of isolation from the Old World, epidemics, conquest, and culture clash. The region followed Mexico and Panama as a scene of violent military conquest and saw similar disruptions, wars, plagues, population decline, and acculturation.

For the purposes of this study, Central America encompasses the vast isthmian stretch which runs from the eastern and southern borders of Tehuantepec, Tabasco, and Yucatan to the Costa Rican border with Panama.[1] The area has a certain apparent unity; it consists of the block of highlands and complementary lowlands between the two great isthmi of Tehuantepec and Panama, and, in historical terms, it was the imperial connection between two of the nodal areas (Panama and Central Mexico) of the Spanish American system. The Spanish Crown, after some early tinkering with the boundaries, decided that Central America should be administered as one unit, and assigned its administration to the President and Audiencia of Guatemala which held court first in Gracias a Dios, and then in the more logical Santiago de los Caballeros de Guatemala (now Antigua). Although the central administration of this area was often more apparent than real, the notion of its political and geographical unity survived the wars of independence and has, to some extent, lasted to this day.[2]

Central America is a relatively narrow isthmian land mass connecting the two greater areas of North and South America, and so its climate is affected by the Caribbean Sea to the north and the Pacific to the south. (The Pacific was always referred to as the South Sea by colonial Spaniards.) Central America lies entirely in the tropics, runs approximately northwest to southeast, and its back-bone is mountainous, a part of the great American chain which runs from Alaska to Tierra del Fuego. Within Central America these mountains reach their greatest heights in the Cuchumatanes in western Guatemala and their lowest around the Nicaraguan lakes. They are still highly volcanic and lie nearer to the Pacific than to the Caribbean so that the Pacific foothills, known as the boca costa in Guatemala, press close to the sea leaving only a narrow coastal plain in most places. Vulcanism has deposited thick layers of fertile vol-canic ash in the mountain valleys and plateaus, and on the slopes going towards the Pacific and the Caribbean, but much of the broad Caribbean coastal plain has been too distant from the volcanic dis-turbances, and the deposits of ash there are sporadic or non-exist-ent.

The Pacific coast and the backbone highlands and valleys also enjoy an advantage over the broad Caribbean coastal plain when climate is considered. The mountains modify the heat of the tropics and the severity of the Caribbean storms. Above 5,000 to 6,000 feet lie areas which the Spaniards dubbed tierra fría (cold land). Nearly all tierra fría lies in Chiapas and western Guatemala, and these high valleys are fertile but subject to frosts. Tierra templada, the temper-ate land, lying between 2,500 feet and tierra fría, is to be found in the lower highland valleys and on the mountain slopes. Much of interior Chiapas, Honduras, and Costa Rica, Guatemala and the boca costa, plus some of northwestern Nicaragua consists of fertile tierra templada.

These mountainous areas seem favored when compared with the Caribbean coast, but it is when the Pacific and Caribbean tierras calientes, or hot lands below 2,500 feet, are compared that the comparative disadvantage of the Caribbean sector is most apparent. The Caribbean trades blow off the sea toward the land all the year round and deposit heavy rains on the poor, easily leached, clay soils (latosols) which cover great areas of the coastal plain. Much of it is swampy and covered with tropical rain forests, especially the stretch of coast which runs from Cape Gracias a Dios to Panama.[3]

Only one section of this coast is relatively favored. The Petén and a projection of it which runs along the coast from Lake Izabal to the town of Trujillo cannot compete environmentally with the Highlands or the Pacific coast, but in parts its mean annual rainfall is less, there are some local deposits of volcanic ash, a better drain-age system near the Gulf of Honduras, and a large area in the Petén composed of less easily leached soils on top of limestone.[4]

This sector is of significance. Its relative advantages help to explain the flourishing Classic Maya civilization of the Petén, long in decline when the Spaniards arrived. Recent studies have shown that careful and skillful application of the "slash and burn" agriculture which the Maya practiced allows a fairly dense rural population to thrive.[5] (If there is an absence, as there was, one must add, of the more virulent European and African imported diseases.) Nevertheless, it has also been demonstrated conclusively that whereas a judicious slash and burn in relatively favorable tropical soils and rain forests can support surprisingly dense populations, and probably did so until well after the Spanish conquest, yet, as we shall see, these densities still fall below those which can arise within the systems of slash and burn, fallowing, and above all irrigation, which are possible in the highland basins and slopes or on the favored soils of the wet and dry Pacific litoral. And of course the poorer areas of the Caribbean coast running south and east of Cape Gracias a Dios, in spite of the patches of mandioc culture, cannot compare ecologically even with the Petén.

Part of this relatively favored part of the environmentally poor Caribbean coastal plain is the section between Lake Izabal and Trujillo, a window to the sea and to commerce with other areas which was vital to the interior both before and after the conquest. Before the conquest, Hernán Cortés, Cristóbal de Olid, and other early settlers found dense Indian populations around Naco and Nito on the shores of the Gulf of Honduras, living in what has been described as a port-of-trade enclave similar to Soconusco and the Tabasco lowlands around Isla de Términos. The enclave on the Gulf traded with the interior of Guatemala and Honduras, and with Yucatan, Tabasco, and areas beyond.[6] These tropical populations disappeared rapidly under the impact of the conquest, as did coastal populations in many parts of Mesoamerica, leaving a demographic vacuum which the new colonists were unable to fill.[7] Deserted as the area was, it was of vital importance to the new lords of the land, because, excepting the difficult and seasonal navigation via the Desguadero from the Nicaraguan lakes, and a few exposed unhealthy ports in Costa Rica, this was the only area of the coast where European ports were barely possible. The rest of the coast was a series of mangrove swamps, open roads, and shallow estuaries. Poor as they were, Lake Izabal, Santo Tomás, Puerto Caballos, and Trujillo were Central America's only exit to the European world.[8]

The Pacific coast tierra caliente, with its fertile volcanic slopes, receives far less rain than the Caribbean. Rain is abundant, but there is a marked dry season which runs from November to May, especially in Guatemala and El Salvador, when the prevalent winds blow off the land. As a result the Pacific tierra caliente is much more favorable for human occupation and its soils are less leached and weathered by natural agencies. In some places, however, its young, fertile, azonal soils have by now suffered heavy damage from human cultivation and erosion.[9]

Geographically then, highland and Pacific Central America were favored zones, and they were the areas which attracted denser populations before and after the conquest. Classic Maya civilization and the Gulf of Honduras enclave were not exceptions to this rule. This settlement pattern has persisted to this day. Central America is an area which naturally faces the Pacific, yet, significantly, its conquerors were to come from the Atlantic and Europe. Throughout the colonial period, elites were to confront this difficulty and they never solved it. The area they controlled was environmentally a part of the Pacific, yet all their economic, political, and cultural preferences were Atlantic.

Culturally, pre-conquest Central America was not one. A line running from Trujillo south to the Gulf of Fonseca, then turning southwest to the lakes of Nicaragua and from there probably to the Gulf of Nicoya, divided high culture of Mesoamerican origin to the north and west from other disparate groups, many of South American origin and of a generally earlier evolutionary level to the south and east. It is surely no accident that, with the possible exception of parts of highland Honduras and Costa Rica, this line separates geographically privileged highland and Pacific Central America from the poorer Caribbean areas of leached soils and tropical rain forests. The high cultures had evolved in the most geographically advantageous half of Central America.[10]

The southeastern frontier of Mesoamerica was, of course, not absolute. North and west of it we find relatively backward areas, such as isolated parts of highland Verapaz and Chiapas; and south and east of the line, in areas of generally low culture, we find the fairly elaborate social structures of the Huetares in the Costa Rican highlands, and enclaves of Nahua-speaking traders here and there on the Caribbean coast.[11]

Present knowledge of pre-Columbian Indian culture south and east of the Mesoamerican line is far from exact. Along the frontier between the two cultural areas were to be found a series of tribes such as the Lenca, Jicaques, and Payas, each living in relative isolation, and all of disputed cultural affiliation. They are probably of non-Mesoamerican origin, although the Lenca especially had been heavily influenced by the neighboring Pipiles and Mayas of Mesoamerica.[12] The multitude of other tribes and groupings in northeastern Honduras, northern Nicaragua, and most of Costa Rica seems to have been mainly of South American origin. Cultures which closely resembled Chibchan were to be found in the more favored highland and Pacific areas.[13]

Maize was grown in these higher areas, and was in fact of importance there, but most of the Caribbean lowlands from Trujillo to Panama are unsuitable for maize culture, and as a result, like many South American cultures, these tribes of generally lower culture lived on scattered plantations of mandioc, pejibaye palm, and arrowroot and supplemented their agriculture by hunting and gathering. The tropical settlement pattern was communal houses, either long houses or kraal-like buildings which the Spanish referred to as palenques, often set in a defensive position on a hill near plantations. Larger villages or defensive walled hamlets were found in areas of denser population.[14]

Recent studies have shown that mandioc tuber cultivation plus hunting and gathering may not necessarily mean sparse human populations, and there is some evidence that the tribes to the south and east of Mesoamerica reached high densities in a few areas of more fertile soil and favorable environments.[15] It is, however, likely that nowhere did these populations reach the densities of the Mesoamerican nuclei, and the nature of their life style and settlement patterns meant that they were far more mobile, far less tied to the soil and to the agricultural cycle than the neighboring Mesoamericans. Moreover, even within areas of relatively high populations such as Talamanca and the Costa Rican highlands, the Indians of northern Honduras, northern Nicaragua, and Costa Rica were surrounded by fairly empty regions of rather similar environmental structure to which they could escape, if threatened, without great threats of their patterns of living.

Of even more importance to their post-conquest future, these less advanced tribes had not evolved to the level of societal complexity, hierarchical structure, or specialization of Mesoamerica. Their organization seems to have been basically tribal, with headmen and caciques leading bands or tribes of relative equals. While enslavement of enemies may well have existed, there is no evidence of the huge classes of slaves and macehuales which were tied to the Mesoamerican soils and performed the agricultural labor in the most advanced parts of that basically sedentary culture. There was, in short, no long history of subjection and servile agricultural labor in most of the non-Mesoamerican areas of Central America.[16]

North and west of the Mesoamerican frontier the advanced cultures which lay within Central America were mostly of Mayance and Nahua linguistic origins, and they shared many of the cultural and historical attributes which have been identified as typically, if not exclusively, Mesoamerican. Although Spanish friars of the sixteenth century were appalled at what they considered to be a wide linguistic diversity, nevertheless, compared to other regions of America the Central American Mesoamericans enjoyed a relative linguistic unity. Nahuat and Nahuatl were used as a lingua franca over wide areas.

Common features included extensive use of the coa or digging stick, the growing of achiote and cacao for chocolate and coinage, and great dependence on maize, beans, and squash. Of course many areas outside Mesoamerica also depended on this great trilogy, but nowhere was it as indispensable, worshipped, or even prepared for food in the manner which was prevalent in much of Mesoamerica.

In warfare Mesoamerica was unique in its use of obsidian-edged swords, cotton armor, and two-handled shields. In architecture it differed from its neighbors in its use of stepped pyramids for ceremonial and religious purposes, and in the construction of features such as stucco floors and ball courts with rings for the ceremonial ball game. Mesoamerica had also developed hieroglyphic writing, symbols for numbers, folded books probably of bark or skin, and historical annals and maps.

The Mesoamerican calendar was also unique. It contained an eighteen-month year of twenty-day months plus five additional days. Years were believed to proceed through fifty-two-year cycles. Fiestas occurred at the end of certain periods, there were good and bad luck days, and people were named according to their birthdays.

Certain forms of human sacrifice were also common, for example, burning people alive and dancing dressed in the flayed skins of victims. A series of gods was found in most parts of Mesoamerica, sometimes differing in name but recognizable as the same individuals. Tlaloc the rain god in his different manifestations was one, and the feathered serpent, variously known as Quetzalcóatl, Kukulcán, Gucumatz was another.

The area had a highly developed market mentality, with a specialized caste of merchants (who sometimes acted as spies), and specialized market places divided according to merchandise. There was also a specific military class divided into military orders with patron animals and birds. War itself was often waged for the express purpose of obtaining sacrificial victims. Cultural elements shared with other areas included terracing and irrigation of crops, the making of ceramics, the tearing out of the living human heart as a propitiatory sacrifice, and the sweat bath.[17]

Social structure was somewhat similar throughout Mesoamerica, varying in complexity according to the development of social cohesion, statehood, size, and other factors. The basis of social organization in most areas was the calpulli (Nahuatl) or chinamit (Quiché), originally, it is said, an extended family leading to an endogamous patrilineal clan, or perhaps only to a localized kin group of related families usually following the same occupation or working the same prescribed area of land. As society became more diverse and a complex class structure was gradually introduced, the calpulli-chinamit may have declined in importance as stratification occurred within the calpulli-chinamit itself and in the society at large.

Decline of the calpulli-chinamit is not, however, an inevitable consequence of growing social differentiation and complexity. Both may coexist and mutually adapt. In Central America there is evidence of various degrees of complexity in both the chinamit and in class structure. The Spanish invaders, who did not quite grasp the true nature of the chinamit and were confused by the subtleties of local sub-types, referred to it as a "barrio," "tribu," or "parentela."[18]

We have seen that same favored parts of the region now called Petén and British Honduras are capable of supporting surprising rural densities. Estimates vary, and should vary, because the area is far from uniform, but figures between 100 and 200 people per square mile seem generally accepted.[19] The crucial factor seems to be the care with which the slash and burn (or swidden) cycle is respected. About twelve hectares should be "resting" for each one or two hectares in cultivation. If this cycle is shortened either because of increased demands for agricultural surpluses from a dominant or trading elite, or because of overpopulation, then, if the technology remains the same, which it did and has, soil exhaustion, a food crisis, and population decline because of famine or emigration will take place.

Such a system with its ecologically prescribed population limits encourages scattered rural settlements, with ceremonial and trading centers in the more favored or strategic spots. True urbanism needs greater densities.

In cooler and more temperate areas, however, the slash and burn system can be considerably intensified, especially if lateritic tropical soils are not present. Barbecho or sectoral fallowing, basically a two-field or infield-outfield system with a two- or three-year usage cycle, occupied parts of the tierra fría and tierra templada of Central America. Yields from such areas were obviously much higher, in fact more than double that of tropical slash and burn. Obviously, too, the rural agricultural population would not have to be so mobile in its search for new lands. Nuclear settlements and rural densities can then be much greater in an area of fallowing.

If barbecho is practiced in good soils either in temperate climates or in wet and dry tropics—that is, the Pacific coast in the Central American context—then its already high agricultural and demographic possibilities can be enormously increased by irrigation.

In Central America irrigation seemingly never reached the great intensities and the intricacies of the chinampas, dykes, and canals of the central valley of Mexico. Yet irrigation was present and in fact essential in the cacao plantations. Often water was "bled" from a river or carried by primitive canals or containers to the fields. If carefully administered, the yields from irrigated fields of this kind can be two or three times as high as those produced by simple infield-outfield fallowing. Also, in tierra templada and especially tierra caliente, irrigation can assure two crops per year, one with irrigation, one during the rainy season. There is little need to rest the soil if it is treated with vegetable fertilizer, and a family of pre-conquest Mesoamericans could have supplied its needs with one hectare or less. The demographic possibilities are obvious. Rural densities are higher, agricultural mobility is less, and large-scale urbanism becomes likely. Finally, irrigation of this particular type, given the technology at the disposal of the Mesoamericans before the Spanish conquest, could only have been possible through the control and organization of large, servile, rural populations. And to these factors we must add what is now known about maize yields in Mesoamerica. Estimates vary, but it is obvious that the yield of maize per hectare far exceeded that of wheat in the European context at the same time. Moreover, Europeans used much of their available land for the raising of cattle and sheep, notoriously poor calorie producers given the agricultural area which they demand, while pre-conquest Mesoamericans did not raise domesticated animals which required extensive grazing and were able to devote much of their available land to the intensive growing of maize.[20] The demographic implications of these yields are important.

This general schema of land use accords well with what we know of settlement patterns in the Central American portion of Central America.[21] With respect to location we find that in formative and classical times ceremonial and trade centers, which with one possible exception may not have been true towns, occupied sites near or on stretches of arable land. In post-classical times the arable valleys held rural settlements with defensively located towns or castle-like centers, very like some European medieval fortress towns, located on high ground, often surrounded by ravines.

More specifically, settlement patterns in the rural areas varied from hamlets of about five to twenty houses oriented to local food supplies, through scattered dispersed villages of less than a hundred houses, to a ranchería system, and to large satellite or market garden villages which, besides growing their own food, also supplied it on a regional or "national" basis. This latter type was often located near a ceremonial center or defensive town.

Some of these large agricultural villages were also minor ceremonial centers in their own right. Many large villages were distributed around "concourse" ceremonial centers, monumental vacant towns to which the common people went on religious and market days. Finally, at least in the post-classic period, some villages supplied genuine towns such as Iximché or Mixco which were populated by administrators, soldiers, priests, and artisans. Rural densities may well have been close to what they are today in parts of Guatemala and El Salvador, and in spite of Spanish congregación and large movements of laboring populations, the above types of towns and patterns of settlement are close to those of today. The conquistadors add further support to our evidence of dense rural populations in Mesoamerican Central America. Everywhere they went they reported large, sometimes astonishingly large populations.[22]

Central American Mesoamerica was intermittently tied to an even greater and more powerful cultural, political, and economic center. The greatest focus of power in Mesoamerica was the central Mexican plateau, and the area which concerns us was heavily influenced by this region before the arrival of the Spaniards. The routes of influence and invasion followed favorable geography and soils. The Pacific coast and foothills which run from Tehuantepec through Soconusco, northern Guatemala, El Salvador, the Bay of Fonseca, and lacustrine Nicaragua were the major access routes,

drawing merchants and invaders to their rich soils, heavy populations, and valuable assets such as cacao and slaves.[23] Another route
went fairly directly from the central valley of Mexico to the trade
depot and center around the Laguna de Términos in the present
state of Tabasco. From there this route followed the settlement
centers of the Choloid-speaking Mayan Indians who occupied a
broad band of territory at the base of the Yucatan Peninsula. Crossing the Petén in this manner, the route terminated at the port-of-
trade enclave on the south coast of the Gulf of Honduras.[24]

These two major routes linked up in Guatemala. From the
south coast of Guatemala easy mountain passes allowed access to
the valleys and plateaus. Similarly, from the Gulf of Honduras rivers
such as the Motagua, Polochic, and Aguán provided routes to the
highlands. These major routes meant that areas such as part of
highland Chiapas, the Cuchumatanes, and western Verapaz tended
to be bypassed. They were emphatically Mesoamerican and Mayan
in culture and language, but in some areas at least they missed many
of the major military, political, and cultural intrusions from Mexico.[25] The same was probably true of some of the more isolated and
mountainous areas of Central Honduras and northern Nicaragua.

The causes of these intrusions are various and probably varied
according to the epoch. Military expansions may well have occurred
because of population pressure, consequent shortages, and unsettled conditions in Mexico. The growth of urban imperialism in the
central valley and elsewhere certainly was part of the story, especially when explaining the presence of Teotihuacán, Toltec, and
Aztec traits. A hunt for extra labor may also have been a feature. It
has been suggested that the northern Petén and Yucatan had little
to offer, apart from salt and feathers, to support the large trade
which these areas obviously enjoyed with Honduras and Mexico.
Either these areas traded some product of which we know nothing,
and this seems unlikely at least for the immediate pre-conquest
period, or they knew how to accomodate a massive and permanent
trade deficit, which is even more unlikely, or they exported skill and
labor, that is, men and perhaps slaves.[26]

One reason for these intrusions, which had been ignored until
recently, is the need for cacao. Both the fertile Pacific crescent,
running all the way down the coast from Colima to Nicoya, and the
relatively favored south coast of the Gulf of Honduras had dense
populations, large groups of traders, and extensive cacao plantations. In fact these areas, plus Tabasco and parts of Veracruz, may
have specialized in cacao to the extent of showing some of the signs

of a monoculture. This would have meant that these areas would have had to import quantities of foodstuffs, especially maize.[27]

Recent research has suggested that Olmec culture may have spread by creating and stimulating a need for cacao, and certainly the central cities of the Aztec empire many centuries later consumed massive quantities of this product. It was also in wide use as a coinage at the time of the conquest and possibly long before then. The petty proto-historical kingdoms of the Guatemalan highlands and boca costa squabbled constantly over control of the cacao-rich Pacific plain.[28] The Pacific coastal route and the route through the Petén to the Gulf of Honduras may, in fact, have been the age-old golden route of the cacao trade similar to the Amber Route of Bronze Age Europe.[29] The colonial period, as we shall see, was to show some amazing continuities in these patterns and routes.

Mexican intrusions in the Central American area and beyond left three principal kinds of manifestations. On both cacao coasts were to be found enclaves of Nahuatl-speaking traders. The town of Naco on the Gulf of Honduras and the famous province of Soconusco before it was actually seized by the Aztecs are the best known examples, but smaller enclaves were to be found as far to the southeast as Costa Rica.[30]

A second manifestation of Mexican cyclical presence was the existence of areas within Central America itself where the resident populations at the time of the conquest or before spoke Nahuatl or its variant Nahuat. The Pipiles of southeastern Guatemala and western El Salvador, and the Nicaraos of Nicaragua are the most significant examples.[31] This would indicate either the migration of large bodies of Nahuas, who drove out the original occupants of these regions, or that the cultural dominance of Nahuat-speaking elites in these areas was such that the original inhabitants gradually gave up their own languages in favor of that of the intruders.

These invasions were obviously of greater geographical significance and extent at the time of their occurrence than the relatively reduced areas occupied by such as the Pipiles and the Nicaraos at the time of the conquest would indicate. Kaminaljuyú, the great center near present day Guatemala City, now appears to have been not only heavily influenced by Mexican culture, but even to have been, during "classical times" at least, an actual settlement of invaders or immigrants from Teotihuacán itself. So also was Tikal at one time.[32] The Cotzumalhuapa culture which occupied much of the Pacific coast remains a puzzle in many ways, but it seems totally Mexican rather than merely Mexican in influence.[33] Finally, we now know that the Pipiles, for example, had once occupied a much larger area than the one in which the Spaniards found them; they may, in fact, have previously dominated much of the region occupied by Quichés, Cakchiquels, and Tzutuhils at the time of the conquest, but had been pushed back to the south and east by resurgent Cakchiquel power.[34]

The third manifestation of Mexican presence in Central American Mesoamerica was the most important in terms of numbers of people involved and historical significance. It was, in fact, so pervasive that some Mayan specialists find it difficult to think of the southern Mayan area, that is, the highlands and Pacific coast, as really Mayan at all.[35] This third type of influence can be called cultural and political, and obviously results from the conquest, or commercial and political dominance, of basically Mayan groups by smaller groups of militaristic Mexican invaders. Thus we find that while the highland Maya had absorbed their invading Toltec masters linguistically, yet as far as architecture, political organization, great traditions, and religion were concerned, the basically Mayan Quichés had been "Toltecized" and appear in retrospect to have been a distinct regional cultural variation, but extremely "Mexican."[36] It is noticeable that Mexican influence of this kind follows the two great routes and the connection between them in the Guatemalan highlands. Backwaters such as Chiapas and Verapaz remained relatively less Mexican.

The historical sequence in the southern Maya area—that is, the part of Mesoamerica which lies within our Central America—can be summarized as follows. The original speakers of the prototype Mayance may have arrived in Central America in the third millenium B.C. Early departures included northward moving groups which settled in Yucatan, in the Huasteca, in the Choloid area across the base of the Yucatan peninsula, and later in Chiapas (Tzeltal and its offshoot Tzotzil).

In the original Mayan homeland linguistic division continued. Mam, which was one of the earliest offshoots, spread to parts of the Pacific coast. Quiché, with its later variations Cakchiquel and Tzutuhil, dominated the Central Guatemalan mountains and the boca costa, and disputed the space with Nahuas and with lesser Mayan groups such as the Pokomam, the Ixil, and the Kekchi, who in post-conquest times have spread northward into the lowlands of the Gulf of Honduras. To the southeast on the Pacific coastal plains of El Salvador, the Bay of Fonseca, Nicaragua, and Nicoya, Nahua and a variant called Nicarao, and little known languages such as Lenca and Chorotega, were to be found.[37] As we have seen, all the above groups, Mayan and Nahua, were influenced to various degrees, and at different times, by the powerful Mexican central area to the northwest.

The chronological history of the region is a long one. After 1500 B.C. simple plot gardeners and hunters began to establish formal agricultural villages with increased densities of population. The Pacific coast may well have led this process.[38] Generally known as the Formative Period, this long span ended with the gradual rise and sudden collapse of the Olmec influence, spreading from its center on the Gulf Coast of Mexico into the Central American area.

The life style of the Formative Period yielded between 100 A.D. and 300 A.D. to various forms of the so-called Classic Period. Once again the Pacific Coast appears to have been the critical area for this gradual evolution. The Izapán culture of the late Formative Period which dominated much of the coast may well be a key transitional phase.[39]

Early Maya Classic culture in the highlands is by no means as celebrated as that of the Maya lowlands. In fact it may have been in some ways a regression, perhaps even a demographic regression from the splendors of the late formative periods on the coast and in Kaminaljuyú.[40] About A.D. 400 these subdued but growing highland areas began to feel the impact of the Mexican empire centered on the city of Teotihuacán in the lacustrine basin of central Mexico. Kaminaljuyú became a city of these invaders, ruling the surrounding Maya agriculturalists. As a result, while the life style of the Mayan peasantry probably remained the same, that of the rulers was decidedly Mexican. It is in fact during this Teotihuacán domination, often known as the Esperanza phase, that the southern area of the mountains and the Pacific coast which had led in the development of so many characteristics later to be thought of as Mayan ceased for good to be typically Mayan itself. In all but the isolated areas Mayan ways gave way to Mexican ones from then until the arrival of the Spaniards.

A common generalization about classical times in Mesoamerica has pictured it as a time of peace, relative plenty, and artistic expression, contrasting sharply with the militaristic, barbaric post-classic period. Some now feel that such a distinction, it it existed at all, is at best relative. Teotihuacán shows many signs of having been a warring imperial center, and the people of that city took their culture with them to Guatemala and Yucatan. Nevertheless, militaristic though it was, classic Teotihuacán may have brought relative peace, a sort of military pax romana, to parts of Mesoamerica.[41]

Classic Maya disintegrated in a time of troubles. In the lowlands of Yucatan and the Petén there are signs of considerable disruption and abandonment of traditional centers. In the already heavily populated Mexican highlands, new waves of invaders from the north disrupted the Teotihuacán and Mayan culture there. Various theories have been advanced to explain the fall of Classic civilization. Natural disasters such as earthquakes and floods, peasant revolts against theocratic oppression, soil exhaustion brought about by abuse of the slash and burn cycle, overpopulation, and pandemics have all been considered as possibilities.[42] The most likely solution of all seems to lie, once more, in the larger demographic center to the north in Mexico. The fall of Teotihuacán in the late sixth or early seventh century A.D. must have been an event of the greatest importance considering the vastness of the area which it dominated. As we have seen, a primary reason for this fall may have been a rapidly approaching population crisis, which, in an essentially agrarian community, would produce severe strains on the food supply, erosion because of abuse of the soil, regional quarrels over sources of food, and, eventually, emigrations of those able to travel in search of new sources of land and food. If such a theory of overpopulation is of any validity, then the Malthusian obverse may follow. After the population-technology crisis had been reached within the agricultural possibilities of the central Mexican region, then severe population decline might follow until eroded lands recovered, better lands became less crowded, in fact until man and land, given the agricultural technology of the times, were once more in technological balance. Another possibility is that population growth, rapid until the ecological crisis, would simply slow down, with "safety valve" emigrations in search of new lands, until new systems such as chinampas and new distribution patterns allowed more rapid growth.[43] Such general theories fit fairly well with what we know of the population history of Mesoamerica and also correspond to events in the Mayan areas of Central America. After the fall of Teotihuacán disruptive militarism and mass migrations swept central Mexico. The times of trouble spread outward and eventually reached the Petén, the Guatemalan highlands, and the Pacific coast in the form of hordes of marauding Toltec warriors emigrating from the collapsed militarism of Tula. As the population crisis arrived in central Mexico and possibly even in the Petén and Guatemala, a severe but temporary population decline caused first invasions and then abandonment of agriculturally peripheral areas, many ceremonial centers, and as a result some relocation of population.[44]

Whether this type of causal explanation is adequate or not, the post-classic and protohistoric history of Mesoamerican Central America can legitimately be seen as a slow rebuilding of a Toltec-dominated society on the shores of the Gulf of Honduras, in the highlands of Chiapas and Guatemala, and down the Pacific coast as far as Nicaragua and Nicoya. The Toltec invaders, having destroyed the hegemony of Teotihuacán, erected their own capital of Tulán in its place, and then destroyed it in renewed warfare; they penetrated Central America; and after years of strife they emerged as the elite classes in various principalities throughout the region. These principalities remained basically Mayan in language, but Toltec-Mexican in the culture of the elites; and by the end of the eleventh century A.D., a new political situation had become stabilized.

For a short while the Quiché rulers of the central highlands managed to establish a fairly large kingdom. It must have controlled much of the Pacific cacao coast, but as populations grew once again the Cakchiquels and the Tzutuhils broke away and achieved their own independence.[45]

In perpetual strife when the Spaniards invaded, it seemed that these disunited kingdoms were about to succumb once more to a new Mexican power from the north. When Cortés arrived the Aztecs had already seized Soconusco and had sent traders (pochteca) and emissaries to the Guatemalan courts. Central America, lying athwart the routes of expansion to the south, was in the path of the new Teotihuacán, Tenochtitlán, or since Tenochtitlán and its population were fast approaching another apex and crisis logistically and demographically, Central America would perhaps have been spared until a new race of Toltecs had exploded from the warring ruins of the Aztec confederation. Whether it would have been Aztecs or people from the ruins of the Aztec empire we shall never know, because the Spaniards interrupted and deformed these long cyclical processes forever.[46]

Central America was the scene of the first European contact with the great high cultures of the Americas. Christopher Columbus on his fourth voyage seems to have been the first European to see the shores of the area. His ships having raised the Gulf of Honduras in 1502, he and his crew saw Guanaja, one of the Bay Islands, and seized a large canoe full of people and produce which was headed for Honduras. Columbus and his men were pleased to see obvious signs of an advanced civilization and of a developed trade in cotton, cacao, and other goods. At last it seemed that they had found the rich mainland civilizations which had been the purpose of the four voyages. If Columbus had turned west or northwest he would doubtless have found much more evidence of dense populations and high cultures in Mayan Yucatan, but inexplicably he turned east to Cape Gracias a Dios, and then down the tropical Mosquito coast. The few Indians which he saw during this trajectory were as primitive as any in the islands, and with the exception of a brief stay in Costa Rica, where the more advanced people he saw may have been an outpost of Nahuat traders, Columbus missed Mesoamerica and probably never knew of its existence.[47]

After the departure of the great discoverer, Central America was largely bypassed for two decades. There is some evidence of slave raids being made in the Bay Islands and possibly even on the mainland of the Bay of Honduras between 1510 and 1520, as Spaniards from Cuba and the other islands searched for ways of filling the demographic vacuum which had been created by the death of most of the aboriginal population.[48] Diego de Nicuesa, moving from Darien up the Caribbean coast in search of Veragua, sighted the Mosquito coast, where he became lost and confused. Pedrarias too sent probing expeditions along the Pacific coast to Nicoya and Nicaragua.[49] With these minor exceptions, however, it would seem that for a while at least, the attention of the first conquistadors had moved elsewhere. Mexico and Darien were the great targets.

The Spanish invasions of Central America, when they finally began, came from these two staging areas, the origins of so many of the conquests. It is significant that these two waves entered Central America in much the same way as invaders and merchants from South America and Central Mexico had done for centuries, using the same routes of penetration up the Pacific coast of Costa Rica and Nicaragua, down the Pacific coast of Soconusco and Guatemala, with a doubling back through the highlands, and across the Choloid area at the base of the Yucatan Peninsula towards the Gulf of Honduras. The invading Spaniards accompanied by their Indian auxiliaries and porters had well-known, established routes to follow.

Central Americans of the early 1520s were singularly unprepared to face the newcomers and the result was widespread devastation, disruption, and mortality. As in Michoacán, and no doubt elsewhere, the Spaniards unbeknownst to them were preceded by their terrible allies, the European epidemics, smallpox, pneumonic plague, and typhus.

Moctezuma's awe and dread of the army of Cortés is well-

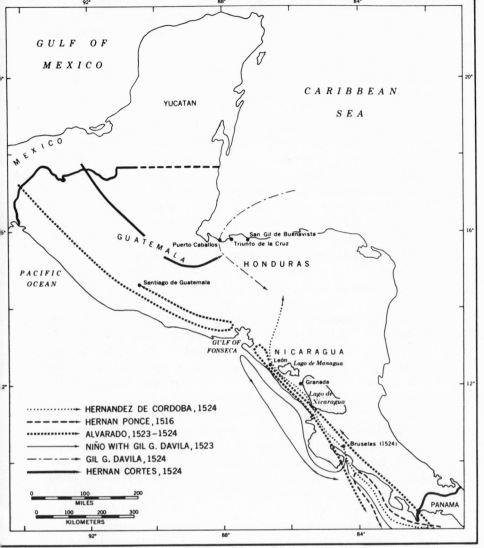

Figure 1 Early Spanish Entradas to Central America

known, but it does not seem to have prevented all initiative on his part. In spite of previous enmities, quarrels over pochteca spies, the recent seizure of the cacao country of Soconusco, and the counterattacks of Cakchiquels and Quichés, there is evidence that Moctezuma tried desperately to persuade his smaller neighbors to the west (Michoacán) and to the east and south (the Cakchiquels, Tzutuhils, and Quichés of Pacific Guatemala) to bury past hostilities and to unite in a common fight for survival against the strange and terrifying new invaders.[50] At any event emissaries were sent with this purpose. In Michoacán these envoys were met with justifiable suspicion and Tenochtitlán had fallen before the ruler of Michoacán had realized that this was not just another Mexican ruse.[51] In Guatemala the evidence is more contradictory. The Mexican envoys seem to have received little response from the Cakchiquels, who then, in their turn, sent representatives to Cortés, hoping no doubt that he and his men would aid them against their traditional enemies the Quichés, Tzutuhils, and Pipiles as Alvarado later did. The Quichés and Tzutuhils also seem to have ignored or rejected the desperate Moctezuma, but knowledge of their attitude towards Cortés has been clouded by conflicting accounts. Cortés, reporting to Charles V, alleges that the Quichés, like their enemies the Cakchiquels, at first sent friendly ambassadors to him and talked of peace, but later betrayed his trust by attacking Aztec outlying areas such as Soconusco. Guatemalan Spanish and Indian accounts, on the other hand, talk of steady Quiché hostility to the invading Spaniards.[52]

Subsequent events seem to support the Indian version. Pedro de Alvarado and his band, advancing down the Pacific coast in 1524, met fierce resistance from the Quichés and the Tzutuhils, but seem to have been welcomed, at least initially, by the Cakchiquels, who willingly supplied soldiers and supplies for Spanish expeditions against the Tzutuhils and the Pipiles.[53]

At any event, the importance of these different attitudes toward the Spaniards and toward each other among the Indian kingdoms of Guatemala was to become greater during and after the first Spanish entrada under Alvarado, whereas the ambassadors from Moctezuma, or some other individuals passing back and forth at about the same time, before the Spanish invasion of Guatemala had begun, brought plague and smallpox to a population in which these diseases had not existed before, and which consequently had no physiological immunities to them. These plagues were in fact the shock troops of the conquest, weakening resistance and reducing numbers.

Indian accounts of these first epidemics in Michoacán and Guatemala are quite explicit. Such diseases had not been known in the region before; the death rate was catastrophic, and demoralization and illness were so widespread that the piles of dead were left untended and unburied for the vultures. Native sources in Yucatan, where a similar epidemic struck, called this time of sickness "oc-na-kuch-il" which is to say "when the zopilotes come into the houses," that is, when the dead lie about everywhere untended. Normal hierarchical and governmental patterns were disrupted, and in Guatemala at least, just as in the fourteenth-century Florence of

Boccacio and the seventeenth-century London of Daniel Defoe, people who could abandoned the towns and fled to the countryside, where many died of hunger or other diseases.[54] Given present day knowledge of the impact of smallpox or plague on people without previous immunities, it is safe, indeed conservative, to say that a third of the Guatemalan highland populations died during this holocaust. Knowledge of past epidemics in Europe and of the aftermath of smallpox and plague can also lead us to assert that those who survived were left at least for a year or so in a weakened condition, with greatly lowered resistance to the minor ills, colds, bronchitis, pneumonia, and influenza which carry off so many invalids. It was then in large part the sickly survivors of a disaster whom Alvarado and his men encountered on the Pacific coast of Central America.[55]

The conquest of the Mesoamerican part of Central America was itself an unusually destructive and protracted process, especially when compared to that of Mexico. This arose from a series of unique conjunctions of circumstances, all of which combined to prevent a quick resolution.

The politically divided nature of the area has already been noted. There was no unifying tributary confederation to compare with that of Central Mexico, where central power had the effect of polarizing the conflict into two sides, those who supported the Aztecs and those who disliked them sufficiently to become steady and reliable allies of the Spaniards. When Cortés destroyed Tenochtitlán, terrible though that siege was, the conquest of Central Mexico was all but over, and the establishment of Spanish government could begin. Circumstances in Central America, unfortunately for both sides, were not such that decisive engagements of that nature were possible. The Quiché empire had long ago dissolved into three or four smaller, mutually hostile kingdoms of approximately equal power, and even when the Quichés had been at the peak of their influence they had controlled only a small part of Mesoamerican Central America. For Alvarado to conquer the Quichés, Cakchiquels, and Tzutuhils was only a beginning. There still remained the Tzendals and Tzotzils of Chiapas; the Mam, Pokomam, Ixil, and Kekchis of Guatemala; and the Pipiles and Lencas of the Pacific coast and El Salvador, not to speak of the many petty kingdoms and tribal units in Honduras, on the Pacific coast of Guatemala, and elsewhere.

Similarly, those advancing up from Darien found no unified structure in Nicaragua. This area too had to be conquered piecemeal. Thus the conquest of the area can be said to have lasted

almost two decades, with all that implies in the way of recurrent
battles, sieges, movements of already conquered populations as
soldiers and bearers, and failure to establish a coherent Spanish
system of social control.[56]

The nature of the Spanish conquest worsened these tendencies. Again the conquest of Mexico is a relevant contrast. With the
possible exception of the Narváez expedition, which was quickly
absorbed by Cortés, the seizure of this area was done by one expedition with a recognizable coherent leadership. Central America, on
the other hand, was attacked from two bases, and by an extended
series of mutually suspicious conquistador bands. Cortés dispatched
Pedro de Alvarado to conquer Pacific Guatemala, and he in turn
delegated lieutenants and brothers to the conquest of areas such as
Chiapas and the Ixil country.[57] The Gulf of Honduras was entrusted
originally to another of Cortés' subordinates, Cristóbal de Olid, but
as the internecine squabbling there increased, Cortés himself invaded the area by crossing overland through Tabasco and southern
Yucatan. After his departure the area fell to Francisco de Montejo,
who disputed possession with Alvarado himself for several years.[58]
From Panama an even longer series of conquistador bands went
out, all emphasizing the priorities of their claims to Central America. The area eventually fell under the control of the ambitious
Pedrarias Dávila.[59] The two groups of conquistador bands, one
from Mexico and the other from Darien, met along a line running
from the Bay of Fonseca, through the highlands of Honduras, to the
Gulf of Honduras near Trujillo. As a consequence, a series of disputed territories (El Salvador east of the Río Lenca, Fonsecan Honduras, and the eastern end of the south coast of the Gulf of
Honduras) came into being along this frontier. The result was more
controversy, more expeditions to be raised and Indians taken away
from home, more campaigns, and a further blurring of the lines of
uncoordinated Spanish leadership.[60]

Circumstances surrounding some of the Spanish conquests further extended the era of warfare and conquest and postponed the
coming of formal Spanish government. Some areas such as Chiapas
and southern Verapaz were conquered by Spanish bands and then
abandoned when more attractive possibilities seemed to lie elsewhere. Regions of this kind then had to be reconquered, either by
punitive expeditions, as in the case of Chiapas, or by the much
mythologized pacific conquest of Verapaz by the Dominicans.[61] The
most extreme example of this kind of partial or recurrent conquest
is highland Costa Rica, which was bypassed when the men of Darien

pushed into more attractive Nicaragua and Nicoya, and where because of the obduracy of the local Indians and the sporadic and halfhearted interest of nearby Spaniards, several ill-equipped and poorly supported entradas were necessary before the area passed effectively under Spanish control in the 1570s.[62] The tardy occupation of the Tegucigalpa region in highlands Honduras may be another example.

A somewhat similar feature was the inability of the Spaniards in Central America to hold the allegiance of their original allies. Cortés found that the Tlaxcalans, once they had submitted, could be relied upon for aid both in good times and bad. Alvarado took some of them to Guatemala and found them to be loyal allies. Either because the Cakchiquels were more recalcitrant than Cortés' Mexican allies, or more probably because the Spaniards of Central America appreciated them less and abused them more, this initially friendly nation rose in revolt. If we are to believe the Cakchiquel account of its suppression, this too was a protracted, bloody, and destructive episode.[63] Similar revolts of originally friendly Indian groups occurred in Honduras, El Salvador, and in northwestern Nicaragua before the era of conquest was over.[64] Many accounts of the Central American conquest emphasize the unusually high mortality associated with it, in the first battles, in the transportation and uprooting of Indian auxiliaries, and in these revolts.[65]

In this long and destructive conquest the personalities and aspirations of the Spanish leaders involved must be taken into account. With the possible exception of Francisco de Montejo, most of the leading conquerors seem to have had no great interest in Central America from the point of view of development or administration. Several of them showed anarchistic tendencies. The most extreme example was the Contreras brothers who murdered Bishop Valdivieso of Nicaragua and revolted against the Crown, feeling that they had not been sufficiently rewarded after the death of their patron Pedrarias Dávila. Pedro de Alvarado seems to have been essentially ambivalent about his new government. At times he spent time and great effort in his attempts to build a personal fortune there, but equally often his restlessness led him to abandon it for fresher pastures, or to plan large expeditions with the express purpose of abandoning them. Nor did he find it hard to recruit like-minded followers. His expedition to Ecuador was staffed largely by Spaniards from Central America and his projected expedition to the Spice Islands brought many volunteers.[66] In fact there was a steady stream of complaints from clerics and administrators during these early days that Spaniards would not stay in Central America, were in fact using it as a way station between Mexico and Peru, and other parts, and that if these emigrations continued the area was in danger of being abandoned. Bernal Díaz del Castillo, the old chronicler, settled down to enjoy the fruits of his encomienda, but most of his fellow soldiers do not seem to have stayed behind with him.[67]

Early leaders such as Alvarado and Pedrarias, besides being preoccupied with building personal fortunes, had singularly little interest in building and running a new society. It is safe to say that even in the key areas of Central America conquest did not finish and systematic government did not properly begin until some twenty years after the first entradas. Religious instruction among the Cakchiquels, one of the first groups conquered and a population residing close by the main Spanish settlement, did not start until 1542.[68]

Part of this delay may have been caused by the nature of their new lands—Central America was certainly no Mexico or Peru—and part of it may have been caused by the characters of the men themselves. At any event, Central America was not conquered by men with the imperial imagination of Hernán Cortés, and the conquest was a difficult, destructive, bloody, and piecemeal task, involving more effort and fewer rewards than the conquests of Mexico and Peru. In fact many parts of Central America, particularly those of the less favored and more sparsely settled Caribbean side, were not conquered at all in the sixteenth century. Some remain unexplored to this day.[69]

By about 1540 ecology, aboriginal history, and the Spanish conquest had helped to stamp certain basic characteristics on colonial Central America. Central America was and is divided between a "backward" Caribbean zone and a relatively advanced zone on the Pacific and in the highlands. Obviously the advanced area was one which would draw conquerors, be they Mexican or Spanish, in search of exploitable populations and resources. Demographically and culturally, Central America was then a Pacific province, yet its conquerors would be Europeans, whose preferred economic ties would be with Europe.

As a cultural area Central America had been influenced by its neighbors. The poorer Caribbean zone had been occupied from South America with populations reaching high densities in more favored spots, but nowhere apparently reaching the size of complexity of the Pacific, Mesoamerican part. This zone had been historically an adjunct of the empires of Central Mexico. Some empires had physically occupied the area, others may simply have influenced it through trade or culture.

Pacific and Mesoamerican Central America had seen long human occupancy, and large rural populations. There is evidence that these technologically poor, but labor and soil sufficient populations had been subject to Malthusian pressures for centuries. Further research may prove that the cyclical nature of Central America's populations was a local phenomenon, not applicable to the entire area, but all evidence is that much of the coast and mountains between Soconusco and Nicoya were heavily peopled when Cortés first landed at Veracruz and that these stratified societies contained large classes of servile agricultural laborers.

Various types of clans formed the basis for Indian social structure in the advanced parts of Central America. In the more elaborate societies a complex social and class structure had been imposed upon the original clan system. The Spaniards could understand hierarchy, or at least its salient and useful features, but they never fully grasped the intricacies of the calpulli-chinamit clan structure.

The petty states which ruled much of Central American Mesoamerica underwent a particularly long and bloody Spanish conquest. Preceded by a great epidemic, the uncoordinated, mutually suspicious Spanish conquerors found the region hard to subdue, and not as rewarding as Mexico once it had been seized. The native peoples there underwent a drastic shock, and large numbers of them died in the epidemics, famines, battles, forced migrations, and dislocations of these early years. Colonial Central America was faced with some difficult demographic and economic patterns and problems from its beginnings as a colony. The attempts of the new conquerors to find solutions to these difficulties, and the efforts of the declining Indian populations to adapt to the pressures imposed upon them while preserving some remnants of their cultural identity, are a large part of the history of the next two centuries.

2

Slaves and Silver: The First Exports

One of the main concerns of Spanish colonizers in the New World, as we shall see, was to find and control large agricultural populations. An equally persistent trait in the sixteenth and seventeenth centuries was the compulsion to seek a raw material or natural product which, because of great demand elsewhere, would rapidly produce considerable wealth if exported to needy areas. Spaniards also found it eminently reasonable to assume that rapid accumulation of wealth could best be accomplished by finding a substance which did not need elaboration or lengthy processing. They therefore concentrated on basic vegetable and mineral products which could be rapidly extracted or packed by servile labor and then shipped out to the consumers. Life was comparatively short in the sixteenth and seventeenth centuries, and the conquistador who wished to become a feudal lord, or even to return to Spain to purchase mayorazgos and a place at court could not afford the time, or the capital for that matter, needed to set up intricate machinery. Nor did he wish to wait for elaborated products to emerge from manufacture. Drying in the sun, boiling, or steeping in vats was as far as any Spanish developer wished to go, and even these processes were to be avoided if possible.

The one exception was precious metals. The conquistadors and their successors saw with great clarity that gold and silver were the desired products, the wealth producers of the day par excellence. Mercantilist Europe was chronically short of these precious metals and considered the possession of them to be the touchstone of success for individuals or nations, In such circumstances Spanish invaders were willing, albeit impatiently, to sink primitive mines to reach the ores and to build equally primitive smelters to extract the metals from the ores.

In short, a good understanding of European demands and priorities led the first Spanish colonizers to concentrate on the much desired precious metals whenever they were available. Given this eager European market and the fact that the New World was a turbulent place of newly subdued Indians, it is small wonder that Spaniards had few thoughts of long-range economic development. Moreover, most of the invading Spaniards probably intended their New World stay to be temporary. Their concern in these early years was to accumulate booty or wealth as rapidly as possible so that they could return to wealth and prestige in Spain. Thus the conquest of Central America and the two decades after it bear more resemblance to a large raid than to an occupation.

Another result of this early, perfectly logical singlemindedness, this urge for rapid accumulation of wealth, was monoculture. Once sixteenth- and seventeenth-century Spaniards found a sure source of rapid wealth, there was a definite tendency to abandon or at least neglect other economic activities in favor of the new dynamic industry. This concentration on one product was not absolute, of course. Some industries and crops survived in various stages of health and decay throughout the colonial period. Others disappeared and then revived when the enthusiasm for another product had passed. Both comparatively and absolutely, however, there is a marked tendency in Central American colonial history towards monoculture—the logical result of a determined drive by the dominant class to obtain rapid wealth from unprocessed natural resources.

Thus the economic history of Central America in the two centuries following the Spanish conquest can be described as a constant search for a single key to wealth, for a "produit moteur" as one scholar has described it, which would provide rapid tangible wealth for large numbers of individuals of the invading groups.

Inevitably raw materials become scarce or exhausted. Then too, labor supplies may dry up—and they did indeed in Central America—centers of demand for a given product may fall away, or rival areas of production may appear. Moreover, with transportation only via small sailing ships, many promising products were automatically excluded because their profit margins when allied to their relative bulk or perishability were too small to pay the freight at such long distance.

Consequently, another feature of economic life in colonial Central America was a series of cyclical "booms" and depressions. (The expression "boom" is not of course intended to mean here a period of general prosperity for all. Only some of the elite would noticeably benefit from such times.) This tendency was further exacerbated by the very nature of the raw materials involved, simple agricultural crops and two minerals, and by the primitive, wasteful technologies employed by the people of the time. Agricultural husbandry would have seemed an irrelevant preoccupation to most sixteenth-century Spanish colonizers, and rightly so in their terms, for the supply of land and of labor, at least at first, seemed limitless. Why then conserve soil, plantations, or indeed, in the early days, the plentiful labor force?

The picture which emerges of Central American economic life during the sixteenth and seventeenth centuries is one of two great systems. Much of the countryside was filled with cattle and sheep and with Indian and Spanish staples such as maize, beans, and wheat. Largely for home consumption and prestige, or for local trade, this agricultural complex was primarily a phenomenon of the highlands, although cattle swarmed everywhere. The Central America of cattle and cereals had its eras of great expansion, prosperity, and decline, but the primary function of this agricultural system was a limited one—the feeding of local populations and the maintenance of the existing class structure. As a result, the declines in this economy were felt mainly by the poorer and less powerful sections of the populace, and had a correspondingly secondary impact on the immediate economic life of the masters of colonial Central America. The system of cattle and cereals was in effect a background economy, a continuing, relatively unobserved support to the other and more brilliant colonial economy of foreign trade, shipping, and quick wealth.

The other great system was the one of the "produits moteurs," the golden keys to wealth, which rose and fell for the first three centuries after the Spanish conquest. Except for the early days of silver and gold production, these products were agricultural and were mostly grown in the Central American "fertile crescent" which runs east and south along the Pacific coast from the isthmus of Tehuantepec to the plains of Guanacaste and Nicoya. Consisting of volcanic soils which were originally of high fertility, this strip was to undergo intensive cultivation in some areas and much of its soil and its peoples suffered damage as a consequence.

It is within this second great economic system, at once more dynamic and more fragile than the background one of extensive farming, that the great "booms" occurred which made fortunes for Central Americans or cast them into despondency. The patterns repeated themselves several times. A product would be discovered, would develop with an amazing rapidity given the technologies of the time (Spaniards could be the most singleminded of men), would enjoy a period of great prosperity in which it was squeezed for every last pound of production and profit, and would then go into profound decline or stagnation.

The disappearance of the boom would then set off a frantic but determined hunt for another dynamic export crop. These periods of depression often saw a fragmentation of the Central American area as different regions which were no longer able to look to the great money-earning product which had united Central America economically each sought new solutions in the most regionally appropriate directions. As a consequence it was normal to find minor booms in one or more small areas of the Audiencia of Guatemala during these depressions, while the rest of the area remained depressed in the aftermath of the last major boom. These minor booms occurred because some small sub-region had found a crop of sufficient dynamism to rescue it temporarily from the general depression, but not sufficiently profitable or in demand to rescue the area as a whole. Such secondary regional solutions rarely lasted for long. Concluding the cycle would be the rise of a new product which was sufficiently organized or commanded enough of an outside market to reunite economically much of the area under the Audiencia, even if only briefly and unequally.

This cyclical pattern was affected by dozens of outside variables. Population loss and soil erosion cut short some booms; lack of outside markets prevented some crops from becoming as profitable as was first hoped. Tastes, fashions, and fads kept some trades from disappearing entirely, and competition from other areas prevented Central Americans from asking high prices and quick profits for others. But the general pattern, even with these distortions, is quite clearly discernible.

The conquering Spaniards entered the areas later to be known as the Audiencia of Guatemala from the two staging areas of Mexico and Panama, the thrusts of the conquest meeting at the bay of Fonseca and in the mountains of southern Honduras.

Immediately the search for a key to riches began. The conquistadors were pleased to find that the two features characteristic of the Mexican area were present to a somewhat reduced degree in many parts of the new region. There were clusters of dense native populations, and the streams were gold-bearing and produced quick profits when subjected simply to panning and gold washing.

Outside factors presented the new conquerors with unique and obvious ways of utilizing the teeming Indian populations. The isth-

mus of Panama and the larger Caribbean islands had suffered drastic losses in population, and the young Spanish communities in
these areas had been totally deprived of the essential laboring force
required for all their activities. To a lesser degree the recent discovery of Peru and the still unfinished wars there presented another
opportunity. The Spanish expeditions there needed large numbers
of porters, servants, and auxiliary warriors until the area was subdued. (Then of course, the native Peruvian populations could be
utilized in these and other tasks.)

The conquistadors of Central America, especially those who
went to Nicaragua, were quick to seize these clear opportunities.
The exporting of slaves began almost immediately via the Pacific
coast of Nicaragua to Panama and Peru and from the north coast
ports of the Bay of Honduras to the major islands of the Caribbean.
All areas of Central America, except unconquered Costa Rica and
distant landlocked Chiapas, were affected in varying degrees by this
trade.

Raiding for slaves on the coasts of Yucatan, among the Bay
Islands, and on the northern coast of Honduras itself had begun
some time before the area was conquered, perhaps as early as 1515.
Indian captives were taken to Velázquez's Cuba and enslaved there.
To judge by some reports these early victims did not make satisfactory workers, and some showed a considerable spirit of resistance.
One group from the Bay Islands seized a ship in Cuba and sailed
it back to their homeland.[1] Satisfactory or not, these inhabitants of
Yucatan and northern Honduras continued to be exported as slaves
after the conquest. Hernando Cortés, during his epic and troubled
expedition to Honduras, claimed to be shocked at this trade and
asked the king to require that all such slaves be returned to their
place of origin.[2]

Such pleas had little effect at this stage. While the export of the
slaves was not comparable to that of the Pacific coast, it continued
in fairly steady fashion for many years after the departure of Cortés.
Officialdom was in no position to stop this no doubt lucrative slave
trade because some of the conquistadors, adelantados, and appointed royal officials were those directly involved.[3]

The trade of Indians to the nearby Caribbean never approached the dimensions of this trade in the Pacific. One writer has
pointed to a basic difference in the nature of the conquistadors and
conquests of Mexico and Panama. Mexico soon arrived at a seig-
noral society of feudal lords, intensive mining, and Indians in encomienda. This stage never really arrived in Panama, where hunting

for booty, pearls, and slaves were of prime importance and were then replaced as basic economic activity by the profits made from the transisthmian cargo route to Peru. These early prizes were seized by roving bands of soldiers and exported to the older settlements on the islands of the Caribbean. Hunting and slaving of Indians lasted longer in Panama then elsewhere on the mainland.[4]

Panama became of ever-increasing importance after the discovery of the rich empire of the Incas. Most persons and goods to and from the new discovery passed across its isthmus. The problem was how to staff these routes. The aboriginal inhabitants of Panama had rapidly disappeared, and the lack of a laboring force threatened the small Spanish settlements with starvation, or at the very least with economic paralysis. Negro slaves were brought in as often as they could be purchased, but this expedient hardly began to solve the manpower problem in the early years.[5] Peru itself also had manpower needs in the early years of conquest and campaigning.

In both cases the Central American area was the most convenient center of large Indian populations, and within Central America itself lacustrine Nicaragua was the closest nucleus. Thus it became the main center of the slave trade in Indians.

The sending of Indian slaves from Nicaragua to Panama started almost at once after the conquest. Nor did the early conquerors feel that there had to be anything furtive about such a trade. Pedrarias Dávila obliged the king by giving him a detailed description of the process—and this as early as 1529. He declared that he had been the first to realize that it was against the royal laws, and had therefore banned such exports of Indian slaves to Panama.[6]

Instead of stopping the trade, Pedrarias was soon involved in the lucrative business himself. Indeed, given what we know of the man, his organizational ability and exclusivist temperament, he probably took over the more profitable parts of the business himself. All pretence of sending only branded, legitimately enslaved Indians had been abandoned by the time Pedrarias began to participate. On April 8, 1529, the alguacil mayor, Alonso Gil, accused two Spaniards, one of them a royal official, of sending great numbers of free, unbranded Indians to Panama as slaves. Many witnesses agreed.[7]

Pedrarias' death in 1531 changed nothing. In fact it is safe to say that in the decade of the thirties slaving was the basic industry of Nicaragua. Indians were simply rounded up as they were found and marched down to the Pacific coast, either to Realejo or to the Gulf of Nicoya. There they were herded onto small ships and taken to the markets in Panama and Peru. Little attempt was made to select only those Indians who had been captured in war, as the royal regulations demanded. Francisco Castañeda and the notorious Rodrigo de Contreras, the two governors who succeeded Pedrarias, were even more interested in the industry than he had been because by their time it had grown even larger. Other famous names were involved; Fernando Ponce de León and Hernando de Soto, for example, both owned and operated slave ships.[8]

The numbers of Indians involved between about 1528 and the late 1540s, when the trade died out, is hard to estimate, but the total must have been large. Between 1536 and 1540, when the Indian exports were at their greatest, there were more than twenty ships sailing regularly between Realejo, Nicoya, Panama, and Peru, perhaps as often as six times a year for each ship going to Panama and once or twice a year to Peru. Even the crews on these ships were mostly made up of Indian slaves. The number of Indians in the cargoes varied according to supply and the size of the ships, but numbers as high as four hundred slaves on one ship are mentioned as being frequent. Ten thousand slaves per year for the decade between 1532 and 1542 would certainly seem to be a low figure, and a total of two hundred thousand Indians for the whole Nicaraguan slaving period appears to be conservative. As early as 1535 it was being reported to the Crown that one third of the aboriginal population of Nicaragua had been enslaved and disposed of in this fashion.[9]

Nicaragua was not the only Pacific area involved in this large undertaking. As demand continued in Peru and Panama the depleted Nicaraguan area was increasingly unable to meet it. As a result areas of dense population further up the coast were brought into the trade in the 1540s or perhaps even earlier. As far as is known the export of Indians from provinces such as San Salvador and Guazacapán never equalled that of Nicaragua in the 1530s, but it was large enough to shock that stern reformer Licenciado Alfonso López Cerrato when he arrived in Guatemala in 1548.[10]

The slaving industry in Nicaragua and Guatemala was a wasteful process. Many Indians were killed resisting enslavement, particularly when the slaving entradas reached previously unconquered areas. To compound the demographic damage the Spanish slavers naturally preferred able-bodied adults, so that family units were broken up, with unhappy results for the young and the aged left behind to tend the milpas.

Figure 2

Population of Nicaragua, Indian Tributaries

Year	No. of Tributaries	Source	Comments
c. 1520	600,000	CDII, XXIV, pp. 389-90.	A rough figure, very much exaggerated, but indicative of very great numbers. See also Fernández de Oviedo's baptismal figures, in XI, pp. 103, 105, 166, 171. See also Las Casas' figures for slave exports between 1525 and 1533 in MacNutt, "The Brevíssima Relación," pp. 340-41.
1544	30,000	CDII, XXIV, pp. 389-90.	In 1533 a count made of the Dominican parishes showed over 7,000 tributaries (AGI/AG 8, Fray Thomas de la Torre to Consejo, May 22, 1553). The Dominicans were not the dominant religious order in Nicaragua, and instructed only a small part of that province's Indians.
1548	11,137	AGI/AG 128	This count, the first great count in Central America, seems to be almost complete for Nicaragua, but it omitted a few villages. The total number of Indians is then slightly too low. See also AGI/AG 50, Alonso de Arteaga to Crown, May 15, 1555, f. 2, which talks of a great decline in the last decade (1545-55).
c. 1560	6,050	AGI/AG 167, "Lista del Obispado de Nicaragua" (no date).	This count took place the year after the reservados (all those such as choristers and sacristans who had previously not paid tribute) were deprived of their exemptions and placed on the tribute rolls.
c. 1570	6,000-6,500	López de Velasco, pp. 314-6.	Probably based, at least in part, on the tribute count mentioned above in AGI/AG 167.
1663	5,100	AGI/AG 40, "No. 2." León, Jan. 2, 1676.	In 1612 a complete count of all the population of Nicaragua gave a figure of 28,490 people. The Indian tributary population of that time would seem to have been just below 6,000. Cf. Boletín del Archivo General de Gobierno (Guatemala), V, no. 1 (Oct. 1939), p. 11.
1674-76	4,540	AGI/AG 40, "No. 2." León, Jan. 2, 1676.	The writer compares each partido in the count of 1663 and the ones of 1674-76. The average drop in population for that period is 10.98 percent.
1685	4,716	AGI/AG 29 Antonio Navia Bolaños to Crown, July 28, 1685.	A very complete count. It includes Indian villages which have just been "reduced" and settled. These villages are not yet paying tribute, but are counted as tributaries against the day when they will begin to pay.

The death rate on the Nicaraguan slave ships was appalling. Undoubtedly those who were against the trade exaggerated to improve their arguments, but even if only part of their claims were true few indeed of those sent off arrived in Panama, and only a fraction survived the long and difficult journey to Peru. The queen was informed that commonly only four in twenty survived the crowded conditions. This is probably an exaggeration, but one ship with four hundred Indians was reported to have unloaded less than fifty survivors, an even lower percentage.[11]

Leaving aside the demographic impact and judging the trade even on its own terms, it was wasteful. "Overheads" in foodstuffs, ships, and maintenance must have been high. The Indians had to be fed during their weeks or months at sea, and the toll on wooden ships was severe in these waters. The high death rate during the hunting down of slaves, and between assembly of the Indians for shipment and their delivery in Panama and Peru, meant that neither the expectations of the slavers nor those of the purchasers were fulfilled. Those who rounded up the Indians received a much lower profit than they had hoped, and the vecinos or citizen freeholders of Panama did not receive the numbers of Indians which they needed to replace the original inhabitants. The murderous trajín or cargo route between Nombre de Dios and Panama quickly reduced the numbers of those who survived the voyage, and only a growing population of Negroes and the expansion in the numbers of draught animals allowed the isthmus route to stay open after 1545.[12] Some rough idea of the proportionate share played by Nicaragua and other areas of Central America in the attempted restocking of the Panamanian isthmus with imported Indians can be gained from the totals of slaves released there when Indian slavery was brought to an end in 1550. Nearly all of the Indian slaves had technically been freed and transferred to other statuses before that date, but of the eight hundred and twenty one surviving slaves involved, some one hundred and seventy five were from Panama or nearby in Tierra Firme, and one hundred and ninety, possibly one hundred and ninety four, were from Central America. Of this subtotal 167 were from various parts of Nicaragua. The only other area which provided more was the small pearl islands off the Venezuelan coast. Cubagua alone supplied 272.[13]

By 1550 the export of Indian slaves had fallen to a trickle in all the areas of Central America which had participated in this trade. The reasons are not hard to find. In Nicaragua and Honduras there were simply no Indians left to send. The teeming populations mentioned by early invaders of the Nicaraguan lake area had fallen to under 10,000 heads of families. Honduras had suffered a similar catastrophe.[14] Slaving undoubtedly played a role in this decline, possibly the major role in the case of Nicaragua, but revolts, famines, overwork, and above all epidemics also contributed. Not only were these remnant populations hardly worth shipping, but they were now being guarded much more jealously by the local encomenderos and officials. The expendable work force of the first years after the conquest was now carefully rationed to the farmers, plantation owners, and miners, who resented attempts to export their much reduced labor supply.[15]

With the passing of the conquistadors and early settlers came the establishment of royal control, and to enforce that control, a new breed of royal official. The two outstanding ones were Bishop Cristóbal de Pedraza in Honduras and especially the severe Alonso López de Cerrato in Guatemala, who was remarkably like his master Felipe II in temperament.

Pedraza's role was small. He fought vigorously against the exporting of Honduran Indians to the Caribbean islands, but the Indians were already so reduced in numbers that the trade was not so much halted by officialdom as extinguished by its own lack of supplies.[16] López de Cerrato, on the other hand, arrived after the great days of the Honduran and Nicaraguan aboriginal slaving had passed, when the Pacific coasts of Guatemala and San Salvador, still comparatively thickly populated, were taking control of much of the declining slave trade to Panama and Peru. By relentless legislation against Indian slavery, which freed all the slaves to which no title existed, and by widespread visitas on the south coast by his Audiencia judges (oidores), López de Cerrato used the powers given to him by the famous New Laws to eliminate the Indian slave trade in Guatemala.[17]

His actions aroused great resentment among the Spanish and Creole populations, and in spite of his determination and forceful actions it is doubtful if his prohibitions would have been obeyed had it not been for other factors.[18] It is significant that repeated royal attempts to have surviving slaves from Panama and Peru returned to their homelands appear to have been unsuccessful.

About 1545 the ecomenderos of the coastal province of Izalcos were beginning to cultivate the large plantations of cacao which were to give them such prosperity in the following two or three decades. One can assume that their reaction to the export of the local servile populations was the same as that of the encomenderos in Nicaragua and Honduras; they did not want to lose their work force. Of course they also resented López de Cerrato's liberation of all Indian slaves.

The factor of greatest importance in the decline of Guatemalan slave exports was, however, the gradual disappearance of demand. By 1548 the first Peruvian conquests and civil wars had ended, and thereafter the local subject populations were employed in the fields and mines. In Panama Indian bearers were being replaced by mules and horses, bred locally and in nearby areas in ever-increasing numbers. The negro population was also rising.[19]

Thus local demands for labor, rapidly declining populations, strict royal officials, the disappearance of the first great generation of conquistadors, and vanished markets led to a rapid decline in Central American exports of Indians. By the early 1550s this industry had disappeared.

There were sporadic instances of the illegal removal of natives from one jurisdiction to another throughout the sixteenth and seventeenth centuries.[20] But with one notable Costa Rican exception in the eighteenth century these cases usually involved individuals, and they never came close to the mass, forced emigrations of the first twenty-five years after the conquest. The era when Indian slaves were the principal export of Central America never returned. It is one of the most tragic and forgotten aspects of Spanish Pacific history.

"During this year [1530] heavy tribute was imposed. Gold was contributed to Tonatiuh; four hundred men and four hundred women were delivered to him to be sent to wash gold. All the people extracted the gold. Four hundred men and four hundred women were contributed to work in Pongan [Antigua] on the construction of the city, by order of Tonatiuh. All this, all, we ourselves saw, oh, my sons!"[21]

The lament of the Cakchiquel chronicler over the events of that year was not only applicable to highland Guatemala. As in Mexico, the invading Spaniards found that many of the streams between Chiapas and Costa Rica contained gold which could be extracted in profitable quantities if large numbers of workers were put to washing and panning. Given the sizeable Indian population which the conquerors found in Central America and the prestige enjoyed by precious metals in mercantilist Europe, the Spaniards of the time adopted the logical course. In the belt of highly mineralized rocks which runs through central and southern Honduras to north-central

Nicaragua around Nueva Segovia, Spaniards devoted a major part of their efforts to fomenting and exploiting gold washing. In Chiapas and Guatemala also, and in Costa Rica after its belated conquest, similar events on a lesser scale took place in the first years after pacification.

Gold washing, then, went on everywhere at first, and large gangs or cuadrillas of Indian slaves and draughted laborers are mentioned as having been moved around the countryside all over Central America. By the mid 1530s, however, it became obvious that the streams and rivers flowing north and west to the Caribbean from the central highlands of Honduras and northern Nicaragua contained far more gold than those of other areas. As a result Spaniards concentrated on them and gave up gold panning in the less productive provinces.

The raising and moving of these Indian cuadrillas caused great dislocations. Some of them were taken from Guatemala on long treks to Honduras and Chiapas.[22] Pedro de Alvarado, second to none in his search for gold, was one of the first to realize that Honduras offered better prospects than Guatemala, which brought about his invasion of Honduras, another conqueror's preserve, his founding of the city of Gracias a Dios, and his intensive gold washing activities in that region.[23]

At the time of Alvarado's Honduran incursion there were twenty or more cuadrillas of imported Guatemalan slaves working there. The average cuadrilla was probably about twenty men, but some contained more than a hundred Indians. The Spaniards who had settled in Honduras resented these activities and the export to Guatemala of quantities of gold. The Indians of coastal Honduras had fallen to a very few, and as a result the local Spaniards were not able to raise cuadrillas to match the Guatemalan ones.[24]

Methods of obtaining labor in these early years were relatively simple. Large numbers of Indians had been enslaved because of their resistance to the Spanish armies or because of previous servitude. These individuals were divided among the Spaniards, who promptly formed them into work gangs and sent them under overseers or mayordomos to the nearest gold-bearing streams. When these slaves were not enough the Spaniards simply demanded tandas, or draughts, of a given number of Indians for a certain length of time from every village or tribal group under their control. The four hundred men and four hundred women mentioned by the Cakchiquel chronicler are one example of this early method.[25]

The areas first exploited in Honduras, besides Gracias a Dios, were Trujillo, San Pedro (Sula), and Comayagua. (Comayagua was important for its silver.) The first exports to Spain were large and encouraging, and these areas seem to have reached their greatest productivity in the years between 1539 and 1542. "In 1540 the figures for refinement in Gracias a Dios were 5,000 pesos, for San Pedro 9,000, and for Trujillo 10,000. In March 1542, 30,000 pesos worth of gold was reported ready for refining in San Pedro, and 15,000 pesos worth in Trujillo. Silver production in the region of Comayagua in 1541 was some 2,050 marcos."[26]

In northern Nicaragua entradas coming from León and from the Guayape River found gold in an area which was named Nueva Segovia. This new field was at first worked by a combination of negro slaves and local pacified Indians. The early days of the Nueva Segovia placers were unsettled. The newly "reduced" Indians revolted in 1529, killing twelve to fifteen Spaniards and several negro slaves, and it was some time before new entradas were able to reopen the fields.[27]

The largest early strike of all was the gold and silver field centered around Olancho and the Guayape River. The area was opened up several years after the other Honduran fields. Like Nueva Segovia, it proved difficult to pacify completely and in 1541 Olancho and the river were temporarily abandoned by all but a holding force of eleven soldiers. It was frequently reported that there were large numbers of Indians in the vicinity, yet the placer work was chronically short of workers and most of the labor seems to have been performed by negro slaves. These slaves, hard-driven in the new fields, themselves revolted in late 1542 and temporarily expelled the Spaniards once again. By this time they may have numbered about a thousand.[28]

Despite this unrest, by the middle 1540s Olancho's Guayape River had become the most important producer of precious metals, in this case gold, within the confines of the Audiencia of Guatemala and Yucatan.[29] In the next ten or fifteen years Guayape produced large quantities of gold for the royal coffers. One estimate claimed that the enormous sum of 1,750,000 gold pesos had been extracted from the river and other deposits near it. Large amounts were paid to the king in taxes. In 1553 alone 26,400 pesos of "good gold" were dispatched to Spain.[30]

By 1560 Olancho-Guayape was in serious decline, and the other lesser areas had sunk to minor status long before.[31] The reasons for this precipitous decline of such seemingly promising fields are familiar ones. Once again a dominant factor was the severe drop in the laboring population. Even the large imports of negro

Figure 3

Population of Honduras, Indian Tributaries, Sixteenth Century

Year	No. of Tributaries	Source	Comments
1524	400,000	Benzoni, p. 99.	A rough figure, but indicative of the great numbers. Numerous witnesses concur that the population at the moment of Spanish impact was very great.
1539	15,000	Bishop Cristóbal Pedraza, "Relación de varios sucesos ocurridos en Honduras," *Relaciones Históricas de America. Primera Mitad del Siglo XVI*, p. 167.	Based on some counts, personal inspection, and approximation.
1541	8,000+	Benzoni, p. 99.	Personal observation. An estimate.
1571-74	8,100+	López de Velasco, pp. 306-13.	Probably based on the count of 1548-49 in AGI/AG 128. I have left out his figure for Olancho, obviously a guess at the number of "unreduced" Indians.
1582	5,106	"Relación hecha a s.m. por el gobernador de Honduras de todos los pueblos de dicha gobernación—Año 1582, *"Boletín del Archivo General de Gobierno* (Guatemala), IX, nos. 1 and 2 (March-June 1946), pp. 5-19.	A good count. By now Tegucigalpa and its mines have been opened up, and some of the Indians there added to the tribute rolls. This count may have been several years old.
1582	4,840	AGI/AG 164, Bishop of Honduras to Crown, May 12, 1582.	A less reliable and more general count than the one above, but more recent.
c. 1590	4,864	R.A.H. 11-4-4-854, Relación Geográfica (Francisco de Valverde).	Choluteca included. Olancho had only 476 tributaries.

slaves could not provide a remedy, and the second half of the sixteenth century saw frequent complaints that the abundant gold and silver of Comayagua, San Pedro, and above all Olancho only needed manpower to become a rich asset to the local inhabitants and the Crown. Panning, then, as carried out by Indian slaves under Spanish supervision, seems to have been even harder on the native populations than underground mining itself.[32]

In addition to the lack of labor there was the gradual increase of royal control after 1540, with increasingly restrictive legislation. As the generation of Pedrarias, Castañeda, Contreras, Montejo, and Alvarado disappeared, royal government came into the hands of appointed royal officials such as Alfonso López Cerrato; together with less compliant ecclesiastics such as Pedraza of Honduras and Valdivieso of Nicaragua, they made it locally difficult to flout the laws against the more extreme forms of Indian exploitation. The forced movement of vast cuadrillas of Indian slaves about the isthmus came to a halt. Branding and chain gangs diminished, and to an increasing degree the survivors of Indian communities came under the control of local encomenderos, clerics, and officials.[33]

Because royal restrictions and changes such as the freeing of the Indian slaves and the prohibition of Indian labor in the mines were the most obvious impediments which they faced, the local Creoles emphasized them most in their complaints to the Crown. Often their complaints and arguments were confused; they found themselves arguing that the Indian slaves were not heavily burdened, and that gold and silver extraction was by then only a minor part of their activities, while at the same time admitting that gold and silver panning was of great importance to them by the extent and fervor of their protests and by the expenses which they were willing to face, such as sending whole deputations to Spain, in order to have the old Indian slave system continue. Even Guatemala City, not one of the gold panning areas, was eager to spend time and money to have the ban on Indian slavery removed. Bernal Díaz was one of the agents (procuradores) dispatched to Spain to plead their case.[34]

With many of the Indians dead and the use of those remaining somewhat restricted, the heyday of gold washing was over. Labor shortages, however, may not have been the root of the problem. In an area such as the Guayape River, discovered and pacified at a relatively late date, intensive placer mining continued after the era of restrictions, and in fact most labor in the Guayape area was performed by negro slaves, who may have numbered as many as

1,500 by 1545. Admittedly, the Spaniards of Olancho also complained that with greater supplies of manpower their output might increase, yet the true cause of the decline of Guayape between 1550 and 1560 would seem to be that the deposits of gold which could be obtained by the primitive methods used by the Spaniards were simply exhausted. Depletion of the readily available sources of the gold and silver may well have been the decisive reason for the decline of the early gold and silver industry rather than the labor shortages or restrictions on slavery.[35]

There are other indications of a short depression in the new Central American export economy in the late 1550s. One observer has called this approximate period "the bottom of a relatively large depression."[36] On the Pacific coast, as we shall see, the Soconusco cacao groves were in rapid decay, and those of Izalcos and Guazacapán had not yet fully reached their years of prosperity. Slaving, once the great trade of Nicaragua, and of some importance in Honduras and Guatemala, had declined to a trickle.

Cacao and slaving were largely Pacific coast enterprises, however. On the Atlantic side of the isthmus, which was more closely tied to the products of the mountains and Honduras, and more reliant on exports to Spain at this time, the years after the falling away of gold and silver panning were difficult ones. Naturally this short recession did not mean a complete falling away of all previous activities. Gold panning continued throughout the sixteenth and seventeenth centuries even in areas such as Guatemala, where it had never been of primary importance. From time to time gold and silver would be found in a previously ignored stream and sand bed, and for a short time thereafter the site would be exploited by local Spaniards. When the superficial gleaning had been cleaned off, the site was usually abandoned.[37] There were also the products of the cattle economy. Great quantities of hides and leather were sent to Spain from Honduras ports throughout the latter half of the sixteenth century. While on a much lesser scale than the exports of hides from the islands and Mexico, this trade was one factor which kept Honduran exports from falling to the levels which were to be reached in the middle years of the seventeenth century. (The trade in hides, of course, was to suffer its own collapse when the cattle crisis began in the 1590s.) The short depression was severe enough, however, to drive local Spaniards to searching for alternative sources of export income, and thus such products as sarsaparilla, balsam, and hides received increasing attention in the 1570s, as is noted below.

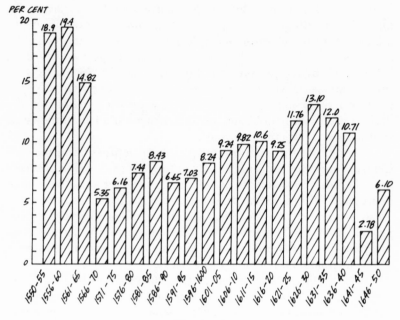

Figure 4

Port Traffic from Honduras Ports as Percentage of Port Traffic of Veracruz.
Derived from Pierre and Huguette Chaunu, *Séville,* 8[1], pp. 850-51. This
chart has only relative value, but it does show a marked falling off in
Honduras' share in the late 1560s. After 1640 comes the collapse of the
Spanish commercial system and the consequent emphasis on Mexican gold
and silver to the exclusion of other imports. Honduras trade holds up a
little longer than that of Veracruz, probably because of indigo, but decline,
when it comes, is even more severe.

This depression of the 1550s was, in fact, more in the nature
of a pause. The cacao industry, so basic to the Central American
economy in the sixteenth century, had far from run its course and
was merely moving on to new areas not yet under full production.
The silver and gold mining before 1560 was simply the run-off, both
figuratively and literally, from the larger deposits of mineralized
rocks in the central highlands of Honduras and northern Nicaragua.
While the laboring population had suffered a catastrophic drop, yet
Central America's natural resources were far from being exhausted,
and the recession of the 1560s represents little more than an early

readjustment to the disappearance of the more obvious and immediate sources of wealth.

In Central America the early stages of the search for a dynamic export product can be divided into two phases. The first one can most conveniently be described as looting, for the invading Spaniards simply took the resources most readily and obviously available and sent them out of the country. Thus human beings and surface gold were exported in large quantities for the first thirty years after the conquest.

The failure of these looting activities was inevitable. Depletion of the resources and a desire to utilize the manpower still remaining for local tasks were two of the principal reasons. As a consequence the second phase can best be described as a search for alternatives. The hunt for silver and gold continued and the result was the sixteenth and seventeenth century mining industry around Tegucigalpa, a local industry at best and a source of wealth for very few. Looking around them further Spaniards found various plants which had aromatic or medicinal uses which could be turned to account, even if only briefly. These alternatives were unsatisfactory as permanent solutions, and many Spaniards continued to search. In the decade of the 1560s Spaniards in Guatemala, San Salvador, and Nicaragua found, to their surprise no doubt, that the new key to great wealth had been present for some time and was a lowly staple in the diet of the subject Indians.[38] Before examining the cacao industry and boom, however, a brief glance at some local failures can illustrate the problems faced by the conquerors.

3

Ephemeral Hopes

The search for new export products following the collapse of slaving and gold panning in the mid-sixteenth century took many directions. Eventually it created a boom on the Pacific coast based on cacao and led to the establishment of a regional economy based on silver mining in the previously unsettled area around Tegucigalpa in Honduras. This fugitive recession of mid-century, however, did not immediately find the solutions or partial solutions mentioned above. Casting around for a cash crop, Spaniards turned to many strange and ephemeral products.

To a group eager for quick profits but unwilling to spend time and effort in manufacture, the plant life of Central America was an obvious place to search for saleable goods. In middle San Salvador, halfway between the towns of Santa Anna and San Salvador and reaching to the Pacific coast, the Spaniards found large stands of balsam trees. The principal villages of the area were Guaymoco and Tonolá. The Pacific plain itself between Acajutla and the present town of La Libertad came to be known as the balsam coast.[1]

Collection of balsam seems to have intensified about 1560, perhaps partially as a result of Central America's first economic pause, when slaving and gold panning had not yet yielded completely to cacao. For several years great quantities were shipped to Peru and even larger quantities to Spain via Mexico and Honduras. From 1560 until the end of the century it was identified as one of the more important products of Guatemala.[2]

Balsam was used as an unguent, a medicine, and a cosmetic, but even under optimum conditions of use it could not aspire to become an item of export sufficiently large to support a vast area such as the Audiencia of Guatemala. There were simply not enough popular uses for it. Moreover, balsam was extracted from a large, slow-growing tree and consequently supplies could not be quickly increased. Nevertheless, it appeared that central San Salvador had found a crop which would be able to provide a fair measure of prosperity for at least that small region. Instead, very quickly, this trade began to fall off. The main reason for the decline cannot be stated definitely, but one of the most important reasons must surely have been the destructive methods used in collecting the product itself.

Balsam had originally been collected like tropical rubber. Slash marks in the bark of the tree allowed the resinous substance to seep through the bark for collection; and oil of balsam, a similar liquid, was extracted from the nuts. As demand increased, however, the local Indians began to "sweat" the balsam trees. Between November and May, the best season for gathering balsam, they would pile brush (zacate) around each tree and set the brush on fire. The heated tree would then exude great quantities of balsam, which after collection were sold to Spaniards in San Salvador and Sonsonate. Of course such violent methods harmed and often killed the trees sooner or later. Even more disastrous for the industry, the Indians took to stripping bark or even branches off the trees and to boiling them with water in large vats. The oily unguent would then rise to the surface to be skimmed off. Balsam produced by heat turned black and was considered less pure than "virgin" balsam obtained by the slash method.[3]

Even with such draconian and counter-productive methods the supply was insufficient. Indians used many devices to increase the volume: "although they try many schemes to increase its bulk, like the women innkeepers in Madrid, putting water in the wine, the balsam will not unite with anything of different nature from its own; in fact it draws apart immediately and becomes recognizable and easy to distinguish."[4] Balsam continued to be a crop of minor importance to central San Salvador until the nineteenth century but by 1600 the days of the "balsam coast" had ended, and it was no longer considered to be a major product of the Audiencia of Guatemala.[5]

Other gums, waxes, and unguents, such as liquidambar, beeswax, copal, and perfumed resins were of occasional importance, but the sporadic nature of their occurrence meant that large quantitites could not be gathered. Liquidambar, for example, was usually found scattered in the very moist cloud forests between 6,500 and 7,000 feet.[6]

Two medicinal and cosmetic plants were found in quantity. Cañafístula, the product of the cassia tree and the cassia nigra of commerce, was used as a cathartic in the seventeenth century, and royal attempts to stimulate its cultivation in Guatemala show that it was considered to be of some consequence as an article of trade. In spite of encouragement, however, it remained a minor item of commerce in Central America. Coastal Honduras and Verapaz seem to have been the main areas of production.[7]

Sarsaparilla far exceeded cañafístula in importance and for a short time this strange product became Central America's most important export to Europe. Sarsaparilla, *aralia nudicaulis,* a species of *smilax,* is a wild plant native to the Americas. In the sixteenth and seventeenth centuries it was held, somewhat erroneously, to be a medicine of great efficacy. Syphilis, scrofula, fever, and plague were all thought to respond to it, and great quantities were consumed in Spain and other parts of Europe. Usually it was infused in water and taken as tea or tonics of various kinds.[8]

Central America was not the only source. The headwaters of the Guayas River in Ecuador were a region of rival production, and several other tropical provinces produced large quantities.[9] One of the areas of greatest production, however, was the ridge of low hills running east from Trujillo in Honduras along the Caribbean towards Verapaz. Here the surviving Indians were diverted from the failing gold panning to the collection of sarsaparilla rootstocks. Trujillo's sarsaparilla was said to be the best in the Indies. The plant was also of considerable importance in Verapaz and on the Caribbean coast of Costa Rica before the rise of the cacao industry.[10]

Once its gathering had been systematized Trujillo exported amazing amounts of this root. At the height of the trade in the 1580s, yearly totals of 3,000 to 5,000 arrobas (75 to 125 thousand pounds) were leaving the Bay of Honduras for Spain—almost incredible cargoes when it is considered that the root was gathered from a wild, uncultivated, scattered plant in swampy, difficult terrain.[11]

The industry was similar to the balsam trade in that it was bound to destroy its own resources if pursued too intensively. After the roots had been removed most of the plants probably died, and the Indian gatherers had to move steadily further away from Trujillo on their gathering expeditions. By 1590 the main sources of the plant were reported lying five or six leagues away from the town.[12]

The gathering of sarsaparilla also required large numbers of Indians, and as a result the industry suffered from their decline in numbers. The Spaniards of Trujillo demanded sarsaparilla as tribute, but their excesses, and the disappearance of tribute payers, caused the authorities to interfere and decrease these forced payments. The Audiencia reported that around Trujillo the "living Indians were paying for the dead" in sarsaparilla and that collecting the root was an unhealthy task. It had to be collected during the rainy season, often by wading in water, and because of this task Indians missed the sowing season on their own milpas and so had no food at harvest time. Honduras was full of young widows because of the sarsaparilla industry, the Audiencia claimed, and food shortages were becoming more acute.

Similar complaints were made between 1599 and 1602 by the Indians of the villages of Yurusti and Barva in Costa Rica. The local Spanish official was working them so hard gathering sarsaparilla for his own benefit that they were failing to plant their staple crops, and some were fleeing to the wilds.[13]

During the early decades of the seventeenth century considerable quantities of the magic root were still leaving Trujillo. In 1608 800 arrobas were sent, and in 1610 almost double that amount, probably two years' harvests; but these were poor figures compared to those of thirty years before, and unstable prices for the product once it reached Spain were a further discouragement. Prices fell steadily between 1625 and 1648,[14] and by the second half of the century sarsaparilla had long ceased to be of great importance.[15]

The minor flurries caused by these exotic plants are in many ways little more than historical curiosities. Yet they are illustrative of a stage of development in colonial Central America, and the destructive methods and circumstances which caused their demise offer, in microcosm, a picture of what was to happen to the major export industry of the area in the sixteenth century.

The drawing off or "sweating" of balsam and the gathering of sarsaparilla roots are an intermediate stage which, historically and technologically, lies between the simple looting and export of the decades of gold and slaves, and the more complicated neo-plantation and intensive farming arrangements of the cacao and indigo industries. Gradually Spanish entrepreneurs were being forced to invest more time, effort, and organization in the products which interested them.

Obviously such crops as balsam and sarsaparilla could not hope to replace gold or slaves. They could hardly even hope to leave much of a profit margin when shipped to the distant European markets. The demand for them was a small, peripheral one, for medicines even in the sixteenth century were not a large item of everyday personal consumption, and the supply could not be organized on a steady basis because of the nature of the plants. Spaniards would have to look elsewhere.

4

Soconusco, A Hint of Things To Come

A product which was to become the preferred beverage of a large number of Americans and Europeans from the sixteenth through the eighteenth centuries provided post-conquest Central America with its first agricultural boom and, after the boom collapsed, with its first crisis in exports and external markets.

The cacao bush, *Theobroma cacao,* is a new world tropical plant of uncertain provenance. It has been suggested that the upper Amazon basin was its first home in its undomesticated state.[1] The fruit of the cacao is a large, fleshy pod containing numerous nibs or "beans." (The Spanish often referred to these seeds as almendras or almonds, and to the pods as mazorcas or ears.) Whatever its origin, cacao has been cultivated by the inhabitants of Middle America since prehistoric times.[2] One authority asserts that the Central American type of cacao "has probably been subject to human selection for three thousand years and possibly much longer."[3] It is a crop of sufficient antiquity among the Quichés and the Cakchiquels of Guatemala to have entered their legends about the creation of man and their mythology of tribal origins.[4]

In pre-conquest Middle America, plantations of cacao bushes were grown for two purposes. Its beans served as a coinage or means of exchange, which was accepted across regional and linguistic barriers and over a wide geographical area.[5] They were also eaten. Cacao beans intended for human consumption played a large part in tribute and commerce before the arrival of the Spaniards, and their use for tribute payments was probably ancient.

Plantations existed on both coasts of Central America. On the Caribbean side the Ulua Valley of Honduras was important and exported to Yucatan, while Tabasco, southern Veracruz, and Campeche sold cacao and paid tribute in it to the Aztec Empire. The main source of cacao in pre-conquest and Spanish colonial times was, however, the belt of highly fertile, volcanic soil which runs along the Pacific coast of Central America from the isthmus of Tehuantepec to the extreme northwestern plains of the Nicaraguan and Nicoyan coast. Along this narrow plain Soconusco and Zapotitlán were the areas where the cacao plantations had been most intensively developed before the conquest, and Soconusco, in fact, was the tributary district which sent most cacao to the Aztecs. The Codex Mendoza shows a tax of 400 cargas, or loads, from Soconusco out of a total tribute of 980 loads from all cacao-growing areas paying tribute to the Aztecs. Other Pacific coastal areas of Central America beyond immediate Aztec pressure, such as Izalcos and Nicaragua, also had concentrated plantations, but they may have been fairly small at the time of the conquest.[6]

The pre-conquest agriculture of Middle America did not supply a sufficient quantity of cacao to make it a popular drink for all classes of the dense Indian population in all parts of Mesoamerica. Yields were low, and there was little monoculture. Also trade was frequently interrupted by local wars which may have prevented wider diffusion of the cacao drinking habit. No doubt it was a general staple in an area of fairly intensive cultivation such as Soconusco, but in the valley of Mexico, a principal center of its consumption, and even in Yucatan and Nicaragua, where it was grown on a small scale, we find cacao and the various concoctions thereof being treated as items of luxury and prestige. There may also have been a reluctance on the part of the common people to imbibe their hard-won coinage, and there are indications that the consumption of aristocratic cacao by the lower classes was forbidden in some areas of Middle America.[7] There are further indications that the Mayan area held the plant and its fruit in considerable awe, and that cacao, perhaps because of its antiquity and its place in mythology, possessed sacred or at least ritualistic attributes for the higher cultures of pre-conquest Central America. It was also used for its supposed medicinal properties.[8]

Thus cacao was a drink often reserved for the nobility and the warriors before the arrival of the Spaniards. At that time it was consumed as a cold or tepid drink. Usually the cacao bean was dried, roasted, and ground to a flour, then mixed with water to form a thin gruel. Various other agricultural products were added to give flavor, bulk, and color. Maize flour added bulk, chili added a certain bite and flavor, while achiote (a red or yellow vegetable dye) gave the beverage a reddish color which many Indians seem to have found pleasing. Several of these ingredients and at times some others were present in most of the pre-conquest cacao recipes which we know

Figure 5

Weights and Measures of Cacao

Name	Approx. Number of Beans	Approx. Arrobas	Weight (Lbs.)
zontle	400		.833
xiquipil	8,000	2/3	16.66
carga	24,000	2	50
tercio	72,000	6	150

Note: 20 zontles equal 1 xiquipil; 3 xiquipiles equal 1 carga; 3 cargas equal 1 tercio. (1 arroba equals 25 lbs.) Sources: Thompson, "Notes on the Use of Cacao," p. 97; Torquemada, *Monarquía*, 2:620; FG, 2:221; Vázquez de Espinosa, *Compendium*, p. 225; Motolinía, *Motolonía's History*, p. 218.

of today.[9] Most Europeans found these early mixtures to be nauseating, and they remain so today to the unconditioned palate. Benzoni described the repugnant brews containing cacao as "better fit for pigs than for men." Others agreed.[10] No doubt there was also prejudice against this "Indian" drink among the first conquerors.

Thus cacao remained a native drink during the early years of Spanish domination. At first the industry seemed little changed by the conquest. The sources of supply and the main centers of consumption remained the same. Tabasco, Colima, and above all Soconusco continued to supply cacao as tribute to the new masters, who, while altering the structure of tribute payments quite radically, altered the nature of the items to be paid very little before the middle years of the sixteenth century.[11] From the beginning of Spanish domination, however, the whole complex of customs and beliefs surrounding cacao was to undergo radical and continuous changes.

The Christian Spaniards cared little for the special and aristocratic position occupied by cacao as a dietary item but quickly realized its economic possibilities. As a result, in a few years the general Indian population was consuming large quantities of the formerly mystic, upper-class potion. Since the Indian population in Mexico, Guatemala, and Nicaragua was declining rapidly during the first decade or two after the conquest, the plantations in Tabasco, Colima, Soconusco, and Zapotitlán seem to have been able to supply the increased demands of the common people without undue strain. By 1545, however, the ravages of disease had decimated the producers of cacao even more than the consumers, and the populations of the cacao areas were rapidly approaching extinction. Soco-

Figure 6

Cacao Tribute and Tributary Population in Soconusco

Years	Official Amount	Alleged Additional Amounts	Indian Population (Tributaries)	Source
Pre-conquest	400 cargas	?	30,000	Codex Mendoza *fide* Molins Fabrega; and AGI/AG 968B. No signature, 1573?
1524-26	?	?	15,000	Bernal Díaz del Castillo, p. 380.
1563			1,600	AGI/AG 968B. No signature, 1573?
1571	400 cargas	200	2,000 "or less"	López de Velasco, p. 303; AGI/AG 9, Lcdo. Arteaga Mendiola to the King, March 20, 1571.
1573	400-500 cargas	100	1,600	AGI/AG 9, Pres. Villalobos to King, May 15, 1573.
1576	650 cargas	100	1,800	AGI/AG 965, a priest to the King, 1576.
1609	1,157 cargas	?	2,000	AGI/AG 60, governor to the King, May 6, 1613.
1613	1,133 cargas	?	2,000	AGI/AG 60; governor to the King, May 4, 1613.

Note: The difference in population between the pre-conquest era and 1524-26 may be a result of the first colonial epidemic.

nusco, the greatest cacao province of all, declined from a population of 30,000 tributaries or more at the moment of impact to one of 1,600 in the 1560s and 1570s. Desperate efforts to recruit fresh labor were made, but the new laborers died as rapidly or more rapidly than the original inhabitants. Large plantations of delicate cacao bushes were abandoned and became overgrown. Sometimes the crop could not be collected. Circumstances in neighboring Zapotitlán, densely inhabited when Alvarado arrived, were equally bad by the 1560s.[12] These two northwestern areas of the fertile Pacific plain of Central America wrestled with the problem of rehabilitating their principal industry throughout the sixteenth and much of the seventeenth centuries without notable success. A closer examination of the history of the Soconusco fields provides the explanation.

In spite of complaints at the time, we can conclude that the work in the cacao plantations does not seem to have been particularly hard, compared, for example, to the *obrajes* or sugar mills, provided an adequate number of laborers was available, which was seldom the case. But large numbers of workers *were* required all year round. The Central American type of cacao is extraordinarily delicate.[13] Consequently the groves needed constant semi-skilled attention. The least wind, cold, or frost killed the trees or destroyed the fruit. Direct sunshine was equally undesirable. To provide shade, large leguminous trees had to be planted between the rows of cacao bushes. On the Pacific plain of Central America, with its marked rainy and dry seasons, water was a constant problem. During the rainy season the Indians were occupied in providing drainage so that the trees would not become swamped or choked. The task was complicated by the luxuriant growth of zacate, tall rushes or hay, at that time of the year, which had to be cut to allow for drainage. The dry season, shorter in Soconusco, presented the opposite problem. Water had to be carried to the trees or irrigation canals constructed and kept open.[14] Occasionally emergency gangs were required to drive off invasions of parrots or locusts. Also time-consuming was the constant work of replanting and renovating the groves. The cacao bush of Central America had and has an extremely high mortality rate compared to the other varieties of cacao, and even the hardiest varieties of cacao are considered today to be delicate plants. Cacao is attacked by an extraordinarily high number of blights and parasites.[15] The delicate Soconusco-Zapotit- lán cacao bushes yielded nothing in their first five years of growth, and very few plants lasted until their twentieth year. Constant vigilance was also required so that the trees which had passed their best productive years might be uprooted and replaced.[16] The close crowding in the plantations, with bushes only ten to twelve feet apart, standing in shade because of the necessary madre de cacao trees, made for poor yields and difficulty in spotting sickly or unproductive bushes. All these tasks consumed scarce manpower.[17]

Groups of highly skilled workers were also needed for the seed starting beds. Such experienced Indian agricultural experts were very hard to replace. The Spaniards probably knew little of apprenticeship and specialization when lowly agriculture was involved. Large gangs of temporary workers were required at harvest times, which came twice a year. (The smaller crop was in November and December and the larger crop around St. John's day, June 29.) The pods had to be picked and emptied, the beans dried and then stored.[18] Some Spaniards, noting this varied, intensive activity, and the disappearance of the local inhabitants, concluded that the two circumstances were related. López de Velasco claimed that the hard work in the cacao industry of Soconusco killed off the Indian population.[19] Others spoke feelingly of bad conditions and overwork on the plantations.[20]

Certainly, one can agree that the Indian porters, or tamemes, were overworked in the years immediately after the conquest, carrying the cacao, as they did, from the Pacific coast to the Central plateau of Mexico and elsewhere. In the cacao plantations themselves, however, the tasks outlined above would not have been murderously heavy, although they were constant, if there had been an adequate labor supply and a certain number of skilled and experienced individuals. Lack of manpower rather than the nature of the work caused exploitation. It would seem, in fact, that overwork in the cacaotales, or cacao plantations, did not begin in a severe form *until* the Indian population had declined so drastically that the labor situation had changed from one of overabundance to one of scarcity. Then indeed the Spaniards forced the remaining Indians to work harder in a desperate attempt to prevent the plantations from becoming overgrown, aged, and gradually unproductive, as they were doing increasingly by the early seventeenth century.[21]

A brief history of the cacao groves of Soconusco after the conquest is illustrative of this and other matters. The invading Spaniards found a flourishing cacao industry when they reached Soconusco and Zapotitlán. Except for urging the Indians to expand their groves, they wisely refrained from interfering in its basic pattern for some time. In the first half of the sixteenth century, for example, while the industry was not noticeably in decline, the Spaniards seem to have made little or no attempt to gain ownership of the plantations. The cacao could be acquired easily enough by two principal methods. These were the collection of tribute, and one-sided "trading" with the subject race which technically owned the cacaotales. At first in Soconusco it was encomenderos who forced Indians to work their own plantations and to pay cacao as tribute, but by 1556 when Soconusco was transferred from Mexico to the Audiencia de los Confines, all or nearly all of the original Soconusco encomienda grants had been assumed by the Crown, which became, to all intents and purposes, the only encomendero in the province. In less important Zapotitlán the old system of private encomenderos lasted well into the seventeenth century.[22]

In an area such as Soconusco, where the Crown collected the tribute, the governor and other royal officials occupied a position of decided influence. They were responsible for collection and, in Soconusco, were far removed from central authorities in Guatemala, Mexico, or Spain. Governors often became involved in illegal activities for personal gain. The principal offenses perpetrated by governors were "trading" with the Indians for cacao, selling them wine or alcohol for cacao, extorting various kinds of gifts or levies of cacao, demanding excessive tribute payments which were then not turned over to the Crown, and working in collusion with the Spanish and caste merchants. A blind eye was turned to many of their activities, and "profit sharing" between royal officials and purchasers was common at the time of sale of the royal cacao tributes. Priests were sometimes accused of the same offenses.[23]

Merchants were guilty of similar practices. Many merchants traded honestly with the Indian cacao growers, no doubt, but many others were accused of extortion, petty trickery, or fraud. The Indians were sold shoddy surplus or worthless goods, alcohol or wine, often at inflated prices, while the cacao was bought at prices far below those of the day.[24] This "trading" was so lucrative that large numbers of merchants and vagabonds came from Mexico and elsewhere to share in the assured profits.

Royal efforts, and occasional more ambivalent efforts on the part of the Audiencia, to force these merchants and vagabonds to limit the duration of their stays in Indian villages or to forbid them from entering villages altogether seem to have yielded no durable results. By the seventeenth century the movement to the countryside was so strong that vecinos in Zapotitlán, living permanently in Indian villages, were able to defy the royal expulsion orders.[25] One reason for the inability to force compliance was that the royal officials responsible for the carrying out of the law were themselves often implicated in the sale of wine and other goods to the Indian villages and to the plantation owners.

Another reason was the ambivalent attitude of the Crown itself. During the days of Soconusco's prosperity the Crown wavered characteristically between dismay at the ill treatment of the aborigines and envy at the amounts of untaxed wealth amassed by the Spaniards, both officials and merchants. Characteristically again, the Crown finally shed most of its scruples and demanded its share of the golden eggs when the goose had already ceased to lay with such frequency. The Crown's first step was to require that all merchants purchase export licenses before sending cacao to New Spain.[26] Then, as late as 1576, the Crown inquired in Mexico and in Guatemala about the feasibility of setting up a customs house in Masatepeque, where a 5 per cent tax would be charged on all cacao leaving for the north. Exporting via Chiapas to avoid payment would be punished.[27] In spite of such attempts, the Crown appears to have obtained little of the profits.

Another device used by the Crown and its local officials to

increase their share of the profits was to increase tribute in the early seventeenth century, when production was low or even falling. Tribute assessments grew rapidly. The Crown and its officials were taking even more of the available cacao for resale to the merchants, thus insuring that a larger share of each crop would pass through their hands, instead of directly from producer to merchants. As was so often the case in Guatemala, tribute collection was varied and had local peculiarities. After 1612, for example, the Indians in Soconusco began to pay two tributes, as had been the practice in Guatemala for many years. One was assessed on the normal basis, and another on the number of cacao trees they owned. The rate was four beans per tree. This second tribute was admitted frankly by local officials to central authorities, who quietly took their share. Such maneuvering on the part of the Crown and its officials partially condoned the activities of the merchants.

The merchant headquarters was Huehuetlán, the only center of Spanish settlement in Soconusco until late in the seventeenth century. During the sixteenth and much of the seventeenth centuries it was an unstable town. The royal government for the province resided there, but many of the inhabitants were transients.[28] In spite of its early foundation by Pedro de Alvarado in 1524, Huehuetlán did not achieve the title of ciudad or villa during the sixteenth or seventeenth centuries, probably because of its shifting merchant population.

Here cacao tribute was collected, stored, and then sold to merchants. Here also merchants collected and weighed the cacao which they themselves had acquired directly from the Indians. Huehuetlán was, in fact, an entrepôt and assembly point from which the cacao was sent on to its New Spain markets.

The routes and methods for taking the cacao to its markets are only roughly apparent. In the early days of the trade the Spanish and mestizo traders who came to Soconusco and Zapotitlán from Mexico, Tlaxcala, Puebla, Cholula, and elsewhere probably sent the cacao on the backs of Indian porters. Later large teams, or recuas, of mules were engaged in carrying the cacao to New Spain. This was done either by the usual route along the coast of Tehuantepec or circuitously through Chiapas to avoid customs payments.[29] Throughout the colonial period the aboriginal system of measuring and counting cacao was used by these merchants and by the royal officials. Attempts to interfere fraudulently with this system were noted and criticized by the Audiencia.[30]

The aging and deterioration of a cacao plantation is a gradual process. Given the absence of severe blights, locust plagues, winds, or floods, a drastic fall in production may not be apparent for several years. The severe reductions in the Indian population of Soconusco and Zapotitlán in the first two decades after the conquest (1524–44) seem to have affected the industry very little. Even the price of cacao at its major destination in Mexico City remained fairly stable during this period.[31] Presumably the population still surviving in the early 1540s was large enough to keep the plantations in production without notable strain. The devastating epidemics of 1545 and immediately after, however, appear to have so reduced the Indian laboring population that within a few years it became obvious that the plantations could not be maintained at the same level, if the wasteful use of large numbers of workers was to be the basis of the cacao industry. Thus we find the vecinos of Huehuetlán writing to the king in 1565 that a new irrigation canal program, sponsored by the governor of the province, had proved to be a success. The vecinos reported that they were well satisfied with the governor's work and hoped that the irrigation system would provide a solution to the problems of the cacao industry. By that stage only some 3,000 cargas per year were being exported to New Spain.[32] As the plantations declined Spaniards also tried to force replanting and maintenance on Indian owners with increasing insistence. From time to time this replanting was supervised legally, and heavily, by the jueces de milpas or agricultural supervisors appointed by local officials with Crown approval. At times when the excesses of these inspectors led to their being banned, private individuals or royal governors did much of the supervision.[33] The Indians, at any rate, were either so harassed, so few, or so apathetic, and so taken up with labor on the cacao plantations that they ceased to plant sufficient amounts of the basic staples such as maize and beans. In some areas, moreover, the available fertile land was so packed with young bushes, most of them no doubt unproductive because of lack of staff and high casualty rates, that there was no space available to grow other crops or to run cattle.[34] This situation forced the Spaniards in the two areas to import basic food and clothing, thus forcing up prices and providing Spaniards with another opportunity to exact high prices when trading with Indians for cacao. There are reports of Indians eating grass and dying of hunger because of inability to pay for their staples. Famine was widespread in 1570.[35]

Much of this forced clearing and planting may have been counterproductive. Alvarado found Zapotitlán's cacao to be planted in heavy forests of other trees. (Vázquez de Espinosa noted the same thing when the Guayaquil groves were flourishing.) As more and more groves were planted much of the original forest must have been cut, thus leaching the soil, increasing erosion, and lowering overall yields.[36] The decision in 1568 to start four cattle ranches to provide local meat at lower prices for the hard-pressed inhabitants, and the increasing number of cattle ranches thereafter suggest that some of the land was becoming grass-covered. By the late seventeenth century grazing became more important than cacao in Soconusco, suggesting that most of the forest cover had been cut or burned. The cacaotales were thus overexposed to sun, wind, and flood, and more susceptible to the sudden disasters of wind or rain which attacked the province.[37]

In an age of little mechanization, irrigation and drainage canals proved inadequate solutions. Nor could the few available Indians be worked or taxed beyond certain limits in replanting, harvesting, or tribute paying. The central problem remained a severe lack of manpower, which became critical twice each year at harvest time. To replace the dead, as it were, the Spaniards of Soconusco began to import large numbers of workers from highland areas, where survivors of the early holocausts were still numerous.

Some Indians came voluntarily, no doubt attracted by tales of wealth and opportunity, as were the casta and Spanish merchants from New Spain, Guatemala, and elsewhere. But the majority of these Indians were coerced either overtly or indirectly. Many were forced to go to the two coastal provinces by the need to earn cacao beans or silver coinage in order to pay their local tributes. The ecclesiastical or civil authorities of several areas, such as Verapaz, Chiapas, and Quetzaltenango, which produced little or no cacao and far less silver, demanded payment of tribute in cacao or silver.[38] Thus we find Indians traveling to Soconusco from Quetzaltenango, Chiapas, and Verapaz in considerable numbers. The long journey, the drastic change in climate, and the exposure to the murderous diseases of the coast quickly killed many of these new arrivals.[39] Of the survivors some remained permanently on the Pacific coast, abandoning their wives, children, and milpas in the highlands and thus accentuating food shortages and mortality in the regions which they had left. Some of these new settlers on the coast remarried bigamously or formed irregular unions, much to the dismay of some churchmen.[40] Other survivors returned home as invalids, carrying infection to their home communities, or at the very least living on as unproductive consumers.[41] Some, no doubt, returned unharmed and duly paid their tributes.[42] Other methods of forcing or inducing Indians to go to work on the cacao plantations of Soconusco and Zapotitlán are not documented, but may have been used.

These new immigrants, arriving steadily year by year in the second half of the sixteenth century, had two immediate effects on the cacao provinces of the northwest. They gradually changed the ethnological structures of the aboriginal population. By 1570 the foreign Indians residing in Soconusco were so numerous that it was necessary to appoint a separate judge to deal with their cases; this individual, like so many others, was also involved illegally in the cacao trade.[43] The demographic effect of the new highland immigrants was to stop the imminent disappearances of an Indian population on the coast. From a low point of some 1,600 tributaries or less in the 1570s, the population increased to about 2,000 tributaries in the 1580s, and stayed at that level into the seventeenth century.[44]

The manpower problem, nevertheless, remained unsolved. Two thousand tributaries were sufficient to conduct a meager holding operation in the cacao groves. A slight recovery from the low levels of the 1560s can be noticed. Exports went up from 3,000 cargas in 1562 to 4,000 in 1573, and 5,000 cargas in 1575. Zapotitlán exported about 1,000 loads in 1576.[45] But the recovery was not nearly sufficient to return the groves to the production levels of the 1530s and 1540s. Officials continued to refer to the high mortality rate in the area throughout the sixteenth century and well into the seventeenth century, while at the same time the tributary population was counted as being "just above" or "just below" 2,000. The immigrants from the highlands, often seasonal workers earning tribute to return to the mountains, were not settling down in Soconusco, surviving, and eventually becoming tributaries there, in sufficient numbers to outweigh the high mortality rate and thus raise the number of workers available. Workers from the highlands poured in every year, yet the population remained static at around 2,000. By the 1570s government officials, often deeply and illegally involved in the cacao industry, had decided that new methods of obtaining manpower were needed. No doubt the flourishing rival groves of Izalcos and Guazacapán spurred them on.

Soconusco, prophetically, was already a devastated and depressed area by the end of the sixteenth century, its plight giving an early and ominous hint of what was to happen elsewhere in Central America. Compared to Honduras gold panning, it had enjoyed the advantage of a nearby market, but like gold panning it had depended on a steady labor force all the year round.

Emptied of its aboriginal population and with its immigrants dying as fast as they arrived, the history of Soconusco after 1570, and indeed throughout the seventeenth century, is one of an unsuccessful fight to restore the province's lost prosperity by trying to find Indian labor supplies elsewhere.

5

The Cacao Boom

The course of Soconusco's cacao industry was later paralleled by a larger phenomenon further down the Pacific coast. Izalcos, the extreme western tip of present-day El Salvador, had been one of the reasons for the extinction of the trade in rival Soconusco. Now it was to undergo a similar series of apparently inexorable events.

Izalcos, with its larger but less important subsidiary of Guazacapán to the northwest, had grown cacao in plantations before the conquest. After the arrival of the Spaniards cacao soon became an important item in Guatemala.[1] Alvarado and the other conquerors realized the importance of the crop, at least locally, and the most favored or fortunate members of the invading bands, especially Alvarado himself, tended to appropriate the larger cacao villages for their own encomiendas.[2]

There is no doubt, then, that Spaniards saw cacao as an item of importance. But the importance was local. Spaniards themselves did not use it, and Mexico, the main market, was still well supplied from its traditional sources. Gold and slaving drew far more attention from the first conquerors. Interest in commercial possibilities was thus slow to develop among the Spaniards during the early period of slaving and gold panning following the conquest. The problem was distance from the main markets on the central plateau of Mexico. By land a journey of several months was involved; by sea the construction of a permanent fleet of small cargo ships would be necessary. And geographically Soconusco was much more advantageously situated.

By 1535 some small beginnings had been made, and Mexican merchants began to import small amounts of cacao from the Izalcos area, perhaps because of lower prices.[3] By the 1540s and the 1550s the cacao plantations in Izalcos had expanded to such an extent that the area was becoming known as the richest in Guatemala.[4] Heavy export had begun to the centers of consumption in Guatemala and to the far northwest in Mexico.[5] No doubt Izalcos took advantage of the failure of the small fields in Tabasco and northern Oaxaca to fulfill the needs of the Mexican market. Above all, Izalcos was well-placed to replace Soconusco after that province's serious decline in the middle years of the sixteenth century. Izalcos' rise parallels Soconusco's decline too closely to be a coincidence.

In its early days of expansion, and especially before royal cupidity was aroused, Izalcos exported very little of its cacao by land. The coastal road to Mexico via Soconusco was the better of the two routes, but it was often impassable during the rainy season and involved a long and hazardous journey in the best of times. The alternate route via Santiago de Guatemala and Chiapas was drier, but it was even longer and passed through extremely difficult terrain. No doubt profit margins were a consideration. Soconusco's closeness to the Mexican market meant that her transportation costs by land routes were lower than those of Izalcos. The Izalcos exporters naturally chose the quickest and cheapest route they could find.

Izalcos was fortunate to find a large fleet of small ships at its disposal. Central American shipping had enjoyed something of a boom during the heyday of slaving in Nicaragua and on the Pacific coast of Guatemala.[6] The Pacific coast of Nicaragua was particularly well-suited to shipbuilding. It was well-stocked with guayacán, a hard but workable wood which is resistant to toredo worms, barnacles, and the other marine pests which the Spaniards knew as barva. Pitch, cordage, cotton, and canvas were readily available in Nicaragua; and the Bay of Fonseca, Realejo, and the Gulf of Nicoya provided good harbors for careening ships and for shelter from bad weather in the Pacific.[7] The only obstacle was that all these good ports lay further down the coast than Izalcos.

When the slaving industry declined in the 1540s and early 1550s because of increasing royal disapproval and the disappearance of a ready supply of slaves, a shipbuilding industry, based primarily on the Realejo shipyards, was available to supply the needs of the cacao exporters of Izalcos. Huatulco also had developed services for supplying and repairing ships. No doubt some of the existing slave ships were simply taken over for the new trade.

Cacao was shipped from the open roadstead at Acajutla to Huatulco in Mexico. It was recognized that Acajutla was a dangerous, exposed port for such heavy use, but attempts to make a harbor at Alvarado's old port of Iztapa further up the coast came to nothing.[8] To carry the cacao further down the coast to the Bay of Fonseca or to Realejo and then to ship it back north again would have added considerably to transportation costs. By 1550, and probably before, a regular shuttle service of small ships was carrying cacao from the Izalcos and Guazacapán fields via Acajutla to Huatulco. From there it was carried to Puebla, Mexico City, and other Indian population centers.[9] Supplying the smaller market in the Guatemalan highlands was relatively simple. The city of Santiago was only two days away by mule. Some cacao was also shipped down the coast to Realejo, Panama, and Peru during the early days of the Izalcos boom.[10]

Although the development, management, and decline of the cacao plantations in the small province of Izalcos paralleled those of Soconusco, there were several differences in emphasis and size. Spaniards quickly realized that the rising prices and demand for cacao in Mexico made the small cacao plantations on the coast near Santiago a potential source of quick profits. The decline in early slaving and gold and silver panning had also left many of the Spaniards, of those who had not gone to Peru, still looking for alternative sources of wealth.

As in Soconusco, the area was soon invaded by Spanish and caste merchants "trading" with the Indians. Attempts to control these merchants varied in intensity and degree of success. One such measure which brought lasting results, although not those intended, was the gathering together of all non-Indians in the area in 1552 and 1553, and their resettlement in a newly constituted Spanish villa called Santísima Trinidad de Sonsonate, usually referred to as Sonsonate. The strong group of encomenderos who controlled the Indians of the province seems to have been responsible for this resettlement through the good offices of their ally President Landecho.[11]

This compromise measure did not solve the problem of merchant exploitation of Indian cacao growers. Some merchants and vagabonds continued to reside in Indian villages for short periods. Royal attempts to force these nomads to settle in the villa, or at least to stay out of the Indian villages during the time of the cacao harvest, met with little success; the Crown was still hearing about the activities of these marauders in the seventeenth century. Operating out of Sonsonate, the main body of merchants traded with the Indians, encomenderos, and vagabonds to the accompaniment of imprecations and legislation from the Crown.[12] The new town grew rapidly. By 1558 it had 150 houses of "merchants and traders." López de Velasco noted in the early 1570s that it had 400 vecinos, not one of whom was an encomendero. All were engaged in the cacao and balsam trade. The port of Acajutla three or four leagues away also harbored a few Spaniards.[13]

The merchants owed some of their ability to survive to the remarkable development of a tight monopoly in the cacao plantations of Izalcos province. Large fortunes were made by the monopolists, and a few individuals became so powerful that the king was warned that it would be imprudent to attack them directly. These encomenderos did not want competition from the merchants, but they needed them conveniently near in order to dispose of the cacao.

We owe our knowledge of this system to a few detailed, generally vituperative reports sent to Spain by men who had been rejected by the group in control of the plantations, and to royal officials who were either fresh from Spain, or too obstreperous or too honest to have been absorbed by the group at the date when they wrote.[14]

The first two of these reports, sent to Spain in 1562 and 1563, were from Francisco de Morales, a relator (clerk) of the Audiencia of Mexico. Morales had been relator and defensor of the Indians in Guatemala and was disgruntled to the point of vindictiveness by the experience. His willingness to name individuals, give dates, and describe events shows that he had sufficient evidence to support even his most inflammatory assertions. Morales described a situation which had been in existence for several years. A small group of interrelated encomenderos were controlling the cacao industry and extorting fortunes from the Indians of the area. These encomenderos enjoyed a situation of unparalleled advantage; he wrote, "for truthfully in any twenty leagues of land and province, there is nothing in the world of more profit and less cost, and all in ready cash, for the Spaniards call the income from the cacao bunches of gold."

Morales' main argument was that all or part of this large income should belong to the King, but that the encomenderos were so strong that reform would be difficult and would have to be done warily or even secretly. The encomenderos and the local royal officials were practically one and the same. Governors and officials, especially Alonso de Maldonado, had placed relatives, retainers, and friends illegally in all the best encomiendas and many were returning to Spain "with their salaries doubled twenty times over." The situation, Morales claimed, had deteriorated since the New Laws and the setting up of the Audiencia de los Confines. Before, when there were only governors, the Indians had been exploited by the small number of Spanish officials. Now, with an Audiencia, the exploiters had multiplied: "for then the few wretched Indians only had to take into account one governor and judge, and now they had to reckon with many." Obviously the situation had to be drastically changed. Yet it was hopeless to attempt reform through the governor and Audiencia then in office; they were men "who are already like encomendero householders and who will secretely disrupt the undertaking [of the reform] because it concerns almost their own interests, such are their family connections in the region." Morales was able to name many individuals as examples.

As for methods of reform, Morales advised caution but an immediate start. The trade had been going on for years and any delay would mean more harm to the Indians and more possible royal revenues lost. A trusted visitador arriving unexpectedly might catch all the malefactors and provide an opportunity for clearing out the whole clique, but it is obvious that Morales himself doubted the wisdom of pursuing this course. He believed that an overly vigorous reassertion of the King's authority might well cause revolt. A new, honest, and experienced governor, however, might be advised to restore royal prerogatives by a system of "divide and rule." Morales pointed out that Guatemala contained many poor vecinos who could be won over by ayudas de costo (pensions for past favors). Most of the cacao encomenderos were "nouveaux riches"; "what they or their ancestors owned in Spain was not much and what they brought with them was less again." At most the large cacao encomenderos numbered twenty, and most of them could not qualify as conquerors or "first settlers." A combination of exploited Indians and poor Spaniards favorable to the Crown might well be enough to defeat such a small group. (The Crown's brief experiment in dividing the Audiencia de los Confines between Mexico and Tierra Firme obviously was an action which might have reduced the power of the cacao group and Morales expressed approval of it in his second letter. But the Audiencia of the Confines was reconstituted soon afterwards.) After the restoration of royal authority, Morales argued, two sources of great income would open up. The King had already decreed that all port areas and principal towns should be repossessed from encomenderos and put under the care of the Crown. Izalcos province, with its town of Sonsonate and port of Acajutla, was such an area, and so its tributes could be taken over legitimately by the Crown. Morales' other suggestion for benefiting from the cacao trade was the setting up of an export tax (almojarifazgo) of 7.5 per cent to be collected at Acajutla on the 50,000 cargas of cacao sent out in an average year. Similarly the

King could expect a large income by taxing the cloth from the Mexican obrajes, the clothing, slaves, horses, mules, and other merchandise which were loaded at Huatulco for Acajutla. A Huatulco export of special interest to Morales was the "great quantity of silk which is carried to Acajutla and to the kingdoms of Peru and Nicaragua." The exports from Huatulco to Acajutla were estimated as being worth 400,000 gold pesos per annum, much of it specie, while Morales thought that the income which the King would receive from almojarifazgo and both Acajutla and Huatulco exports might amount to 150,000 ducats each year. Nor should the King feel any qualms about imposing such taxes; the trade, Morales said, had been going on for forty years and so far it had never paid any dues to the King.[15]

Morales was exaggerating. Izalcos cacao paid various minor taxes. Viceroy Luis de Velasco had already placed an import tax on Guatemalan cacao. The ayuntamiento of Guatemala City protested vigorously in 1553 through an agent in Mexico City.[16] The Crown had already anticipated some of Morales's ideas. A royal cédula of February 4, 1560, decreed that a license had to be purchased before cacao could be exported from Sonsonate, Soconusco, or Guatemala. Illegal trading between Sonsonate and Mexico was rife and was to be stopped. Almojarifazgo, however, did not start until 1577.[17]

Morales' complaints were echoed by reports from various others. Obviously many believed that the monopolistic situation in Izalcos was dangerous. In any event, the Crown took drastic action in an apparent attempt to correct the situation. President Licenciado Juan Núñez de Landecho was deposed by royal decree on May 30, 1563. He was fined 30,000 gold pesos for multiple abuses as a governor, and Licenciado Francisco Briceño was ordered to go to Guatemala to conduct a full inquiry into Landecho's government.[18] By the end of the year even more drastic counsels had prevailed and the court dissolved the Audiencia of Guatemala (Los Confines) and divided it among its jurisdictional neighbors. Drawing a line roughly north and south through the Honduran city of Gracias a Dios, the Crown awarded the northern part (Chiapas, Soconusco, and Guatemala including San Salvador) to Mexico, and the rest (Honduras, Nicaragua, Nicoya, and partly settled Costa Rica) to Tierra Firme. The Audiencia was removed to Panama City and a new governor was provided for Guatemala. Morales was delighted with this action, as we have already seen, and felt that it would restore royal authority to the area.[19]

The attempted dismemberment of the Audiencia was a failure. The new governor, Luis de Guzmán, died before leaving Panama. Briceño, who had investigated Landecho's conduct, was reinstated as governor. And on December 21, 1566, under pressure from Fray Bartolomé de las Casas and the cabildo of Santiago City, working together for once, the Council of the Indies restored the Audiencia to Santiago. The royal decree was issued on June 28, 1568, and by January of 1570 the Audiencia was installed once more in Santiago de los Caballeros (Guatemala City).[20] The attempted disruption of the cacao monopoly of Santiago and Izalcos province failed almost as badly. Landecho had been removed, but new reports from offended royal officials in the 1570s and 1580s show that the encomendero group, while reduced in numbers, was still firmly in control of the system of tributes and exactions on the fertile plain around Sonsonate.

The most complete history of the evolution of the system was provided in a long report written to the King and Consejo by President Valverde and the members of his Audiencia in 1584. They began by warning the Crown that what they had to relate was more extraordinary and unbelievable than anything coming from the Indies. After discussing the uses of cacao past and present, the documents state that the plantations on the Pacific were small when the Spaniards first arrived; there was just about enough cacao to supply the province of Guatemala itself.

Three encomenderos had been installed in Izalcos province, the richest area of the cacao coast. They were Juan de Guzmán, Francisco Xirón, and Juan Vázquez de Coronado, all from Salamanca. The President at that time was Alonso Maldonado de Paz, also from Salamanca. Juan de Guzmán was related to the President and had accompanied him to Guatemala. Many of the other encomenderos of influence were Salamancans. None was a conquistador. All had arrived in the 1540s.

As the price of cacao rose these three and some twenty others began to amass considerable fortunes. Guzmán distinguished himself. A man of "extraordinary covetousness," he returned twice to Spain taking 70,000 pesos with him. All of this fortune appears to have been produced by his encomienda. In Spain he set up two entailed estates (mayorazgos), which were later consolidated into one. He also arranged good marriages for two of his children. The document proceeds to explain how the three encomenderos managed to accumulate such wealth. In the early days of the Izalcos cacao industry the encomenderos forced the Indians to begin a

rapid expansion of the groves. The document talks of Indians planting "day and night," which may be an exaggeration. Most of the
Indians were from other areas and were hired by the Indian tributaries of the three Spaniards.[21] Other testimony corroborates these
assertions. The labor supply was recruited in a manner very similar
to that employed in Soconusco.

It must be remembered that cacao was labor intensive. By 1556
most of the original inhabitants of Izalcos province had died, and
the expanding cacao plantations were already suffering from a serious shortage of native labor. To solve this problem large numbers
of Indians were coming to Izalcos. Some came from as far as forty
leagues away, from provinces such as Comayagua and Verapaz.
Great numbers of these Indians died, and Spanish officials blamed
the change of climate. One official said that "this land is a general
sepulcher for all these Indians who come to it, for great numbers
of them die and others of them forget their wives, whom they leave
in their home villages." Once again there were complaints that the
need to earn tribute to be paid in mountain areas was driving Indians to the coast in large numbers.[22]

Legally speaking, much of the land and the cacao plantations
on it remained under Indian ownership. The Indian owners desperately needed the labor from other areas in order to grow and harvest
enough cacao to meet the exactions and confiscations of the encomenderos. In order to attract labor these Indians paid surprisingly high wages. In the early 1570s Indians from Verapaz were
earning two reales a day for their work and were going to Sonsonate
in large numbers. "This going forth [from Verapaz] is necessary for
them, for here they do not have work nor employers to pay a day's
wage, and if one [Indian] hires himself out to another here he earns
forty cacao beans daily which would be worth ten maravedis,
whereas for the same work they earn two reales a day in Sonsonate,
one for living expenses and the other for saving; so all go there and
they cannot be held back, for they argue that they are going to earn
the tribute, their shirts and their pantaloons."[23] This accurately
sums up the mixture of compulsion and eagerness which drove the
Indians of the highlands to the cacao coast in search of work.

The three original Spanish encomenderos and their descendents obtained their wealth by extortion under the guise of tribute.
The tribute which they levied was of two kinds. One was the formal
tribute required of most married Indian households in the Audiencia of Guatemala. The other tribute was levied on property and,
more significantly, on the cacao plantations according to their size

and productivity. "Thus the tribute assigned to an Indian would be according to the milpas and family inheritance that he had and could work with the help of his sons, and could rent by using his inherited wealth." And any other Indians who bought or inherited the property had to pay the tribute attached to it, even if he were paying another full tribute, or several other tributes, elsewhere.[24]

It is obvious from this and other reports that the formal ownership of a plantation meant little to the small group of encomenderos. If an Indian failed to pay his tribute, his plantations were simply taken away from him and given to someone who was thought to be more likely to pay.[25] Cacao was peculiarly adapted to a flourishing encomienda system, especially if it was not closely supervised. So the extraordinary situation was created whereby ownership of vast cacao plantations did not bring wealth to the owners during a time of heavy demand for cacao. "Rich" Indians often did not have enough surplus to clothe themselves.[26]

Because of the high mortality in Izalcos there was an unusually large number of orphans and widows. A widow was held responsible for the full tribute on her late husband's property. Such women had great difficulty in working their plantations efficiently enough to avoid the punishments inflicted for non-payment of tribute exactions. Relatives avoided them, and Indian males were reluctant to marry these seemingly wealthy heiresses, since such a marriage would mean assuming the heavy tribute burden attached to the widows' properties, in addition to the one which these males already had to pay. The Church complained that consequently many of these widows remained unmarried or lived in concubinage, thus lowering the birthrate and adding to the problem of the disappearance of the Indians.

Orphans were in a similar predicament. When a child was orphaned it was the practice among the Spaniards to appoint a "tutor" or legal guardian. This hapless individual then became responsible for the tribute on the cacao groves inherited by his orphan ward. The inevitable result was a great unwillingness among Indian men to serve as guardians. Some tutors, says the report, developed violent hatreds toward their charges. Many orphans were found dead or starved.

Various other examples of the social abnormalities caused by the tributary systems were offered as evidence. When a baby was left an orphan at birth, it was noticed that female relatives and local wetnurses were wont to flee the neighborhood to avoid ruinous tribute payments and overwork. When the owner of a cacaotal died without legal heirs, a similar panic was apt to seize his native village.

And technically some Indian owners were very wealthy. Indians were often forced to assume ownership of vacant plantations and the tribute which went with them. And if parents had fallen in arrears in tribute payments, children were obliged to inherit the debt—an early variant of the later institution of debt peonage.[27]

The tribute payments made by some Indian cacaotal owners were extremely high. A few paid as much as one hundred ducats a year. The village of Xicalapa contained only twenty-five Indian survivors by 1584 but was paying a tribute of 40 cargas each year. Forty cargas were worth 1,200 tostones at that time so that the individual Indian tributary was paying 50 tostones.[28] In some cases the exactions were such that the Indian paid more each year than he could obtain through the sale of his holdings. Indians were extremely reluctant to buy or rent cacao groves.[29]

The encomenderos had two main concerns: the careful collection of all the available cacao, and the distorting and rearranging of information about the condition of the province and its inhabitants. Confiscation of the cacao harvests was managed by two methods. These were collection of alleged past debts and personal supervision of the work in the plantations by representatives of the encomendero. By 1584 Caluca "owed" 1,100 cargas and Naolingo some 600 cargas. Gonzalo Vázquez de Coronado, Diego de Herrera, and Pedro Xirón, the principal encomenderos in the two villages, simply seized each cacao crop as it was harvested because the villages were in arrears.[30] Juan de Guzmán was the encomendero for Izalcos, the principal Indian village of the province of the same name. A true son of his father, he had proved "most extraordinarily diligent" in collecting the yearly harvests. He employed four Indian alguaciles or calpisques to act as inspectors. These individuals would go through the cacao groves and assess the likely size of the harvests. Later they would inspect the drying tables (paseras), set aside a small quantity of cacao for the Indians of the village, and take all the rest as tribute.[31]

The falsification of information was also arranged by two methods. Guzmán relied on terror to discourage the Indians from making complaints. Terror and bribery were also used to ensure that Indians gave suitable answers when questioned by visiting royal officials. Even allowing for exaggeration and atrocity stories, it was obvious that the Indians subservient to the group of encomenderos were treated with great brutality.[32]

The other method for managing information from Izalcos was bribing royal officials. The local officials, such as the alcalde mayor at Sonsonate, were willing accomplices at times and were themselves accused of extortion and fraud.[33] The high cost of living in Izalcos imposed a strain on the honesty of poorly paid local alcaldes mayores. After a short residence in Sonsonate officials were faced either with bankruptcy, which did in fact happen to one official, or with the need to accumulate outside income. Thus they were rendered susceptible to the blandishments of local merchants and encomenderos.[34]

Visitadores, arriving suddenly from Santiago de Guatemala or more distant places, were more of a threat to the group which dominated Izalcos. They had not been "conditioned" by life in the area, and they arrived with little advance warning. Usually they were oidores, or judges, from the Audiencia in Santiago, where other opportunities for wealth had been open to them. On the other hand, it was to the encomenderos' advantage that they were limited by their lack of knowledge of the region and by their normal human cupidity. Since few oidores had either the time or the inclination to count trees in the cacao groves or the number of tributary Indians, they were forced to rely on careful questioning of local Indians. These terrorized Indians, even the caciques, had been supplied with appropriate answers. There is also evidence that bribes were accepted by these judge inspectors. The well-known oidor Diego García de Palacios "visited" Izalcos in 1575 as part of a larger mission through San Salvador and San Miguel. He was a military man who showed a marked preference for a military career whenever possible. His attitude toward Indians can be judged by his reports. He believed that they needed discipline and firm guidance but showed a genuine interest in their customs and religions.[35] Nevertheless it seems evident that he was either duped while in Izalcos or was acting in collusion with the local encomenderos to present a false report of conditions in the province. It is known that his tour of inspection of the area was extremely rapid and that his questioning of a small number of Indian witnesses was brief. Some reports to the King state that he was deceived by Diego de Guzmán. Others say he was bribed.

At the time of his visita there were only 520 survivors of the 700 tributaries counted in López de Cerrato's day, but García de Palacios was obviously persuaded to include imported Indians in his count, and the tributary totals and assessments were not changed. Indian witnesses had been bribed or terrorized by Diego de Guzmán, as was usually the case. Any Indians who attempted to see García de Palacios were taken away for punishment. One was severely beaten outside the house where the oidor was staying, and when he inquired about the noise he was told that an obstreperous vagabond was disturbing the peace. García de Palacios was also misled about the number of cacao trees in production.[36]

Such visitations were infrequent in the heyday of the Izalcos and Guazacapán cacao fields. The Audiencia of Guatemala was chronically understaffed and on one occasion was reduced to the President and one oidor. In such circumstances, as the Audiencia repeatedly pointed out to the King, this tribunal could not send its judges on protracted tours through the distant regions of the large kingdom of Guatemala.[37] Encomenderos used the law to good effect in this situation. Guzmán insisted that only oidores were legally entitled to make such visitas and would receive no substitute officials for such purposes. As a result the powerful encomenderos were rarely troubled by outside interference and conducted the affairs of the area as if it were a private fiefdom until the 1580s.

As in Soconusco, the factor of greatest importance in the history of the cacao fields of Sonsonate was Indian population decline. All indications point to a peak of expansion and productivity in the early 1570s. At that time the province was "so full of people that it looked like a street."[38] The area had all the typical characteristics of a monoculture boom. It was so packed with cacao trees that other crops could scarcely be grown. Food was imported and prices were high. Cattle had been banned for a distance of twenty leagues from the villa of Sonsonate. Indian farmers' complaints that cattle intrusions were harming their crops met with sympathy from the Spaniards, for once, because cacao was the crop involved.[39]

The poor port facilities were proving a small handicap. There were always two or three ships loading off Acajutla. Royal intrusion on the lucrative trade was disposed of by suborning local officials or evading their ordinances, but even so the almojarifazgo totals in Acajutla were impressive.[40] From about 1562 until the late 1570s the Izalcos area seems to have exported about 50,000 cargas a year by sea to New Spain. This can be compared with some 3,000 to 4,000 in Soconusco and about 1,000 cargas in Zapotitlán. Izalcos' total production was much higher than 50,000 cargas. Some cacao, perhaps as much as 1,000 cargas per year, was exported to New Spain by land, and Izalcos also supplied Guatemala, and to a lesser extent Panama and Peru. To avoid alcabala, the purchase of licenses, and excise taxes, large amounts of cacao were being exported by land along the coast. Guazacapán in particular used this route. As we have noted, all efforts to provide that area with a port had failed, and the inconvenience of sending the cacao by mule train down the coast to Acajutla, and then by ship to Huatulco was even greater than that of sending it by land through Zapotitlán, Soconusco, and occasionally Chiapas, a route, moreover, which was occasionally tax free.[41] Sporadic efforts by the Audiencia or the Crown to force compliance with the laws, or to ascertain the true state of the province and its subject Indians were parried with little sustained effort.

Yet the beginnings of decline were already present, and the decay of the industry, once it began, was precipitous. The near extinction of the original inhabitants of Izalcos and the high mortality among the immigrants from other areas meant that a steady replacement of manpower was essential. The tasks of harvesting, watering, weeding, ditching, and replacing unproductive trees were constant.[42]

By the late 1570s the outside sources of manpower had dried up. The epidemics and high death rates in these areas had drastically decreased the population. Large numbers had gone willingly or unwillingly to the coast and had not returned. And above all Spaniards in the sierra were becoming concerned that their own labor force was being destroyed for the benefit of others. Consequently they began to prohibit Indians from going to the coast. Royal laws were invoked forbidding the movement of Indians to different climates.[43]

The report of 1584 examines the manpower situation in the three principal villages of Izalcos province at that time. Izalcos, which had 800 to 900 tributaries when first assigned to Juan de Guzmán, by then had only 100 native tributaries and 400 to 500 Indians from other areas. Naolingo had been reduced from 600 to 40 or 50 native tributaries, and 250 "foreign" Indians had been added. Caluca, with an original population of 700, had 60 native tributaries and 240 immigrants remaining. The work force therefore amounted to somewhat over 1,000 Indians. But this number was falling fast, and new arrivals were increasingly scarce. The alarmist Audiencia forecast that if the trend continued the province would be totally depopulated within ten years. As it was, many Indian cacaotal owners could not find the labor to keep their plantations in full production despite energetic recruiting attempts by the encomenderos. Consequently their arrears in tribute were piling up year by year; the groves were becoming overgrown with weeds and were gradually declining in yield. Yet tribute levies had not been lowered and, as the reports succinctly put it, "dead Indians" were paying tributes.[44] The few Indians from other provinces who were

Figure 7

Indian Tributary Population, Verapaz, Sixteenth Century

Year	No. of Tributaries	No. of Villages	Source	Comments
1544	12,000 to 14,000		AGI/AG 10, Audiencia to Crown, April 23, 1582. AGI/AG 163, Bishop Antonio de Hervias to Crown (1583).	Seven languages spoken.
1561	6,000 to 7,000		AGI/AG 965, Viceroy Luis Velasco to Bishop Angulo, (1561?); Frs. Viana, Gallego, and Cadena, "Relación de la provincia....de la Vera paz," *Guatemala Indígena*, II, no. 3 (1962), p. 158.	Two languages now spoken. Tribute counting began about this time.
1566	3,856		AGGG, A3. 16, exped. 26371, legajo 1600 (1571).	
1571	3,135 to 3,329	15	AGGG, A3. 16, exped. 26371, legajo 1600 (1571); Viana, Gallegos, and Cadena, "Relación," p. 158.	The AGGG source mentions 4,214 vasallos, (all males including caciques and other reservados). The figure of 3,135 is too low because it includes three villages which were counted by houses.
1573	3,864	15	AGI/AG 9. Dr. Villalobos to Crown, May 15, 1573.	A new tasación, just completed. Yet may be a reference to the one of 1566.
1578	3,135	15	AGI/AG 39. Dr. Villalobos to Crown, March 15, 1578. See also AGI/AG 10. Dr. Villalobos to Crown, March 17, 1578.	A curious document. Villalobos is obviously using the count of 1571, in spite of the new one made in 1573.
1583-84	c. 3,000	15	AGI/AG, 10 Lcdo. Velásquez Ramírez to Crown, April 15, 1584; AGI/AG 163, Bishop Antonio de Hervias to Crown (1583).	These are rough figures in both cases.
1590	1,948	12	AGI/AG 966, "Cuenta de los indios tributarios de la Verapaz," April 10, 1590.	
1598	1,948	12	AGI/AG 11, "Testimonio sobre los indios tributarios que ay en la provincia de la Verapaz," April 8, 1598.	Obviously relies on the count used in 1590.
1664	2,105		BPR Miscelanea de Ayala, XXXV (1664).	Refers to "Cobán and its partido," so may be low.

coming to Izalcos by this time had often been deceived by promises of complete exemption from tribute. When the new arrivals found that tributes and other payments were expected from them after all, many fled.[45]

The growing labor shortage in the Izalcos cacao groves led to even heavier exactions by the encomenderos. The surviving Indians were called and recalled with ever increasing frequency for tandas or cyclical work gangs. Other injustices increased as the encomenderos' determination to maintain production led to mounting pressure on the Indian population. The devastating plague of 1578 pushed the labor shortage to a critical level.[46]

By 1582 the situation had become so scandalous, and the stories of extreme oppression so numerous, that the Audiencia instigated a full-scale investigation of the conduct of Diego de Guzmán, the leading encomendero. One report tells of a quarrel between Guzmán and another encomendero. In a spirit of revenge the rival encomendero "told all" to the Audiencia. No doubt the Royal Decree dated Lisbon 27 May 1582, which arrived in Guatemala the following year, demanding that the taxing of dead Indians must stop, also pushed the Audiencia to more forceful action. Guzmán was a powerful figure. While serious charges against him were being investigated he was elected alcalde of Santiago City by its ayuntamiento. The Audiencia refused to permit him to take office, and the ayuntamiento protested interference.[47]

The amazement and dismay of the Audiencia at what it found is obvious. Guzmán was living like a feudal lord, maltreating his wife and surrounded by mistresses. After putting up a spirited defense, it became obvious to Guzmán that he would not escape conviction on the three major charges—overcollection of tribute, maltreatment of the Indians, and deception and bribery of government officials. Guzmán fled, having carefully arranged changes of horses along his route of escape. His wife, who had sought refuge in a convent, was granted a small pension by the Audiencia, and Guzmán's fiefdom was ordered broken up. Tributes were lowered by as much as three-quarters in the district which he had dominated.[48]

The removal of Guzmán did nothing to halt the decay of the cacao industry. Evidence of increasing decadence follows lines similar to those of Soconusco. Indians were unable to pay tribute and asked to be allowed exemptions, postponements, or permission to pay in other goods. Groves grew old and overgrown, but little replanting was done. Merchants and sometimes local priests continued to defraud Indians by using alcohol and other methods.[49]

Fresh fields for new groves were opened up further down the coast in San Salvador, San Miguel, and northwestern Nicaragua. At times these new fields seemed to have reached considerable sizes. Initially at least, their output was surprisingly high, better than that of Izalcos.[50] But the large fields had declined for good, and by 1600 the great days of the cacao coast had passed.

Although demographic catastrophe had played a major role in the decline of the cacao fields on the Pacific coast, there were several other major causes, as in Soconusco, which cannot be ignored. The cacao trees were particularly susceptible to natural disasters. Cold northerly winds known as "papagallos" would sweep across large areas, parrots and locusts could cause extensive damage, and the fields of Izalcos were damaged by heavy falls of ash from a nearby erupting volcano on at least one occasion.[51]

Improvident agricultural methods were also a factor in the decline. The Central American varieties of cacao were delicate to begin with, and there was little improvement in ways of irrigation, harvesting, and maintenance throughout the period. The destruction of surrounding protective vegetation, the overcrowded plantations, the careless harvesting and inattention to renovation shortened the lives of many trees. The heavy cutting and burning of forests and tall grasses caused erosion, leaching of the top soil, and flash flooding. Land was plentiful compared to labor and capital on the cacao coast, and the Spaniards saw no reason for maintaining its quality or fertility. The restoration of eroded, leached soils for cacao plantations is an extraordinarily long and difficult task even today. The Central Americans of the sixteenth and seventeenth centuries did not have the technology or the patience to attempt it. Cattle or brush often filled the poor pasture lands left behind by the exhausted cacao groves.[52]

Cacao did not drop from sight, however; it had created too many fortunes to be quickly forgotten. During the seventeenth century many battled to revive the industry and to protect what was left of it from the threats of outside competition.

6

From Conquest to the Emergence of Order and Pattern

Before examining the lives of Central American Spaniards and Indians between 1524 and the middle of the 1570s it would be well to evaluate once more the aims and ambitions of those of the Spanish group. The traditional picture has been that economically and socially speaking, the conquerors and their followers were fired by emulation. Mostly of lower class derivation, or at best from the minor regional nobilities of Spain, they envisioned themselves, we are told, as feudal lords, a status which could only be gained by obtaining large quantities of precious metals or money, or by ownership of large cattle or sheep estates worked by semi-servile labor. Ownership of such estates, this traditional version continues, gave Spaniards the self-image and prestige which they desired and the surplus capital so produced allowed them to live as nobles in the courtly and administrative capitals, the most desired of which were Valladolid and later Madrid.[1]

Certainly many Spaniards of the sixteenth century were motivated by such general notions, and some of them, upon coming to the New World and failing to find sufficient gold and silver at once, soon directed their energies to the accumulation of land.[2]

In general, however, the feudal-land set of motivations would seem to have waned by the sixteenth century. Although the settlers lived in the New World, their main ties were with the Old, at least in the first few decades; and because of this, one of their ambitions was to take or send wealth back there, and thus to accumulate capital. The primary economic purpose of the colony to them, and to the Crown, was to provide exportable wealth which would improve the economic situation of the individuals concerned or of the nation as a whole. In general, it would seem that Spaniards, rather than engaging in activities which can be recognized as feudal, moved in preference toward what could be described as early modern entrepreneurialism.

In the Central American case we have seen that the first activity of consequence was a rush toward the gold and silver bearing streams which might yield the precious metals which were in great demand in Europe, which would pay the freight and other costs of sending them there and would still show a handsome profit. Failing these precious metals, and Central American extraction of gold and silver soon did fail, the next best option was to use local products which were in demand, not in Europe, but in other American markets. If such enterprises were sufficiently successful, the profits which they produced could then be transferred to Spain and exchanged for mayorazgos, noble titles, or other advantages. Some of the large cacao encomenderos were able to do this. The export of Indian slaves from Nicaragua and Honduras and cacao from Soconusco and Izalcos represent these kinds of activities. Unfortunately for the Spaniards, disease, overwork, and the export of slaves reduced the work force, outside competition challenged their prices, and these industries too declined.

Thus the economic history of sixteenth century Central America can best be described as a desperate and fairly successful search for a key to wealth from exports, a search for a cash crop or "produit moteur," as the Chaunus have called it, which would bring rapid accumulations of wealth to many individuals of the conquering groups.[3] These entrepreneurial ambitions made control of labor more important than control or ownership of land. Slaves, silver mining, cacao, and, as we shall see, congregación, or the gathering of Indians into centralized large villages, and encomienda, the assigning of given numbers of Indians to specified Spanish individuals for service and tribute, were far more important features of the years before 1580 than the acquisition of land or title to land. Only in areas very close to major Spanish towns, such as Santiago de Guatemala or Granada-León, where there was a fair market for European agricultural produce, or in regions where the Indian population had quickly disappeared, for example around San Miguel and Trujillo, was there any early interest in taking possession of land.[4] Even during the brief economic pause just after mid-century, the two leading reactions of Spaniards were to search for a new cash crop to replace slaving and silver, a search which led to the Izalcos cacao monoculture, or to flee to better areas such as Peru. Relatively few had yet reached the stage of resignation which would push them toward farming or stock raising as a principal livelihood.[5]

Figure 8
Pandemics in Central America, 1519–1750

Years	Location	Origin	Illness Identified or Symptoms	Comments	Sources
1519-20	Guatemalan highlands	Cuba	Nosebleeds, pains in the side, rapid death. Smallpox in New Spain. May have been accompanied by pulmonary plague or typhus in C. America.	Very high mortality, 1/3 of general population. This epidemic probably covered most parts of Mesoamerica, but it is pre-conquest in most areas. Therefore we have few sources.	Annals of the Cakchiquels; FG, I, p. 338.
1529-31	Nicaragua Honduras Chiapas	Panama?	peste (pneumonic plague) tabardillo in Chiapas. Followed by famine.	Very high mortality, 1/3 to 2/3. Several sources talk of more than 1/2.	Lic. Castañeda to Crown, CDI, 24, pp. 182-83; AGGG, A1. 37, exp. 41234, legajo 4777; Pedrarias to Crown, Jan. 20, 1520, CS I, 456.
1532-34	General	Mexico	"sarampión"	High mortality. Some 6,000 deaths, 1/3 of Indian population in Nicaragua. Indians said in Nicaragua that this disease and the one of 1530-31 were unknown to them. Measles?	Lic. Castañeda to Crown, CDI, 24, p. 193; Alvarado to Crown, Sept. 1, 1532, *Cartas del Perú;* Oviedo, VIII, p. 151.
1545-48	General	Mexico	"peste" (pneumonic plague) "gucumatz" (cocoliztli)	Very high mortality. Several villages disappeared.	FG III, 425; Isagoge, p. 290.
1576-77	General	Mexico	"peste" (pneumonic plague) and viruelas, "matlazáhuatl," gucumatz	High mortality. Several villages disappeared.	Isagoge, p. 290; AGI/AG 10, Lcdo. Salazar to Crown, March 15, 1578. Several other letters in this legajo.
1600-01	General		Killed in 3 days.	Killed in 3 days. High mortality. In Verapaz, smallpox also.	Bancroft, II; p. 656; Asturias, p. 87; AGGG, A3. 16, exped. 40493, legajo 2801 (1600).
1607-78	General		Nosebleeds, "tabardillo," (typhus and/or plague).	Worst in highlands, less deadly on coast. Did not greatly affect Spaniards, but did affect all Indians, even those "ladinoized." Came after a good harvest. Suggests fleas or lice as a vector. 30,000 deaths.	Alonso Criado del Castillo to Crown, 1608 in *Boletín,* XI, nos. 1 and 2 (1946), pp. 20-21; Ayón, I, p. 15.
1631	General		Typhus	"Many deaths"	Molina, *Memorias,* p. 254; Gage, p. 291.
1686	General		Typhus and/or pneumonic plague	"dolores del costado," "peste." Killed 1/10 of Santiago. Indians and poor had highest mortality.	Pardo, *Efemérides,* pp. 103-4; Bancroft, II, p. 656; FV, 4, p. 253; Espinosa, *Crónica,* p. 547; FG, I, p. 151.
1693-94	General		Sarampión, viruela, tabardillo	High mortality	Pardo, *Efemérides,* p. 115; AGGG, A1. 6-7, exp. 30980, leg. 4026 (1694); ANCR Cartago 098(1699).

Figure 9

Local Epidemics in Central America, 1520–1700

Years	Location	Illness Identified or Symptoms	Sources	Comments
1563-65	Guatemala	drought, famine, followed by an epidemic	Batres, *La América Central*, 2:318; Bancroft, *History of Central America*, 2:367, 375.	Link between malnutrition and disease
1570[a]	Verapaz Soconusco	local famine, then fevers	Diego Garcés to Crown, November 30, 1570, AGI/AG 9.	Many deaths in Soconusco
1571	Guatemala Verapaz	"peste"	AGGG, A1. 23, legajo 1512, f.416; Viana, Gallegos, p. 150.	
1573	Costa Rica Nicoya	fevers	Thiel, "Datos Cronológicos," p. 57.	300 deaths in Nicoya
1585	North of Granada	famine, weakness, and disease	Ponce's *Relación*, p. 358.	
1598	Verapaz	"peste"	"Testimonio sobre los indios tributarios que ay en la ... Verapaz," AGI/AG 11.	
1610	Nicaragua	famine, then illness	Ayón, *Historia de Nicaragua*, 1:15.	
1614[b]	Reventazón valley, Costa Rica	"peste"	Thiel, "Datos Cronológicos," pp. 73-76.	Atirró left with only 12 inhabitants
1614	Guatemala	an epidemic	AGGG, A1. 23, legajo 1514, f. 237.	Illness confined to Indians
1645	Costa Rica	"peste"	Thiel, "Datos Cronológicos," p. 95.	
1647	Santiago	"peste"	Pardo, *Efemérides*, p. 59; FG, 1, p. 151.	Flight to countryside, over 1000 deaths
1650	Guatemalan highlands	gucumatz, bubonic plague	FG, 3:401-2; Molina. *Memorias*, p. 106.	Villages disappeared, great death
1654	Quepo, district	smallpox	ANCR, Cartago 041.	Tribute reduced
1660	Santiago	smallpox	Molina, *Memorias*, p. 106.	
1666	Guatemalan highlands, San Salvador	"peste," "tabardillo," typhus?	Pardo, *Efemérides*, p. 74; AGGG, A3. 16, 26390, 1600 (1670); AGGG, A1. 1, 50569, 5911 (1667).	"Many deaths"
1676	Santiago	"peste"	Molina, *Memorias*, p. 132.	
1690	Costa Rica	smallpox	Thiel, "Datos Cronológicos," p. 134.	In the valles, or Spanish rural settlements.
1695	Guatemalan highlands	smallpox	Pardo, *Efemérides*, p. 118.	

[a] Origin, Mexico.
[b] Origin, a ship.

Figure 10

Local Epidemics in Central America, 1700–1750

Year	Location	Illness identified or symptoms	Source	Comments
1704-05	Guatemalan highlands	"peste"	Pardo, *Efemérides*, pp. 131, 133.	
1707	Santiago	smallpox, complications	Pardo, *Efemérides*, p. 134.	
1708-09	Guatemalan highlands	"peste"	Pardo, *Efemérides*, p. 135; AGGG, A1. 23, legajo 4597, f.50.	Limited to the Indian population
1710-11	Guatemalan highlands	"peste"	*Isagoge*, p. 291.	Small villages extinguished
1723	Santiago	smallpox	Pardo, *Efemérides*, p. 159.	
1728	Santiago	"sarampión"	Pardo, *Efemérides*, p. 165.	Indians especially affected
1733	Guatemalan highlands	"peste," smallpox, typhoid	Asturias, p. 88.	Many deaths, in one month alone 1,500
1737	Costa Rica	plague	Thiel, "Datos Cronológicos," 182.	
1741	Guatemalan highlands	"tabardillo," typhus	Pardo, *Efemérides*, p. 189.	Pains in the side
1746	Guatemalan highlands	"tabardillo," typhus	Pardo, *Efemérides*, p. 198.	

The first two decades after the conquest were ones of great confusion in Central America. Labor was absurdly plentiful at first and was used capriciously and wastefully. The few surviving Indian accounts tell of arbitrary seizures and forced movements of Indian populations, of Indians dying in unfamiliar climes while performing unaccustomed tasks, of anarchy in the countryside and on the highways.[6] The old Indian routes and trading patterns from village to village were severely disrupted and this, together with the catastrophic mortalities of the twenties and thirties, effectively shattered the greater political fabric of Indian society. When order of a kind was restored in the 1540s the Indian kingdoms and confederations had disappeared; Quichés, Cakchiquels, Nicaraos, or Chorotegas had ceased to be nations and had become linguistic classifications. The royal houses or paramount chiefs had gone (partly as a result of deliberate Spanish policy), and the village chieftain had replaced them, leading at best a large village or two with a few anexos or subsidiary hamlets.[7]

In the Spanish society of the twenties and thirties the anarchy was almost as prevalent. Rumors of new conquests and El Dorados would set groups of men campaigning across the length and breadth of Central America. Disgust at their disappointments in Central America and exaggerated reports of the wealth of Peru led other groups to abandon Central America altogether. Alvarado is reported to have taken 400 men—which sounds like an impossibly high figure, since the total Spanish population of Central America in the 1530s cannot have been much higher—to meddle in the conquest of Ecuador and Peru, and it was conquistadors from Guatemala who became, in the main, the first settlers of Quito.[8] (Alvarado also took Indian auxiliaries with him, a small matter compared to the vast numbers rounded up, branded, and shipped to Panama and Peru from Nicaragua.)

Other factors added to the chaos of the first two decades. Royal government was distant, although it may well be doubted if it could have accomplished much anyway at this early stage. The conquest was not a unified enterprise, and the conquerors soon fell to quarreling over spoils and boundaries. The result was more campaigns. The forced marches and campaigning which Indians were obliged to do to help one Spanish conqueror against another or to reach some distant gold-bearing stream may have been as baneful to the indigenous peoples as the original conquests. Alvarado, when he went to Honduras to establish his claims against Montejo and to find gold, took large groups of Indians with him, Guatemalan warriors of an unidentified group known as the Achíes, who savagely attacked their Honduran counterparts. He also took cuadrillas of slaves for gold panning.[9] When he was finally bought off and new rumors of wealth elsewhere sent him rushing back to Guatemala, he took large numbers of Honduran Indians back with him.[10] In the same way raiding parties from Nicaragua sponsored by Pedrarias, which attempted to assert claims to the Caribbean coast of Honduras, brought armies of Nicaraguan bearers, auxiliaries, and gold-panning cuadrillas. Once again the results were disastrous.[11] Other Indian groups were used in the peripheral entradas made throughout the first half century of Spanish rule. Every Spanish expedition to Costa Rica or against the Chol-Manché and Lacandones of Upper Verapaz required large numbers of impressed Indian auxiliaries, and more threats to their numbers and to the villages and dependents which these predominantly male groups had been forced to abandon.[12]

The restlessness and migratory urges of many Spaniards, the forced migration of large numbers of Indians, the lawlessness practiced upon Indian communities, the quarrels between the various

groups of conquistadors, and the absence of governmental control
are all major features of the two decades of conquest. All these
features, moreover, are related to the nature of Spanish conquistador leadership during this period. With the exception of Francisco
de Montejo, who, whether in Yucatan, Honduras, or Chiapas,
showed a compulsive urge to organize, control populations, and
stabilize institutions—like Cortés, he was essentially a post-conquest, administrative type as well as a conqueror in his own right—
the major conquerors in Central America exacerbated the chaotic
atmosphere of the early years by the nature of their temperaments
and ambitions.[13] If men such as the Alvarado brothers, Pedrarias
Dávila, Francisco de Castañeda, or the Contreras family are considered, with their followers, as a group, two salient facts about their
post-conquest activities soon emerge. First, most if not all of them
were not basically interested in Central America per se. They
thought of it as a staging area, or an asylum, or at best as a part of
a whole complex of interlocking source materials, which if fitted
together in the proper conjunction might produce capital. Second,
these men were entrepreneurs, not administrators and certainly not
statesmen. Others were thus potential rivals, and such matters as
colonial institutions, the founding and location of Spanish cities, the
administration of a given law, or the distribution of benefits such as
encomiendas and land grants were seen primarily in terms of how
they could best be used to produce capital for the individual conqueror.

Pedro de Alvarado is the most extreme example. Guatemala
was to him what Cuba might have become to an unsuccessful Cortés.
He was always traveling: to Spain to "mend fences" or to arrange
a money-making enterprise with the clique around Francisco de los
Cobos; to Peru to try to capture part of the spoils generated by the
Pizarros, Almagro, and Benalcazar; or to the Spice Islands, which
death prevented him from reaching, to tap the legendary riches of
the Orient.[14] He did return each time to Guatemala, and he did
indeed establish many new enterprises there, but his returns were
not those of a chastened man or of an aging warrior seeking an
agreeable and well-earned niche for his old age. His Guatemalan
lands were a reserve, a bank of Indian labor, of persuadable, restless, and ambitious Spanish soldiery, of goods produced by his
many slaves and encomiendas, of gold and silver from its streams
and those of Chiapas and Honduras, only to be tapped fully when
previous capital ran out or an enterprise abroad failed, but then
tapped with all the single-mindedness of which he was so awesomely
capable.[15]

Pedrarias Dávila showed similar traits. Old age kept the Justiciador from personally wandering around the New and Old Worlds like an Alvarado, but the Isles and Tierra Firme failed to hold him, and Panama and Nicaragua produced a restlessness which exacerbated his customary ferocity. Instead he sponsored and financed overseas enterprises, up the Pacific coast to Nicoya and Nicaragua, down the same coast using his subordinates Pizarro and Almagro to search for the rumored Inca empire, and once he was established in Nicaragua, into El Salvador and Honduras. In all these enterprises the necessary capital was produced by a ruthless manipulation of salaried offices, encomiendas, slaves, export of slaves, gold, silver, and Spanish soldiers.[16]

Thus it is possible to interpret the first chaotic quarter century of Guatemala's existence as a Spanish colony in terms of the arrivals and departures of Alvarado and men like him. His departures to Spain or on a new entrada would leave Guatemala exhausted, drained of many Spaniards, some Indians, and all of the capital in gold, silver, supplies, and ships which he had been able to accumulate. At the same time he would leave behind a collective sigh of relief, a group of resentful and ambitious men, including his two brothers Jorge and Gonzalo, whom he exploited as extensively and rewarded almost as meagerly as others. No doubt hoping that Pedro would find great wealth elsewhere and not return, those left in Guatemala would begin an extensive redistribution of encomiendas, offices, and other advantages.[17]

Upon returning, armed with new rights and privileges, and sometimes accompanied by new and hungry soldiers and settlers, Pedro would be as ambitious as ever, but capital-starved. His arrival would therefore bring a reversal of many of the previous decisions, the voiding of encomienda grants made by Jorge de Alvarado or others, and a new intensive campaign to raise the men, ships, supplies, and money needed for his next foreign enterprise.[18] The instability which these departures, absences, and returns caused can well be imagined. The average Spanish settler could not be sure of his tenure of encomienda, house plot (solar), land allotment near the city, or much else. Little wonder that so many settlers left in disgust or were so ready to follow the next leader to raise a new enterprise of exploration or conquest.

The deaths of these entrepreneur-conquerors of Central America brought similar consequences and are equally revealing about their activities. When Alvarado died in the Mixton Wars in 1541, far from Guatemala and in the final stages of preparing a new expedition, the settling of his estate led to a new distribution of wealth, partly because the contrite Alvarado felt burdened by past sins and asked that this be done, and partly because so much of his estate in Indian slaves, encomiendas, and lands had been acquired and held through such patently illegal or ruthless methods, this in spite of the attempts of his executor, Guatemala's Bishop Francisco Marroquín, to justify and gloss over many of his past transgressions.[19]

The deaths or removals of the early governors of Nicaragua, Pedrarias Dávila and Rodrigo de Contreras, brought even more extreme readjustments and redistributions. At the time of his death Pedrarias seems to have held over half of the available encomiendas in the province.[20] His death may have brought a more egalitarian distribution of encomiendas and other perquisites, but if it did, this was temporary, for Castañeda and Contreras were accused of accumulating almost as much of the available encomiendas as had Pedrarias. Contreras was able to evade the spirit of the New Laws (1541) by distributing many of his encomiendas among his family, retainers, and close followers. At his death he too seems to have held at least a third of the available Nicaraguan encomienda Indians, and a new distribution once again took place.[21] The picture which emerges is one of the granting, voiding, and regranting of encomiendas, land titles, and other privileges; this was a chronically unstable society, and would remain so while it was under the domination of that first generation of enterprising conquerors.

Even in these two turbulent decades some important patterns began to emerge. Everywhere the Indian population declined catastrophically. The wars of conquest and the skirmishing between conquerors, overwork on gold panning, exorbitant Spanish demands for tribute and labor, the dislocations brought to the food supply and marketing systems by deprivations and forced migrations, the rapid shattering of the native culture, all played a part. On the Pacific coast around San Salvador, on the Caribbean coast of Honduras, and especially around the Nicaraguan lakes there is no doubt that the export of large numbers of the indigenous population caused serious demographic losses. In Nicaragua this seems to have been the leading cause of depopulation. None of these factors, however, can explain the magnitude of the disaster, outside Nicaragua, except the pandemics of 1519–20, 1530–34, and 1545–48. And to these must be added the local epidemics which raged almost everywhere in Central America at some time or another during the colonial period.[22]

The effect of these demographic catastrophes varied according to the region. By the late 1540s, Soconusco, Nicaragua, and Caribbean Honduras, in short much of the lowlands, had been reduced to areas of sparse Indian populations. Most Spaniards there had either left, taken to the countryside themselves to begin small farms, or had carefully gathered the few remaining Indians around the tiny, isolated Spanish settlements.[23] Where there was no export industry of consequence, as around San Miguel, there was little to do except live off the expanding populations of domestic animals.[24] In regions where there still remained a possibility of extracting precious metals, or of exporting a cash crop—as in Soconusco, Sonsonate, Trujillo, and to a lesser extent Granada and León— attempts were made to induce or force Indians to come in from the highlands of Chiapas, Verapaz, and Guatemala. Some Spaniards resorted to expeditions to previously unconquered areas, either hoping to settle there and abandon the depleted sites previously occupied, or to "bring out" captured Indians and thus rebuild the labor force. All three kinds of attempts to repopulate the emptied zones were, in the long run, failures. As populations decreased in the highlands Spaniards living in Ciudad Real de Chiapas and Santiago de Guatemala became less willing to allow their servile labor to leave for the coasts. The Indians were no longer such a surplus commodity and were more and more needed where they were. Nor could the attempts to bring Indians out of previously unconquered sectors or to settle there hope to accomplish much. Part of the reason why these peripheral areas had remained unconquered was that they were not desirable for Europeans. With the exception of the Costa Rican highlands they were regions of poor soils, tropical rain forests, and relatively sparse, nomadic populations. Hopes of settling in these tropical forests were frustrated, the Indians were hard to catch, and when brought out to previously occupied Spanish areas they either proved unsuitable for the labor assigned to them or died from disease and shock, perhaps even more rapidly than had the original Indian inhabitants.[25] Nevertheless, this method of "entrada y saca" was to continue throughout the sixteenth and seventeenth centuries, and indeed it intensified and spread to new areas as the Indian populations continued to decline.[26]

In these lowlands, however, although the Indian populations had declined so remarkably, the volume of complaint about the lack of a labor force did not reach the crescendo which it was to do between 1580 and 1630. This was still an optimistic era of conquest, and there still seemed to be many alternatives which, once explored, would bring wealth. In some areas such as the Olancho valley, the profits of the first years could be used to import negro slaves to replace the vanished Indians. In San Salvador and Olancho there were large negro slave populations by 1550.[27] Above all, this was still an era of mobile, indeed somewhat transient, Spanish populations, and the Indian populations, although much reduced, still had not fallen to their nadir and could support a small elite class. Spanish populations in the lowlands, therefore, tended to adjust themselves downwards before 1545. Those who could not find encomiendas, slaves, or other situations to their liking could still leave for other regions with fair hopes of something better, leaving those behind with a few Indians each with which to maintain a moderate town existence. In the future, as Indian populations headed inexorably downward and as the other regions of Spanish America became filled, pressures and complaints would increase and settlers would be forced to look beyond the Indians for a source to supply their basic needs.

In the highlands of Honduras, Guatemala, and Chiapas the population decline had also been precipitious, and this was noted by Spaniards before 1550, but the original numbers of Indians had been so large and the numbers of Spaniards were still so small that the situation still seemed to the dominant group to be one of plenty. Individuals complained that Alvarado or others were denying them an adequate number of Indians, and that the division of labor supplies was partial and unjust, but in the highlands there was still a surplus of Indian labor.[28]

The Costa Rican highlands were still to be conquered, there were various seventeenth-century forays into Taguzgalpa and Talamanca, and the Petén would not be subdued until the late 1690s, but these were peripheral areas. By the late 1540s the conquest was over. There are other reasons for considering the late 1540s as a decisive turning point in the most important areas of Central America. By then the first individualistic conquerors were all dead. The highest posts were now filled by royal administrators appointed from Spain and more interested in administration than in warfare and exploration. These royal administrators first began to make their presence felt in the same years as the first great missionary effort by the monastic orders. (In Central America the Dominicans, the Franciscans, and the Mercedarians led the sixteenth-century "spiritual conquest" in about that order of importance.)

Priests and friars had accompanied the conquering bands of the 1520s, but these men recruited by and subservient to the great conquerors emerge as compliant figures, ministering to the occasional spiritual needs of the Spaniards and living in the Spanish cities. Francisco Marroquín, the first bishop of Guatemala and a close friend of Pedro de Alvarado, is a typical example. He arrived in Guatemala early in the 1520s and lived in Santiago serving the Spanish community. He attempted to persuade the local Spaniards to modify the worst of their abuses against the Indians, but he does not seem to have felt any urge in these early days to condemn such activities from the pulpit, or to report the offenders to the authorities in Mexico or Spain. In Marroquín's defense it can be argued that his approach to maltreatment of the Indians was a realistic one given the economic and political forces which he encountered in the colony.[29] The early priests and friars in Honduras, Nicaragua, and Chiapas were even more inconspicuous than Marroquín.

In the late 1530s and early 1540s these faceless men found themselves under pressure from a new kind of cleric. Apostolic, ascetic missionaries similar to the famous twelve who came to Mexico with Motolinía began to arrive in Chiapas, Guatemala, and Honduras in some numbers.[30] They claimed that their express purpose was to convert the Indian masses to Christianity, and in order to do this effectively they established themselves in Indian villages, where they vigorously opposed the excesses of the Spanish slavers and encomenderos.[31]

Of even more political moment was the arrival of a new kind of bishop. Bishops Pedraza in Honduras and Valdivieso in Nicaragua wasted little time in friendly persuasion. In letter after letter to the Crown, and in repeated harangues from the pulpit, they condemned what they felt to be the greed and cruelty of the local conquerors and settlers.[32]

The death of Valdivieso seems to provide further evidence of the realism of Marroquín's tactics. Valdivieso's condemnations of the activities of Governor Rodrigo de Contreras sent Contreras back to Spain to defend himself, and in his absence the bishop's continued attempts to bring about drastic reform provoked his two sons to such extremes that one of them, Hernando Contreras, murdered the bishop and then with his brother led an unsuccessful revolt which for a short time held Nicaragua and threatened Panama.[33]

Even more emphatic were the activities in Central America of the great "apostle of the Indians," the Dominican Bartolomé de las Casas. Appointed bishop of Chiapas in 1543, he brought a zealous group of Dominican monks from Spain with him to his new episcopal seat in Ciudad Real de Chiapa. The result was a decade of struggle between the Dominicans and the local encomenderos, in which the Dominicans tried to curtail the unrestricted rights which the encomenderos enjoyed over the Indian population.[34]

The dedication of these early apostles to improving the lives of the Indians is beyond question, but there is little doubt that the struggle was also, at least in part, a fight for the allegiance and services of the Indians. As a result the Indian cacique class, as usual, found itself caught in the middle, unable to serve both of the contending forces.

In Chiapa de los Indios, one of the largest villages of the province, the death of the cacique provoked a bitter contest. The local encomenderos picked a candidate who had proved amenable to their demands and the Dominicans tried to install a protegé of their own, who was probably the "legitimate" heir. The encomenderos then jailed the Dominicans' candidate and the Dominicans pursued the other, no doubt unwilling, contender and his sponsors with ecclesiastical sanctions.[35]

The Central American journeyings of the restless Las Casas were not confined to his own diocese. He visited Santiago de Guatemala several times and traveled as far as Nicaragua at least once. In Santiago he roundly condemned the local Spanish inhabitants and all their relations with the Indians. The citizens, who interpreted such attacks as a danger to the economic foundations of their way of life, were outraged. The cabildo wrote to the Crown condemning Las Casas as "a friar unread in laws, unholy, envious, vainglorious, unquiet, tainted by cupidity, and above all else a troublemaker."[36] The mild and compromising Bishop Marroquín was also embarrassed by this obstreperous guest and obviously felt him to be a misguided pest.[37]

Rightly appalled by what he had seen, Bishop Las Casas left his charge in Chiapas and returned to Spain to press for more vigorous enforcement of the legislation forbidding Indian slavery and the worst abuses of the encomienda system. In 1542 the proclamation of the New Laws in Guatemala created dismay. "We are as shocked as if an order had been sent telling us to cut off our heads," the cabildo wrote in 1543.[38]

Now, not content with the effects produced by humanitarian bishops such as Las Casas, Pedraza, and the unfortunate Valdivieso, the Crown sent a reformist administrator, Alfonso López de Cerrato, as stern and humorless a man as the master who sent him, Phillip II, to apply the New Laws to Central America to the fullest extent possible. López de Cerrato began by moving the seat of the

Audiencia from the isolated Gracias a Dios to Santiago de Guatemala, the most important town in Central America and the home of its wealthiest encomenderos. He then began to free the remaining Indian slaves, and announced that he would enforce the provisions in the New Laws directed against the worst abuses of the encomienda system.[39] The result once again was uproar.

Although slaves were no longer a major part of the Indian labor force, Spaniards in Central America fought against abolition with every weapon at their disposal. The King was informed that those who had won new kingdoms in his name were now reduced to beggery; dark hints were sent to Spain, pointing to the civil wars in Peru and the assassination of Bishop Valdivieso in Nicaragua as examples of what could happen even among loyal vassals if they were pushed too hard by overzealous and unsympathetic administrators. A delegation was sent to Spain—the old chronicler Bernal Díaz, by this time an encomendero, was one of the delegates—but it had no effect.[40]

A case has been persuasively made that López de Cerrato and the whole generation of more reformist administrators of the forties and early fifties made a lasting impact on colonial life in Central America. More specifically it has been said that these stricter and more honest men, with López de Cerrato again the exemplar, brought about an improvement in the position and welfare of the Indians. Those who have advanced this interpretation of the mid-century turning point put forward as evidence the freeing of the slaves, the first thorough counting of Indians and readjustment of the tribute to a more reasonable level, and the attacks, verbal and otherwise, made on the most flagrant abuses against tamemes (bearers) and encomienda Indians.[41]

The first impression which such claims make is that in a general way there may be some truth to them. Obviously if a reformist President such as López de Cerrato were residing in Santiago, Spaniards living in the city or hard by it would probably try to check the more flagrant and visible abuses which they had been inflicting on the subject population. If this is true, however, it would also suggest that the further away the Spanish encomendero or merchant was from the reformer and those around him, the more likely he would be to abuse his position and inflict hardships upon the Indians. These are perhaps logical generalizations, but they seem to bear little relationship to the more important changes which were taking place in the colony. To assess López de Cerrato's impact properly it is necessary to take a closer look at his activities, and even more to compare those activities with what can be discovered about the social and economic situation of the colony.

First comes the question of Indian slavery. This system had certainly been an important one for the organization of Indian labor in the days of Alvarado, Pedrarias, and Contreras, but it is obvious that by the time of López de Cerrato's reforms it had already fallen to a minor position, far surpassed as a method of controlling labor by the now flourishing encomienda. Indian slavery was particularly suited to certain economic conditions. It was ideal for the Spaniards in the days when the main industries were the extraction of gold and silver and the exporting of the slaves themselves. Complete ownership of the slaves meant that they could be moved at will from one stream to another, from one province to the next; and industries such as the panning of gold and silver had large enough profit margins so that the Spanish owners could afford to feed and clothe their large cuadrillas. (Not that there is any evidence that Spaniards spent more than an absolute minimum on such food or clothing.)

Slavery, however, proved to be an extraordinarily wasteful system. Indians died in great numbers when moved from one climate to the other, and the work on the rivers took an equally heavy toll. The effect of the constant uprooting of Indian men from their native villages cannot be specifically demonstrated, but many accounts speak of the demoralization and even death which occurred when men were removed in this fashion, and there is even more frequent mention of the disruptions which these forced migrations caused among those left behind. Milpas were often abandoned and families were left to starve.[42] In brief, Indian slavery as a system of using Indian labor effectively was best suited for conditions where there was a large surplus of labor, where labor had to be mobile, and where the profits were such that the capital used in caring for the slaves still left a considerable margin for the owners.

By 1548, however, all these conditions no longer obtained. The Indians alive in that year had survived the epidemics of the early 1520s, the 1530s, and the matlazáhuatl of 1545-48. The number of the inhabitants cannot have been more than half of what it was in 1520. While the population was still large in the Guatemalan, Chiapan, and Honduran highlands, Spaniards could no longer assume that Indian labor existed in limitless supplies. As a result they tended to move to labor systems which were less wasteful than slavery.

Moreover, for reasons explained above, most of the gold and silver mining districts had been abandoned by 1548. Except for

Olancho and the Guayape River, which was still producing large quantities but where the labor was performed by imported African slaves, the heyday of gold and silver was over. (The Tegucigalpa mines, not yet opened up, are a case apart.)

Gold and silver had been replaced by enterprises which depended on neo-plantation systems or the gathering of local plants or plant products. Preeminent among such activities after 1550 was cacao raising. As a result there was no longer such a great need to move Indians from their villages (although such a need would return as the cacao growing areas grew increasingly short of labor), and pressure grew to find a system whereby Indians would take care of their own basic needs when not performing the tasks assigned to them by their masters.

The encomienda satisfied most of these conditions. It supplied labor and tribute when it was required, and for the rest of the day or week the Indian returned to his village and fed himself from his own milpa. In the monocultural areas it proved no more difficult to drain off all profits from Indian cacaotales under encomienda than under slavery. In fact expenditures under encomienda were probably much less. So Spaniards had simply found more convenient and less curtailing ways of using Indian labor.

What we find in 1548, then, is that Indian slavery was no longer the most important method of organizing and coercing Indian labor. It had given way to the encomienda. The Guatemalan petitioners themselves admitted as much in their appeals to the Crown. Those who still relied on slaves were the few who remained dependent upon the dying gold washing industry for their livelihood.[43] It is noticeable that not one of the powerful private individuals in Guatemala, men such as Juan de Guzmán, Francisco Xirón, Juan López, or Francisco Calderón, were deeply involved in the campaign to stop the abolition of slavery.[44] When slavery was abolished in Chiapas some of the settlers protested that such a change would bring them poverty and worse, but others in the Spanish community enthusiastically helped local friars to settle the newly "freed" slaves in encomienda villages. One man's poison was thus another man's meat.[45] Further confirmation comes from the ever moderate Marroquín. He did not object to the freeing of the slaves. In fact, he said, he had been trying to obtain such action for the few surviving slaves for many years. What did annoy him was that some of the freed slaves were given complete liberty! They should have been assigned, he claimed, to old or new encomiendas.[46] So in abolishing Indian slavery López de Cerrato was not attacking the powerful in

Central America, nor was he improving the lot of the majority of Indians who were by this time nearly all in Crown hands or private encomiendas.

It is when López de Cerrato's supposed attacks on the encomienda are examined that the superficial nature of his changes becomes more apparent. In the early years of his presidency he fulfilled all the hopes of Bartolomé de las Casas and those others who had admired his strict and just government in Hispaniola. He and his oidores went on distant visitas, counting Indians, modifying tributes, and condemning and punishing guilty encomenderos and officials.[47] López de Cerrato, oidores Rogel and Herrera, and the Church orders supervised, as we shall see, the huge and largely successful regrouping of the Indians into large villages which was known as congregación. The new President certainly cannot be accused of lack of zeal or energy, at least at first.

It is upon more detailed examination of specific reforms and localities that the failure of this early enthusiasm becomes apparent. In areas somewhat distant from the government seat in Santiago, areas such as the Chiapas highlands where local encomenderos were very powerful, loyal government officials were haunted by the civil wars in Peru and by the Contreras uprising and the murder of Bishop Valdivieso in Nicaragua. Because of these fears government officials quickly became not firm administrators of the laws but brokers of them. In each province they applied only as much of the laws as the local situation would bear. They also became brokers for those below them, interpreting and gauging their discontent and informing the Crown of it.

A typical example of this was López de Cerrato's attempts at reform in Chiapas, a peripheral province distant from the aegis of Santiago. In spite of the years of bitter skirmishing between the settlers and the Dominican friars brought to Ciudad Real by Bartolomé de las Casas and Tomás de la Torre, when López de Cerrato's appointed judge, Gonzalo Hidalgo de Montemayor, began his reforms, he found a shocking situation. Violence, robbery, beatings, murders, and extortions were rampant.[48] The law was clear and he applied it. Seventeen encomenderos lost their encomiendas and others were fined or otherwise punished.[49] As opposition mounted, however, the zealous judge retreated. "[Since] the faults had been committed some time ago, and by people who had not known the law, and since such things were common in all the Indies, and had been perhaps even worse in Guatemala and other parts than they had been here [Chiapas], and seeing that many of the encomenderos would have been destroyed, and that Peru was in rebellion, and that from rigor many evils might result, great clemency was later shown."[50] Those who had lost property had it restored. Plainly the powerful had not been affected, nor had their abuses been modified by the reforms in Chiapas. In fact, those who had been punished suffered little more than a fright, and must have realized that from then on they had little to fear from central authority if they acted cohesively and avoided the more blatant forms of exploitation when officials were around.

One of the main grievances which López de Cerrato was supposed to rectify was inequity in the distribution of encomiendas and other privileges. By the late 1540s two groups had emerged among the Spaniards of Central America. We shall examine the origins of these two groups later, but for the moment a general description of them is of help in gaining an understanding of López de Cerrato's place in history. Those who had capitalized on their original encomienda grants to diversify into many lucrative activities, and those who had enjoyed family or dependent relationships with Alvarado, and especially with Alonso de Maldonado, and thus had received disproportionately large grants, formed a rich, entrepreneurial class. Those who had not diversified and had simply lived off their encomiendas, or those who had received small grants of Indians in the first place, formed a much larger, poorer, and discontented class. As the Indian population declined the situation of this latter group deteriorated. Their small encomiendas became even smaller, and they had shown an inability to diversify their economic activities. Many of this resentful group were conquistadors or first settlers, or their sons, and they felt with good reason that the Crown and its local officers had not rewarded them equitably. The Crown agreed and instructed the President to favor such people and to attempt to restore some balance to the size of encomienda grants. At the same time López de Cerrato was ordered to apply the New Laws by eliminating abuses, by avoiding illegally obtained encomiendas, and by returning them to the Crown after "two lives." (That is, after two generations, such as a father and son, had held one.)[51]

Not enough is known about López de Cerrato's personal life and opinions during his years in Central America, but it is obvious that a gradual but drastic change in personality and outlook overtook him. In Hispaniola and at first in Central America he had been considered a just, correct, and exemplary official, reflecting in appearance and conduct his stern, ascetic master Phillip II. Disillusionment with his reforms or bitterness that his long years of service had not brought him greater preferment or a comfortable retirement may have caused his later cynicism. Whatever the reason, toward the end of his life a different picture of the man emerges.

As a judge he had been correct and severe. He now became sarcastic, vindictive, and abusive. Discontented poor Spaniards who petitioned him to give them better encomiendas and distribute the fruits of the conquest more evenly were told to desist, that they had already stolen enough for any one man.[52] This churlish behavior seems to have been reserved for the poorer petitioners among the Spanish population. There is evidence that he applied the New Laws only to those who lacked power in the community and that he completely ignored his other charge, that of breaking up the large encomiendas and distributing them among the poorer Spaniards.

Of course much of the written evidence is biased. Those who complained about him were his enemies. But it is remarkable that the most powerful encomenderos of the region found little to complain about during his regime. Decisive evidence comes from the pen of Bishop Las Casas. The great defender of the Indians had little affection for Central American encomenderos, rich or poor. Indeed, his relations with the Spaniards of Central America had been little more than a series of mutual accusations, insults, and threats. Because of his anxiety over the Indians of Central America and his hostility to the Spaniards there, it was in fact Las Casas who had proposed and supported Alonso López de Cerrato for the post of President of the Audiencia of Guatemala.[53]

In 1552, astonishingly, Las Casas reluctantly informed the King that the evidence from Guatemala was overwhelming. He had made a mistake in his judgment of López de Cerrato and was sorry for it. López de Cerrato had not tried to redistribute encomiendas or to impose the justice of the New Laws upon the powerful; in fact the clique which controlled the region around Izalcos had grown more powerful. And the individuals whom he mentioned were none other than the members of the cacao clique of the 1570s or their fathers. Obviously López de Cerrato's reforms had little impact on them. Many of the poor encomenderos of the region, Las Casas added, had only 20, 30, 80, or a few hundred pesos per annum of income, and they lived squalid lives of poverty. In other words, the President had in no way altered the economic structure of the colony. He had not attacked the rich class created by Alvarado's favors nor the cacao-rich clique left by Maldonado.[54]

If this had been the extent of Las Casas' complaint, then López de Cerrato could only be criticized for negligence or for a fear of attacking the powerful—a justifiable fear given what had happened in Peru and Nicaragua. But Las Casas goes on to accuse him of attempting to join this powerful group, or at least of trying to insert his family and friends into it, by the most flagrant nepotism.[55]

Here again we must judge cautiously. All those who hated López de Cerrato accused him of favoring his family, and it is logical to believe that this was in many cases a last resort on their part. He was applying the New Laws; his personal life was beyond reproach. So he was accused, *faute de mieux*, of placing a swarm of relatives and dependents (the infamous paniaguados), which every colonial and ecclesiastical official brought with him to his post in the New World, in vacant encomiendas, in newly created encomiendas, and in minor salaried offices. It must be remembered that this was general practice in the sixteenth century and was in effect the Crown's unofficial way of compensating for the poor salaries which it paid its officials. To accuse the President of nepotism, then, might normally be considered a thin reed to support the many allegations of dishonesty and malfeasance.

It is when the extent of López de Cerrato's nepotism is tabulated that it becomes obvious that the poorer colonists and Las Casas had a solid case. A few examples will suffice. Diego Robledo, secretary to the Audiencia and therefore disqualified by his position from holding Indians in encomienda, was given a grant of Indians worth 400 gold pesos a year. An individual who is referred to in all documents simply as Dr. Cerrato and who turns out to have been the President's brother, was given Nindiri, one of the few remaining encomiendas of any size in Nicaragua, which must have enraged the settlers there, starved of labor as they were by the 1550s. Las Casas' claim that Dr. Cerrato derived an income of 6,500 pesos per year from this encomienda may be an exaggeration, but the presence of cacao plantations there suggests that the exaggeration may not have been too great. To add insult to injury, the President of the Audiencia also appointed his brother to the salaried post of Protector of the Indians for Nicaragua, a job which for obvious reasons encomenderos were not allowed to hold. Nicolas López, who some claimed was Portuguese and who was married to López de Cerrato's niece, was granted two towns in San Salvador, both on the fringes of the cacao monoculture. One of these towns, Santa Anna, was very large. Las Casas estimated the income from these two encomiendas as 5,000 gold pesos per annum. Many other family members and servants received similar largesse.

One concession which caused particular distress was given to a notorious and detested man known to Central Americans as Vallecillo. López de Cerrato had brought Vallecillo with him from Santo Domingo, and according to López de Cerrato's enemies he had been accused of robbery and assault in Panama, and had been detained and put on board a ship for Spain. In Santo Domingo he jumped ship and escaped. López de Cerrato took him in and seems to have used him as a bully boy or bodyguard. No doubt he needed such protection; the colonists of the poorer class abused him and harassed the old President publicly. Finally he was ostracized completely. This Vallecillo was granted two encomiendas in Comayagua, Honduras, which gave him a yearly income of 500 gold pesos. The rage of the poorer encomenderos can be imagined.[56]

Even López de Cerrato's attacks on the heavy and abusive uses made of Indian tamemes or bearers may not have been the main reason for the gradual diminishing for these illegalities. He is said to have opened new roads and to have improved others to encourage Spaniards to use draught animals rather than Indians, and this may be the clue. The decline in the use of tamemes is probably largely due to the huge increases in the equine and bullock populations, which literally and figuratively shifted some of the burden from the tamemes.[57]

The results of the López de Cerrato years, then, were mixed. Indian slavery disappeared, but it was a secondary and dying system when he arrived. Minor abuses were corrected, and many of the smaller encomiendas reverted to the Crown; but the richer encomenderos were not attacked, and in fact consolidated their power, and López de Cerrato, while personally honest, attempted to place his extended family in positions which would enable them to become rich, just as Maldonado had done before him.

The question of whether the position of the Indian improved in the second half of the sixteenth century can never be correctly or precisely answered, but reform even to the extent that López de Cerrato encouraged it died with him. The abuses suffered by the Indians of Izalcos-Sonsonate between 1560 and 1580 and the compliance of governors such as Landecho are proof enough. Even the prosecution of the leading offender, Diego de Guzmán, helped little. He fled and in a few years had returned to his former station and was subsequently elected regidor of the ayuntamiento of Santiago de Guatemala. The cacao boom and the abuses which accompanied

Figure 11

The Richest Encomenderos of Central America, c. 1550
(the cacao clique in formation)

Name	Income per annum in pesos de oro	Comments
Juan de Guzmán	4,000	"Plus what he collects illegally." This is the father of the notorious cacao *encomendero* of the 1570s, Diego de Guzmán. Juan de Guzmán was from Salamanca, and was either the cousin or nephew of Gov. Alonso de Maldonado, also from Salamanca. A Maldonado grant. Cacao.
Martín de Guzmán	2,000	A cacao *encomienda*. Maldonado's brother? A Maldonado grant.
Francisco Xirón	4,000	One of the great cacao *encomiendas* of the 1570s. A Maldonado grant.
Juan López	2,000	Both were probably Maldonado grants. Calderón's *encomienda* was in the cacao area.
Francisco Calderón	2,000	
Viuda de Becerra	1,600	
A younger son of Sancho de Barahona	2,000	Originally an Alvarado grant. The father then quarreled with Alvarado and lost several grants. He won his case and received further favors under Maldonado. He controlled one-half of Santiago Atitlán, the cacao trading point between the coast and Santiago. Atitlán also dominated parts of the cacao coast of Guazacapán.
A younger son of Gaspar Arias	2,000	An Alvarado grant?
Gómez Díaz de Reguera	1,500	A Maldonado grant?
Younger son of Gonçalo de Ovalle	1,700	A Maldonado grant?

Source: Bartolomé de las Casas to Crown (1552?), AGI Indiferente General 1093. (Reported in Bataillon, "Las Casas et Le Licencié Cerrato.") See also *Cartas de Indias*, pp. 38-44; CDI, 24:561-3.

it were not destroyed by reform but by demographic collapse, plant disease, soil exhaustion under monoculture, and by outside competition from Guayaquil and Caracas.

In 1602 another Dominican reformer appeared in Central America, Bishop Juan Ramírez de Arellano. His observations confirm for us that nothing in the treatment of the Indians had radically changed. Double tribute and more was being collected in the dwindling areas of cacao prosperity. Indian women were being overworked as permanent house serfs, and the draught labor system (repartimiento) was excessive and its officials corrupt. Above all, Bishop Ramírez was outraged at the conduct of local officials at the corregidor and alcalde mayor level. Some of these were Spaniards, many Creoles. Ramírez accused them of extortion, theft, fraud, physical cruelty, and infliction of forced labor, all at the expense of the Indian population. The Audiencia, he felt, was not guilty of such crimes, but just as in the days of López de Cerrato, it either could not or did not want to interfere.[58]

When an attempt is made to assess the condition of the Indians, then, it would seem that humanitarian laws and officials are of some importance, but they cannot be considered critical variables. Changes in Indian conditions can be measured much more effectively by using two other great variables, population decline and the presence or absence of an economic boom. As population in Central America fell off drastically sources of labor dried up, and the survivors became more valuable to and therefore probably better treated by their employers. Wherever boom conditions existed, however, and whenever Spanish entrepreneurs found a profitable export product, pressures on the Indian population intensified and all the old abuses returned. It was not until the deepest trough of the seventeenth-century depression that highland villages in Central America were left relatively unmolested to recreate what was left of a shattered culture and life style.

It can be argued, in fact, that the vociferous reformism of Bishop Las Casas and the outrage caused by President López de Cerrato's attempts at reform led to a reaction among the Spaniards of Central America. Bishop Las Casas, great reformer and humanist though he was, had insufficient power at his command to affect the relationship between conquering Spaniards and conquered Indians in Central America; and the extreme nature of his attacks on the conduct of the Spaniards, and the transient threat to their way of life posed by men such as López de Cerrato, seems to have driven the colonists to such defensive extremes that even moderate reformers were unable to disseminate their views for more than a century after Las Casas and López de Cerrato had vanished from the scene.[59]

Because López de Cerrato the reformer was in office in the last years of the forties and in the early fifties, and because these years were a decisive turning point in the colony, it has been widely assumed that there was a solid connection between the two events. This was not so to any important degree. Yet these years did see important changes. If they were not brought about by individuals such as López de Cerrato or Bishop Cristóbal de Pedraza, then what were these changes, and what caused them?

We have already noted the passing of the generation of the conquistadors, the brief recession which took place between the decline of Indian slavery and its replacement by the encomienda. The late 1540s were also a turning point demographically. The great epidemic of 1545-48, matlazáhuatl or cocoliztli in Mexico, gucumatz in Guatemala, perhaps pneumonic plague in both areas, reduced the Indian population drastically. The tiny surviving populations in Nicaragua and along the tropical coasts were decimated again, and in the highlands of Chiapas and Guatemala, Spaniards realized for the first time that Indian labor was a commodity which had to be carefully husbanded. It was after the plague of 1545-48 that real counting and rationing of Indians, their labor, and their tribute began. If the plagues, conquests, and forced migrations of the preceding years can be said to have reduced Indian labor in the highlands from superabundance to abundance, then this new disaster which began in 1545 brought matters from abundance to a general state in which, if labor distribution and utilization were fairly well managed, then there would be a sufficiency and no more for many of the still tiny group of Spanish settlers.[60]

Thus in 1550 Central America presents an important conjunction of events. Government passed from the adelantados and conquistadors to the administrators and the audiencias, the church entered the region in force both as a defender of the Indians and as a rival power which would wish to capture some or all of their diminishing services from the encomenderos and other Spaniards. The exporting of slaves ended, and with it slavery and gold and silver panning. Spaniards had to search for new ways of making their livelihood, and the pandemic of 1545-48 made it plain to all but the most obtuse of them that even in areas where Indians had been numerous their services and numbers would have to be more carefully managed if the level of living of the new elites was to be maintained. For all the reasons described above, then, after mid-century we see a more settled, established colony, less anarchy, and more perceivable long-term trends and developments among all sectors of the new society.

7

The Two Republics, Indians and Spaniards, in the Age of Encomienda

In the more ordered, regulated, and careful society which emerged after 1550, a major interest of the dominant Spanish-speaking group was what to do about the labor supply. The first concern of each Spaniard, of course, was to obtain his fair share, or better, of this supply. The next concern was to organize Indian society in such a way that it could be used effectively. Slavery had been a failure, but for some at least the encomienda was still satisfactory. The needs of the settlers to obtain better control over the remaining Indian workers coincided with that of the missionary orders. After years of intermittent friction the friars, encomenderos, and officials could at last work together.

The Dominicans, Franciscans, and Mercedarians first entered Central America in any numbers in the 1540s, and they found the evangelical task awaiting them to be a formidable one.[1] Unscrupulous encomenderos like the famous one in Chiapa de los Indios and uninterested officials like Contreras were only part of the problem. They were also faced with a multiplicity of Indian languages. The result was a magnificent outpouring of grammars, dictionaries, and catechisms in these languages. The number and excellence of these works cannot fail to impress.[2] Yet another obstacle was an Indian population which was already hostile and suspicious because of the treatment it had received over the previous twenty years. Above all, the missionaries found the Indians in a settlement pattern which, from the missionaries' point of view, was an impossible one. Some Indians lived in towns and large villages, but even more lived in dispersed, scattered settlements called rancherías, visiting the otherwise empty concourse or ceremonial centers only for festivals. Still others lived in sparsely settled areas in isolation from one another. Some of the natives who had formerly dwelt in towns or villages had fled to the monte to escape the depredations and exactions of the conquerors.[3] Thus the missionaries, aware of their lack of manpower, realized that they had little hope of Christianizing the Indians, or of bringing them to an orderly, regulated Christian life (policía), while these patterns persisted. The Franciscans, Dominicans, and, to a lesser extent, the Mercedarians decided on a profound and difficult reorganization of Indian society. It was felt that the Indians could never be "reduced" to a "politic," that is, civilized life, unless they were "congregated" into villages or towns. Obviously such a system would also help to Christianize them, because friars would be able to address themselves to large numbers of Indians in one place and would not be forced to spend days travelling about a mountainous and dangerous countryside, only to talk to a handful of Indians. It was also felt that the physical care of the Indians would be simplified, especially during times of food shortage and epidemics. (It seems probably that congregación, unintentionally, may have had the opposite effect; communicable diseases are of course more virulent in areas of dense population than in those of scattered settlements.)

The civil authorities and the settlers agreed. Many of the pre-conquest villages had been on defensive sites, on hills, or surrounded by ravines, quite far from the valley bottoms and basins where most agriculture had developed.[4] Spaniards may have felt that these defensive sites represented a danger if the Indians should ever rise in rebellion, and they preferred to congregate the Indians near the towns or in the valleys where agricultural labor was performed. Hastening this desire on the part of the Spaniards was the fall in the native population which made them seek better utilization of the services of the survivors. Still another motivation may have been to seize Indian lands by moving the former native owners off them.

As a result, with few exceptions, the Spanish populations assisted the friars in "reducing" the scattered Indian populations to "congregaciones" or centralized villages.[5] The process began in 1543, and accelerated in the late 1540s. It was led enthusiastically by Bishop Marroquín and the Dominicans.[6] In some cases smaller villages, the so-called anexos or parcialidades, were moved into a central one or one convenient to the missionaries. In other cases the whole population was moved, sometimes a fair distance, to a new site, where the Indians were given the task of building a new village and church.[7]

It is hard to tell what the Indians' reactions were to congregación. Most of our information comes from reports written by friars
or other clerics and these are usually little short of rhapsodic in
tone. The whole massive operation, they felt, had been conducted
with a minimum of fuss and disruption, and the centralization was
greatly helping the evangelical effort.[8] They were correct. The operation was surprisingly successful throughout Chiapas, Guatemala,
Verapaz, and Honduras, and its rapidity and completeness aroused
the envy of those in neighboring regions. One chronicler claimed
that its success when compared with congregación in Mexico was
because the movement had been led, not by civil officials, but by
friars, who had attempted to persuade the Indians to move and had
explained the benefits of congregación to them.[9] Nevertheless,
some accounts admitted that not all the Indians were that easily
persuaded. There seem to have been three basic reactions. Some
Indians moved willingly, others moved reluctantly after coaxing or
persuasion, and some resisted until threatened or coerced.[10] In all
this campaign it is obvious that the friars and civil officials worked
through the Indian caciques or village chiefs.[11] These unfortunate
individuals were to find themselves trapped again and again between two incompatible pressures—that of the Spanish class who
wished to use them as its representatives in the villages, and that of
the Indians, who felt that the caciques should defend their interests
against the dominant Spaniards.

Whatever its popularity among the Indians, congregación was
at least a temporary success for the Spaniards. For the friars it made
the evangelical task, the "spiritual conquest," much easier; and at
a more material level, it allowed them to organize labor for such
tasks as church building. For the Spanish laymen and officials it
centralized and organized such matters as tribute collection and
control and distribution of labor.

Congregación was over by 1550, but its impact was widespread
and long lasting. It seems to bear a particularly close relationship
to the matter of land ownership and land use, at once clarifying and
obscuring these questions. On the one hand, since it gathered the
Indian population into a much smaller area, something that population decline must have done even more effectively, congregación
freed land for Spanish crops and cattle. One Mexican observer
certainly believed that it did and asked that a similar policy of congregación be followed there in order to free lands for Spanish use
and occupation.[12] On the other hand, since land was a surplus
commodity in the early and middle sixteenth century anyway, and

since congregación emptied even more, it further reduced the necessity to acquire title to land. If there was so much of it, and it was so worthless compared to silver, cacao, or Indian labor, then why bother formally claiming it? Thus congregación adds to the difficulty in describing the Spanish land tenure picture before the late 1570s.

Much of the parts of Central America which interested Spaniards had been Mayan or Nahuatl in speech, that is, Mesoamerican. In this area as already noted, the basic unit of social organization, little understood by the Spaniards, was the patrilineal, exogamous clan known as the calpulli in Nahuatl, and as the chinamit among the Quiché-Cakchiquel. The degree of importance of the chinamit varied from nation to nation and from region to region within Central America, but chinamit-like organizations existed almost everywhere, and they were an important, if not the key unit in the social structure.

In some cases the chinamit occurred as an important step in the hierarchy. Just as the individual and the family formed part of the chinamit, which in turn was a part of the lordship (señorío), the city, and the state, so, in many cases land tenure moved through a hierarchial arrangement of individually held, chinamit, noble, and state lands.[13] In other cases the chinamit as a land tenure unit seems to have been all-embracing. A certain number of clearly defined clans made up the entire nation and inside each chinamit there might be noble land, stateland, freeholders, sharecroppers, and so on.[14]

The agricultural techniques applied to the land varied, as already described, all the way from primitive hunting and gathering in tropical rain forests on the Carribbean coast of Nicaragua and Honduras to intensive irrigation and specialization in the Guatemalan highlands and on the Pacific piedmont and plains. Outside of the Mesoamerican culture area tubers of various kinds seem to have predominated, with maize, beans, and other crops also used west of this area. In Mesoamerica itself, the great crops were maize, beans, and squash, supplemented by chiles, cacao plantations, various fruits, and domesticated animals such as the edible dog and turkey, which made few demands on the land base. Cotton and a few other fibers were also grown. Means used to produce these crops in Mesoamerica varied from slash and burn in the thinly settled, lowland areas, through various degrees of barbecho or fallowing, to intensive huerta or irrigation agriculture to feed the denser populations gathered in cities. The greater the intensity of agricultural production, the greater the degree of specialization. While this never approached the exaggerated monoculture which the Spaniards were to bring, nevertheless we find that certain areas tended to be associated with certain products in pre-Columbian times; cacao in Soconusco and cotton in Nicaragua are two examples.[15]

In all cases, in so far as the systems are known, the agriculture was intensive, with high personal care and attention being given to rather small plots. With a total lack of domesticated grazing animals, the Indians of Central America had not developed any form of extensive agriculture, unless hunting and the gathering of undomesticated produce can be included.

The Spaniards who invaded Central America and who devoted most of their attention to the Mesoamerican high cultures had come from a different agricultural tradition. Early sixteenth century land tenure and use in Castile, Andalusia, and Extremadura were going through a time of important transitions. The wheat farming of Castile, once important enough to produce a large export surplus, was in steady decline, yielding lands and fueros to pasturage as it sank. Sheep had become the dominant agricultural product, with the raising of cattle not far behind. The raising of animals has two dominant characteristics when compared with cropping. It requires far more land to be productive, but needs less labor for its day to day functioning. Castile and Extremadura had been lands of large estates and poverty-stricken peasants since the reconquest. The change to ranging and stock raising reemphasized this pattern.[16]

Private ownership of lands was also increasing in Spain during the early sixteenth century. The medieval custom whereby herds of cattle belonging to townsmen were grazed on common or royal pastures was slowly giving way to the privately owned large "ranch," the whole process being accelerated by usurpation, pressure from the powerful, rewards from the King, and other means. When the conquistadors arrived in Central America they already knew a system of "seigneurial estates devoted to large scale stock raising"; a dual system of liberal pasturage rights to common lands; and large, privately owned estates, with private ownership increasing at the expense of common grazing.[17]

It is obvious that the invading Spaniards never fully understood the Mesoamerican chinamit. It was alien to their experience, they were culturally egocentric with few exceptions, and things which they found alien were usually explained in terms of something familiar. In any case there was no social or economic need to try to understand the chinamit. The invaders were the conquerors and could impose what they wished. So writers of the colonial period referred to the chinamit as a barrio, a tribe, or even rarely as a parentela or clan, perhaps the closest guess of all.[18]

It is equally apparent that the early conquerors or settlers were little interested in either understanding or preserving the various systems of Indian land tenure, except to the extent that they served their purpose. Besides, few of the first invaders came as settlers, and the commercial activities which they started in the first decades did not involve much interest in the acquisition of land.

In any event, the conquest of Central America was an anarchic and destructive one. Where Spaniards needed land in these years, they simply took it, assuming that they had this right through conquest. At the time of the setting up of the first and second cities of Santiago de Guatemala, at Trujillo, Puerto Caballos, and Gracias a Dios, years later at Cartago and Santiago de Talamanca in Costa Rica, the Spanish vecinos simply chose the best available site, set up a town, and divided it into lots (solares). A large common grazing field or ejido was traced nearby, and those who wanted them were assigned gardens or small farms outside the city. Few if any questioned the legality of this.[19]

The things which Spaniards in the New World, or more particularly in Central America, found to be worth reporting give us a rough idea of their order of priorities. Political and military affairs were a constant preoccupation as was the availability of a labor force, but the early soldiers and settlers showed little interest in reporting agricultural conditions or land tenure patterns except in the most general terms.[20] When the Spaniards arrived labor in most areas was superabundant, and it is perfectly clear that where the labor supply was plentiful land became a minor consideration. There were few quarrels of significance before 1560 over the ownership, or even the usufruct of lands, such as were to develop later in the century. There were, however, bitter disputes over the disposition of Indian labor, especially when the time came to assign encomiendas.[21] (The whole process was repeated at a much later date when Costa Rica was finally occupied. There is no mention of problems over land division, but when Perafán de Rivera assigned the first encomiendas in 1569, favoring some followers and inevitably slighting others, complaints to Nicaragua and Spain were numerous.)[22]

In Guatemala, Chiapas, and Nicaragua, and possibly in Honduras, there seems to have been no prolonged shortage of foodstuffs in the first fifteen years after the conquest. Indians were being persuaded or compelled to turn over agricultural surpluses to the conquistadores, who, being few, found such quantities more than enough for their needs. There was little compulsion to take up and plough land when food was so easily procured.

Spanish usage where grazing was concerned also postponed the necessity to acquire land titles. Although the great latifundia were a growing feature of central and southern Spain, nevertheless the tradition of common grazing, the right held by all to pasture their animals on vacant or royal land (tierras baldías and tierras realengas) was taken as granted. Besides, the early cattle multiplied at such extraordinary speed that there was little need to ration them. Semi-feral and seldom herded, they roamed at will and were killed when caught, as needed. If they did invade Indian lands there were few visitadores or clerics to notice and report on it before 1546.[23]

Thus the paucity of information of land tenure before the 1560s: a long and anarchic period of conquest, unsupervised and highly authoritarian leaders, a desperate rush from gold panning and slaving to Peru, and a plentiful supply of labor, all produced an emphatic lack of interest in the possession of land among the first Spaniards in Central America.

What little information that there is, however, does show the small beginnings of processes which became important later. There are in fact complaints, albeit only a few, that Spanish cattle were invading and destroying Indian crops.[24] It is obvious that a few Spaniards were persuading, forcing, or tricking Indians into selling or giving away their lands.[25] A very few Spaniards, Pedro de Alvarado very prominent among them, concentrated on the setting up of great estates from the very first. Many of them later left for Peru or lost their hastily acquired domains in the period of reorganization following Alvarado's death. His own estate in the valley of Guatemala was broken up at that time.[26] But cattle invasions, land usurpations, and the setting up of large haciendas are revealing only because of our knowledge of later days in the colony. They were not dominant features in the reporting of the first two decades.

In the pause which occurred in mid-century, when gold, silver, or slaving failed or when a latecomer Spanish immigrant found that a monopoly of encomiendas or other privileges had been established which excluded him, the response was sometimes to petition and obtain a merced or royal grant of land. A far more usual course in these early, still optimistic years, however, was for such individuals to look for a new boom crop to replace the one which had failed or to leave for Peru, Mexico, or Darien.[27] Thus, compared to the first two decades of Spanish occupation there was more interest in obtaining land titles, but compared to other factors such as cacao or encomienda it was still a very minor affair.

A feature of continued importance was the growth of cattle, sheep, and pig populations. From their introduction via Mexico, Panama, and the Gulf of Honduras in the late 1520s, these animals multiplied with astonishing rapidity, their numbers apparently increasing until the late sixties and seventies.[28]

The reasons for this population explosion must remain speculative. The vast savannahs and grasslands of Central America had never been grazed, and these virgin areas must have provided excellent fodder for herds. The good agricultural land vacated by dead or exported Indians in areas such as Nicaragua and the tropical coasts also presented fine ecological conditions for grazing animals. Then too, there was an almost complete absence of natural predators on cattle. The occasional jaguar or poisonous snake was all they had to fear beyond man. And in the case of man himself there was at first little demand. In the years following the conquest the Indians were terrified of these unfamiliar, large, and often horned animals, and they, the vast majority of the population, did not become large consumers of meat until late in the century. The Spanish population consumed very large quantities per capita, but it was a tiny group of a few hundred originally and grew only slowly throughout the century. Since these domesticated animals quickly grew to numbers far beyond the needs of the human population, and since most Spaniards were more interested in activities other than stock raising, many of these herds were not tended, culled, or branded, and were left to wander at will. Cattle and pigs often reverted to a feral state, only being rounded up and killed when required.[29]

In Europe in the century after the Black Death, we noted a dramatic tension between a declining human population and a growing one of grazing animals. In Central America this phenomenon was even more marked, for the Indian population declined even more rapidly than the European one and the animal population grew much faster. These two somewhat rival forces are inextricably connected. Cattle invasions of Indian plantings, which became a predominant feature in the second half of the sixteenth century, were one of the causes of Indian hunger and death. Afraid of these animals or their owners, and despairing of any answer to their complaints, many Indians abandoned their destroyed milpas or sank into apathy. The decline in their food supply then left them even more susceptible to the next epidemic. Conversely, the abandonment of prime lands by dead, apathetic, or fleeing Indians was one of the reasons for even greater increases in the herds. As Simpson and Chevalier have shown in sixteenth-century Mexico, the two processes are almost inseparable.[30] And of course the fact that cattle and meat were readily available and ridiculously cheap helped to turn many Spaniards away from stock raising and land acquisition and towards other enterprises. Land was a surplus, almost useless, commodity.

Just as in the first half of the century, so between 1550 and the 1570s Indian labor was the prime interest of the Spaniards, and thus it is to the encomienda which we must now turn our attention. Alvarado, Pedrarias, Contreras, and the other early leaders used encomienda as a personal weapon. They kept the best ones for themselves and rewarded friends, family, allies, or reliable paniaguados with what was left. The anarchy and economic concerns of these early years were such that not many of these early encomienda grants persisted or were the basis for later fortunes. The avarice of conquistadors such as Alvarado and Pedrarias was such that it created great enmity among others powerful in the colony, and it also caused the Crown to fear that they were erecting private feudal kingdoms of their own. As a result, we find that on the death of men such as Alvarado, Pedrarias, and Contreras, their encomienda holdings were broken up and either taken over by the Crown or redistributed among powerful men.[31] Moreover, the early industries of slaving and gold and silver panning were not closely linked to encomienda, so that some of the early entrepreneurs made their fortunes without encomienda. Then again, Spaniards between 1524 and 1545 could not know which parts of Central America were going to be really rich and productive areas of the second half of the century. They were unfamiliar with the region geographically, and cacao, while useful as a tribute item, was still thought of as a lowly and despised Indian drink. Nor could Spaniards of the first two post-conquest decades know that some encomienda populations would disappear entirely, others would barely survive, while some, relatively speaking, would continue to be quite large. Thus some of the early large encomiendas simply disappeared or turned out to be economically useless areas, far from the cacao boom. Spaniards had little use for tribute paid in quetzal feathers or copal, no matter how plentiful.[32]

By the 1540s the necessary adjustments had been made. The

new elite had not as yet altered the basic structure of the Indian tributary system, but they had changed the nature of the tributary items. Indians who could not provide items desired by Spaniards or which could be turned into cash were ordered to pay wholly or partially in money. This seems to have had two contradictory effects. It forced Indians to wander far from home to earn the money for their tribute payments, thus helping the plantation areas which were short of labor and severely damaging the householders and villages they had been forced to leave. On the other hand, this forced traveling may have helped revive Indian local trade and village specialization, which had been all but destroyed by the conquest and the insecurity and destruction of the first two post-conquest decades.[33]

Of still more importance, by mid-century Spaniards were more familiar with the country geographically, knew exactly where the major population concentrations were still to be found, and by then had a fair knowledge of which items and which regions were to be profitable and which were to be economic backwaters.

As a result, the decisive period for the formation of the great encomiendas was not the period of gold panning and slaving, not the days when Alvarado and Pedrarias were distributing or withholding their favors, but rather the time of López de Cerrato and especially Alonso de Maldonado. It is the encomiendas granted to Maldonado's relatives and favorites, particularly in Sonsonate-Izalcos, in Guazacapán and San Salvador, which became the basis for the cacao clique and its wealth. Many of López de Cerrato's grantees became minor members of this group, and a few individuals, such as the descendants of Sancho de Barahona, found that their grants dating from the time of Alvarado had turned out, by accident and coincidence, little else, to be strategically placed so that the owner could benefit from the new ways of accumulating capital.[34] Sancho de Barahona's grant, half of the large Tzutuhil village of Santiago Atitlán on the southern shore of Lake Atitlán, commanded a major pass between the highland capital of Santiago and the cacao growing areas of the Pacific coast. He and his son were thus able to demand much of their tribute in cacao.[35]

The nature of a Spaniard's encomienda grant was as crucial to his future fortunes as the way he used it. If a Spaniard was paid tribute in worthless items or in common foodstuffs such as maize or poultry, or if his grant were small, then he had difficulty in using it for much more than maintaining a fairly satisfactory but uncommercial existence. An equally vital ingredient was the amount of imagination and energy he put into the use of tribute goods and Indian labor, which up to the 1560s was an ingredient of the encomienda tribute owed to him. Many encomenderos took to running cattle or sheep near the village or villages which they held in encomienda. This had some major results. In highland Chiapas and Huehuetenango and Quetzaltenango, where entrepreneurial possibilities for Spaniards were few, it meant that a close link was forged between encomienda and hacienda. The land owned by a Spaniard, and to which he finally sought a title, was likely to be close to his encomienda and sometimes he would actually encroach on his encomienda village and absorb it, thus owning the land on which his Indians lived.[36] In most cases, however, to employ encomienda labor to look after sheep and cattle was not an imaginative way to use it and did not build a fortune for the encomendero. The few cases where the contrary was true were where a powerful man, with a large encomienda, was able to use the presence of a nearby urban market to sell sheep and cattle as a large-scale commercial enterprise. One individual, Juan de León, raised such a business northwest of Santiago in Tontonicapán and Quetzaltenango. He raised thousands of sheep and forced his Indians to care for them and then buy the wool which they produced. The meat he disposed of in the city.[37]

For most encomenderos of this type, however, that is, for those who owned small, poor, or unproductive villages or parts of villages, or those who did not use their Indian labor in imaginative enterprises, the encomienda turned out to be a trap. Grants that in the 1550s had provided an adequate but somewhat vegetative existence for a Spaniard were by the 1570s leaving him in desperate straits, often in poverty. While the number of his family and relatives had grown, the number of Indians in his encomienda, and with it the amount of their tributes and services, had declined. This pattern tends to be the more typical one. It is Indian depopulation, plus royal interference, which first tamed and then finally killed the encomienda as a major force in the last half of the sixteenth and early seventeenth centuries.[38]

A document dated 1582 illustrates what was happening. Between 1578 and 1582 the new president, Lic. Valverde, revised the tribute counts. Some of them had not been changed in fifteen or twenty years. The list of villages is long and representative. It includes highland villages from Guatemala and Honduras, some from the boca costa and San Salvador, and several from the coastal areas of Soconusco and Izalcos. In all, the number of tributaries had fallen

Figure 12

Decline of an Encomienda Village (population of a
highland pueblo, Santiago Atitlán)

Year	Tributaries	Adults	Est. Total Population
1524	12,000[a]		48,000
1545	1,400[b]		5,600
1585	1,005[c]		4,020
c. 1660	1,000[d]		4,000
1689		1,900[e]	2,280
1770	200 families[f]		800

[a] "Relación de Santiago Atitlán, ano de 1585," *Anales de la Sociedad de Geografía e Historia* (Guatemala), 37 (1964): 87-106.
[b] *Ibid.*, pp. 97, 105.
[c] *Ibid.*, p. 97.
[d] FV, 1 : 170-71.
[e] *Ibid.*, 4 : 46-47. The term used here is men and women "de confesión." Those younger than confessional age are estimated here at 20 per cent of the population.
[f] Pedro Cortés y Larraz, *Descripción Geográfico-moral de la Diócesis de Goathemala,* 2:279.

from 10,027½ to 7,730 in the period between the counts, a fall of just under 23 per cent.[39]

Far less usual, but of great importance, was the group of encomenderos who, because of the large size of their grants or because of opportunity or imagination, used the capital from them to diversify into more productive areas. Juan de León is one example. The cacao encomenderos were another, with Juan de Guzmán as the leading case. This man used the profits from his cacao encomiendas to buy and build ships which extended the cacao trade by sea to New Spain. He then took further profits and invested them in mayorazgos in Spain. A device used steadily from the 1540s onwards was to copy the methods used to dispose of the produce collected on the Crown's encomiendas. This was auctioned off publicly to convert it into cash, which was then sent to Spain. Encomenderos also used the auction system to turn maize, cacao, hens, and other products into money. Alvarado, as in so many things which had anything to do with gathering capital, is the supreme example of the diversified encomendero. He turned tributes into cash, which he then used as capital for paying soldiers or for mounting his next overseas exploration. He used encomienda labor to build his ships, houses, and his hacienda near the city. Even the few poor encomiendas which he held near Comayagua in Honduras, minor affairs compared to the ones he owned in Guatemala, were turned to good account. The maize, beans, and fowls which they paid in tribute were used to feed the cuadrillas of Indian slaves which were panning gold in the nearby rivers.[40]

The Indians who technically were not in private encomiendas but who were "in the Crown," that is, who paid their tributes and other services directly to the Crown, were often used in similar fashion by royal officials and merchants. When Soconusco definitely became part of the Audiencia of Guatemala in 1556 all the Indians there were placed in the Crown's hands, but the regional governors, officials, and priests, all of whom were more merchants than functionaries, and the other merchants from Mexico who lived in the village of Huehuetlán, were all able to draw off large sums from this cacao-rich area by tricking the local Indians, trading with them, or holding back part of the royal tributes. Royal officials and merchants in the cacao capital Sonsonate used similar devices. López de Velasco reported that the merchant population of Sonsonate was about 400. Not one of them was technically an encomendero, but by using the labor and tributes of the Izalcos Indians, these intruders were able to accumulate capital for expenses or for reinvestment in other enterprises.[41]

The enterprises of the first fifty years, the nature of the encomienda, and the various uses made of it help explain the character of Spanish cities and Spanish society in Central America in the third quarter of the sixteenth century. The richest men were those encomenderos who had managed to capture the cacao areas, or merchants and merchant-encomenderos who had diversified their enterprises and had interests in trade with Mexico and Spain, in feeding the cities, or in a multiplicity of small enterprises. Many of them were not descended from conquerors or first settlers, but rather from the Salamancans and other entrepreneurs who had arrived with Maldonado. A remarkable number were foreigners, Genoese or Portuguese merchants with connections abroad.[42]

Most of these men lived in Santiago de Guatemala. Magnificent houses had been built in the barrio of Santo Domingo, and this section of the city remained the elite quarter until the middle years of the seventeenth century. It is obvious that by 1560 these men were the most powerful people in the colony, and that officials of ambition such as President Landecho and his followers tended to gravitate towards them, rather than vice versa, by marrying into their families, establishing ties of compadrazgo, performing large or small favors, and overlooking minor infractions of the law. In the third quarter of the sixteenth century those in commerce and trade clearly dominated the colonial bureaucracy.[43]

Groups similar to the one in Santiago, often connected to the powerful encomendero merchants of the capital, but sometimes lesser elites in their own right, existed in Granada, Realejo (a heavily Genoese port), Sonsonate (center of the cacao boom), San Salvador, and Huehuetlán.[44] Realejo, Sonsonate, and Huehuetlán were little more than ports and warehouses. They depended entirely upon trade for their existence. But in the larger towns of Santiago and Granada the powerful merchants and merchant-encomenderos were outnumbered by a Spanish class of encomenderos and petty farmers, who still lived in towns, but in increasingly straitened circumstances. They had not received large encomiendas or privileges at the right time, or had not known how to turn them into profitable directions. Such men, often the descendants of conquerors, constantly petitioned royal officials and the distant Crown, telling of the "merits and services" of their fathers and asking for favors as a consequence. Often such pleas would bring a small pension or gratuity which would enable these families to survive at a low level. Bernal Díaz is a typical example of this class.[45] Below these classes were the artisans, a growing class of mestizos who were often petty merchants or local traders, the Indians who had abandoned their villages or lived nearby, and a very small group of negro slaves.[46]

In the other towns of Central America, those not connected to international trade or too far from the boom to benefit, the few wealthier people were traditional encomenderos who had begun to take up land. They still lived in town; but by the 1570s in towns such as San Miguel, Comayagua, Gracias a Dios, and Ciudad Real de Chiapas the poorer encomenderos had already started to move out of the cities to a poor existence on small farms, the notorious chacras y bohíos. There, removed from the eyes of officialdom, they could make use of the services of the remaining Indians without interference, and they did not have to keep up the style and pretensions of town living. Some descended to working small farms or running a few cattle themselves with two or three Indians or mestizos to help them. Such individuals, and by 1570 they were probably a majority of the vecinos of minor cities such San Miguel and Gracias a Dios, visited town only for festivals, for trading, or for mass. These lesser towns were left to the friars, government officials, and a few petty merchants.[47]

To conclude this brief review of the structure of the Spanish community, it is still apparent that the towns with prosperous classes—Realejo, Sonsonate, San Salvador, Granada, and above all

Santiago—were of far more importance than peripheral ones such as San Miguel or Gracias a Dios. Most Spaniards, even those caught in the trap of the undiversified encomienda, still thought of the age as one of possibilities, still had a rich class of ruthless entrepreneurs to envy, and were aware of a still sizeable Indian population. Compared with later years, 1550 to the 1570s appears as a prosperous age.[48]

An examination of the Indian communities gives a much more depressing picture. The devastation caused to their numbers and culture by the conquest has already been described. The relentless pressure exerted on the dwindling population by capital-hungry conquistadors, slavers, cacao encomenderos, tribute exactions, and congregación can also be seen in previous chapters.

Indian society was faced with three assertive intruders: alien diseases; the Spaniards, who insisted that they change many aspects of their way of life and their religion, and who extracted labor and goods to the extent that they were able; and thirdly the rapidly multiplying semi-feral animals, cattle, horses, sheep, and goats and pigs, which the conquerors had brought from the Old World.

These three agents moved toward the same ends. High mortalities and falling populations mean that hierarchical structures become severely disrupted. Recent observations in Brazil conclude that a group undergoing such times of hardship does not willingly change its social organizations, but that the exigencies imposed upon these structures by severe population loss serve to change, if not their form, then at least their intrinsic nature.[49]

We know that in many parts of Mesoamerican Central America at least some of the offices in each community were assigned on the basis of prestige plus age; that is to say, the concept of government by at least the advisory "elder" was strong. Falling population disrupts such a pattern severely. Older men are killed off by many epidemics more rapidly than men of a more vigorous age, and even the young decline in numbers. The result is premature promotion and the arrival of younger men in positions of prominence far earlier than had been the custom. The consequences of such a change are not precisely measurable, but it is obvious that two phenomena must logically follow. Younger men will arrive in offices of greater or less responsibility before they have the experience to cope with them, or at least before the social system has finished the process of molding them to the behavior and symbolic actions associated with these offices. The second phenomenon follows equally logically. Since the scarcity of men with respect to the number of offices means that younger men hold such offices, the offices themselves, and those who occupy them, lose respect and prestige in the eyes of the general community. The result is a general leveling, a blurring of the sharper power and class lines.

The next stage is amalgamation. The shrinking community logically tries to preserve its cultural identity by all possible means against intrusive diseases or other humans. As a result it will resist giving up any of the many hierarchically structured offices which civilly or religiously govern the community. Sometimes of course, circumstances such as isolation force the village or tribe to simply adapt to a less numerous or less complex hierarchy, but more often the clan, tribe, or village combines with a neighboring one to form a large unit which can thus continue to maintain the former governmental scale and complexity. Thus groups which in the 1520s had enjoyed a multitude of patrilineal clans, were, by the 1570s, reduced to two or three.[50] It is also worth noting the role which Spanish-induced congregación must have played in this process. In many instances several shrinking or disappearing villages were forcibly or willingly combined, and were thus able to maintain and support as much of their complex structures as the Spanish friars, encomenderos, and officials found unobjectionable.

The result of this amalgamation was also a lessening of complexity and variety. Vastly different villages and clans, each with its idiosyncrasies, its religious and economic peculiarities and specializations, were forced to adapt to one another and to the Spanish friars, and the consequences, inevitably, were increasing sameness.

The conquering group's activities hastened these processes. In the first place Spaniards did not understand, or did not need to understand, the subtleties and diversities of social organization in Central America. We have seen their inability to grasp the basic organization of the calpulli-chinamit. They found it equally cumbersome to deal with a variety of governmental and social control systems. In the islands of the Caribbean the hereditary cacique or village headman had proved to be a convenient means, and the same institution had worked with a fair degree of success in Mexico and Panama, the previous points of reference for most of the Central American conquerors. Besides, to a superficial observer the same system seemed to exist in most parts of Central America. So it was simply imposed. In one part of Nicaragua at least, where such a system did not exist, where elders seem to have been the strongest form of government, the Spaniards, finding such an aberrant system to be a governmental and tributary inconvenience, simply abolished it and imposed a new class of caciques on the local Indians.[51]

Yet it would be an oversimplification to say only that Spaniards continued the cacique system where they found it and imposed it where they did not. In many parts of highland Guatemala the question of succession to the chiefdom had been an intricate matter and did not always or necessarily pass from father to son. In some cases the brother of the deceased chief was chosen to succeed him, in others the most suitable or popular male within the royal clan. Spaniards preferred the simple rule of inheritance from father to son and this became the rule almost everywhere.[52] In addition, Spaniards had little regard for a widespread use of the idea of communal property, and in many cases land which had once belonged to a principality, village, or patrilineal clan became the private property of the chief and his family, often, no doubt, with that individual's enthusiastic complicity.[53]

Even the cacique system which the Spanish conquerors themselves preferred was not left unaltered. To begin with, the invaders dismantled the national states and destroyed the royal families at the top of the social and political hierarchies, the kings, princes, and great paramount chiefs (tlatoani). In part this process was logical enough. The kings and princes of the Quichés, Cakchiquels, and Pokomams led the resistance to the conquest and the uprisings which followed it. So they were the principal enemy and were killed in battle, deposed, or executed soon afterwards.[54] In part, however, their removal was calculated. The conquerors could not afford the continuance in office, or perhaps even the continued existence, of such symbols of the old pre-conquest days, of such potential rallying points for large-scale revolts, possibly on a nationwide scale. The Tzutuhils, a smaller group territorially and numerically than the Cakchiquels and Quiches, and therefore not so dangerous, may have been somewhat of an exception. In the 1570s Santiago Atitlán, formerly the capital of the Tzutuhil kingdom, still dominated a large group of anexos and parcialidades, probably all the villages of Tzutuhil speech on or near the lake, and the chief, surrounded by a court of lesser chiefs, seems to have belonged to the pre-conquest ruling house.[55] But even in this case it is obvious that his essential authority had been destroyed, and as a general rule the Spaniards dismantled the states and principalities and reduced Indian government to a local and village level. In similar fashion the traditional religious hierarchy was dismantled. Spanish friars demanded that the Indians became Christians, and the former priests were deposed or converted.

As in much else in Spanish American colonial government, over questions of the treatment to be accorded to the cacique class a large gap existed between Spanish royal theory and local settlers' actual practices. The Crown held the caciques to be señores naturales, that is, rulers by natural law, and thus to some extent by divine right, of their domains.[56] As such, once they had proved to be loyal vassals of the Crown they had the right to be considered members of the local nobility and were supposed to be accorded the rights and privileges associated with such a rank. There can be no doubt that the Crown sincerely wanted to create a strong and vigorous Indian nobility. The advantages were obvious. Such a group would to some extent act as a countervailing force to the new brash Spanish nobility arising from the conquest, a class which the Crown distrusted deeply—and with good reason.

Moreover, the existence and encouragement of a loyal Indian nobility helped to justify the conquest to its perpetrators and sponsors. It could then be argued that the conquest had not disrupted the natural, and thus God-given order of things, but had instead enhanced it by imposing order (policía) and Christianity, and by stamping out practices such as human sacrifices and sodomy which Europeans found abhorrent. And an Indian nobility brought the new society which was being created more into accordance with what the Spanish Crown considered to be the ideal order for an earthly society, that is, a divinely appointed monarch, responsible via the agency of his loyal aristocracy and officers for the welfare of of his free but lowly vassals. The Crown also had other pragmatic reasons. A loyal Indian nobility would be less likely to rebel than a uniformly suppressed race, and the caciques could be used as agents of social control among the Indian population.

Much of the royal will on this matter was circumvented. In the first two decades after the conquest the Crown had little control over Central America, and Spanish conquerors simply removed caciques whom they found to be reluctant or intractable. They had, of course, good reason for this. The conquest and the subsequent Indian rebellions were too recent to allow recalcitrant chiefs to continue in office. Likewise, Spaniards also imposed caciques as they saw fit, often bringing in usurpers because they had proved to be more friendly or more easily coerced. As a result many caciques lost their legitimacy and prestige both to their subjects, the Indian villagers, and according to the Spanish governmental system. Both

the conquered and the conquerors could clearly and cynically see
that the new caciques were little more than subordinate agents of
the real lords of the land. López de Cerrato reported to the king in
1552, no doubt with some exaggeration, that so many chiefs had
been killed and deposed, and so many usurpers raised up and imposed, "that, in all this province, there is not a natural or legitimate
cacique."[57]

In the following three decades when royal government was at
least officially in control the Crown proved equally unable to develop its idea of an Indian nobility free from coercion. Caciques
complained to the Crown about violations of their rights, and the
King usually responded by insisting that Spaniards desist, and by
ordering his officials to ensure that they did so. But the complaints
continued, a sure sign that little was being done.[58]

The Crown also sought to reward loyalty. Indian chiefs were
given coats of arms, were permitted to bear arms and ride on
horseback, and their sons were encouraged and helped in achieving
a superior Spanish schooling.[59] Such matters did not usually conflict
with the economic interests of local Spaniards, and consequently
they passed off without much uproar. It was a different matter when
the Crown attempted to aid loyal and helpful chiefs more tangibly.
In 1543 the king rewarded the caciques of Santiago Atitlán, Tecpanatitlán, Chichicastenango, and Rabinal for the help which they
had given to the two future bishops Bartolomé de Las Casas and
Pedro de Angulo in their preparations for the peaceful conquest of
Verapaz. He awarded them freedom from private encomiendas and
put them in direct vassalage to him. Part of Tecpanatitlán always
seems to have been vested in the Crown anyway, and it continued
to be so. Other encomiendas, another part of Tecpanatitlán, Rabinal, and half of Santiago Atitlán, were part of Pedro de Alvarado's
vast holdings. (They are also a good illustration of the extent of
these holdings.) These did not revert to the Crown until after his
death. The other half of Santiago Atitlán belonged to Sancho de
Barahona, one of the richest and most powerful men in Guatemala.
In spite of the royal decree, half of Santiago Atitlán continued in his
hands and at his death was duly passed on to his son. Chichicastenango continued to belong to two encomenderos until at least
1613. The village of Sacatepéquez, accorded a similar privilege,
belonged to the conquistador Pedro de Portocarrero, and his descendants kept it.[60]

In short, it is a generalization, but a fairly safe one, to say that
the cacique class obtained the trappings but not the substance of

nobility. The Crown was unable to give them real economic privileges when these conflicted with the needs of the encomendero class.

The position of the traditional hierarchies was further weakened by some attempts at reorganization made by both the clergy and the Spanish civil administrators in the 1550s and the 1560s. After congregación was over, the three leading orders began a vast program of church building, the goal being to have a parish church and at least one friar or priest in each major village. The leading religious chroniclers, Remesal, Ximénez, and Vázquez, assert that the newly converted Indians performed the labor required of them for this task, quite willingly, indeed enthusiastically, which may well have been true in at least some cases.[61] Certainly Indians must have found the early generations of evangelical friars a welcome alternative after the attentions of the conquistadors and first encomenderos; but the building of such churches, some of which still dot the Guatemalan and Honduran countryside, incongruously large even today for the villages which they serve, must have made heavy demands on the Indians, already harried by epidemics, wars, and tribute collections. The point here is, however, that labor and the collection of goods for the new churches was entrusted by the friars to the caciques, and thus whatever animosity was created by the church building program was partly turned on the cacique class.

More significant than this, however, was the situation created in the villages which did build churches after congregación was completed. One of the most privileged positions which a sixteenth-century Indian might hope to occupy was that of reservado, a person who, because of birth, tribal association, or office, was exempt from tribute. Around the church and its friar or priests a totally new group of reservados was created—sacristans, altar boys, choristers, and flautists among them, and these individuals, or at least some of them, were able to rise socially and economically.[62] Some of them, on the lowly scale which is being considered here, may have constituted a class of nouveaux riches to challenge the supremacy of the old elite.

Even more serious for the traditional cacique class was the sporadic but gradually increasing Spanish policy of making Indian village government conform to the elective ayuntamiento or town council pattern which was prevalent in Spanish ciudades and villas. In some villages this was not started until late in the sixteenth century, in others the old caciques and sub-caciques (or principales) automatically and with the support of the Spaniards became the new alcaldes and regidores of the village cabildo or ayuntamiento, but in still other cases the new ayuntamiento was composed of reservados from the church, lower principales, or even commoners. At first many of these new ayuntamientos were subservient or deferent to the cacique, but in others the two were rivals from the start. Sometimes Spanish officials encouraged this rivalry, especially where they felt that the cacique and principales were too "traditional," or were suspected of idolatry. One specific letter of instructions to the villages of the valle of Guatemala (the large jurisdiction around the city of Santiago) ordered the Indians to obey their ayuntamientos and to break away from their allegiance to their old leaders.[63]

The ways in which the violence of the conquests interrupted the everyday commerce of the highways and marketplaces has already been remarked upon. We have also seen how Indian petty trade and specialization gradually revived as order and stability returned in the late 1540s. Inter-regional trading may also be linked to the standardizing of the tribute by the Spanish encomenderos. Their demands that this tax be paid not in the speciality of a given region, but rather in goods to their liking, eliminated regional handicrafts but also forced Indians to travel in search of these goods, or in search of work which would yield cash pay. These travels had extremely harmful effects both on the travelers, who were forced into climates or conditions of work which either killed them or sent them homeward as invalids, and on the abandoned families, usually wives and children, who were left behind.[64] But such travels in search of tribute may have had other effects. They may have helped revive commerce, and, to a minor degree, they may have also helped create a small group of Indian petty merchants who constituted yet another novel element in the social structure, thus further distorting it from the pre-conquest form.[65]

Equally harmful to the cacique class, and indeed to the whole Indian community, were the persistent and illegal visits to the villages of petty Spanish and casta merchants. There these men traded with the Indians, used up their food, tricked them, sold them wine and alcohol, and bullied them. All the Crown's efforts to stop these activities failed.[66]

All these factors, nevertheless, all tending to upset Indian social structure and most leading to a leveling downward of social classes, were minor compared to the overriding fact of Indian colonial life: the Indians were a conquered and, therefore, a subject people. Although their numbers were rapidly shrinking it was expected that they fulfill the demands of the conquerors. Thus, to refer once again to the cacique and principal class, it was impossible to perform traditional roles. Caciques were ideally considered by both Indians and Spaniards as intermediaries, translating the needs and cultures of each group to suit the other. But because of the steady or growing pressure on ever smaller numbers, few caciques were really able to act as true cultural and economic "brokers." In the early days of the 1540s it is true that some chiefs were able to pay the Spanish tribute demands and still keep back sufficient money or goods to sustain their social position.[67] As time went on, however, they were caught in a remorseless squeeze. To be true brokers they had to convey demands both up and down the two-class structure, but increasingly demands were only from the top down. Caciques were thus placed in the invidious position of being mere tax collectors or recruiters of forced labor among their own people. Tribute both in goods and labor was adjusted downward throughout the sixteenth century, but these adjustments were not made yearly and were always well after the fact. Tribute counts were often ten or even twenty years apart and would show population losses of ten or fifteen per cent.[68] During the long years between counts tribute remained the same or even increased illegally. If the caciques or calpisques failed to produce the required quantities they were blamed by the Spanish encomenderos or officials. Some of these offenders were then jailed or otherwise punished.[69] Yet, in order to produce the amounts required they had to extort excessive quantities of goods and services from their Indian subjects, which of course did not endear them to these subjects. Abuse of their own Indians, paradoxically, could also on some occasions cause them trouble with the Spanish authorities. So, inevitably, the cacique class was forced to assuage the hostility from above and below by reducing the amount of goods and services which it had kept back for itself to maintain its social position. Without the trappings, the comforts, and prestige of chiefdom the cacique class had little left. By the 1570s many were despairingly complaining to the King that their people no longer respected them and that the system was still abusing them.[70] Dispassionate Spanish observers reported that it was often hard to tell any more which were the caciques and which the macehuales. All had sunk to the same level of poverty. Chiefs were living in squalid huts and were cultivating and working their own milpas.[71]

The two institutions, Indian cacicazgo and Spanish encomienda, were tightly connected, and both declined together because of population loss. Some few Indians rose above this general impoverishment. Some caciques, merchants, and reservados were able to escape from village life and to build enterprises of their own. A few caciques were rapidly hispanized and became large landowners and employers of servile labor.[72] In general, however, the result of the first half century of Spanish domination is quite clear. The demands of the encomienda, above all tribute in cash or useful goods, introduced the European money economy to Indian society and drove Indians to the coastal plantations, usually of cacao, to get money. Thus we have the transformation of a varied and tribal people into a kind of peasantry. The Indians were to be part of the economy, influenced and depressed by the alien Spanish cities, yet dependent on them and not sharing in their profits.

Highly complex and stratified Indian societies had been reduced to a common demoninator. There were still a few rich Indians. There were still some differences among Indians because of prestige, office, or religion, but in general variety had gone, and the Indian survivors of these terrible years had become the peasantry of the newly formed agrarian society.[73]

PART II

Years of Trial and Much Error; The Economics of Search and Diversification (c.1576-1635)

8

Attempts to Revive Declining Industries

Soconusco had been the first of the cacao fields to decline, and the merchants and officials there, living in the warehouse village of Huehuetlán, were the first to search for solutions to their problems. They saw clearly that one of the leading causes of the falling away of the cacao groves was the insufficient labor force. The local Indians had long since disappeared and those brought in from the highlands of Guatemala and Chiapas died at such a pace that the old systems of recruitment barely sufficed to keep the tributary population at the very unsatisfactory level of about 2,000.[1]

The dominant groups dependent on cacao decided that what was needed was a larger labor force, and they began to look covetously at the still relatively large neighboring populations of the highlands. They now began to request large, systematic transplantings of highland populations. These officials and the private Spanish vecinos of Soconusco realized that such extensive organized movements of Indians to the coast would necessarily involve the Audiencia at the very least. And the Audiencia would in all likelihood refer the matter to Spain because a basic, legalistic question of Indian welfare was involved. The Indians would have to be moved from tierra fría to tierra caliente, which was against the law, and would then be put to work in an industry which had the reputation, rightly or wrongly, of killing them off.[2] Obviously such large-scale operations could not be conducted surreptitiously, so the Spaniards of Soconusco decided on boldness and attempted to win royal approval and even support for the transportations. In the years between 1570 and 1605 the Spanish officials of Soconusco presented a series of ingenious plans to the Crown and its consejo. At first these plans were deferential and modest. The area of recruitment was to be decided by the Crown. One official suggested New Spain, Chiapas, Verapaz, and Guatemala as possibilities—that is, every area of significant Indian population within reasonable distance by land from Soconusco. In selecting the putative Indian immigrants the petitioners also sought not to offend the King and consejo. One petition suggested that all criminals, vagabonds, slaves, and Chichimecas be sent to Soconusco to work out their sentence or to settle permanently in the area.[3] (How it was intended to police and control this presumably volatile population is not mentioned. Perhaps Soconusco's diseases and work in the cacaotales were expected to do that.) Another official attempted to overcome royal qualms by suggesting that Indians be imported only from areas of similar climate such as Tehuantepec or coastal Verapaz. Yet another suggested that volunteers be solicited by proclamation throughout New Spain and Guatemala, with suitable inducements offered.[4]

The King's response was to ask the Audiencia in Santiago for more information.[5] Meanwhile he was sufficiently convinced to allow a half measure. On November 15, 1585, he decreed that Indians from other areas should be permitted to go to Soconusco if they so desired—a far cry from the suggestions of large-scale recruitment in the petitions. It was also stipulated that such Indians should be exempted from tribute for one year as an inducement.[6]

A new series of petitions in the first two decades of the seventeenth century is significantly more specific and daring. By that time the largely lay government of underpopulated Soconusco had begun to show resentment against the "unused" pool of labor in Dominican-dominated Chiapas immediately to the north and east. In these seventeenth-century petitions it was repeatedly pointed out that Soconusco had the resource, cacao, to provide large tax and tribute revenues for the royal treasury, but had only 2,000 tributaries; whereas Chiapas, with more than 24,000 tributaries, had no great source of revenue beyond the tribute itself.[7] All talk of impressing only undesirables for service was dropped.

The new urgency felt at the beginning of the seventeenth century was partly brought on by a drop in production. But even more it was because of the rise of the Guayaquil industry, which by 1610 was exporting significant quantities to New Spain. The new source of cacao quickly eclipsed both Soconusco and the larger Izalcos.[8] The Soconusco officials seem to have realized that a sop to the King's conscience was needed to persuade him to break his own laws. The petitioners suggested that the desired immigrants be subsidized and exempted from tribute for various periods until the plantations revived.[9]

Some of these petitions were very specific and told the King just how much hard cash he might gain through reviving the cacao industry in Soconusco. One of them, which requested 2,000 Chiapas Indians, pointed out that apart from "restocking" the province, the newcomers would double the tribute from Soconusco after the period of exemption was over. They would pay 1,133 cargas of cacao, 2,000 fanegas of maize, and 2,000 hens. Each carga would be sold for 24 pesos and when shipped north, would revive trade with New Spain.[10]

Another official, even more enthusiastic and addicted to figures, proposed that 2,000 Indians be imported from Chiapas and exempted from tribute for eight years, except the tostón tribute to support the Barlovento fleet. Every year, however, each Indian should be obliged to plant 300 trees. After eight years each Indian would have planted 2,400 trees, and there would be 488,000 new cacao bushes in Soconusco. How the official meant to arrest the high mortality of both Indians and bushes for eight years is not explained.[11] One official daringly requested the importation of 8,000 Indians, but the suggestion had no effect. The royal officials in Soconusco continued to point to the sparse 2,000 in their province and the teeming 24,000 in Chiapas and continued to suggest that various quantities of the latter should be "translated" to the coast. There they would be given land, cacao plantations left empty by the dead, and tax exemptions until the long-hoped-for revival of the cacao industry took place.[12] It was pointed out that many of the Chiapas Indians were so poor that they came down to Soconusco to find temporary work as it was. Why not move them permanently?[13] No royal plan for mass movements to the coast was forthcoming. The Soconusco groves continued to rely on seasonal labor from Chiapas and Quetzaltenango; and, in the course of time, even this source began to dry up.

The level of production and the exports of cacao in Soconusco seem to have remained undesirably low but at least fairly constant between the slight revival of the population in the early 1570s and the last years of the sixteenth century. In the first decade of the seventeenth century it became apparent that years of understaffing in the cacaotales, continuing decline in the population centers of the highlands, and ever-increasing competition from other areas was causing a new economic decline in the Soconusco and the subsidiary Zapotitlán areas, this time occasionally described as "decadence" or complete "falling away" of the industry.[14] The imaginative campaign of petitions designed to repopulate Soconusco and its cacao groves with Indian laborers from the highlands had come to nothing. The area now sank back to a minor position, decadent economically and ignored by Audiencia and court alike.

The search for new export products which had followed the decline of slaving and gold panning had taken several directions. One great discovery had been the cacao groves of Izalcos and Guazacapán. Other regions sought revival through balsam, sarsaparilla, and other small crops.

In one area the solution was found in a continued emphasis on precious metals. In highland Honduras miners leaving the emptied Caribbean coasts made the first major silver strike at Guascarán in 1569, and this was followed soon after by several others in the wild, mountainous, and only partly conquered area to the south and east of Comayagua, which was known in Tegucigalpa. By 1580 some thirty small silver mines were working in that area.[15]

Silver had been mined on the coast since the first conquests, and in the mountains themselves the valleys around Comayagua had been fairly large producers since the 1530s, but these new discoveries of the late sixteenth century were different in nature and scale and were to change the center and emphasis of Honduran economic life and settlement. Honduras became a mountain province, like the rest of Central America closer to the Pacific than to the Caribbean, and after 1570 the Caribbean coastal area, now emptied of most population and of its gold and silver, sank back to a secondary position, kept alive only by the gathering of sarsaparilla near Trujillo and by the need for access to the Caribbean and to Europe through its ports.

The early strikes in Guascarán and Tegucigalpa were followed by a rapid rise in silver production. The capital produced by this infant boom was invested in negro slaves, who were shipped into Honduras and brought to Tegucigalpa in considerable numbers. The local Indians too, some of them now subdued for the first time, and so still relatively numerous, provided a supplementary labor force for transportation and smelting. They were also used as a source of foodstuffs once the encomienda system started. This rapid and easy expansion reached its peak in 1584, when a total of 12,500 marcos of good silver was officially and legally mined.[16]

After 1584 decline began. From time to time a new strike would cause a flurry of excitement and would improve the situation for a

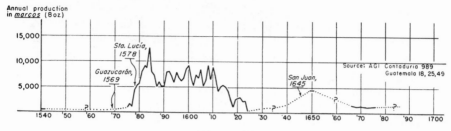

Figure 13

Production of Silver in Honduras, 1540–1700

year or two, but as the vein ran out or as excavation in the new mine proved more difficult, production would revert to approximately its former level.[17] The problems faced by the miners of Honduras at the turn of the century were many and varied, and together they prevented the area from becoming a major producer of silver. As it was, however, a relic, so to say, from the days of the conquest, and sunk in a frustrated stagnation, Tegucigalpa-centered silver mining was by far the most important industry of backward central Honduras in the seventeenth and eighteenth centuries. The story of Honduras and its mines, however, properly belongs later in this study. For the moment it is appropriate to examine the reasons why the potential boom of the late sixteenth century did not develop.

One of the main problems faced by the miners of colonial Honduras was their primitive technology. The rocks of central Honduras are particularly hard, and the poor tools used were inadequate for the task of mining them. The water table was also quite high in the Tegucigalpa area, and it was soon reached, but the miners knew little about systematic drainage or pumping. Even worse, the local veins were often intermittent or uneven in quality, which caused discouragement and the suspension of mining after the first easily extractable ores had been worked out.[18]

One of the most intelligent and global views of the Honduran mining situation came to the King in 1581 in a letter from the alcalde mayor of Tegucigalpa at that time, Juan Cisneros de Reynoso. There were some thirty mines, he reported, but only two had any real possibilities because the others all belonged to poor men who lacked the capital to develop them. Guazucarán [sic,] with its Enriqueña Pit, offered the greatest opportunity.

A great problem, he said, was a shortage of negro slaves, which was a direct result of the lack of capital. The nature of the mines and the rocks was even more of a hindrance. The rocks were hard and rough and had to be worked by fire in most cases. Miners knew where very rich veins were to be found but were simply unable to work them.

A shipment of 500 negro slaves and of 3,000 or 4,000 quintals of mercury would be a swift and dramatic cure for many of the problems which ailed the industry, but much of the cost would have to be borne by the King until the miners could afford to pay back the loans. Such aid would do little to alleviate the main problem, Cisneros warned. The area was one of wild pine woods and a high water table. Mining in Honduras could be made profitable by heavy investment, but it would always be difficult.[19]

Attempts to improve local methods met with little encouragement. Unlike Peru and Mexico, Tegucigalpa had few local capitalists or merchants who would lend money to improve smelting machinery or to buy slaves, and the total output was not impressive enough to attract much money from the financially straightened metropolis. So many of the pleas to the government in Spain for additional supplies of slaves contained the proviso that the local indigent miners would have to be allowed to pay for them over several years, and this discouraged the Crown.[20]

There was also the vital question of mercury supplies. The greatest advance which took place in silver smelting following the opening of mines in Middle America was that developed in the second half of the sixteenth century, whereby ore was extracted by means of a mercury amalgamation process. Known generally as the "patio process," it required, if it were to be used in Honduras, the importation of large quantities of mercury. There was no local source of supply. The two legal sources of mercury within the Spanish imperial system were Almadén in Spain and the Huancavelica Mine in highland Peru. Pleas from officials for steady imports of mercury from Spain began almost at once.[21] The Crown, eager to encourage the mining of precious metals above all else, promised to supply the Honduran mines with 100 quintals a year in addition to its longstanding concession to Honduras of a tax of one-tenth instead of one-fifth (the famous quinto) on all gold and silver mined there.[22] For some years the embattled Spanish monarchy made strenuous efforts to send the stipulated quantity. Given the distance from Spain its performance was adequate at first, but the decay of Spanish shipping in the 1630s and 1640s destroyed all hopes of a steady supply, and periods of several years passed in which no mercury at all arrived in Tegucigalpa.[23]

A further complication was an unwillingness on the part of some miners in the neighborhood to use mercury. Many small miners simply could not afford to buy it. Those who did buy royal mercury frequently complained that the cost was exorbitant and asked the Council of the Indies to freeze the price. Royal efforts in the thirties and forties to do so, at 60 ducats the quintal, had little effect. Miners often had to borrow money from the Crown to buy its mercury, which they were subsequently unable to repay. Thus they became, in effect, royal mining employees.[24]

Part of this reluctance to buy mercury also doubtless reflected attachments to traditional ways, or simply ignorance; but the main reason for avoiding the "patio process" was fraud. The Crown held a monopoly on the mercury supply; and by recording the quantities assigned to each mine, royal officials could estimate fairly closely how much silver any given mine using the "patio process" should smelt. Thus taxes on silver smelted by the "patio process" were much more difficult to evade than those on ore smelted using the old methods of combining fire and amalgams such as litharge. The government saw the implications, but its prohibitions against silver extraction by the old methods seem to have been completely ignored.[25]

One royal treasurer for the province of Honduras lost a whole year's supply of mercury through negligence. He was accused of extortion, theft of royal tribute moneys, buying and selling on a large scale (illegal for officials), and even of sacrilege. One of the main charges was that when the fleet arrived he had used all the available mules for carrying his own trading goods and had left the mercury from the fleet lying in the port for two years (the demand for it in Tegucigalpa cannot have been high) until finally it was seized by English pirates. The treasurer was very popular in Honduras, however, and local Creoles came to his defense.[26] Obviously the loss of the mercury was not severely felt. Its disappearance may have been a convenience which saved embarrassment.

Fraud was fast becoming a permanent feature of colonial mining in Honduras, and it took many forms. All the classes and groups involved in mining took part, and most of it obviously went undiscovered. The great age of fraud, however, was to be the era of depression after 1630, and it is in that context that it will be more fully examined.

Only the two most important attempts to revive dying or stagnant industries have been examined here, but neither one, cacao or silver, succeeded. Central American entrepreneurs would have to look elsewhere to replace cacao and silver.

9

The Search for New Industries and Trades

By the early seventeenth century the Spaniards residing in Central America were again faced with the collapse of a basic dynamic product. Cacao had not produced quick profits for all the elite groups, but it had been of sufficient dimensions as an industry to engage the efforts of most of those in the dominant class between Soconusco and Nicoya interested in acquiring wealth. Citizens of Santiago, Sonsonate, San Salvador, San Miguel, Granada, Realejo, and León had all been involved in the trade.

Nor was the new depression at all comparable to the brief pause of the 1550s. That ephemeral period of difficulty occurred in an atmosphere of optimism, when the freshness of discovery had not yet completely dissipated, when the new land's riches had barely been touched by the invaders, and when the native populations were still relatively large. Fresh alternatives such as cacao in Izalcos, mining in Honduras, and lesser exports such as balsam, hides and sarsaparilla opened up almost immediately. The difficulties of the 1550s brought only a healthier if narrow diversification and produced in toto even greater wealth than gold panning and Indian slavery had ever done.

The depression caused by the disastrous decline of cacao and other features was a different matter both in nature and in degree. Whole populations of laborers had vanished, soils and other natural resources on the Pacific coast had been depleted, the mother country was proving increasingly unwilling and unable to help its colonies, and above all, the best and most persistent efforts of the local Spaniards to preserve the industries had proved unavailing. When the rival fields of Guayaquil and Venezuela came into production in the 1620s the gloom deepened still further.

The depression, which became increasingly ominous between 1610 and 1630 and which increased in severity until the 1660s, later became in fact the first serious prolonged economic crisis encountered by the Spaniards in Central America. Its impact was to be profound and lasting, and the search for an escape from this seemingly endless time of troubles proved frustrating, tortuous, and painful.

Two basic reactions to the depression are discernible. Many Spaniards, and an overwhelming majority of the castes, abandoned the more overt commercial activities which had engaged them, and, as we shall see, withdrew to a rural life of stock raising, sugar growing, and occasional agriculture. Some became hacienda owners in an impressive way and converted themselves into fair imitations of feudal lords. Most were reduced to a miserable peasant existence of chacras and bohíos, the rounding up of scrub cattle, and the growing of plots of maize. The remaining Indians, relieved from the strain of sustaining major intensive industries such as cacao, found themselves more in demand than ever, carefully rationed out among the Spaniards, either in the old systems of encomienda and repartimiento or in the new forms of naboría—debt peonage. Thus most of the inhabitants responded to the contraction of the early seventeenth century by a withdrawal and a reduction in activity of their own. They became less involved with the outside world, with government, and with trade. These individuals, and by extension the area as a whole, learned a certain self-sufficiency of poverty which weakened ties with Spain, deemphasized the city, and helped to give rise to the self-contained rural hacienda, the economy of cattle and corn in the mountainous zones.

A minority of Spaniards and Creoles refused to follow this way of adapting to their new circumstances. Their basic attitude remained much the same as that of the early conquistadors. They felt that the discovery of a product which was popular but scarce in other lands was the key to wealth, mayorazgos, and possible return to an opulent and prestigious life at court. If cacao had brought wealth to some, then surely other products could do the same for others. Such individuals, government officials, merchants, and plantation owners for the most part, conducted a prolonged search for a "produit moteur," a new and dynamic export product, in the early years of the seventeenth century. Their search was an intensive one. In fact, the period between the epidemics of the 1570s and the collapse of the late 1630s was the most dramatic era of experimentation and adjustment until the mid-eighteenth century. The entrepreneurial leaders of the colony had not yet admitted that decline was irreversible. They contrast sharply with those of the period after 1640, when officials, merchants and landowners withdrew from economic engineering and social legislation. By that time they had unwillingly accepted the depression and adjusted accordingly.

These leaders of the early seventeenth century exhibited a strange mixture of optimism and conservative refusal to adapt to new circumstances. Their activities, dreams, and plans illuminate the economic life of the Audiencia of Guatemala until the 1630s, a story of many attempts and few successes in an area too much susceptible to the pressures of an outside world which it could not control.

A major difficulty faced by many Spaniards in the Audiencia of Guatemala who wished to develop trade with the Caribbean or with Europe was the nature of the Audiencia's Caribbean coast. The north coast of Honduras or the east coast of Nicaragua were the areas which had to be used by ships from the east because Costa Rica's and Mexico's Caribbean coasts were distant from the major production areas of Guatemala, San Salvador, and Nicaragua. But the Honduran and Nicaraguan coasts, especially the Nicaraguan one, had many disadvantages.

On the whole, the two areas had been sparsely occupied before the conquest, and by 1600 these coasts were practically devoid of population. The Spaniards occupied the area between the Golfo Dulce and Trujillo to some extent, but the coast from Trujillo to the mouth of the Desaguadero in southern Nicaragua was never effectively reduced during the three centuries of Spanish rule; it remained a refuge for hostile Indian tribes, especially the notorious Mosquitos, who often allied themselves with English pirates or other adventurers.

In addition to the sparse hostile populations, there were other problems in these areas. They were notoriously unhealthy. The heat was accentuated by the heavy rainfall, the dense vegetation, and the poor drainage of the swampy coastal lowlands. They were an ideal breeding grounds for malaria, yellow fever, and other plagues. All of this was a poor contrast to the Pacific coast, which although hot and wet did enjoy the advantages of dense populations, a dry season, good drainage and soils, and nearby mountains.

The most difficult aspect of all on the Caribbean coast was the lack of adequate defensible ports, compounded by dangerous and difficult seas. The Gulf of Amatique and the Golfo Dulce, a small port at Puerto Caballos, and the rather open bay at Trujillo were all harbors of some advantage; but Nicaragua's export coast, the mouth of the Desaguadero, had no proper anchorage at all. And even the best of these ports, the Golfo Dulce, had extremely hazardous approaches, poor soundings, shifting sand banks, and above all, difficult surrounding terrain; for there was little point in using a good port if the routes of access to it from the productive hinterlands were prohibitively long and expensive.[1] Once again these circumstances compared unfavorably with the situation on the Pacific coast. On that side of the isthmus the Bay of Fonseca, Realejo, and the various inlets on the Gulf of Nicoya all provided excellent harbors close to the respective centers of production. The port situation was, in fact, simply one more accentuation of the basic Pacific orientation of Central American demographic, social and economic life.

After the collapse of the cacao industry Central Americans once more turned their attention to the situation on the Caribbean coast. After all, the lack of facilities there had hampered exports, and perhaps, they thought, it had been a major cause of the decline of the area. Apart from the fact that much of the cacao was exported along the Pacific coast, the reasoning was quite sound, for if a new, dynamic export crop were discovered it would almost certainly be sold to European markets.

This reconsideration of the Caribbean harbor problem was further emphasized by the arrival of a new and energetic governor in 1598. Alfonso Criado de Castilla was interested to an inordinate degree in development, defense, and the improvement of communications. Mercantilist notions of trade, the role of colonies as suppliers to the mother country, and the movement of goods between the two areas preoccupied him to a far greater extent than it did most governors, with their habitual emphasis on keeping the peace, building a personal fortune, and maintaining the status quo in the colony.[2]

Criado de Castilla made a few brief and unimaginative attempts to restore the lost prosperity of the cacao industry. He reinstated the much debated jueces de milpas, or inspectors of Indian crops, but their presence did nothing to halt the decline.[3] Thereafter he devoted his attention to encouraging the growing indigo industry and to improving port facilities.

The development of indigo can be described, somewhat hesitantly, as a fairly successful venture, and will be examined separately. The attempt to develop an adequate port and transportation facility on the Caribbean coast caused a brief flurry of excitement and ephemeral improvements but provided no solutions to the deepening depression.

The first port used on the Caribbean coast had been Trujillo, but very soon the increasing importance of Guatemala and the coeval decline of Honduras after the decay of gold panning demanded that the port be moved westward. Despite some grumbling from the vecinos of Trujillo, the port was moved to Puerto Caballos, otherwise known as San Juan, some forty leagues away. It quickly proved to be an unsatisfactory port. The harbor was shallow and dangerous and the seas off Puerto Caballos were notorious for marine parasites, barva to the Spaniards, which soon ate away exposed timbers. Even worse, the place was a pest hole comparable to Nombre de Dios and Veracruz, but without their great wealth. Sailors hated the place and were reluctant to go there. In an arrangement similar to Caracas and La Guaira the inhabitants of Puerto Caballos and the royal factors responsible for the port took to living in the salubrious San Pedro Sula, the former gold washing camp some leagues inland. For most of the year Puerto Caballos was simply a depot with a few warehouses and a handful of sickly negro and mulatto slaves.[4]

Nor was Puerto Caballos of any real advantage to Guatemala. The road from the port to Guatemala via San Pedro Sula was a long, tortuous one. Much of the wine and oil brought from Spain in the sixteenth century must have been spoiled or lost before reaching Santiago. In spite of these glaring disadvantages Puerto Caballos was the principal European port of the Audiencia from the 1570s till 1604. Ships coming from Spain anchored briefly at Trujillo and unloaded some goods for Honduras, then continued along the coast to Puerto Caballos, to discharge wine, oil, iron, manufactured goods, and furnishings, and to load hides, indigo, a little silver, sarsaparilla, cacao, and cochineal.[5]

Even before Puerto Caballos had become the major port of the Audiencia, local merchants had begun to develop alternative routes in order to compensate for the disadvantages of Trujillo. Small ships would meet the galleons and urcas from Spain at Trujillo and later at Puerto Caballos, load the produce for Guatemala, and continue westward along the coast to the Golfo Dulce. After crossing the shallow bar there, the goods were unloaded and stored in a few warehouses, or bodegas, on the shore, to await transportation. Then the imported goods would be taken upstream via the rivers

Gualán or Polochic until met by mules, which completed the long journey to Santiago via Verapaz. Also used was the short mule trip east from the lake to near Gualán on the river Motagua, which could be followed almost to the capital either by water or trail. Sometimes the Honduras ships themselves, after their stop at Puerto Caballos, would continue westwards to the Bay of Amatique and the entrance of the Golfo Dulce area, where, for want of warehouses, they would unceremoniously dump the precious imports on the beach until the canoes and small frigates of the Golfo Dulce came out across the bar to pick them up. Increasingly, as the seventeenth century advanced, the pirate-harassed ships for Honduras, when they sailed, would stay with the main fleet from Spain as long as possible and then creep down the Yucatan coast, staying close in shore. When this occurred, the Golfo Dulce was again the first anchorage off Central America, and again the merchandise was left on the beach there. Small wonder that by 1600 the exasperated merchants and royal officials were blaming Puerto Caballos, albeit erroneously, for the decline in trade.[6]

The last straw was two pirate raids in 1591 and 1596, which thoroughly sacked the miserable port and deepened the dissatisfaction with it.[7] When the energetic Criado de Castilla arrived he was beseiged with complaints about Puerto Caballos, and his own inclinations prompted him to do something about it. He addressed himself to the problem in a systematic fashion, first sending a pilot named Francisco Navarro to the coast near the Golfo Dulce to survey it, take soundings, look for defensible areas, and report to him. The engineer duly suggested that the most favorable spot was in the Bay of Amatique just outside of Golfo Dulce, and he proposed the erection of a new port there.[8] After obtaining the necessary royal permission, Criado de Castilla set about the construction of his new port, named Santo Tomás de Castilla in his honor. Shrill objections from Honduras, which saw the new port as an attempt to exclude it from new trade with Spain, were overruled by the enthusiastic, dogmatic president of the Audiencia.

By 1604 a small fort and several warehouses had been built, the inhabitants of Puerto Caballos had moved, not unwillingly, to the new town, some Indians had been "reduced" and settled in the locality, official naming and founding ceremonies had been conducted, and optimistic reports to the King had obtained his permission to transfer the Honduras ships to Santo Tomás. Enthusiasm was infectious. For a short time the port grew rapidly, and thanks to the expanding indigo industry, the volume of exchanges increased too. Between 1606 and 1610 legal exports and imports reached a record level, never attained again until the eighteenth century.[9]

The effervescence was transient. Decline in Spain, renewed pirate attacks, stagnation in the indigo industry, further decline in cacao, the merchants' increasing tendency to send goods via Veracruz, where the fleets were better protected, all led to a falling away of volume. And in the final analysis Santo Tomás de Castilla was not such a wonderful port. Much of its prestige had been based on the enthusiasm of its founder, Criado de Castilla, and once he was removed from the scene the true nature of the new town became clear. Disease soon followed the inhabitants from Puerto Caballos to Santo Tomás, the few local Indians were lethargic and inclined to run off, the port was hard to defend (it was sacked in 1607), and the seas outside it were very difficult and capricious.[10] Communications with Santiago were better no doubt than they had been from Puerto Caballos, but they were still appallingly difficult. The building of the road from Santiago to Amatique had been an expensive undertaking and had been wasteful in Indian labor and lives.[11] After the completion of the road it proved to be too long, lonely, and dangerous. Cimarrones (runaway black slaves) were a constant threat, and the empty desert-like stretch over Mica Mountain exacted a heavy toll in mules. Attempts to erect way stations along more difficult and deserted stretches caused further hardship to local Indians, who were forced to build them and supply them, and seem to have alleviated the situation very little.[12]

By 1617 Criado de Castilla's successor, the Count of La Gómera, was reporting that the port was a liability. It would be far better, he claimed, to revert to the more natural route discovered by Guatemalan traders many years before. Goods should go directly into the Golfo Dulce to be unloaded there, then up the rivers to Verapaz or Santiago, with recuas or mule trains being employed for the last stages of the journey. As for Santo Tomás, Gómera concluded, it was an inconvenient, inaccessible, indefensible pest hole.[13]

Ships continued to call there sporadically for the rest of the century as indeed they also did at Puerto Caballos; but by 1618 the pattern of trade in the Gulf of Honduras, when there was any, had become set. First a secondary stop at Trujillo or Puerto Caballos when circumstances or cargoes so indicated, then a general unloading either at Puerto Caballos itself, at Santo Tomás, or at the mouth of the Golfo Dulce. Then small ships would meet the urcas at these ports and take the unloaded cargoes into the Golfo Dulce itself past

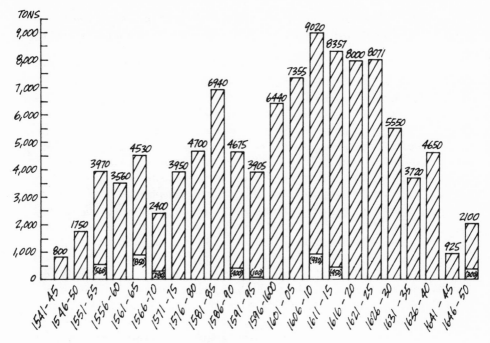

Figure 14

Tonnage of Ships between Honduras and the Seville Ports Complex (round trip) by Five-Year Periods. Derived from Pierre and Huguette Chaunu, *Séville,* 6², p. 664, table 8. Numbers in parentheses give the tonnage lost to shipwreck or pirates; for example, 560 tons were lost in the period 1550–55, so only 3410 of the 3970 tons actually completed voyages.

the fort guarding its mouth. From there it would be taken inland by canoe and mule train.

Defense, part of another history, adapted to these changes as best it could. To the dismay of local merchants and officials, poor port facilities on the Caribbean side of the colony had not proved to be the major reason for the great depression which was fast coming upon them. The building of a new port had cost money and the lives and labor of many Indians, but it had provided only an ephemeral solution to the growing problems. Obviously the roots of the matter lay elsewhere.

While searching for other solutions to the economic problems of the colony, Criado de Castilla and those who shared his interests had hit upon an idea which had been explored several times already in the previous century. Central America's isthmian position made it a natural area of contact between the two great oceans, the Atlantic and the Pacific. As Peru gradually became Spain's greatest source of silver after the discovery of the mines of Potosi and Huancavelica, the strategic importance of the isthmian regions of Central America increased. Panama, the first isthmus to be settled, and otherwise lacking in valuable resources, was able to capitalize on its position by providing transit facilities for the Peru trade and fleets on both coasts of America. In part Panama's very existence and whatever wealth its occupants possessed was a direct result of the trajín, the costly transfer of goods between Panama City and Portobelo. Nevertheless, Panama's ownership of the lucrative portage trade was not always secure. Portobelo and its predecessor, Nombre de Dios, were notoriously disease-ridden ports and poor harbors to boot, while Panama itself, with its tropical climate, was thought of as being unhealthy compared to Mexico City and Bogota, or more to the point, to Santiago de Guatemala, Comayagua, Granada, and León. Panama was also lacking in certain important resources needed for the trade. It grew few crops to feed sailors in port, its shipyards were poor, it bred few mules to do the carrying and had to import nearly all of them from Costa Rica, Nicaragua, and beyond; and the native Indians had nearly all disappeared so that recurrent labor shortages and steady imports of expensive negro slaves were permanent features of life on the isthmus.[14]

The expense and inconvenience caused by these disadvantages were apparent to the Crown and its councils, who were thus ready to consider alternative routes for the Peru trade if such routes could be found. The only route which was at all feasible outside of the Audiencia of Guatemala was the isthmus of Tehuantepec, which was used in the early days in a fashion similar to Panama for the conveyance of heavy cannon from Veracruz to Acapulco and thence to the Philippines.[15] Otherwise all of the alternative routes proposed lay within the jurisdiction of the Audiencia of Guatemala.

Apart from the minor attempts on the part of Costa Ricans and Chiapans to suggest that their provinces might be the best alternative to Panama, the Central American routes proposed can be reduced to two. One route was Nicaraguan. It involved the use of the San Juan River or the Desaguadero, the lake of Nicaragua, and a short overland journey from the lake to the minor Pacific port of San Juan del Sur. A variation on this theme was the suggestion that a canal be cut from Lake Nicaragua to the Pacific at San Juan del Sur.

The other route was Honduran. It consisted of a proposed road between the ports on the Gulf of Honduras and the Gulf of Fonseca, with Comayagua acting as the principal way station. Once in a while Iztapa, Pedro de Alvarado's old port in Guatemala, or Realejo, the important Nicaraguan port, would be suggested as alternative Pacific terminals for this route.

That either proposal should be seriously considered as more appropriate than Panama, given Spanish technological capabilities in the sixteenth and seventeenth centuries, seems ludicrous today, yet both routes were studied in detail, and one, the more difficult of the two, was in fact approved by the Crown and might have gone into operation had not other extraneous events intervened.

Three circumstances helped to blind Central American merchants and the Crown to the obvious disadvantages of the Honduran and Nicaraguan routes. The seventeenth century preferred to trade by water whenever possible. Movement of goods by land, especially in difficult terrain, was slow, expensive, and destructive. Hence the long search for a water passage through the American continent, and the attention given to suggestions of a Nicaraguan route which would have been almost entirely, or entirely by water.

Panama's sickly climate and lack of human labor and draught animals made the healthier highlands of Comayagua, the mule farms of La Choluteca, and the comparatively dense Indian populations of Guatemala and San Salvador seem more attractive than they were, and inclined the Crown to consider the Honduran route. Most important of all, ignorance, enthusiasm, or guile, and no doubt a measure of desperation, led Central American entrepreneurs into the most amazing exaggerations when describing local amenities. Silted little estuaries such as Iztapa were described in terms which conjured up visions of a port such as Rio de Janeiro; pest holes like Puerto Caballos and Trujillo were described as swept by healthful sea breezes; the difficulties of negotiating the rapids in the San Juan River were brushed aside; and the highlands of Honduras were depicted as being packed rather than inhabited by healthy, hard working Indians. What living space was left, it was alleged, swarmed with mules and oxen. Little wonder that the Crown found itself persuaded by such panoramas.

The proposals to use the Audiencia of Guatemala for the Peru trade began before the Audiencia itself was established. Bishop Marroquín was suggesting it as early as 1536, and much of the early exploration of Nicaragua was inspired not only by a search for gold but also by an eager hunt for a way across the isthmus. That other and even more famous Central American bishop, Bartolomé de las Casas, had been attracted to the idea of a Nicaraguan route during his visit there in 1537. As trade began via the River San Juan between lacustrine Nicaragua and the Spanish Main, the local Spaniards and the Crown continued to show interest in this route as a possible alternative to Panama.[16] In several ways, after all, Central America was proving to be a major route to Peru. The Central American area, particularly Honduras and Nicaragua, experienced great difficulty in holding its original colonizers, who were eager to rush off to the riches discovered by Pizarro. Cattle and horses were also sent to Peru from Nicaragua as early as 1535, and towards the end of the decade Nicaragua was supplying Peru yearly with men and provisions in addition to its exports to Panama.[17]

Such activity and the great prosperity of cacao in the 1550s and 1560s led to the first concerted attempt to win the Peru trade for the Audiencia of Guatemala, still known as Los Confines. The original proposition came from Juan García de Hermosilla, who brazenly suggested that Trujillo serve as the principal port both of Peru and New Spain. The King asked for a lengthy study of the matter and his instructions seem to have been carried out. In 1560, after much debate, the Crown decided that the Peru trade should indeed be conducted through Trujillo and Fonseca, an astounding decision. Habit was already too strong, however, and Spain was involved in war. The ayuntamiento of Santiago was still talking hopefully of the project in 1561, but by the time the matter was considered again in a serious fashion Guatemala's great opportunity and much of its prosperity had passed. The idea was mentioned on several other occasions during the seventies and eighties but never generated the great interest of the 1550s.[18]

The next major attempt to ascertain the true nature of the proposed Guatemalan route was made in 1590. An intensely partisan reporter, Francisco de Valverde, made an optimistic report to the Crown. Traveling southward from Puerto Caballos to the Bay of Fonseca and Realejo he compiled a detailed study of harbors, soundings, Indian populations along the route, Spanish towns in each region, the availability of fodder, grain, pitch and cordage, and the size of the local herds of cattle and mules. Much of what he had to say was favorable, untruthfully so perhaps, especially in his description of Puerto Caballos; but even Valverde could not ignore the obvious and appalling difficulties posed by the length of the route and the broken mountainous nature of the terrain. The cost of building bridges, maintaining roads and way stations, importing two thousand negro slaves, and buying the thousands of mules involved would be enormous. Valverde preferred to avoid this discouraging matter, and left the decision on cost to others.[19]

The others were, in fact, three inspectors sent by the Crown in 1589 for the express purpose of studying the proposed route. Juan

Batista Antonelli and his aide, Diego López de Quintanilla, submitted a report on the same area covered by Valverde, but by emphasizing costs, came to completely opposite conclusions. The route was long and would prove very expensive, there were few Indians, negroes would have to be imported, and Puerto Caballos was indefensible. Antonelli reported that at least 10,928 oxen, 2,000 negro slaves, and 400 to 500 Spanish farmers would be needed to make the route possible. The cost in money would be enormous, and the outlay would be at best a long-term investment, for little return could be expected for several years. The royal agents warned the Crown not to trust the optimistic, self-serving accounts submitted by local inhabitants, and concluded: "it appears to us that it is not a thing which is of advantage to Your Majesty's service or to the common good of your subjects."[20]

Such accounts of appalling expenses were enough presumably for the ever-indigent Spanish Crown. At first glance it would seem reasonable to assume that the reports of the 1590s had brought all hopes for the project to an end. It is, therefore, a measure of the degree of desperation of the first two decades of the seventeenth century that local officials and Creoles should turn once more to this already exploded scheme for sudden and easy wealth.

Halfhearted suggestions that the Peru trade be moved to Guatemala were a prelude to the main assault.[21] The opening of Santo Tomás de Castilla, and the brief expansion of trade which took place immediately thereafter, further encouraged the promoters; and for a few years a little merchandise and a number of people were sent to Peru via Santo Tomás and Guatemala. In 1605 seventeen passengers, including the newly appointed corregidor of Quito, arrived on one ship at Santo Tomás, bound for Peru.[22] From 1607 to 1610, led by Criado de Castilla and the ayuntamiento of Santiago, a concentrated effort was made to bring the trade to Guatemala and Honduras. The old arguments about the unsuitability of Panama and the ideal nature of the Audiencia of Guatemala were paraded once more, with increased exaggeration and vehemence. The ayuntamiento threw in 1,000 pesos of its meager funds for the improvement of the old port of Iztapa. But the moment had passed, and Guatemala's prosperity had disappeared. The King remained uninterested in this and all sporadic references to the matter in the seventeenth century.[23]

The Nicaraguan route, in many ways a less improbable alternative to Panama than Guatemala-Honduras, attracted much less attention. The most coherent exponent of the Nicaraguan route was a Flemish vecino of Guatemala, who reported to the King on January 23, 1620.

After condemning Nombre de Dios, Portobelo, Panama, and Perico as uninhabitable swamps, he praised San Juan del Norte and San Juan del Sur as healthy, safe ports with plentiful supplies of fresh water. He asserted that the trade between Granada and the Caribbean was already well established, with ten or twelve frigates plying between Granada and Cartagena via the Desaguadero with fowls, maize, pitch, and similar agricultural supplies which they exchanged for wine, cloth, and other Spanish imports. Admittedly, the Desaguadero was a difficult river, but here surely was a base to which could be added the Peru trade. The four rapids could be cleaned and smoothed during the dry season, and the worst rocks removed with explosives.

On the Pacific side there were many good ports; San Juan del Sur itself was adequate, and even better were Realejo, the Gulf of Fonseca further to the west, and the various ports of the Gulf of Nicoya to the south. Above all the route would be almost all by water and thus would save on handling and damage. Even the heavy artillery which had been sent to China and the Moluccas via the isthmus of Tehuantepec, at the cost of many Indian lives, could in the future go much more expeditiously via Nicaragua.

In Nicaragua, he claimed, there were many experienced navigators who could testify to the suitability of the route, "such as Gaspar de Palacios, Spaniard, Jácamo Premontorio, Venetian, and Simón Bacarias, Flemish, and many others." (Presumably the presence of so many foreigners was not considered a handicap.)

Another advantage was the proximity to Havana, the gathering place for the fleets. On the other coast, San Juan del Sur was closer to Peru in sailing time than Panama. Because of contrary winds and currents, ships sailing from Panama often found themselves obliged to head west northwest up the Central American coast, and then out into the Pacific, before heading south.

The optimistic surveyor first began to wander seriously from the truth when he came to describe the interior of Nicaragua. It was, he asserted, a fertile province of large crops and many Indians, a patent falsehood. Ship stores were plentiful and cheap and Costa Rica could supply additional foodstuffs, which was true enough. And, he continued, engineers claimed that to cut a canal from the lakes to the Pacific would be an easy task. In fact, the lake would increase in size, being lower than the Pacific.[24]

The King's immediate response to this document is unknown, but no attempt was made to move the Peru trade to this route, nor was any start made on the proposed canal. The attempt to win the Peru trade from Panama had failed, and Central Americans would have to look elsewhere for a solution to their crisis. What could not be accomplished by legal means was often attempted by subterfuge. The hope of attracting the rich trade of other areas was not limited to the idea of seizing Panama's lucrative trajín. Another enterprise which caught the attention of Central Americans was the rich China trade, whereby silks and other Oriental goods crossing the Pacific from Manila in the Philippines to Acapulco in New Spain were exchanged for Peruvian silver and ended up in Callao and Lima.

The history of this Chinese-Peruvian trade in the sixteenth and early seventeenth centuries is one of expansion and increasing royal restrictions. Spanish authorities felt the lack of the Peruvian silver which was directed to China instead of to the metropolis; and the Spanish merchants, represented by the Consulado of Seville, found their New Spain and Peruvian markets filled with Chinese goods, with the result that they were unable to sell the merchandise which they had sent to Peru and Mexico. Cédulas of 1604, 1609, and 1620 gradually reduced the legal trade from Callao to Acapulco to a trickle, and in 1631 the trade was banned completely.[25]

Massive evasion of royal restrictions was the response. With the connivance of royal officials, ships smuggled Chinese silks up and down the Pacific. Guatemalans who were aware of this situation, and it was increasingly obvious after 1610, apparently saw it as an excellent opportunity to act as an entrepôt. If Acapulco and Huatulco were carefully watched to prevent the reexport of Chinese goods, then the best alternative was to dispatch these goods by land to Guatemala where the entry of Chinese goods from Mexico was not forbidden, so that they could be loaded for Peru at Acajutla, Fonseca, or Realejo. Because it was illegal, the size of this trade is impossible to estimate; but if the interest displayed in the business in Guatemala is at all indicative, it may have been considerable.

The region's interest in the Oriental trade was first apparent in the 1570s or earlier, the first step being an attempt to seize the Manila-Acapulco branch of the trade outright. Pedro Venegas de los Rios, treasurer of the province of Nicaragua, wrote a long letter to the King about 1576 on shipping and sailing routes in the Pacific. His main proposal was that ships from "China" should sail directly to the magnificent port at Realejo. From there Oriental goods could easily be transferred to Granada, thence down the Desaguadero to Nombre de Dios to await the sailing of the fleets for Spain; this would be far simpler, he claimed, than using the involved Acapulco–Mexico City–Veracruz route. Realejo had other advantages too; nearby it had many Indian villages which paid tribute in henequen, the cañamo or fiber from which xarcia or caulking for ships was obtained. There was cotton for sails, good hardwoods, and plenty of grains and cattle for provisions.[26] No response from Spain is on record.

The exclusivist approach whereby Central America unsuccessfully proposed itself as an alternative to the Acapulco–Mexico City–Veracruz route having failed, the next step was to attempt to obtain at least part of the Manila trade. In 1575 the ayuntamiento of Santiago, with the support of other groups, petitioned the Crown for permission to trade directly with the Orient, only to have their request refused the following year.[27] For a few years thereafter the evidence is confusing. There are indications that Guatemala was given permission to open a China trade in 1579,[28] and again in 1597, when the Crown approved an auto acordado by President Sandé, recently appointed from the Philippines, authorizing sailings to the Orient.[29] But if any ships did in fact sail directly to Manila there is very little record of it, and there are many indications that between 1582 and 1597, and certainly thereafter, Guatemala's Oriental goods arrived via Acapulco, and that any other way of importing them was considered illegal.[30]

All attempts at obtaining the China crossing having failed, some Guatemalans took to living on the margins of the trade. As royal restrictions on trade increased, Guatemala became one way of evading customs officials and local port authorities in Acapulco and Huatulco. This method of sending Oriental merchandise was in existence by 1590, but it accelerated after the complete ban on Mexico-Peru trade in 1631. The main ports used were Acajutla and Realejo. Some merchandise reached as far as Nicoya by land, but authorities were inclined to discount the importance of smuggling of Chinese goods south of Realejo. There were also hints of Chinese goods passing through Granada and down the Desaguadero on the way to Cartagena and Portobelo.[31]

As usual, royal prohibitions had little effect, and royal officials themselves were deeply involved in the smuggling. The governor of Costa Rica, Alonso de Castilla y Guzmán, was accused of various illegalities by his predecessor, Juan de Mendoza y Medrano, among others trading and selling "one thousand pesos worth of merchandise from China and other parts."[32] The President of the Audiencia, Francisco Sandé, who had come from the Philippines and showed great interest in the trade, was accused as early as 1591 of taking large quantities of Chinese goods with him to his post in New Granada when he was appointed there in 1596. His large following of retainers and relatives also took their share, and all obviously hoped to sell the merchandise in Bogota and elsewhere for high profits—much to the disgust of the royal master. (As late as the 1640s accusations of complicity in the illegal Chinese trade were still being made against oidores of the Audiencia of Guatemala.)[33]

Attempts to legalize the trade were rebuffed. In a published report on the indigo industry in 1642, Francisco Romero Valtodano briefly turned his attention to what was happening. Chinese goods were being exchanged for Peruvian wine in Guatemalan ports on a regular basis. Legalizing this trade, which seemed impossible to stop, would earn the King 20,000 or more ducats per year in tax, and many other "inconveniences" would cease. The King was adamant and replied that the royal laws prohibiting the trade should be enforced with great zeal.[34]

The extraordinary voyage of one of the Manila galleons illustrates some aspects of this marginal trade in Guatemala. Nuestra Señora de la Victoria, the almiranta or the smaller of the two Manila ships, sailed from the Philippines on July 20, 1656. After some eight months of sailing, it first raised the American coast at Salagua in Tehuantepec. Allegedly the ship's officers then misread their landmarks and sailed down the Central American coast as far as the small harbor of Salto in Guazacapán. After anchoring there for a short time, the galleon continued until it anchored in the Bay of Fonseca in mid-April.

The ship and its crew were in sad condition. Most of the survivors were sick and 150 were dead, the vessel was demasted and leaking, and stores of food and water were either spoiled or had been consumed a long time ago. The survivors (one of whom was obviously an Englishman) were gaunt and unable to continue. The alcalde mayor of San Salvador helped the ship with food, water, and medicines and informed the Audiencia in Santiago.

It is obvious that trading and unloading began almost at once. The events in the Bay of Fonseca naturally drew the curious, and soon many of the local inhabitants were on board, and many of the ailing crew were on shore. The Audiencia, concerned that the situation would deteriorate to open smuggling or even pillage, then dispatched its fiscal, Oidor Juan Francisco Esquivel, to look into the matter. His orders were to prevent illegality and to dispatch the ship to Acapulco as expeditiously as possible.

When he arrived at Fonseca it was probably already too late to prevent most of the trading. Esquivel himself never admitted as much, but he noticed immediately that "more care was needed because of the many canoes which I saw from my lodgings, going and coming from the ship." He put a guard on the vessel "so that nothing could be taken off it or mislaid," but shortly thereafter two coasting frigates arrived from Realejo, ostensibly to help. News of the windfall had traveled fast.

According to the oidor's report, extraordinary precautions were taken for over a month, while the ship was being refitted and the crew restored to health. Suggestions that the ship be unloaded then and there because of its wretched condition were firmly rejected "because of the fact that it would cause very great annoyance and inconvenience to the service of Your Majesty, and because of the proximity of the ports of Peru." Once again no mention was made of the unloading which probably took place before the oidor appeared on the scene.

The people from Realejo, who had not had the opportunity to obtain goods from the ship before Esquivel's arrival, were obviously a problem to him. The shipwrights and carpenters who repaired the vessel were all from the Nicaraguan port and took an inordinate amount of time, well over a month, to repair it. Then there was the problem of the frigates which had come from Realejo to "help" and to convey the almiranta to Acapulco. Esquivel was intensely suspicious of their motives. He decided that the galleon should sail to Acapulco alone, for after all, he reasoned, it had just been repaired, and the remainder of the crew nursed back to health, and he wanted to make sure that there were no "chance encounters" at sea. The Realejo frigates were sent back to their home port before the Manila galleon set sail from Fonseca, and the port officials of Realejo were ordered to refuse sailing permits to all ships until the 20th of July, "by which time it could be hoped that the said almiranta would be very close to finishing its voyage." The galleon finally limped into Acapulco at the end of July, causing general rejoicing and the ringing of all the church bells in Mexico City.[35]

The arrival of a Manila galleon in Guatemala waters illustrated the demand for Chinese goods, the elaborate precautions and regulations which surrounded the China trade, and the overall failure of authority to prevent Oriental goods from reaching their markets.

Yet Guatemala's participation in the China trade was marginal and in the general decline of shipping between the 1630s and the

1680s the Guatemalan share probably became still less.[36] Even the Oriental goods which did not pass through Guatemala had to be brought from Mexico at high prices and then resold to Peruvian agents; sometimes the merchandise may even have been brought directly to Acajutla by Mexican traders themselves, so that only the muleteers and a few people at the ports benefited and the trade profited Guatemalans very little.

The Oriental trade from Acapulco to Peru via Guatemala was a factor in the flood of debased Peruvian coinage, which to the disgust of Mexican authorities poured into Mexico in the 1630s and 1640s (one document specifically mentions that this coinage was arriving by way of Guatemala),[37] but a transit area such as this was not likely to garner much of the profits. In spite of the restrictions, moreover, most the the trade continued to flow from Acapulco directly to Peru. Some Guatemalan ships were involved in the carrying, no doubt, but many others were Peruvian or Mexican. A seventeenth-century document gives a good description of the process involved. Philippine goods worth two million pesos and more were reaching Peru every year. The main ports of New Spain which were involved were Acapulco, Huatulco, Acajutla, and Realejo. The one or two authorized ships which sailed from Peru to Mexico every year before 1631 were allowed to carry 100,000 ducats for the purchase of merchandise. Instead they usually sailed loaded with wine, a forbidden export, and carried over a million ducats in gold and silver.

By far the most important port of the four mentioned was Acapulco and its small subsidiary Puerto Marqués. To allay suspicion the Peruvian merchants usually bought Oriental goods after they had reached Mexico City, then took them back to Acapulco and Puerto Marqués where they were loaded onto Peruvian ships at night. With the connivance of the royal officials the goods were sometimes, after the payment of minor taxes, labeled as local produce.

After the voyage south much of the Chinese merchandise was unloaded in northern Peru at the mouth of the Piura River, which is navigable as far as the town of Paita for some months of the year and provides a small harbor. From Paita a runner was sent on to Lima to inform local agents of the ship's arrival. Soon afterwards the goods were dispatched by night on muleback, and were quickly disposed of on arrival by the well-prepared Lima merchants.

An alternative method was for the limeños to send a fleet of small coastal ships north to Paita to meet the smugglers. There in the port or on the high seas the forbidden Chinese merchandise was transferred to the vessels from Lima and then later landed at coves north and south of Callao. Still another method was to transfer the forbidden goods to the "timber ships" from Guayaquil which carried lumber down the coast to Lima. These ships were usually allowed to pass customs in Callao after a cursory inspection. A visitor summed it up that "even though there are such stern prohibitions against carrying it, the profits are so excessive that the risk is taken, and there are so many ways of hiding it, and introducing it into the city, and there are so many that turn a blind eye"[38]

With the easing of royal restrictions in the later years of the century Central America's tiny share in this trade increased. In 1678 Peru was given the right of sending two ships per year to Guatemala for the purchase of local products. In 1685 a limited trade in wine was allowed for an experimental period. On the fringes of these slowly awakening trades some contraband Oriental goods on their way to Peru began to move through Central America again, and Realejo and the Bay of Fonseca became smuggling depots for these goods once more. Local monasteries, not so subject to official search, were sometimes used as warehouses for the Chinese contraband.[39]

Nevertheless, no matter what efforts were put into this trade by local merchants, friars, and officials, providing an alternative route for contraband Chinese goods between Mexico and Peru was not enough in an era of growing strain to solve the economic problems of a large area such as the Audiencia of Guatemala.

Mercantilist ventures had failed, and the entrepreneurs of Central America turned once more to an inventory of their own resources. Noticing the decline of one plant product, cacao, after a period of great prosperity, it was natural that those concerned with such matters should look for a similar product or series of products for a solution to the growing depression.

Cochineal, known to the Spaniards as grana cochinilla, or simply as grana—thus the English expression "engrained"—is a fast, scarlet dye which comes from a most unique series of plants, insects, and processes. The cochineal insect which produces the dye, coccus cacti, is raised on the leaves of the Mexican nopal cactus, opuntia cocconellifera. This cactus was known to the Spaniards as the nopal or the tuna. Only the wingless female insects yield dye, but fortunately they outnumber the males by some two hundred to one. The hatched insects live on the sap of the cactus, lay eggs, pass through a chrysalis stage, and are then gently brushed off the plant into receptacles to make dye. It was a tedious process in the sixteenth and seventeenth centuries; and the drying of the insects, either in the sun or in artificial heat, required vigilance and a fair measure of expertise. Skill in manufacturing cochineal was passed from one generation of Indians to the next and does not seem to have been easily learned by newcomers to the business. One authority mentioned that it took some 25,000 live insects to weigh one pound, and some 70,000 dried ones to make one pound of dye. As is to be expected, the uninformed Spaniards left such slow and painstaking work to the Indians.

Cochineal was of two types. The main type, grana, was grown in nopalerías, large regular plantations where the cactus plants were placed in the manner most convenient to the owner. Uncultivated cochineal, known to the Spaniards as grana silvestre or wild cochineal, was gathered at random in the monte. The insect gathered from wild tunas was smaller and less succulent, and some claimed that as a result the dye made from grana silvestre was inferior, but it was much hardier and did not need the constant attention which had to be given to the domesticated variety.

Grana had been cultivated before the conquest in the Mixteca, in Oaxaca, and around Puebla. It was an article of tribute and trade in Moctezuma's empire.[40] In Central America cochineal was of slight importance before the conquest. Plantations may well have existed in northwestern Chiapas and western Nicaragua, but they were not even close to the importance of those of Mexico.[41]

Just as happened in the Central American cacao industry, the Spaniards of Mexico were slow to realize the potential profits to be made from this dye. Thus in the first years after the conquest cochineal was transferred from the Aztec to the Spanish tributary system but little attempt was made to develop the enterprise any further.

It was not until the second half of the sixteenth century that expansion took place. By 1575 annual production in Mexico was estimated at 175,000 pounds, and by 1600 the trade was a large and very profitable one, with shipments of between 250,000 and 300,-000 pounds flowing regularly from Veracruz via Spain to the European cloth makers and dyers centered in the Netherlands.[42]

Central America had remained very much a poor relation in this burgeoning trade. Puerto Caballos exported fair quantities of grana at times, and some was also marketed at Granada. From there it was sent down the Desaguadero to Cartagena and Portobelo where it was loaded onto fleets for Spain.[43] The exports of the small Chiapas fields, mostly grana silvestre, were sent down the Río Grijalva and then by sea to Veracruz. Sometimes it may have been sent from Chiapas overland by muleback to Puebla and beyond.[44]

As the Mexican exports grew, envious Central Americans sought to emulate them by increasing their production. In 1575 Nicaraguan growers talked of increasing their plantings and expressed hopes for a bigger trade. President Villalobos in Santiago is reported to have caused quantities of tunas to be planted along the Zapotitlán coast at the same time. In both cases there was little apparent growth.[45] The King was also interested in this lucrative trade and saw no reason why Central America should lag behind Mexico. After some prodding, the Audiencia ordered by a decree of 1595 that all appropriate attention be given to the intense development of large nopalerías in Nicaragua, "for the greater benefit of the local inhabitants and the royal treasury."[46]

If these attempts to promote grana in Central America did achieve anything, then it must have been slight. Mentions of cochineal exports from the area continue, but always in a minor key, and it is obvious that grana was not considered a major export of Central America up to the second decade of the seventeenth century.

The search for new solutions and export crops which followed the collapse of cacao and mining inevitably turned Spaniards in Central America to thinking once again of this minor export. The arrival in Santiago in 1611 of a second dynamic and above all acquisitive governor, the Conde de la Gómera, added enthusiasm and governmental authority to this reawakened interest in cochineal. If his predecessor, Alonso Criado de Castilla, for whom Gómera had little respect, had failed to stimulate flagging industries or to lure away lucrative enterprises from other regions, then the new president would attempt to create a new and vital industry of his own.

The result was the largest promotion and developmental campaign which Spanish-dominated Central America had seen. Beginning in 1617 large nopalerías were planted at Gómera's orders. The favored area was the warmer foothills of the Pacific coast of Guatemala, the ever-fertile boca costa which has been the basis of so many of Guatemala's ephemeral periods of wealth. Within this area the new plantations were to be found in the lower parts of Totonicapán, in parts of Suchitepeques, Guazacapán, and south of Atitlán. No doubt similar efforts took place in other areas, especially northern Nicaragua.[47]

At first, hopes were high and glowing; enthusiastic reports were sent to the Council of the Indies and the Crown. Gómera wrote that on his orders, and backed by his authority, "great quantities" of the proper kind of cactus had been planted and were doing well. Soon they would be at the stage when the insects could be harvested. Detailed instructions had been given to local growers on the proper care of the plants.[48]

Obviously this kind of activity and optimism represents an important stage in the socioeconomic history of the colony. It represents a stage in which there is a recognition that a time of difficulties has arrived, but there is no admission that such difficulties are beyond resolution; or, to put it another way, there is an optimistic naïveté about the complexity of the problems to be faced. It is also the age of governmental intervention and social engineering in Central America. Both private individuals and officials seemed to feel that while the mounting problems were perhaps beyond individual attempts at solution, yet a concerted, well-organized effort coupled with the proper laws and sanctions, could still restore lost prosperity. As a result it was an age dominated not so much by the activities of great entrepreneurs, the Alvarados and the cacao encomenderos of the first fifty years, but by government officials who tried, with the entrepreneurs, to restore the days of the boom economy.

The grana euphoria lasted for about two years, and happy reports to the Crown continued to leave Central America. Detailed reports were sent to the King about the nature of the insect and the techniques to be used in its husbandry. Gómera wrote as if cochineal did not exist in Mexico and as if the Crown had never heard of the whole business before. A map of the area under cactus was forwarded together with other drawings.[49]

It is safe to assume that this operation must have taken considerable time and government capital. There was an unusual emphasis on central direction, planning, and investment for the future. It is also safe to assume that the project must have proved an onerous one for the Indians. They, of course, performed the labor of planting and tending the cactus—yet another task to keep them away from their subsistence milpas.

The great grana promotion died as quickly as it had come into being. After 1621 the enthusiastic reports cease. Indeed all mention of the new plantations and the insects disappears from the documents in a most mysterious fashion. One can only speculate on the reasons for this anticlimax. Perhaps the main reason for failure was locusts. The worst invasions of the two centuries following the conquests took place in the two barely separated years, 1616 and 1618. All efforts to control them—burial pits for the young locusts, fires, and early harvesting—failed, and for three growing seasons they consumed everything in their path. In spite of Gómera's still enthusiastic reports of 1620, it is likely that the locusts had already destroyed many of the young cactus plants and all the maize of the Indians who were obliged to look after them. Cochineal insects are also vulnerable to heavy rain, and many of the areas may simply have had too much annual precipitation for them and for the cactus.[50]

As always, by this time, there was the problem of labor. The reduced Indian populations could not grow maize, tend the delicate and aging cacao bushes, perform the labor on the increasingly important indigo works, and also learn the skills and tasks necessary for the development of intensive nopalerías. Even more important than lack of labor was lack of skilled labor. The care of cochineal insects, the drying techniques, and the conversion of them into blocks of dye were intricate processes for that age, little understood by most Spaniards and mestizo merchants involved in the dye trade, and inherited from generation to generation by the Indians of the pre-conquest cochineal areas such as Oaxaca and the Mixteca. It is unlikely that the local Spaniards and government officials of Central America were able to develop these skills among a sufficient number of Central American Indians. Most of the cactus plants and insects which survived the locusts and the tropical downpours probably died because of inadequate care.

Most important, Central America did not have a monopoly of the product. Mexico was the great colonial producer of cochineal, and the existence of such a formidable and nearby rival inhibited the expansion of the Central American fields. In spite of a rapid decline in the seventeenth century, Mexico's exports of cochineal even exceeded those of Central America's most successful crop of the period, indigo, except for a brief period from 1608 to 1614. After the developmental flurry had passed cochineal returned to its old place in Central American economics. Once in a while the local growers or wild cochineal gatherers would have a particularly good year, and exports would reach fairly significant dimensions. Remnants of Gómera's plantations may have been the reason for the entry of a few new areas after the 1620s. Totonicapán, for example, was growing a few tunas commercially in the late seventeenth century, but does not appear to have done so at any time in the sixteenth century.[51]

In the minor areas where grana or grana silvestre had always been a product of some importance, the Indians were exploited in ways similar to those already discussed elsewhere. They were allowed to remain as the owners of many of the nopalerías, but they were largely excluded from the trade. In the northwest of Chiapas, on the border with Tabasco and Tehuantepec, Indians were forced to sell their grana to Spaniards at absurdly low prices or to exchange it for worthless goods which they did not need. In Monimbo and Managua in Nicaragua, petty traders who tricked the few remaining local Indians out of their grana were known pejoratively as quebrantahuesos (bone breakers), or mercachifles (swindlers). In Chiapas royal officials also attempted to play a part in the trade and export of grana. Some tried to control it. In other words, it soon reverted to a secondary regional product outside central control or interest.[52]

Cochineal was no solution to Central America's search for a replacement for slaves, silver, and cacao. It remained in the seventeenth century a crop of some importance in a few minor subregions within the territory of the Audiencia. Not until the third decade of the nineteenth century were Central American entrepreneurs able to develop local cochineal into a major profitable industry in the way that the Conde de la Gómera had dreamed of so many years before.

As the economic and demographic crisis continued in the third and fourth decades of the seventeenth century, it became increasingly obvious that the developmental schemes of Presidents, local governors, silk merchants, and Flemish pilots had come to very little. The depression had been caused by factors outside their control.

10

Indigo, 1580–1720; Possibilities and Frustrations

Those who looked for quick wealth through trade in a dynamic product seemed to be in a hopeless position when cacao exports collapsed. Not only had this and other major industries disappeared, but Central America could not even buy the goods which it needed from outside, and its currency was unstable and debased. Most of those in the dominant classes withdrew from commercial activities connected to areas outside Central America.

Central America's currency troubles and the withdrawal of its elites from international commerce will be examined later; first it is pertinent to examine the last of Central America's great colonial trades, indigo. For some time it seemed to have replaced cacao. Indeed between 1580 and 1620 it enjoyed great prosperity. Although it stagnated thereafter and remained in a backward condition for over half a century, there were some indications that this new trade would provide under favorable conditions the key export which was sought.

This stagnant yet promising industry was the principal factor which kept a small group of Central American entrepreneurs agitating, experimenting, and hoping, even during the leanest years of the mid-century depression.

Like most of the commercial agricultural products grown during Spain's domination of Central America, indigo dye had been in use before the conquest. Little of its early history is known. There appear to have been few areas of intense cultivation in Central America, and the plant seems to have had little religious or symbolic significance. Human sacrifice may have been one exception. Blue was the traditional color for sacrifice in the Mayan culture, and probably indigo was used to make this sinister paint. The humdrum daily activity of dying cloth was the principal use for indigo, however, and consequently it received appropriately little mention in pre-conquest sources, which are mostly concerned with ritual and religion.[1]

Unlike cacao, however, a market for indigo existed in the Old World even before the conquest. Indigo of various kinds had been imported from the East by both land and sea for centuries. Woad had been used to produce blue dye in northern Europe but was expensive and unreliable. As a consequence of these movements and activities Europeans were aware of the value of fast blue dyes.

Spain had not been able to share in these trades. She had little early commercial contact with the East compared to nations such as Venice, Portugal, and Holland. Often she was obliged to buy blue dye through intermediaries at high prices. As a result the home country was most interested in early reports from Mesoamerica of an excellent fast blue dye. In 1558 the King asked that samples of the dye-bearing plant be sent to Spain, accompanied by a description of its cultivation, the climate most suitable for it, and the techniques used by the Indians for its extraction.[2] Later in the century an unsuccessful attempt was made to grow Mesoamerican indigo in Spain itself.[3]

Given this enthusiasm on the part of home authorities, local American interest in the commercial possibilities of indigo was slow to develop. Probably there was enough readily available to accommodate early demands. The plant grew in a wild or semiwild state, and the dye-bearing leaves were simply gathered as needed. No doubt slaving, silver, and cacao diverted Spanish attention elsewhere.

Nicaragua is the region within the Audiencia of Guatemala which was most frequently mentioned in early reports. It seems to have had considerable quantities of wild indigo. By 1568 local Spaniards there were becoming somewhat more interested in the dye and were encouraging Indians to gather large quantities of it. By 1576 small shipments were being exported to New Spain, presumably via the Pacific, for use in the textile obrajes of that province. In 1575 Nicaragua was reported to have produced some 100 quintals.[4]

Nicaragua and the nearby area around San Miguel on the other side of the Gulf of Fonseca had also begun to export the dye to Spain by this time. John Chilton, an escaped pirate, wandering somewhat hopelessly through San Salvador in 1571 and 1572, found that "annile" was the solution to his financial problems. He bought a quantity of the strange substance, which, as he said, "is a kind of thing to die blew withall," and crossed the isthmus to Puerto

Caballos. There he found stores of indigo, cochineal, silver, gold, sarsaparilla, and hides awaiting shipment to Spain.[5]

At this stage there is no evidence of organized plantations. Although the industry was flourishing, the leaves needed to make the dye were still being collected from wild bushes. Much of the production was being left in the hands of Indians, who knew the process and could be induced to work. With rare exceptions Spaniards showed little curiosity about the plant and the techniques used to extract the indigo.[6]

The success of early Nicaraguan exports soon changed these haphazard beginnings. Once the profits to be made from indigo had become obvious, a transformation took place in the Spanish methods and attitudes. As we shall see, Spaniards rented, seized, or otherwise acquired land along the Pacific coast for the specific purpose of growing indigo plants. Facilities were built to extract the dye and interest in the technical aspects of its production increased greatly. It is probably no coincidence, of course, that the upsurge of interest in the indigo industry took place at a time when the cacao industry of Izalcos and Guazacapán were showing increasing signs of collapse. Once these new developments began the industry expanded rapidly. By 1600 indigo production was the major export industry of Central America. Much of it was being grown in planted groves along the volcanic lowlands under plantation conditions, and obrajes or dye works were numerous and well-organized.[7]

After the establishment of indigo as a major commercial crop, information on its cultivation and use became more detailed, and by the early seventeenth century the process whereby the plant was cultivated and yielded its dye had become fairly standardized. In spite of the availability of other techniques from time to time, the methods used by the Central American producers evolved very little until the industry collapsed in the nineteenth century.[8]

Linnaeus identified four indigo plants, and there is some disagreement over which one was used in central America. Most agree that the type should be identified as *indigofera suffructiosa,* with *indigofera tinctoria* a later introduction.[9] The plant itself was known to the colonial Guatemalans by the Nahuatl word xiquilite, although the spelling varied. The finished product, indigo dye, was called añil or "tinta añil" from the Arabic *al-nil* (blue).

The xiquilite bush is from three to six feet in height. It is a leafy tropical perennial and grows rapidly on well-drained soils. In its wild state it is found on tropical savannahs and along river banks. Many of the early plantations were in such areas or on gradual slopes where natural drainage provided good conditions for growth. Swampy or rocky ground was unsuitable. Seeds were usually sown in broadcast fashion in freshly burned-over fields. The best time in Central America was thought to be after the first two or three downpours of the rainy season, which usually occur in April or May. Sometimes fields were plowed before planting, but such extra pains were thought to be superfluous. After planting, large farm animals were released into the fields to tramp down the new seeds and to crop off the extra grasses. Horses and mules, when available, were preferred to cattle because they did not crop so closely, and cattle were apt to root with their horns. A careful weeding was needed when the plant grew to a foot high, but after that the hardy xiquilite needed little attention. Some growers grazed cattle and horses permanently in the sparsely planted fields in order to keep down the weeds; apparently these animals did not eat or harm the indigo plants.

Guatemalan growers began to cut xiquilite when it was five or six months old although better results were obtained by waiting until its second or even third year. (After reaching three years of age most indigo plants gradually lose their quality.) Harvesting of xiquilite took place once a year, usually in July. The leaves contained most of the dye, and in many countries they are the only part harvested. The Central Americans, in their eagerness to obtain as much dye as possible, often cut twigs, stalks, and branches with the leaves.

Usually the xiquilite was cut in the early morning and loaded into small carts for transportation to the obrajes. As soon thereafter as was possible the vegetation was placed in vats, which were then filled with water for several hours of steeping. In the early years of the industry the small troughs were known as canoas. As the industry grew, large vats known as pilas were installed in the dye works.

Freshly cut xiquilite yields much more indigo than withered or dried-out leaves, and consequently the Central American growers preferred to have their dye works close to the fields and near a water supply such as a stream or spring. For the same reason, it was preferable to have the cut vegetation transported to the vats before the sun had reached its full intensity. The length of steeping varied. Usually it was continued until the following morning, making a total of about twenty-four hours. Some dye works owners attempted to hasten the fermentation process by using warm water from volcanic springs and by stirring occasionally to break up matted vegetation. Swamp water was also thought to be especially efficacious.

After the initial fermentation period the vats were watched closely for changes. Once the water had turned blue and begun to bubble the first stage was over. The water was then drawn off into large beating vats, leaving a mass of malodorous vegetation in the steeping pilas. In these second vats the slimy liquid was exposed to oxidation by constant beating of the surface with wooden poles. In the early days of the industry when canoes were still in use, this was often done by individual workers standing in the canoes, and it involved short periods of intense physical labor. Later, especially in the larger obrajes, water wheels drove the beating poles, while horses or mules provided the labor in smaller works. By the seventeenth century nearly all the obrajes were mechanized in these ways.

After some three to five hours of steady beating the liquid reached a crucial punto or point; to decide when the "point" had arrived was the most important part of the process. Ending the beating too soon, or continuing it after the "point" had been reached, reduced both the quantity and the quality of the dye. Various signs were awaited. Some punteros, or "point watchers," a skilled and respected group of professionals, were able to distinguish subtle changes in color and thus to decide on the correct moment. Others simply waited until the frothing produced by the beating stopped, showing that coagulation was taking place. Some punteros withdrew pailfuls of the liquid at certain intervals to see if the lumps of tinta añil were forming and sinking to the bottom.

Once the puntero had made his decision the beating was stopped and the liquid was left to settle. Then the water was drained off leaving a thick sediment in the vats. This was scooped out with bowls and emptied onto coarse cloths where the water was strained out. After a period of drying on long tables in the open air, the indigo was cut into solid bars, put into bags or boxed, and shipped to the cities and ports for distribution. It was a haphazard and wasteful process. One observer said that each wagonload yielded about one pound of dye. Quality fluctuated considerably according to the age of the plant, its freshness when steeped, the care taken in processing, and the skill of the puntero.[10]

The new indigo plantations, spreading up and down the Pacific coast of the Audiencia, were to occupy roughly the same area as the cacao plantations had occupied shortly before. But the indigo plant was hardier than the cacao tree and could be grown on most cleared land. This hardier nature and greater resistance to cold also meant that it could thrive at higher elevations than cacao, and that it could survive on less frequent attention. Thus indigo plantations were established in areas such as Gracias a Dios, Comayagua, and Chiapas, as well as on the fertile coastal plain.[11]

On the Pacific plain itself it is significant that the area of most intense cacao cultivation, Izalcos, never became important for its indigo. Of course this was partly because some of the cacao groves were still in place, but the main reason may have been soil exhaustion. The same was true of Zapotitlán. Significantly also, the jurisdictions which became most important to the indigo trade, San Salvador and San Miguel, were the Pacific areas where cacao had been least intensively cultivated. Nicaragua, the other area of importance, was similar in that it had never seen the intensive cacao cultivation of an area such as Izalcos.[12]

The making of indigo, then, did not demand much labor, except for one or two months per year. The plant was hardy and could be grown in any well-drained area below 5,000 feet. Even when it was grown intensively, in neoplantations, it could be combined with cattle grazing. Compared with cacao it was especially suited to a time of sparse populations and depression.

Between 1590 and 1620 the new industry expanded rapidly. Land was acquired in the area by Spaniards. Large numbers of obrajes were opened, and considerable acreages were planted to xiquilite. Land was plentiful, and profits seem to have been high. By 1620 there were over two hundred "obrajes de tinta añil" in the jurisdiction of San Salvador, more than forty in the corregimiento of Esquintepeque, over sixty in Guazacapán, and many more in San Miguel, Tecpanatitlán, La Choluteca, and Nicaragua. Certainly large numbers of Spaniards and Creoles were investing their capital and their efforts in the acquisition of land and the building of obrajes.[13]

There were other reasons for optimism. Some of these new obrajes were directed by absentee owners living in Santiago, but a greater number lived in San Salvador near their obrajes. By 1620 the non-Indian inhabitants of Central America had started to move to the countryside in large numbers. This was especially true in the San Salvador region after the city had been devastated by earthquakes, and Vázquez de Espinosa noticed that most Spaniards there were living permanently on their farms or obrajes.[14] Thus many of the plantations and obrajes received personal attention from the owners themselves.

Royal interest remained high. On several occasions careful processing instructions were sent out to different parts of the Audiencia, and the authorities of areas where the industry had not yet started were urged to stimulate local indigo plantings. It was indicated that royal cooperation could be expected and that the production of indigo was considered important.[15]

By 1620, therefore, it seemed at first glance that a replacement for cacao had at last been found. The indigo industry of the Audiencia of Guatemala had expanded very rapidly and was expected to continue to grow. Land was readily available, interest and enthusiasm were high both in Central America and in Spain, and the dye was very much in demand in Mexico, Europe, and even Peru. The industry was not labor intensive, and the plant was hardy.

In spite of all these favorable circumstances, the history of indigo in seventeenth-century Central America is one of frustration and unrealized potential. The industry did remain considerable. It continued to dominate economic life in Central America, at least for the Spaniards and Creoles, and it sent large amounts of indigo to Europe, Mexico, and Peru. Yet Central Americans throughout the century felt with considerable justification that the industry was unnecessarily stagnant.[16]

Many believed that a reorganization or new approach would give it the impetus needed to make all involved into wealthy exporters. Some añileros, their vision limited by the times or perhaps showing a legalistic approach typical of Creole society, believed that a change in this or that restrictive law, or an easing of an employment prohibition, would be sufficient to bring an era of great prosperity for the industry. A few, as always happens, tried fraud.[17]

The reasons for the stagnation of the indigo trade were more complex than most commentators realized. Local conditions, laws, demography, natural phenomena, markets, and conditions in the mother country and in Europe all combined to keep a potential boom in check. Central America's indigo industry continued in a classic state of arrested development almost to the end of the seventeenth century. Once slow changes had taken place in some of the conditions which were inhibiting its growth, indigo began to enjoy the boom which those involved in the industry had so long desired, but the beginnings of this new growth become apparent only at the end of the seventeenth century, and the period of prosperity itself occurred in the eighteenth.

Production figures are confusing. Some refer to total production, others to total exports, and still others to legal exports, a very different matter. Totals also varied widely according to the source, and depended, it would seem, on whether the writer was complaining about backwardness and asking for help or painting a favorable picture of the industry's potential if suitably stimulated.

Imports through Seville averaged 240,000 pounds annually from 1606 to 1620, but this figure no doubt included Mexico and excluded the massive frauds and evasions both in Spanish America and in Spain. In 1631 some four to five thousand quintals were being exported yearly from the province. (At that time each pound of indigo was worth some eight reales or less at the place of production, but prices fluctuated greatly.) Of this total the fraction which was going to Spain in a legal way may not even have reached half, suggesting little growth, or even regression since the twenties. Other figures throughout the century, although often vague or subject to other interpretations, suggest a fairly stagnant level of production.[18]

The number of obrajes in operation tends to support this belief. After the early, hasty proliferation of indigo obrajes noticed by Vázquez de Espinosa, their number seems to have soon declined to about 200 for the whole province of Guatemala, and it remained there for the rest of the century. Most were small establishments.[19]

A significant change was noticed by an observer just after the turn of the century. Around 1700, some 600,000 pounds of indigo per year from Guatemala were passing through Veracruz; another writer said that 1,000,000 pounds per annum were manufactured in Guatemala itself. These figures suggest rapid growth at the very end of the seventeenth century.[20]

Unfortunately for the would-be entrepreneurs and the planters of colonial Guatemala, most of the factors inhibiting growth were completely beyond their control. Natural disasters are frequent in geologically unstable Central America. At times the area would be rocked by severe earthquakes, with heavy destruction of housing and obraje equipment. One volcanic eruption destroyed all the xiquilite in the region around it by covering it with a deposit of ash. A delayed rainy season, or an overgenerous one, could also ruin the crops.[21]

One of the greatest fears in colonial Central American was locusts. These insects devastated huge areas, and the Spaniards could do little to stop them. Many different methods of killing locusts and their larvae were tried but they seemed to make little difference. The locusts came according to patterns and circumstances which were beyond the ken of the human inhabitants. One particularly severe series of "plagues" of locusts from 1616 to 1619 may well have been the principal factor which first decisively halted the expanding indigo industry. In some areas the locusts consumed all the available xiquilite to be found.[22]

Human labor and the laws governing its use in Central America were the two factors which most frequently concerned the indigo growers and other interested individuals in the seventeenth century. Indigo reached importance, unlike cacao, after the Indians had all but disappeared. By 1600 the once teeming populations of the isthmus had been reduced to a demoralized remnant. One of the main problems of the seventeenth century was to exact sufficient labor from this group without further reducing its numbers. The indigo industry found itself faced with this dilemma almost from the beginning.

The work to be performed on a typical indigo obraje in the seventeenth century was different in nature and intensity from that of a cacao plantation. Very little field work was required because the xiquilite plants required minimal care, and cattle did the weeding.[23] Nor did the vegetation require a significant number of skilled or technically competent individuals. One good "puntero" and a foreman or mayordomo were sufficient to supervise even the largest obraje. For most of the year the xiquilite plantations and añil obrajes were deserted, while the local Indians worked on their own crops or tended cattle.[24] Thus far it would seem that indigo was an ideal crop for an area with a shortage of labor. Certainly indigo's labor requirements were not as high as those of cacao, and, as we have seen, they were far less than those of mining. Nevertheless, even if indigo was an appropriate crop for the labor-starved seventeenth century, it still had fairly substantial seasonal needs.

During the months of July, August, and September a considerable force was needed. Xiquiliteros were needed to cut down the bushes and load them into carts. Muleteers and wagoners were required to take the harvested xiquilite to the obrajes, and in the obrajes themselves gangs of laborers were needed to load the vats, empty out the dye, and cut it up and package it when it was dry.[25] For a short period, often only about two months, large numbers of ordinary laborers and draught animals were required. For the other ten months, except for a few people to do the planting and maintenance, the obrajes could be left unattended.[26]

These peculiar seasonal labor needs made the use of negro slaves difficult and costly. Slaves were expensive and in short supply. To purchase them for one or two months' labor per year was impossible for all but the wealthiest añileros, and only those who could use their labor elsewhere for the rest of the year would be likely to consider this solution. So the obraje owners were thrown back upon vanishing Indians for their labor needs. In any event obraje owners often preferred to use inexpensive Indian labor whenever and wherever it was available. There were several reasons for such a preference. An encomienda Indian, either naboría or a debt peon, could usually be hired or forced to abandon his own small milpa for the obraje whenever his services were needed. His salary was low and often it was possible to obtain his services without salary. At the end of the dye-making season he could be returned to his milpa or even at little cost kept on the premises to look after the cattle. There had been no original capital investment to obtain his labor, and the cost of his upkeep was insignificant. He was available when required and could support himself, after a fashion, for the rest of the year.

Unfortunately for the obraje owners, the indigo industry developed during a period of acute government concern about the decrease in the Indian population. The severe epidemics of the 1570s, second in intensity only to those of the 1540s, had drastically and suddenly dropped some Indian populations by as much as 40 per cent.[27]

Adding to this growing concern on the part of the Crown were early reports on the unhealthy nature of the work in the dye works. In the first obrajes, where the canoas were small and water or horsepower was not available, the Indians performed the labor of loading, draining, and above all beating. These tasks were often performed standing in canoas of warm, fermenting liquid, and Indians were reported to be susceptible to pneumonia and other respiratory diseases after three or four hours of intense physical effort in these conditions. For those Indians who had been brought from the highlands it was even worse.[28] Although the later system of several vats, drainage areas, aqueducts, and water- or horse-driven beating apparatus eliminated this hazard almost completely, it was too late. The complaints and detailed reports were already in.[29]

Another unhealthy aspect of the obraje method of dye extraction was the residue of rotting vegetation which was left in the steeping vats after the first part of the process. Bad air and vapors were thought to be responsible for disease. Moreover, because of this malodorous, fermenting bagasse, obrajes were always plagued by large swarms of flies, which constantly stung the workers and also spread disease. For many years the bagasse was hauled to nearby fields and spread there as fertilizer. Since this did little to alleviate the problem, a royal order of the eighteenth century commanded that all bagasse be burned. During the seventeenth century, however, the authorities remained convinced that the añil works were unhealthy for Indians.[30]

Royal orders against working Indians in textile factories and other obrajes had existed since the 1550s. Upon receipt of a report in 1580 that añil obrajes were also harmful, the Crown specified in 1581 that these were to be included in the prohibitions.[31] Such bans seem to have been ineffectual and unheeded in the wave of expansion up to 1620. The Crown's main response to such disobedience was more forceful and specific legislation. In 1601, for example, it was decreed that the prohibition against using Indian laborers applied even if they were volunteers.[32] The colonists then began to resort to special pleading. They claimed that the work on the obrajes, per se, was being performed by slaves, free negroes, and castes, and that the Indians were employed only as xiquiliteros to cut the bushes and to haul them to the obrajes. Another form of evasion was to pass on hiring responsibility to intermediaries. The obraje owners would commission or allow casta agents to find labor for them and would then refuse to be held responsible for the fact that Indians had been hired or coerced by their agents.[33]

Sometimes Indians themselves grew añil for profit, either individually or on their common land. Creoles took advantage of this. Indians could hardly be prevented from working their own añil.[34] Royal concern over the possible unhealthiness in the obrajes continued in spite of all evasions, denials, and assertions that the bad, old days of canoes and manual labor were gone.[35]

As a further measure to halt this use of Indian labor, the Crown established a system of obrajes inspectors. Suspected offenders were visited by royal officials, their misdemeanors reported, and punishments meted out after prosecution. By 1592 visitas were being made along the Guatemalan coast. By 1607 the system was established in La Choluteca, San Miguel, and San Salvador, all major areas of production. In at least one area, however, the system was not instituted until late in the century: in Tegucigalpa first discussions about imposing a system of visitas did not take place as far as is known until 1676, when fines began to be levied in a regular way. No doubt Honduras' poverty and the relative unimportance of its indigo works were factors in this delay.[36]

In the early days of the visitas in the major areas, there seem to have been some genuine attempts to eliminate the use of Indian labor. There were several quick prosecutions and some remarkably

severe fines. To reinforce the visitas several prohibitions were
added with the intention of preventing conflicts of interest. Obraje
owners were forbidden from holding offices in the Santa Hermandad and from the posts of alcalde ordinario and royal lieutenant
(teniente de oficial real).[37]

In seventeenth-century Creole society such firmness was quite
unusual, and accommodations and subterfuges soon took the place
of severity. Royal officials were paid too poorly, indigo was too
profitable, and there was too little real concern for the welfare of the
Indians for the visitas and fines to long hamper the use of illegal
labor in the obrajes. Very shortly after the visitas began, they, and
the resultant fines, became a well-organized, unwritten system
whereby local officials exacted their share of the profits from the
indigo industry in return for their silence and forbearance.

Sometimes an honest official would report home. Rarely, an
official would demand too much, or an obraje owner would prove
obdurate about payment of his normal fines or bribes. Then the
system would falter, and reports of the true state of affairs would
reach the King's ears.[38] Nevertheless, for some eighty years and
throughout most of the seventeenth century, the collusive visita and
fine arrangement between local officials and obraje owners ensured
that those few Indians who had survived could be used on the
obrajes, and that poorly paid officialdom could accumulate some
extra capital for the eagerly awaited return to Spain.[39]

Typically, a visita would function as follows. The visitador, with
a few followers whose silence also had to be purchased, would arrive
at the town or village nearest to a group of obrajes. Warnings of the
visita were sent in advance, no doubt, and appropriate local arrangements were made. Since the visitador and his entourage seldom visited the obrajes themselves, their "investigations" were
usually perfunctory. Most of the evidence was collected by calling
on one or two witnesses from each hacienda, who would duly con-
fess that they had worked in indigo dye works. But, it was often
stipulated, they had been treated kindly, had worked on obrajes
voluntarily, and were part of only a small group of Indian laborers.
Another plea often advanced claimed that the Indians did not set
foot in the obraje themselves, but confined their part of the process
to cutting the xiquilite and bringing it to the pilas. Thereafter, it was
alleged, the work was performed by slaves and "free" negroes,
mulattoes, and mestizos.

After brief deliberation each obraje owner would be found
guilty, but only mildly so. He would be fined at a fixed rate (usually
an insignificant amount), the visitador and his followers would be

bribed (often in indigo rather than money), and the inspection team
would move on to the next group of obrajes.[40] All secrecy surrounding this system disappeared very quickly. Complaints were not frequent, but they were made. Moreover, the fines were simply too
regular, at too fixed a rate, and too willingly paid to deceive even
the most uninterested members of the Royal Audiencia in Santiago
or the Royal Council of the Indies.

The responses of both institutions to such blatant illegality
were predictable and typical of seventeenth-century reactions from
such institutions. Since their inception the visitas to the añil works
had been undertaken by local officials in most areas. The most
important of these officials was the alcalde mayor of San Salvador,
which was the center of the industry. The Audiencia alternated
between pompous scoldings and attempts to seize the lucrative
privilege of conducting the obraje visitas for itself. The tenacity with
which local alcaldes mayores in San Salvador fought these attempts
by the Audiencia shows that the añil visitas, far from constituting
one more official burden, were considered a very lucrative and
desirable set of privileges, not to be surrendered without a struggle.
With the help of the Crown the alcaldes mayores were able to resist
the intrusive Audiencia, and they retained the right to conduct the
obraje visitas until the whole system was abolished.[41]

If the duties of the visitas could not be taken from the alcaldes
mayores by the Audiencia, then the next step was obviously to
capture the office itself. Powerful interests centered in Santiago who
were financially interested in the indigo industry, the most lucrative
trade in Central America, used their influence and proximity to
royal officials to obtain the office for themselves or for their trusted
representatives. This capturing of the office of alcalde mayor of San
Salvador accomplished two main purposes. The post itself was a
source of considerable income, and it allowed the powerful interests
to engage in illegal activities on the obrajes with impunity, since the
official inspector was one of them. The most blatant example of this
kind of nepotism took place during the presidency of Diego de
Avendaño (1642–49) and was the object of a complaint to the King
which was later printed.[42]

One of the richest families in Santiago in the first half of the
seventeenth century was the Justiniani Chavarris, Genoese entrepreneurs with many ties to officialdom. Antonio María Justiniani
Chavarri, the leader of the clan and a close friend of Avendaño,
obtained the alcaldía mayor of San Salvador for his nephew, who

was totally inexperienced and only nineteen years old. The complaint protests that the youthful alcalde mayor was little more than an agent for his uncle in the indigo trade. Other Justinianis were accused of similar wrongdoings. All were accused of being extremely wealthy, largely because of tax evasions. Some, for example, had defrauded on composiciones. The family agent in Panama, another nephew called Juan Vicencio Justiniani, had not even bothered to become naturalized.[43]

The Crown's response to the "fine-bribe" system was similar to that of the Audiencia. There were infrequent reproofs, and more frequent reiterations of the decree against the use of Indian labor. Nevertheless, the fines, such as they were, produced a respectable total when accumulated and deposited in the royal treasury. In the indigent Spain of the seventeenth century few steady sources of revenue could be ignored. Quite the reverse, such sources were guarded and protected with something approaching reverence, whatever their origins.[44]

Thus the Crown became, in effect, a silent partner in the illegal visita and fine system of Indian labor in the obrajes. By 1659 a separate division or ramo had been organized in the royal treasury at Santiago to take care of the fines. Royal urgings to increase the size of the fines no doubt came from mixed emotions. The Indians might be helped, and royal revenues increased.[45] Indigo producers realized that fines were of value and interest to the Crown, and their letters reflect this. When official exactions became too severe or the payment of bribes too offensive, their complaints to the King against the system always made allowances for the King's "share." Thus, in 1630, when Juan Ruiz de Avilés of San Salvador, speaking for some two hundred obraje owners, protested to the King against the system, he offered, in effect, to "buy out" the King's interest in it. The obraje owners, he promised, would contribute 40,000 pesos to the royal treasury if the system of visitas were stopped and the prohibitions against the employing of Indians rescinded. Obviously the bribes and fines together, while not exorbitant, were adding significantly to the cost of production, and were reducing the margin of profit obtained from the sale of the finished indigo. Thus the visita system was in its own way preventing the expansion of the añil trade, and the more farsighted producers wished to escape from this trap.[46]

Suggestions of immediate cash payments were appealing to the bankrupt monarchy. In 1670 the Court, writing to the Audiencia in

Guatemala, indicated that objections to the visitas and the prohibition of Indian labor seemed to have some validity and asked for
advice.[47]

Yet the system continued. Inertia and insufficient powerful opposition perpetuated it. In spite of sporadic attempts, the prohibition against Indian labor was not removed until 1738 when the new
Bourbon kings began to effect their reforms.[48] By that time, however, labor relationships and the groups involved had changed.
During the seventeenth century itself, the main effect of the prohibition was plainly to hamper the growth of a potentially rich industry
and keep production at unnecessarily low levels.

The long argument over the use of Indians in obrajes assumes
even greater importance when it is realized that even an exhaustive
use of the local Indians in an industry with relatively low labor
demands still left the obrajes short of labor. Once the añileros had
obtained as much Indian labor as they dared, they were forced to
turn to two other sources of supply. Both were expensive and one
was unreliable.

Slaves were one possibility, but even if the dye works owner
could use them elsewhere for the ten months of the year when
indigo production was dormant, he was still faced with the high
purchase prices. Most indigo works were small until near the end
of the seventeenth century, and it is unlikely that many of the owners were able to accumulate large reserves of capital. Central America in general suffered from a great shortage of coinage, and slave
traders may not always have been willing to accept boxes of indigo
or other goods for their slaves. On several occasions the impecunious obraje owners or the governors asked the Crown to lend them
the necessary capital or to supply slaves on credit. The Crown's
financial straits were such that it could be of little assistance.[49] Even
if the dye-maker did decide to purchase slaves, he was faced with
problems of supply and legislation. Slave ships called infrequently
at the Caribbean ports of the Audiencia. Apart from the deserted
nature of that side of the isthmus, Central America was not a good
market compared to New Spain or Tierra Firme. Slavers had an
assured sale in these areas and came to Honduran ports only when
they could be sure of disposing of their cargo.[50]

Furthermore, the central authorities within the Audiencia were
not enthusiastic about large importations of slaves. The empty
tropical areas of the Caribbean coast provided refuge for a growing
number of cimarrones, or runaway slaves. Their harassment of communications with the Caribbean coast was a nuisance, and the possi-

bility of their collaberation with foreign powers hostile to Spain worried the Audiencia and the Crown throughout the century.[51] Small groups of cimarrones also established themselves in the more remote areas of the highlands and the Pacific coast, and from time to time costly expeditions had to be sent against them.[52] Above all, the authorities dreaded slave revolts. There had been one serious outbreak early in the sixteenth century in San Pedro Sula, and rumors of new conspiracies caused great uneasiness from time to time.[53]

Thus the indigo growers, when they did have the capital and the opportunity to buy negro slaves, often encountered indifference or even hostility from the authorities in Santiago, who felt that the slave population was already dangerously large.[54] Adding to the Audiencia's fears and reluctance was the ever-increasing number of castes. These groups, "free" negroes, mulattoes, mestizos, and declassé white vagabonds, were held under suspicion because of their very origin. Because of their anomalous "free" position they were less amenable to control than slaves, and the authorities often felt uncertain and confused about the proper way to control them. Technically they were free, but they were not the social or legal equals of Creoles or peninsulares.[55]

The castes themselves, being aware of their anomalous position, responded in many cases, as might well be expected, with asocial or even antisocial behavior. They showed a tendency to keep away from the centers of control as much as possible, and to avoid recruitment to the more exigent forms of labor.

The attitude of the authorities, on the other hand, was that labor was scarce and necessary for the public welfare and that individuals of lowly status, free or not, should be productively employed.[56] And these castes, oppressed and alienated, were potentially hostile. Particularly feared was the possibility that they might join with or incite Indians or slaves to revolt.[57] Thus Spanish authorities worked constantly to force the castes to "settle down." Repeated laws forbade vagabondage, the milder form of caste rejection of society. To sporadic brigandage and rustling, the more violent forms, the authorities could only respond with an occasional use of force and spectacular punishment of offenders.[58]

Vagabondage and criminal activities remained permanent features of caste behavior during the colonial period, but a large number were persuaded or forced to accept an informal compromise with Spanish authorities. This compromise was essentially the performance of the more individualistic and responsible tasks in the

cattle-dominated countryside. As a result many of the early herders
and range hands were of mixed blood. So too were many of the
hacienda mayordomos and small rural entrepreneurs such as mule-
train managers and Indian labor recruiters.[59]

Often local Spaniards would attempt to stabilize these caste
roles by entangling individuals in one or more of the devices collectively and loosely known as debt peonage. These arrangements
gave a certain amount of individual freedom and leisure to the more
independent members of the castes, yet helped to satisfy the authorities that they were productively employed.

The system, if it was ever formalized enough to deserve such
a name, was subject to frequent breakdowns. Ranch hands often
turned to rustling, raiding, indiscriminate slaughter of cattle for
their hides, abuse of Indians, and other criminal activities.[60] Far
from central authority, or even from the owner of the hacienda, the
castes often became skilful horsemen with a remarkable, independent mode of life. Authorities expressed fears about this situation
regularly.[61]

Breakdowns in the social control system for rural castes were
even more frequent in the indigo obrajes. Dye work was probably
not a preferred task, especially compared to the relative freedom of
herding or driving mule trains. (Of course there were no strict
differentiations according to employment. Some herders and muleteers were probably impressed for work in the obrajes for two
months every year.) Within the obrajes themselves some tasks were
especially scorned. Driving carts of xiquilite to the obrajes or working as mayordomos or punteros were probably acceptable roles, but
the hard labor of loading and unloading pilas, beating the vats, and
carrying the zurrones of indigo were tasks hated by all. Consequently it was more difficult for obraje owners to induce free castes
to work on the obrajes, and once there, to hold them to their tasks.
Even debt peonage did not always work. Village-oriented Indians
could often be found, punished, and brought back if they fled their
contracts or debts. The more individualistic castas, familiar with the
handling of horses and mules and often brought up to a nomadic
rural existence, could disappear quickly and permanently whatever
the size of their alleged debt or the stipulations of their contracts.[62]

As a result castes performed many of the supervisory and transportation roles on the obrajes. On most of these establishments
there was a nucleus of free negroes or mixed bloods which was
entrusted with the effective running of the establishment.[63] But as
a permanent labor force castes presented many problems, and the

labor shortage remained chronic throughout the seventeenth century.

In terms of a replacement for the decadent cacao industry, then, indigo cultivation presented certain advantages as far as labor supply was concerned. The hardiness and adaptability of xiquilite and the seasonal nature of work on the obrajes meant that indigo was a more viable industry than cacao for an area of drastically reduced populations. It simply did not need so many workers. Nevertheless, such was the shortage of labor that even undemanding indigo could not find an adequate supply of manpower. Indigo was, in fact, only a partial solution to the problem of finding a dynamic export item which did not depend on the work of vanished populations. The change from cacao to indigo was a typical seventeenth-century adaptation. It allowed exports to continue and provided a little financial support for the local Spaniards, but true prosperity, even for a few, had to wait for a revival in population.

In spite of the shortages, it is obvious that lack of labor was not the critical variable in the stagnation of the indigo industry. Nor was it held back by outside competition. Mexico's production never matched that of Central America, and the indigo booms of Brazil and South Carolina were essentially eighteenth-century phenomena.[64]

Taxation was another factor in the stagnation of the indigo industry in the seventeenth century. Taxes were visible, resented, and paid in hard-earned coinage or merchandise. As a result they were frequently mentioned in complaints. (After all, tax injustices are quickly and simply solved by doing away with the taxes involved. So protesting Creoles tended to concentrate on this soluble problem rather than becoming involved in discussions of the bewildering labor and market situation.)[65]

In spite of the volume of complaints, taxation was probably even less important as a restrictive factor than labor or outside competition. One suspects that more tax was evaded than paid in many areas. Moreover, the rates were not so appallingly high as some complainants alleged. Taxation increases in the seventeenth century were, in large part, a result of the monarchy's increasing financial predicament. Every war in Europe cast the Spanish Crown into desperate straits and forced it to resort to ever more counterproductive and hasty methods of collecting revenues.[66] Moreover, Spain's lack of funds made her incapable of helping the colonies, especially the minor ones, so that all local emergencies had to be met out of local funds.[67]

Because of these factors there were really two types of taxation. One was the fairly regular normal taxes such as the alcabala or sales tax, the import and export taxes, the tithe, the port dues, the official paper tax for all documents, and so on.[68] It was the other type of taxation which was probably more inimical to the long-term development of any activity or industry. This second kind of taxation can be roughly classified as emergency levies. These were imposed for many reasons and for all kinds of emergencies both within the New World and in Spain. They were capricious, sudden, and no doubt demoralizing to those forced to pay. Because indigo was the foremost export product of Central America, it was particularly susceptible to this kind of taxation.

The indigo industry had its beginnings when Spain's financial troubles were becoming obvious, and from the start it found itself subject to special taxes. As early as the middle 1570s the viceroy had agreed with the archbishop of Mexico that a tithe be put on all boxes of indigo weighing 25 pounds or more. The bishop of Guatemala was instructed to impose a similar tax. The president of Guatemala objected in 1578, and referred the matter to the King.[69]

Another example occurred in 1629. On January 25 of that year the cabildo of Santiago received a royal cédula which asked the viceroyalty of New Spain and the kingdom of Guatemala to provide 250,000 ducats for "grave necessities." Such a sum was to be paid annually for 15 years. Santiago, without the provinces, assigned itself an annual quota of 4,000 ducats and decided to raise it by taxing imports and exports of wine, cacao, and indigo. Nor did the unlucky obraje owners escape the many composiciones, ex post facto fees or forced purchases of recently invented licenses, which the Spanish kings used throughout the seventeenth century as a device for raising extra funds.

On March 26, 1689, the King ordered that all obrajes of añil and all sugar mills had to be "composed." Clear titles, pardons, or exemptions had to be bought. President Jacinto de Barrios Leal questioned this order, pointing out that most of these obrajes and mills stood on lands which had already paid such fees. The King was adamant. Even if the owners had a good title to the land, they still had to purchase a license in order to have an obraje or ingenio on that land. Dye works owners were, in effect, being forced to purchase and legalize their titles twice over. These and other tax abuses were frequent. The King doubled the alcabala in 1631 as an emergency measure. Quick sales of juros, solicitations of voluntary donations, and even confiscations continually threatened the indigo growers' profit margins throughout the seventeenth century.[70]

If the beleaguered obraje owner did manage to find sufficient Indians or castes to cut his xiquilite fields and produce some indigo, if he did buy off the official visitador, and if he succeeded in either evading his taxes or paying them without too much loss, he was still faced with the problem of disposing of his valuable product. The problem of markets may well have been the most crucial of all to the seventeenth-century industry.

Quantities of indigo were consumed locally, but the amount was probably small, and it was obviously a minor market. No doubt small quantities of Central American indigo also found their way to other colonial markets, such as Panama, Cartagena via Granada, and Havana via the Honduras ports.[71] There were also exports southward to the viceroyalty of Peru. The traffic is frequently mentioned but there are few statements as to quantity or frequency. One suspects that the trade may have been large. At times Central America had some substantial items to exchange for the wine, oil, and silver coming from Peru, all of which came to the ports of La Caldera, Nicoya, Realejo, Fonseca, and Acajutla throughout the seventeenth century. Yet these items do not seem to have been sufficient to balance ledgers. Obviously cacao was not a large item after the growth of the Guayaquil plantations. Exports of Guatemalan cacao to Peru in the seventeenth century were probably limited to small quantities of higher quality or aromatic chocolate for the upper class. The export of "brea," or pine pitch, was large for many years but the trade was confined, as we shall see, to one region of Nicaragua. Chinese goods, mostly luxury textiles avoiding prohibitions or taxes in New Spain, were also sent in fair quantities but could hardly have accounted for the bulk of the shipments. Various medicinal plant products, local handicrafts, timber, and ship stores together added up to considerable bulk and quantities but individually earned little in return.

Moreover, there seems to have been an industry with a considerable demand for indigo in the large textile obrajes of the Quito highlands. Various sources refer to this area as an important producer of cheap cloth, and presumably at least some of it was dyed.[72] Unfortunately there are few lists of typical cargoes, so that quantities of indigo shipped down the Pacific coast are unknown. The few available often mention indigo.[73] New Spain also received large quantities of Central American indigo, much of it for transshipment, and some for local use in its own infamous obrajes de paños. But New Spain was itself a small producer of indigo, indeed a rival to Central America, and thus did not require large imports.[74]

It is obvious, in fact, that the New World in the seventeenth century did not afford enough markets to sustain a large dye industry. The indigo traders of Central America were inevitably forced to look to Europe for their major markets. By relying on that distant area, and particularly on Spain, which the cacao industry had not been obliged to do in its heyday, indigo exposed itself to all the problems and turbulence of Atlantic shipping and seventeenth-century Europe.

Piracy was a constant threat. Like taxation, its role as an inhibitor of trade, while total at times, was probably overestimated by the terrorized people of the time. Nevertheless, pirates destroyed some stocks of indigo and made off with others. They seized ships at sea or appeared in such numbers that no ships dared to sail. Above all, they drove trade inland from the decks of small coastal canoes and frigates to the backs of mules. In the seventeenth century such a method of transportation was more expensive and much slower, especially in the highland terrains of Middle America.[75]

Even more important than piracy was the role of Spain itself. Spain was the presumptive market for Central American indigo. Legislation forbade the colonies to trade with other areas or intrusions of any kind by foreign vessels.[76] Yet, as the seventeenth century advanced, Spain was increasingly unable to fulfill her roles vis-á-vis the New World possessions. The depressed nonindustrial Spanish economy was unable to absorb the products of the New World other than precious metals and even these were quickly reexported to pay debts. The textile industries which needed indigo had almost disappeared.[77]

The decline in Spanish manufacture meant that Spain's production of finished products also dried up. By 1600 the mother country was hard pressed to supply the New World with the goods it required. By the end of the century she was unable to export such essentials as iron, oil, and wine and had long ceased to be a major source of cloth and other finished articles. Since Spain's coinage came from the New World, and then drained off to Flanders, Italy, and elsewhere, she could hardly pay for the produce of the New World in gold and silver. So Spain did not have the wherewithal to buy indigo, even if she needed it.[78]

Added to Spain's inability to absorb or pay for a product such as indigo were a number of minor hindrances which further discouraged trade. Spanish officials were prone to indulge in confiscation of cargoes in particularly lean years, repayment often coming, if at all, in the form of long-term juros or pensions promised against future collection of revenue by various sections of the Spanish treasury. Capricious taxes at the port system around Seville, sudden devaluations and revaluations of a debased vellón (copper) coinage, low prices for dye after 1625, and the frequent inability of Spanish merchants or factors to pay as promised all added to the hazards of trade, made the Spanish market less inviting, and thus reflected on the production of indigo in the Audiencia of Guatemala. At times the Crown would attempt to restore confidence by proclaiming an end to arbitrary confiscations, and promising regular fleets in the future, but the next emergency would cause a relapse.[79]

Until about 1630, however, Spain maintained her fleet service with impressive regularity. Secondary areas did not suffer much more than the major ones of New Spain and Peru from the occasional interruptions in traffic.[80] Ships called at the three ports used by Central America for its direct European commerce as a regular part of the New Spain fleet system.[81] Guatemalans complained that the ships which called were too few and of insufficient tonnage to transport their imports and exports to and from Spain, thus causing dangerous overloading. The ownership of the ships and cargoes also aroused dissatisfaction because of its monopolistic nature, but in spite of these objections the ships transported large quantities of indigo and other Guatemalan products across the Atlantic with fair regularity.[82]

After 1630 the Spanish fleet system began to show signs of great strain and occasional collapse. Spain experienced ever-increasing difficulty in keeping her shipping lanes open. Partly this was because of pirates or hostile foreign navies in times of war. On rare occasions these marauders seized all or part of major Spanish fleets. The famous coup by Piet Heyn in 1628, when he seized most of the New Spain treasure outside Havana, meant the loss of the entire year's export of indigo for the Guatemalan producers and merchants. The following year the almiranta ship was sunk by the Dutch off Havana after a stiff engagement. Fleets were also lost to pirates in 1656 and 1657, when the economic depression may have been at its worst.[83]

The export of indigo to Spain reflects this situation. From 1608 to 1614 the exports of indigo, largely Central American in origin, surpassed even those of cochineal, one of New Spain's most prized exports. And when decline in shipments came it was less rapid at first in Honduras than in New Spain. The Honduran traffic's relative strength vis-à-vis Veracruz between 1625 and 1640 was no doubt created by the large indigo industry. But by 1640 the character of the fleet system changed, priority was given to silver ports, and Honduras calls became infrequent, to the detriment of the indigo trade and its growth.[84]

In addition to the pirate threat which kept ships in port, there was a frequent inability to gather enough produce in Spain to make the sailing of the fleet worthwhile. Sometimes the process of gathering cargo for a sailing would take several years. At times there was a lack of money to fit out the ships and to provision them for the voyage to the New World. In some years, as the Spanish navy declined and as ship building disappeared as an industry, there would be insufficient ships to even send a fleet.[85]

Recent investigations into the ships, cargoes, and routes used in the sixteenth and seventeenth centuries have established some of the determinants which decided which trades were to flourish, and which were to stagnate or be stifled.

The small, cumbersome, wind- and sail-propelled vessels of this period required an irreducible minimum of hands for their functioning. These crews had to carry most of their food and water with them, and some of it—the water itself, and the ever-present weevily ships' biscuits, salt pork, oil, and wine—was subject to spoiling, especially in the tropics. Because of these factors long voyages were enormously expensive. On a long voyage much more of the cargo space had to be taken up by the provisions which the crew itself would eat, and the risk of food spoiling and thus of the crew dying and the ship becoming undermanned grew correspondingly. This meant that the longer the voyage from Spain and back to Spain, the fewer the products which could pack enough profit into their bulk and weight to pay the freight and still leave something over for those who had dispatched them.

For example, the long trade route from the Seville-Cadiz ports to distant Manila took about a year. It involved four long voyages and two overland transshipments between Veracruz and Acapulco, difficult terrain for mule trains. The factors of ship capacity, crews and provisions, and the factors of bulk, weight, and profitability meant that only the most luxurious, light, and exotic goods could pass from Manila to Seville and still show a profit. As a result, the trade was confined to silks and exotic goods for the upper classes. And on the return journey from Acapulco to Manila only gold, silver, and precious stones could pay the freight.

In the smaller Atlantic world these determinants were not quite so limiting, but they were still in effect. What has been called the "near Atlantic," that is, the large islands of the Caribbean, northeast Brazil, and the coasts of Venezuela could turn a profit from plantations and cattle, and as a result their monocultural exports to Europe were built on such products as hides, tobacco, cacao, and above all, sugar. In the "far Atlantic" distances killed such trades as major exports. In Mexico, in interior New Granada, and especially in Peru only gold, silver, and precious stones were sufficiently profitable exports to become major industries.

In an area such as Mexico, therefore, the general economic prosperity and the state of shipping was crucial for minor products. In prosperous times ships arrived frequently enough, and profits from gold and silver were large enough, so that exports such as hides, cochineal, and even dye woods could flourish on the margins of the greater industry. In times of depression, when the Spanish market was drying up or when Spanish shipping was falling in numbers and in frequency of sailings, emphasis increased on loading only very profitable goods, and the secondary trades—and regions —fell away.[86]

Central America's position in this pattern of Atlantic trades was an intermediate one. It was not part of the "near Atlantic." The Gulf of Honduras was a sail of a week or so beyond Havana in the seventeenth century. It was, however, somewhat closer to Spain in sailing time than Veracruz. Central America was also fortunate in that two of its first three great exports did not have to cross the Atlantic. Indian slaves were sent to Peru and Panama, cacao to Mexico. The third great sixteenth-century trade, gold, could show a profit no matter how great the shipping distance.

Indigo was a different matter. As long as Spanish Atlantic shipping remained healthy and the exports of Peruvian and Mexican silver mines remained high, then Central American indigo exports could benefit, even if profit margins were relatively low when compared with precious metals. When Spanish seaborne commerce went into severe decline, however, the old determinants of distance, time, weight, and profitability applied with all their rigor, and indigo exports from Central America stagnated.

Inevitably the result was Spanish neglect of Central America. When the fleets did sail they had to take care of the greatest priorities and so they disregarded the minor colonial areas. The purpose of the exercise, to a blatant degree, became the conducting of the past year's output of silver and gold from Mexico and Peru to Spain.

If this great task, so vital to royal finances, could be completed, then such other tasks as the maintenance of communication and supply to minor provinces or the shipping of their products to the Spanish market were left for the future, when perhaps there would be more numerous fleets and more prosperous times.

An extraordinary meeting of the town council of Santiago was called on May 23, 1709, to protest this neglect. It was one of the many such meetings between the 1640s and the early eighteenth century, and it will serve here as a typical example. The embittered but still loyal cabildo pointed out that in the previous twenty years only two registered and licensed ships had come to Central American ports. To make matters worse, the authorities in Spain kept raising people's hopes to no good purpose. Two years earlier, for example, the local merchants had been cheered when they heard that a registro ship was being prepared for a voyage to Honduras. But once again, the cabildo complained, these hopes had been dashed. The ship in question had put in at Veracruz for fear of pirates. The town council agreed to petition the viceroy of Mexico to forbid the unloading in Veracruz of ships which had been bound for Honduras because with the additional transportation from Mexico to Guatemala, the Spanish goods, already exorbitant in price, "would become even more expensive."[87]

The cabildo was complaining about an old situation which was by then thoroughly established. As early as 1649 it had become obvious that the Spanish authorities were paying little more than lip service to the idea of a steady trade between the metropolis and the Gulf of Honduras. In fact the Crown was not prepared, or able, to do anything about maintaining or reviving these somewhat marginal concerns. The royal decree of 1649 is typical. The King ordered that the port of Trujillo was to be defended with care, but added that he could not help, and that local defense costs were to be held down by the strictest economy.[88]

Guatemalan merchants had occasionally sent their goods and letters to Spain via Mexico and Veracruz since the beginning of regular trade between the colony and the mother country. Another route had also been used from time to time. Goods were sent from all parts of the region to Granada in Nicaragua, and from there to Cartagena or Portobelo via the San Juan River and the Caribbean coast to await sailings of the Peru fleet for Spain. The Granada route, however, was full of difficulties, and because of the small ships and canoes which navigated the San Juan River the shipping of large or bulky commodities was wasteful and expensive. No doubt the use of such extended and inconvenient routes as the ones through Veracruz and Granada was originally little more than a safety valve indicating that thriving trades were finding a scarcity of cargo space on the regular Honduran flota ships. The use of such routes from time to time may also have been an indication of occasionally highly favorable prices in the Spanish market. Such an upward fluctuation of prices would result in a high but temporary margin of profit, and so Central American merchants would attempt to dispatch as much produce as possible while the high prices lasted. In some sailing seasons when reports of pirates off the coast were numerous, merchants doubtless preferred to lower their profit margins and to absorb the extra cost of the roundabout route through Mexico or Panama in return for the added security of shipping their goods in large protected fleets instead of in the two or three ships of the small Honduras flotilla.[89]

As time went on the sporadic use of these tortuous routes increased, and by mid-seventeenth century they had become the rule rather than the exception. The King's great concern for the arrival of his New World silver helped to force Central American exports to Veracruz. Sometimes the Crown was quite explicit about this. As early as 1606 Central Americans were ordered to send the royal silver and taxes overland to San Juan de Ulloa (Veracruz), when there was the slightest doubt about security in the Caribbean.[90]

After 1630 the Veracruz route become more important than the old one via the Gulf of Honduras. The calling of ships there had become so haphazard and unreliable that merchants with perishable goods began to ignore it altogether and to use regular mule trains on the long overland journey to New Spain. There are also some indications that the Granada-Desaguadero-Portobelo route was used more frequently after about 1630, at least for the sending and receiving of news.[91]

In addition to the heavy cost of the long journey by mule train, the use of the port of Veracruz raised the cost of sending Central American indigo and minor products to Spain in other ways. The Veracruz authorities and merchants, themselves heavily taxed and suffering from shrinking markets and profits, saw the yearly arrival of Central American indigo as a source of extra income. Despite Guatemalan protests, in 1669 the Veracruz ayuntamiento imposed a tax of 10 pesos per case on Guatemalan indigo. Other products from Central America were also assessed at various rates. Costs of shipping were given even more importance by a gradual but definite fall in the price of indigo in Spain between 1625 and 1648, a further squeeze on small profit margins.[92]

The additional costs of the Veracruz route caused the ayuntamiento of Santiago to ask the King in 1606, 1684, and 1685 to insist that the Barlovento squadron, which was partly sustained, after all, out of Guatemalan taxes, should protect the Honduras ports from pirates instead of confining its activities to the Gulf of Mexico. Otherwise, the ayuntamiento insisted, the exploitations of their trade by Veracruz interests would ruin it. But the King's main concern was not the restoration of trade to the Honduras ports, but rather the exorbitant fees charged by the muleteers for conveying royal moneys from Guatemala and Honduras to Veracruz.[93]

Disposal of the indigo by legal means was then a constant problem throughout the century. Even if scarce labor and capital could be found, there was little point in planting larger acreages of xiquilite or sinking scarce capital in better obrajes if the final product could not be transported or guaranteed a market.

A legal case in 1708 illustrates the market problems faced by indigo traders who tried to obey the law in the early years of the eighteenth century and the decades immediately before. Two merchants sent 42 sacks of indigo to Oaxaca by mule train. News reached them after the departure of the mule train that prices in the viceroyalty of Peru were very high, so they sent a messenger after the muleteer to recall him. The indigo was then redirected to Sonsonate for reshipment to Peru. The two merchants claimed that they did not have to pay export taxes again since they had already paid them in order to send the dye to Oaxaca. After litigation the case was decided in their favor, but the affair illustrates the hazards of fluctuating prices, shifting distant markets, poor communications, and inhibiting taxation which so hampered the colonial dye industry.[94]

As a crop, therefore, indigo had promised well as a way toward solving some chronic seventeenth-century problems. Xiquilite was a hardy plant which did not require the best of soils or constant care. Its demands on labor were seasonal and were not as high as other major industries in Central America; and what labor it did need had been, for the time, fairly efficiently obtained by the manipulations of a "fine-bribe" system and through the peculiar social position of some of the castes. In addition, obrajes did not require huge initial investments. Yet the industry stagnated from the 1620s until the last years of the seventeenth century. Spanish ships had all but disappeared from the Bay of Honduras, and the cost of hauling the indigo to Veracruz was high. In short, there was little point in producing more indigo than could be disposed of. A lack of convenient markets was the main factor stiffling an industry which otherwise showed signs of potential prosperity. The colonial dye industry's struggle to find markets was a long and frustrating one which took over half a century to resolve, and the solution, when it came, was found without the legal commercial system of the Crown.

11

The Effects of the Crisis on Local Populations and Economy

The late 1550s had represented a turning point, a pause in the growth of the economy of the sixteenth century. The exhaustion of the early "looting" industries, and the fall in the superabundant Indian laboring populations, had led Spaniards to a more regulated life, to industries where labor could be controlled through encomienda and tribute. Spaniards had been forced by changing circumstances to turn to exports which required a neo-plantation form of production, and, to the great advantage of some, cacao with its adjacent Mexican market had proved to be a solution. Pressure on the Indian population and shrinking numbers had molded this group into a more uniform, regulated, and obedient peasantry.

In the late 1570s and the 1580s the Spanish, casta, and Indian populations of Central America were again faced with a conjunction of events which together constituted a crisis. This time, however, the nature of the crisis was far more complex, and the crisis itself was more fundamental. As a result the solutions which people adopted, or were forced into, were more radical, and consequently more disturbing.

The Indian population had been falling since the conquest. Each year saw a further inexorable shrinking of numbers, but such demographic losses were fairly constant, and they were gradual enough so that Spanish encomenderos, merchants, and officials, Indian caciques, calpisques, and town councils, could adapt, albeit reluctantly, to the slowly falling labor force and tax base. The great epidemics of the 1550s severely challenged these adaptations, and in coastal areas such as Soconusco and Izalcos it was only by importing highland Indians that Spanish activities were kept going. In Nicaragua and coastal Honduras the few Indians who had survived until the 1550s shrank to an even smaller remnant. In the highlands of Central America, however, in Chiapas, most of Guatemala, Verapaz, and highland Honduras—that is, in the most populous parts of Central America, both in Spaniards and Indians—the epidemics of the 1550s, for all their ferocity, had still left enough labor for the new upper class, if it were used efficiently.

Now, between 1576 and 1581, the chronology of the disease varying according to subregion, a new and dreadful wave of cocoliztli-matlazáhuatl spread south and east from Mexico. Once again its main impact was among the Indians. Spaniards escaped relatively unscathed. Obviously the explanation, as in the Europe of the sixteenth century, must reside in the complex relationship between the physiological well being and immunological preparedness of human groups. Reporters of the time doubtless exaggerated the impact of the pandemic, but when these reports, the failures to pay tribute, and the downward revision of tribute counts, are all taken into account, it becomes obvious that the total number of Indians moved suddenly and sharply downward.[1]

This epidemic also affected newly conquered Costa Rica. Previous epidemics in Mesoamerica, those of 1520, 1531, and 1545–48, no doubt reached there too, but we have no record of how they affected the population. Spanish entradas in the late 1560s found, to their satisfaction, that the area was still fairly densely inhabited. It did not approach the totals or the densities which had first been found in Chiapas, Guatemala, Honduras, or Nicaragua, but it was felt that the numbers would provide a satisfactory living for a small group of conquistadors. Certainly many found it preferable to empty Nicaragua, and in fact the permanent occupation of Costa Rica may well be linked directly to the disappearance of the Nicaraguan Indians.[2]

The early conquistadors of Costa Rica, led by the admirable Juan Vázquez de Coronado, responded to the demographic situation which they found in two ways. The optimists, Vázquez de Coronado among them, reported favorably to the Crown and encouraged the sending of more settlers. There was room enough and Indian encomiendas enough for all. Others, remembering their experiences in Nicaragua, and feeling that the people of the expedition were more than enough already, sent pessimistic reports to the King and tried to discourage further migration. Even they, however, found a considerable population.[3]

The pandemic of 1576–81 proved the Costa Rican pessimists to be correct. At one blow it reduced the Indian populations of highland Costa Rica to a very few, and from then on the area was to become chronically starved of labor.[4]

Accompanying this pandemic and closely tied to it was the failure of the great cacao boom in Izalcos and on the boca costa of Guazacapán. In the new mining area of Tegucigalpa the 1570s and 1580s were years of new hopes. Decline there was not to come for some thirty years more. But even in the silver mines the epidemics imposed a severe shortage of labor on the new fields from the start.[5]

The new drop in labor supplies caused radical reorganization of the rationing and use of Indian workers. All but the wealthiest encomenderos found that their grants were no longer sufficient to maintain even a meager level of city living. The encomienda as an institution had suffered from increasing royal restriction and from a steady fall in the number of Indians subject to it since the 1540s. The epidemics of the 1570s were the final quietus for the undiversified encomienda. The institution itself would linger on for nearly two centuries more, but it changed radically in nature and purpose after 1575. As the encomienda had decreased in importance, an increasing number of tributary and encomienda Indians had reverted to the Crown. Some encomenderos had left Central America, others died without heirs, and still others abandoned the failing institution and sought their livelihood in other directions.[6]

From the beginnings of the colony the Crown had permitted its Indians to be used as a labor force for certain approved tasks. The first and most important, as far as the Crown was concerned, was that the Indians perform sufficient work to ensure their payment of royal tributes. Secondly, the Crown had no objection to the Indians being put to work on bona fide public works projects. Thus Indians "in the Crown" had been drafted throughout the sixteenth century for the building of cathedrals, town halls, roads, aqueducts, and bridges. The cities of Central America had called them for cleaning the streets and for other petty tasks of municipal government. In the performance of these tasks, the Crown insisted, the Indian laborers were to be treated fairly, and paid a just wage.[7]

As the labor supply grew smaller and the number of Spaniards grew larger, the Crown came under increasing pressure to permit its Indians to be used in a greater variety of jobs. The Crown found itself broadening the tasks which it could define as public works. Thus the labradores, the wheat farmers near the larger Spanish cities, found that they were able to argue that they were performing a public service, since the Spanish vecinos would be deprived of their daily bread were it not for them. Even over the most onerous tasks the Crown found itself forced to compromise. Officially, at least, the Crown steadfastly refused to allow its Indians, or any Indians for that matter, to be worked in certain industries which it felt to be especially detrimental to their health and welfare. Among these proscribed industries were textile mills, indigo plantations, and the underground work in mines. Indigo growers, as we have seen, circumvented this prohibition by turning the fines levied against them for using Indian labor into an unofficial but formalized system whereby the fines were in effect unofficial licenses purchased from suborned local officials to permit them to use Indian laborers on añil. In the mines, too, the Crown was forced to compromise by its own need for silver. The miners of Tegucigalpa complained repeatedly that shortage of labor was preventing them from developing the industry, and from exporting to Spain the amounts which they would like. In 1602 the Crown ordered the President to make a secret inquiry to find out if labor underground was really so harmful to the Indians.[8]

In general the Crown compromised with the settlers' urgent need for its Indians by extending its system of drafting Indians for specific tasks. This draft system came to be known in Central America as repartimiento. In theory the system worked as follows. A given village was ordered to supply a given number of its able-bodied males for a certain number of days per month. Within each village liability for this draft was to rotate among the villagers regardless of rank or wealth. The Indians drafted from the village were ordered to report to a predetermined place, usually the main plaza of the nearest Spanish town. There they would be met and counted by a Spanish official, the juez or judge of the repartimiento. It was this official's responsibility to ensure that the draft was fair, and that the village was not excusing its more privileged members by sending the same macehuales time after time.

Spanish landowners and agriculturalists would then each request the services of a certain number of Indians for the prescribed number of days of work. The juez de repartimiento was supposed to prevent Indians from being assigned to illegal tasks, and to make sure that they were treated according to the laws governing repartimiento. These laws specified the kinds of work that repartimiento Indians were supposed to perform and the conditions which they were to be given. Indians were to receive a fixed wage, the tools required for their work, an adequate diet, and satisfactory housing while they were in a Spaniard's employ. The time which the Indian had to take to come from his village to the Spanish city, and the time needed to walk back to his village at the end of his service (Indians sometimes had to walk two or three days to reach their destinations) was to be deducted from the length of service required. After the Indians had been assembled in the plaza some would be sent to public works in the city and nearby, and the others would be divided out (repartidos) among the Spaniards who had petitioned and were competing for their services.[9]

Repartimiento grew into a major supplier of labor after the epidemics of the 1570s, and during the half century of transition between then and the 1630s it was widely used. To some extent, although the two coexisted, repartimiento succeeded and replaced the encomienda system. In essence it was a system whereby Spaniards gained access to non-encomienda Indian labor, most of which was "in the Crown."

Encomienda had been a system which in its heyday had worked successfully for some Spaniards. Repartimiento, a system which reached its full development during much more difficult times, never really worked to anyone's satisfaction. The Indians detested it, and with good reason. The Crown found it impossible to make the system fair, and became alarmed at the many abuses which crept into it, and the Spanish employers found that repartimiento seldom granted them enough Indians for long enough, and at favorable enough terms so that the work was done to their satisfaction.

In the Indian villages the heaviest draft requirements often fell at times when Indian agriculturalists most wanted to remain at home. Spanish farmers needed Indians more at planting and harvest, and these were the seasons of the year when Indians had to tend their own milpas. Because of this Indians were willing to pay their local caciques or alcaldes so as not to be drafted. Thus the wealthier Indians were often able to evade their turn, and the poor were called repeatedly. For these poorer agriculturalists the repartimiento was a disaster. They spent much of their time on the road to and from the repartimiento, working in the city, or on Spanish farms. This often meant that they missed planting and harvesting time on their own plots, and their fields became overgrown. If they did not have able bodied dependents to do the work, they and their families suffered from hunger, and were then more susceptible to disease. The repartimiento also disrupted village life. Caciques and alcaldes lost their subjects, parish priests and friars lost their flocks, and the local petty merchants lost part of their market. These losses were all temporary, but they were nonetheless resented.[10]

Nor did the jueces de repartimiento perform their duties as the law prescribed. The post of juez repartidor was a minor one, although it was often coveted because of its lucrative possibilities. Each occupant held the job for a limited number of years, and like most minor bureaucratic positions in the colony, it was poorly paid. The post was nearly always filled by local Creoles, who were, it is logical to suppose, tied by bonds of family and interest to other Creoles in the locality, including some of those who would be requesting Indian labor from the repartimiento system. With only a few years in which to extract capital from the post, the typical juez repartidor was an ideal subject for a bribe. Thus wealthier Spaniards were able to obtain more than their fair share of Crown Indians, were able to retain their services for longer than the prescribed time, and were also able to evade their responsibilities to the Indian workers while they were in their employ. Indians were forced to bring their own tools and food with them, were tricked out of the pay which they were supposed to receive, and were forced to work the full term of the repartimiento on the farm in spite of the time which they had spent coming from their village. In some cases Indians were told that they would be permitted to return to their villages before the end of their repartimiento spell if they did not demand payment for the reduced time which they would be required to work. Many Indians, detesting repartimiento labor, and only too anxious to return to their own neglected milpas, readily agreed.[11]

Even with this wide range of abuses Spanish farmers found the system irksome. Jueces de repartimiento had to be bribed, or, if the juez was incorruptible, the Indians had to be paid and fed. One could never be sure of obtaining a sufficient number of laborers, and worse still, repartimiento supplied only a non-resident transient labor force which was not on call when needed for the day to day labor of a farm. Spanish farmers also found themselves competing with one another, which only served to raise the cost of the bribes which had to be paid. Thus Indians, the Crown, and Spanish users of the repartimiento system all found it unsatisfactory. Only a few local officials were able to turn it to any permanent benefit.

Another result of the epidemics of the 1570s was a drop in the total volume of foodstuffs produced by the Indian economy. Inevitably, as their numbers fell, Indian milperos were less able to produce the maize, hens, wood, fish, and other items which they had paid as royal or private tribute, and which via auctions and other devices had finally found their way into the city markets. Thus the growing cities found that their supply of basic agricultural produce was decreasing, and that prices were rising concurrently.[12]

One obvious solution was to force the Indians to plant more. Even as early as 1550 Spaniards had assigned this task to petty officials who became known as jueces de milpas. These Spanish overseers were supposed to inspect the fields to make sure that Indians were clearing, planting, weeding, and harvesting them adequately. The system never seems to have worked, and one of the two basic rationales for it was an absurdity: this was that Indians were lazy, and were simply not working hard enough. Higher officials and the Crown saw clearly that most Indians were working as hard as possible to feed themselves and to fulfill their many obligations. Indeed the administration knew that Indians were subject to multiple abuses, and that overwork rather than laziness was a cause for the decline in population. Consequently the Crown repeatedly banned the appointment and the activities of jueces de milpas. After the epidemics of the 1570s new and more strident appeals and attempts were made to obtain government approval for this institution, but once more the Crown was adamant.[13]

Part of the Crown's opposition came because royal officials understood the second reason why Creoles wanted to legalize the institution. It would create another stratum of offices, paid either by the Crown or by the Indian communities. Even during the short periods when jueces de milpas were appointed, many of them limited their activities to going round their jurisdictions collecting produce. One individual did not even visit the villages which he was supposed to supervise, but confined himself to writing pious letters of exhortation to the Indian milperos, and to drawing his salary.[14] Jueces de milpas were not authorized by the Crown during the crisis of the late sixteenth century, and even when they functioned illegally they had little effect on the steadily diminishing supply of Indian produce to the cities. It seemed that Spanish vecinos would have to rely increasingly on the few labradores who had established wheat farms around the cities, and that they would also have to compensate by increasing their already heavy consumption of beef, which until the 1570s had always been cheap and plentiful.[15]

The cyclical nature of pre-industrial demographic patterns in Europe has already been mentioned. A similar pattern may also have existed in preconquest Mesoamerica, although in this case it is more debatable. At any event there is one cyclical pattern which is beyond question. Mesoamerican populations rose to a maximum at the time of the conquest and then fell precipitously.

In Europe and Mesoamerica cattle and sheep populations rose as the human populations fell, and, as we have seen, the two demographic movements were interrelated. Now, however, beginning somewhere in the third quarter of the sixteenth century, the cattle population of Central America began to proceed through a mysterious demographic cycle of its own. (A similar phenomenon has been noted in Mexico.) Before the 1570s part of the reason for the rapid expansion of the animal population was that dead or fleeing Indians, or ones who had been brought into *congregaciones*, had left behind fertile plots and valleys which these animals filled. Also, Indians had great difficulty in preventing animal invasions of their crops because they initially feared these unfamiliar beasts, and because the beasts themselves belonged, even if only vaguely, to the dominant conquering class, the Spaniards. After about 1570, however, although the Indian population was still declining and cattle were still invading their crops, it is obvious that cattle had begun to decline in numbers too.[16]

This created a serious situation for the city dwellers. Compared to Spain and other parts of western Europe, meat continued to be very inexpensive in Central America throughout the seventeenth century, but to Central Americans its price, once absurdly low, rose alarmingly between the late 1570s and 1635. Even worse, meat began to show seasonal and local supply shortages.[17]

Spanish officials felt that they knew the reason for these reversals. Just as in the case of the great export crops they were still optimistic enough, or, to make the matter more general, the age was still optimistic enough, to believe that better organization and control would rectify the matter. They blamed the fall in the cattle supply on four things: indiscriminate slaughtering of animals, the demands of the export trade in hides, lack of proper pastoral care for the herds, and a disorganized system for the urban marketing of meat.[18]

There was some truth in this reasoning. When the cattle populations were numerous rural people had killed them as they needed them. Officials particularly blamed the castas for this. The rapidly growing mulatto and mestizo groups took to the countryside in large numbers to avoid the pressures put on them by the dominant whites of the cities. In the rural areas they became petty traders in the Indian villages, mayordomos on some Spanish estates and indigo plantations, and cowherds. Their intermediate social position meant that they had few opportunities for achieving positions of importance in the Spanish cities, but it also would not allow them to descend to the inferior status of Indian milperos, making a living from the lowly cultivation of maize, beans, and squash. The alternative for these cowboys was then meat, and they slaughtered cattle as they needed them. Renowned for their horsemanship, one of their most noted methods for bringing down a fleeing steer was *dejarretar*. Armed with long knives or lances, they would simply slash the tendons of the rear legs. Dismounting, they would skin the animal for its hide, and cut off a day's supply of meat. The rest of the carcass was left to the buzzards and wild animals. Very often, when the day's ration of meat had already been collected, cattle were killed for their hides alone.[19]

Obviously such practices were extremely wasteful, and as soon as it became apparent that numbers were falling cowhands were forbidden to kill cattle by *dejarretar*.[20] As was the case so often in colonial Central America, however, the crux of the matter was how to enforce the legislation.

Several difficulties stood in the way. A complaint to the King from a vecino of Santiago in 1646 is revealing, not only as to the racial attitudes and fears of colonial Spaniards, but also because it reveals much about the problems which urban officials faced when they wished to exert social control in the rural areas. The writer was a firm believer in the old European metropolitan canard that colonial life was debilitating. There was, he informed His Majesty, something in the air or atmosphere of the New World which in a few generations, or even in one lifetime, reduced fine, martial, Spanish stock to city-dwelling sybarites surrounded by retainers and sunk in indolence. This in itself was deplorable, but from the imperial point of view much worse was to come. The only skilled soldiers, the only people left who could handle horses and who could fight on horseback were mestizos, mulattoes, and negroes of the countryside, who lived a free life of tough self-reliance. These groups were growing far more rapidly in numbers than were the city Spaniards. They were far more to be feared than the depressed, humble, and rapidly disappearing Indians. If the test were ever to come they would clearly be more than a match for the decadent Spaniards. To make matters worse these rural castas were natural rebels. They had no knowledge of Spain, paid no attention to the law, and had little acquaintance with the Christian religion. They were also, the writer believed, inevitably resentful in that they had Spanish blood yet were denied equal status with the Spaniards. The castas were then an ideal breeding ground for sedition from abroad. What, for example, if Portugal were to encourage revolt in the Spanish colonies? There were many Portuguese residents in Guatemala, and they could easily spread disaffection among the castas. An even greater threat was the influence which some members of the castas exercised in the Indian communities. They terrorized and dominated many Indian villages. If the castas and the Indians were to combine, then the conflagration would be general, and the colony inevitably lost.[21]

This document is from half a century after the first legislation affecting the activities of the casta cowherds, but the situation which it described—somewhat hyperbolically—was already in existence by 1590. An unwritten contractual understanding had been elaborated between these groups and Spanish officialdom. The castas would perform certain minimal tasks in the countryside, the herding of semi-feral cattle, the supervision of Indian work gangs at the planting and harvesting of xiquilite, the work of muleskinning on the long journeys made by the requas between Santiago and Veracruz, between Santiago and the Gulf of Honduras, and up and down the Pacific coast linking the cities of Cartago, Realejo, León, Granada, San Miguel, and San Salvador. In return they could escape from the harassment of the laws of the cities, laws such as those against vagabondage, and laws arising from the shrinkage in the labor force which tried to coerce all unemployed or partially employed people into prescribed and usually unpleasant tasks, such as mining or laboring on the construction of buildings. In short, if the somewhat undisciplined casta cowherds did not tend the herds, then who would? It was several years later before Spaniards began to retreat in any numbers to a permanent rural life.

Officials tried to solve these problems, and the problem arising from the poor care given to the herds, by insisting that the herds be domesticated. Formal ownership should be asserted by those who had proper title to the animals, activities such as rounding up, branding, and culling should be done regularly and at the proper time. There were attempts to organize a formal mesta, or corporation of cattle and sheep owners, and the ayuntamiento of Santiago started to keep a book in which owners might register their official brands. This would also, it was hoped, lessen the widespread rustling, another practice which was adversely affecting the size of the herds.[22]

The most difficult problem of all was to ensure a regular and reasonably priced supply of meat to the cities. The cities, with the encouragement of the President and Audiencia, began to set up supervised slaughterhouses where the supply and quality of meat to the towns could be regulated. In Santiago slaughtering outside the city limits for the purpose of selling meat in the city was forbidden, and all private, unsupervised slaughtering within the city was banned.

The ayuntamiento also began to look for an assured supply of meat. Each year the position of meat supplier to the city was auctioned. The highest bidder was awarded the job, and he had to agree to provide a specified and sufficient quantity of meat for the city's needs. In return he was given, in effect, a monopoly of the supply of meat, and could thus be sure of a satisfactory price. The ayuntamiento had, then, sacrificed price control in order to maintain the level of supply, a policy not designed to appeal to the poorer classes of the city.[23]

If a boom creates greater regional cohesion, then the obverse is equally true. A recession creates regional rivalry and hostility, and sends local economies on widely divergent paths. This law of economics held firm when the cattle population of Central America entered its demographic recession. By the 1570s a regular trade in cattle had developed between the Honduran highlands around the small cities of Comayagua and Gracias a Dios, and central Guatemala with its larger city of Santiago.[24]

The opening of the new silver mines at Tegucigalpa and Guascarán coincided with the recession in the numbers of cattle, and as a result highland Honduras seems to have found itself, at least in some years, less able to supply distant Santiago because of the demands for meat nearer at hand. Santiago was the seat of the Audiencia, legally if not actually the central government. The Audiencia tried to use its authority to oblige the cattle owners and drovers of Honduras to supply Santiago first. It is easy to imagine the resentments which such a high-handed and selfish policy created in the provincianos of Honduras. Probably the owners and drovers of Honduras did not mind this legislation. Prices were higher in Santiago than in Comayagua, Gracias a Dios, or Tegucigalpa. But local Honduran officials, especially those of Tegucigalpa, concerned with the welfare of their own citizens, and with supporting the new and still promising silver mining industry, reacted to these exports of needed foodstuffs. They informed local herders that cattle must not be exported from the province until its own needs had been met. Thus new resentments and strains were placed upon an already fragile interregional cooperation and integration.[25]

Officialdom had failed to understand the true nature of the commercial crisis facing Central America between 1576 and the 1630s. New ports and new industries and new laws had not revived the export economy. Similarly, we must conclude that the official reasons and solutions advanced for the decline in cattle populations were only partly correct. The cattle cycle had other causes in addition to those which the people of the times had seen.

Cattle in Central America may have gone through a Malthusian cycle of their own. The growth in numbers was so swift after the conquest that it is possible that by the 1570s this population, too, had outgrown its food resources. Overgrazing and erosion quickly destroy pasture, and biological deterioration is one of the results.

Another cause, probably less important, may have been the rapid growth in meat consumption among the human populations of Central America. During the sixteenth century the Spanish and casta population grew very rapidly. Times were generally propitious for these groups, and this encouraged large family size, and, after stability was achieved around 1550, steady immigration from Spain.[26]

More important than the growth of the Spanish population, however, was a gradual change in the dietary habits of the Indians, still a majority of the population even on the coasts and in Nicaragua, and an overwhelming majority in the highlands. For several years after the conquest Indians continued to use their traditional foods. Maize, then as now, made up some 90 per cent of the diet, and was supplemented by beans, squash, chile, cacao, fruit, turkeys, and edible dogs. Also important to Indians as a source of protein was the monte. Each village had a right to some uncultivated land, and indeed such lands were an indispensable part of the ecological conjunction in which Indians lived. On these lands Indians gathered brush, timber, and reeds for construction, and nuts, roots, and grubs for food. They trapped and hunted deer, birds, and jaguars for meat, skins, and ceremonial plumage. On the coasts fishing was another supplementary activity.[27] As their numbers were reduced Indian villagers found it to be increasingly time-consuming to cultivate their own milpas, plus those required for the payment of tribute to the encomendero or the Crown, those required for the upkeep of the local church, the caciques, the village treasury, and the religious sodalities. Thus the monte, while it remained important to the Indians culturally, religiously (Indian places of worship were often the summits of hills near their villages), and as a source of building and food supplies, could not play as much of a part in their daily and seasonal round as it formerly had. To some extent Indians were forced to search elsewhere for protein. As time went on cattle, and especially sheep, became more familiar and less dreadful animals.

Indians first took to keeping European poultry. Within twenty years of the conquest, some few were paying tribute both in gallinas del país (presumably muscovy ducks) and in gallinas de castilla (Eurasian hens). Then, many became familiar with European domesticated animals because of the services they owed under the early tributary system. In the Cuchumatanes Mountains, the highest area of Central America, many Indians from Quetzaltenango and Huehuetenango were employed in sheepherding. Very quickly in these higher and colder areas the carding and weaving of wool replaced traditional cotton weaving, and by the seventeenth century woolen garments had replaced cotton ones in several parts of western Guatemala. Some Indians were also employed in herding cattle. Thus, because of necessity and increasing familiarity, Indians gradually adopted the eating of beef, mutton, and pork as part of their diet. By the 1620s observers such as the English renegade priest and pícaro Thomas Gage, were remarking on the great amounts of jerky consumed by Indian villagers.[28]

Overgrazing, increased consumption of meat, indiscriminate slaughtering of animals, and lack of animal husbandry all played a part in the fall of the cattle populations in the decades after 1570. Spaniards understood only some of the causes of this decline, and so could do little to rectify the situation, but the results—more expensive and scarcer supplies of meat in the cities, and smaller exports of hides to Spain—were apparent to all those involved in such matters.

As the crisis of labor and food supply failed to improve after 1600, President Alonso Criado de Castilla, the governor who had done so much to improve Guatemala's port facilities, tried new and energetic methods of improving the situation. He renewed legislation which was designed to apply more careful administration to the supplying and butchering of meat, and sought also to regulate labor. Recognizing that the repartimiento system was not filling the needs of employers, and rejecting the growing system of debt peonage via adelantos (advances) as unjust, Criado nevertheless sought to tie down labor and wages, and to increase the size of the work force. His ordinances bear a striking resemblance to the Ordinances of Laborers promulgated by Edward III of England in 1349, the year after the first catastrophic visitation of the Black Death or pneumonic plague. And indeed circumstances were similar. In both cases the plague had reduced the work force and emptied agricultural land. In both cases free labor could now expect to have multiple offers for its services, and thus to increase its wages. The main difference between the two cases is that Central America was still very much a post-conquest society in which two culturally and racially distinct groups lived in a dominant and subordinate relationship. Nevertheless Criado tried to inhibit what little competition there was for free, salaried Indian labor. Artisans were to cease traveling about seeking more advantages. The wages paid for specific jobs of work were to remain at the former level, and anyone demanding more was to be punished. Equally, employers who were discovered bidding against one another for workers, and thus driving up wages, were to be fined. It was also forbidden for employers to entice workers away from one another by promises, or to solicit for workers at the church doors in the villages. Just as Edward had done, Criado tried to solve the problem by increasing the work force. All vagabonds or unemployed persons, whatever their race, caste, or station, were to be jailed and put to work. Wandering from place to place was forbidden.[29]

Such decrees had little chance of success in times such as these. There was only a small and uncoordinated police force, the Santa Hermandad, to enforce the law, and technically its members were not allowed to visit Indian villages, where many of the Spanish and casta vagabonds and petty criminals went for asylum. Added to this inability to police the countryside were the poor communications and vast distances between settlements. Thus an unemployed vagabond evading work could move between Spanish towns and jurisdictions and might confidently expect that it would take weeks or months for his past to catch up with him. Laws made by the President of the Audiencia, therefore, had an ever-decreasing impact the further away one got from Santiago de Guatemala. The decrees which attempted to control and coerce labor were no more successful than were the repartimientos or the jueces de milpas. Spaniards living in the cities, or those in the countryside dependent on official supplies of labor, found themselves between 1575 and 1635 chronically short of an effective work force.[30]

All the pressures, social and economic, which city-dwelling Spaniards encountered between 1576 and the 1630s pointed in one direction. All these pressures but one were negative, but negative or positive they added up to a clear situation. Life in town had become for most too expensive, too regulated, and without opportunity. Lack of opportunity in town, and the expenses of town life had driven Spaniards to the countryside before the 1570s. In smaller and peripheral cities such as Ciudad Real de Chiapas, Gracias a Dios, San Miguel, and La Choluteca, many had become

Figure 15

Spanish Population (in vecinos) of Central America, 1550–1685

City	1550	c. 1565-75	c. 1620	1657-59	1675-85
Santiago de Guatemala	100	500	1,000	1,000	1,000
Ciudad Real (Chiapas)	50-60	250	250	50	50
San Salvador	50	150	200+		
San Miguel	25-30	130	100+	50	
Sonsonate	150 houses (1558)	400	200		
San Vicente	N. F.[a]	N. F.[a]		50	
Comayagua (Valladolid)	29	100	200+	100	
Gracias a Dios	29-35	50	60	50	
San Pedro (Zula)	32	50		30	
Trujillo and Puerto Caballos	40	140	100+	30	
La Choluteca	N. F.[a]	30	60	"few"	
Granada		200	250+	400	200
León		150	80	50	
Nueva Segovia		40		50	187
Réalejo		30	100	46	77
Olancho		40	40	20	
Cartago	N. F.[a]	60	100+	300	600[b]
Esparza		3-4			100
Huehuetlan		60		30	100

[a] Not founded.
[b] Includes all those living in the countryside.
Note: Principal sources used were Sherman, "Indian Slavery," p. 7; López de Velasco, *Geografía*, pp. 283-333; Vázquez de Espinosa, *Compendium*, pp. 204-63; BNM, 3023 (Díez de la Calle), ff. 291-326.

small farmers, raising cattle, maize, and wheat. In Chiapas such farmers, and the local Indians, became famous for raising fine horses which they exported to Mexico. Farmers in Gracias a Dios, on the plains around La Choluteca and the Bay of Fonseca, and around San Miguel, became noted for the numbers of mules which they raised. Many of them went to supply the mines of Tegucigalpa and Guascarán. Others were taken in muletrains along the Pacific coast all the way down to Panama, where the murderous trajín, the bearing of goods across the isthmus between Panama City and Portobelo, devoured large numbers of these pack animals.[31]

Now, however, Spaniards from the more important cities, Santiago, Granada, Sonsonate, and San Salvador, began to leave the cities in increasing numbers. The failure of the encomienda meant that those who relied upon it for income had suffered heavy losses. Its decline also meant a lack of foodstuffs for these individuals, and for the cities. Even meat was increasingly scarce and expensive. Repartimiento labor was little more than a temporary relief, supplying only intermittent and transient labor to a favored few. Besides, encomienda and repartimiento were becoming more and more rigidly supervised. In the rural areas, away from the watchful eyes of higher officials, more work could be extracted from the labor force and expenses could be cut. And Spaniards would no longer have to rely on the food supplies of the cities. They could grow their own

Figure 16

Sums Paid in 1636 for Cabildo Offices in Central America (a rough guide to the comparative wealth of the Creole communities)

Name of Town	Sum paid
Santiago de Guatemala	76,764
San Salvador	22,875
San Miguel (last of the cacao boom)	12,376
Ciudad Real (Chiapas)	10,614
Granada	10,122
León	9,825
Sonsonate	9,300
Gracias a Dios	6,050
Valladolid (Comayagua)	5,325
San Vicente de Austria (a new town)	5,200
Realejo	4,350
Nueva Segovia (brea not yet started)	3,395
Cartago	2,820
Trujillo	2,035
Xerez de la Frontera (La Choluteca)	716[a]
San Pedro Zula	465
Olancho	175

[a] Incomplete.
San Juan de Puerto Caballos and Esparza are not mentioned; both were very small.
Source: García Peláez, *Memorias,* 1:221-22.

maize and wheat, optimally with Indian servile labor, and they could raise their own cattle and pigs with little effort. The decline of the cacao industry had also ruined many. These individuals also found themselves unable to afford the expensive life of the larger cities, and fled to the self-sufficiency of the countryside.[32]

Most depressing of all to the beleaguered vecinos must have been their inability and the inability of their officials and Crown to remedy the crises which had descended upon them. Official attempts to revive old industries, to stimulate new industries, to increase the food supply, and to ration the labor supply more equitably had all patently failed. There was little point in looking any more to the government for solutions.

This flight to the countryside has so far been presented in its negative aspects. Spanish vecinos reluctantly abandoned the cities and retreated to the countryside because they could no longer afford city life. In the decades before 1630, however, there was at least one positive reason for going to the countryside, and that was indigo. As we have seen, indigo was well adapted to a time of falling sparse populations. It was not a heavy consumer of labor, and most of its requirements were seasonal. Another advantage was that it was not as monocultural as cacao, cochineal, or sugar cane. It could very easily be combined with cattle, which could even graze in the same fields where the xiquilite had been planted.

Thus indigo permitted the poorer vecinos of Santiago, San Salvador, and Comayagua to speculate on the possibility of a new boom product and still survive. If indigo turned out to be a profitable crop they would extend the areas planted to it and reduce other crops. If it failed they would not be caught in a monocultural trap and could extend the acreage of these other crops. In both systems there was also the self-sufficiency of running a few cattle.

Their petitions for title to their new lands tell the story of their doubts and hopes. In the 1570s and 1580s a few optimists were asking for land to set up indigo mills, nothing more. But as time passed more and more of these petitions asked for land so that the petitioner might feed his family on maize and cattle, and also, circumstances permitting, grow some indigo.[33]

On the other hand, indigo postponed the flight to the countryside for a few successful entrepreneurs. Between 1580 and 1620, when indigo was being exported in large quantities, the wealthy merchants of the barrio of Santo Domingo in Santiago de Guatemala, many of them foreigners, who had had the foresight to move out of cacao and other declining trades into indigo, were able

Figure 17

Changing Occupations in Santiago, 1604–26

Occupation	1604	1611	1620	1626
Merchants, traders and shopkeepers	144	107	137	100
Encomenderos	75	27	33	43
Indigo and sugar mill owners; wheat and cattle farmers	147	55[a]	96[a]	96[a]
Artisans	102	?	?	80

[a]Only those living in the city were counted. The rest were living permanently in the countryside, although still classified as vecinos. Places of residence identified include Petapa, Pinula, Mixco, Xalpatagua, Gualán, and Río Redondo.

Sources: Many authors have used parts of this document, and some have misinterpreted it. The document is numbered AGGG, A1. 2-6, 11810, 1804 (1604-26). (30 of 84 wheat farmers lived out of town, so did 14 of 19 cattle ranchers). See also, Milla, *Libro sin nombre*, pp. 213-5; Milla, *Historia de la América Central*, 2:293-4; García Peláez, *Memorias*, 1:203-7; Hussey, "Analysis of a document," pp. 705-6.

to maintain an expensive city life and to keep up their palatial houses. A few in Granada survived equally well. Some of this small group of great merchants no doubt grew indigo extensively, but most made their profits by buying it from a number of small growers and then shipping it out to Europe via Veracruz, the Gulf of Honduras, and the Nicaraguan Desaguadero.[34]

This group of wealthy men was thus able to postpone adjustments in its way of life until the 1620s or even later. It was not until indigo failed to develop because of transportation costs and the falling away of the European market that the rich indigo merchants abandoned Santiago and Granada. Some of them also took to the countryside, but more seem to have simply left Central America altogether.[35] It is readily apparent that the first great flight to the countryside in the 1580s and 1590s was not caused by the same kinds of optimism as the changes of the 1550s. Most of the reasons which vecinos had for moving were ones which they cannot have liked. Indigo represented a hope, but few trusted such hopes.

Now, for the first time, Spaniards were taking up the tierras baldías and realengas which had been abandoned by dead or "congregated" Indians. Now also, the first heavy intrusions on Indians' land began. Indians had been tricked or forced from their lands since the conquest, but never on the scale which developed at the end of the sixteenth century. The number of complaints, petitions for title, and lawsuits increased rapidly.[36]

Indians were at a great disadvantage when it came to defending their lands against Spanish intrusions. They were, after all, the subject race, and thus their access to law and the money needed for law and lawyers was more limited than that of Spaniards. Many of those in the more isolated areas, it is safe to assume, did not know that they had any rights, and local Spanish landowners saw no reason to tell them.

Another reason for Indian loss of land was the failure of Spanish officials, even when they were well intentioned, to understand the economic and ecological basis of Indian society. In some petitions for land, particularly those in the lower altitudes where indigo grew best, Spanish vecinos would request title by claiming that nobody lived on or used the land in question. In fact, such petitions often continued, Spanish-owned cattle had wandered and grazed over the area for decades. Spaniards and mestizos living in the neighborhood corroborated these statements. Nobody had lived on the stretch of land in question for as long as they could remember, and it was not under cultivation. It was true despoblado and monte. The petitioner would then conclude with a plea designed to please officialdom and the Crown. The taking up of such vacant and unused stretches could only help to increase trade, and would increase the food supply, royal taxes, and the general well-being of the colony.

Indian villagers would reply that the land had been recognized as part of the village since time immemorial. In former days, when the village had been larger, it had even been cultivated on a rotating basis. Nowadays, although it appeared unused, the monte was still of great importance to the village. It supplied thatch, wood, game, dye, and wild cacao for the villagers. If a Spanish farm were set up there the woods would be cut down, the game would disappear, and the Indians would have to pay for any kind of usufruct. Spanish judges were familiar with the concept of the ejido, the common grazing land near each village and town, but this idea that each village should also have a large stretch of wild and overgrown land nearby was not part of their picture of a properly managed and governed society. Indian appeals against the usurpation of their monte were rejected as sheer contrariness or as representing a "dog-in-the-manger" attitude. It would be far better for them, because it would provide jobs and food, if the land were cleared and cultivated by a responsible Spanish farmer. The title was then awarded to the Spanish petitioner.[37]

The desperate financial straits in which the Spanish state found itself in the 1590s also played a minor part in alienating Indian village lands. Since the conquest the Kings had thought of themselves as protectors of the Indians, and had repeatedly though unsuccessfully forbidden Spanish purchase or acquisition of Indian lands.[38] Thus Spanish invasions and usurpations of Indian property, while largely unrestrained, were at least illegal. Now Felipe II's bankruptcy forced him to compromise and lower his standards. In 1598 he began to demand payment for land grants. In 1631 Felipe IV declared himself ready to accept a fait accompli and to legalize titles acquired by a variety of good and questionable means, if he were paid for it. The result was composición, a system whereby Spaniards purchased titles or paid fines for past wrongdoing in order to have it forgotten. Once the composición was paid, and the title was issued, Indians had little chance of ever regaining their alienated lands.[39]

Composición has generally been considered a peripheral phenomenon. The Crown simply raised a little money by placing its seal of acceptance on an unfortunate set of circumstances which it could not prevent anyway. But the implications were, at a more intangible level, very serious. Once the impecunious Spanish Crown discovered a means of raising money it could seldom afford to give it up until the source was milked dry. Spanish landowners and would-be landowners might confidently expect that there would be many more rounds of composiciones. And indeed there were. Throughout the seventeenth century, as the Crown faced crisis after crisis, new waves of composiciones de tierra were periodically announced. This meant that after 1631 Spaniards could drive their cattle into Indian fields, trick Indians out of their land, or simply seize it, knowing all the while that a small payment would settle the matter at the next royal bankruptcy. Certainly composición must have made opportunism over land easier for many Spaniards.[40]

Composición in some cases also seems to have been applied to Indian titles. This caused already overburdened Indian villages to have to pay yet another tax. And in their especially disadvantaged position it was always safer to be "plus royaliste que le roi." So some Indian villages "composed" their titles every time there was a composición, just to be on the safe side. Those who did not, either because of ignorance or because they believed that they had already gained a clear title by a previous composición, were in grave danger of losing their lands.[41]

Some observers have expressed the opinion that the decline of the encomienda represented an improvement in the position of the Indian. To some extent this may be true. It may be more accurate to say, however, that the years between 1576 and 1635 represent rather a period of radical change in the forms of exploitation to which the Indian was subject. In the first place encomienda did not relax its rigors overnight. Double tribute and more was still being exacted in the declining cacao areas in the seventeenth century, and caciques and alcaldes were jailed for arrears in tribute payments throughout the seventeenth century.[42] Encomenderos did not willingly relinquish their privileges and tributes. Nor can the repartimiento system of labor be considered as an improvement on encomienda. We have already seen how much it was abused and the stresses which it placed on Indians and on their villages. Cattle continued to invade Indian milpas destroying and devouring crops, and for the first time a major attack was made on Indian lands. Spaniards fleeing from worsening conditions in the cities usurped and encroached upon the village and reduced its productive base. To the extent outlined above, therefore, it would seem that there was no discernible improvement in the treatment of the Indians; in fact, in areas such as land tenure their situation worsened appreciably.

Yet the impression remains that some Indians found better conditions because of the Spanish drift to the land. The answer may lie in the changing employment relationships between Indians and Spaniards during these years of transition. In the waning years of the sixteenth century Spanish employers of Indian labor noticeably tried to move away from formal and regulated systems of labor and tribute such as encomienda and repartimiento. Instead they became involved in more informal, individual, and extra-legal arrangements. The manipulation of debt was one such arrangement. Indian workers were advanced pay against future work, often for as much as the following six months, to induce them to hire themselves permanently to one Spaniard. By the end of the contractual agreement the Indian usually found that he was still in debt and so was forced to accept another adelanto (advance). Officials at first opposed this system of debt labor, and tried to prevent Indians from accepting adelantos, and Spaniards from giving them; but the government's attitude was always ambivalent. It was equally annoyed at those laborers, usually disaffected members of the castas, who took advantage of adelantos, accepted advances, and then decamped for other parts of Central America. Failure to pay just debts was a criminal offense and debts were inheritable upon the death of the debtor. The government never seems to have considered relaxing or changing these laws, and by 1610 or shortly thereafter it had ceased trying to prevent the development of debt labor.[43]

By 1600 the system was well established. It took several forms. The most familiar one to students of Latin American colonial history is debt peonage, under which the debtor, usually an Indian and an agricultural laborer, resided permanently on the hacienda or farm, and became in effect a serf there. Many other variations existed in Central America; indeed debt peonage may not have been the most prevalent form in the early seventeenth century. Indigo growers would often entrap many of the alcaldes and young men of a neighboring pueblo in a series of petty debts and obligations, debts as small as three to five pesos, which the debtors would be obliged to work off at planting or harvest time. Then they would be allowed to return to their villages, only to fall once more into debt before the next indigo season came around. Similarly merchants involved Indian muleteers in debt, sheep ranchers obtained shepherds, and builders obtained artisans and day laborers (gañanes). An examination of the wills and inventories made after the deaths of Spanish settlers between 1585 and 1620 shows that many were at the time of their deaths creditors for a multitude of petty debts. One farmer in Huehuetenango seemed to have had all the males and some of the females of an Indian village tied up in petty obligations to him. One Portuguese merchant recruited his muleteers by similar methods. There are many other examples.[44]

Another informal system which rural Spaniards adopted for obtaining a small but steady labor force was sharecropping. As the Indian villages lost land in the early seventeenth century some of the villagers found themselves obliged to seek land from neighboring Spanish owners. In some cases an arrangement was agreed upon whereby an Indian family would be assigned a plot on the hacienda, and there the family would be allowed to build a hut (bohío) and start a small plot. In return the Indian man and his wife were obliged to work a specified number of days per week for the landowner.[45]

Perhaps the most usual system of all was one in which Indians and castas simply became attached to a hacienda or plantation by a multitude of interlocking arrangements. The owner would provide them with food, clothing, and housing, and sometimes with a small wage. He would pay their tribute to the authorities and protect them from other intrusive forces. In return the laborer became attached to the hacienda and became part of its tangible assets. Such people, sometimes known as adscritos or peones could be bought and sold with the estate on which they lived.[46]

Although it may seem incongruous at first sight, there is evidence that systems such as debt peonage, sharecropping, and adscritos ad glebam did represent some improvement for some Indians. For many Indians the pueblo had become an oppressive and hostile place by 1600. The demands for their produce and labor were constant. Tribute and maize were demanded by the encomenderos or the Crown, by the Church, by the village cabildo and by the few remaining caciques. Repartimiento made further demands on their time. Merchants and vagabonds tricked or bullied them into selling at low prices, cattle invaded their plantings, and Spaniards usurped their land. To some life on a hacienda must have seemed preferable. There, if cattle or sheep were the main concern, the work was light when compared with the intensive agriculture of the village. If indigo was the main product of the hacienda then the work was seasonal and demanded intensive labor for only about two months each year. There are many cases which clearly show where many Indians' preferences lay. Indians would run away from their villages and hire themselves out to Spanish landowners. The village alcaldes would then appeal to the authorities, pointing out that if such flights continued the villages involved would be unable to meet their tribute obligations, and the Spanish cities would suffer even greater shortages of foodstuffs. Invariably, if the Indian was given a free choice at these hearings, he opted for the hacienda.[47] Of course it is reasonable to argue that such individuals were the ones who had been most influenced by Spanish culture. Where the village had preserved a proportionately large part of its precolumbian culture such flights may have been fewer.

The movement of some Indians from their villages to the new Spanish landholdings casts further light on the nature of the late sixteenth-century encomienda, and points up the aforementioned division between those encomenderos who had remained entrapped in the dying encomienda system, and those who had diversified out of it in time.

Many Spanish encomenderos, those who still relied mainly on the encomienda system, shared the concern of the Indian village leaders. If Indian commoners deserted their villages for Spanish farms then the meager tributes would shrink still further. As a result

there are signs of competition between minor "undiversified" encomenderos who had not obtained land, and the new and growing
group of landowners. (The result of this peripheral squabbling was
never in doubt. The "undiversified" encomienda was a dying institution after 1576).

Some encomenderos had made the shift to the land in time, and
these men tried to ease the Indians which they held in encomiendas
toward the new forms of peonage. Some used arrears of tribute as
a device. The judges of the Audiencia complained to Madrid in 1584
that Indians who were unable to pay their tributes found that their
arrears had been marked down as debt, "which is a thing which
much afflicts the Indians, and which is done by the encomenderos
in order to obtain payment in other things, such as on their cattle
farms, or in the repairing of their houses, or in the produce of a
fertile year, and to enforce this they molest them and often jail
them."[48]

Thus, to a much lesser degree than we observed in Europe,
upper-class Central Americans between 1576 and the 1630s were
forced by demographic losses among their work forces into the
same position as the lords of the European fourteenth century. To
obtain a reliable and steady labor supply they had to allow a marginal improvement in the conditions of some members of the lower
classes.

Lest repeated mention of haciendas give the impression that
most Spaniards, fleeing from the depressed cities, became large and
successful landowners, it would be well at this point to discuss the
nature of these early Spanish farms. Some, about 200 or 250, grew
indigo, at least up to about 1630. Others produced horses, mules,
cattle, wheat, or maize for export to Mexico and Panama or for the
markets in the local Spanish cities. In general, however, most Spaniards and castas in the countryside had neither the resources, the
manpower, nor the capital to mount large-scale agricultural enterprises. Above all, there was a lack of large internal markets. Santiago
was a large enough market so that some dozen wheat farmers
around Pinula and Mixco were able to profit. Thomas Gage described one barbaric individual who lived a simple but self-indul-
gent life, surrounded by slaves, which he maintained by raising large
numbers of mules. Granada and León seem to have sustained a belt
of market gardens around them, although many of these small holdings belonged to the vecinos themselves. In general, however, it
must be noted that very profitable holdings were relatively few
compared with the miserable, self-sufficient chacras and bohíos

Figure 18

Population of the Jurisdiction of Cartago, 1625–99

Year	Total	Spaniards and Ladinos	Indians	Mestizos	Negroes	Mulattoes	English	Unknown
1625	665	436	144	16	41	12	0	16
1644	690	365	181	13	98	33	0	0
1675	1,746	1,114	190	70	55	145 / 89	2	170
1699	2,353	1,769	111	43	89		0	252

Source: Thiel, "Datos Cronológicos," p. 181.

where so many Spaniards lived after 1630. When indigo declined there were simply too few internal consumers for many capitalist enterprises to exist. All the Spanish landholdings were potentially capitalistic in that the owners would have been eager to join in any new boom, and many of them were asylums to which Spaniards had reluctantly retreated to await better days. But most Spanish holdings in the seventeenth century were not large-scale developmental enterprises. They were self-sufficient food suppliers to a few rural families, and did not provide more than a bare level of living.[49]

Some of the effects on the Indians of the Spanish and casta exodus to the countryside have already been noted. In many ways, moreover, the processes observable in the villages were simply those noted before 1576. The general blurring of class distinctions continued. The traditional caciques and the recently installed alcaldes and regidores of the Indian villages continued to be jailed and otherwise harassed for failure to collect the prescribed amount of tribute, for defending their subjects too vigorously against Spanish intrusions, or for not defending them enough.[50]

Now, however, toward the end of this period of transition, perhaps in the 1630s, it becomes possible to see that what would happen to a given Indian village would depend very much on a series of critical variables. Some of them, of course, had been operant since the moment of first Spanish impact, and it is appropriate to start with them.

Comparative demographic strength is, of course, the most important single factor. Where the Indian population had been sparse before the conquest, it stood little chance of survival as a culture or tribe. Numbers became so small that there was not a sufficient base for regeneration and the few survivors were absorbed by the invading Spaniards. The two coasts of Costa Rica are an example. (Talamanca is not really the exception which it first appears, since colonial Spaniards were never able to conquer and hold it).

From this stage, absorption by the invaders, there is a whole gamut of other processes. The intermediate ones may be generally described as occurring in areas where there was a large population, but, because of heavy population loss or intensive intrusion, the Indian culture was "ladinoized." Typical examples of this would be most lowlands, where death rates seem to have been higher than in the mountains. Other examples would be areas which drew great numbers of Spaniards or great economic interest and activity. Thus areas near Spanish cities, or regions where Spaniards established monocultural plantation or export crops were ones in which Indians rapidly became cultural mestizos or ladinos. Soconusco (cacao), the region today called El Salvador (cacao and then indigo), and the villages next to Spanish cities (Comayaguela, Mixco, Chimaltenango are typical examples) all lost their "Indian" appearance relatively quickly before demographic, cultural, and economic pressures.[51]

At the other end of the scale are those formerly Indian communities which, originally large in population, were relatively neglected by Spaniards because they did not present opportunities for intensive cash crops. It is true that much of the preconquest culture of these areas was also destroyed, and that populations in them were often taken out of them seasonally or permanently to areas of more intensive Spanish activity. Indians from Quetzaltenango, the Cuchumatanes Mountains, and Chiapas were forced or persuaded to go to the Pacific coast because of successive cacao, indigo, cochineal, banana, and coffee industries from the sixteenth century to the present. Nevertheless, compared with areas of intensive Spanish activity, or areas where Spaniards settled, these relatively neglected zones were able, especially in times of depression, to rebuild, or rather create, a new and different culture from a synthesis of their former culture and that of the Spanish and African incomers.

The Spanish flight to the countryside between 1580 and the 1630s helped to accentuate these differences. In most of Nicaragua and El Salvador, and on much of the Pacific coast of Guatemala, the issue had already been decided. The Indian populations had been overwhelmed, and were well along the path to becoming "bleached out" to form a part of a westernized, Spanish-speaking, "ladino," rural peasantry, basically mestizo in racial origins.[52] In Guatemala proper, however, and in highland Honduras and Chiapas to a lesser extent—in short, in the mountain blocks which together contained most of the Indian and Spanish populations—the issue had remained in doubt until this period. The areas to which the Spanish vecinos retired in numbers to set up their chacras and bohíos came under pressure to ladinoize; those which Spanish settlers neglected did not.

Altitude, indigo, and communications seem to have been the basis of many of the regional choices made by Spanish rural settlers. The higher and colder an area was, especially above 6,000 or 7,000 feet, the less likely it would be to attract Spanish settlers. Part of this reluctance was, of course, because indigo would not grow where it was cold or very wet. Spanish settlers also preferred, if possible, to be on easily cultivated land, and near to communication routes or cities. As a result the period between 1580 and the 1630s sees the beginnings of a basic division in highland Guatemala. South and east of the present city of Guatemala the mountains are lower and the topography is less extreme. The taking up of land titles in this region far exceeded that in the area to the north and west of Guatemala City, which is higher and colder and where the terrain is difficult. Thus, today, eastern Guatemala is largely ladino, with a few pockets of "Indians." Western Guatemala is basically "Indian," that is, seventeenth-century reconstituted Indian, and the few ladinos are confined to the towns and larger villages.[53] In present-day Chiapas we have a similar division in settlement patterns. The so-called "Chiapas depression" and the foothills leading toward the Pacific and toward the River Grijalva are Spanish-speaking. The mountains and higher plateaus are Tzotzil and Tzendal in speech.[54] Highland Honduras, with its lower altitudes, small population, and demanding mining industry quickly ladinoized the remaining Indians there.[55]

Another feature of this period was a gradual change in the geographical distribution of the secular and regular clergy. It has been suggested that this was because of a gradual weakening of evangelical enthusiasm and general morale. For whatever the reason, after the turn of the century we find more and more of the clergy living in the Spanish towns, or in the fairly ladinoized villages near them, and correspondingly fewer living and proselytizing in the poorer, remoter, and higher Indian villages.[56]

One result was a new growth of religious or ceremonial practices which smacked to Spaniards of preconquest or pagan religions. These rituals, incantations, and dances had existed secretly since 1524, but now the more distant villages, less inhibited by the presence of a Spanish friar, began to combine them with what they knew of Christianity, into a new syncretic religion.[57]

In the civil sphere also it is apparent that relative isolation and peace meant important changes for some Indian communities. The old cacique class and even some of the town ayuntamientos had been seriously weakened or destroyed by the leveling down of the sixteenth century. Now new kinds of institutions, first introduced by Spaniards, but then changed by Indian cultural survivals, began to replace them as cultural barriers or "brokers" to defend the gradually emerging and distinctive cultural style against Spanish intrusion. The most important of these newly developing institutions was the caja de comunidad, the Indian village treasury, and above all the cofradía or religious sodality-fraternity.

The new syncretic "idolatries" and the new kinds of broker institutions were only possible in the areas which Spaniards tended to ignore in an unprosperous era. Their consolidation is, therefore, more a feature of the seventeenth-century depression, and it is in that context that they will be examined.

The failures of remedial legislation, the continuing decline of sixteenth-century industries, the frustrations experienced in the new indigo industry, the decline in Indian and cattle populations, the Spanish flight to the more favorable parts of the countryside, and their partial abandonment of higher and less favored zones, the growth of informal debt and peon relationships, the rapid decline of encomienda and repartimiento, and the beginnings of a new syncretism in the isolated villages together constituted such a radical shift in emphasis that by 1640 Central America was very different from the colony struck by the matlazáhuatl of 1576. The new equilibriums and styles developed after this time of transition, in short, the age of the seventeenth-century depression, shall be the next subject of study.

PART III

The Seventeenth Century Depression and the First Signs of Recovery (c.1635-1720)

12

The Aftermath of a Boom; Seventeenth-Century Cacao

The great cacao industry had dominated the second half of the sixteenth century in Central America, and it did not disappear overnight. After the epidemics of the 1570s, and until the 1620s, Spaniards in Soconusco, both officials and private individuals, continued in a rather hapless and despairing fashion to request additional drafts of manpower from the highlands. The King, offhand about such a valueless province, usually shelved the matter by asking his Audiencia in Santiago de Guatemala for more advice, urging it to take "appropriate measures" in view of the "new decadence" of the cacao fields. The Audiencia, no longer interested in the small, empty, distant province to the west, and seriously worried by the start of a precipitous decline in the larger and nearer plantations of Izalcos, and by the increasing competition from Guayaquil, did little or nothing to comply with the royal order.[1]

By 1675, in fact, most of these forced movements of Indian populations had ceased, at least for that era, and in that year a royal cédula (decree) forbade all further importation of outside Indian labor.[2] It is significant that by 1684, after less than a decade without Indian migration to the province, Soconusco's tributary population was again in serious decline, numbering only 800 in that year. (Against this new drop must be weighed the increase in the size of other groups. In 1684 Soconusco held 100 or more Spanish vecinos, and some 259 mulatto, mestizo, and negro heads of families.)[3]

After Soconusco cacao had receded to the minor position which it was to occupy for the rest of the seventeenth century, local mestizos, Spaniards, and church orders began to assume ownership of the plantations. This taking of the groves from their dead or living Indian owners was in response to several general kinds of pressure previously outlined, but one local inducement was the hope that

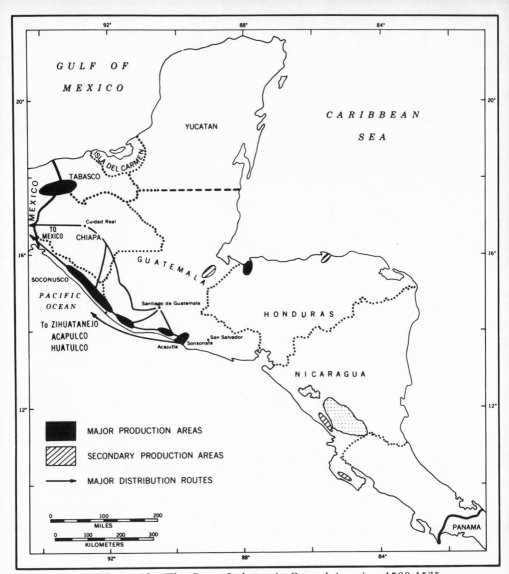

Figure 19 The Cacao Industry in Central America, 1500-1535

personal management by the Spaniards might halt the decline of the few large cacao plantations left. As a consequence we find increasing numbers of plantations in the hands of Spaniards and castes, and above all in the possession of the vecinos and Dominicans of Ciudad Real de Chiapas, during the seventeenth century.[4] (No doubt this was part of the more generalized move to the countryside). Nevertheless, while closer personal supervision may have helped sporadically and locally there is no evidence that any decided reversal came about.

Despite the slump at the beginning of the seventeenth century, and the long failure to revive, the high-cost Soconusco and Zapotit-

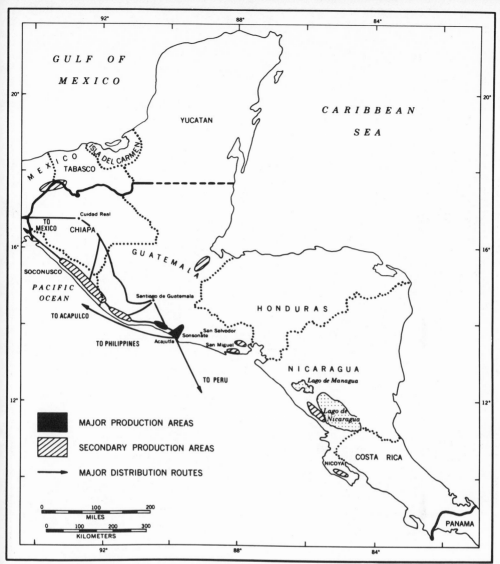

Figure 20   The Cacao Industry in Central America, c. 1575

lán cacao was able to keep a minor place in the lucrative Mexican market throughout the seventeenth century.[5] It benefited from its relative proximity to Central Mexico, and allowances were made for its high price by the increasing numbers of Spaniards in New Spain and Europe who were becoming fond of chocolate drinks. Soconusco cacao was generally held to be the best available.[6] Whether it was in fact the best, or whether it was a question of conditioned tastes dating from the days when Socousco supplied the major part of the cacao consumed in New Spain, or whether it was merely a matter of snobbery arising from the small supplies and high prices of Soconusco cacao, it is hard to establish. Whatever the reasons,

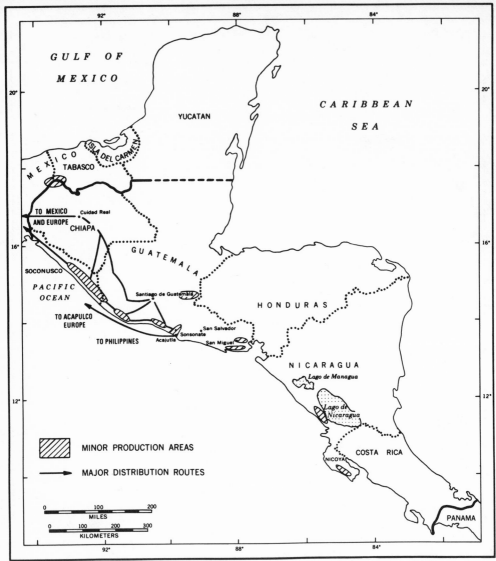

Figure 21 The Cacao Industry in Central America, c. 1640

small quantities of Soconusco cacao found their way to Mexico, Europe, and the Philippines.[7]

The understaffed and aging cacao groves of Soconusco were particularly susceptible to the effects of natural disasters. Hurricanes in 1641 and in 1659 further reduced many of the surviving plantations, and if it had not been for the rising demands for high quality cacao among the upper classes in both New Spain and Europe during the second half of the seventeenth century, there is no doubt that the cacaotales in Soconusco would have disappeared.[8] The few remaining Indians often found themselves unable to pay tribute.[9] As it was, only a few Spanish and church-owned, carefully

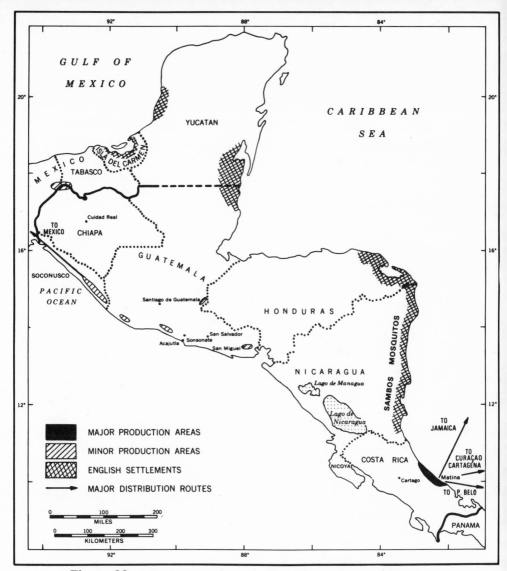

Figure 22   The Cacao Industry in Central America, c. 1700

tended, fragile groves survived into the eighteenth century. Long before then the empty spaces of Soconusco had been seized by non-Indians, and the dominant occupations had become the herding of cattle and to a much lesser extent the growing of wheat. The province never overcame its manpower problem, and was still being described as "a land of few people, very hot and unhealthy," at the beginning of the eighteenth century.[10] Here and there, especially in the neighboring subsidiary province of Zapotitlán, the eighteenth-century visitor could just discern abandoned, overgrown cacao groves among the exuberant second growth of tropical woods.[11]

Soconusco, however, had obviously failed long before the seventeenth-century depression. What of Central American cacao in general, and the Izalcos industry in particular? The sixteenth-century cacao boom advancing south eastward from Soconusco to Nicaragua between 1525 and 1600 left depleted populations and exhausted soils in its wake. Such an extensive and intensive agricultural complex did not disappear overnight; vast areas continued to be cultivated throughout the seventeenth century. Yet the nature of the industry had changed, and in commercial and economic terms it was frail and catered to luxury tastes. It was high priced and undependable. It had great difficulty in withstanding any competition, and the Spaniards of Central America spent much time and effort erecting protective economic walls around their fragile industry.

Internally certain patterns are discernible in the seventeenth-century cacao fields. Low yielding plantations occupied a large part of the available agricultural land along the Pacific coast from Soconusco to Nicaragua. Cultivation had also spread inland through areas such as Chiquimula de la Sierra and Zacapa. The lower valleys of some rivers running north and east into the Gulf of Mexico and the Caribbean through Chiapas, Verapaz, Guatemala, and Honduras, also contained small plantations, as they had before the arrival of the Spaniards.[12] But labor shortages and the rise of other activities kept these fields short-staffed. Occasionally bursts of activity would improve the fields to some degree, especially during the periods when the notorious jueces de milpas were allowed to force the Indians to plant vacant fields. At other times, when the jueces were banned or when the Indians could not dispose of their crop, slumps would occur and the cacao groves would become even less productive. The older groves would go out of production entirely, and the Indians of the cacao region would fail to pay tribute or plead for exemptions.[13]

The same kind of injustices as the sixteenth century, such as overcollection of tribute, the collection of two kinds of tribute, counting "the absent and the dead," and fraudulent trading plagued the Indian communities. But the frequency and extent of these extortions were lower, at least in the cacao groves.[14] On the other hand royal taxes increased as the century advanced, and Spain's financial crisis deepened. Both Indians and merchants were affected.[15]

It is doubtful, however, if either exploitation or taxation were decisive factors in the seventeenth-century cacao industry when compared to labor, inferior plantations, and outside competition. The revivals and declines of the seventeenth-century were relative.

The plantations never approached their sixteenth-century levels of production, but only occasionally did they lose their small but important position in the New Spain and European markets.

The people involved in the trade were also of a radically different kind by the first decade of the seventeenth century. The era of the great cacao lords of the encomienda system disappeared as the cacao fields declined and the encomiendas lost their importance. Increasingly, cacao was bought from the Indian, caste, and occasional Spanish grower by numerous groups of petty local traders, often Indians, based in Sonsonate or Santiago. These traders sold the cacao to corrupt government officials, or to the agents of large concerns who came from outside the Audiencia to Santiago to make the purchase.[16] That the cacao fields of Guatemala survived at all, in the face of the heavy competition from Caracas, Maracaibo, and Guayaquil, can be attributed in the main to three fortuitous circumstances.

Guatemala's geographical position afforded her exports to New Spain some protection. The market was close. As Pacific shipping declined and Caribbean piracy increased Guatemala was advantageously placed to send her produce to New Spain by land. Central America's geographical advantage also became apparent during disasters or minor depressions in rival fields, such as the one of the 1620s and 1630s in Guayaquil. But similarly, when large Guayaquil exports glutted the Mexican market even geography could not help the costly Central American cacao. At these times much of the Guatemalan cacao was unsaleable.[17]

Another advantage was custom and tradition. The Indians of New Spain and Guatemala had been drinking Guatemalan cacao for some time and seem to have preferred it. When Spaniards first began to drink cacao in large quantities in the 1590s they also became accustomed to the taste of Central American beans. There is strong evidence that beans from other areas tasted quite differently. "Criollo" cacaos from Guatemala are smooth and mild. "Forastero" varieties, Guayaquil cacao especially, were often described in disgusted terms as bitter, repugnant, and even poisonous. Indians in Central America had been accustomed to drinking patlaxtli, a wild cacao, when no other was to be had. So they took more kindly to the drinking of the Guayaquil cacao, with its bitter taste, which was also grown in a semi-wild state along the Guayas river. When cacao from Venezuela began to be exported to Europe in large quantities in the 1630s Creole and European tastes became more eclectic, but until the end of the century Guayaquil cacao tended to be cheaper and drunk by Indians, while Guatemalan and

Soconusco cacao was more appreciated by Spaniards. No doubt questions of snobbery and prestige were also involved.[18]

The greatest single reason for Guatemalan cacao's precarious survival into the eighteenth century was the increase in the demand for chocolate drinks among Indians, Creoles, and Europeans. When Venezuelan and Guayaquil cacao first reached New Spain it caused the price collapse which so disturbed the cacao interests in Soconusco and Guatemala. The result seems to have been that cacao passed from being an expensive drink enjoyed by Indians when they could afford it, to being a basic food staple, drunk in huge, if not incredible quantities by Indians, and enjoyed by the poorer Creoles. The growing inability of Spain to provide the New World with the wine it needed, and the prohibitions against Peruvian wine, however ineffective, probably forced Spaniards to turn reluctantly to chocolate. Until the 1580s, at any rate, cacao was still very much an Indian drink, but by the end of the century it was being accepted by other Americans and some Spaniards with slowly increasing relish. By the 1630s it was reaching Spain, Holland, and even England in fair quantities, and by the mid-seventeenth century it was the preferred drink of the upper classes and the club and teahouse society of all the capitals of western Europe. Recipes had changed, of course. Indians continued to drink cacao, maize, chile, and achiote mixtures, but Europeans had experimented with vanilla and cinnamon flavoring, and had sweetened the brew with sugar. Cacao in paste or blocks was also coming into fashion as a medication, a confection, and a cosmetic.[19] The constantly growing demand after midcentury kept prices high, and allowed Guatemala to occupy its precarious and artificial place as a cacao exporter. The prestige of Central American cacao crossed the Atlantic and still exists today. (Central American cacaos are held to be superior in flavor but are very delicate. Hardier types are preferred for commercial plantations, and the Central American "Criollo" cacaos have all but disappeared.)[20]

To maintain Central American cacao's unsure footing in Mexican and world markets, local Central American authorities were forced to fight a desperate protectionist battle throughout the seventeenth century. Before and after recovery from its depression of the twenties and thirties Guayaquil cacao was so cheap that it could successfully compete with the Central American product within Central America itself even after a long sea voyage.

Venezuelan and Caribbean cacaos, which first began to appear in sizable plantations about 1622, also represented a serious threat to the Central American export. But Venezuelan and Maracaibo

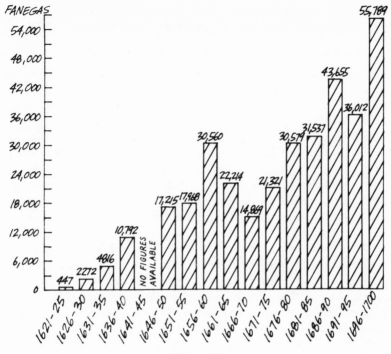

Figure 23

Five-year Totals (in fanegas) of Cacao Exports from Venezuela to Mexico. Compiled from a list of totals by years in Arcila Farias, *Economía,* pp. 96-98.

Figure 24

Cacao Imports to Mexico City, 1638–39

Year	Guayaquil	Guatemala	Suchite-peques	Caracas	Maracaibo	Tabasco	Soconusco
1638	337	633	113	143	296	53	78
1639	341	499	137	307	378	67	104

Note: *Alhóndiga* figures in *fanegas.* It should be borne in mind that some, perhaps a great deal, of the Guatemalan and Suchitepeques cacao may have been "relabeled" Guayaquil exports. Also, Guayaquil cacao, unlike that of Guatemala and Venezuela, usually arrived on illegal ships and was smuggled in unregistered and unreported at Guatemalan and Mexican ports so that the Guayaquil figures above probably represent only a fraction of the true total. Source: Arcila Farias, *Comercio,* 78.

cacaos were seldom if ever seen in Central American ports or cities. They were exported directly to Veracruz, and thence to the highlands of Mexico. The rest was sold to Spain or to the Dutch after the seizure of Curaçao. Consequently poorly informed officials and merchants of the Audiencia of Guatemala seldom complained about the threat of Venezuelan cacao.[21]

The cacao from the Guayas river area was a different matter. The plantations were begun about the same time as those of Venezuela and were developed in entirely new groves among thinned tropical forests.[22] According to one authority the Guayaquil Spaniards started the groves with the specific purpose of seizing the Mexican market, which was then seriously undersupplied because of the decline of the Guatemalan fields.[23] In any event competition between the two areas was open and bitter from the start. When large quantities of Guayaquil cacao first began to appear in the Mexican market in the early 1600s prices dropped rapidly. Soconusco complained and asked to have Guayaquil cacao excluded.[24]

Throughout the century the commercial rivalry continued. The royal limitations on shipping between Peru and New Spain of the 1620s, and the complete ban of 1631, meant that much of the Guayaquil cacao destined for New Spain was unloaded at Acajutla, and sent from there to Mexico by large mule trains. Santiago's ayuntamiento and Audiencia pestered the Crown with complaints and unilaterally banned Guayaquil cacao from Guatemalan ports in 1628. They alleged that it was noxious to the Indians, and even held it responsible for their disappearance. It was further argued that it was worthless stuff at best, and that Guatemala, a strategic province, needed its cacao industry to survive, whereas isolated Guayaquil had other incomes. Above all, if Guayaquil cacao ruined the Guatemalan fields, royal tributes would fall drastically and deplete the treasury.[25] To the existent bans and limitations on Peruvian shipping, local and royal decrees added specific bans on Guayaquil cacao both in Guatemala and in Mexico in the seventeenth and early eighteenth centuries.

In spite of these restrictions Guayaquil cacao poured in. The market existed and the Guatemalan and Soconusco fields could not satisfy it. Up until mid-century, however, Guatemala's share of the market remained considerable. Supplies from other sources were irregular and prices fluctuated greatly. Guayaquil's temporary cacao depression of the third and fourth decades of the century probably helped Guatemala to hold a good share of the Mexican market. An alhóndiga, or government warehouse, was set up in 1636 in Mexico City because of hoarding and other attempts to drive up the fluctuating local prices.

In the 1680s supplies from Guayaquil and Venezuela increased still further and the Guatemalan industry lost considerable ground.

The ships from Guayaquil used various routes. Often they called at Huatulco, Zihuatanejo, and above all Acapulco after passing provocatively along the cacao coast of Guatemala. Occasionally, and increasingly after 1680, Guayaquil cacao was shipped to Panama, then to Portobelo by land, and then by sea to Veracruz. In New Spain and Guayaquil royal officials connived with shippers to allow exit and entry by both these routes.

Frequently the cacao was landed at Realejo, Fonseca, or Aca-jutla, ports of the Audiencia of Guatemala, and then carried by mule train to Mexico or Santiago de Guatemala or distributed locally. Often the ships had legal papers for Panama or elsewhere, and came into Guatemalan ports as alleged "arribadas" or weather-driven ships.[26]

This illegal trade is difficult to measure. It was persistent, profitable, and probably very large. In 1626, for example, just before severe prohibitions started, one individual asked for a monopoly of the importation of Guayaquil cacao. (The Audiencia rejected his petition in the name of free trade!) Individuals at all levels participated in the new trade. Indian, mestizo, and negro muleteers carried the contraband cacao from the ports, and royal port officials surreptitiously or openly allowed its entry. Often it was introduced without the knowledge of any officials, particularly in the large harbor of Realejo. Sporadic attempts to enforce the law caused the seizure and burning of an occasional shipment, but even seized shipments were sometimes wholly or partly restored to their owners upon the payment of appropriate fines and bribes.[27] So considerable was the trade that it seems fair to suppose that substantial local interest groups were involved in it.

Although written evidence is limited, it appears that Guayaquil cacao, while passing through Central America, was used to adulterate higher quality Central American cacao, and then sent to Mexico as Guatemalan or Soconuscan cacao. Certainly fraud of this and other types was no novelty, either before or after the conquest. Probably the local petty merchants were involved in this kind of activity.[28]

The inability of the authorities to enforce even partial compliance with the ban on Guayaquil cacao had deeper reasons than the cupidity of local port officials and cacao merchants. The several provinces of the Audiencia of Guatemala disagreed on this question of Guayaquil cacao, as on so many others, and acted accordingly. The groups controlling such export areas as the Chiapas plantations along the lower Río Grijalva, the Caribbean plantations in Honduras and Verapaz, and the expanding Matina valley plantations in

Costa Rica at the end of the century already enjoyed access by sea
to major areas of consumption such as Veracruz, Cartagena, or
Europe. They appeared to have been little interested in the issue.

Soconusco, Suchitepeques, Guazacapán, and Izalcos, the major
cacao provinces of the Pacific coast, were generally in favor of the
ban, for obvious reasons, and enjoyed the professed support of the
Audiencia and ayuntamiento in Santiago.

Indians, who appreciated the lower prices of the Guayaquil
cacao, muleteers, and some merchants engaged in the trade, no
doubt dissented when they dared. Nicaragua, the only major Pacific
province not under the direct control of Santiago, objected completely to the ban. Since Realejo, the best Pacific port, lay near León
and Granada, this was an important dissent. Effective policy for
exclusion was impossible while divergencies of attitude existed between the provinces.

Nicaragua's most coherent and massive dissent came between
1627 and 1629, the years after the Conde de la Gómera and the
Audiencia banned Guayaquil cacao from the Audiencia of
Guatemala (1626). All Nicaraguan agencies of any importance,
royal, local, and religious, united to protest that the prohibition was
unjust and ruinous to the welfare of the province.[29]

Nicaragua had long resented the dominance of the officials of
Santiago.[30] For a while it appears that Nicaragua did not expect the
prohibitions to be rigorously enforced, but almost immediately they
were. A ship named Nuestra Señora de la Concepción was seized in
Realejo harbor laden with wine and cacao. Both were forbidden
imports; the wine had been forbidden by royal decree in 1625, and
cacao in an auto acordado by the Audiencia in the following year.
The Audiencia threatened to burn and destroy the whole cargo.
Luis Gómez Varreto, the captain, and a vecino of Lima, hired lawyers for his defense, and quickly enlisted the support of local royal
officials. They insisted on the necessity for the trade. The exchange
of wine and cacao for pitch, indigo, tobacco, and other agricultural
produce was the basis of Nicaragua's economy and was "the trade
which most engages the Spaniards of the area."

All Nicaragua's resentment against Santiago de Guatemala
flared up. Guatemala often obtained wine from Spain, they argued,
Nicaragua hardly ever; Realejo depended on the wine and cacao
trade, Acajutla was a different case with different conditions. Nicaragua with four populated towns was, they claimed, the biggest nucleus of Spanish population in the whole jurisdiction, but
depopulation would take place if the prohibitions continued.
Nicaragua needed the cacao desperately, the petitioners added, for

although Granada grew a little the rest of the province had none. Since reales were the smallest coins, all minor transactions involved cacao beans.

As for Guatemala, it would not be adversely affected by Nicaragua's imports from Guayaquil, since all of Guatemala's cacao was sent to New Spain because the prices were higher there. Guatemalan cacao was 80 to 100 tostones (80 at Realejo and 100 inland) per carga. For the same price Nicaraguans could buy more than five cargas from Peru.

Every cabildo in Nicaragua protested, but, as might be expected, Realejo was the most vehement. The city's petition, dated January 16, 1628, warned that it would simply disappear as a trading port if the ban was continued. Peruvian ships would cease to sail to Realejo, Nicaraguan pitch, indigo, and tobacco would have no outlet, these industries would decay, and the King would lose revenue on almojarifazgo, alcabala and tributes. Above all, the town cabildo warned, these restrictions would simply give rise to increased smuggling. "Item: this port of Realejo is so large and open that ships are wont to arrive and anchor in it while still two leagues from town, and they cannot be seen from land as they enter. And if there were some ships stormbound in the port loaded with the said cacao and wine, or if one came openly with such a cargo through ignorance of the prohibition, they might well unload all the cargo which they wished in the port and on the beach without giving notice to the royal officials and justices, and with nobody to prevent them. And thus they would send it inland via the haciendas, and thus find markets for it, and after having done so then tell the royal officials to come and conduct inspections and thus lose his majesty's royal dues, or they would bring it in occultly altogether and thus lose the alcabala which the merchants have to pay also. For there is no doubt whatsoever that the sales and exchanges will be hidden. . . . and it will be impossible to remedy the above." The city of Realejo was giving due warning that the trade would continue illegally and that local authorities would do little to stop it. The area, they added, would soon be out of coinage and wine if the ban continued, then small business transactions would cease and the saying of mass would be suspended.

Many Realejo vecinos were called upon to confirm these assertions. The governor also concurred, concluding that "in the time which he has governed this province of Nicaragua, he has noticed and thus affirms, that the business and trade in wine and cacao from Peru sustains it, and if these two products fail, the trade and contact will fail between this province and Peru, and no silver will come."

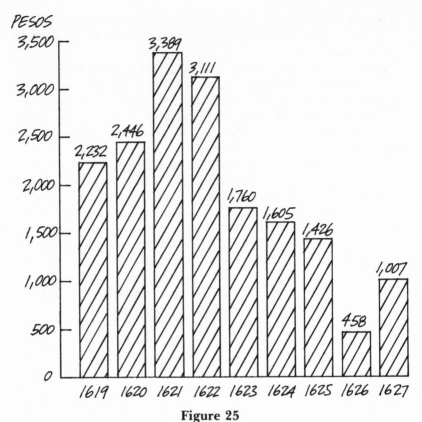

Figure 25

Almojarifazgo Paid at the Port of Realejo, 1619–27. Source: AGI/AG 43
pieza 21, ff. 31-31v

Corregidores, ecclesiastics and vecinos all agreed that the prohibitions would ruin the province. Some added that the Guayaquil
cacao was healthful and delicious despite all the allegations from
Guatemala about its pernicious nature. Others noted that the poor
would suffer most if the cacao imports failed.

The Audiencia in Santiago was adamant. It reiterated the royal
cédula forbidding Peruvian wine and its own decree banning cacao.
Ill feeling between the two provinces, pleas to the King, and smuggling via the large, unsupervised port of Realejo continued throughout the century.[31] The royal authorities in Guatemala never
succeeded in overcoming local Nicaraguan opposition.

Guayaquil cacao also helped exacerbate internal rivalries in
Nicaragua itself. Granada with its own small fields had sufficient
cacao to maintain a local coinage. León, dependent on imports,

Figure 26

Price of Cacao per Carga in Guatemala

Year	Price in reales	Area Within the Audiencia	Source
1524-25	32-40	Soconusco	Torquemada, II, 620.
1541	62.5-75	Soconusco and elsewhere	Motolinia, Tratado III, Chapter 8
1549	80-90	Guatemala	R.A.H. Muñoz 85, 169 v.
1552	80-88	Guatemala	A.G.G.G., A1. 23, legajo 4575, 121.
1553	137.5	Guatemala	A.G.G.G., A1. 23-173, legajo 1512, 253.
early 1560	200	Soconusco	A. G. I., Guatemala 968 B, No date.
1562	160	Soconusco	Morales, 155.
1574	160-176	Soconusco	A. G. I., Guatemala 40, 19 Jan., 1574.
1576	120	Izalcos	Ponce, I, 296.
1613	192	Soconusco	A. G. I. Guatemala 40, 4 May, 1613.
1619	280	Guatemala	A. G. I., Guatemala 22, Audiencia to King, 7 Sept., 1666.
1621	about 110	Guatemala	Vázquez de Espinosa, 642.
1622	136-140	Guatemala	A. G. I., Guatemala 22, Audiencia to King, 7 Sept., 1666.
1647	120	Soconusco	U. T., G19. 137, 351.
1651	240	Guatemala	A.G.G.G., A1. 11-15, expediente 48954, legajo 5801.
1652	216-240	Guatemala	A.G.G.G., A3. 1, expediente 38942, legajo 2716.
1659	176	Guatemala	A.G.G.G., A1. 7-4, expediente 12020, legajo 1819, 122.
1661	168	Guatemala	A.G.G.G., A1. 7-4, expediente 12022, legajo 1820, 105.
1663	104-144	Guatemala	A.G.G.G., A1. 7-4, expediente 12022, legajo 1820, 122.
1681	240	Guatemala	A. G. I., Guatemala 28, Sarrasa to King, 6 Jan., 1683.
1682	96-120	Guatemala	A. G. I., Guatemala 28, Sarrasa to King, 6 Jan., 1683.

often had little and suffered severe inflations because its transactions were in silver.[32] Bickering between the two cities over this and other issues was frequent during the seventeenth century.

A study of available prices shows that Guatemalan cacao seldom had a stable one. No doubt the long sea voyages caused great fluctuations in supply and thus the variations in price. As each

Figure 27

Some Cacao Prices in Mexico, Reales per Carga

Year	Price	
1525-26	80-96	Torquemada, II, 620. Stable until mid 1540s.
1550	c. 187.5	Official price, Borah and Cook, *Price trends,* 36-37.
1551	250	Official price, Borah and Cook, *Price trends,* 36-37.
1588	200	Ponce, I, 296.
1589	256-72	Suárez de Peralta, *fide* Thompson, *Cacao,* 98.
1610?	400-480	Torquemada, II, 620.
1625	176-200	Gage.
1647	480	U. T., G19. 137, 351.
1652	400	A.G.G.G., A3. 1, expediente 38942, legajo 2716.

successive source became depleted, its cacao would become more expensive. Then a new vigorous source of supply would open up and prices would drop sharply. Thus Soconusco's cacao in the early 1560s reached a price of 200 reales per carga in the province itself, only to fall sharply as the Izalcos fields began to export large quantities. Izalcos local prices had crept up to 192 reales the carga in 1613, and 280 reales the carga in 1619, only to plummet downwards to 110 or 140 reales the carga in 1621 and 1622, no doubt after the Venezuelan and Guayaquil exports began.

Seventeenth-century fluctuations are even more erratic and are typical of a marginal industry. Local prices depended on how much Guayaquil and Venezuelan cacao was reaching Guatemala and New Spain. In one year alone, 1663, cacao prices ranged from 104 to 144 reales the carga in Santiago de Guatemala.

The few Mexican prices studied confirm these general tendencies. Stable prices between 1524 and 1525 and the middle of the 1540s suggest a dependable source of supply. Then came an extremely rapid rise until the middle of the 1550s. This would coincide with the epidemics of the middle and late 1540s and the resultant decline of Soconusco, Tabasco, and northern Oaxaca plantations.

By 1588, thanks to Izalcos no doubt, prices were down to between 200 and 300 reales, but by 1610, as Izalcos supplies dried up, they reached the level of 400 to 480 reales the carga. By 1625, with new supplies from Venezuela and Guayaquil reaching the New Spain market, prices had dropped to 176 and 200 reales. By 1647 prices were again over 400 reales. In all the price history of cacao in Middle America, the main factor seems to have been the question of supply. Legislation against hoarding, government warehouses, and attempts to set prices seem to have accomplished little and affected prices hardly at all.

The increased demand for cacao during the seventeenth century led to the export of some subsidiary products from peripheral areas of Central America. These products were flavorings or spices for chocolate, and as such were fairly profitable. But they were seldom required in sufficient quantities to give rise to intense cultivation. Some of them flourished only in a wild or semi-wild state and the gathering of the crop was haphazard and time-consuming. Others were needed in such small quantities that an occasional search through the forest was sufficient to meet demands. The one exception, sugar, was cultivated for a variety of reasons, such as curing meat and distilling alcohol, and owed its cultivation only marginally to the use made of it in chocolate by Creoles and Europeans.

Arnatto or achiote *(bixa orellana),* the pulpy part of the fruit of the Central American arnatto tree, had been used for coloring Indian chocolate since pre-conquest times. Its use is also well documented in the sixteenth century, and increased somewhat in the seventeenth century as consumption rose. It seems to have been used mainly by Indians, who liked the red color which it gave to the chocolate. No doubt like maize and chile it also provided bulk to the drink.[33] Most Europeans did not favor it. Arnatto's dying qualities are fugitive, but it was exported to the Philippines to be used for dying cloth.[34] The tree flourishes in tropical humid areas or cloud forests. Thus the most productive regions were the wetter, lower parts of Verapaz and Eastern Chiapas. From there it was exported to Mexico and Guatemala by land. Occasionally quantities crossed the seas to Europe as well as Asia, perhaps for coloring butter and other edibles. Small amounts were sometimes gathered in other parts of Central America.

For the poverty stricken province of Verapaz, with its low Indian population and almost complete absence of Spaniards, the crop was sometimes the most important commercial product. Traveling merchants, and the Dominican friars who controlled Verapaz and much of Chiapas, obtained it from Indian gatherers by purchase of as a contribution of various kinds.[35]

Vanilla (*vanilla planifolia*), in contrast, was predominantly a Spanish flavoring. It had been used as both medicine and flavoring in Aztec times, but was not recognized as a plant of value for some time after the conquest. It did not come into vogue until chocolate became an accepted drink among non-Indians.

Vanilla is a wind-born epiphyte of the orchid variety, and does not lend itself easily to extensive human cultivation. Like achiote it was often gathered where encountered. It prefers a hot climate, with rainy and dry season, and grew on many parts of the Pacific coast of New Spain and Central America. Central America was the leading producer of achiote, but it was only one of several jurisdictions which produced vanilla. New Spain, for example, produced far more.

By the second half of the seventeenth century vanilla was being produced in fair quantities on the Atlantic coast, particularly in Campeche.[36] Despite this heavy competition, vanilla cultivation was profitable on Guatemala's Pacific coast. It appears to have followed in the wake of the cacao industry as it moved south eastward along the coast. By 1600 it was a crop of importance in Soconusco. By Gage's time (the early 1620s) it was growing in Soconusco, Zapotitlán, and Guazacapán. Later it became of some importance in San Salvador and Izalcos.[37]

Thus vanilla, to a very limited extent, provided an alternative source of wealth after the cacao boom had passed. It grew on the abandoned cacao bushes or was planted on the madre de cacao tree by the Indians.[38] Fortunately for the Guatemalans involved, the competition of New Spain and other areas did not mean that sufficient amounts of vanilla were produced to meet the demand. Vanilla remained a luxury product. As chocolate production and consumption rose rapidly in the New World, vanilla failed to keep pace because of its sporadic growth and informal harvesting. By the end of the seventeenth century it commanded very high prices in New Spain and Europe. Thus the small amounts which Guatemala and San Salvador did produce were easy to market.[39]

The cacao trade in seventeenth-century Central America was living in the wake of a collapsed boom. It had all the characteristics of a marginal, luxury industry. Large imports from stronger, rival areas seriously affected its profit margins. For a small place in the market it had to depend on fads and changing tastes, and if it had not been for the growing fondness for chocolate in Europe and among non-Indian Americans it is doubtful if Central America could have continued to produce even the small quantities which it did export in the seventeenth century.

13

Honduran Mining; The Emergence of a Local Industry and Culture

After the depression of the seventeenth century began, the Honduran mining industry became more and more dominated by fraud. Evasion of the Crown's laws became almost complete and fraud was, in fact, the mechanism whereby the Honduran mining industry escaped from the Spanish imperial export system to become a semi-autonomous, locally oriented industry and culture. Fraud of a local nature, although it did not much affect the monarchy, was the basis for more elaborate schemes in which Indians, with their subject social position and their commercial naïveté, were, as usual, the easiest prey for trickery and extortion.

A typical example took place in 1652. Cristóbal Gómez, an Indian ironmonger, claimed that Blas Ferrer, a creole miner, had criminally defrauded him. The plaintiff stated that he had found lumps of silver on his milpa, which was two leagues from the village of Comayaguela, today a suburb of Tegucigalpa. To find out if this silver was of good quality Gómez innocently took some of the lumps to Blas Ferrer to have them assayed. Ferrer told them that the samples were of poor quality, but asked to be shown the place where they had been found. Again the unsuspecting Cristóbal Gómez obliged.

After visiting the milpa Ferrer took away some new samples. He also advised the Indian not to tell anyone about the discovery. When Ferrer then registered not only the new "mine" but also the milpa as his own, Gómez complained to the authorities. He asked that the intruder be ordered to withdraw the men who had already started to excavate in his fields. He further complained that Ferrer and his men were trying to evict him from his house on the milpa and concluded by asking the alcalde mayor of Tegucigalpa to "make a great demonstration [of justice] by favoring my cause so that as a result the other Indians will be thereby encouraged to declare and disclose the mines which they have." Blas Ferrer argued lamely that the new mine was next to Gómez's milpa, not on it. He lost the case. Such an assertive Indian was a rarity, however, and much of the fraud of this nature may have succeeded.[1]

The success of this kind of local chicanery led to more general evasion of the laws. Other kinds of fraud included the failure to register new mines as was required by law; the sale of silver privately without the payment of royal taxes; the employment of Indians underground, which was forbidden for much of the seventeenth century; the bribery of royal officials; and a general disregard for the legal safety standards in the mines.[2] Most brazen of all was the deliberate misinterpretation of the laws by local officials. One regulation stated, for example, that certain officials from Tegucigalpa had to visit all the mines within the jurisdiction so that the Crown could then make a fair estimate of how much silver each mine was really producing. Thus the administration would have a reasonably accurate way of knowing how much in taxes these mines should legally pay. On one occasion, in reply to a royal request for information of this kind, the officials sent a long and outwardly innocent report on the safety standards in each mine which they had inspected, one more instance of "se acate pero no se cumple."[3]

Evasion of the use of mercury and the "patio process" continued throughout the seventeenth century. Mercury was a royal monopoly and so its sales were a means whereby officialdom could estimate silver production. Miners preferred to submit their own estimates. Several times during the century the available supply of mercury was so little used by the Honduran miners that the Crown ordered it to be sent on to Mexico. There is also evidence that surplus mercury from Honduras was illegally shipped to Pachuca and other parts of New Spain for resale, because local miners did not wish to use it.[4]

The Crown's ambivalence must have dismayed any genuine reformers or honest officials. The financial crisis of the 1630s in Spain caused the financially embarrassed government to lower its standards and beg for money whenever it was available. One obvious way was new composiciones. On May 28, 1632, the Crown sent an order to the Audiencia in Santiago de Guatemala, which then passed it on to the provinces, ordering that all those who had been evading the royal "fifth" by hiding the gold, silver, and precious stones which they had mined would be absolved of all criminal guilt if they now declared these effects. As a further inducement the Crown added that such tardy declarations of former deceits would be taxed at the rate of one tenth instead of one fifth.[5] It is easy to guess what effect such pathetic begging and connivance on the part of the Crown would have on the morale of the officials and miners who had been obeying the laws or declaring their gold and silver regularly and openly.

The failure of the miners to declare their gold and silver for tax was not all pure deception. By the middle years of the seventeenth century Central America was suffering from a critical shortage of coinage. Much of it had been drained away to Spain, New Spain, and Peru. The Tegucigalpa area was as hard hit as other parts, and as a result many of the poorer miners were forced to use their bars of crude silver as coinage in order to buy foodstuffs and basic mining equipment.[6]

During the growth of this new culture based on evasion, some of the best evidence on what was really happening was provided by government inspectors or visitadores, sent from Guatemala or Spain to report on the state of the Tegucigalpa mines. Such men had usually spent some time in the Indies, and many were sophisticated or even cynical men who were not given to naïve outrage at minor offences. Many were not beyond accepting bribes to overlook petty illegalities. Their amazement at the audacity and extent of fraud in Tegucigalpa is therefore convincing evidence.[7] Two detailed visitas are worth examination here because of what they reveal about the mining industry.

Oidor Gerónimo Gómez, sent from Santiago de Guatemala, arrived in Tegucigalpa in late 1672 charged with the task of conducting a thorough visita. On examining the royal account books to check the collection, stamping, and taxing of silver, a step he was required to take before setting off on an extended tour of the local mines, he found, to his astonishment and dismay, that according to these books and therefore according to recent and incumbent Spanish officials in Tegucigalpa, only 12,500 marcos had been collected in the previous eight years, "it being certain that a much greater quantity has been extracted; in spite of the penalties which those who sell silver without paying the royal 'fifth' may incur, it has been diverted and hidden, and miners have refused to use the mercury which is in the royal treasury on his majesty's account to be used for silver, for the abovementioned miners say that the metals which are taken out from the said mines cannot be extracted by mercury but

rather by fire, whence results the hiding of the said silver and the
lack of royal fifth, to the grave harm of His Majesty's royal treasury."[8]

Gómez went on to point out that although it was possible to
differentiate the silvers smelted with mercury from those smelted
with fire, it was impossible to enforce the ban against fire smelting
by this method because all those who could so differentiate were
financially involved in the mining industry and could not be trusted
as a consequence. Unfortunately, reported the oidor, smelting by
the old methods could be done anywhere in the countryside and was
hard to trace.

The visitador, who obviously felt that the situation was almost
hopeless, confined himself to ordering a stricter enforcing of previous laws. In the future all persons entering or leaving the pueblo
of Tegucigalpa were to declare all that they had with them. Any
evasion or fraud would bring seizure of all the goods accompanying
the individuals involved and forfeiture of these goods to the royal
treasury. The criminal himself was to be jailed and then sent to the
Audiencia of Guatemala in Santiago for judgement and sentence.
Obviously the oidor did not place much trust in local royal officials.
They, he added, were to follow these rules without any deviation
under threat of the gravest penalties.

For a short time after the Gómez visita there was some attempt
to enforce the laws, and a few malefactors were punished as examples, but such waves of reform were halfhearted and ephemeral, for
too many local people were committed to illegal methods. Soon the
frauds surrounding the mining undustry were as prevalent as ever.[9]

Another visita in 1695 and the years immediately following was
sponsored by President Barrios Leal and his successor Sánchez de
Berrospe. Most of the inspection was done by Francisco del Valenzuela Benegas. One of the richest mines in the Tegucigalpa area was
the Mineral de Corpus and the immediate cause of the visita was a
series of disturbances and uproars in and around the Corpus mine.

The visitador found that the rules for registering new mines
were largely ignored. Many of the mines which were functioning
were extremely dangerous and half-flooded, but no safety rules
were in force. The alcalde mayor of Tegucigalpa seemed to have
little authority, and the visitador ordered that when the alcalde was
not in the Corpus area himself he had to name a lieutenant there
as his personal representative.

The Corpus settlement had all the typical features of a raw
mining community. The region swarmed with vagabonds and petty

tricksters. Valenzuela Benegas ordered that all Spaniards, negroes, mulattoes, and mestizos should have a permanent job in the settlement or else leave. Gaming was widespread and was forbidden.

As usual, there were many reports of abuses to the local Indians. The repartimientos made by the alcalde mayor and other officials were exceedingly corrupt, with officials accepting bribes to favor certain mines and mine owners, who received in return more than their alloted share of the limited local supply of Indian labor. Indians were often ill-treated by miners. Royal justices were ordered to ensure that all Indians received the basic pay of one and a half reales per day, and that they were given appropriate days of rest and time to eat and sleep. Many local Spaniards were obtaining repartimientos of Indians under the guise of being miners, and then putting the Indians to work at other tasks.

Local monopolists were extorting high prices for foodstuffs and thus driving the local miners even deeper into debt. Royal officials were either participating in or ignoring the situation. All such monopolists were to be expelled from the Corpus settlements, the visitador ordered, and royal officials were to fix fair prices and to ensure that all food sales were made openly in public. Royal officials and clerics were deeply involved in the mining industry, which was against the law. Some actually owned mines. Any association between officials or clerics and any part of the mining industry was to stop. Gold was to be taken to royal officials for the payment of the royal fifth, and attempts at evasion were to be properly punished. Profiteering over mercury was widespread, and the visitador ordered that it be sold only to miners and only at the official price.

The main outcome of this lengthy investigation was not reform of the mines at Corpus, but intensive pursuit and prosecution of those who were held to be responsible for the uproars which had caused the visita. One Felipe de Cevallos was held to be the ringleader. After Valenzuela Benegas arrived he provoked fresh disturbances and then fled to New Spain. Other malefactors were captured. Some were sent to the coastal castles as prisoners, others to Spain. Several were minor royal officials. As was to be expected, the visita found itself unable to change the basic system at the mines of Corpus, but it was able to control and punish offenders whose activities were so extreme as to approach sedition. Given the weakness of royal authority in the seventeenth century, the Crown had to be content with such modest accomplishments.[10]

A major cause of corruption at Tegucigalpa and Corpus was the labor shortage. Miners could not afford to buy large numbers of negro slaves and the Crown was unable to supply many on extended credit. Negroes never numbered more than a few hundred[11] and attempts to round up vagabonds and idlers for work in the mines seem to have had very limited success.[12] So the result was a reluctant reliance on the local Indian populations. As far as can be known these groups had never been large, and by the time the Tegucigalpa-north Choluteca area had been pacified in the 1570s many had probably died from the various epidemics which swept through Honduras between 1520 and 1570. In 1582 there were some 740 Indian vecinos living in the area between Agalteca and Guascarán, hardly an adequate supply for a large mining industry.[13]

The miners and the officials of the Tegucigalpa and Guascarán district attempted to solve this problem in three principal ways. They sought changes in royal legislation protecting the Indian, they attempted to use the local supply of Indians to capacity, and they tried by legal and illegal means to bring Indians from other areas into the mining districts to be used in the work of the mines.

Mining had been quickly recognized as one of the forms of labor most harmful to the Indians, and accordingly the Crown had speedily sought to prevent the use of Indians for this work.[14] Mining interests petitioned to have the ban removed by pointing out that the industry could not flourish, and the King would be starved of bullion, as long as there was insufficient labor to develop the mines. The argument was a telling one as far as the impoverished Spanish government was concerned, and various compromises were attempted leading finally to an almost complete erosion of the prohibition.

The Crown's first concession was to permit repartimientos or drafts of local Indians for agriculture and supplementary labor in the mines. This involved growing food, cooking it, making charcoal, cutting and dressing pit props, drawing and carrying water and supplies, and tending outdoor smelters.[15] The King further weakened his position by asking the President of the Audiencia of Guatemala to undertake a secret enquiry to ascertain if a year's extension should be granted to those employing repartimiento Indians in the mines themselves.[16] Finally, on April 9, 1650, after many more petitions, the King gave permission for the use of 100 Indians in the mines themselves. From then on Indians were probably used underground whenever they were available.[17]

The local Indians were made to feel heavy pressure both before and after 1650 because of these repartimientos. This pressure took several forms. Some villages were assigned the task of supplying nearby mines with foodstuffs, and in times of shortage were subject to harassment and imprisonment for failure to provide the stipulated amounts. The heaviest requirement, however, was the repartimiento itself, and most of the immediate pressure fell on the caciques and other village leaders who were responsible for producing the Indians at the mines at the appropriate time. These Indian leaders found their situation further aggravated by the conduct of their villagers, who showed great unwillingness to work in or around the mines and fled from their villages whenever possible. Indian caciques and alcaldes were then blamed by the Spanish authorities for a lack of vigilance and enthusiasm. On one occasion the exasperated Spaniards simply burned the Indian huts found outside the village and forced all the rural Indians to return to it.[18]

The overzealous or acquisitive Indian leader was not free from interference of another sort. In 1708 Diego González, alcalde of San Antonio de Texaquat, was accused of causing harm to his charges by cooperating in the sending of Indians to the mine at Corpus, "many leagues distant," thus exceeding the requirements of the repartimiento.[19]

Attempts to bring in new Indians from areas beyond the jurisdiction of Tegucigalpa were constant. Petitions to the Crown repeatedly suggested that this was the only way to solve the problems of the mines and proposed ways of conducting this resettlement which would not impose undue hardship on the Indians involved. The most daring request of the series asked for 1,600 Indians from neighboring provinces who would be settled in four villages of 400 vecinos and their families. All would be exempt from tribute and each village would supply 100 workers for the mines at any given time.[20]

Far more success was achieved by less official methods of recruitment. Numbers of Indians seem to have been taken from the lowlands around the Bay of Fonseca to the highland mines to the northeast. Raids were also made into areas inhabited by "unreduced" Indians. A report of 1698 stated that 700 Payas plus an unspecified number of children had just been "taken out" of the wilds near Comayagua and had been added to 100 Indians of the same tribe previously captured. All these Indians were to be moved to the jurisdiction of Tegucigalpa, near the Corpus mine, to become part of the repartimiento system, which was clearly stated as still going on. There was probably much of this type of activity which went unreported.[21]

The early gold mining in Nueva Segovia had continued after the depression of the 1540s and 1550s but in a much reduced state. This area, which was a peripheral part of the Tegucigalpa mining complex, also suffered from severe labor shortages and belonged politically to the province of Nicaragua. Debt peons from Nueva Segovia, fleeing across the boundary to Honduras, were of course welcomed by the Spaniards in Tegucigalpa, and attempts by their counterparts in Nueva Segovia to recover these Indians caused ill-feeling between the two groups from time to time.[22]

Labor shortages, social and caste distinctions, the poor quality of many of the mines discovered, primitive technology, and the high price of mercury led to the development of two different, coexistent mining industries, indeed two different mining cultures. By the last quarter of the seventeenth century these two cultures were clearly distinguishable to the people living in the area, and mutual hostility was to be a feature of relations between the two groups involved from that time forward.

The group of greatest economic importance was the one based on the formal system of large or fairly large registered mines. These mines used slave labor, repartimientos of Indians, a little mercury when it suited their owners or was available, and they produced most of the silver and gold sent out of the province. Mines such as Santa Lucía, La Enriqueña at Guascarán, and the cluster close to the village of Tegucigalpa were typical of this group. The miners who owned or leased this type of mine were closely linked to government. They were visible and therefore more subject to visita and quinto. Their frauds and evasions were the ones most likely to be discovered. They felt themselves to be a valuable and productive part of society and thus appropriate recipients of royal favors, loans, and encouragement. They were overwhelmingly Creole in origin and were the writers of complaints, reports, and petitions to the Crown about the mines of Honduras. They represented, in fact, the official mining industry of Honduras, the economic group which controlled the mines and interacted with royal officials.

The other group was composed of the guïrises, the folk miners of Honduras. Despised and hounded by the owners of the larger mines, they were in no position to inform the Crown and local authorities of their grievances, so most of what is known about them is pejorative. Many of them were Indians or members of the castes, and all were poor. Consequently they could seldom hire labor of any kind. Most worked alone and there were seldom more than three in any team. Some of them opened small mines of their own and registered them in the hope that later they would turn out to be rich strikes worthy of greater development. Great numbers of these small strikes were registered during the seventeenth century, but few if any rescued the guïrises from their poverty.[23] Other guïrises were wont to explore abandoned mines and to reregister them in the hopes of finding veins which had not been fully utilized.[24] By far the greatest number of guïrises, however, seem to have been little better than scavengers, if one can believe their enemies the owners of the larger mines. One petition requested that the guïrises be prohibited from registering or owning mines, for all they did was "ruin" them so that they were of no further use to any miners. Many of these guïrises did not register the mines which they were working, far fewer paid taxes on the small quantities of silver and gold which they extracted. Since they knew and cared little about safety or maintenance their operations were extremely dangerous. One favorite trick used by some of the poorer guïrises was to enter an abandoned mine and remove the pillars of ore which had been left in the tunnels to support the ceilings, a habit which effectively barred any future exploitation of the mines thus "ruined."[25]

In spite of the hostility of the "better" classes—even the chronicler Fuentes y Guzmán, who knew little about mining had unkind words for them—the Honduran folk miners and ore scavengers continued to exist as basic native figures throughout the colonial period. There are many in the Tegucigalpa region today.[26]

The relatively small mining complex around Tegucigalpa moved the center of Honduran economic life from the Caribbean shores south into the central highlands. It created towns such as Tegucigalpa, which did not become a villa until 1762, and changed the function of the provincial capital at Comayagua. Both of these settlements became storage towns for the replenishment of food and equipment.[27]

Mining encouraged the further development of stockraising in central and southern Honduras. The mines needed steady supplies of meat, leather sacks, tallow, and mine candles. The mules which grazed on the plains around La Choluteca and the Gulf of Fonseca were sent up to the mines in the mountains, and also on the long journey along the Pacific coast to Panama. Large quantities of lead and litharge were needed as reagents for smelting, and lead mines were opened at Agalteca and in Chiquimula in the province of Guatemala. Salt was needed in considerable quantities for the amalgamation process associated with smelting, and this encouraged the development of a salt industry on the shores of the Gulf of Fonseca. Salt pans just behind the mangrove swamps along the shores of the bay provided most of the amounts needed. These salt pans are worked to this day.[28]

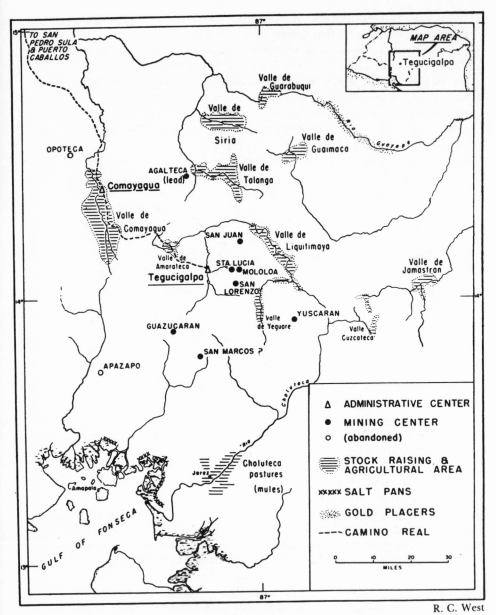

R. C. West

Figure 28

Mining Activity in Central Honduras, Mid-Seventeenth Century

Another offspring of the Tegucigalpa mines was the typical brawling, lawless, mobile society which always seems to come into being in mining areas. Gaming, riots, concubinage, and financial swindles troubled inspectors and conscientious local officials. They were constant features of seventeenth-century Tegucigalpa.[29]

The mining industry of Honduras presents something of a paradox. Founded after the days of intensive gold panning and slaving had passed, it enjoyed only a fleeting and relative prosperity. At its ephemeral heights of success it was never an industry of sufficient dimensions to provide the main export product of Central America. During most of the seventeenth century it was a poverty-stricken industry, starved of mercury, often unwilling to use it, short of manpower, ignored by central authorities in Spain and Guatemala, and unable to solve the problems presented by the terrain and the local rock formations.

Yet it must be granted that this small mining industry had a certain dynamism. Although the mines of Tegucigalpa occupied a poor, unimportant section of depressed Central America, overshadowed by Guatemala, San Salvador, and even Nicaragua, nevertheless they were responsible for the settlement of central Honduras, they founded and supported a series of supplementary activities, and gave rise to a whole pattern of folklore and culture. Without its poverty-stricken mining industry Honduras might have been abandoned to a few herders and hordes of cimarron cattle after the early conquerors and slavers had passed from the scene.

14

External Trades in the Depth of the Depression

By the late 1630s the economic depression affecting Central America and its export trades had deepened markedly. Old elites based on the export trade were disappearing, and only those based on officialdom, land, local markets, or the Church showed any permanence. In the face of this prolonged and seemingly insoluble crisis, the official and private remedial legislation and searching for solutions of the years between 1580 and 1630 died down. More and more, the survivors of the years of dynamic exports tended to turn away from recognized and legal systems towards illegality. Smuggling, both on the Pacific and the Caribbean coasts, seemed to be the only way of keeping any trade open at all, and at that smuggling was a meager business until late in the century.

Reduced as they were, these small trades do yield useful information about society in Central America during the depression. Moreover, islands of relative success in the general picture of stagnation show how, from the economic point of view, certain areas remained more viable than others, even during the periods of lowest activity.

Related to these small exchanges were some of the features to be expected in times of economic difficulty. Central America suffered all the strains of shortages and sudden rare gluts, of insufficient and debased coinage, of sudden devaluations, and of lack of confidence in government on the part of the common people. Within Central America the performance of government had been far from inspiring. Its policies had fluctuated between laissez-faire and intervention—intervention which was often little better than petty meddling. In times of prosperity the attitude was generally one of laissez-faire. As the depression increased economic tinkering of a rather panicky kind began, an essentially defensive attempt to preserve the commercial and monetary status quo. As difficulties continued and multiplied year after year, however, and as none of the governmental measures seemed to have even the most minimal success, a new kind of laissez-faire born of despair returned, and the government, cutting its losses as it were, again withdrew from intervention in the economic sphere.

Even in times of the greatest depression some trades survive, some capital is accumulated by the fortunate, and some fortunes are even made. Such successes are rare, however, and struggling trades are more familiar. By examining such activities we can learn much about the nature of the Central American depression itself.

Two important commodities for non-Indian society in the New World were wine and oil. Used for cooking meats and fish, and in some houses for heat and light, olive oil was a staple for most Spaniards. Wine was drunk by all Spaniards when available. Water was regarded as unhealthy, as indeed it often was, coffee and tea were unknown, and chocolate, being an Indian drink, was only taken by men in the absence of wine. It did not become a "fad" among all classes until late in the century.

Both oil and wine were also consumed in large quantities by the Church. They were used for daily household food and drink in the many monasteries and convents, and also sacramentally in the mass and in extreme unction. Olive oil was also considered to be the only proper fuel for the sanctuary lamps which burned on all altars. Because of these many uses, then, wine and oil were needed in large quantities in all parts of colonial Latin America.

Except for an ephemeral viniculture in northern Honduras immediately after the conquest, Central America was totally lacking in both oil and wine.[1] Oil could be produced from many other sources, of course, but melted pig fat, beef suet, or liquid wax were thought to be poor substitutes for the genuine article. As a result of these cultural preferences Central America was obliged to import almost all of its requirements in wine and oil. Not only did these imports have to be large, they also had to be regular. Both wine and olive oil were subject to spoiling and damage when transported over long distances in the tropics under the poor technology of the seventeenth century. More than once vinegar and rancid olive oil was all that reached Central Americans who were eagerly awaiting the arrival of overseas produce in Santiago.

For most of the sixteenth century wine and oil supplies seem to have been sufficient to satisfy most Spaniards. The ships from Spain brought enough to provision the small non-Indian populations of that time, and as we have seen, there was even a surplus at times to be used for paying, bribing, or tricking Indians who had cacao, cochineal, or other products to sell.

Two factors were to complicate this economically tranquil situation. After 1570 the valleys of southern Peru began to develop a wine and olive oil industry of their own, which, since Peru was a steady trader to Mesoamerica, was bound to compete with the Spanish exports to the same area. By the 1630s, moreover, great strains were beginning to appear in the Spanish economy, and as a consequence, in the Spanish fleet system. Sailings became increasingly irregular thereafter, and the arrival of a fleet to the ports of Honduras was the exception rather than the rule from then until well into the eighteenth century. All this time, of course, the wine and oil consuming population of Central America was slowly rising.

The Peruvian vineyards and olive groves began to offer significant competition to the Spanish products some years before the fleet system entered its period of noticeable decay and reaction from Spain was typical. The merchants in Seville represented by their consulado exerted pressure on the Crown to have Peruvian wine exports barred from New Spain and Central America.

At first such efforts did not trouble those in Central America who took an interest in such matters. Castilian wine was more expensive, but the supply of it was still large and steady enough. Royal officials found that they were able to give the protectionist efforts of the consulado their support, and the Conde de la Gómera for example actually suggested to the Crown in 1611 that Peruvian wine be denied entry to the area under his jurisdiction, because it was strong, raw, somewhat noxious, especially to the Indians, and the cost of importing it was leaving Guatemala short of coinage to send to Spain.[2]

The request from Guatemala, soon to be bitterly regretted by those of that province, met with an enthusiastic response in Spain. The export of Peruvian wine to Guatemala was forbidden in 1615, and the ban was emphatically and frequently repeated up to 1685.[3]

Nicaragua's response to this curtailment of trade was the same as that already noticed in the case of cacao. Very little Castilian wine was received via the Desaguadero from the cities of Cartagena or Portobelo, which had their own needs and other wealthier areas to supply, so Nicaragua depended almost entirely on the Peruvian exports and much of the traffic of Realejo in particular was a result of this trade. The province therefore resented the "selfishness" of the Guatemalan authorities in suggesting the ban, and frankly warned the Crown that the wine suppliers and local buyers would quickly turn to smuggling, particularly in the many coves and inlets of the large Realejo outer harbor where constant surveillance of ships was impossible.[4]

Chiapas and Costa Rica, in this as in much else more closely tied to neighboring jurisdictions than to the Guatemalan center, expressed no opinions. Chiapas probably received its small supply from Mexico and Puebla, or by sea from Veracruz via the river Grijalva. Costa Rica's wine and oil supply—some Castilian and some Peruvian, no doubt a negligible quantity in all—entered the region from Panama through the many harbors in the Gulf of Nicoya, principally the official one at La Caldera. Sometimes such shipments obeyed the law. At other times the small coastal frigates evaded some or all of the taxes, or simply smuggled, with or without the help of local officials in Nicoya and La Caldera.[5]

As wine or oil supplies from Spain dwindled in the 1630s and 1640s, the authorities and Spaniards of Guatemala realized what they had brought upon themselves. For about half a century, petition after petition was sent to Spain alternately demanding and imploring that the ban be removed. Wine and olive oil were absolute necessities, they claimed, all religious ceremonies would have to cease if the shortage continued, no wine was coming from Spain, the ban was only causing smuggling, royal officials feared for the maintenance of public order, and so on. The fact that Peruvian wine was allowed entry to Panama after 1670 caused particular resentment. An attempt was even made to obtain an independent consulado de comercio for Guatemala, but it was rejected by the Crown.[6]

The Crown was in a quandary. Pressured by Spanish merchants, it usually obeyed the dictates of seventeenth-century mercantilism, sacrificing the interests of the overseas kingdoms (read colony), however urgent, to those of the mother country. Yet obviously it was of importance to keep the colony supplied with basics such as wine and oil. The Crown's role as guardian of the Church demanded as much. But the enfeebled monarchs could do little except try to increase the supply from Spain. Ships of the Honduras flotilla were ordered to consign at least one-third of their cargo space to the carrying of wine, oil, and other vital items for the colony.[7] There is no sign that these orders were carried out, and for years at a time the Honduras flotilla simply did not sail anyway - with or without wine and oil.[8]

Another solution tried by the Crown much later was removal of the ban for an experimental period. In 1685 limited wine imports from Peru were at last permitted for a period of three years. By means of extensions and renewals this free trade lasted until 1713, when at the urging of Spanish interests, still jealous of their illusory monopolies in the colonies, the ban was reimposed, not to be lifted again until 1774.[9]

The response of the colonists to these bans could only be smuggling and probably the Crown expected it, grumbling and reiterating prohibitive legislation more on principle than from any hope that the law would be obeyed. Contraband trading in wine and oil became one of the main economic activities of the Pacific coast of Central America. Even the period of relatively free trade in these commodities between 1685 and 1713 when the ban was lifted, did not stop it, for the Crown could not resist the temptation to impose immediate taxes on Peruvian wine in 1685, there was still officialdom to be avoided, and smuggling had become customary after so many years.[10]

Contraband was conducted by a variety of techniques, and some were of course improvised as circumstances arose. Many of the methods used, however, became standardized, almost rigid, and were so well known by all segments of the community, Church, state, town and country, Indians, castes, and Creoles, that it is obvious that wine and oil contraband involved a tacit understanding between officialdom, perhaps even the Crown, and those interested in obtaining wine.

The first and most blatant form of avoidance was that which took place on the registro ships, those which sailed from Callao, Acajutla, and Realejo with royal permission to buy local Central American produce. In the very year in which the Crown first permitted these ships, 1620, three sailed instead of the statutory two, well loaded with wine, which was sold at Acajutla as vinegar. At other times ships passed off their cargoes as oil, olives, or chile peppers, which were not forbidden imports.[11] In addition these ships often returned to Callao loaded with Chinese goods, purchased with large quantities of silver, far exceeding the 200,000 ducats legally permitted. There was little that could be done: By 1631 the trade between the regions of New Spain and Peru had been stopped entirely by the exasperated Crown. Protests and petitions brought no results for two decades.[12]

During this period from about 1640 until the middle or late 1660s the depression seems to have been at its height. Even smuggling fell off and became a sporadic matter. Basically Peru did not seem to need or want any of the products which Guatemala had to offer. Chinese goods were to be had in Acapulco and Mexico City in far greater quantities, indigo was still a minor requirement in Peru, local Guayaquil cacao was plentiful, and only pine pitch was eagerly sought. As a result few ships came, and those that did received a great welcome. The situation was one of such need, and the eagerness to obtain wine was so great that royal regulations were often quite openly flouted.

Once in a while wine and cacao, for they often came together, were confiscated; but then they were quickly sold at public auction. It was suggested occasionally that severe penalties would be imposed for smuggling. More often the wine was simply admitted with few questions asked. A ship which arrived in Acajutla in 1655 without any licenses for any ports was typical. The captain scarcely took the trouble to invent an adequate excuse; he simply stated that he had lost all his papers.[13] Even royal officials openly disobeyed the law. One official in 1643 quite frankly explained his position to the Crown, with no subterfuge or special pleading.

Called to Acajutla because of the arrival of a ship, he found that it had already sailed on to Realejo without waiting for permission. In Acajutla the ship had unloaded 490 botijas of wine. Some 300 had been found by officials on a recua of mules, and had been confiscated. The owner of the remaining 190 botijas had stored them in a warehouse and refused to surrender the keys to the officials, for which stubbornness he was arrested. The people of the villa of Sonsonate were dismayed and sent a deputation of eight leading vecinos to tell the official that such activity would ruin the place and halt all remaining trade. He admitted to the King that he found himself in a dilemma. The vecinos were threatening to abandon the villa, which would cause the whole province to suffer, yet he had to maintain the dignity of his office as pesquisador and uphold the authority of the Crown. In addition, wine was so scarce and so badly wanted that there was a danger of unruliness. There had been no supplies from Castile for a long time. The pesquisador finally resolved the problem by declaring that all wine which was declared within an hour would not be removed. Over 200 botijas appeared within the hour, and when the period was extended a certain Captain Carasa, master of a ship called *San Francisco Javier* arrived to declare 2,500 more, some in a warehouse, "and some hidden in a gully." An agent also came forward to declare that the ship which had continued to Realejo without permission had 500 more botijas on board for that town, "so that all together . . . more than 6,000 botijas" were declared. Taxes were paid on all this quantity and it was then returned to its owners. The Crown was rewarded with 20,000 pesos in taxes, the villa rung all its church bells in relief, and a deputation was sent to thank the pesquisador in the name of the town. Yet all the wine was contraband, and the actions of the official were illegal. "Of course," he admitted, "a contradiction is implied. But to deprive the province of urgent necessities is foolish." Public order, he said, was the first responsibility of any official. Whether he was reprimanded or punished is not known—probably he was not.[14]

In the 1670s the wine and oil trade slowly began to increase. The reasons can only be guessed. Guatemala had solved some of its financial and currency problems by that time and the obrajes of the highland basins of Ecuador were growing in importance, thus requiring more indigo and perhaps cochineal. There may have been a new growth in the trade in Chinese goods after the depression in Mexico, and the slow growth in smuggling on the Caribbean coast was probably providing some Central Americans with increased funds to buy the luxuries they wanted. Whatever the reasons there are signs of an increased interest in trade with Peru about 1667. Sailings seem to have become more regular, and shortages of wine and oil in Central America less frequent.[15] In 1667 and possibly earlier, the Crown permitted the reestablishment of the two ships per year system, whereby sailings from Callao to load Central American produce were allowed so long as no wine or cacao were taken to Central America. Steps to restart the legal trade were initiated very quickly in Guatemala, as one might expect, and by 1668 trade was under way again.[16] The only other concession which the Crown made before 1685 was to allow the number of ships to increase from two to three.[17]

The usual smuggling techniques continued. Wine was introduced as vinegar or as preserved peppers or simply not declared. Ships which were not part of the recognized flotilla smuggled in Acajutla and Realejo almost at will. From time to time an enthusiastic official would cause severe strains in the system by obeying the law and confiscating wine and punishing smugglers, but most royal officials gave the trade fairly open support. Finally the Crown surrendered and legalized a small wine trade.[18] Smuggling did not stop and continued into the eighteenth century.

Some indication of the expansion of Peruvian trade to Central America can be gained from noticing the routes by which Peruvian news arrived in Mexico. After 1675 mail came to an increasing degree via Guatemala. Evidence from the pirates is similar. Those who penetrated to the Pacific in the 1680s seized a considerable number of wine ships, some bound for Central America.

Most significant of all was the revival of two trade routes which had fallen out of use. In 1680 trade was reinitiated between Iztapa and the Mexican ports of Huatulco and Acapulco, the glories of former cacao days being by that time so remote that this sea lane was described as a "new route of navigation . . . worth promoting." New interest was also shown in the local trade between the Honduras ports and the Caribbean islands, with Havana receiving most emphasis. This trade had been banned in 1676 at the urging of the consulado of Seville, for a trial period of five years. Thereafter the trade had languished. Now at the turn of the century, vigorous efforts were made to revive it and remove the ban. The building of heavy ships of 300 tons and more on the Pacific coast was also started in the last years of the century.[19]

Once Peruvian wine had arrived in Guatemala or Nicaragua it affected local life in many ways. The price fluctuated wildly, especially in the middle years of the century. Within a period of months, the price could double or fall by fifty per cent depending on the arrival of ships from Peru.[20] Naturally these wild fluctuations caused official concern, but sporadic attempts to regulate prices seem to have had little success.[21] Such rapid price changes also attracted profiteers, and their monopolistic tactics sometimes contributed to the shortages.[22]

The wine trade involved many in high places. Ximénez the chronicler mentions one President who refused to take a bribe from a Peruvian wine importer as an outstanding exception.[23] During the period between 1667 and 1685 when ships were permitted to sail between Callao and Central America, but without wine or cacao, the ayuntamiento and the Audiencia quarrelled over which body should have the right to inspect the incoming ships—an ideal post for accepting bribes.[24] The transfer of wine from the coast to the cities, particularly to Santiago, was another process which involved many prestigious institutions. Indians in villages such as Escuintepeque, Petapa, San Juan, and San Cristóbal Amatitlán were ordered to watch for illegal mule trains, especially at night, but they seem to have slept instead. Churches and monasteries a few miles outside the city were used to store smuggled wine which was then transferred to the city as needed. Sometimes officials allowed wine to enter upon payment of a small duty, as if it were perfectly legal. The wine, whether admitted improperly by royal officials or simply smuggled, was sold to all conditions of men, including oidores and Presidents of the Audiencia of Guatemala, hospitals, and leading Creoles. Some merchants in the main towns appear to have lived almost entirely from the proceeds of this illegal business. In the early 1680s three Basques controlled much of the Peruvian import trade. Two lived in Santiago and one in Realejo. Eventually their success became too flagrant and they were prosecuted, fined, and saw their goods confiscated.[25]

Statistics on the Peruvian wine trade are sparse. After all, the trade was illegal and few figures were kept. But the few figures available give us an idea of its relative size. Between 1673 and 1679, while Peruvian wine was still illegal, only three official ships arrived in the Gulf of Honduras from Spain. They carried only 4,598 botijas of wine which paid 827 pesos and 4 reales in duty. In these same years at least 15,954 botijas entered Guatemala alone from Peru, paying 16,319 pesos and 7 reales in tax. Almost certainly the 15,954 Peruvian botijas were only a fraction of the quantities which were smuggled in.[26] By the 1690s royal permission to bring in wine plus smuggling had solved the problem of supply. New attempts to restrict the trade after 1713 were unsuccessful.

A persistent excuse used by apologetic officials when explaining their tolerance of the Peruvian wine trade was the need for wine and oil for the use by the Church. Under the terms of the patronato real, the Crown and its local representatives had undertaken to provide the Church with its needs in wine, oil, and wax. The Crown was careful to point out that such help was to be given only when needed, and that the orders and other religious entities were to buy their own wine when they could afford it, and when it was easily available.[27] Local officials, however, were able to claim that in Central America wine was nearly always scarce, so that they were obliged to heed the pleas from the monastic orders and to buy up whatever wine was available at public sales or auctions for the use of the Church. On at least one occasion, when a ship from Spain did arrive, the whole cargo of wine and oil was seized for the use of the Church. In rural areas shortages were so severe that religious establishments had to do without.[28]

On rare occasions fraud crept in here too. While on a visita to Costa Rica in 1710, the bishop of Nicaragua found that the fuel in the sacramental lamps was manteca (suet, no doubt), because the local provincial of the Franciscans was misappropriating the funds given to him by the royal treasury for buying olive oil.[29] More usual than this, however, was strict accounting on the part of the orders, and insistence that wine provided from royal funds not appear on refectory tables.[30]

The needs of the Church, while large, were probably partly an excuse on the part of royal officials in Central America, but the royal charity in wine, oil, and wax, not abolished until 1729 and 1742, was one more reason why the shortage of these commodities was so great and so vitally concerned the Spanish community.[31]

The great significance of the Peruvian wine trade is that once the worst of the seventeenth-century depression had passed it provided a solution, and an illegal solution, to a problem which the mother country had obviously created and proved unable to solve. Wine smuggling was a signal lesson to the Creoles, a forerunner to the contraband culture which was to govern Central America in the eighteenth century.

Used by the Church and by the elites, wine and oil was one of the most crucial trades during the seventeenth century. It was at once an illustration of Central America's Pacific orientation, of Spain's inability to supply her colonies and enforce her laws, and of the course of the depression, deepening gradually until the middle years of the century, and beginning to show definite signs of recovery by the last decade of the century.

A well-tested economic law holds that inequalities and consequently frictions increase between regions in direct proportion to the persistence of economic stagnation. We have seen how Nicaragua became disaffected over Guatemala's protectionist policies against Guayaquil cacao and Peruvian wine, how Honduras quarrelled with the Audiencia over the moving of port facilities from Trujillo to Puerto Caballos to Santo Tomás, and how Chiapas and Costa Rica, because of neglect at the center, looked outward to other regions for their basic economic ties.

Another result of the depression was the fragmentation of the search for solutions. As the possibility of finding a single, unifying crop, trajín, or trade grew more remote after 1630, some of the peripheral regions began to turn inward to seek local remedies, if such existed. This gave rise here and there to minor, regional "boomlets," even during the years of deepest depression, small ephemeral surges of economic activity in no case strong enough to reunite the area, but which some observers, with a touch of exaggeration, have called exceptions to the seventeenth-century depression. Some examples of these regional flurries will illustrate this type of activity.

Chiapas, known for its wild cochineal and patlaxtli (wild cacao), also developed something of a trade because of the quality of its horses and mules. These horses, raised around Chiapa de los Indios, the largest village in the province, were exported to Mexico where they enjoyed a high reputation.[32] In the main, however, Chiapas simply retired from most interregional trading and became, to an ever-increasing degree, a very isolated, rural community living a self-sufficient agricultural life centered on the basins around Ciudad Real and on the upper waters of the Grijalva River.

Several areas off to the south and east of Guatemala itself were able to add to their agricultural self-sufficiency by supplying Panama. The most extensive trade of this kind was in mules, which were sent to Panama from as far away as Gracias a Dios.[33] One of the main regions involved was the riverine plain around La Choluteca on the Nicaraguan-Guatemalan provincial boundary at the Gulf of Fonseca. Vast numbers of mules were raised there both for the nearby mines of Tegucigalpa and for the more distant trajín of Panama.[34] Nicaragua also sent many mules to Panama, as did Costa Rica, but Costa Rica's role in this trade was more that of a way station. The mule route ran over easy terrain along the Pacific coast from Honduras and La Choluteca to Granada. After leaving the city the trail crossed the broken, almost uninhabited country between the Lake of Nicaragua and the Nicoya Peninsula. Cartago, the principal Spanish town of Costa Rica, was able to provide food and pasture for the transient mule trains, and even obtained permission to levy a tax on each mule passing through, thus obtaining a further share of profits from this trade.[35]

After resting in Cartago the mule trains crossed the most difficult part of the long trail to Panama. Staying close to the Pacific coast the recuas passed through Quepo and Boruca, areas of partially reduced Indians. The trains were often attacked by recalcitrants, and at the best of times the route was long and difficult. Given the hazards of the route, the mortality of the mules which must have occurred, and the no doubt wretched appearance of the animals upon arrival in Panama, the profits from this trade, so vital for Spain's Peruvian fleets, must have been very small.[36]

Important to Costa Rica, which was never much more than an appendage to the more vital zone at Panama, was its role as a supplier of basic foodstuffs for the merchant population of that city, Portobelo, and Cartagena. Much of the provisioning of the fleets in biscuit and pork was also done with supplies brought in from Costa Rica. Nearly all of this trade was by sea, and it started soon after the permanent establishment of the colony in the 1570s. Small ships usually described as frigates came to the open roadsteads of Punta Blanca, Suerre, and Moín on the Caribbean coast to load live pigs, flour, maize, and hens. On the Pacific side the favorite port was La

Caldera on the northern shore of the Gulf of Nicoya. Nicaragua also participated in food exports to Panama in a small way via the port of Realejo. From La Caldera tallow, suet, hides, biscuit, and flour were the main exports, and small vessels plied up and down the coast with fair frequency. By 1640 the two valleys of Landecho and Bagaces, lying between the small town of Esparza and La Caldera, were teeming with cattle. Vast numbers of these animals were slaughtered for their tallow and suet, the carcasses being left to rot "for want of people to eat the meat."[37] Some larger outside trades crept into these grocery supply routes from time to time. Wine from Peru and Chinese goods from New Spain certainly appeared in the Gulf of Nicoya, and Spanish goods, especially cloth, came in the ships from Cartagena to Panama, often in exchange for the food-stuffs sent to the isthmus ports.

Serious difficulties began to disrupt these small but busy exchanges after 1640. No doubt factors such as overgrazing, indiscriminate slaughter of animals, disappearing Indian workers, pirates in the Caribbean, and lack of supplies from Spain played a role, just as they did earlier in Guatemala and Honduras. The main factor, however, was probably the slow growth of agriculture in the Peruvian coastal oases and in the Audiencia of Quito. Surplus wheat, wine, cloth, and oil were flowing from Peru to Panama in a regular fashion by mid-century, and by the 1680s Peru was Panama's chief food supplier. This meant less demand for Costa Rican agricultural produce and lower prices, while Costa Rica's needs in such commodities as cloth, iron, oil, and wine remained fairly constant. The result was an unfavorable balance of trade, the disappearance of silver coinage in the locality, and its replacement with cacao beans, and Costa Rica's little margin of prosperity was gone, not to return until the rise of the cacao plantations and smuggling at the end of the century.[38]

Even smaller industries than the groceries of Costa Rica brought intermittent activity to small areas up and down the Pacific coast. The occasional discovery of a new oyster bed in the Bay of Fonseca or in the Gulf of Nicoya would cause some brief pearling and enriched a few Creole administrators.[39] The preconquest activity of making purple and blue dyes from the excretions of sea snails, a process known also to the Phoenicians, was revived in the Franciscan mission in Boruca in the Nicoya area in the 1680s. The industry was small and seems to have been controlled from the start by whoever, alcalde mayor or corregidor, was governing Nicoya at the time. The Indians of the area, by then a mere handful, were worked hard at this industry and finally revolted against their treatment in 1760.[40] It is evident that pearling and snail dye were marginal activities. An astute local Creole or administrator might make his fortune out of such articles if there was no interference and some docile Indians nearby, but there was seldom enough profit to enrich more than one or two exploiters.

The only industry which, while not large enough to benefit the whole region under the Audiencia, did bring a significant surge of prosperity and external trade was the export to Peru of pine pitch from Nueva Segovia in Nicaragua via the nearby port of Realejo.

Nicaragua had always been noted as a center for all the trades and products required for seafaring. Early observers just after the conquest noticed large quantities of cotton cloth and canvas for sails, large stands of hard timber and pine for planking and pitch, henequen, cabuya, pita thread, maguey, and other fibres for rigging, cordage, and tackle. In addition the large harbor at Realejo was one of the very best on the west coast of South America.[41]

As a result, when slaving, the China trade, and other seaborne commerce began to expand in the Pacific in the middle years of the sixteenth century, the area was admirably equipped to become one of the most important shipbuilding centers, outfitters, and suppliers for Spanish navigation in the Pacific. Realejo was the center of these activities, a small town of shipwrights, dockers, riggers, and outfitters, desperately short of accommodation, often crowded with travelers waiting for ships to and from Peru. Large ships were built there, including some for Acapulco and the Philippines.[42]

After 1610 Realejo began to experience growing difficulties. Guayaquil had been a major rival as a shipbuilding center for some years, but now that shipping was becoming increasingly restricted between New Spain and Guatemala and Peru, while Peru's trade with Panama was growing, Guayaquil was totally eclipsing the Nicaraguan port. Cotton, fibres, and timbers were still products of some importance, but contraband in wine, cacao, and silver began to replace the legal trades which had brought the town prosperity.[43]

This declining port was revived by the rise of a new industry, also in Peru. The vineyards in the valleys of southern Peru required large quantities of pine pitch or resin for lining the large storage barrels and the tuns or botijas in which the wine was shipped. The area around the vineyards, however, was almost totally lacking in woods of any kind.

One of the greatest stands of pine in early America seems to have been the one which stretched from the region around Tegucigalpa, southeastward into the Nicaraguan region known as Nueva Segovia. (While the pine woods of this area are only a remnant of what they were, they remain impressive today.) The town of Nueva Segovia had been an early center for gold washing, settled by miners and their slaves, both Indian and negro, advancing north from León. After the mining stage had passed, Nueva Segovia sank into obscurity, perhaps the least known city of colonial Central America. It was a small agricultural center and a supplier of pitch and resin, usually known in Spanish as brea, to the port of Realejo and Granada.[44]

The wine industry of Peru brought a new if brief prosperity to this backwater. The rising demand for brea caused a massive attack on the pine woods of Nueva Segovia, and, to a lesser extent, those of Tegucigalpa. The pitch was extracted in primitive ovens and then sent on muleback to Realejo and Fonseca, where it was shipped to Peru. By the time Vázquez de Espinosa visited Nicaragua and Peru around 1620, the trade was flourishing, and it was making large profits for the middlemen of Realejo.[45] A quintal of pitch, sold in Realejo for 20 reales, brought 96 reales or more at Callao and some 120 reales in the vineyards, and "with the low original cost and the expensive consumption of it in Peru, the trade is very profitable, for it has made many men rich." Vázquez estimated that after freight and duties were paid, the Realejo middlemen were clearing 30 reales of profit on each quintal.[46]

By 1647 the pitch trade had reached startling proportions. It had become so large that officialdom and the Crown had become interested and were searching for ways to share in the profits. The production around Nueva Segovia alone was between twenty-two and twenty-three thousand quintals per year. If Tegucigalpa is included the total production probably exceeded 30,000 quintals. The bishop of Nicaragua was the first to show interest. He complained that Nueva Segovia had always been such a poor town that little effort had been made to collect the tithes there. Now, with the enormous profits made there, the Crown, the bishop, and the cathedral were all losing money.[47]

The following year a secret report on the industry was sent to Spain. It was proposed that a royal contract asiento for brea be established. The author of the report, an Augustinian friar called Hernando de Abreu, stated that some 20,000 quintals of brea per year were exported to the vineyards of Peru to line the wine jugs and barrels. Some was also used in the shipyards. The King was losing significant amounts of revenue through his failure to monopolize and tax this industry. Besides, the friar believed, price and profits on brea were too high, and the King should lower them for the common good. A government monopoly would certainly lose money, for such monopolies, claimed this early defender of free enterprise, always did. The Crown should, therefore, seize control of the industry and then lease it to private individuals for a fee or a percentage. Abreu believed that a fairly useful control could be established for counting the amounts of pitch involved. One pound of pitch was needed for each botija or jar of wine. Peruvian botijas, usually about four times as large as those of Castile, carried approximately one arroba of wine. So one pound of brea was needed for each arroba of wine. Such calculations gave Abreu his total of 20,-000 quintals. Peru was supplying many regions, he argued. To supply Chile, Paraguay, Tucumán, La Plata, Santa Cruz de la Sierra, La Paz, Arequipa, and the distant parts of the bishopric of Lima must have taken, he believed, a million arrobas. Above that there was the brea needed for ships twice a year and home consumption in Peru, so 20,000 quintals was probably a conservative figure. And apart from a little in Campeche, Huatulco, and Nicoya, all this pitch was Nicaraguan. The highest price he had seen was 36 reales the quintal, of which 8 was freight and the rest production costs and pure profit. Often merchants were paid for their pitch in wine, which they then took back with them to sell in New Spain for another large profit. Such extravagant trades needed royal regulation.[48]

As far as is known little was done except for a few attempts to tighten the collection of export and import duties. The trade continued to be large, and in time began to create its own social institutions. The vecinos of Nueva Segovia gradually assumed tight control of the brea industry. In 1663 the city and its jurisdiction was described as having 1,127 tributary Indians and many Spaniards, most of whom spent much of their time on their farms. A corregidor or alcalde mayor was badly needed, this report said, because Nueva Segovia was far from the central authorities of Nicaragua in León, and the local vecinos had stepped into the governmental vacuum and had gained "such power that they are the government, so that there is none of the necessary equality either in justice or in the distribution and election of offices." Moreover, the report added, the town had become the "most commercial" part of the province, yet little sales tax (alcabala) was ever collected and an inspector was sent about once in five years.[49]

Some officials managed to obtain a share of the profits by extra-legal means, but otherwise little was done to break up the vecinos' control. In 1677 the alguacil mayor of the city, obviously a member of a dissident faction, was complaining that of the five regidores of the city three were close relatives, and these three dominated elections and other functions. The Audiencia ordered this clique to be broken up.[50]

Another feature of the Nueva Segovia brea industry was heavy pressure on Indian labor. These Indians, by this time debt peons for the most part, escaped in large numbers into Honduras, where they settled in the jurisdiction of Tegucigalpa. Although the unwitting Indians had leapt from the brea frying pan into the silver mining fire, the Tegucigalpa Spaniards, even more pressed for labor than those of Nueva Segovia, often gave the refugees a kind welcome, and sought to protect them from those in Nicaragua who tried to obtain their return. Some, of course, were probably put to work in the same brea industry which they had hoped to escape, for Tegucigalpa was second only to Nueva Segovia in the trade.[51]

The destruction of the pine woods involved meant that the pine pitch industry was to be short-lived. The invasion of the Pacific by the English and French pirates in the 1680s only emphasized the decadence of the trade. As usual, the pirates were given undue credit for the fall in commerce. It is noticeable that after their departure the industry did not revive. By then Peru had probably found other sources of supply.[52]

Nueva Segovia's moment of prosperity had gone, and it soon joined the other depressed areas of the Audiencia as a rural area of maize and cattle. Trade in Realejo, and indeed on the whole stretch of coast between the Gulf of Fonseca and Panama, was to revive somewhat in the last years of the century.[53] So too did the sailings between Granada and Cartagena-Portobelo via the Desaguadero, a route in use since the early days of Spanish settlement.[54] But Nicaragua had failed to find a dynamic product and had in fact become little more than a larger Costa Rica, an appendage and supply center for the more vital, busy area at Panama.

15

The Currency Crisis

By the middle years of the seventeenth century the economic depression had reached its greatest intensity. Trade even in wine and olive oil had slowed down to a trickle, and contact with the mother country, indeed between the various parts of Central America, had become infrequent and often indirect. The disappearance of trade and exportable products, plus the continuing, even if diminished need for imports from Europe and Peru, precipitated a currency and coinage crisis which conveniently marks the most severe part of the depression.

The minting of money in the New World began officially in 1536 with the setting up of a royal mint in Mexico. This institution coined silver pieces of 4 reales, 2 reales, 1 real, medios, and cuartillos, all approximately circular coins with the arms of Castile and León stamped on one side. Peru began to mint coins 32 years later in 1568, followed shortly thereafter by Potosi.

In the early years of the seventeenth century, perhaps because of lack of molds and other equipment at first, and then later from habit, coins of irregular shape and varying weights began to be issued. These were the famous macacos or macuquina money. On these crude coins the stated value and a rough coat of arms were often hammered in or punched on bit by bit, rather than being imprinted by a mold.

Mexico, closer to central control and probably more carefully governed, soon returned to more or less legal and respectable methods of producing coinage. Peru, in spite of repeated royal admonitions, continued to issue macacos and other crude coins for more than 150 years (until about 1774).

Also circulating in seventeenth-century Spanish America was moneda cortada, fractions of pieces of eight. This "cut money" had been divided by means of a cold chisel or other implement into 4 parts to make values of 2 reales. Below moneda cortada was moneda recortada, usually worth a real but sometimes, because of its battered and debased condition, even less. Central America did not obtain a mint of its own until 1774 and all these coins circulated there.[1]

While trade was flourishing, with cacao flowing to New Spain and hides, indigo, silver, and other lesser products leaving for Europe, there seems to have been an adequate supply of coinage for normal marketing and payroll purposes. As the depression worsened, however, Central America experienced the problem of finding a supply of money. Basically colonial economies of a rather small scale such as that of Central America depended on gold and silver currency. Token coinages such as cacao beans could not fill the gap unless strongly backed by precious metals. Nor was there a temporary buffer such as is provided today by paper money and letters of credit. Other types of negotiable credit instruments were still relatively new, and in any case they required a scale of economic transactions beyond that of seventeenth-century Central America. In short, the supply of money necessary to keep commerce and the general economy at an acceptable level was the same thing as the supply of gold and silver. If these two metals could not be mined or imported in sufficient quantities, the flow of monetized goods, and then the economy, was bound to turn down.

Central America's first problem was that the precious metals tended to drain away. As in Mexico, large quantities left the area for Spain as the Crown took its revenues not spent on local administration, derived from its share of mining, the tribute, monopolies, fines, and other taxes. Royal officials, amassing wealth as quickly as they could, also remitted large sums, much of it no doubt coming from royal moneys not taken to Spain by the Crown, in the hopes of one day returning to the metropolis to enjoy their wealth. Creoles and Spaniards not directly connected with the Crown or with officialdom also sent large sums in the hopes of one day visiting the mother country or settling there. Juros and other pensions payable out of the royal treasuries of Central America to persons who had never lived there further increased the drain of specie. Moreover, Central America's mining industry, mostly centered around Tegucigalpa by this time, was tiny compared to that of Mexico or Peru, so that Mexico's lack of coinage in the seventeenth century was never as severe as that of Central America, small though the region's remittances were in comparison.[2]

To compound this unfortunate state of affairs, Central America's balance of trade with Mexico gradually swung from being an extremely favorable one at the height of the cacao industry in the 1570s to being a very unfavorable one. The decisive era seems to be the 1620s, after the entry of Guayaquil cacao as a major source for the Mexican market. Central America, especially Guatemala, continued to look to Mexico for many items, particularly cloth from its obrajes and Chinese goods, whereas Mexico, except for the famous horses of Chiapas and a little indigo, needed very little in return. Moreover, after the Spanish fleets stopped calling regularly at the ports of the Gulf of Honduras, many of Central America's exports were forced to travel to Spain and other parts of Europe via Veracruz, and these goods were forced to pay freight and taxes, often in specie, as they passed through. Mexican traders who found little to interest them in the Santiago market visited with far less frequency after the second and third decades of the century. Instead they began to demand payment in coinage for the goods which they sent there. In the case of cloth Central America was at a great disadvantage because the availability of abundant, cheap Mexican cloth seems to have inhibited the local development of textile mills.[3]

Central America found, then, that its exports were unwanted in Mexico, the area where reliable coinage was minted, while at the same time the small amounts of gold and silver which were mined locally were drained off to Spain and Mexico.

The other alternative was Peru, which had a superabundance of silver. Large quantities seem to have arrived in Central America in the sixteenth century. Peru had not yet diversified economically. Its only product of any significance was silver, and it had to pay for slaves, cacao (before about 1590), ships' stores, and indigo. By 1600, however, Peru was rapidly becoming self-sufficient in many items. Cacao and wood were being exported from Guayaquil, cloth was a growing industry in the Quito, Ambato, and Riobamba basins. And as Peru grew less dependent on produce from North America, it also began to produce goods other than silver, such as wine and oil, which Mexico and Central America urgently needed.

This shift in Peru's balance of trade was a slow process. Large sums of silver were shipped to New Spain and Central America before 1630, and between 1630 and 1660 wine and oil did not wholly pay for Peru's imports from the north.[4] But for Central America the implications were serious. It had enjoyed an abundance of silver and consequently of coinage up to 1630, but at the same time as it found that this supply was dwindling, Peru became increasingly capable of paying for her Central American imports with agricultural products of her own. Furthermore Peruvian coinage was often falsified, particularly after the establishment of a mint at Potosi, so that what little Peruvian currency Guatemala did receive after 1630 or so was often debased, sometimes even falsified, and inferior to that of Mexico.

By the middle years of the century the Audiencia of Guatemala was suffering from a severe shortage of coinage, and what little there was came from Peru and was of suspect quality. Coins less than a real disappeared entirely and increasingly the Audiencia of Guatemala was suffering from an inability to find a product which Peru was willing to pay for, just as in her trade with Mexico; this in part explains Guatemala's attempts to capitalize on the illicit nature of the large Chinese trade.[5]

In the Tegucigalpa area the situation was similar but the presence of silver mines created some peculiar difficulties and solutions. Payrolls had to be met periodically in the mines, but there was no local coinage, not even cacao, with which to do so. Beginning about 1649 local miners took to shaving thin slivers off bars of unstamped silver and using these illegal parings to pay workers and buy supplies. Once again the royal treasury found that it was the biggest loser, and promptly prohibited the practice; but banning these silver slices did nothing to solve the problem, so the Crown turned to more reasonable measures. The Nicaraguan treasury was instructed not to remit its moneys to Santiago for shipment to Spain, but to send them instead to Tegucigalpa for the purpose of buying up silver shavings, thus neatly gathering this illegal currency for the Crown, and providing a local currency. The coinage supply of the Nicaraguan treasury having proved inadequate, the Guatemalan treasury itself sent 6,000 pesos to withdraw the silver parings from circulation, but the official real of Tegucigalpa informed the Audiencia that at least 30,000 pesos in coins would be needed to complete the task. This large sum was not forthcoming and the local illegal currency of Honduras continued in use throughout the seventeenth and much of the eighteenth century.[6]

By 1650 the general situation in Central America was such as to involve the royal treasury and the officials of the Audiencia in Guatemala. As in Spain, tinkering with the coinage was assumed to be the most logical method of correcting difficulties. Since the Peruvian money found within the provinces of Central America was base and often imperfect it was decided to devalue it. The perulero peso worth 8 reales was declared to be worth only 6 thereafter, and the 4-real coin, usually known as the tostón, if from Peru to be worth only 3. This reform was first promulgated in 1650 but did not go into effect fully until 1653.[7]

The Crown's interest had been particularly drawn to the Central American case by an aberrant working of Gresham's law. ("When two coins are equal in debt-paying value, but unequal in intrinsic value, the one having lesser value tends to remain in circulation and the other to be hoarded or exported as bullion.") True, the superior coinage, the Mexican, went out of circulation through export and no doubt through some hoarding, and the inferior coinage, the perulero, remained in local circulation. After all there had been much more of it since Peruvian exports to Central America began. But through a variety of local circumstances the Peruvian coinage was also the one exported to the Crown in Spain, much to the disgust of that body. Part of the problem was that by the middle years of the century, most of Central America's legal exports went through Veracruz, and Mexican goods enjoyed a market in Central America while that area had little that was desired in Mexico. The merchants of Veracruz, Puebla, and Mexico, however, would only accept Mexican money, and not the debased perulero variety. As a result much of the perulero money was "dumped" on the royal treasury as the only means of disposing of it. The Crown complained that the need of the royal treasury for good coinage should take precedence over those of Mexican merchants, but supply and demand continued to dictate otherwise.[8]

A solution proposed by the fiscal of the Audiencia was to send all the perulero money to Tegucigalpa, where it could be refined into silver bars of adequate purity. The King would have to wait for his money, but at least when it finally did arrive in Spain he would not lose "one-third or more" of its face value. The same writer suggested that the King pay all of his debts in debased perulero coinage and thus foist it off on third parties.[9]

Other suggestions to solve the crisis were that tribute goods for sale at public auction be sold only for Mexican coinage or that tribute goods be sent directly to Spain in lieu of coinage. (If American produce such as indigo, cochineal, or cacao were auctioned off in Spain by the Crown instead of in the colony, the Crown would obtain much higher prices and profits from its tribute.) The most sensible proposal, perhaps, was that Peruvians should be obliged to stop producing and exporting such inferior coinage. Mexico, which could afford to take such a step, simply banned inferior perulero money and recalled it all for new refining, alleging that much of the poorest perulero money was actually made in Germany and elsewhere in Europe "with very little silver and much alloy."[10]

The problems associated with perulero money were compounded for the merchants of Central America by the unwillingness of their counterparts in other areas to accept it in exchange for goods. One of the few ways of getting rid of it was via the royal treasury. And of course it was put into the royal treasury worth 8 pesos but upon being melted down in Spain it lost at least one-quarter of its value. Yet if the Real Caja had not provided this outlet, many in Central America would have been totally ruined, with disastrous consequences, so some royal officials believed, for the general well-being of the republic. 1652 was a particularly bad year for the royal treasury in Guatemala. A slowly accumulated total of 100,000 pesos was sent to Spain, the King assuredly losing at least one-quarter of that amount. That same year, possibly as a reaction, the King ordered strict monetary reform in Peru.

Hence, then, the devaluation of 1653. The Crown felt that it could not afford to carry the trade deficits of the colony year after year. At the same time the Real Caja began to refuse to accept perulero money. The results were disastrous. Trade fell off as merchants lost confidence in coinage, for many refused to accept Peruvian money if the King would not and if it could not be dumped on the royal treasury. People began to hide good money for their Mexican needs "in such a way that there is none to be found in the markets or in trade." As a special concession, however, the Crown decided not to refuse Peruvian money from Indians, so as not to cause these lowly sectors of the population undue distress. This provided an outlet of a kind for the merchants. Perulero money was foisted onto the Indians and ended up in the royal coffers just as before.[11]

These early measures having failed, the next step was to declare the perulero money, increasingly known as moclones by this time, to be illegal and suppressed. Many who owned large hoards of silver lost heavily.[12] Coinage shortages increased as a consequence, and the authorities wavered between permitting the outlawed Peruvian coinage to be used, and prohibiting the export of all coinage of any kind beyond the confines of the Audiencia of Guatemala, with further loss of confidence in coinage as a result. On one occasion the ayuntamiento of Santiago asked permission to send its annual payments in tinta añil to prevent the shortage of coinage from becoming more acute. Local people were capriciously prosecuted for using some coins and hoarding others. Finally, after several twists, moclones were banned altogether in 1661.[13]

The period from about 1655 until about 1670 saw Central America's coinage shortage at its height. Only 2-real coins were permitted, and the moclones from Peru, besides being illegal, had lost in prestige to the point of being worthless. Further royal decrees ordering their confiscation did little to help. Government nervousness reached such an extreme in 1663 that it was proclaimed that even the recognized Peruvian 2-real coins were to be suspended from use until they had been retested, the good ones separated from the bad, and restamped. The 2-real coin had been the one most widely used in the region after the official disappearance of the moclones.[14] The mid-century wave of debasements, suspensions, and revaluations of the coinage, during the period of deep economic depression, further exacerbated the situation, and helped to provoke a profound crisis which damaged exports, destroyed internal trading, and even weakened security and confidence in the governmental order. Little wonder that when the crisis passed people began to look outside the Spanish commercial system for their coins and imports.

After the desperate situation of the 1660s the situation eased. Peruvian money continued to come in, legal or not, and the Crown, increasingly desperate for money of any sort, gradually relaxed restrictions. In a cédula of 1677 the king declared that the royal moneys shipped to Spain could be either Mexican or Peruvian, and could include the suspect 2-real coins, where before such shipments had been limited to tostones of 4 reales, and pesos of 8. The ayuntamiento and the Audiencia began to encourage the use of Peruvian moclones, the worthless macaca money, because it was "usual and current."[15] A "take what you can get," laissez-faire attitude superseded the previous one of attempted supervision.

Guatemala continued to have severe monetary problems, basically a lack of coinage, with much of what there was in a debased, unreliable state. A shortage of some dimensions seems to have struck the region between 1719 and 1729, but the difficulties of this nature were never again as severe as they had been during the depths of the depression in the seventeenth century.[16]

By the late 1630s, then, the economic depression had become obvious to all. Cacao had declined irreversibly, the silver mines of Honduras were obviously not going to compete with Zacatecas or Potosi, indigo was not as yet fulfilling the hopes of its developers, lesser crops such as sarsaparilla, vanilla, or cochineal were too minor or too heavily cultivated in other regions to bring prosperity, and attempts to steal the entrepôt trade of rival areas, such as the trajín of Panama or the China trade of Acapulco, had failed. Even the coinage was increasingly suspect and attempts to correct it only made the situation worse.

The Audiencia of Guatemala had proved unable to find a strong unifying export product. Not only that, but attempts to halt the steady decline had further fragmented the area under its jurisdiction. Guatemala's protectionist attempts to exclude Guayaquil cacao had enraged the merchants of Nicaragua and further exacerbated the growing rivalry between Granada and León. Criado de Castilla's attempt to provide the Audiencia with an adequate port on the Caribbean had dismayed the settlers of Comayagua, San Pedro, and Gracias a Dios in Honduras. Neglect had so annoyed the few settlers in Costa Rica that they repeatedly asked to be transferred to the jurisdiction of Tierra Firme.

Many of the subregions withdrew into rusticity, with the self-contained small landowner or hacendado as a dominant feature of social and economic life. Such areas exported little, and what was sent outside their confines usually consisted of domesticated animals, basic crops, or their immediate by-products.

In one or two localities the search for a wealth-producing export crop continued, and in some of these areas such a product was discovered; in no case, however, was this discovery of sufficient importance to transcend the needs of the circumscribed locality where it was grown or elaborated. Pine pitch in Nueva Segovia and Realejo was not an export of sufficient dynamism to restore the lost prosperity of Izalcos or even Santiago, but such regional or provincial exports do account for the one or two local exceptions which we find, thus explaining isolated areas of relative commercial prosperity in a time of general economic depression.

The period between mid-century and the 1680s found Central America fragmented, rural, agricultural, and isolated. The search for wealth had failed, and nearly all Spaniards and Creoles had admitted it. Any new prosperity would have to be based on some vast new readjustment, and, above all, on the introduction of new sources of demand and new methods of disposing of produce.

16

Men and Land in Mid-Century; Contraction and Isolation

By the 1650s Central America was the result of a long series of problems. Early slaving and gold panning was less than a memory. The area's greatest resource as far as the conquerors were concerned—its large autochthonous populations—had all but vanished on the coasts and in the lowlands, and, while still far more numerous than the Spaniards, Creoles, and castas in the highlands, even there they were but a remnant of their former numbers. Central American entrepreneurs and farmers found that as a result the encomienda was a precarious source of wealth, but those who depended on the Crown's Indians for labor were also disappointed. Some had sought to solve their problems, at least in part, by switching from cacao to indigo; but while this change had the advantage of avoiding the labor trap—indigo required less labor than cacao—at the same time it extended trade routes to the other side of the Atlantic. So indigo, unlike sixteenth-century cacao, had to be sent such a distance to market that it had great difficulty in showing a profit. Most of Central America's other products, hides, arnatto, or cochineal to name but three, faced similar problems, or were held back by the competition of cheaper, more abundant rival producing areas. To make matters worse, the mother country compounded these problems by failing to produce enough ships and fleets, by declining economically and thus failing to provide satisfactory markets or enough manufactured goods for the colonies, and by proving unequal, at least before the late 1680s, to the task of keeping the Caribbean free from the freebooters and pirates who made use of the unoccupied islands and empty beaches.

These difficulties brought on a prolonged period of experimentation. Indigo growers sought freedom from taxation or escape from the restrictions imposed on the use of Indian labor. Government officials, both in Santiago and in the provincial cities, cast

Figure 29   Political Divisions in the Audiencia of Guatemala, c. 1685,
Showing Spanish Towns

around for alternatives to the dying trades, which would bring back
prosperity. Still optimistic, they tried to sponsor new plantations, to
capture trades or trade routes from other colonies, and to regulate
the use of ports and labor more carefully. They failed. By 1635 it
was apparent that the forces which were bringing these problems to
Central America were largely beyond the control of the people of
that day: Social engineering and governmental intervention and
regulation had little discernible effect on the declining trade patterns.

Within the colony itself the new elites were caught in a demographic and price scissors similar to that of medieval Europe after 1348. While they, still mostly city dwellers, increased in numbers because of immigration and a high birthrate, the food suppliers, the Indians, became fewer. City Spaniards had begun to complain about the Indians' inability to supply the cities with maize, beans, charcoal, and cloth as early as the 1550s. After the epidemics of the late 1570s the situation became much worse.

Some of these supply difficulties should have been soluble by altering the Spanish diet. Even more meat and less cereals was one possibility. Cattle had grown rapidly in numbers since the conquest; indeed their demographic advance was related to the decline of the Indians: both competed for land and nutrients. In the last quarter of the sixteenth century, however, there is evidence that the cattle population had also passed a demographic crisis and was falling. Indiscriminate slaughtering and poor husbandry no doubt contributed to this turn of events, but many of the reasons for it remain mysterious.

At the very time when city Spaniards found that their incomes from encomiendas, cacao, indigo, and other trades were shrinking, the price of foodstuffs in the cities rose rapidly, and the supply shrank. Once again the response was regulation. Municipal ordinances tried to fix prices and wages. Herds were better tended and municipal warehouses and slaughterhouses were built, but governmental intervention had as little success as in the export trades.

City dwellers set about finding individual solutions to the many problems posed by the age in which they lived. Many escaped the high prices and food shortages of the cities, and the inability of the Indians to supply them with a comfortable level of living, by leaving the cities and taking up rural land for subsistence or semi-commercial farming. Much of the countryside was without landowners because of the deaths of so many of its former inhabitants; in such cases the new occupants were able to buy title by paying the indigent Crown. In other cases the settlers tricked, bullied, or persuaded Indians into yielding their lands.

Related to this flight to the countryside was the beginning of a change in the labor relationship between Spaniards, the castas, and the Indians. To an increasing degree the subordinate classes and races became related to their places of work on an individual rather than an official basis. Informal arrangements such as debt peonage or "adscritos" tended to replace encomienda and even repartimiento. It can be cautiously asserted that sometimes Indians may have preferred these new relationships to the former burdened life of the tributary village.

As yet the flight to the countryside had not produced the manorial estate. A few wheat and cattle farms and sugar plantations were able to profit from the proximity of larger cities and thus to run commercial operations. Most Spaniards, however, retired to a rather squalid self-sufficiency on the chacras y bohíos, supported by a few mules and a handful of peons.

Flight to the countryside added another important variable to the question of which Indian groups were to survive and which were to be absorbed. The higher and poorer the land, the more Indians were left to themselves during the depression. Western Guatemala, Verapaz, and Chorti and Pokomam pockets in Eastern Guatemala probably felt less pressure from Spaniards than they had in the sixteenth century. The inhabitants of fertile and lower areas may have felt more pressure than ever—on their lands, religions, and cultures—although the new pressures differed from those of the sixteenth century.

If further evidence is needed of the decline it can be found by examining local and coastal commerce. As mid-century approached Spanish officials and settlers found themselves unable to maintain a steady supply of such essentials as oil, wine, or currency. The lack of currency, and the debasement and falsification of what little that was present, led to devaluations and restampings. These measures were carried out in a halfhearted manner by a badly shaken government, which led to a loss of trade confidence at the local level. The result was a fall in volume and a return to cacao and barter, the latter a much less efficient method of trading. Money hoarding and coinage dumping (usually on the royal coffers) heightened the crisis and constrained entrepreneurial activity.

The approach of the depression fragmented Central America economically and socially. We have already seen its differential effect on Indian society. Now the various Spanish subregions began to go their separate ways. Contacts between the large centers of Santiago and Granada and peripheral colonies such as Chiapas, Soconusco, Nicoya, or Costa Rica became even less frequent than before. Some areas, notably Nueva Segovia, discovered local trades which brought a fair measure of local and transient prosperity. Other areas, emphasizing local activities, began to develop coherent, divergent local cultures. Central Honduras became an area of folk miners, no longer dependent on Guatemala or Nicaragua, and increasingly different from either.

By the middle of the century, then, the various parts of Central America had drawn apart. Government had lapsed into a new laissez-faire. Much of the area had developed a new agrarian self-sufficiency of poverty, and international and interregional trade and communication had all but disappeared.

Previous chapters have indicated that the flourishing encomienda of the third quarter of the sixteenth century was severely weakened as an institution by heavy population loss. By 1600 it was no longer a major source of wealth or even labor for the dominant Spanish and Creole class. Yet the encomienda did not entirely disappear. As the depression in Central America deepened and sources of income disappeared, desperate Creoles were eager to turn to the encomiendas, meager though they were, to add to their slender incomes. Those who tried this solution, of course, were Creoles of the poorer sort who were afraid of slipping back into the despised, rootless middle group of artisans, rural mayordomos, castas, and vagabonds.[1]

The appeals to the Crown for help from this class caused a change in the nature of the encomienda and, after a fashion, revived it as an institution. In the early part of the seventeenth century it is obvious that royal policy was to stifle the encomienda so that it would gradually disappear. The number of new encomiendas granted fell with each decade as encomienda holders died or moved away and the vacant grants reverted to the Crown. Between 1602 and 1612, about 55 new grants were made. In the following decade this total fell to 34, and between 1632 and 1642 only 9 awards were made. In the second half of the century, however, the trend was reversed. Between 1662 and 1672 the authorities awarded 29 grants, and in the following decade 25. An examination of these grants shows that they were not true encomienda grants of the sixteenth-century kind. Rather the institution had become a means whereby the King swelled the rolls of those to whom he gave grants of ayudas de costo. The encomienda system, or at least new grants of encomiendas at the local Central American level, had become a way of giving pensions to indigents of the conquering class. Of the 25 grants between 1672 and 1682, 8 were to widows of deserving beneméritos.[2]

It is not to be thought that such occasional benevolence on the part of the Crown satisfied the poorer class of Creoles. For one thing the encomienda compared most unfavorably as a source of income with the major posts which the King and his higher officials could award. For another, even at this late date the local petitions were not receiving all, or even the best, of the available encomienda grants. There were two reasons for this.

Many of the larger grants were never allowed to fall vacant. The original owners renewed them far beyond the prescribed "two lives," or the King reawarded them immediately when they became vacant. When these large encomiendas did become vacant, however, the King usually did not reassign them to Central Americans. Sometimes the awards went to powerful Mexicans to provide them with supplementary incomes or pensions.[3] More often they were given to courtiers or members of the great noble houses in Spain itself. As a result of this policy, by 1650 many of the larger encomiendas in Central America were owned by rich and powerful men in Spain, a fact that caused great complaint and resentment among indigent Creoles.[4]

Even the larger encomiendas were but a shadow of what they had once been. Not enough detailed study has been made of the institution in the seventeenth century, but one revealing document about Chimaltenango allows us to see some of the factors which were causing decline.

The cabecera and anexos which formed the parish of Santa Ana Chimaltenango had once been very large and populous but had lost population throughout the sixteenth century. By the late seventeenth century it was still one of the largest villages in highland Guatemala, and indeed in Central America, but the income to be derived from it was much less than it had been. The encomienda was owned by Luis Nieto de Silva, who had inherited it from his mother, the Countess of Alba. Neither the countess nor her son had ever seen Guatemala and the resident administrator, Captain Joseph Aguilar Rebolledo, was therefore obliged to give an accounting every so often. In the sixties collecting the tribute had been extremely difficult. There had been locust invasions and general economic depression. At one time (1664) he had found that the tribute was three years in arrears and had collected what was owing only after "great difficulty." In fact the good captain had used the usual Creole tactic of jailing the Indian caciques and principales until the debt was paid up by the villagers.

After 1670 it appears that the Indian population began to recover, but this was of little help to the countess or her son. During the lean years of mid-century, when the Indian population and the fortunes of the royal house of Spain were both at their nadir, all the Central American encomiendas had become encumbered with various payments, taxes, and obligations. Every needy institution that had the power to do so had taken a slice of encomienda income during these years; and once such practices were started by the financially embarrassed Crown, it seldom stopped them. As a result

a high percentage of the income from the Chimaltenango encomienda was disbursed and dispersed to other sources before
reaching the encomendero. Nor did the encomendero enjoy the
freedom of action and decision which he had in the sixteenth century. Restrictions were numerous, and supervision from the authorities was more careful. In 1667, for example, a plague had struck
Chimaltenango, and the mayordomo had found himself responsible
for the cost of the doctor and medicines. He was also forced to feed
the invalids during the epidemic. As Captain Aguilar explained
bitterly to the absentee owner, "I state further that I performed this
service, not only because it was my duty, but because I was ordered
to do so by President [of the Audiencia] Don Fernando de Escobedo."

In the 1680s there was a new plague of locusts, and several of
the Indians ran away. No doubt they were fleeing to nearby haciendas. As a result tribute payment again fell in arrears. In spite of
jailings and threats it was impossible to collect all the arrears for the
years 1684–86. Part of the problem had been, of course, that as the
population slowly grew, the encomendero and the government had
tried to derive more income from the encomienda. This might have
been possible in the sixteenth century, but in the 1680s there were
too many haciendas to which an overburdened Indian could escape.[5]

In short, by the middle of the seventeenth century, indeed long
before in most parts of Central America, the large encomienda had
been "tamed." Most tribute income was going to the Crown and the
Church.[6]

The second factor which annoyed the poorer Creoles of Central America was that even the smaller encomienda grants were not
all distributed in the way which they would have liked. Preference
tended to be given to those near the centers of power within Central
America. Chiapas and Costa Rica, the two most distant and peripheral provinces of Central America, were the most outraged. They
protested repeatedly that when new encomienda awards were made
near Cartago or Ciudad Real, they should be given to local people.
Instead many of them were going to influential vecinos of Santiago
or Granada. Such injustices added further to the growing friction
and inter-provincial rivalry in Central America. Localism and sepa-
ratism received new support.[7]

After the early 1680s the granting of encomiendas, even in the
"second life" began to fall once again. The granting of an encomienda was still one way of giving a royal pension, but by the late

seventeenth century there were better ways of doing even that.[8]

Other sources of recruiting labor also changed character during the depression. The repartimiento system suffered from the same basic problem as did encomienda, a declining labor force, and it had been unsatisfactory from the start. The same abuses continued. Many Indian villagers were reluctant to take their turn in the draft and illegally evaded it by bribing caciques or Creole recruiters. As a result commoners (macehuales) were called repeatedly, some to go great distances before they arrived at the appointed place of work.[9] Spanish officials, farmers, and other would-be employers of repartimiento labor found themselves in a quandary. As their needs grew the laboring population remained static or fell, and the royal laws prohibiting the employment of Indians in specified industries remained in force. These contradictory pressures were not resolved completely, but there were several attempts. The size of the legal draft in some Indian villages rose until it was sometimes as high as one quarter of the Indian male work force.[10] The effect that the absence of one quarter of the work force for 49 weeks per year would have on village agriculture can be imagined. Spanish employers resorted to various subterfuges to circumvent royal laws. Wheat farmers, who had a clear right to repartimiento labor, sometimes applied for a quota of Indian workers and then "rented" them to others in more doubtful industries for the week or two weeks which the repartimiento was supposed to last.[11] Others, the owners of indigo obrajes, textile obrajes, or sugar mills, where the use of repartimiento labor was illegal, masqueraded as wheat farmers in order to receive a quota of workers.[12] As had been the case before 1635, the compliance of the officials in charge of the repartimientos was a factor in all the frauds throughout the remainder of the seventeenth century. The post of juez de repartimiento remained one of the most lucrative possibilities for an aspiring Creole bureaucrat.[13]

Within each Indian village the repartimiento discriminated against the poor. It is also obvious that it discriminated geographically. In spite of the many complaints that Indians were forced to go great distances to their repartimiento work it is clear that the nearer a village was to a major Spanish city or agricultural settlement the more subject it would be to the pressures of the labor draft.

The implications for acculturation are apparent. Indian settlements distant from cities, such as those of Huehuetenango, or the more isolated mountain villages of Chiapas, did not bear a burden similar to that of the villages near Santiago or Ciudad Real, and so came into contact with Spaniards, their language, their crops, food, and agricultural techniques, far less frequently.

The seventeenth-century labor repartimiento of Central America, and especially of Guatemala, is a somewhat paradoxical institution. It never functioned smoothly, seldom legally, and from the beginning it was unpopular with employees and employers alike. Nevertheless, it seemed to have had a certain vitality when compared, for example, with the same institution in Mexico.[14] It may be that a proportionately greater number of Guatemala's Indians were in the Crown's hands rather than in the possession of private individuals. Or perhaps the need for repartimiento labor was greater in the valle around Santiago than it was in the valley of Mexico. Whatever the explanation, regular drafts of labor for farming and public works, and extraordinary drafts for such work as earthquake repairs or portering for an expedition into the Petén were prominent and frequent features of the entire seventeenth century in Central America. (A major attempt to abolish all repartimientos in 1671 seems to have failed, for there is firm evidence of large-scale official drafts in the 1680s and after.)[15]

As for the various types of peonage-debt, sharecropping, or tenant farming on the hacienda, it is obvious that these forms of labor grew in importance, and in the numbers of people involved in them, throughout the seventeenth century.[16] Moreover, it is also evident that the Crown and its administrators either became accustomed to the practice of adelantos—the advances of money or goods which brought on debt peonage—or resigned themselves to it, because the volume of legislation against adelantos which was such a feature of the 1620s and 1630s died down to a trickle.[17] Increasingly, officialdom's only concern became that Indians should not be tricked or coerced into signing contracts before or after mass. The thought of running such gauntlets was keeping Indians away from church. In this the civil officials were of course urged on by the clergy, particularly the energetic—indeed obstreperous—Bishop Andrés Navas y Quevedo.[18]

Other legislation favored peonage. The Audiencia reiterated its orders that Indians were to live where they wished as long as they paid the tribute.[19] Such laws meant that the efforts of village caciques and alcaldes or the efforts of encomenderos to force Indians to return to their villages could have little effect as long as their new masters, the landowners, paid the tribute. It is also obvious that Indians from many villages took advantage of such an ability to move away from the village. Just as in the early part of the century, when Indians were offered a choice between village and hacienda they usually chose the hacienda—obviously the lesser of two evils.[20] Of course if the Indian could not find a protector, usually a Spanish landowner, and was a true vagrant, then the law would support his being forced to return to his village—if he could be caught.[21]

On the margins of these greater systems—encomienda, repartimiento, and the various forms of peonage—there survived a series of local obligations and labor impositions, which while not general in character must have caused strains for the villages on which they were imposed. Some priests in the rural areas, for example, continued to make use of Indian tamemes or porters on their long pastoral journeys through the mountains. Gage himself found this to be common practice in the early years of the century, and frequent admonitions against it thereafter seem to have had little effect.[22] An occasional friar went even further and made use of his position in the village, not only to profit from the usual tributes of money and goods which the Indians and their ayuntamiento were obliged to pay, but also to acquire a retinue of unpaid and badly overworked personal servants. The priest of the village of Nacaome was accused of these kinds of abuses in 1672.[23]

Officials also used their positions to impose personal and private services on the Indians, and because the offenders were officials it was often several years before such injustices were discovered and abolished. These impositions ranged all the way from regular extortions to trivial exactions. On May 5, 1713, for example, the Indians of the barrio of La Candelaria of the village of Santa Inés del Hortelano complained that for some time they had been forced to provide weekly supplies of butter and suet to all the alcaldes and officials of the ayuntamiento of Santiago. They had realized that such a tribute was not legal and were now appealing to have it done away with.[24] Similar, but more nearly legal, was the requirement imposed by the ayuntamiento of Santiago on the villages of San Juan Amatitlán and Petapa. They were to bring Friday's supply of mojarras (a fresh water fish) to the city every Thursday. The Indians of Jocotenango were charged in a like fashion with keeping the city supplied daily with its needs in suet.[25]

Other officials broke the repartimiento laws more flagrantly. On April 10, 1681, three prospectors from Cartago, Juan Sáenz (a relative of the governor), Francisco Fernández de Miranda (the alguacil mayor of the city), and Juan de León informed the governor, Juan Saénz Vázquez, that they had discovered new and important gold washings in the appropriately named Río del Oro in the

valley of Santa Clara. They officially registered their strike as a mine
and asked that they be assigned a repartimiento of Indians to work
it. (The three prospectors obviously knew that such a request was
against the law; they were most fervent in promising to pay their
Indians a good wage and see that they received a proper diet.)
Governor Sáenz Vázquez insouciantly and officially acceded to this
illegal petition and granted the three men the services of 8 Indians
from Pacaca, 6 from Barba, 8 from Asserí, 8 from Curridabat, 2 from
Orosí, 2 from Ujarraz, and 2 from Güaicaci [sic]; 36 Indians in a
labor-starved colony for an illegal activity.[26]

One of the more interesting of the petty illegal impositions was
discovered in 1686, and so scandalized the King that he issued a
royal decree on the subject. "The custom should cease entirely,"
said Charles the Bewitched, whereby Indians of the village of Man-
guera had been obliged to supply several free fanegas of oysters at
Lenten time to the alcalde mayor of Tegucigalpa. The response of
the isolated epicurean to this sign of personal disfavor from his
monarch is not recorded.[27]

In a time of labor scarcity there was, as is to be expected,
attempts to recruit outside labor. On the question of importing
African slaves, Central Americans remained as ambivalent as ever.
At times individuals or institutions would hesitate. There were more
than enough lawless castas in the countryside, they felt, and to add
to them and to the troublesome cimarrones made little sense. On
other occasions local officials saw the importation of slaves as one
solution to the depression. If only a reliable work force could be
created, then, they argued, decayed industries such as gold panning
or silver mining could be revived. Using these kinds of arguments
the ayuntamiento of Santiago petitioned the Crown to subsidize the
importation of 500 African slaves per year.[28]

The decline of Central America's export industries has already
been examined, and it was obviously caused by a series of connected
phenomena. The importation of slaves would have been at best a
partial solution. At any event the plan was not possible. The Crown
was too financially embarrassed to pay for 500 slaves a year, and few
Central American entrepreneurs of the 1660s or 1670s had the
capital to pay for them or the resources to support them during the
dead season on the indigo plantations. As a result, the importation
of African slaves dropped to almost nothing after 1635 and did not
revive until the last decade of the century.[29]

The other obvious solution was to incorporate previously unconquered Indian groups into the laboring population. Such a prac-

tice had been common since the conquests, which were of course the leading examples of this method. These new conquests, known by some as entrada y saca, had some advantages and several disadvantages when compared with the purchase of African slaves. First of all there was no initial purchase price. Then the Indians who had been "brought out" could be settled near Spanish cities or farms in their own agricultural villages. Thus when they were not working for Spaniards or Creoles they could be returned to these villages where their food, clothing, and housing would be their own responsibility.

In a time of depression, however, the disadvantages must often have been greater. Expeditions into unconquered, unknown areas, most of which were tropical and unhealthy, were expensive to prepare and conduct. Arms had to be bought; soldiers had to be recruited with cash or promises of future advantages; Indian porters who were usually reluctant to leave the safety of their villages for encounters with indios bravos had to be obliged to join in. Even more important than initial cost was the results which these entradas y sacas were likely to yield. The "unreduced," tropical forest Indians were not to be compared with the sedentary, agricultural Quichés, Tzendales, or Pipiles. Attempts to make them live in villages often failed, either because they ran off at the first opportunity or because they died of the cultural or microbial shock of meeting the Western world for the first time. Even if they survived in their new villages, these tropical Indians did not make good workers.[30]

The greatest problem of all was the antipathy of the Crown and the Church to such poorly disguised slaving expeditions. Would-be adelantados or leaders of such expeditions found it hard to recruit Creole soldiers unless they promised them an encomienda of the newly captured Indians. The local missionary orders detested such conquests. They believed, correctly or incorrectly, that the only true conquests were peaceful ones, and that soldiers should not enter the unconquered areas unless the friars had already tried and found the Indians to be unchangeably hostile. The Crown was somewhat less idealistic but believed in peaceful conquests if possible, and in exempting newly pacified Indians from tribute and other obligations as a means of winning their allegiance and of making the transitional period in the new village less traumatic for them. Because of these strong objections from Church and Crown it was difficult to raise entradas of this kind. Most of them before the last two decades of the century were opportunistic, barely legal sorties which advanced feeble excuses, usually of the revenge kind, as reasons for their existence. Thus, if a friar were killed on the frontier or while on a missionary venture among "wild" Indians, if some soldiers or settlers were attacked on the frontier between the unsettled and the pacified areas, then an opportunistic local governor or alcalde mayor might hastily raise a band, punish the Indian ringleaders, and "bring out" a few dozen or a few hundred Indians to be settled nearby, all before instructions had arrived from the Crown. The King could hardly object to his loyal subjects avenging the brutal murder of a saintly missionary, and so such punitive expeditions usually won reluctant ex post facto approval from the central government.[31] On at least one occasion there were serious allegations of fraud. One governor of Costa Rica was accused of having invented an Indian rebellion so that he could attack and secure a fresh supply of Indian laborers.[32]

Entrada y saca was never a major method of recruiting seventeenth-century labor. It was obviously less efficient then the various forms of peonage and it was always of doubtful legality and morality. When the need for a larger labor force increased in the last decade of the seventeenth century and in the first twenty years after 1700, the number and intensity of these slave raids—for they were little better than that—increased, but, as will be seen, increased effort did not bring appreciably better returns.

After 1635 the patterns of land occupancy closely followed those of the previous half century. The former occupants of the cities continued to take up rural land by a variety of methods. Some simply petitioned for title to empty lands and were usually given what they wanted for a small consideration.[33] The Crown was too short of ready capital to raise strong scruples about such an outwardly harmless custom and was assured of a small income from these requests via the long series of composiciones.[34]

Other farmers expanded their holdings by encroaching upon neighboring land, some of it occupied, some vacant. Farmers were adept at filling in the unoccupied gaps between their holdings or at running cimarron cattle through a neighbor's maize plantings, especially if he were an Indian or an insignificant member of the castes. Cattle invasions brought protests throughout the seventeenth century, and no doubt many small holders lost heart, settled with the intrusive neighbor, and moved off.[35] Many farmers encroached on Indian lands. Probably most of these cases never came to court. If they did Creoles tried to take advantage of the lack of sophistication of the villagers. Spanish or Creole litigants would petition the courts to oblige the Indians to show their titles or their latest certification of compliance with the most recent composición decree, knowing full well that in a high percentage of cases the guileless Indians would be unlikely to possess either kind of paper.[36]

The movement to the countryside seems to have eased the problem of food supplies in the cities, at least until the new and different crisis of the last two decades of the century. At any event, officials were obviously less worried about the problems of supply and distribution. The reasons for this slight improvement can only be guessed at, but part of the explanation may have been better organization. Warehousing, price controls, inspection of food markets, and the prohibition of hoarding, monopolizing, and the indiscriminate slaughter of cattle may well have helped to improve the situation, at least marginally.[37] Most of the explanation may be much simpler. After many of the Spanish vecinos had moved to the countryside, either temporarily or permanently, many of them began to be able to feed themselves. Thus the quantities which the Indian communities and the commercial farmers had to send to the cities became less crucial.

By the middle years of the century it was obvious that most Spaniards were no longer living in cities. Only Santiago and Granada were showing any signs of growth, and that was slow considering the expanding Spanish populations.[38] Some of the cities, León in particular, may have fallen in numbers.[39] Most Creoles and castas lived in the countryside or in the Indian villages where their presence caused great vexation to the Indians and to the colonial authorities.[40] In general, the Crown and the Church deplored the flight to the countryside. It meant not only new and unobserved exploitation of the Indians, but also a decline in culture and formal piety on the part of the "Old Christians." Friars complained that isolated rural Spaniards were postponing baptism, living in concubinage, and sometimes dying without the consolations and extreme unction of the Church.[41] A local official replied to the Crown's questions about the emptiness of Cartago and the absence of its vecinos by pointing out that "they have nothing there but the bones of their ancestors and the treasury of your majesty."[42] The economic pressures which had driven so many to live in the countryside were more powerful than the admonitions or threats from the secular or religious authorities.

By a strange turn of fate, many Spanish cities now came to resemble the great ceremonial centers of the preconquest Maya. They remained empty during the week except for officials and the priestly caste, and filled up for one or two days per week as people arrived to exchange goods, drink alcohol, and attend obligatory festivals or religious ceremonies.

Once again it is worth emphasizing that most of the new farmers did not turn their holdings into commercial enterprises, at least not in the seventeenth century. They had retreated to these chacras and bohíos—both essentially derogatory terms denoting wretchedness and poverty at that time—to await better times and to survive hard ones. (In this they were, perhaps, microcosmic haciendas, in as much as the undeveloped hacienda has always played a major role as an asylum for non-developmental capital.) Moreover, most of the settlers had neither the available labor force or the capital necessary to mount profitable enterprises. Above all, there was an absence of large markets for commercial goods. The Central American cities were not manufacturing centers and were largely consumers of foodstuffs, but because transportation was slow most perishable foods could not be carried far. Except for cattle and sheep which could be driven to the cities on the hoof, this meant that most commercial farms had to be close to the Spanish cities. A distance of more than three or four day's journey meant that anything but animal husbandry or a little indigo was likely to be unsuccessful. Even indigo, as already noted, was usually mixed with subsistence crops or cattle. For many years in mid-century the ships from Europe did not arrive, and in still other years Spanish dye prices were so low and taxes on imports and exports so high that it was scarcely worth sending the indigo to the Gulf of Honduras, Granada, or Veracruz.

Most land grants were fairly small—4 caballerías might be about average—especially when compared with the much larger ones asked for and granted after 1695.[43] Most general pictures and descriptions of rural establishments describe poor housing, scrub cattle, a few plots of maize, rough food and clothing, a large Spanish family, and a few peons. This seems to have been the condition of most rural Spanish families until late in the century.[44]

Certainly some of the large wheat farms and sugar plantations near the villages of Amatitlán, Pinula, Petapa, San Pedro and San Juan Sacatepeques, and Mixco, all of which were dependent on the Santiago market, produced wealth for some. Gage was duly impressed in the twenties and thirties, and other observers throughout the century considered that they were solid enterprises and that their owners were among the wealthiest in Guatemala.[45] Raveneau de Lussan, Dampier, and the other pirates from the South Sea who sacked Realejo, León, and Granada in the 1680s praised some of the farms near Granada and the buildings on them.[46]

One group was able to find enough capital for agricultural development. The great monastic orders do not appear as major landholders until about 1600, but thereafter the growth of their establishments was rapid. The Mercedarians were granted sixteen caballerías near La Choluteca in 1607, a very large grant for the early seventeenth century.[47] Usually, however, the orders inherited their lands through the wills of the faithful. They also gained interest in some estates by lending money to indigent farmers. Some churchmen also bought or inherited farms as private individuals and then willed them to their religious order.[48] The Dominicans were also adept at "denouncing" tierras realengas and taking them over by means of composición. These growing estates were efficiently managed compared to those of private individuals—perhaps the availability of developmental capital made the difference.

The Jesuits seem to have been particularly enterprising. Their favorite combination was sugar, slaves, and day laborers. Their account books show no evidence of debt peonage. The slaves and day laborers seem to have been fed cheaply but efficiently on maize, beans, and salt. Wages for the free workers were low, and after they had paid for their food they left the Jesuit haciendas with precious little in the way of savings. Yet they did leave at the end of their contracts and there was no overt attempt to retain them. The sugar and its various derivatives went to Santiago.[49]

A sugar mill required far more initial capital than an indigo obraje or a cattle estancia, and as a result the great orders had established a near monopoly of the ownership of sugar plantations by the end of the century. The chronicler Fuentes y Guzmán, somewhat anticlercial at times, especially if peninsular priests or friars were involved, noted that of the eight sugar refineries in the Mesas valley (near Santiago) five belonged to the Church and only three to laymen. "As in all the other kinds of enterprises the greatest and best possessions are found in the hands of ecclesiastics, and few in the hands of laymen, so that men can scarcely find work for themselves."[50] Francisco Ximénez, a peninsular Dominican, resented such cuts and said defensively that it was not the fault of the orders that the faithful were wont to leave them such lands. It is obvious that Ximénez heartily wished that the orders would get rid of their estates. To him they were an encumbrance and an embarrassment.[51]

Complaints from indignant or jealous Creoles such as Fuentes y Guzmán seem to have reached the King's ear, however, for by 1687 he was expressing concern to the Audiencia at the quantities of lands and buildings belonging to the orders. How, he asked, could the wealth of the region be better distributed to allow Creole laymen to have a share in it?[52]

Yet, with the exception of a few farms close to the two major cities, and some heavily capitalized sugar plantations owned by the monastic orders there was little sign of entrepreneurial, capitalist enterprises in the Central American countryside in the seventeenth century. (Not a lack of will, to be sure; there was simply no way.) Most holdings were small and poor, and even many of the larger ones were deceptive. They did not yield much tangible income.

A case near Trujillo on the Caribbean coast startled a new arrival from Spain. A vecino of Trujillo, Mateo Ochoa, owned some thirty leagues of savannah and these grasslands held vast herds of cattle, so many that Ochoa could not guess at their numbers. Ochoa was obsessed with the dream of every good colonist. He wished to leave the colony and return to the metropolis, but to raise the cash for a life at court he had to sell his great estates. Nobody in Guatemala or Honduras could pay such a price, even when Ochoa reduced the price drastically and offered to throw in 100 slaves for nothing. The cattle were useful only for their hides, and Central America with its trade deficits had a shortage of coinage and other means of exchange. The factor which trapped some apparently wealthy men in the Indies was the problem of convertibility. Ochoa could find no way of converting "paper" Central American wealth into wealth that would be recognized in Spain. To buy land, houses, position, and titles in Castile he needed coin of the realm, silver, or gold. He could not find these things, and so Mateo Ochoa with his large untended estate was left to brood over it in the sickly port of Trujillo.[53]

Six large haciendas near the villa of Xerez de la Choluteca were in an even poorer situation. These six estates between them owned some 30,000 head of cattle. There was only a small local market for meat—even Granada and León were a little too far off, and they had their own herds. San Miguel and Tegucigalpa were small settlements. So hides were the principal product of value. La Choluteca, however, was on the "wrong" side of Central America for this trade, and the transportation of hides across the isthmus added to the costs and cut into profits. Moreover, the owners could not be sure when the fleets would arrive, or how many hides had been collected in any given year in Hispaniola, Cuba, and Jamaica. These six farms were therefore of a marginal importance in spite of the impressive size of the herds. The owners, although one can only guess, probably lived rustic lives devoid of the luxuries they craved, much as their less spectacular neighbors of the chacras y bohíos.[54]

Two results of the continuing occupation and use of the land by Europeans become increasingly obvious after 1635. The Spanish cities of the sixteenth and seventeenth centuries made new and different demands on the countryside. They consumed great quantities of wood for charcoal, and for furniture and decoration. Around Santiago, for example, the demand for wood was so constant that some Indian villages specialized in supplying it. One of the main employments in Almolonga was cutting wood for the city. In Tecpán-Guatemala carpentry was a leading trade and Santiago was the market. It was the Indians of this village who fashioned the large, rough, cedar boxes which were used for packing and dispatching indigo. The Indians of the village of San Cristóbal Amatitlán, who were rapidly becoming ladinos, specialized in providing heavy cedar beams for building construction. Such trades as the pine pitch exports of Nueva Segovia and the balsam extraction on the coast of San Salvador caused further destruction of tall ground cover. No doubt clearing of woods for cacao and sugar plantations also took place.[55]

The results of these new demands for wood were apparent by the late sixteenth century. Especially around the leading Spanish towns and the larger Indian villages the forests which the Spaniards had seen at the time of the conquest began to disappear. By the late eighteenth century it was noted that Tecpán-Guatemala was still supplying wood and carpentry work to Santiago, but the overburdened Indians of that village were now having to go "too far" to cut it.[56]

Yet another change to the landscape caused by the coming of the Spaniards was the damage caused by deep ploughing (for example in the wheat growing, hilly areas near Santiago and Cartago). Even more radical was the introduction of cattle and sheep. These animals grew remarkably in numbers and cropped the grass closely, especially the sheep. In the neighborhood of Santiago the damage caused by grazing was further exacerbated by a local variant of transhumance called "agostar." Just before the beginning of the rainy season it was the practice to burn off the vegetation cover in the valley bottoms. This destroyed old, tough, and dead grasses and brush, supplied the soil with nitrogens, and provided fresh new grass for the cattle when the rains came. While the valleys were being burned and until the new grasses sprouted, the cattle were grazed at higher elevations, usually on steep slopes.[57]

It can also be supposed that the Spanish occupation of the better lands in the hilly sections of eastern Guatemala pushed Indian cultivation to steeper slopes where soil was thinner. Sheet erosion and gullying were bound to result.

Evidence of these changes occurred first in the larger mountain towns which were set in small, poorly drained valleys. Santiago and Ciudad Real de Chiapas were little bothered by flooding in the sixteenth century, or if they were nobody reported it. Increasingly in the seventeenth century the diminished ground cover and vegetation, and the increased sheet erosion and exposure of hardpan meant that heavy rains could not be quickly absorbed. Both towns began to be plagued by flash flooding. Ciudad Real was particularly threatened because it was situated in a bottleneck at the narrow end of a valley. It was flooded in 1592, 1651, 1652, 1662, 1672, and 1676. In fact scarcely a rainy season went by without the threat of inundation.[58] Santiago suffered almost as badly. There were major floods there in 1685, 1688, 1691, and 1693. Each flood there meant extra labor for the Indians of the local villages, because special repartimientos were ordered to clean the streets after each flood.[59] Obviously the situation had reached a crisis by the early 1690s. The catastrophes were almost annual. Either the city would have to be moved to a new site or a solution to the flash flood problem would have to be found. In early 1699 the ayuntamiento of Santiago ordered the Indians of the barrio of Candelaria, adjacent to the city, to stop cultivating the slopes of the Cerro de Candelaria, "because they are destroying the trees and because the lands which they till are carried off by the rains, and the streets of the town get swept off."[60] A similar edict of 1701 was sent to the villagers of Magdalena Milpas Altas and San Miguel de las Milpas Altas, both close to Santiago. They were to stop cultivating the steep hillsides because they were disturbing water flow and causing streams to either dry up or flood.[61]

Erosion first became a problem in the mountainous parts of Central America in the seventeenth century, a time of demographic recession. Normally such a time would have allowed the recovery of populations and soils. But the destructive animals and techniques, plus the new indigo boom of the eighteenth century meant that Central American slopes were not granted a breathing space similar to the exhausted marginal fields of fourteenth-century Europe.

In the period before the 1630s some of the more significant variables affecting the degree of acculturation to which Indians would be subjected were: the comparative demographic size of Indian and Spanish populations in a given area; the presence or absence of a monocultural boom such as cacao; proximity to or distance from Spanish cities; intensive plantations, or much frequented routes of communications. To these factors must be added elevation, for Spaniards generally shunned the higher and colder parts of Chiapas, western Guatemala, and to a much lesser extent, central Honduras. Yet another critical variable, as we have already seen is where Spaniards chose to settle when they first started to occupy the rural areas in large numbers between 1576 and the 1630s.

Between the 1630s and the last decade of the seventeenth century the land settlement tendencies which were apparent earlier received new emphasis, indeed became irreversible. By mid-century it had become apparent that certain parts of Central America were destined to be Spanish-speaking and ladino, while others, the mountain redoubts, would remain, not exactly Indian but at least modified, colonial peasant, speaking Indian languages.

The issue had been decided on the coasts and in Nicaragua long before the seventeenth century. There, the slaving of the first twenty years and the epidemics of the thirties, forties, and seventies had reduced the number of aboriginal inhabitants to a remnant which was too small to be a basis for future recovery. When Spaniards, mulattoes, and mestizos began to occupy the rural areas at the turn of the century the remaining Indians were soon absorbed into the general mestizo or ladino populations. Seventeenth century descriptions refer to these areas as Spanish-speaking and ladino. Nicaragua was usually described as the most hispanized area of them all.[62]

In highland Honduras and Costa Rica the impact of the European conquest and its sequelae may have been less, but it was still enough to reduce these relatively small populations to a remnant. There too, relative demographic sizes dictated that a mestizo or Spanish-speaking population would start to emerge as soon as Spaniards began to live in the countryside. In the seventeenth century there were still Indian villages around Tegucigalpa and Cartago; Indians still spoke their own languages, paid tribute, and were accused of "witchcraft and superstition," that is, of preserving some elements of their preconquest religions; but it was already obvious that these communities were too small, dispersed, and demoralized to withstand the conformist pressures of the town, the mines, and the hacienda.[63]

On the boca costa and in San Salvador and San Miguel a different set of conditions obtained. There the main factor was that this band of fertile foothills was the economic heartland of Central America. The original population disappeared or fell to a small fraction of its former numbers, but large numbers of highland Indians were brought in to replace them. Such uprooting from their homes started the process of acculturation. Coming from many disparate tribes and linguistic groups, these migrants became Spanish speakers. This was also the area of cacao, cochineal, sugar, and indigo, and thus of pressure on the laboring populations. European agriculture and the plantation quickly transformed the Indians into cultural mestizos, and the fact that this was an area which because of its wealth also attracted relatively large numbers of Spaniards, Creoles, and castas reinforced this tendency. In the seventeenth century much of the population of present-day El Salvador was already living in the countryside, and many non-Indians were living in the surviving Indian villages. By the late eighteenth century, although racially the greater part of the inhabitants may well have been Indians, their culture was mestizo or ladino.[64]

In the mountains of Central America, in highland Guatemala, Chiapas, and to a lesser extent Verapaz, the Indian populations had been large at the time of the conquest, and in spite of the ravages of warfare, disease, forced migrations, and exorbitant tribute, a relatively large remnant survived. In these districts, therefore, the areas which Spaniards chose to settle was critical. Just as before 1635, they preferred the outskirts of the cities, the lower, flatter, and more fertile parts of the mountains, and the areas where indigo could be grown. Santiago and present-day Guatemala City became the dividing line between ladino eastern Guatemala and "Indian" western Guatemala.[65] In Chiapas also, the higher the elevation the more Indian the population remained.[66] All these processes were accelerated by the depression-caused flight to the countryside, and the changes in the eastern hills of Guatemala were well under way by mid-century. It was not until the 1670s that Spaniards and mestizos began to farm in the more favored parts of Huehuetenango, Totonicapán, or Verapaz in any numbers.[67]

The Central America of the seventeenth-century depression was rural, self-sufficient, poor for the most part, fragmented politically and economically, and culturally introverted. It was during this period that the basis was laid for the modern Central American land tenure structure, for the modern political and economic divisions of the area, and for the cultural cleavage between "Indian" and ladino which hampers Guatemalan nationhood to this day.

17

The Two Republics
in the Years of Depression

The seventeenth-century depression, running from the fourth decade almost to the end of the century, forced many Spaniards to sharply revise their way of life. The Indian population changed little. In some areas it had become small and continued to fall. In others there are a few signs of stabilization and even of the beginnings of recovery. Because of this scarcity of labor, and also because of lack of markets, profit margins, and shipping, Central America's trades and export industries had disappeared or stagnated.

Many Spaniards and Creoles found city life more and more difficult. Encomienda and repartimiento no longer supplied enough goods and services to sustain everyone, and, a lesser but annoying matter, regulation of these institutions grew more and more restrictive. To make matters worse, domesticated animals did not seem to be as numerous as before. Even meat became scarce. These pressures forced many city dwellers to the countryside. Many retained their vecino status so it is hard to guess at the real size of Spanish towns at mid-century. Many reports, however, describe vacant centers occupied by clerics and officials only, which filled up once a week or even more seldom for festivities or religious ceremonies.

At that time there was little point in occupying vast tracts of land. Spaniards lived on a few caballerías, grew a little indigo and ran some cattle, and tried to supply their labor needs by coming to individual arrangements with a handful of Indian workers. The usual result was one of the various forms of peonage, and this, a result of labor scarcity, gradually replaced the older forms of labor recruitment such as encomienda and repartimiento which had dated, particularly the former, from days of greater abundance of workers.

Lack of international and interregional trade—for there was, of course, continuing marketing at the local level—meant that the separate regions of Central America tended to draw apart economically and go their separate ways. Rivalry and hostility between the regions, and the resentment of all of them against the central government in Santiago de Guatemala, increased.

Such circumstances produced two obvious results. The fact that more and more people were living off a declining or stagnant base meant that many Spaniards and Creoles were forced to lower their expectations and their standards of living. More important, these circumstances dictated that competition for the few advantages left would become harsher. And, because greater insecurity and rigorous competition meant that the individual could not afford to display the least symptoms of social slippage, questions of prestige, the symbols of prestige and station, and protocol became more important. Spaniards and Creoles alike became extraordinarily sensitive about questions of personal dignity and formal precedence.[1]

Secondly, the absence of some of the population of the cities for all or part of the week, and the new economic circumstances under which everyone was living, meant significant changes in the nature of the cities. Many became emptier, of course, but there were subtler changes in the prestige accorded to certain groups, and in the aspirations of socially mobile Spaniards and Creoles.

In the first place, then, the overriding factor of Creole or Spanish life was the need to find an occupation or source of income which would prevent the individual's falling in status and retreating into the despised and declassé groups of castes, vagabonds, hired hands, and petty artisans. Farming or trade could still provide the answer for a few. Wheat farmers near Santiago, for example, built large fortunes based on the needs of the city market. Before 1680 or 1690, however, most Central American farms produced little more than the foodstuffs needed by the owner and his workers. Markets, internal or abroad, were not sufficient or available. A still smaller group still profited by sending indigo, hides, and other goods to Europe or to other parts of the Indies.

The only practical answer for most was public office. A governmental post provided two advantages. It gave the person who held it a small cash salary, which was of some importance in an era of scarce, debased coinage, and a desperate struggle for social position; and even more important, it gave him one small and transient opportunity to accumulate some capital. Few thought any more of returning to Castilian noble titles or mayorazgos, but if enough money could be extracted from a few years as corregidor or juez de repartimiento, and the capital accumulated invested wisely, social position and way of life could become more secure.

This need for public office and its advantages and opportunities produced several effects on social structure and group politics, effects so central to many lives that it is obvious that the desire for public office is a critical factor for reaching an understanding of Spanish and Creole life at the time.

In the sixteenth century the Spanish towns had dominated the countryside. In the towns, after all, lived the conquerors and their retainers, and the conquered, subject race lived in the countryside. To a certain extent towns continued to dominate. They remained the centers of government, the places where larger quantities of desired goods such as food and clothing were stored and sold. Nevertheless, as Spaniards moved to the countryside, and as the hacienda, chacra, and bohío became important factors in economic and social life, the balance shifted somewhat. It was not only the fact that more of the relatively powerful were not living in town. Capital was shifting from trade into the refuge of land, just as it had done in the great European depressions of the fourteenth and seventeenth centuries. The rentier and landlord class became more significant than the merchants.[2] Moreover, the town, bluntly put, was much more at the mercy of the countryside. In the days of abundant foodstuffs in the sixteenth century the town imposed the prices it wished. Now it was engaged in a hard struggle to prevent inflation of food prices and had to exert considerable pressure to oblige the countryside to send enough food to the city for its maintenance.[3] To a certain extent neighboring Spanish settlements began to compete and to bid against one another for the resources of the countryside.[4]

More important than the shifting of capital and resources from town to country, a relative and small matter at best, was the shift in the structure of the upper classes in the Spanish and Creole cities. The age before 1550 had been that of the conqueror. The years between mid-century and the great plagues of the seventies had been dominated by the entrepreneurial encomenderos. In the case of Central America most of these men had been in the cacao trade or close to it. In this third quarter of the sixteenth century these men were the ones who exerted "gravitational pull." Ambitious Presidents, oidores, or governors such as López de Cerrato or Landecho tried to attach themselves or their families to the cacao group.

In the half century or so between the epidemic of 1576–78 and the collapse of Spanish shipping and trade in the 1630s the encomendero class declined. This era was the one of the merchants, those who lived off the still large trades with Spain and Mexico, and of the reformist, active, innovative governor—Criado de Castilla and the Conde de la Gómera come immediately to mind—who tried to solve the growing commercial difficulties of the region. These two groups worked together and exchanged favors.

During most of the remainder of the seventeenth century, elite society was dominated by the government official, and above all by the positions which could be given out by Crown and Audiencia. Upwardly mobile people no longer sought alliances or friendship with encomenderos or merchants, for the most politically and economically significant posts were now in the royal administration.[5]

The main attraction of governmental office for the ambitious Spaniard or Creole was not the salary but rather the capital which could be accumulated by using government office. By and large extra capital could be extracted from these positions by fraud or other illegalities, and it is no coincidence that this is the greatest age of petty fraud, bribery, and governmental corruption. These frauds took several forms. At the upper levels, in the series of seventeenth-century Presidents and oidores of the Audiencia, and to a lesser extent among the governors and alcaldes mayores of the major jurisdictions, extra capital was accumulated by accepting bribes for services and jobs, and by placing relatives, no doubt for a percentage of the profit, in lucrative offices. Accusations of nepotism were a constant feature of Spanish colonialism, but these charges were particularly frequent and bitter in the seventeenth century.[6]

At a lower level there were offices such as juez de repartimiento, market inspectors, or, in the short spells when they were legal, the jueces de milpas. These officials had great opportunities to show favoritism, or not apply the law, in return for cash or other favors.[7] Of course the ability to extract cash from such an office depended not only on the particular daring and proclivities of the individual involved, but also on the wealth of the people and the region which he helped to administer. It is obvious, for example, that one of the most lucrative and sought-after posts was visitador to the indigo obrajes. Men in such posts, as we have seen, accepted bribes to ignore the illegal employment of Indians in obrajes, and other irregularities. These "fines" or bribes were collected on a regular basis in San Salvador, and the possibilities for capital accumulation were often excellent.[8]

Many of the above positions were basically ones which extracted surplus and "bribe" capital from the Spanish and Creole community. Of course ultimately such bribes may well have been paid indirectly by the lower classes, especially the Indians. A Spanish farmer, forced to bribe a juez repartidor so that he might keep his draft labor for an extra day or two, recovered part of his outlay from Indian labor. Most posts, however, involved much more direct exploitation of the Indian communities than the ones which have already been mentioned.

Most Creoles and many of the Spaniards who were seeking governmental positions could not hope for a post such as juez repartidor or visitador de obrajes, posts which, so to say, "automatically" produced extra income. If they were fortunate enough to be awarded such a job it was likely to be for only one year.[9] Rather they might typically expect a three-year appointment as teniente de gobernador in some minor place, or as corregidor de indios in a rural section. Salaries for such posts were ludicrous. Even in the depressed seventeenth century, when barter was almost as usual as coinage, when government officials gave change in cacao beans rather than reales, these salaries, usually under 500 pesos per annum, would not have been enough for ordinary living expenses.[10] Yet there was little to be earned from the Spanish or casta community. In such isolated regions these people were usually poor farmers, living in a self-sufficient manner with a few peons. They had little need for the approval or disapproval of any royal authorities. And so, inevitably it would seem, the only resource for these minor Creole officials was the Indian.

Capital was extracted from the Indian communities in a variety of ways. Creole corregidores and tenientes usually only had a few years in which to pile up a reserve of capital for the future, and they had no assurance of ever being rewarded with such a post again. (The fact that they had been appointed to a rural corregimiento was often evidence in itself that they were not of the most powerful economic or social group.) Such pressures were spurs to their ingenuity, and Indians were tricked or coerced in a myriad of ways. Some of these methods of extortion had been in existence on a smaller scale since the sixteenth century, and the most frequently used methods began to fall into a few well-recognized categories.[11]

One of the most common but probably least onerous was the obligation forced on Indian villages to care for, house, and feed officials, or indeed any travelers, as they passed through.[12] Parish priests had the right to expect their parishioners to supply them with a certain amount of maize, beans, chocolate, firewood, and so on, but many of them, under the same kinds of economic pressures as the minor Creole officials, added cash to these tributes. Some priests took to collecting a small payment from each village as they went on their pastoral rounds. (These payments were over and above the normal charges for ceremonies such as baptisms, confirmations, marriages, funerals, extra masses for the dead, or the blessing of new equipment or houses.) In Verapaz, where the local variant of this illegal tax was known as the salutación, it seems to have been especially systematic and resented, perhaps because the Indians of Verapaz were notoriously among the poorest in Central America.[13]

This offense also seems to have been widespread in Chiapas.[14] There, rarely, it reached rather large proportions. From time to time the bishops of Chiapas would pay a pastoral visita to their whole diocese. Usually Indians were delighted to see such men, and were only too willing to provide them with food and lodging if that would give the alcaldes and regidores of the village an opportunity to pour out their many real, and some imagined, grievances to the sympathetic prelate. It has been generally held that the Central American Church in the seventeenth century displayed little of the evangelical fervor of the first fifty post-conquest years, but the Church was still the best protector of the Indians. A few of the long line of bishops of Chiapas were more mercenary and turned their visitas to the villages into little more than cash-collecting forays into the countryside. In these cases Indians dreaded the arrival of a new visita and fled to the monte to avoid them; and, naturally, the salutación to be paid to a bishop far exceeded that expected by a simple cura. Even in graft the amount must fit the station.

The most notorious example of such a visita, although the question was highly partisan and there were conflicting reports, was the one held just before the Chiapas rebellion of 1712. A kindly and respected bishop, Francisco Núñez de la Vega, was succeeded by Bishop Alvarez de Toledo. This man collected the tithe with great enthusiasm, raised other ecclesiastical taxes, and then set out on a long and detailed visita, one of the main purposes of which, according to some, was the gathering of money for himself. Several observers, including the chronicler Francisco Ximénez, felt that the rage and desperation caused by this heavy tax-collecting tour was one of the main reasons for the huge Indian revolt which broke out in the Chiapas highlands shortly afterwards.[15]

Civil officials were not supposed to depend on the Indian communities for free supplies or labor, even when not traveling, yet in many cases they did.[16] Such practices, however, did little more than help with living expenses. Two other devices were far more productive of capital and were criticized repeatedly by the Crown. They were derramas and repartimientos (not to be confused with the labor repartimiento).

The derrama was a system whereby the local official became a merchant. He purchased goods cheaply in the cities and then sold them to the Indians whether they wanted them or not. Usually the prices were inflated. The reverse of this practice was to buy goods from Indians at very low prices and then resell them for a handsome profit. The only serious factor inhibiting such activities, apart from royal disapproval and occasional jealousy and informing by resentful or law-abiding Spanish or Creole neighbors, was finding the right goods and the right markets. Cases of derramas were widespread, and a few spectacular cases in which delinquent officials were punished did little to stop the practice.[17]

Sometimes the local official transformed himself into an illegal manufacturer, or rather a cottage industry supervisor. This practice, known as repartimiento, often involved the making of cotton cloth. Typically, a Creole corregidor in western Guatemala would buy raw cotton on the coast or at the Santiago market. He would then have it taken to his jurisdiction in the mountains and oblige the local women to spin it into thread and then to weave it into mantas (pieces of cloth). These could then be sold back to the Indians, to local Creoles or mestizos, or back to the cities, at a high profit. Again, there were several prosecutions, but probably most of the cases went undiscovered.[18]

The attitude of the higher authorities in Central America was ambivalent. The Audiencia, for example, knew the law and was probably aware of how essentially counterproductive exploitive methods such as derramas and repartimientos were. On the other hand, the granting of these lucrative rural offices was one of the few devices left to a President and his oidores for taking care of their relatives, friends, and dependents who had arrived from Spain with them, or for turning aside the importuning swarms of indigent Creoles who constantly demanded their rewards as descendents of conquistadors or first settlers. So the Audiencia preferred to turn a blind eye, only bestirring itself to reprimand, arrest, or prosecute after insistent urging from Spain. At times this complicity on the part of the Audiencia when faced with a really blatant case would arouse the ire of the Crown. In 1680, for example, the King fined each member of the Audiencia 300 pesos for having tolerated, and even given interim approval via an auto acordado, to repartimientos of cotton thread in Zapotitlán, where the corregidores were forcing Indian women to weave it into cloth. As in so many other matters, however, the Crown's lack of funds forced it to lower its standards. One of the Crown's devices for raising money was to solicit "voluntary" donations from the wealthier inhabitants. It was strongly implied that the amount given was a good gauge of the donor's loyalty and patriotism. Sometimes the King suggested appropriate amounts for individual people according to his estimate of their financial worth. Colonists responded reluctantly, and as requests for donativos graciosos became more frequent some refused to contribute. In 1717 the desperate King offered a bribe: he promised to send no inspectors or judges to zones that would pay up! This was, of course, disguised royal permission for all kinds of illegalities, so long as they were paid for.[19]

Such a system of providing Creoles and newly arrived Spaniards with a means to accumulate extra capital would seem to have been capable of preserving the social status and levels of living of these groups, if it had existed freely. The distribution of minor offices, however, was itself subject to many pressures, and as a result there were chronically too many applicants for too few posts.[20]

The Crown had several reasons for wishing to prevent the growth of public positions, or even for trying to reduce them in number. One was the problem of the royal treasuries in the various cities of Central America. These collection agencies should have been sending remittances back to Spain to support the King's wars, armies, and bureaucracy, and to finance his large debts to foreign bankers. Instead, these treasuries were themselves heavily encumbered. Widows and orphans of deserving Spaniards had to be maintained through encomiendas vacas or other ayudas de costo, royal forts and armaments had to receive some minimal maintenance, especially in the second half of the seventeenth century, the great age of piracy, and above all there was the growing weight of juros, pensions large and small which the Crown had promised when demanding loans or confiscating moneys to ward off bankruptcies. On top of all these burdens were the salaries of the various kinds of officials. The Kings, with their historical interest in preventing the worst abuses against their Indian vassals, saw clearly that the suppression of many of the local offices and subterfuges such as the jueces de milpas, would at one blow lessen the burden on the royal treasury and on the Indians.[21]

After 1635 a long, seldom-declared battle was waged between the Crown and colonial officials. The Crown constantly tried to keep down the number of appointments, while the colonists just as persistently tried to expand the number, either by "featherbedding" already existing varieties of employment, or by making largely spurious cases for the creation of new kinds of jobs to handle imaginary or exaggerated crises.[22]

The question of the jueces de milpas discussed in an earlier chapter is a case in point. The Crown steadily declared that such a title and post was abolished, that it served no purpose other than the enrichment of the holders, the diminishing of royal funds, and the infliction upon the Indians of one more layer of parasites. After a suitable pause local officials would tell the Crown that a new crisis had arisen, that once again the "naturally lazy" Indians were not producing enough food to feed the towns, or even themselves, and that they had decided to recreate the position of juez de milpas. Pending royal approval they had appointed several of them. After due deliberation the Crown would once again order the abolition of the post.[23]

Once again the Crown was hampered by its penury. During the seventeenth century it made heavy use of the sale of public offices to collect money. Obviously, then, if the Crown reduced the number of offices too sharply, the revenues from sales would fall off.[24]

In general, then, the positions which the Crown kept in its appointive control, the better positions in the colony such as President, oidor, alcalde mayor, and governor, and to a certain extent all the higher positions in the religious hierarchy, actually declined in number throughout the seventeenth century. The lesser posts such as corregidores de indios, tenientes, local jueces, visitadores, and inspectors fluctuated wildly in numbers as the Crown would react to proliferation, or as the Audiencia and other higher authorities would allow the numbers to creep up again "behind the King's back."[25] By and large, then, the number of governmental offices in Central America did not grow much in the seventeenth century, whereas the class which urgently sought these offices did.

Of more importance than the number of available offices, however, was the increasing downward vertical pressure which was placed upon their restricted number. Each office holder appointed by the Crown—most were from Spain, a few were Mexican Creoles, hardly any were Central Americans—brought with him a large retinue of relatives, friends, and paniaguados (retainers).[26] The higher the post, generally speaking, the larger the dependent group around the official. Presidents and some bishops might have thirty people of ascribed upper class status with them in addition to ser-

Figure 30

Major Local Offices in Central America, 1548–1785

	1548	1550	1570	1600	1650	1700	1785
Corregimientos (posts were usually within the appointive power of the president of the *Audiencia*.)	29	27	22	19	20	8	5
Alcaldías Mayores (usually appointed by the Crown.)	2	1	4	7	7	9	12
Gobernaciones (usually appointed by the Crown.)	1	1	4	4	4	4	4
Totals	32	29	30	30	31	21	21

Note: (1) The total number of these offices declined after 1650. (2) The offices which were subject to local appointment, i.e., those for which Creoles and *paniaguados* competed, declined steadily over the whole period. (3) Offices to which appointment was made in Spain gradually increased in number. These were almost all filled by *peninsulares*. Source: Carlos Molina Argüello, "Gobernaciones, Alcaldías Mayores y Corregimientos en el Reino de Guatemala," *Annuario de Estudios Americanos* 17 (1950): 105-32.

vants, personal family, and slaves.[27] Many of these noble officers had to borrow heavily to reach the New World and to establish themselves in a manner befitting the office. They were consequently under great pressure to rapidly accumulate wealth to pay off creditors and to accumulate a reserve which would support them on their return to Madrid. (Many of them never achieved their goals. They died at sea, in office, or during their residencia; or, realizing that they had not accumulated enough wealth, they compromised and chose to live an upper class life in the colony. In their early years in office, however, their aspirations and desire for rapid wealth were as described above.) Above all, the new President, oidor, or governor had to get rid of, or place, his crowd of relatives and retainers as soon as possible so that they would not hamper his personal acquisitive efforts. This was done by following a custom already established in the early sixteenth century. As offices became vacant he filled them with his own people. If he were unscrupulous or rushed by creditors he might remove incumbents before their terms ran out in order to get his personal appointees off his private budget as soon as possible. Naturally, such usurpations by newcomers, and newcomers charged with preserving the welfare and tranquility of the colony, aroused the greatest bitterness among the Creoles, who saw themselves excluded from offices, dispossessed, or at the very least pushed down to the rung below the one occupied by the President's favorites.[28]

Thus, in the ladder of appointive offices, there was constant pressure from new and politically powerful influxes at the top. The result, throughout most of the seventeenth century, was persistent downward mobility in the harried Creole class. Typically, a President arriving in Santiago would appoint sons, brothers, nephews, and friends to the corregimientos, juzgados, and other posts at his disposal. Upon his death or replacement by a new President his sons and other appointees were rapidly or gradually replaced by new appointees. But they were, after all, the sons of a former President, and the King usually rewarded them with encomiendas, juros, or grants of land. By the third generation, however, the royal connection had become vague. As like as not, the King had changed. The grandchildren of the original President or his brothers were regarded as pure Creoles. We find them as members of ayuntamientos of Santiago or Ciudad Real, as petitioners for minor posts, and as minor hacendados. The descendents of Criado de Castilla, the Conde de la Gómera, Martín de Mencos, Lara y Mogrovejo, and other seventeenth-century Presidents all followed this seemingly inescapable path.[29]

Not only the descendents of top royal appointees felt this decline. The grandfather of the chronicler Francisco Antonio de Fuentes y Guzmán had arrived in the New World early in the seventeenth century as alcalde mayor of Sonsonate, still, even then, a very lucrative post in the heart of the cacao country. The grandson, a member of the ayuntamiento of Santiago, and proud of his descent on his mother's side from Bernal Díaz del Castillo, never rose higher than minor posts such as corregimientos in the west of Guatemala. He even failed to gain the appointment of royal historian for the province, although he sought the post vigorously.[30]

A similar downward path can be seen in the descendents of some of the powerful merchants of the early years of the century. A typical case, once again, is the Genoese clan of Justiniani Chavarri. In the 1640s the leading members left with their capital for Spain and elsewhere. Later in the century members of the clan were scattered throughout the colony as petty traders and minor officials.[31]

This downward mobility and nepotism in Santiago further exacerbated the growing regionalism of Central America. The provinces complained that these new officials and usurpers always came from Guatemala. This was not strictly true. Many of them were newcomers from Spain who had simply passed through Santiago. Whatever their origins, it seemed to the local Creoles of provinces such as Nicaragua that these intruders were appointed and imposed on them from Santiago, and so the resentment of the periphery against the center grew accordingly.[32]

The seventeenth-century depression brought great changes to the cities of Central America and to the Spanish and Creole vecinos. Industry and commerce died down, and as they did the cities became less marketplaces and more conventual and administrative centers. Spaniards and Creoles found that they could not support their level of living on trade or export, and they tended to move toward a combination of land and public office. The ownership of land provided security and subsistence in hard times, and also served as an asylum for capital. Public office was one of the few means of accumulating capital, and much of that, as in the sixteenth century, was at the expense of the Indians. Creoles found themselves at a permanent disadvantage because of fresh arrivals at the top of the official and prestige pyramid. Bitterly resented downward mobility was a feature of the age.

More than against Santiago, Creole hostility came to be centered increasingly on the detested new officeholders who continually usurped, to the Creoles' way of thinking, the posts which rightfully belonged to them. During the seventeenth century, the deprived Creoles came to detest the wealth and the assumed superiority of the peninsulares, and during the period between 1640 and 1680 they carried on a long struggle to obtain the privileges which those fresh from Spain already enjoyed. (Partly, of course, such rivalries and jealousies are inherent in any metropolitan-colonial relationship.)

These growing dissensions manifested themselves in a variety of ways, and in a time of economic difficulties it is obvious that access to economic opportunities would be a particularly sore point. On the peninsular side there was the feeling that Creoles were country bumpkins, inexperienced, lacking in intelligence, and indolent. When the King asked the governor of Costa Rica in 1648 to prepare a list for him of those in the colony who showed the proper qualities for administrative office, the good governor, with typical peninsular superiority, answered the following year that in all of Costa Rica there were only two suitable men, and one of them was Portuguese and thus inappropriate. Similar reports on the "weakness" and dissolute nature of the Creoles were regularly sent to the Crown.[33]

Creoles were very sensitive to such allegations, but the most notable manifestation of such implied superiority was in the matter of public offices, and it was there that the battle began. One refuge which was open to many financially embarrassed families, both in Spain and in the colonies, was the Church. Large numbers of men and women entered the regular orders throughout the hispanic world. Now, a reasonable argument could be made that the King might prefer to appoint to secular offices only people whom he knew, or people who had been trained at court in the great traditions and methods of Spanish bureaucracy and government. In spite of the fact that the Crown constantly claimed that colonials should get preference for new appointments, and then blithely ignored its own edicts, the repeated awards to peninsulares, even though resented, were partly understandable to men of the seventeenth century.[34] That Spaniards from the mother country should claim greater piety or sanctity, however, was not. Most clerics found it much more difficult to advance arguments of inherent superiority for peninsular friars, although some did.[35] Moreover, the Church was an international organization and aggrieved friars could complain to their superiors in Rome, who might have little sympathy with claims that Spaniards were superior to Creoles. Above all, the clergy were the intellectuals of the age, and were therefore the ones who were most able to mount the campaign of arguments and debates which was needed. Competition for the few available posts was just as keen as in the civil bureaucracy. Within the Dominican and Franciscan orders in Central America many impoverished members of the upper classes had found shelter. Yet all or nearly all of the best appointive positions, those of prior and provincial, went to peninsulares.

These tensions existed in all the Spanish American colonies, although the relative proportions of Creoles and Spaniards varied greatly. The King was constantly urged to provide a solution to the problem. In Central America the Franciscans were the first to approach a solution and in the general chapter held in Toledo in 1633 the King agreed to the imposition of a political compromise known as the ternativa.[36] Under this arrangement the leading offices rotated in turn between peninsulares, hijos del país, (friars born in Spain but educated and received into the order in the New World), and Creoles. This still was hardly satisfactory to the Creole majority, and in the next general chapter it was agreed to reduce the arrangement to the alternativa, with offices "alternating" simply between Creoles and peninsular Spaniards.[37]

Grumbling in the Franciscan order was much less than it was among the Dominicans. In that order the fight to obtain the alternativa was a long, vituperative, and bitter one. There had been a few Creole provincials in the Franciscan order before the alternativa, but not even one among the Dominicans. (Ximénez, a peninsular, argued lamely that Creoles had, however, occupied other important posts.)[38]

The winning of the alternativa for the Creole Dominicans of Central America was reported to be the work of one man. (The way in which he was either reviled or revered, depending on the geographical origins of the writer, shows what a divisive and important issue this matter of access to offices was to the people of the times.) Fray Francisco Morcillo, a native of Sonsonate, was from a wealthy family. When the Franciscans applied for the alternativa in 1633 he hastened to Rome, and after some time obtained a papal statement in favor of a similar arrangement for the Dominicans. In Spain the change was resisted, and it was several years before the King issued the appropriate royal decree extending the alternativa to all the monastic orders. Among the Dominicans the alternativa did not go into effect until 1647, and the first Creole provincial, Fray Jacinto de Cárcamo, a nephew of Bernal Díaz del Castillo, was not elected until 1651.[39]

Occasional bitterness recurred for the rest of the century. Creoles were accused of disloyalty and worse, Spaniards of greed and pride.[40] To a great degree, however, the alternativa did calm the atmosphere. Rivalries continued, but in Central America it would be hard to consider the fight over the alternativa as the beginnings of an independence movement. It was rather a symptom of a general malaise and of great economic pressure, and in this case the question was soon resolved.

The success of the alternativa encouraged the King to use it elsewhere. By the 1670s the King was ordering the ayuntamiento of Santiago to alternate the posts of alcalde ordinario and alcalde de la Santa Hermandad between Creoles and Spaniards, and when the ayuntamiento met in March 1679 to choose a delegation to send to Spain it carefully chose three Spaniards and three Creoles.[41]

In civil life, however, the alternativa was a hollow victory. Spaniards were far outnumbered by Creoles in a city such as Santiago, and the ayuntamiento, perhaps because of its economic and political unimportance, had always been a Creole stronghold. There, then, the alternativa may have even decreased the number of posts available to Creoles.

Above all, access to the best secular jobs continued to be denied. By the last years of the century it is obvious that many Creoles were bitter, and in their casting around for new avenues to wealth, a hint of disloyalty and desperation had crept in. The way was now open for contact with the foreigner. The chronicler Fuentes y Guzmán complained that distance made the King deaf to the pleas of his most loyal subjects, that it was little wonder that new conquests brought little enthusiasm and few volunteers. Creoles saw how the great exploits of their fathers had been rewarded. "Others who did not wear themselves out win the prize earned by the merits of still others, a cause, perhaps, of the decay of our Republic. Because from the inequality of subjects is born the desolation of peoples." And again, "an old sickness of those of us who are born here is the sickness of Tantulus; we fast in the sight of nourishment, and are parched with thirst near to water, water which is poured out in abundance for those of other parts."[42] The psychological change behind such words is clear.

It is even less accurate to generalize about Indian society in the seventeenth century than it is in the sixteenth. The degree of impact of the conquerors, their diseases, presence, and labor exactions had varied widely from region to region and had produced different results as a consequence.

Figure 31

Revision of Tribute in Nicaragua, Seventeenth Century

Jurisdiction	1663 Count	1674 Count
Realejo	430	380
Subtiaba	1,100	950
Sebaco (including 3 Chontal villages)	520	460
Monimbo	1,900	1,750
Nueva Segovia	1,150	1,000
Totals	5,100	4,540

Note: Indian population thus fell 10.98% in this decade. Source: *pieza* 2, Nicaragua 1536-1692, AGI/AG 40.

On the coasts, in Nicaragua, and in areas where the Indian populations had never been dense, the aborigines continued to be absorbed by the Spanish population. Most of these areas, and the region around the mines of Tegucigalpa, were well on the way to becoming ladino-mestizo and Spanish-speaking by 1650. Another series of important variables had to do with altitude and export industries. Wherever Spaniards settled, or formed profitable crops —and these tended to be in the lower mountains—Indians were subject to acculturative pressure.

As the depression deepened the plantation industries fell away, so that Indians were less moved about. There was no longer any great need to bring Indians to the cacao coasts or to the indigo plantations of the boca costa. So plantations ceased to be the critical variables in acculturation which they had been before 1635. The important variable which remained, therefore, especially in highland Guatemala, Verapaz, and Chiapas, was where Spaniards had settled, either in cities or when they fled to the countryside in the age of crisis and experimentation (1576 to the 1630s). In Guatemala, as already indicated, the area to the east came under strong Spanish influence. In Chiapas, the valley of the Grijalva River and the Chiapas depression attracted settlers; the higher plateaus and mountains did not.

As the Spaniards and Creoles of the cities took up the better land in the zones of more equable climate they began to arrange for a labor supply outside of the formal systems of encomienda and repartimiento. The result was Indian and caste peonage on the chacras and haciendas which these new country dwellers built up.

In eastern Guatemala and temperate Chiapas this process, which many Indians seem to have welcomed as a lesser evil, further weakened the Indian village and hastened the acculturation process. It may also have meant, in some localities at least, a marginal improvement in the living levels of some of the more fortunate Indians. They found protection from tribute and, to some extent, from local Spanish officials.

In the tierra fría of western Guatemala and highland Chiapas peonage also existed but it was much less prevalent, at least in the period before 1690 or so. Since there were no labor demands from outside, the Indians of these regions now traveled only as petty merchants, not as plantation workers. There was also a decline in missionary zeal in the seventeenth century. Friars tended to congregate in the cities or larger villages, and to avoid the more difficult and isolated posts.[43]

Economically the picture was different. The tribute still had to be paid, and so did the various other royal and local financial impositions which were levied regularly or sporadically. Above all, there was intense pressure for goods and cash from impecunious local officials—corregidores, jueces of various kinds, tenientes, and visitadores, all of whom had few opportunities to obtain money and precious little time in which to do it. Moreover, all the old abuses still existed. Indians were used illegally as porters, even by presidents, and traveling Spaniards lived off their generosity while passing through. Villagers still complained at times that their own Indian authorities, alcaldes or caciques, were extorting labor or cash. The kinds of pressures to which these more isolated villages were subjected changed radically, however, as the depression worsened. Socially and culturally the pressure lessened; economically it remained high.

Indian society in western Guatemala, mountainous Chiapas, and in the few enclaves scattered throughout the rest of Central America can best be considered between the 1630s and the last decade of the century as undergoing a gradual and partial reconstruction. It was not a return to precolumbian culture, although some elements resurfaced. The destruction of the conquests and epidemics, and the century or more of Spanish acculturation had been too radical.[44] Rather it was a synthesis of the elements of European culture which Indians had accepted or which had been especially strenuously forced upon them, plus the precolumbian cultural components which Spaniards had not found objectionable, or which Indians had stuck to persistently despite prohibitions and persecutions. This synthesis which gradually emerged was not uniform, but varied from region to region according to the "mix." It was also new, in that it was neither Indian nor Spanish but an autonomous synthesis. In culture and religion it was, in fact, a culture which can best be defined as "conquest peasant."

Much of this slow rebuilding of a culture did not please Spanish governors, especially the religious authorities. There were frequent complaints of "idolatry" and a return to "superstitions."[45] Yet, if the Indians were circumspect and not too blatant, the authorities were too removed to do much about these deviations. What begins to emerge in "Indian" society is a series of "broker," or even "barrier" institutions which seem intended, perhaps not consciously, to turn aside weak cultural and religious intrusion while giving in to economic exactions and trying to prepare for them.

One of these "broker" institutions was the caja de comunidad, roughly translatable as the community chest. Created by the Dominicans, the institution spread to many of the more Indian parts of Guatemala and Chiapas.[46] At first it was intended to act as a bank or credit union for Indians, but gradually it became a way in which the village cooperated so as to be ready for Spanish and Creole imposts and seizures. Sometimes tribute was even paid out of the caja, but above all it was useful for paying sudden exactions from priests, merchants, or local officials.[47] It was also useful in buying off wrath. A visiting bishop or government inspector could be mollified by a substantial payment, and thus prove less strict in religious or political matters such as the elections of Indian alcaldes. In effect, then, by giving in to pressure economically, and by cooperatively preparing for such pressures, the cajas de comunidades indígenas acted as a barrier institution which allowed new religious and village political institutions to become fixed without too much outside interference. Examinations of Indian cajas show no fixed pattern. Some consistently balanced their books; others were chronically in debt.[48] All, however, made substantial payments to outside agencies or individuals, and these cajas were especially prevalent and important in the regions where a more Indian culture survived.

A similar institution in these villages was the cofradía, or religious sodality. Again, this institution enjoyed the advantage of having been introduced by Spanish clerics; indeed, there were Creole counterparts in the Spanish-speaking communities, and so the cofradías began life with a cachet of authority and respectability.[49] Many cofradías were founded for the veneration of a specific saint and to perform a specific charitable or mutually beneficial function for its members. Some of them, for instance, seem to have begun as funeral cooperatives. Every member if he contributed properly was assured of a decent burial with appropriate ceremonies.[50]

In the second half of the seventeenth century the Spanish community became suspicious of the Indian cofradía. Why this huge Indian enthusiasm for the institution? In some villages a dozen or more were founded.[51] Spanish officials ordered that the numbers should be curtailed and that cofradía activities should be scrutinized for irregularities.[52] And "irregularities" there were. Spanish officials complained of wild dances, processions, drinking, and idolatry.[53] They were particularly concerned about the dance known as "El Tun," which was banned repeatedly—with little effect.[54] In short, the cofradía had been a cloak of respectability which had allowed the more isolated villages to pursue religious practices which Spaniards would normally have considered unacceptable. It was another "barrier" institution which helped to recreate village society, and it was closely related to the return of idol worship and other "superstitions." It was no accident that there were several reports of pagan idols hidden behind Christian altars.[55] In these cases, and in some of the cofradías, the Indian appeared to be performing usual devotions. Instead he was turning, by subterfuge, to his new syncretic and officially banned religion.

Similar processes were taking place in Indian civil government. The Indian town councils (ayuntamientos or cabildos) with their regidores and alcaldes, were gradually transformed into not only office-holding institutions but also religious ones. Alcaldes, and such of the caciques as had survived without becoming hispanized, now became both civil and religious leaders, as many similar offices had been no doubt before the conquest.[56]

These defensive villages became conservative and suspicious of any intruders. The old hispanized caciques found that they were now true aliens in their former villages. One cacique in Chiapas in 1716 had to ask for protection from the government in order to visit his own home village. He dressed in Spanish clothes and spoke Spanish, but the village by that time had recreated its own nativist leadership out of adapted, transformed Spanish institutions.[57]

Indians tended to revert to what was more regionally appropriate or traditional in a variety of ways. In many parts of western Guatemala, for example, the "congregated" village began to break up as Indians in some localities reverted to a scattered "ranchería" type of settlement, leaving the village as an empty "concourse" and religious center.[58]

The seventeenth-century depression had some strange and unexpected effects on the two societies of Central America. Spaniards and castes fled the expensive, restrictive cities and began to build the first haciendas in the countryside, using a combination of cattle and indigo, and employing a much reduced and scarcer labor force as peons. There on their farms they learned a certain self-sufficiency born of isolation. Those who did attempt to maintain status found that the only avenue available to them, public office, was often denied them by an absent Crown. In spite of concessions such as the alternativa, Creoles developed a great hatred for all those who came from Spain, and to a lesser extent, for the Spanish government.

The Spanish flight to the countryside and the decline of major export crops meant a variety of things to the survivors of the Indian demographic collapse. In areas where Spanish speakers settled the process of acculturation continued. In areas where they did not, Indian communities were less imposed upon socially and culturally than they had been at any time since the conquest. These villages slowly built a new synthetic culture and erected a series of broker or barrier institutions which, while yielding to the cash demands of the cities and Spanish-speaking officials, protected the nascent religious and political governments then emerging.

Obviously the years of the seventeenth-century depression, from the 1630s to the late 1680s, cast a long shadow. Many of the social and economic patterns created then have only begun to disappear in the last thirty years.

18

Costa Rican Cacao

One more area must be discussed before the story of the Central American cacao cycle can be closed. After the collapse of the Pacific fields, with their exhausted populations and soils, one minor area attempted to create new cacao plantations to take advantage of the great rise in demand in the seventeenth century, both in Europe and in America. Although not exactly a success story, the career of the new fields of Costa Rica does, at least, relieve the atmosphere of gloom and disaster which descended on the Pacific coast cacao areas in the seventeenth century. Moreover, Costa Rican cacao encountered some very typical seventeenth century problems, and its early history provides a useful illustration of the economic and social circumstances of that age.

The area in question was the Matina Valley on the Caribbean coast of Costa Rica. The Matina Valley was tied commercially and culturally to the Cartagena, Portobelo, Panama, complex of ports. (As we have seen, Costa Rica felt much more affinity for nearby Panama, or Tierra Firme, than it did for distant Guatemala, throughout the colonial period.) Consequently its economic history belongs only marginally to that of the Audiencia of Guatemala.

Cacao was present in Costa Rica for many years before its commercial possibilities were explored. The unconquered "Botes" or Votos Indians living south of the San Juan river, or Desaguadero, near its Caribbean mouth, or along its tributaries, had traded cacao for many years with reduced Indians or with travelers on the river. Often these Indians gave the cacao in return for wine, of which they were inordinately fond, and which did them much harm according to one report.[1]

On the opposite side of the province of Costa Rica the Pacific fields advancing down the coast from Soconusco had gradually spread all the way to the Guanacaste lowlands and the Nicoyan Peninsula. By the 1630s some cacao was being collected as tribute from the Quepo area. But the supply was erratic.[2] There was enough, seemingly, to encourage some Spaniards to engage in the familiar false trading and extortion to obtain cacao, but the Pacific groves of Costa Rica did not become important and exported little.[3]

By 1660 Spaniards from Cartago had begun intensive cacao plantations in the hot, Caribbean, coastal areas around Suerre, Matina, and Moín. The estuaries of the River Reventazón, the River Chirripó and others had been used as ports for Portobelo and Cartagena since shortly after the conquest. For almost a century after the final settlement of Costa Rica in the 1560s these shallow estuaries had been used to send grains, tallow, and other animal products in small ships to the large isthmian market in Tierra Firme. According to one report the planting of the first commercial cacao groves in this coastal area was an attempt by Spanish merchants and hacendados to find an alternative product when the prices of other agricultural exports collapsed. A 1691 report says "Captain Gerónimo Valerino and the other said hacienda owners, having recognized the little trade and commerce which this province has with the cities of Portobelo, Panama, and Cartagena, because the fruits of this province have no value, while they formerly had, they sowed and cultivated in the said valley of Matina more than 140,000 cacao trees, which are all bearing fruit today, and what with the great demand and consumption, their harvests increased daily with the passing of time and the cultivation of the said haciendas."[4] The development of the coastal plantations was probably not so carefully planned as was reported thirty years later, but otherwise the report seems accurate.[5] Soon the Matina valley became the principal center for Costa Rican cacao, but other groves were established around all the anchorages in the region. Although none of the ports was safe or deep, transportation from the groves, at least, was not a problem.

With available ports, a ready market nearby, fresh undepleted soils, and local enthusiasm, it seemed that many of the conditions were present for the growth of a prosperous and intensive industry. But although the early growth of the plantations was rapid, the infant industry soon encountered some familiar seventeenth-century problems.

By the 1660s the Indian population of Costa Rica had dwindled almost to extinction. The coastal areas of the Caribbean were either empty, or their aboriginal populations had proved so recalcitrant that attempts at conquest had not succeeded. Costa Rica was not a wealthy area. The few Spaniards who exported agricultural produce to Tierra Firme seem to have had low profit margins, and there were

Figure 32

Population of Costa Rica, 1563–1720

Year	Indian Tributaries	Indian Population	Spanish and caste families	Source	Comments
1563	20,000	80,000?		Juan Vázquez de Coronado, *Cartas de Relación*, 25, 27, 38-39, 56. See also Thiel, "Datos Cronológicos," p. 178 (11,800).	Several entradas were made before this one, and epidemics may have reduced the population before 1520-1563. One informant who plainly wished to discredit Vázquez and to prevent the arrival of more Spaniards painted a poor picture of the province and its possibilities. But even he admitted that there were at least 7,000 tributaries (28,000 people?). See Peralta, ed. *Costa-Rica, Nicaragua y Panamá*, pp. 395-410.
1573			55	Fernández Guardia, *Historia de Costa Rica*, pp. 235-36.	At this stage the two towns of Cartago and Esparza were little more than forts. There were few women and children present, if any at all.
1581		7,000		Peralta, ed, *Costa-Rica, Nicaragua y, Panamá*, pp. 608-11.	Over 7,000 Indians baptized. In a visita of 1611 a total of 7,708 persons of all races was counted. See Thiel, "Datos Cronológicos," p. 72.
1583	1,126	4,504		Thiel, "Datos Cronológicos," p. 59.	
1645	800	3,200	200	CDHCR, 5:71.	Less than 200 Spaniards, and altogether less than 1,000.
1655	620			Thiel, "Datos Chronológicos," p. 103.	
1665	400	1,600			N.B. Indians were constantly being "brought out" of unconquered areas and added to the population. E.g, Thiel, "Datos Cronologicos," pp. 79-80, 105.
1675	500	2,000	500-700	CDHCR, 5: 360-62; Thiel, "Datos Cronológicos," pp. 122-23.	
1681	400	1,600		Thiel, "Datos Cronológicos," p. 180.	
1714		999		Thiel, "Datos Cronológicos," p. 183.	A careful count.

frequent complaints of extreme poverty from diverse sources. Consequently, few could afford to buy slaves, and the negro slave population was small between the conquest and 1660.

The only solution for the new cacao merchants and growers was the tapping of new sources of manpower within reasonable distance. At least one report claimed that it was no coincidence that a new and vigorous effort was made to subdue the Indians in the previously unconquerable Talamanca area. Two governors, Dr. Juan Fernández and Rodrigo Arias Maldonado, led armed bands into the area in the 1640s and 1650s. While their success was limited, some previously "wild" Indians were "settled" in the newly pacified areas, and others were "taken out" of the Talamanca area to be settled elsewhere.[6]

The area around the new village of San Bartolomé de Urinama on the northern fringe of Talamanca proved to be the best source of labor for the cacao fields. For more than twenty-five years the Urinama Indians were moved permanently or seasonally to the cacao groves to perform the work there. The numbers were not large, but sufficient Indians were involved, when combined with resident slaves and owners, to allow the fields a moderate growth and prosperity.

Such constant use of Indians, with forced removals consisting of several days' journey to the place of work, was patently illegal, but for some twenty-five years the Audiencia and Crown either ignored the situation or were unaware of it. The first objection on record came in 1690 from an indignant friar. Realizing that local officials would be unsympathetic, he appealed to the President in Guatemala and sent the letter from León, Nicaragua. The friar, Diego Macotela, asked the President to order the governor of Costa Rica to forbid the taking of Indians from Urinama for work in the cacao haciendas of Matina.[7] The President's compliance was rapid. By October of the following year the vecinos of Cartago were already complaining. The prohibitions against taking Urinama Indians from their villages to work on the cacao haciendas of "Matina, Barbilla, and Reventazón," were ruining the groves. The President was told that 130,000 trees were involved, and that about 100 owners depended on them. Now work had ceased, and the groves were deserted. Cacao was the major product of the province, the President was told, and ruin would result from the prohibition. There were no Indians near at hand.[8] Soon after the ban, however, many of the Urinama Indians who had fled to the monte to escape forced labor in Matina returned to their villages.

Labor shortages continued. Gradually, the number of slaves, "free" negroes, mulattoes, and mestizos on the coast increased. A few Indians also continued to work in the area, sometimes as owners, but more often as laborers.[9]

Apart from labor shortages, the main inhibitors of expansion on the coastal plantations of Costa Rica were problems of satisfactory disposal and public safety. The Caribbean coast of Costa Rica is an exposed, extremely rainy area. The rainy season brought almost yearly damage to the groves. Nor was it a healthy area. The hot climate and sickliness of the place was such that most owners preferred to live in Cartago or Turrialba and to visit their plantations only at harvest times. At other seasons of the year negro and mulatto caretakers, either slaves or freedmen, were left to tend the bushes. Understaffed and left to the care of a few individuals who had little reason, either physiological or psychological, to be enthusiastic, it is likely that the plantations were inadequately maintained.[10]

The Pacific groves of Guatemala and San Salvador had flourished before Spain's decadence had become obvious. Costa Rica's Caribbean groves were planted and extended during Spain's most anxious times, the mid-seventeenth century. The resultant burden of taxation, although certainly not a decisive factor, further increased the cost of Costa Rican cacao and decreased the already small profit margin. Costa Rican cacao was the subject of new taxation almost from its beginnings. Not only was the cacao sent to Portobelo and Cartagena subject to the usual host of almojarifazgo and barlovento impositions, but local trade was also burdened. One of Costa Rica's natural advantages was the nearby Nicaraguan market, which suffered from a chronic shortage of cacao. The perils of a sea voyage could be avoided and the overland journey was short. As difficulties arose in the Matina, Portobelo, Cartagena sea route, the records begin to show large numbers of individuals engaged in the trade of transporting cacao by mule trains to Nicaragua. By 1680, however, no lucrative trade long escaped the hungry eyes of officialdom. The Costa Rican cacao mule trains to Nicaragua were made subject to a new tax in 1685. The cabildo of Granada proposed putting a tax of one peso, a heavy sum, on each tercio of cacao leaving Costa Rica for Nicaragua. After some hesitations the Audiencia of Guatamela approved the request. The money was to go toward the depleted treasury in Granada and to defense.[11]

Money for defense was a constant need in seventeenth-century Costa Rica. Little could be obtained from the impoverished Crown; Guatemala was distant and uninterested to the point of merely

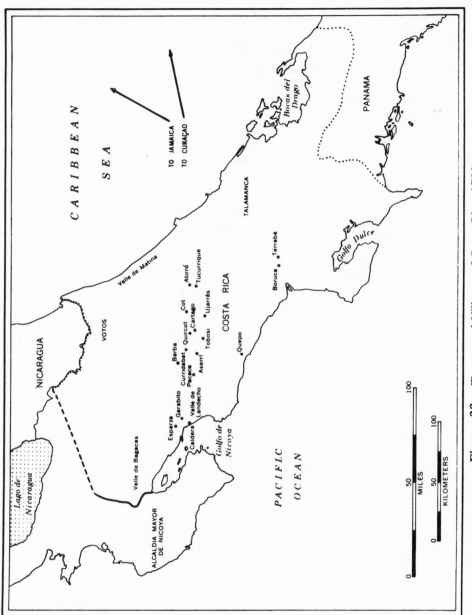

Figure 33 Towns and Villages of Costa Rica, 1700

token support; Panama did help on occasion but had its own troubles with pirates and felt, logically enough, that Guatemala should either attend to the financial needs of its own regions or transfer them to other jurisdictions. On one occasion financial help came to Costa Rica all the way from Lima.[12] Since outside help could not be obtained Costa Rica was obliged to fall back on raising her own defense funds. (The impecunious Crown favored such "self-help.") The cacao industry was the only apparent taxable enterprise. In 1675 a tax of one real per cacao bush was suggested in order to support a detachment of 200 soldiers. The President renewed the suggestion in 1680. The King approved of this and more export taxes in a cédula of the following year and deplored Guatemala's tardiness in helping. At the same time he made clear his own unwillingness to give financial aid. Such measures were counterproductive. Plantation owners were being accused of fraudulent under-counting of their own cacao trees less than two years later. Others were insisting that the tree tax had to be paid only once per tree.[13]

Costa Rica's plantations were on the "good side" of Central America as far as commerce with Europe and the Caribbean was concerned, but such an advantage was more than outweighed by the susceptibility to pirate attacks in such a position. Ships were often seized between Costa Rica and Panama. Pirate incursions in the Matina valley and other cacao plantations were persistent, disruptive, and destructive. The pirates frequently burned housing and equipment. They killed or carried off slaves and free negroes, causing further depletion of the labor force. Sometimes they maliciously destroyed trees and cacao stocks. At other times they would carry off all the cacao they could find. They knew when the harvests were gathered. On one raid they seized the whole crop, which had been destined for Cartago.

Toward the end of the century a second group joined the pirates and increased the frequency of the depredations. Sometimes allied to the English, sometimes alone, the Zambos Mosquitos inhabited the Caribbean coast between northern Costa Rica and the eastern tip of Honduras. Punitive expeditions were difficult to mount against their scattered settlements in the tropical forests, and the Zambos Mosquitos were excellent seamen. Their sudden attacks in large canoes were usually successful. Such frequent setbacks further raised the cost of producing cacao and its price in foreign markets, and encouraged absent plantation owners to live in Cartago, not on the dangerous coast.[14]

All of these factors slowed the development of the cacao industry of Costa Rica and kept its product at a high price. This price, together with the danger of pirates, caused difficulties in selling the cacao crops. With Venezuela, Maracaibo, Trinidad, and other areas already supplying the Caribbean, Holland, England, and Spain, and with plentiful supplies of Guayaquil cacao in Panama and New

Spain, Costa Rica faced intense competition. The high quality of the Costa Rican cacao and the convenient proximity of the province to large markets were some compensation and helped the Matina fields in this struggle.[15]

Nevertheless, the problems of governmental restrictions, insecurity, labor supply, and markets were not solved to any extent during the seventeenth century. It is obvious, for example, that few people were obtaining more than a meager living from cacao. Records show that while cacao and mules were the largest sources of income for the vecinos, only a small number owned enough trees at any one time to rise above the general poverty, as we shall see.

An individual in Cartago who did wish to acquire wealth through cacao was faced with multiple difficulties. The case of Antonio de Acosta Arévalo is illustrative. By 1678 he was the largest plantation owner in the Matina area. Only one other vecino, Gerónimo Valerino, had holdings which came close to the size of those of Acosta. Other plantations were considerably smaller and probably provided only meager incomes.[16]

By birth Acosta Arévalo was a Greek, and this was to complicate his life further. After living in Cartago for over twelve years, marrying there, and raising three daughters, Acosta found himself under attack by the governor in 1672. A royal cédula of September, 30, 1670, ordered the expulsion of all foreigners. This cédula was one which was often reissued and seldom heeded. One suspects that Acosta's Greek origin was merely a pretext, and what was really annoying and arousing the cupidity of officialdom was his success. At any rate other poorer foreigners in Costa Rica seem to have had little harassment of this kind.[17] Acosta appealed. He had served the King of Spain as an artillery officer in the navy for many years.[18] To allegations that he had dealings with English pirates and smugglers, he replied that he had been acting as a mediator in the case referred to and had been treated roughly by the English. Witnesses agreed. If, as seems likely, Acosta had been engaged in smuggling, he was probably only one of several in the colony. The governor, Juan López de la Flor, ordered his expulsion in spite of the testimony. Acosta withdrew to Guatemala where he appealed to the Audiencia. His appeal was upheld. It was pointed out that the cédula of 1670 exempted these foreigners who had lived in the Indies for more than ten years and had married locally. The governor was ordered to molest Acosta no further. Acosta Arévalo's complaints that he had lost large sums through selling cacaotales to raise capital for his hurried trip to Guatemala were exaggerated, but the expense must have been considerable.[19]

An ambitious cacaotero was subject to other hazards. If he were to develop his groves adequately and dispose of the crop, personal supervision was needed. If the enterprise was large he needed collaborators. Acosta had a close collaborator in a fellow Greek, Juan Antonio Foto, or Soto, a "native of Escopilo in Greece and a vecino of Costa Rica." Acosta brought Foto into the family by giving him one of his three daughters in marriage. But the necessity of going frequently to the coast, with its diseases, marauding pirates, and treacherous seacoasts, could not be avoided. The ambitious Acosta took the risks for the sake of his groves and suffered the consequences. He was lost at sea in 1691. His nephew, traveling from Portobelo to Matina in the same boat, managed to reach the shore. At the time of his death Acosta owned 8,176 cacao trees, several slaves, goods from Italy, Holland, Brittany, and Germany and other signs of wealth.[20] His nephew inherited the cacao groves and continued the same hazardous life of commerce. In July 1695 he reported that in April of 1693 pirates at Matina seized an entire shipment of goods imported from Portobelo.[21] Foto died in 1699 and left property similar to that of Acosta. His cacao groves were large, and he had luxury goods from European countries.[22]

The brief history of Acosta and Foto graphically illustrates the predicaments of any ambitious Costa Rican cacaotero in the late seventeenth century in Costa Rica. Rapid acquisition of wealth aroused the cupidity of royal officials who had only a few years in which to become rich. Personal participation in coastal agriculture and commerce left one open to disease, shipwreck, and pirate attacks. There is strong evidence from the inventories made after the deaths of the two Greeks and in other mortuales of the period that smuggling and other illegal activities were the only way to avoid taxation, to find profitable markets for cacao, and to buy luxury goods to accompany acquired wealth.[23] Most Cartago vecinos wisely refused to take up such a hazardous existence. It may be of significance that the two examples used here were foreigners, "unconditioned" perhaps to the restrictions, "style," and tacit understandings of Creole life. Significantly too, there are other examples of foreigners becoming involved in lawsuits in Costa Rica at this period because of overassertive or illegal commercial practices. And there were few foreigners in Costa Rica between 1675 and 1700. Of course local chauvinism may have been part of the problem.[24]

Under such restrictive circumstances cacao did not become the dynamic export product that some Costa Ricans had hoped. By the end of the century it was obvious that Costa Rica was facing a grave

Figure 34

Cacao in Costa Rica

Year	Fruitful Trees	Young Trees	Total Trees	No. of Haciendas	Sources	Comments
1675			About 200,000		C.D.H.C.R. VIII, 349.	Probably too high. An estimate.
1678			136,130		C.D.H.C.R. VIII, 376-77.	
1680			130,000		C.D.H.C.R. VIII, 381.	
1681	60,000				A.N.C.R. Cartago 1078, 270.	An estimate.
1681			About 150,000		C.D.H.C.R. VIII, 397.	An estimate.
1682	28,700	76,700	105,600	55	C.D.H.C.R. VIII, 399-605. Fernández Guardia, *Crónicas*, 211.	The C.D.H.C.R. report bears the marks of fraud. Cacaotal owners counted their own trees for taxation purposes. Thus both the no. of fruitful trees, and the total no. of trees are probably too low. In C.D.H.C.R. VIII, 428.
1683	40,000	110,000	150,000		C.D.H.C.R. VIII, 428.	See above (1682).
1691			About 130,000		A.N.C.R., Cartago 085.	
1691	21,500	122,900	144,400	56	An estimate. See also Lijia Estrada Molina, *La Costa Rica de don Tomás de Acosta* San José: Ed. Costa Rica, 1965), 54.	No source mentioned by Estrada Molina.
1719	80,000				C.D.H.C.R. V, 476; García Peláez, III, 30-31.	
1738	137,848	99,290	237,138	89	C.D.H.C.R. IX, 321.	See also Estrada Molina, 53.
1747			189,869	144	A.G.G.G., A1. 17-1, exp. 5003, leg. 210 (1760).	61 of the haciendas were new and not yet in production.
1752				142	Salvatierra, I, 352.	

crisis in currency and foodstuffs. Flour, meat, tallow, and other agricultural produce had declined as export commodities, and by the 1680s were in short supply in Costa Rica itself. The usual stratagems of controls and forced plantings were tried with the usual lack of success.[25]

At the same time the cacao growers encountered increased difficulties in selling their products to the legal markets outside the province. One document of the second decade of the eighteenth century complained that it cost twenty-five pesos per zurrón to grow cacao and to send it from Matina to Nicaragua via Cartago when all costs and taxes were included. But the best price to be obtained in Nicaragua was twenty pesos.[26] And Nicaragua, except for its home-grown supply, had less access to other sources of supply than Panama and Cartagena.

The result of the lack of exports was a disappearance of all silver currency at the beginning of the eighteenth century. Before then cacao had been used as small change in Costa Rica just as elsewhere in Central America. Now various petitioners asked the governor to declare cacao beans to be the official means of exchange acceptable as currency in all circumstances. Such was the eclipse of all commerce that the governor and other officials were obliged to comply. Cacao became widely used as money.[27]

The Costa Rican cacao merchants and growers adopted the only course left to them in these circumstances. Spain and the other colonies could no longer supply favorable markets, goods, security, or coinage to Costa Rica. The cacaoteros were forced to look elsewhere. Smuggling had existed on the coast since the beginning of the plantations there. Occasionally pirates and Zambos Mosquitos traded instead of looting.[28] Curaçao and especially Jamaica were prepared to pay high prices for quality chocolate and were themselves emporiums of a variety of European goods. After Costa Rica's crisis of the 1700s smuggling increased rapidly. English traders from Jamaica took the place that other provinces could no longer fill. The groves grew and Matina became a smuggling depot. Occasional prosecutions could do nothing to stop the exchange of goods, and by mid-century royal officials had tacitly accepted that fact. A system of regular small fines was ensuring that royal officials could share in the new profits and increased prosperity.[29]

Smuggling had provided a partial solution to Costa Rica's cacao problems. Once the illegal trade had passed from a sporadic occurrence to a regular system, including official bribes, the plantation began to enjoy a fair measure of the prosperity which had eluded them in the seventeenth century.

19

Signs of Strain and Change
(c. 1685-1720)

Previous chapters have examined the new equilibriums established during the depression. Central America became rural, self-contained, and isolated. In Costa Rica there was the completion of the great cacao cycle, and, at the beginning of the eighteenth century, the hint of a solution to the problems of markets, profits, cargo space, and transit time. Caribbean cacao plantations near Matina, Moín, and Suerre began to sell their produce to Jamaica and Curaçao by means of contraband with the English and the Dutch.

In most things Central America continued in ways which had become recognizable in the previous half century. Creoles and castas lived predominantly in the countryside, living for the most part on self-sufficient farms, growing a little indigo, and running a few cattle. Few of these holdings developed into recognizable haciendas or great estates in the period which concerns us. In the areas where these people settled, Indian communities came under heavy pressure, and many became peons on the Spanish farms. In the areas which the Spanish-speaking settlers did not favor, mostly the high country west of Santiago, Indians remained subject to the same economic pressures as before, but socially and culturally they found themselves left alone more than at any time since the conquest. The result was that these communities, sheltering behind a series of broker institutions, were able to recreate an individual society, not Indian yet not Spanish or ladino.

The society of the cities, dependent on the countryside, and no longer tied to any great industry or trade, became preoccupied with the advantages to be gained from public office. There were no other real opportunities for accumulating capital. Creoles had to face the fact that most of the major offices were dominated by people from Spain, which meant that many of the minor posts went to their

Figure 35
Size of Indian Families in Costa Rica, 1713–14

Village	Date	Population	Number of Families	Childless Couples	Couples with 1 child	Couples with 2 children	Couples with 3 children	Couples with 4 children	Couples with 5 or more children
Garabito	1713	27	7	1	3	1	—	—	2
Barba	1713	205	58	23	4	15	15	1	—
Pacaca	1714	204	47	9	10	10	7	6	5
Aserrí	1714	154	40	11	8	11	6	2	2
Curridabat	1714	137	36	11	6	8	7	4	—
Quircot	1714	57	14	3	2	3	3	3	—
Tobosi	1714	75	16	4	3	2	2	1	4
Cot	1714	40	12	5	2	3	—	1	1
Ujarrás	1714	45	17	11	4	2	—	1	—
Naboríos	1714	55	17	5	4	5	1	—	1
Totals		999	264	83	46	60	41	19	15

Thus: (1) About one third of Indian families were childless.
(2) Average size of Indian family was 3.78.
(3) Average size of Indian *naborío* family was 3.24.

Source: Thiel, "Datos Cronológicos," p. 183.

retainers. The result, in spite of some attempted solutions such as the alternativa, was great bitterness against those from Spain.

As soon as these new systems became recognizable, however, they began to show signs of new strains. At first these new tensions were minor. The depression was a long one, and the social arrangements which it helped to produce became firmly rooted. By the end of the century, however, it was obvious that the society formed at mid-century was undergoing slow but radical change. In most cases these tensions, strains, and signs of disequilibrium and change had existed before. It is the intensity and frequency of occurrence, and the conjunction of these events in the same span of years which gives them their significance.

The most noteworthy of these changes was that reports on Indian population began to be slightly conflicting. Reports of decline continued to predominate, especially in the area where pressure had continued to be intense. One of the few studies of differential fertility available, from Nicaragua, shows that Indians were simply not replacing themselves at a sufficient rate, especially when compared with the other racial groups in the countryside.[1] Tribute counts from Tegucigalpa show that family sizes there were also too small to maintain the population at its level.[2]

In some of the villages of the western highlands, however, there were a few sporadic reports of population growth. A village priest would ask for help because his parish was becoming too large, or an encomendero would request an increase in tribute to reflect a growth in the number of potential tribute payers.[3]

First of all, it is noticeable that most of these reports of the reversal of the demographic trend come from western Guatemala or Chiapas. It is therefore reasonable to suppose that isolation from Europeans and their diseases plus a diminution of cultural pressure may have had much to do with it. Moreover, the population was relatively sparse compared to what it had been in the sixteenth century, and the Indians' abandonment of their congregación villages and return to a ranchería, or dispersed, type of settlement pattern meant that infection did not travel so readily. As a result epidemics remained localized.[4]

When searching for reasons for the demographic revival, however, one is again faced, just as in fourteenth- and fifteenth-century Europe, with the little understood intricacies of human adaption and immunology. After a hundred years the new peasantry had become more psychologically and physiologically prepared to face the new environment. We have already noted the new institutions, cajas de comunidad and cofradías among them, which enabled the communities to fend off some of the impositions of the dominant society. Physiologically too, the surviving Indian communities at last had the strength to outlast the onslaughts of alien diseases.

The first signs of Indian population revival, local and sporadic though they were, are not only important in themselves but also in the way in which they relate to what was happening in the "Indian" communities. Population growth was a mixed blessing for some villages. More mouths to feed meant more land was needed, and some villages found that the best agricultural lands near the village had been taken up by outsiders. Indian villages had little hope of winning lawsuits against Spaniards, although some tried and a few were successful. What is apparent after about 1680, therefore, is that neighboring Indian villages began to compete with one another far more than before for available land.[5]

In the half century or so between the 1630s and the late 1680s Spanish cultural invaders such as priests and labor recruiters seem to have withdrawn from the higher and more rugged parts of western Guatemala and Chiapas. At the same time, however, economic pressures had remained intense. In a time of economic depression the large "Indian" agricultural populations of these areas remained one of the few sources of capital for the increasingly indigent elites. Spanish officials in Totonicapán, Huehuetenango, and Verapaz were repeatedly accused of the worst kinds of derramas, repartimientos, and extortions during this period.[6] After the early 1680s, however, in spite of the Indian population increase, which should have made the situation somewhat easier for them, Indian communities in western Guatemala and Chiapas began to find these pressures unbearable. There was a series of riots and local disturbances culminating, in 1712 and 1713 among the Tzeltal Indians of Chiapas, in a large, anti-Spanish, nativist rebellion which was put down with considerable expense and great difficulty.[7]

In short, the exactions of alcaldes mayores, corregidores, and local friars were no longer simply borne or protested to the authorities. In some cases they were met with physical violence, the killing of abusive Spanish officials, and of course, inevitably, with severe punishment and repression.[8] If it is argued that Spanish economic pressure was enough of a provocation to cause such disturbances, then the question becomes why such outbreaks had not occurred before. The question which naturally follows is, what had changed in the forms and methods of Spanish intrusion in the late seventeenth century which turned resentment and petitions into riot and finally insurrection?

In the last two decades of the seventeenth century a wave of religious revivalism swept the Spanish religious communities of Central America. New, puritanical, evangelical friars entered the area, .traveling constantly, destroying vast quantities of idols, and vituperatively condemning lack of piety, "superstitions," and paganism among both Indians and non-Indians.[9] Sometimes these puritanical evangelists were welcomed. In some Spanish cities and Indian villages there were outbursts of religious fervor accompanied by processions, asceticism, mass recommitments to a reformed life, and so on.[10] In other communities the friars were met less enthusiastically. For fifty years some villages had been left to reconstitute a religion and culture of their own. What had evolved was often a syncretic mixture of precolumbian beliefs and Christian impositions. Such a religion, which the Indians had been able to defend with a fair measure of success by giving in to the economic demands of uninterested Spanish officials, now suddenly came under severe attack from the horrified Spanish friars of the reform movement. The cultural independence for which the nativist communities had surrendered so much was now under attack. Here and there resistance was passive. Idols were quietly rescued from ravines where they had been dumped, and restored to places of honor. Indians disappeared into the monte until the bearers of the new dispensation had carried their message elsewhere. In a few localities the religious revival, or rather the resistance to it, was one of the reasons for riot or rebellion.[11]

Another reason for the riots and violence, even more frequently mentioned, is an increase in economic pressure from the Spanish community. This took two forms. Indians complained that the frequency and heaviness of the usual forms of exactions were increasing. Visitas from avaricious clerics and derramas from unscrupulous corregidores were occurring more often and were demanding more. They also complained that older forms of pressure were being revived. Indians were encouraged or forced to leave their villages or dispersed milpas to go to work on Spanish farms. There was a revival in the use of adelantos or advance payments as a means of obliging Indians to perform tasks not normally to their liking. There is also a notable increase in the entrada y saca method of recruiting fresh labor. Sometimes these expeditions followed missionary activities, sometimes they were more blatant.[12]

The great Tzeltal rebellion of 1712 seems to have been caused by a combination of these circumstances. A new bishop increased the exactions and taxes collected from the Tzeltal villages, vecinos of Ciudad Real continued to use the debt contract as a means of entrapping Indian labor, and the Indians began to emphasize the nativist aspects of their syncretist religion as a retort to the Spanish attempts to weed out "superstitions."[13]

One possible explanation for increased pressure is an increase or an intensification within the non-Indian parts of the Central American economy. The new pressures can be interpreted as a search for new labor or new investment capital because there were better opportunities for investment or expansion than had existed previously.

To a certain extent, then, using the seventeenth-century depression and the eighteenth-century trade revival as evidence, it can be claimed somewhat hesitantly that economically favorable times in the Spanish "republic" meant more hardship for the Indian "republic," while depression in the entrepreneurial economy run by the elites might mean easier conditions for some Indians. Again, the resemblance to the fourteenth- and fifteenth-century Europe is striking.

Further evidence of a change comes from the larger Spanish towns, especially Santiago de Guatemala. Since the 1630s the supply and distribution of foodstuffs in these towns had always required regulation and fairly strict supervision. Sixteenth-century abundance never returned because the Spanish population grew while that of the Indian fell, stagnated, or grew very slowly. Similarly, cattle populations never returned to their old superabundance after the fall in numbers of the last quarter of the sixteenth century, so that meat was no longer so plentiful and cheap. Nevertheless, after the crisis of the 1630s the supply situation had ceased to be critical. Many of the vecinos became self-sufficient farmers, which relieved some of the pressure, while regulation, supervised slaughterhouses, warehousing, and price controls made supply and distribution more predictable and manageable.[14]

In the 1690s and the early years of the eighteenth century, however, Santiago and other Central American population centers were hit by new food shortages. Two or even three consecutive crop failures or bad harvests cannot be the explanation because the crisis lasted far longer than that.[15] The population of the Spanish cities was probably growing but so was the rural population of food producers, both ladino and even perhaps Indian, and farms were growing not only more numerous but also larger, as unoccupied monte came under cattle and crops. Demographic explanations are therefore unsatisfactory.

One possible conclusion is that farmers who had previously supplied the cities now increasingly chose not to. If that was the case, it was obviously because they had found more profitable markets elsewhere. These markets, however, were not for Central American foodstuffs. Maize, beans, wheat, and meat could not be carried beyond the confines of Central America in any quantity under the technological conditions of the seventeenth and early eighteenth centuries. Central American rural entrepreneurs had then found markets for a commercial crop other than the foodstuffs which they sent to the nearby cities. As we have already noted, this crop was indigo. The crisis of food supply in the cities before and after 1700 came about because entrepreneurs in some areas were planting more land to indigo, and thus taking acreage out of foodstuffs. Although expansion of indigo plantations did not necessarily mean a fall in the cattle populations—both could exist to mutual advantage because cattle were used for the weeding of indigo fields —yet it is likely that some of the scarce labor supply was totally or seasonally taken out of cattle herding and put into indigo production.

If Central American landowners were indeed increasing their acreages planted to indigo then it is obvious that they must have found markets where the determinants of weight, cargo space, transit time, and profitability could be overcome. The search for markets had been a long and difficult one for the would-be entrepreneurs of Central America, and the final result of this search will be examined in the next chapter.

20

The Growth of a New Solution; The Rise of Smuggling

After 1600, except on the Caribbean coast of Costa Rica, indigo had replaced cacao as Central America's dominant export crop. Yet the times had prevented those involved in añil from developing the trade to the extent that they had wished. Labor had been a problem, but to a much lesser degree than in the case of cacao because indigo was not labor intensive. Royal legislation, taxation, piracy, and natural disasters such as gales, earthquakes, volcanic eruptions, and floods had all stunted the growth of plantations from time to time. None of these factors, however, was insurmountable, and even together they did not seem to be the critical factors which prevented the expansion of indigo. The main difference between cacao and indigo was that indigo's major markets were in Europe, not America; and to make matters worse, the indigo industry began to expand just as Spain was sinking into a profound decline. The result was difficulties in communications, allied to the logistical factors already mentioned—ship size, distance of journeys, and the weight, bulk, and profitability of goods. If Central American indigo was to be sold in Europe, then in the seventeenth century it could never truly flourish unless two circumstances were changed. The first was the close tie to Spain. The mother country could no longer supply the market which indigo needed and had little to send in return. The second problem was volume of shipping and logistics. Indigo could only show a profit if ships called often, and if the problem of distance-time-weight-profitability could be overcome.

Despite all the marketing difficulties experienced by the plantation owners and merchants of Central America, it is probable that they preferred, whenever possible, to sell their indigo and other exportable products to the other Spanish dominions in America or to Spain. Patriotism and loyalty to the king, if strictly interpreted, demanded this course. To break the laws of trade while selling to Spain and its possessions, or worse still to sell to foreigners, had been repeatedly forbidden, and infringement of the law might bring retribution. Trading with foreigners, especially the hated English and Dutch "luteranos", must have been especially distasteful. These were the nations which had produced many of the feared and detested pirates. Besides, the foreigner was not to be trusted. News of peace treaties or the outbreak of fresh hostilities in Europe were often delayed by as much as a year, and the colonials might find to their astonishment that a peaceful trader was now an enemy. Even in times of peace, foreign smugglers could certainly be counted upon to seize stocks of merchandise rather than purchase them if the occasion presented itself, if the local Creole merchants were naïve and could be duped, or if they appeared for parleying or the exchange of goods with insufficient numerical or military strength.

If patriotism and fear of the law strongly suggested to the Central American entrepreneur that he should not smuggle, then why did he do it? It seems apparent that contraband was the result of desperation. The longer the depression and the lack of large markets lasted, the larger grew the group that was prepared to flout the law, and the more determined it became. Quite simply, it must have been obvious to the average merchant by 1680 that if he was at all ambitious, commerce with foreign markets, as directly as possible, was the only way to achieve relative prosperity and a reward for his past labors.

Besides, the law was not as terrifying as it appeared. If one was of sufficiently high station, penalties and prohibitions could be circumvented, then as now. Creoles knew that frequent repetition of a given royal decree was an admission of royal inability to enforce it.[1] Beyond that there was always legal entanglement. A criminal case could be prolonged, or endlessly re-argued and appealed, back and forth across the Atlantic, if the accused were of sufficient status and means. Beyond that, there was composición. Almost any infringement, not to say major crime, could be "composed" in the seventeenth century. The state was so desperately in need of ready cash that it would accept payments to forget most past infractions which did not affect its immediate security.[2]

Another factor which encouraged commercial illegality was the regular complacence, and occasionally the enthusiastic participation, of local officials in Central America. As we shall see, all ranks from the lowliest lieutenant to the President of the Audiencia were involved at one time or another during the seventeenth century.

The principal reason behind this local official ambivalence toward the illegal trade was the heavy pressure on royal officeholders.

Those who came from Spain bearing royal letters of appointment had often paid dearly for them through bribes or "voluntary" donations to the royal coffers. Some of the lesser posts were openly sold by the Crown. Many of these new officeholders were forced to borrow heavily to find the money needed to obtain the offices which they desired. So some new appointees would arrive in Latin America little better than paupers, having left in Spain unsympathetic creditors who had heard of the fabulous wealth of the New World and adjusted their expectations about repayment and interest accordingly. In face of this situation the new appointee's responsibilities were heavy. He was a member of the nobility, and even in impoverished seventeenth-century Spain he would be expected to live at court in Madrid without overtly engaging in commerce or in industry, and in a style befitting a nobleman and former royal appointee. Yet he often had only a fixed number of years in the New World to pay off his debts and accumulate enough capital to live as was expected upon his return.

To further complicate his predicament, he was underpaid while in office, sometimes severely underpaid given the fact that he was expected to live in the principal cities during his stay in the New World, and was expected to represent royal dignity and majesty while there. Living in the manner which was required by the office was cheaper in the New World than in the Old, but it was still not possible to do so on many of the salaries paid to royal officials.

Most burdensome of all was the new official's responsibilities to those closest to him. It was expected that any official worthy of his post would take a body of slaves and servants to the New World. Not to do so would bring disrespect on the individual and his office. These individuals had to be supported in food, clothing, and lodging. Even more bothersome was the crowd of sons, brothers, cousins, close friends, and retainers from the minor nobility, the famous paniaguados, who usually accompanied important new officeholders to the Americas. All had to be found posts as quickly as possible after their arrival, and once all the posts were filled, the remainder of the retainers could only look to their original benefactors for sustenance. Officials appointed locally, usually by the President or governors, faced similar problems. They had bought their offices, paid bribes in some cases, and in return were receiving underpaid minor offices for a short period of time. Capital had to be accumulated rapidly. To make matters worse for locally appointed officials, many of the posts which they filled, besides being minor in nature and prestige, were corregimientos or tenencias de gobernador in especially backward or heavily Indian areas. The Indian was a failing resource as far as extortion of funds was concerned. Local officials no doubt turned to other methods of making money whenever they could.[3]

As a result royal officials engaged in corruption, extortion, and evasions of all kinds. One of the most frequent temptations was illegal commerce. It produced ready cash, high profits, and was hard to discover. With so many royal officials engaged in trade and smuggling, it is little wonder that Creole indigo growers and merchants in Central America were able to engage in similar practices with fairly calm consciences.

The seventeenth-century Creole or official who was perturbed about breaking the laws of his nation must have found added solace when he considered his country's recent commercial history. Since shortly after the discovery of the Americas, foreigners had played major roles in Spanish American trade, and despite prohibitions they had continued to do so throughout the sixteenth century. By 1600, foreigners in Seville, or their Spanish agents, the formerly powerful Sevillian merchants, controlled nearly all trade both legal and illegal through that port.[4] From the beginning of the seventeenth century and increasingly thereafter even the fleets were Spanish in name alone. Nearly all were financed by foreign businessmen, who used agents, often "peruleros", or made large loans to Sevillian merchants, who were little more than factors of foreign companies. If such was the case why should the local Central American merchants be concerned when blatant illegality was flourishing in Spain's most important port, under the King's very nose? And it was only one step more for the Creole merchants who had been trading with foreign interests in Seville to eliminate this illegal "middleman" and trade directly with eager foreigners off his coast, especially since their goods would be cheaper than those coming in via Seville.

It can be seen, then, that the commercial situation which existed in the Indies trade during the late sixteenth and seventeenth centuries was a complex one with many subtle nuances. It was not simply a question of trading legally, or trading with the enemy. Between these two extremes there was a whole gamut of possibilities, each slightly less legal than the one which had previously predominated.

When legal trade proved to be nonexistent or unprofitable illegal trade with Spain or Spanish nationals was obviously the next possibility. The aim was tax evasion, so that the numerous petty imposts in America and at the Seville-Cadiz ports complex would not eat away all profits. This flouting of the law, but not of national loyalties, was a transitional stage which lasted for many years in Central America; in fact it existed in a minor way from the moment when trade started between Honduras and Seville. Tax avoidance seems to be a universal impulse.

The next step in this progression toward treason—for smuggling with hostile powers must have appeared treasonous to the Crown—was to ship goods obviously destined for markets in Holland, France, England, or elsewhere, via Spain, using merchants or agents in Seville or Cadiz who were in touch with foreign commercial interests.[5] These agents were little more than the paid representatives of foreign bankers and companies, with few autonomous powers of their own. The last stage to develop fully, both chronologically and in terms of the degree of illegality, was deliberate smuggling with enemy ships in the ports and on the coasts of the Spanish kingdoms in America.

In this progression from legal trade to contraband the methods were not successive to the point of being mutually exclusive; none of the three principal methods of exchanging goods disappeared completely. Legal trade continued intermittently, whenever the peninsular authorities could send a fleet, until the partial revival of trade with Spain in the eighteenth century. Illegal trading with the great markets of northern Europe via the legal port of Seville remained important. Smuggling on the Caribbean shore of Central America, however, gradually left these other two systems well behind.

In part, this was a deliberate evolution on the part of those Central Americans who were involved in trade. As the seventeenth-century depression advanced, they moved, perhaps reluctantly but also consciously, toward the most logical trading solution—direct trade, carried by ships from northern Europe, between the producer and the consumer.

In part, however, Central American entrepreneurs found themselves, once again, in a situation which was beyond their control. Cacao had been destroyed by demographic losses and outside competition, indigo had stagnated because of market logistics and because of the ceiling on sailing and cargo technology of the shipping of the period. So Central Americans could not solve their market problems simply by shifting from a decaying market, Spain, to a dynamic one, Amsterdam and London, because Dutch and English ships involved in Atlantic trades faced the same problems of time-weight-distance-profitability as did Spanish ships. So Central American merchants, even those most anxious to trade with Dutch and English smugglers, had to wait until the general situation changed. It was not until the building of English and Dutch trade depots in the Caribbean, and the rapid growth in the numbers and speed of English and Dutch shipping in the late seventeenth and early eighteenth centuries, that Central Americans were able to seize market opportunities.

Another point about Central American smuggling is that it had many local quirks and oddities, just as other Caribbean areas had. Profitable disposal of goods after time and money have been spent preparing them is obviously a great spur to human ingenuity, and in situations where markets are reduced competitive disposal of these products often overrides such passions as patriotism and xenophobia and also, to some extent, recognized methods of contraband. Thus, while Central America was part and parcel of the growth of the Latin American contraband industry in the seventeenth century, yet it retained its own peculiar variations on the theme of smuggling.

A further reservation which must be made in any study of contraband comes from the very nature of the trade. It is above all illegal, so all evidence is piecemeal, and we should regard what little material we have as the sailor regards the iceberg; after all, we can examine only those cases which were discovered. Royal authorities, both in Seville and Central America, often acted in collusion with law breakers or broke the laws themselves by enthusiastic participation. In other instances royal governors had to protect the peace and tranquility of their provinces, and the clamor for manufactured goods from Europe was so great that some governors deemed it advisable to turn a blind eye to smuggling in order to avoid public unrest or sedition. Even had officials wished to punish all smugglers and illegal traders their police forces were small, amateur, and primitive. Add to these factors the difficulty of terrain, the emptiness of the Caribbean coast, and the fear of pirates, and the only possible conclusion is that the known cases of illegal trade represented only a small fraction of it.

One case in Honduras graphically illustrates the difficulties faced by law-abiding authorities. Two men bought nine cargas of woolen goods from a foreign ship near Omoa in 1675. (Some said the ship was Dutch, others English.) By the time reports reached royal officials in Comayagua and Tegucigalpa the contraband goods had been loaded onto a recua of mules and transported inland. The authorities organized a chase. At times the pursuers came within an hour's travel of the fleeing smugglers, but they finally escaped by crossing into the jurisdiction of Nueva Segovia in Nicaragua. A complaint was then made to the Audiencia in Guatemala, which had jurisdiction over the whole province. By the time Guatemala had issued orders for the capture of the two delinquents it was 1677, and the goods in question had somehow diminished from nine loads to six. The trail was cold. It seems to have been common knowledge in Honduras that the two men involved were only employees, and that the goods belonged to Alonso de Castro, a vecino of Comayagua. Yet there is no record of any punishment.[6]

When examining Central American illegal trading it is also necessary to consider some characteristics of the area which differentiate it from other Latin American territories. Smuggling was comparatively slow to develop in Central America. It was not part of the "near Atlantic," so it suffered the disadvantages of the time-weight-distance-profitability determinants; and among those of the far Atlantic it was something of a poor relation. It lacked the silver of Veracruz and Panama (Peru), and the gold of New Granada. So it was not an obvious port of call for a European smuggler. (Cacao did not become an important luxury beverage in Europe until the seventeenth century was well advanced, and by that time only the Costa Rican fields were of any importance. They, too, had marketing difficulties and finally resolved them through organized, systematic smuggling.) Apart from indigo, which was far less profitable than gold, silver, precious stones, or even cochineal, foreigners had little reason to call.

Another factor which delayed the rise of Central American smuggling was the inhospitable nature of the Caribbean coast of Central America. Not only were the seas of that coast notoriously difficult and the anchorages unsafe and few, but there was little Spanish settlement on the shores. Much of the coast was occupied by unreduced Indians such as the Jicaques and Zambos Mosquitos. Spanish settlements were small and isolated, with few subservient Indians to supply the labor. Central America was, in fact, largely a Pacific area both economically and demographically.

For these reasons, smuggling with Europe was exceptionally slow to develop in Central America. There are few incidents before the decadence of the fleet system in the 1630s. No doubt the Dutch and other European traders who purchased the indigo and hides were content to do so through Seville despite the extra cost. Certainly sixteenth- and early seventeenth-century smuggling in Central America could not rival activities in the Caribbean islands, or the massive Dutch intrusions on the Venezuelan coast in the late sixteenth century.[7]

Central American trading illegality, therefore, lagged in its stages, and before 1630, while the fleet system was still functioning adequately so that disposal of goods was not yet a great worry, it usually amounted to little more than evasion of duties and taxes. Thus typical cases of the times are not spectacular. People in Central America were prosecuted for introducing undeclared goods among registered goods,[8] for smuggling out illicit goods on the two official Honduras ships,[9] and for calling at the ports of Honduras when their licenses specified other ports. All these devices were well established before 1605.[10]

The situation altered significantly after 1630 as it became obvious that the flota system was decaying and the Spanish economy declining. Between 1630 and 1680 there seems to have been a slow increase in the volume of smuggling, and gradually smuggling became more important than simple fraud, but during this half century, the depth of the depression, it was not enough to provide a dependable exit and entry for goods. Foreigners were still pirates rather than illegal traders.[11]

So Central American merchants and indigo plantation owners in the middle years of the seventeenth century found themselves with a fairly viable export crop, although one of minor importance compared to silver, and few means of disposing of it. True, solutions to major difficulties within the industry such as recurrent locust plagues and labor shortages, and to minor irritants such as local interference and royal taxation, had been partial ones at best, but now the industry faced more than stagnation. Drastic decline would take place if ways to the major markets of Europe could not be found. Legal trade to the official ports in the Bay of Honduras had fallen away to a trickle, and smuggling had not developed either in volume or method as in other areas of the Caribbean. Transportation of the indigo and royal silver to Veracruz had increased, but this did not help when Veracruz was itself cut off from Spain for several years at a time. Between the early 1630s and the 1680s Central America searched desperately, often beyond the law, for ways of disposing of export crops while obtaining money or goods in exchange. That it took so long before a fairly regular system could be instituted is in part a reflection of the relative unimportance of Central America to the major European traders. Piracy and wars and the difficult coastal geography also played a part. The devices

used during this period of economic exigency also reflect desperation and little long term planning; if the crop of the current year
could be sold, future crops and produce were left to care for themselves.

A case in the 1660s illustrates the problems of the trade, and
also, conveniently, shows us the difficulties faced by royal officials
at that time. Don Martín Carlos de Mencos was one of the most
respected Presidents to govern the Audiencia of Guatemala. He had
been some fifty years in the royal service before he was appointed
to Central America. In all this time he had not been able to become
wealthy. To come to the New World, he claimed, he had been
obliged to auction off his few movable possessions to pay for the
passage, such had been his lack of material rewards. To add to his
poverty his wife had died of fever in Panama after the crossing,
bequeathing a sum of money to a convent in Navarre. As a result,
Mencos was obliged to send two silver bars to Spain shortly after
his arrival in Guatemala.[12] Such was the essence of his defense when
he was accused in 1663 of engaging in commerce with Hollanders.
It is significant that the complainant was Nicolás Justiniano, a Genoese merchant, who just ten years before had seen his own indigo
shipments seized by the Crown, which had then shipped them to
Holland. Justiniano, a member of the powerful Justiniano Chavarri
family, had been paid off by the Crown in almost worthless juros,
and having been thus shabbily rewarded for his rectitude, he was
particularly incensed to find royal officials profiting by illegal
trade.[13] He alleged that Mencos had sent 400 cases of indigo dye
and eight bars of silver to Holland via an agent in Seville. A Seville
merchant, when challenged, agreed that the allegation was substan-
tially correct and admitted forwarding the goods in question to
Holland.

It is obvious that the Consejo knew him to be guilty but at the
same time felt that he was a remarkable public servant. Accordingly
they refused, in effect, to pass judgment, and turned the whole
matter over to the King.[14] The case dragged on. New allegations
were advanced. Gold had also been sent, and some of the shipment,
besides being unregistered, had been sent on unlicensed ships. The
mayordomo of the warehouses at the Golfo Dulce named the ships
involved, and testified to having seen the 400 cases of indigo dye.
In another affixed report it was alleged that the amount involved
was 800 cases.[15]

Mencos pleaded guilty but advanced many extenuating circumstances. He argued, indirectly, that this was the only way to raise the

money necessary to pay his late wife's bequest to the Navarrese convent. And surely, it was implied, the King and the Council would not stand in the way of such a holy cause, or deprive the good nuns of their badly needed funds.[16] By 1668 Mencos' patience had run out, and the Council's anger, if indeed it had ever been very great, had cooled. Mencos complained to the Council that many of his goods were still under embargo by Juan de Arrellano, the juez de arribadas or smuggling judge, and requested that the case be concluded as quickly as possible. The King agreed, scrawling on the cover of Mencos' letter that the Council should "do justice, with all brevity."[17]

The Council presumably found Mencos guilty, but its punishment must have been extremely light for it cast no shadow at all on Mencos' career. At the end of the same year, 1668, Mencos was requesting that an encomienda which he held in Guatemala be extended for one more life. The Council which so recently had been his judge noted that the situation was somewhat irregular, for a President could not by law hold an encomienda in the province which he governed, but the encomienda had been given to Mencos by the King to provide him with an income, and it was in indios vacos, or unassigned Indians, so the Council recommended that the request be granted. They pointed out that Mencos had proved to be a worthy governor! He had just finished his first term and was to be continued in office, a sure sign of royal approval. The King agreed to Mencos' request for the renewal of the encomienda grant.[18] Further proofs of royal favor were manifested to the Mencos family. After the death of Martín Carlos his brother, Gabriel de Mencos, was permitted to assume ownership of the encomienda in "second life." A year later, after Gabriel's death, his son Joseph Carlos de Mencos took over the encomienda.[19]

The reasons for the Council's tolerance of Mencos' illegal trading are fairly obvious. The man had proved himself an efficient yet unspectacular public servant over a period of years, he was popular with most segments of the Spanish population in Central America, and he kept the royal peace. In the seventeenth century such men were rare, and minor indiscretions were overlooked accordingly—yet another adaptation to a time of need.

The lessons to be learned from the Mencos case were surely not ignored by the local Guatemalan merchants. Justiniano Chavarri had lost heavily by trading within the law. His indigo had been confiscated, he had been repaid in juros of little value, and his indigo had ended up in the Low Countries just like that of Mencos.

Mencos, on the other hand, while he had been forced to suffer the inconvenience and the indignity of a long enquiry, had emerged from his illegal activities only to find further rewards and evidences of royal favor. The lesson was not lost on Nicolás Justiniano Chavarri, at any event. About this time he was accused of trading with a Dutch vessel named La Guera, captained by Adrian Andriansen.[20]

Naturally care was needed if one invested in contraband. There was a distinct difference between smuggling via Seville and direct trade with the enemy. Much depended also on the rank and influence of the people involved. Just three years before the Mencos case was so quietly disposed of in Madrid, three men were tried for "relations and commerce with a Dutch pirate ship." Mateo de Rivera Calderón and Domingo de Acosta were sentenced to death, and Francisco Martín Muñoz to life imprisonment.[21]

Despite such occasional ferocity on the part of the authorities, it is obvious that direct smuggling with foreigners in the Bay of Honduras was going on in a sporadic but fairly frequent fashion during the middle years of the century. The Dutch were the most frequent visitors at this time. Certainly large quantities of Central American produce such as indigo and logwood were finding their way to Dutch islands.[22]

A favorite device used by both Spanish and foreign vessels was the arribada maliciosa. The arribada was a device whereby ships claimed that they had been forced into ports where they were not normally permitted by unseaworthiness, lack of supplies, or storms at sea. Such arribadas were very hard to disprove, and common humanity dictated that ships in distress not be turned away from safe anchorages. Time and again the Spanish authorities laid down strict rules for the control of arribadas. Local officials were ordered to verify that any ship which did arrive with this pretext really was in distress or in need of supplies. Once in port arribada ships were to have as few contacts as possible with the shore, and every landing and loading was to be closely watched by local officials. Little could be done about such a situation.[23] Sometimes an honest official in Santiago or Comayagua would attempt to control it, but the capitals were too far removed, "over 140 leagues," and at that distance personal supervision was impossible.

One exasperated President, in an attempt to stop all illegal trade, tried to bring all commerce to a halt in the Gulf of Honduras. The vecinos of the cities of Guatemala and Honduras complained to the King and asked him to restrain the President from such a drastic line of action.[24] The King ordered the President to desist, and said that legitimate trade in the Golfo Dulce, Santo Tomás, Puerto Caballos, Trujillo, the Desaguadero, and Portobelo should be left unhindered.[25]

In their search for solutions the Kings were sometimes led to blame foreigners residing in the Indies. Even those that had resided there for some time fell under suspicion, and all were frequently forbidden to trade, especially with compatriots.[26] Even if foreigners were guilty of smuggling, their expulsion could change the situation little when so many Creoles and peninsulares were involved. Foreigners had little need of local agents from the home country when local officials were willing to undertake this role. One of the most emphatic cases is that involving don José Barón de Burruez (sometimes written Joseph Varón de Berrieza).

This man was treasurer of the Santa Cruzada in Guatemala from December 1673 until December 1689. Almost immediately there were accusations of fraud and illicit commerce against him, but little was done. Finally by royal decree dated May 26, 1686, the King ordered that an enquiry be started. It took two more royal decrees in September of that year before anything was begun by local officials. The inquiry, commenced so reluctantly, proved that the treasurer of the Santa Cruzada had systematically engaged in illicit trade for many years. He had acted as local factor or agent (Spanish, testaferro) for a foreigner called Don Juan Baptista Goli. An inventory found that Barón de Burruez had defrauded the Crown of 18,735 pesos and 7 1/2 reales in taxes, (alcabala, alcabala de Barlovento, and derechos de entrada) on goods brought into Guatemala, the above total being probably not more than 5 per cent of the total value of the goods in question. He had also evaded payments of 4,869 pesos and 7 1/2 reales on taxes on goods leaving the country, giving a grand total of 23,605 pesos and 7 reales. He had been dealing primarily in indigo, pita thread, and cacao.

The treasurer put up a spirited defense. Part of his defense was a list of other tax evaders and smugglers in Guatemala City, the argument being, in effect, that he should not be held responsible for a common practice in the colony. Another excuse was that many of the taxes evaded were simply local ones and thus, presumably, not so important. Much of the indigo was being sent to New Spain for transshipment to Spain or elsewhere.

An interesting point was the double fraud involved in his cacao transactions. Of the 403 tercios of cacao involved, 310 were from Guayaquil, and only 93 from the provinces of Central America. The introduction of Guayaquil cacao compounded the illegality. All evidence and conclusions were sent to Spain, and the King ordered in a decree of 2 June 1691 that justice should be done. A heavy fine was imposed on the culprit, which his widow paid out of his estate shortly after his death.[27] The case is revealing. The reluctance to start an investigation on the part of local authorities, the official position of the culprit, the goods involved, their provenance and destination, the list of other smugglers presented as a defense, and above all the defendant's role as a representative of a foreigner, all show that smuggling was fast becoming a permanent feature of Creole society in Central America.

There was little the Crown could do in face of such widespread and such pervasive illegality. A junta was called by the King in 1677 to discuss the question. The Duke of Medinaceli presided and one of the major figures consulted was the Marquis of Mancera, who had just returned to Spain after serving as viceroy in Mexico. After some discussion the Marquis of Variñas made proposals which reflect the feeling of futility which possessed the members of the junta. The only answer which Variñas could find to the problem of arribadas was to have better governors and ministers and to punish wrongdoers more severely. On smuggling in Honduras itself Variñas had little to suggest.

"On the trade of the coast of Honduras in hides, cacao, cochineal, sarsaparilla, indigo, jalap, arnatto, suet, and many other products, the only solution which was proposed was the tightening of the orders prohibiting the trade with foreigners, and the committing of the investigation and punishment of any infraction, however slight, to an oidor in Guatemala, which is 140 leagues away, or to the Bishop of Comayagua." Further restriction was tried. Decrees of November 4, 1661, and December 21, 1677, ordered that in cases of arribadas maliciosas, forbidden foreign traders, or unlicensed Spanish shipping, one accusation from a public official or person would be sufficient for a formal proceeding to be started against the accused.[28]

In spite of the apparent pervasiveness of smuggling it is obvious that it had not yet reached sufficient dimensions to allow indigo and other industries large enough markets to support expansion of production. Several circumstances postposed its expansion. After the first quarter of the seventeenth century the political and economic situation in the Caribbean was gradually but radically altered by the seizure of islands and the establishment of naval bases on them by European powers, the two most important acquisitions from the commercial point of view being Curaçao, seized by the Dutch in 1634, and Jamaica which fell to the English in 1655.[29]

These new bases for smugglers helped the Central American exporters very little at first. Curaçao was not geographically of immediate use to Central America. Ships from that area put into Costa Rica, and even the Bay of Honduras at times, but the trade was not extensive. The main interests of the hordes of Dutch smugglers lay elsewhere in the Caribbean.[30] Jamaica was a natural center for trade leaving the Bay of Honduras, and it was eventually to become a large emporium of goods for Central America. But for the first few decades after its seizure by the British the future of Jamaica was the subject of a long and acrimonious debate between two very different factions on the island.

One group composed of merchants and slave-trading interests was in favor of peaceful trade with the Spanish islands and mainland, and believed that placation of Spanish suspicions was the proper course for the island to follow. The opposing group believed that wealth could be accumulated more rapidly and England's national interests served more readily by constant armed hostility to Spain. This group was composed of the pirates and their backers and outfitters, and, to a lesser extent, of the local Jamaican planters who saw the produce of the Spanish dominions as a potential threat to their crops if allowed unlimited access to Jamaican and English markets.[31] In spite of the effort of some enlightened early governors, the second faction was in the ascendency in the early years of the colony. Precedent was on their side. Providence Island, a temporary English possession off the coast of Nicaragua, had made a precarious but profitable industry before 1641 out of preying on Spanish coastal traffic between Cartagena, Portobelo, and the ports of Honduras and Yucatan. The high point of the activities of the Providence islanders was the seizure of Trijillo in the late summer of 1639. Trujillo paid a ransom of 16,000 pesos, partly in bullion and partly in indigo.[32]

1660-85 were the great years of English piracy in the Caribbean. Henry Morgan's famous raids took place at this time, and in Central America itself the famous sackings of Granada, Nueva Segovia, Puerto Caballos, and Trujillo were well known.[33] On the empty Caribbean coast between Trujillo and the Desaguadero the English from Jamaica had established friendly relations with the Mosquito Indians and with bands of cimarrones, both groups with long histories of hostility to the neighboring Spanish settlements. In addition small groups of pirates or privateers, mostly from Jamaica, began to settle in semi-permanent fashion on that part of the coast, on the Bay Islands, especially Roatán, and, to a lesser extent, on the equally empty stretch between the Gulf of Amatique and Cape Catoche. At Cape Gracias a Dios, Captain Abraham Blew-field or Blauvelt, a Dutchman in the English service, was reported in 1663 to be "living amongst ye Indians," and in possession of a bark with three guns manned by an English, Dutch, and Indian crew of fifty men. In the second half of the century small groups of whites with negro and some Indian laborers had settled here and there all along what was later to be called the Mosquito Coast, first to do a little small-scale planting and trading with the Indians, and later, after about 1665, to engage in piracy.[34] Obviously pirates were a great hindrance to trade. They made the seas dangerous, and major sackings such as those of the Nicaraguan city of Granada caused heavy temporary damage to the local economy. Smuggling did go on. Piracy did not stop it, but it could help to prevent its expansion. After all, smuggling is to some extent the antithesis of piracy. The two coexist with difficulty. Piracy and trading can be disguises for one another, and sometimes were, but usually piracy prevents the modicum of mutual trust which is necessary even between smug-glers before an effective exchange of goods can be attempted. With the Caribbean coast of Central America a principal haunt of pirates, it was difficult for smuggling to become regular and intensive.

Even after the advocates of peaceful trade gained the ascen-dency in Jamaica and made sincere attempts to end piracy, they found that the establishment of large-scale trade with the Spanish mainland was a slow process. Official encouragement of pirates and looters in Jamaica had built up too much suspicion for the situation to change overnight.

On the Mosquito shore the English reaped the harvest they themselves had sown. By the 1680s the heavy influx of English-led negroes had changed the coastal Sumus or Miskitos into the dreaded Zambos Mosquitos so feared by the Spaniards. The English taught these allies the arts of piracy, and when contraband became the English preference, they found that the Zambos Mosquitos had been taught their lesson only too well. It was quite some time before the inhabitants of the Mosquito Coast learned the new ways, and the Spaniards, especially in the Matina valley of Costa Rica, found them to be very unreliable contrabandistas.[35]

Governor Lynch and other pro-trade governors complained of the difficulties in overcoming this Spanish suspicion. And every relapse into piracy, every English ship which was sighted by Span-iards cutting Brazil wood off Cape Catoche or Honduras, reinforced Spanish doubts about Jamaica's real willingness to trade.[36]

Yet another factor was to postpone the development of a large trade between Central America and Jamaica. Spanish Colonial America had a constant need for negro slaves for its plantations, workshops, and mines. Certain areas needed or could afford more than others. In Middle America, Mexico's mines and the isthmus of Panama, with its trajín or Peru trade from Panama to Portobelo, could outbid any part of Central America for slaves, and needed them in far greater quantities. Moreover, Central American authorities did not always want more slaves even when they were available.

Spain had no slave depots in Africa and so the authorities supplied the colonies with slaves by contracting with private agencies. After the collapse of Spanish trade these agents had to be foreigners. The need for slaves was often the thin end of the smuggling wedge. Foreign control of Spain's slave trade was certainly a major factor in weakening Spain's control of her own American markets. (Before 1580 slaving within the Spanish domains was an ad hoc, individual matter. Scarcity was not much in evidence, perhaps because labor needs in America could be supplied by the Indians before the 1570s. All conditions of men, Francisco de los Cobos and Pedro de Alvarado among them, were engaged in the buying, transportation, and selling of African slaves.)

Portuguese concessionaries had held this royal contract or asiento since about 1580, but their hegemony came to an end with the Portuguese separatist revolt of 1640. During this early period few Portuguese slave ships visited Central America, and there is no evidence that they played a significant part in Central American trade, either legal or illegal. After the Portuguese revolt the asiento system was allowed to lapse for twenty years. The Dutch, and to a much lesser extent the English and the French, filled the gap. Curaçao became little more than a gigantic slave pen and clandestinely supplied Spanish American needs. Once again there is no evidence that these Dutch ships visited the Caribbean shore of Central America more than sporadically.[37] Probably Central Americans could not afford to buy many slaves.

In 1663 the Crown revived the asiento system, no doubt out of a desire to participate in the profits of the slave system. The first asiento was granted to a pair of Genoese bankers and merchants, Domingo Grillo and Ambrosio Lomelin. The Lomelin interest soon died out, and this asiento, which lasted until 1678, is usually known as the Grillo asiento. While the principal business of the Grillos was slaves, it is obvious that they, like other earlier slavers, also dealt in

contraband goods.[38] Their sources of supply of slaves had to be
Curaçao and Jamaica, since there were few others readily available,
and from these two islands and others such as St. Kitts and Bar-
bados, they shipped slaves and contraband goods to their main
Spanish markets, Cartagena, Portobelo, and Veracruz. Once again
this system worked to the disadvantage of any Jamaican-Central
American trade. The Grillos preferred Curaçao to Jamaica because
Jamaica suffered from problems of supply from time to time and the
Dutch offered lower prices.[39] Moreover, the Grillos concentrated on
Tierra Firme and Veracruz, where they could be sure of good prices
for the slaves, and they visited other parts of Spanish America less
often. Not that Central America was totally ignored; there is evidence that Grillo ships and agents did call, particularly in Costa
Rica, where the coastal cacao plantations needed slaves and provided an important export crop to pay for them.[40] But such trade
was a minor matter compared to that with other areas. The net effect
of the Grillo asiento, therefore, was to undersupply Central America
with contraband goods because it was not a major market for the
sale of slaves, and to inhibit the development of direct contraband
trade from Jamaica. Governor Lynch complained of this. There was
little point in trying to start trade with Spanish America, he wrote,
because the Grillos always flooded the market before the English
arrived, and the Grillos had the decided advantage that their entry
to the principal ports was legal.[41]

The succeeding asiento was little better from the Jamaican and
Central American point of of view. After a short period under Spanish control (1682–85) the asiento passed as a bad debt to the ownership of a Dutch banking and trading company called Coymans. The
Coymans asentistas (1685–89) naturally preferred Dutch sources of
supply and continued to indulge in much the same kind of combined slave-trading and smuggling as their predecessors.[42]

Jamaica, then, did not become the Central American emporium
with the speed which all would have desired. From its conquest in
1655 until about 1685 its development, and consequently the development of a large contraband trade in Central America, was inhibited by many factors. As one observer has summed it up: "Too many
pirates and too few negroes, too many disappointments and too
much distrust, prices too high and jealousies too fierce."[43] Central
American frustration at the failure to replace the decadent fleet
system with a large contraband trade was a basic feature of the
mid-seventeenth century. The period of restrained smuggling
lasted from the 1630s until the late 1680s, and there seemed little

that Central Americans could do to develop contraband or seek fresh alternatives. Such matters were too much at the disposition of outside forces in the Caribbean and Europe. The extent of this frustration in Central America can only be guessed. There were many complaints to the Crown, but complaints were not new. Perhaps most revealing of all were two extraordinary events which carried commercial illegality close to the point of rebellion.

The first such event took place early in the mid-seventeenth century depression. One of the two royal ships which sailed with the fleet for Honduras in 1647 was owned by a merchant in Hamburg. There was little of note in this; most Spanish ships were foreign-owned by this time. What was extraordinary was the boarding of the ship by the owner on the high seas some time after it left Seville. Presumably this took place somewhere off the Spanish coast.

The owner accompanied the ship to Honduras, where it was unloaded, and then reloaded with indigo, hides, and sarsaparilla. (One source says 800 cases of indigo, another 1,000. It was obviously the major part of the cargo.) While most of the Spanish members of the crew were ashore, the Hamburger, whose name was Vannesen, a Dutch name surely, seized the ship with the help of the many foreign sailors among the crew.

The ship then weighed anchor and sailed directly to Holland, touching briefly at an English port on the way. Immediately diplomatic activity began. The Spaniards requested the return of the ship and its cargo. The Dutch talked of keeping it as a prize. The Spanish complaint mentioned the great loss sustained by the owners of the cargo, but it was obvious that the Crown's main concern was the loss of the import tax which would have been paid if the cargo had passed through the custom house at Seville. The solution arrived at was satisfactory to both parties. The Count of Peñaranda reported to the King from Brussels on March 2, 1649, that the ship had been unloaded and sold in Amsterdam, and that a compensatory payment was to be made to the Spanish Crown.

Many notes in the whole affair ring false. There was no talk of compensatory payment to the owners of the indigo, hides, and sarsaparilla, in spite of the royal complaint that these owners had suffered heavy losses. Nor is there any known complaint from these owners themselves, either to the Crown or to the local Guatemalan authorities. Such silence is indeed strange. Seventeenth-century Guatemalan merchants were not given to stoicism when faced with losses and abuse of this sort. The truth must be that the whole affair was known to most of the parties concerned. The sailors who were so conveniently ashore no doubt had been informed of the matter and had decided to remain in the New World or to return with another ship. They must have been few, for the ship had enough crew left to sail back to Europe without apparent difficulty—and Spanish seventeenth-century ships did not carry many superfluous crew members.

The series of events was, in fact, a deliberate plot by the owner, and probably the Central American merchants, to eliminate the middleman—in this case the wasteful and expensive port and taxes of Seville—and to save the cost of reshipment of the cargo from Seville to Holland. One guesses that profit margins must have been low, and Central American frustration fairly high, before such blatant illegality was attempted.[44]

The other event occurred in 1688. In that year the Spanish fleet did sail, and two ships put into Trujillo in Honduras with wine, oil, and other goods. The ships were met at Trujillo by the governor of Honduras, don Juan Tomás Milut. (Elsewhere he is named as don Juan José Milutum). The governor allowed only a small quantity of wine to be unloaded. The prices, he claimed, were ridiculously low because of the poverty of the people and the amount of wine, brandy, and munitions which were being smuggled in from Jamaica and Roatán. (Perhaps there had also been a recent shipment of Peruvian wine.) At any rate, the good governor felt these low prices to be sufficient justification for his abandonment of his charge. The governor assumed command of the ships, against all regulations, and sailed them off to Veracruz, where the market was larger and the prices higher.

Once again the elements of a plot were present. There were two Dutchmen on board. One, identified simply as "John of Ostend," was the condestable or chief gunner of the almiranta, or second ship. The other Dutchman, Fernando Masibradi [sic], was commander of the almiranta, and second-in-command of the two ships. He was a former member of the Armada Naval of Flanders. Both fell under suspicion of plotting with the governor. The governor of Honduras died in Mexico before he was able to enjoy his profits and before charges had been brought against him.[45]

The case of the absconding governor illustrates the lengths to which some royal officials would go in order to accumulate capital. Even more, it is symptomatic of some radical changes taking place in Central American trade as the decade of the eighties came to a close. The Spanish enquiry into the theft of the ships mentions several times that a smuggling trade with Jamaica and its offshoots on the Mosquito Coast was fast becoming a permanent feature of the Gulf of Honduras. English ships were coming regularly to the Gulf with wine, brandy, and munitions, then loading up with local produce or sailing north to cut palo de Campeche (dye wood) for the return trip to Jamaica. Roatán was being used as a local depot and refitting port and had a permanent English colony, as did Belize and Cape Gracias a Dios. So the low prices for Spanish wine and oil in the ports of Honduras were not entirely a result of local poverty or Peruvian wine imports. The market was satisfied, perhaps even saturated, by smuggled Jamaican goods.[46]

Several factors were responsible for this new growth and systematization of the smuggling trade. Most immediately important, perhaps, was the ascendency of the merchant class in Jamaica and the consequent suppression of piracy. Governor Lynch, who had always favored trade over piracy, was restored to office in 1681, replacing the notorious Henry Morgan, who was, as might be imagined, anti-asiento, anti-trade, and pro-pirate. Lynch's successor, Hender Molesworth, shared Lynch's ideas. The Duke of Albemarle, who became governor in 1687, represented some return to former policy and was more favorable to local planters and pirates. But his attempt to change policy was brief. Albemarle died after a short term of office, and the English government quickly ordered a return to the encouragement of slave supplying and peaceful trading.[47] Mutual trust was not restored overnight, but by the late 1680s it was clear that the great days of piracy on the Caribbean coast of Central America had gone. The Central American merchants acted accordingly. As their confidence in British efforts to control piracy increased, so did their eagerness to trade with their foreign enemies.

As attitudes in Jamaica changed it became obvious that English possession of the island had been part of the solution to the problem of time, weight, distance, and profitability. Jamaica was part of the "near Atlantic," and therefore many agricultural goods could be shipped to Europe and still show a profit. (The same was true of Curaçao and other islands engaged in smuggling, such as Saint Eustatius, St. Kitts, and Tortuga). Jamaica was also close, the closest large island, to the Gulf of Honduras. Goods such as dyes, sarsaparilla, cacao, or log wood could be shipped on small, undermanned boats which were either too old or too leaky for longer trade routes such as the Atlantic. Then the goods could be stored at the Jamaican way station and entrepôt until fast ships were available to take them to the countries of northwestern Europe. Jamaica also helped take much of the risk out of smuggling goods into

Central America, or indeed into any part of the Spanish possessions on the Caribbean. Goods for sale in Spanish America could be stored on Jamaica in bulk until they were needed in the various markets,[48] and at the same time Jamaica provided a stepping stone to the welcome European markets in Amsterdam and London.

Yet Jamaica answered only part of the difficulty. The volume and speed of shipping had been an even greater difficulty, and one Central American entrepreneurs were helpless to affect. Here again the local dye makers had to wait until situations beyond their control changed in their favor.

The total volume of English shipping changed radically between 1660 and 1730. The total English fleet was about 90,000 tons in 1663, rose to almost double that tonnage by 1688, and had reached 261,222 tons by 1701. A good proportion of that enormous increase went to the American, including Caribbean, trades, which expanded with amazing rapidity at the turn of the century. Accompanying this growth in tonnage was a change in the technology and speed of sailing. The result of these changes as far as Jamaica and Central America were concerned was that both places might expect much more frequent visits from faster and more efficient ships.[49]

English trade figures show that a trade revolution had taken place. England saw a huge growth in its re-export trade between 1690 and 1710, mainly because of reshipped imports from the Americas and the Far East. England's sources of supply and markets, in a remarkably sudden way, had fled from the traditional, nearby ports of Europe to distant parts, especially America.[50]

Dye imports from America rose from an average of £3,000 per year in London in 1663 and 1669 to £71,000 per year from 1699 through 1701, and £85,000 per year for England as a whole during the same years. Granted that some £35,000 of the latter totals represented logwoods which the English themselves had cut in Campeche, Yucatan, and Honduras; nevertheless the rise in American imports is very large. And the rise was purely American. Dye imports from Spain and Portugal, mostly cochineal anyway, remained static in this period, and imports from Holland and other parts of Europe, which in any case were also deriving some of their supplies from America, rose only slightly. Even more significant was the decline, by more than half, in the imports of indigo from the East Indies. The East Indies were still the only other major source of indigo. Brazil and South Carolina were not to enter the market as large competitors until the middle of the eighteenth century.[51]

In fact the great increase in English interest in Central America was largely because of a huge rise in the demand for dyes. Deliveries from India were failing, and even at their former levels they no longer satisfied the expanding textile industry. Central America was the only place to which the needy British could turn. At last the frustrated añileros of the Pacific coast had found the large market which they had sought for so long.

Evidence is spotty, but it is obvious that the new expansion of indigo also helped lesser Central American products. In the nine months between Christmas Day 1697 and September 21, 1698, for example, Jamaica sent 914 barrels of cacao (Costa Rican no doubt) and 83 bags of sarsaparilla to England. Perhaps as much again may have been sent illegally, for the English, too, had their problems with contraband.[52]

The change from the slow growth of contraband in Central America between 1630 and the 1680s to the rapid expansion in the three decades thereafter is hard to document, yet obviously it took place. When President Jacinto de Barrios Leal arrived in Central America in 1687 with his father, several relatives, and the usual retinue of paniaguados, they all brought luxury merchandise of various kinds from Europe. Later, undeclared and untaxed, these contraband goods were sent to Peru to be sold at high profits.[53] Less than a decade later, however, such minor transgressions and petty frauds would scarcely have been noticed. Direct contraband with foreigners had become a major source of income, if not the largest single source, for Central American officials at all levels. The Spanish government was aware of this and knew the names of the individuals involved, but it could do little when all protected one another.[54]

By 1695 smuggling was the major item of news in the colony. Governors or oidores writing to Spain could find little else to report.[55] As we have seen, Costa Rican cacao had been one of the first industries to take advantage of the new conditions in shipping, in Jamaica and in England. Here, too, officials were deeply involved, and heavy punishment of those who were infrequently caught and convicted seemed to be no deterrent to others.[56]

Other factors of a minor nature also acted upon the growing trade. After the expiration of Coymans' asiento the contract passed into the hands of a Portuguese company called Carcau. This company was closely linked to English and Dutch interests, indeed dependent on them. The Portuguese asiento holders even lacked sufficient ships. So from 1694 until 1701, the period of the Por-

tuguese contract, the asiento presented even less hindrance to English and Dutch contraband trade than had Grillo and Coymans,
who themselves had been porous barriers at best.[57] To the extent
that Central America needed slaves in the 1690s, it probably
brought them where it found the prices to be most favorable.

The intrusion of the events of the outside world on Central
American contraband was to continue. The death without issue of
Charles "the Bewitched" in 1700 precipitated a European conflict
over the succession to his crown. England and the Spain of Phillip
V were on opposite sides of this conflict, which at first glance would
appear to be an unfavorable circumstance for the rapidly expanding
Central American contraband trade. The war brought just the opposite effect. English smuggling from Jamaica and elsewhere maintained its position, albeit with some difficulties, in spite of the war.

Central America was no exception. Incidents of English smuggling to Central American ports did not decrease between the years
1700 to 1713. In fact, if anything, they tended to increase and local
officials were heavy offenders.[58] This was particularly true of Costa
Rica, where the cacao plantations had at last found the export market which they had needed in order to expand. Smuggling became
the universal method of trade in that part of the isthmus, and most
non-Indian vecinos seem to have been involved.[59]

While the English held their own, the period of the War of
Spanish Succession saw the entry of a new power into the lucrative
business of Caribbean contraband. The French had no doubt traded
clandestinely with Central America before 1700, but their activities
up until then were not as sustained as those of the English or the
Dutch.

The War of Spanish Succession, whereby a French Bourbon
came to the throne of a thoroughly impoverished Spain, had cast
Spain into the arms of France. Philip V depended on French power
for his very continuance on the throne. In such circumstances pro-
testations that Spain was a separate power, which intended to maintain its exclusivist New World policy intact, were little more than
fond hopes on the part of the Spanish government.

The first sign of the new commercial entrée which the French
had gained was the granting of the slave asiento to France in 1701.[60]
Central America's indigo industry, now expanding at last, had a
renewed and urgent need for slaves, and made full use of this
asiento. Slaves and the accompanying contraband were imported
into the Audiencia of Guatemala in large numbers during the first
decade of the eighteenth century—some legally and many illegally.[61]

Most valuable to France was the Spanish recognition of the weakness of its own navy and its lack of merchant ships. To remedy this Spain's new ally was given the privilege of conveying the Spanish ships to and from the New World, which inevitably entailed the giving of permits to these French ships to allow them legal entry to ports in Spanish America. On other occasions, admittedly fewer, French merchantmen were given licenses for one voyage to carry specific goods to a specific port.[62] Such privileges were cracks in the already tottering dam against foreign trade erected by Spanish imperial exclusionism.

French traders took advantage of their semi-legal status and French goods flooded into Latin America. The Crown sought in vain to point out the distinctions to the deliberately obtuse colonials. That France was Spain's close ally and her protector on land and sea did not mean, the Crown insisted, that France could trade freely with Spanish America. The old laws were still in force. No foreign ship was to enter Spanish American harbors without a proper permit. But the Spanish American merchants and the officials in the colonies continued to profess confusion about this distinction.[63]

Trade increased rapidly. The French, led by the merchants of St. Malo, began to appear in the Pacific off the coasts of Peru and Chile, and even reached the Pacific coasts of Central America on a few occasions.[64] The Caribbean and the port at the Golfo Dulce was, however, France's main entry to the Central American market. For more than a decade Central America and France enjoyed a profitable partnership.[65] And, as ever, the Dutch in Curaçao were engaged in the trade. Jamaica experienced difficulty, particularly in the years after 1700, in competing with the low Dutch prices.

The ending of the War of Spanish Succession gave further advantages to the entrepreneurs in the Audiencia of Guatemala and to the foreign interlopers. By the terms of the treaty of Utrecht in 1713 the English gained the coveted asiento, and from then on their trading activities in Central America gained a quasi-legal official status. True, the treaty meant a decline in French trade, but the expansion of English activity in Jamaica and elsewhere more than compensated for this.[66]

The following examination of a revealing document shows to what extent contraband trade had solved the market problems of Central America by the first decade of the eighteenth century. As the story was first told to officialdom, the watch at the castle of the port of Golfo Dulce observed two ships on November 2, 1705. On November 10 a frigate anchored and sent a license ashore for approval. The license or registro, it was initially said, showed that the ships had left Portobelo with local produce. (What if any was the local produce of Portobelo, and why should it find a market in Guatemala?) All the sailors on board were Spanish. The ship, with the imposing name of La Anunciación San Francisco Xavier y las Animas, asked for permission to unload and was allowed to do so.

As usual, our knowledge of what really happened derives from dissension among those involved. On February 1, 1706, a free negro named Marcos de la Cruz told the authorities that he had been present for the twenty-two days that the ship was unloading, and had himself worked on this task. For his work he had been paid only eleven pesos, instead of the twenty-two pesos promised. All efforts to recover his money having failed, he was appealing to the Audiencia.

Marcos de la Cruz had participated in the unloading of not one ship, but two. The second ship was a balandra from Curaçao. The goods unloaded from the two ships had consisted in large part of foreign cloth. The man in command of the two ships was Francisco da Costa Pego, "of the Portuguese nation, a man well known in the Windward Islands, and who consequently had changed his name to Manuel Diez."

For unknown reasons the affair was not hushed up. Perhaps Marcos de la Cruz was more vocal and emphatic than had been expected. Undoubtedly some Creoles or Spaniards felt that they had been too much excluded from this lucrative business. Whatever the reasons, the affair rapidly grew to such dimensions that it was impossible to ignore it or keep it from the ears of the authorities in Spain. The seizure of the imported goods was ordered, and as much as possible was collected from the various parts of the province. Also seized was "some of the cargo which was awaiting the return of the same frigate, for example 106 crates of indigo."

The first and obvious step was the removal of the commander of the castle at the Golfo Dulce, who was obviously implicated. Yet others were surely involved and enquiries grew more searching. The scandal was further inflamed when the returning ship fell into the hands of the waiting authorities. The sailors on board were nearly all English or Dutch, "with some two or three Frenchmen." The Portuguese captain escaped, fled to a monastery for asylum, and died there soon afterwards. Shortly afterwards the disgraced commander of the castle also died. The enquiry decided that "many people of the city and the province of Guatemala are involved in this case." Several were jailed or fined, including the sailors. The artillery from the frigate was dragged to Guatemala City to help with defense.

Most damaging of all was the information which began to emerge from those already convicted. Members of the Royal Audiencia were deeply involved. Oidor Juan Gerónimo Duardo, a close friend of the disgraced castellaño and a former interim President, was most closely implicated, but other oidores did not escape suspicion. The corregidores of Sacapa and Chiquimula were removed from their posts. Enquiries were made about the dead Portuguese captain. It was found that he was a steady trader in Jamaica, Curaçao, Santo Domingo, and Caracas. He had been calling at the Golfo Dulce regularly for a number of years.

The Crown did not seem overly astonished at the dimensions of these activities. The frigate, old and unseaworthy, was burned. No doubt it had been used for coastal work only. The confiscated goods were sold at royal auction, and the Crown awarded one-third of the profits to the judges in charge of the enquiry. The Audiencia, including some of those under suspicion, was warned that much more enthusiasm would have to be shown in the future to discover and prosecute this type of offense. The Crown took its profits and hoped for the best; perhaps the frightened royal officials might behave better in the future.[67]

Add to this systematic, regular, and organized contraband trade, which involved vecinos and officials at all levels, the impetus subsequently given by the English asiento, and it is obvious that the Audiencia of Guatemala had by 1715 found a market for its goods, and a source of luxury goods for its own consumption, as it had so long desired. "In 1737, the captain-general of Guatemala . . . declared that the ports of this shore were used for no other purpose than as shelter for foreign ships and that the inhabitants of the whole territory, including the clergy and the highest government officials, were interested solely in illicit trade." Forts built to protect the coast had become warehouses for contraband goods.[68]

The solution had been found, outside the Spanish commercial system, and after so many years of stagnation and frustration it was a solution which Central Americans would not willingly relinquish. Central America had belatedly joined the organized intensive international contraband of the Caribbean. Massive smuggling was to become a part of the local way of life for many years.[69] Contraband had proved a major part of the solution to the seventeenth-century depression.

Conclusion

Europe in 1348 and Central America in 1520 were in the process of solving a crisis which was largely Malthusian in origin. Both were struck by alien invasions and both suffered, it has been suggested here, in similar ways. Central America suffered more and underwent greater transformations partly because its isolation made it more vulnerable to its unseen invaders, the diseases of the Old World, and partly because it, unlike the Western Europe of the fourteenth century, was invaded by alien humans with new economic and social goals which were very different from those of the previous inhabitants.

Certain assumptions, based on the evidence, run throughout this study. There seems to be a necessary and close relationship in agricultural, conquest societies of poor technology between the gross size of the laboring or conquered population and the general economic well-being of the colony. As the population collapsed the economy became depressed. When it revived, although by then population was no longer the critical variable, the economy did, too.

Colonies, by definition, are much influenced by their ties with the metropolis. Economic life is heavily affected by how, when, and with what measure of profitability colonial goods can be sent to market. Such factors will be especially important in deciding the nature of the colonial elite, its relationship to the mother country, its relationship to the classes below it in the colony, and its own adaptability. Finally, it is obvious that the Spanish conquerors in the New World were not men dominated by feudal ambitions. They were first and foremost entrepreneurs and merchants. Only when mercantile activities and the exploitation of the work of others failed did they turn to the land and the formation of the great estate.

Within Central America itself the historical evidence has suggested the following periodization. After the conquest came the sixteenth-century extractive period, ending with the great epidemic

374

of matlazáhuatl-plague in 1576–78. This was followed by an era of crisis and experimentation from about 1580 to the late 1630s, in which Spanish laymen and officials sought solutions to their economic' and social problems. The third phase, running from the 1630s to 1690, and in many ways even beyond, was the great depression. Finally, in the last years of the seventeenth century and up until about 1720, we see the beginnings of a new phase in which there are some signs of a revival in trade (through contraband) and native populations.

The economic history of sixteenth-century Spanish Central America can best be described as a desperate search for a key to wealth from exports, a search for a cash crop or "produit moteur" as the Chaunus have described it, which would bring rapid wealth to many individuals of the conquering group. (As a consequence control of labor was more important than control of land.)

The conquistadores and those who came immediately after them saw with great clarity that of all the desired products in mercantilist Europe gold and silver were most in demand. Possession of them was held to be the touchstone of success for individuals or nations. So early Spaniards in the New World soon abandoned most areas where there were no precious metals for distant Perus or New Granadas. The most extended land grants could not hold some of them.

In Central America the conquistadores were pleased to find that two of the features characteristic of central Mexico were present to a somewhat reduced degree—dense native populations and gold-bearing streams which produced quick profits when subjected to simple panning and washing. As a result the economy of the first two decades was dominated by gold panning and slaving. Large numbers of Indians were rounded up for the gold-bearing streams (negro slaves were even imported for the best of these streams), and even greater numbers of Indians, especially those of Nicaragua and Honduras, were shipped off as slaves to fill the population vacuums of Cuba and Panama. Many were even sent to Peru.

These booms proved to be ephemeral. Nicaragua and Honduras were soon emptied of their aboriginal populations both by export and by devastating epidemics. The surface gold and silver were rapidly creamed off, and the settlers found no Central American equivalents of Guanajuato or Zacatecas. The silver strikes around Tegucigalpa caused some minor flurries of excitement in the second half of the sixteenth century, but silver mining there

never developed beyond the stage of being a secondary employer
and producer.

Here, then, in the 1550s, we find Central America's first depression, a minor affair to be sure, but a revealing one. Casting about
for a replacement for gold, silver, and slaves the Spaniards of Central America reacted in several ways. Some took to the land, desert-
ing the cities and attempting to become cattle barons, but at this
stage these would-be feudal lords were comparatively few in number. Many more simply abandoned Central America, leaving their
encomiendas, land grants, and positions as conquistadores and
primeros pobladores to go to lands where gold and silver had been
found or seemed likely to be found, fleeing in such numbers that
some local administrators complained exaggeratedly to the Crown
that the land stood to be totally emptied of Spaniards if the exodus
continued. Most Spaniards, however, took neither of these solutions. Instead they searched stubbornly and widely for a new cash
crop to replace gold, silver, and slaving. Some tried balsam; others
sarsaparilla, much in demand in Europe as a medicine, hides, cochineal, and fibers. But the solution to the problem, a solution
which brought a boom to Central America in the second half of the
sixteenth century, proved to be an Indian beverage previously almost ignored by Spaniards, so bizarre in concoction and taste that
the first conquerors in Central America had dismissed it as "filth,"
"fit only for pigs."

Cacao had been exported from Soconusco and its satellite area
of Zapotitlán-Suchitepeques to the Aztec centers, and from the Bay
of Honduras to Yucatan before the conquest; and some marginal
Spanish petty merchants and officials had attached themselves to
this trade from the beginning. Early and catastrophic population
decline in these two hot coastal areas, however, had diverted the
interest of the more imaginative Spanish entrepreneurs elsewhere.
Now, in the 1550s and 1560s the decline and even disappearance
of the cacao fields in Tabasco, Colima, and Soconusco and the
continuing demand for large quantities of chocolate by the Indians
of central Mexico forced the price of the product rapidly upward,
thus making it economically feasible to bring even more distant
areas into production.

The opportunity was seized by the mercantilist Spaniards of the
Audiencia of Guatemala. Small but flourishing groves in Izalcos
(Sonsonate), formerly used mainly to supply Guatemala itself, were
rapidly expanded. Labor was brought in from the highlands, even
from as far away as Verapaz; a fleet of small ships was bought and

built to carry the cacao from the port of Acajutla to the Mexican ports of Huatulco, Zihuatanejo, and even Acapulco; and by the early 1570s Izalcos had all the appearances of an area undergoing a monocultural boom.

Cacao groves were extended to the east around the town of San Miguel, and the minor fields of Nicaragua were expanded. The Guatemalan district of Guazacapán was added to the Izalcos fields, and a new town was built for the driving cacao merchants in a vain attempt to keep them out of the Indian villages. In the years after the founding of this town, Santísima Trinidad de Sonsonate, it did not contain even one encomendero or landowner.

The main wealth from the cacao boom soon fell into the hands of some three or four favored encomenderos of Santiago de Guatemala who were able for two generations to accumulate massive wealth and transfer much of it to Spain. But the boom was large enough to provide handsome profits for some one hundred to two hundred Spanish and mestizo merchants, and its wealth attracted the Spanish administrators of the cities, many of whom, including a President, several oidores, a Genoese family, and a host of minor officials, attached themselves to the wealthy encomenderos and merchants by graft, friendship, compadrazgo, and marriage. This cacao clique became so powerful that at its height it could ignore the authority of the King, overcome a royal attempt to break up the territory of the Audiencia, and preserve the positions of its most powerful members in spite of massive illegalities and prosecutions. It seemed for almost two decades that if this group could accommodate itself to metropolitan and royal pressures for a share of the profits it had at last solved the problem of the Spanish entrepreneurs of Central America.

The cacao areas, however, were showing signs of strain and a basic unsoundness in structure even in the days of their greatest prosperity. As in the case of Soconusco, Izalcos had not been spared from the terrible Indian population decline which affected all of Central America, and labor shortages hampered the industry from the start. The attempted solution was importation of Indians from the highlands—in the case of Soconusco from Chiapas, Quetzaltenango, and Verapaz, and in the case of Izalcos from Guatemala, Honduras, El Salvador, and, once again, Verapaz. Most of the inhabitants of Soconusco by 1560 and of Izalcos by 1570 were foreign-imported Indians, but the population was still declining. Worse still from the point of view of the cacao industry, the highland sources of replacements were themselves drying up either because, in areas such as San Miguel and Honduras, the Indians had all but disappeared or because, in areas such as Chiapas, Verapaz, and highland Guatemala, local encomenderos or Church orders needed the labor supply which remained and refused to allow it to be enticed or coerced into going down to the cacao coasts.

The response of the great cacao encomenderos and the merchants was increased pressure on the remaining Indians in Izalcos, pressure which reached unbelievable and brutal proportions. The results were predictable. Indians fled elsewhere, refused to marry or bear children, and continued to die from overwork. In spite of the frenzy of the Spaniards, cacao groves became overgrown and neglected. The great chocolate boom in Izalcos was over.

The coup de grâce was administered by the entry into the Mexican market of new and rival areas outside Central America. Shortages of Izalcos cacao drove the price of chocolate still higher in Mexico, and Spaniards were beginning to find it to their taste, thus further increasing the demand and making it profitable to import it from still greater distances. Caracas and Guayaquil, sources of inferior but hardier cacaos, began to export their beans to Mexico in bulk and destroyed what was left of the high-priced Soconusco and Izalcos industry. Some Spaniards in Guatemala fought a rearguard action which ranged in tactics all the way from claiming that Guayaquil cacao was noxious, even poisonous, to obtaining royal legislation banning the shipping of Guayaquil cacao to Mexico, but such opposition accomplished nothing. Central America was not destined to have a major share in the enormous profits made from chocolate when it became a fashionable "fad" drink among Europeans in the seventeenth century.

Once again Central American Spaniards were left in a situation which forced them to search for solutions. The period between 1585 and just after 1630 is dominated by this search. This time, moreover, the government in Santiago de Guatemala joined in. The great age of governmental interference in the economy is 1585–1635.

Some officials felt that the problem rested in Central America's demographic and economic orientation toward the Pacific side of the isthmus and that a solution to this would be to build a good road to a safe, new Caribbean port. The result was the construction of Santo Tomás de Castilla and the temporary abandonment of Trujillo and Puerto Caballos, but all this caused no noticeable long-range change in trade.

Other governors, notably the Conde de la Gómera, attempted to promote new industries to replace cacao. Gómera's sponsored plantations of cactus for cochineal were a complete failure. Guatemala and Nicaragua had no chance of competing with Oaxaca.

Presidents and governors between 1590 and 1630 also sought to reorder the internal situation. By manipulation of the repartimiento system of Indian draft labor they hoped to distribute what manpower was left as fairly as possible. Criado de Castilla felt that trapping Indians into extended obligations by means of debt was particularly harmful and tried with conspicuous lack of success to restrict the practice. By around 1600, however, food was becoming noticeably scarcer in the cities. Fewer and fewer Indians meant fewer fields planted; even forced plantings by the notorious jueces de milpas did not help, and Spaniards had not yet set up many of the large wheat farms which were to appear around Mixco, Pinula, and Petapa twenty or thirty years later.

Worse still, the cattle population was diminishing. Cattle and to a lesser extent sheep seem to have gone through a mysterious cycle of their own between 1530 and 1650. After the conquest the imported cattle population of Central America increased at a phenomenal rate as savannahs devoid of most natural enemies and highly fertile, recently abandoned Indian milpas were grazed for the first time. But somewhere in the decade of the eighties or earlier this population seems to have peaked, perhaps because of overgrazing, biological deterioration, or indiscriminate slaughtering for hides; and by 1600 Spaniards became aware of meat shortages and a rapid rise in prices. The government's response was to try to stop unsupervised slaughter of animals, to forbid the export of cattle on the hoof to other areas, to provision the cities systematically, and to fight monopoly and inflated prices. While these measures may have helped from day to day they did little to reverse major trends.

Individual Spaniards, faced by the cacao disaster, slowly becoming aware of the new weaknesses in the local food supplying economy, at last recognizing that they might well lose the remains of the once huge laboring population, and fearing with some justification that government could do little about any of these threats to their welfare, searched for solutions in a variety of ways.

Some of the wealthy left, including most of those of foreign origins. Others attempted to live off smaller trades such as collecting vanilla in abandoned cacao groves; exporting arnatto, a poor and fugitive vegetable dye; or exporting pine pitch from Nueva

Segovia via Realejo to the growing wine and shipbuilding industries of Peru and Ecuador. A few tried to live on the margins of greater trades, such as the small number who made profits by acting as smugglers and middlemen in the illegal Manila-Acapulco-Callao trade, bringing Chinese goods from Acapulco to Guatemalan and Nicaraguan ports and then reexporting them illegally to Peru.

Most Central American Spaniards, however, turned to the solutions which had helped during the minor pause of the middle years of the sixteenth century. Some gained title to tracts of land, retreated from the cities to live on their haciendas, chacras, or bohíos, and visited town less often. Even more continued to search for a new "produit moteur" to bring rapid wealth as chocolate had done.

For a brief period between 1610 and 1630 it appeared that the basis for a new boom had been found in indigo, known in Central America as añil or xiquilite. Given the situation, it presented several apparent advantages. It was easy to cultivate and could grow almost anywhere on the boca costa or in the warmer tierra templada. It was hardy and did not demand the constant attention needed by the cacao groves. Work on indigo was seasonal. A brief and easy planting season, and an intensive month of harvesting, vat work, and packing were all that was required. On even the larger estates a mayordomo from the castas and two or three Indian workers were sufficient for most of the year. Large resident populations were not needed. So Indians could be engaged seasonally through contract, debt obligation, or coercion and returned to their own villages or plots for the rest of the year, no longer the responsibility of the indigo grower. Granted, shortage of manpower hampered the development of the indigo plantations, and the Crown added to the difficulty by claiming that the effluvia from the vats and bagasse were noxious and that because of this it was forbidden to employ Indians on indigo plantations. Seventeenth-century archives in Central America are full of the records of prosecutions and fines against añileros who employed Indians. Generally, however, labor shortage from population decline was not the critical variable in the seventeenth-century indigo industry to the extent that it certainly was in the case of sixteenth-century cacao. Besides, indigo is grown in cooler climatic areas than cacao, and in the cooler regions much larger Indian populations had survived the sixteenth-century holocaust and were at hand without being brought great distances.

The greatest advantage of Central American indigo cultivation was that it could be combined with cattle raising or agriculture. Cattle could be grazed in the very fields where the xiquilite plant was growing; in fact, they were even used to tramp in the seeds, so rudimentary was the technology. Thus indigo was ideal as an insurance. Badly frightened by the collapse of cacao and worried at the general worsening of the economic situation, Spaniards hoped that indigo would restore prosperity, but they could hedge against its possible failure to do so by running cattle on large acreages.

The period 1590 to 1630 is then the first great era of land occupation and title acquisition by Spaniards in Central America, far exceeding that of the original seizures around the cities immediately after the conquest or that of the minor depression of the 1550s when some had abandoned the small Spanish cities for the land.

All the variations mentioned above can be found in the Spanish applications during these years for *composiciones* or new land titles. Some said that they wanted to set up cattle or wheat farms, this type usually adding that they were poor, could no longer afford to stay in the cities, and must now try to feed their families themselves. Others said that they wanted to grow indigo for export. By far the greatest number said that they wanted to grow indigo and run a few cattle or grow some maize, beans, or wheat. It is noticeable and adds emphasis to what has been said about the importance of indigo that most of this Spanish occupation of the land occurred in land suitable for indigo, that is, in southern and eastern Guatemala, in El Salvador away from the coast itself, and in the areas of Honduras between Tegucigalpa and the Bay of Fonseca. Higher areas such as Quetzaltenango and Chiapas, where indigo would not flourish, witnessed a much slower taking up of the land.

Significantly, too, this era (1590–1630) was the one of greatest pressure on the surviving Indian communities in southeastern Guatemala and El Salvador. Frequent land usurpations and annexations, attempts to lure Indians away from their villages to various forms of peonage on the haciendas (attempts which many Indians welcomed, it should be noted), and Spanish or mestizo occupation of the best parts of that region created the classic division of present-day Guatemala. To the south and east of Guatemala City in the lower mountains and foothills we find ladinos and large estates; in the higher tierra templada and fría to the north and west of Guatemala City, Indian communities which were subject to less seventeenth-century pressure from would-be Spanish indigo growers and cattle ranchers have survived linguistically and culturally to a far greater extent.

The infant boom did not exactly collapse. Rather it remained until the last decade of the seventeenth century in a state of arrested development. The critical variable, as we have said, was not in this case population decline—that was already almost over and indigo was not such an intensive user of labor as gold panning, slaving, or cacao plantations—nor was indigo held back by outside competition. Mexico's production never matched that of Central America, and the indigo booms of Brazil and South Carolina were essentially eighteenth-century phenomena. Central American indigo's failure to develop is directly attributable to lack of transportation and markets. The decline of Spain in the seventeenth century, especially after 1630, meant that the mother country was unable to absorb or pay for Central American indigo, and the decline of the Spanish flotas forced Spain to concentrate on the areas which produced precious metals, with the result that long periods passed in mid-seventeenth century, in one case over a decade, in which no ships from Spain put into the ports on the Bay of Honduras. Much of what trade there was had to travel via the monopolistic Mexican port of Veracruz.

These factors in themselves might not have stultified the growth of the indigo industry if there had been a possibility of getting the dye out to the eager markets of northwestern Europe. We know, for example, that there was an indigo market in seventeenth-century Amsterdam, and it is apparent that the English wool trade, in spite of its attempts to exclude foreign dyes, suffered a serious shortage of them until late in the century. The technological capabilities of seventeenth-century shipping, however, meant that size of cargo space, time in transit, and profitability, when taken together, created a situation in which products could not be profitable if too far from Spain. In favorable times indigo survived on the margins of gold and silver. In harder times it was too far from Europe to show consistent profits.

The Dutch seized Curaçao in 1634 and smuggled intensively on the Venezuelan and Tierra Firme coasts even before then. Foreign smuggling took place up and down the Caribbean coasts of Central America itself in the sixteenth and the first half of the seventeenth centuries. Nevertheless, most of northern Europe's trade with the Spanish American colonies was still funneled through the Seville-Cadiz complex of ports using Spanish merchants there as "strawmen" or agents. Similar merchants, little more than agents of foreign companies, were present in Central America also, but there too it was obvious before about 1685 that most of them were working through the Andalusian ports. Central American indigo entrepreneurs would have to wait for a change in the volume and speed of shipping and for the development of northern European entrepots in the Caribbean islands, and especially in Jamaica, before they could hope to expand their sales. And 1660 to 1685 was the great age of Caribbean piracy. (Piracy destroys the minimal trust needed even in smuggling between the two sides.)

The halting of the growth of the indigo industry around 1630 brought on the trough of Central America's seventeenth-century depression. The Indian working population was approaching its lowest point in numbers, and there was no cash crop to provide the capital to buy African slaves. More and more, Spaniards and mestizos began to live for most of the year on the lands which they had acquired so enthusiastically between 1590 and 1630 for indigo growing. The very wealthiest, and they were few in Central America, still maintained town houses, but many visited the Spanish towns only once a week for mass and festivities, or even more infrequently. Most of these landowners still grew a little indigo as a cash crop, but generally the rural Spanish holdings began to assume the characteristics of the typical Latin American hacienda, self-sufficient, devoted largely to cattle, worked by small staffs of semi-servile, often indebted peons who had been attracted or induced away from the tribute-paying Indian villages.

Financial life was further wrecked by a vacillating policy on coinage. By 1630 or so the Audiencia of Guatemala was suffering from an unfavorable balance of trade with Mexico and to a lesser extent Peru. The good coinage fled and the region was left with debased or falsified exchange from Peru and a scarcity even of that. The steps taken to remedy this situation destroyed what little confidence remained in the coinage. Merchants began to refuse it and many returned to simple barter.

The Indian communities also began to settle into a recognizable mold after 1630. In Nicaragua they had practically disappeared. In the areas of heavy Spanish intrusion they became "ladinoized," losing even their native languages. In areas to the north and west of Santiago, in Quetzaltenango, Huehuetenango, Verapaz, and Chiapas, where they were relatively unmolested, and where the need to fill labor repartimientos for the coast was now greatly diminished because of the death of the great cash crops there, the communities drew in upon themselves, erecting brokerage systems such as sodalities with the outside world and struggling conservatively to preserve the synthesis of some Spanish and much Indian culture which they now considered to be theirs.

The Spanish cities also changed in character between 1620 and mid-century. From a mixture of merchants, encomenderos, and officials, they became largely governmental and clerical centers in which the major sources of income were salaried offices, taxation, and minor graft. By this time those of wealth were almost all peninsular officials, not merchants. They and the high members of the Church were surrounded by large groups of relatives and hangers-on, the infamous paniaguados and validos so resented by the Creoles. Some Creoles also managed to join officialdom at the lower levels and sought to become corregidores, jueces de milpas, and tenientes de gobernador to supplement their meager cash incomes from haciendas or decadent encomiendas. Because the scarcity of such offices was great, the competition for them intense, and the average tenure of them only about four years, many Creoles and paniaguados treated their terms as their only opportunity in life to accumulate any capital. As a result corruption was massive and pressure on the Indian laboring communities intense. This period between 1630 and 1690 is the one par excellence of the derrama, in which minor government officials, often Creoles, forced Indians to buy unwanted goods at inflated prices or forced them to produce goods for nothing or for a pittance. Such strains and excesses show that at least some of the Creoles were still capital hungry, used their nascent haciendas as insurance or as a small capital reserve, and were always ready to join any new enterprise or cash crop system which seemed to promise quick returns.

Such an opportunity was long in coming, and the revival of the dormant indigo trade had to await changes in Europe and the Caribbean. By the late 1680s the long debate between pirates and traders in Jamaica had been won by the traders. England, Holland, and to a lesser extent France had relegated trade via Andalusia to a minor position and were now beginning to trade directly and frequently with the Spanish colonies themselves. The rapid expansion of English overseas trade, shipping, and textile industries between 1680 and 1720 created demands which the Spanish route was patently unable to satisfy. The great age of direct contraband had begun, and the various little ports on the Bay of Honduras such as Golfo Dulce, Santo Tomás, Trujillo, Omoa, and below it San Juan, and Matina became smugglers' havens. Everyone in the Spanish community of Central America joined in enthusiastically, from Presidents, oidores, and bishops to humble mestizo traders and peddlers. Indigo, thus stimulated, moved to the Caribbean coasts in increasing quantities and from there in foreign ships to Jamaica, Curaçao, and northern Europe. By 1715 contraband dominated all forms of commerce in Central America and had revived a stagnant industry. At least some of the Spanish entrepreneurs of the Audiencia of

Guatemala had escaped from the seventeenth-century depression by abandoning their economic allegiance to Spain and by joining the systems of supply which fed the growing industries of northwestern Europe.

Nevertheless, the seventeenth-century depression had made its mark. Although trade had revived and the peasant population now began to grow slowly, the Spaniards of the area had learned their lesson well. The backdrop, insurance economy of large, self-sufficient cattle estates worked by peonage, and the other system of conservative neo-indigenous villages resisting intrusion was to survive each succeeding boom and depression, whether it was indigo in the eighteenth century, cochineal in the nineteenth, or bananas and then coffee in the twentieth.

The processes described here illustrate certain historical problems. Central America was, and has remained, a classic case of monocultural dependence. No matter how the people of the area tried, through legislation, adaption, or flight, there was little that they could do, either personally or collectively, to change unfavorable times or even to affect them. As long as they were dominated by their particular ambitions and cultural necessities, and as long as the economy remained monocultural, first under slaves and precious metals, then under cacao, and then under indigo, Central Americans of all races would be at the mercy of impersonal and little understood forces in the outside world. This feeling of helplessness is exactly the one felt today by citizens of small countries, producers of unprocessed raw materials, when the world price for their product collapses.

It has been argued, in fact, that Latin America's economic independence arrived long before the political struggles of independence. In the Central American case, following this reasoning, the rise of smuggling and the resultant revival of the indigo industry could be considered as Central America's declaration of economic independence from Spain. A more accurate way of summing up this change would be to say that Central America gradually shifted in the second half of the seventeenth century from being an economic dependency of Spain to being tied to the rapidly advancing countries of northwestern Europe. What is remarkable throughout is the persistence of the pattern of dependence.

Within the colony itself monoculture was and is a very important historical phenomenon. If the industry in question is important enough, as cacao and indigo certainly were, and if it is pervasive enough, then it becomes a historical and cultural determinant of

great significance. A case can be made, for example, for attempting
to discuss the sixteenth-century history of Central America in terms
of its great cacao monoculture.

It is not to be expected that the cultural phenomena created by
such a dominant crop and industry, which involved so many people
of different races and classes, and which lasted so long, would disappear after its decline. Because of long conditioning before the European invasion and during the sixteenth century, and because of
other circumstances such as a lack of silver coinage and a poor
supply of cheap foodstuffs, Central America used increasing quantities of cacao, both as money and as food, during the seventeenth
and eighteenth centuries. Indians in particular drank enormous
quantities, and the shortage of a reliable gold and silver coinage
meant that both republics were forced to use it as coinage. At one
stage, in Costa Rica, it was declared to be the official coinage of the
province.[1] Groups such as the Chortis of the Guatemalan-Hondu-
ran border, which did not share in any of the subsequent cyclical
waves of prosperity which have swept over Central America, continued to use cacao as coinage until the middle of the twentieth century.[2]

The mystico-religious aspects of the cacao culture also survived. One reason, no doubt, is that the use of cacao did not seem
an especially reprehensible part of the surreptitious "pagan rites"
which were often uncovered in many Indian communities. After all,
the Creole clergy were heavy cacao drinkers themselves. At any
event, ritual use of cacao by such groups as the Mams has survived
in astonishingly unadulterated form to the present day—calcified
evidence of the great precolumbian and sixteenth-century importance of chocolate to Central America.[3]

The most remarkable feature of all in the history of Central
American cacao is the perseverant nature of many of the patterns
and traits which it helped to set. Cacao was the first great colonial
boom. Monoculture, cyclical booms and depressions, exchange
difficulties, heavy dependence on outside markets, and the attitudes
which accompany these phenomena have been predominant features of Central American life since the sixteenth century. Cacao
and its seventeenth-century collapse played a large part in creating
the colonial ambiente in the region.

Central America has shown a remarkable tendency to persevere
in once-successful patterns. There was even a small recrudescence
of an export industry based on Indian slaves. This took place in

Costa Rica, where so many of Central America's economic cycles seem to end.

Encomienda and the various labor devices which followed it seem to have been thinly disguised forms of total servitude in Costa Rica, more than elsewhere in Central America, but the local Spaniards were nevertheless dismayed to find that in the last years of the seventeenth century and during the first three decades after 1700 that real slavery and Indian slave exports existed in Costa Rica.

The English in Jamaica and on the Mosquito Coast took to recruiting Indian labor along the Caribbean shores and especially in the Talamanca region of Costa Rica. Most of this forced recruiting was done by rounding up unconquered, "wild" Indians. The English rarely performed this task themselves. They purchased the Indian slaves from their ubiquitous agents the Zambos Mosquitos.

Sometimes these slavers simply seized Indians from Spanish plantations in Matina, and most Spanish vecinos were anxious to put a stop to the raids. Actual or potential labor was being taken away. Governor Francisco de la Haya Fernández led the protests to Jamaica and by the 1740s most of this activity had ceased.[4] At best, this late Indian slaving was a marginal activity, but it too rounded out an epoch. It never approached the size of the Nicaraguan trade before 1550, but slave exporting also went through a full cycle.

Another feature of Central America which was to play a dominant role was its basically Pacific orientation. From the point of view of soils, climate, resources, and demography Central America has been an area which, from the logical and natural point of view, has looked toward its southern shore since long before the conquest. Because of this it could be argued that the Spanish invasion and subsequent connection, indeed the continuing commercial and political ties with the Caribbean and the Atlantic, have been to some extent an "unnatural" development, yet another example of the long-lasting distortions and unbalanced emphases which alien conquest can impose on a region. Central America never solved the problem of the clash between its basic Pacific orientation and its Atlantic ties during the colonial period. New ports and roads were built; the Desaguadero of Nicaragua was used, abandoned, and used again; goods were sent overland to Mexico and Veracruz or down the Pacific coast to catch the trajín at Panama; but every alternative was expensive and difficult.

Of course, the Pacific orientation was an advantage from time to time. Central American entrepreneurs learned from the wine and cacao smuggling trade, by which necessary products were brought from Peru and Guayaquil, how to survive and obtain scarce goods in difficult times. Later, on the harsher and emptier Caribbean shore, Central Americans were able to apply the same smuggling methods to restore their economic prosperity.

The existence of a seventeenth-century world depression and of a similar phenomenon in many parts of the New World has been part of scholarly literature for some time. Of course the concept has been progressively refined, both geographically and chronologically. In some parts of Europe, for example, the depression occurred later than usual, or indeed hardly appeared at all. In the world in general similar delayed conjunctures or absences have been noted and acknowledged by many scholars.[5]

In recent years, however, the very existence of a depression has been denied, both for Latin America and for Europe. At the rawest level, the existence of such a phenomenon is a philosophical inconvenience to some Marxist scholars and should therefore be exorcised. Others, using more sophisticated analysis, have observed that there was much prosperity in the mid-seventeenth century and have noted also that the economic activities of colonies such as New Spain were changing in nature. They have therefore concluded that what had formerly been considered as the depth of a great depression was in fact a reorganization and redirection of developmental and entrepreneurial capital.[6]

Certainly there is at first sight little wrong with such explanations. In the seventeenth century money moved from mining and plantation industries into the hacienda and similar kinds of operations. Some hacienda owners did become wealthy and powerful, and definitely used their haciendas as enterprises rather than asylums for capital. It would be hard, after all, to imagine a depression in which no profits were made and in which no capital accumulated. One has only to mention the large growth in the deposits of the United States Post Office Savings Bank during the Great Depression.

Nevertheless, it is obvious that the view which has been gained of the seventeenth-century hacienda is partial and somewhat erroneous. Too much attention has been paid to the commercial enterprises near the big cities. Concentrations of urban people must eat, and money will be made from such circumstances in the worst depression. Most seventeenth-century farms in New Spain and Guatemala, however, were not close enough to large cities to benefit. They were not the dwellings of people who had rushed to the countryside seeking opportunity. The chacras, bohíos, hatos, and estancias were humble places to which vecinos had fled to escape hard times. This is not to deny that such places were potentially commercial. It was simply that they did not have enough captive labor, capital, or markets to mount commercial enterprises. In other words they were depressed.

Elsewhere it has been persuasively argued that the decline of Spain was to the advantage of the New World. Economic power was shifting from Spain to the colonies. To a degree, and if the statement is kept in proportion, this is no doubt true. Hard times create collapse or self-sufficiency. But before one celebrates the independent, vigorous economic life which was allegedly being constructed in the New World, it would be well to consider how closely these new affluents were attached to it. When prosperity returned to the Atlantic, New World entrepreneurs were only too glad, as we have seen, to forsake their erstwhile autonomy, an autonomy of stagnation to this observer, and to become dependent parts of an expanding world market. The New World returned to dependence on the Old with indecent haste.[7] If Central America is at all typical then the impression of a profound depression is hard to escape.

As for the Indians, the depression may indeed have brought some small benefits to some of them. With their cultures and societies shattered by the conquest and the new elite of entrepreneurs, the depression forced those in the agriculturally favored areas to yield still further. By 1740 most of Central America's Indians had disappeared and the inhabitants were Spanish-speaking ladinos.[8] In the poorer and more isolated regions, however, the easing of pressure brought by the depression allowed some peasant communities to erect "broker" institutions which gave them the time and relative tranquility to build a new, hybrid, neo-Indian culture. Like so many New World Celts, the Indians who partly survived were those who were pushed to the poorer and higher lands.

These communities, however, were but a remnant of what once was. In a world which was becoming economically united for the first time, the deaths of their ancestors may have been of more significance. Europe's seventeenth-century crisis and the resultant and still largely unknown processes called the rise of capitalism seem to have had some New World origins.[9] There is a bitter irony to be found in the connection between modern capitalism and the deaths of so many Indians in the War of the Worlds of so many years ago.

Appendix

Presidents and Captains General of the Audiencia of Guatemala (Central America), 1542–1724

1542–48, Lic. Alonso Maldonado, visitador (1536–39), then President, first in Comayagua, then in Gracias a Dios.

1548–55, Lic. Alonso López de Cerrato, President of the Audiencia de Santo Domingo before arriving in Central America. Moved the seat of the Audiencia to Santiago in 1549. Very much involved in the freeing of the Indian slaves and in the application of the New Laws. Died during his residencia (1555).

1555–58, Dr. Antonio Rodríguez de Quesada. After his death oidor Lic. Pedro Ramírez de Quiñones took over ad interim, and led a large expedition to the Lacandones.

1559–63. Lic. Juan Núñez de Landecho. Removed from office for malfeasance. Heavily involved in the cacao trade, and with the cacao encomenderos. He was imprisoned and escaped and the Audiencia was dissolved and partitioned between Mexico and Panama.

1565–69, Lic. Francisco Briceño. After the Audiencia was removed to Panama, he remained as local governor and captain general of Guatemala. Juan Bustos de Villegas died while traveling to Guatemala to replace him, and Briceño was continued in office for four more years.

1573–78, Dr. Pedro de Villalobos, died during his residencia (1579).

1578–89, Lic. García de Valverde. Long-serving, a mild reformer of tributes, but liked by most colonists.

1589–92, Lic. Pedro Mallén de Rueda. Unlike his predecessor, was a contentious, perhaps even unbalanced personality. His presidency saw widespread litigation, factionalism, and complaint. A visita was sent under Francisco de Sandé, who deposed Mallén de Rueda. He then became insane and died shortly thereafter.

1593–96, Dr. Francisco de Sandé, an experienced administrator, deeply involved in the illegal China trade. In 1596 was appointed to New Granada.

1598–1611, Dr. Alonso Criado de Castilla. Arrived in Central America some time after his appointment. Oidor Alvaro Gómez de Abaunza had served (1596–98) until he arrived, and had quarreled with the ayuntamiento of Santiago. Criado also disagreed with that body. He attempted to augment Central American trade, and opened a new Carribbean port. He died during his residencia in 1611.

1611–26, Antonio Pérez Ayala Castilla y Rojas, Conde de là Gómera, a man of the high nobility, and the first military man appointed President. He was accused of corruption, and at one stage was suspended from office. The uproar forced the Crown to reinstate him. He made costly efforts to restore the stagnant economy.

1626–33, Dr. Diego de Acuña, a quiet presidency.

1634–42, Dr. Alvaro de Quiñones y Osorio. Made efforts to settle castas and Spaniards, who were living in the rural areas, in towns. Founded San Vicente de Austria. Died at sea while going to Peru.

1642–49, Lic. Diego de Avendaño. Noted for honesty, piety, and self-effacement. Was an invalid for much of his term. Died in office. An oidor, Lic. Antonio de Lara y Mogrovejo, governed ad interim until 1654, which caused resentment among the other members of the Audiencia.

1654–57, Fernando de Altamirano y Velasco, Conde de Santiago de Calimaya. Sided with the Mazariegos faction in a long feud which disturbed the capital. Died in 1657 without resolving the issue. His replacement, the Conde de Priego, died in Panama, and the badly divided Audiencia then governed collectively (1657–59).

1659–68, General Martín Carlos de Mencos, a very popular governor. Was involved in illegal commerce. Tried to improve coastal defenses on the Caribbean.

1668–72, Sebastián Alvarez Alfonso Rosica de Caldas. Went on a tour of Nicaragua against the wishes of his own Audiencia. Rebuilt the cathedral in Santiago. Died during his residencia. During his last year of office Dr. Juan de Santo Matía Sáenz de Mañosca, Bishop of Guatemala, governed as visitador. He was popular among the Creoles. English intrusions became serious.

1672–78, General Fernando Francisco de Escobedo. He traveled to Nicaragua to inspect fortifications. Tried again to exclude Spaniards and castes from Indian villages, without success. He left to assume the title of Great Prior of Castile of the Order of Malta. His visitador, Lic. Lope de Sierra Osorio, governed 1678–82.

1682–84, Lic. Juan Miguel de Augurto y Alava. Was inhibited by the presence in Guatemala of the two previous Presidents. They both left for Spain before the end of his term.

1684–88, Enrique Enríquez de Guzmán. Reorganized the hospitals of Santiago. Put an end to disputes between ecclesiastical and civil officials in Chiapas and Soconusco.

1688–95, General Jacinto de Barrios Leal. Was the cause of great dissension, and was subjected to a three-year residencia (1691–94). He was then reinstated. He organized and led the early entradas to the Itzáes and Lacandones. After his death he was replaced ad interim by oidor José de Escals.

1696–1701?, Gabriel Sánchez de Berrospe. He fortified the Petén garrison and encouraged colonization there. His visitador, Francisco Gómez de la Madrid, also known as Tequelí, brought Guatemala, Chiapas, and Soconusco to the brink of civil war. The regions divided between Berrospistas and Tequelíes. Armed conflicts led to the flight of the visitador. Oidor Juan Jerónimo Heduardo governed ad interim.

1702–3, Dr. Alonso de Ceballos y Villagutierre, had been President in Guadalajara. He was a compromiser and pacified the two sides.

1703–6, Dr. José Osorio Espinosa de los Monteros. Sent to help calm the uproar caused by Gómez de la Madrid. Succeeded to the presidency.

1706–16, General Toribio José de Cosío y Campo. Helped to suppress the Tzeltal uprising (1712–13).

1716–24, Francisco Rodríguez de Rivas. Opposed moving the city of Santiago after the earthquakes of 1717. Santiago was not moved to its new site until late in the century.

Abbreviations

ACNL	Ayer Collection, Newberry Library, Chicago.
AGGG	Archivo General de Gobierno de Guatemala, Guatemala City (Now Archivo Nacional de Centroamérica).
AGI	Archivo General de Indias, Seville.
AGI/AG	Archivo General de Indias, Audiencia de Guatemala.
AHN	Archivo Histórico Nacional, Madrid.
ANHH	Archivo Nacional de Historia de Honduras, Tegucigalpa.
ANCR	Archivo Nacional de Costa Rica, San José.
AR	Antonio de Remesal, *Historia General de las Indias Occidentales y Particular de la Gobernación de Chiapa y Guatemala*. 2 vols. Madrid, 1964, 1966.
BM	British Museum, London.
BNM	Biblioteca Nacional, Madrid.
BNP	Bibliothèque Nationale, Paris.
BPR	Biblioteca del Palacio Real, Madrid.
CDHCR	*Colección de documentos para la historia de Costa Rica*. León Fernández, comp. 10 vols. Barcelona, 1907.
CDI	*Colección de documentos inéditos, relativos al descubrimiento, conquista y organización de las antiguas posesiones españolas de América y Oceanía, sacados de los archivos del reino, y muy especial del de las Indias*. 42 vols. Title varies. Madrid, 1864–84.
CDIE	*Colección de documentos inéditos para la historia de España*. Martín Fernández Navarrete et al., eds. 112 vols. Madrid, 1842–95.
CDIU	*Colección de documentos inéditos, relativos al descubrimiento, conquista y organización de las antiguas posesiones españolas de Ultramar*. 25 vols. Madrid, 1885–1932.
CS	*Colección Somoza. Documentos para la historia de Nicaragua*. 17 vols. Madrid, 1953–57.
FG	Francisco Antonio de Fuentes y Guzmán, *Recordación Florida: Discurso Historial y Demonstración natural, material, militar y política del Reyno de Guatemala*. 3 vols. Guatemala, 1932–33.
FV	Francisco Vázquez, *Crónica de la Provincia del Santísimo Nombre de Jesús de Guatemala*. 4 vols. Guatemala, 1937–44.

FX   Francisco Ximénez, *Historia de la Provincia de San Vicente de Chiapa y Guatemala de la órden de Predicadores.* 3 vols. Guatemala, 1921–31.

HMAI   *Handbook of Middle American Indians.* 9 vols. to date. Austin, 1964—.

Isagoge   *Isagoge Histórica Apologética de las Indias Occidentales y Especial de la Provincia de San Vicente de Chiapa y Guatemala de la Orden de Predicadores.* Guatemala, 1935. (Most of the references will be to the *Colección de documentos antiguos* published herein as a lengthy appendix, and first published by Rafael de Arévalo in 1857.)

RAH   Real Academia de la Historia, Madrid.

UT   University Library, Univeristy of Texas, Austin.

Notes

Preface

1. Simpson, "Mexico's Forgotten Century," 113-21; Borah, *New Spain's Depression;* Phelan, *The Kingdom of Quito.*
2. Borah, *New Spain's Depression;* Chaunu and Chaunu, *Séville et l'Atlantique, 1504–1650;* Chevalier, *La formation des grands domaines au Mexique.*
3. Chaunu and Chaunu, *Séville et l'Atlantique,* 8^1: 848.

Introduction

1. Ganshof and Verhulst, "Medieval Agrarian Society at its Prime," pp. 291, 295-98; Rusell, *British Medieval Populations,* p. 235; Titow, "Some Evidence of the 13th Century Population Increase," 220-22.
2. Lucas, "The Great European Famine of 1315, 1316 and 1317," 355; Carpentier, "La peste noire," 1075-78. For an illustration of the ties between famine and disease, see Cousens, "Regional Death Rates in Ireland from 1846 to 1857," 55-56.
3. E.g., Burckhardt, *The Civilization of the Renaissance in Italy,* vol. 2, pp. 470-72; Tenenti, *Il Senso della Morte e L'Amore della Vita nel Rinascimento (Francia e Italia),* pp. 58-60, 68-69, 91, 99.
4. Delatouche, "Agriculture médiévale et population," 13-23.
5. E.g., Postan, "Some Evidence of Declining Population in the Later Middle Ages," 221-46; Duby, *L'économie rurale et la vie des campagnes dans l'Occident médiéval,* vol. 1, pp. 317-31; vol. 2, pp. 539-71.
6. Postan, "Medieval Agrarian Society at its Prime, England," vol. 1, pp. 549-632. See also his "Some Evidence of Declining Populations," p. 246; and Saltmarsh, "Plague and Economic Decline in England in the Later Middle Ages," 24-25.
7. Postan, "Medieval Agrarian Society," pp. 549-52, 558-59; Genicot, "Crisis: From the Middle Ages to Modern Times," vol. 1, pp. 670.
8. Mitchison, *A History of Scotland,* pp. 377-78. See also Mackie, *A History of Scotland,* pp. 315-18. This author feels, however, that population pressure was the main factor. It is also obvious that he is somewhat of an apologist for the "clearances." Both Postan ("Medieval Agrarian Society," p. 568) and Genicot ("Crisis: From the Middle Ages to Modern Times," p. 664) examine arguments based on better technology, sociopolitical factors, and growing urbanization. They decide that these factors are secondary.
9. Slicher van Bath, *The Agrarian History of Western Europe,* pp. 78-80, 88-89, 132-36. The material already cited by Titow and Postan is also appropriate.

10. Slicher van Bath, *The Agrarian History of Western Europe*, pp. 89, 142-43; Chaunu, *L'Expansion Européenne du XIIIᵉ au XVᵉ Siècle*, pp. 337-38; Abel, "Wandlungen des Fleischverbrauches und Fleischversorgung in Deutschland seit dem ausgehenden Mittelalter," 411; Postan, "Village Livestock in the Thirteenth Century," 248.

11. Genicot, "Crisis: From the Middle Ages to Modern Times," p. 666. See also Lewis, "The Closing of the Medieval Frontier," 475-83.

12. Brøndstad, *The Vikings*, pp. 28-36, 318-21. (Note that Brøndstad generally discounts population pressure.) See also Sturluson, *Heimskringla (Part Two)*, pp. 160-241.

13. *The Vinland Sagas* ed. and trans. Magnusson and Pálsson, pp. 50-51, 78.

14. Mowat, *Westviking*, pp. 66, 109, 184-85; *The Vinland Sagas*, pp. 18-21; G. J. Marcus, "The Greenland Trade-Route," 71-80.

15. Mowat, *Westviking*, pp. 41-45, 302, 316; Skelton, "The Vinland Map," map on pp. 170, 186-88.

16. Mowat, *Westviking*, pp. 66, 300, 302, 314-6; Skelton, "The Vinland Map," pp. 185-89.

17. Mowat, *Westviking*, p. 477; *The Vinland Sagas*, pp. 22-23; Marcus, "The Greenland Trade Route," p. 80.

18. Utterström, "Climatic Fluctuations and Population Problems in Early Modern History," 3-47 and especially 10-16; for a very complex interpretation, but somewhat similar conclusions, see, Ladurie, *Histoire du climat depuis l'an mil.*

19. A summary of some of these arguments is in Slicher van Bath, *The Agrarian History of Western Europe*, pp. 88, 137, 165.

20. Ziegler, *The Black Death*, pp. 13-15.

21. *Ibid.*, pp. 15-16.

22. *Ibid.*, p. 17.

23. See, for example, Bowsky, "The Impact of the Black Death upon Sienese Government and Society," 18; and especially Carpentier, *Une ville devant la peste*, pp. 33, 63, 79-95, 127-35, 222.

24. For rural urban differences, see Renouard, "Conséquences et interêt démographique," 459-66; and Biraben, "Certain Demographic Characteristics of the Plague Epidemic in France, 1720-22," 540, 543.

25. Ziegler, *The Black Death*, p. 62.

26. Emery, "The Black Death in Perpignan," 612, 615, 619; Wolff, "Trois Etudes de Démographie Médiévale en France Meridionale," vol. 1, pp. 498-99, 502-3; Renouard, "Conséquences et interêt démographique," 459-66. Above all, see Baratier, *La Démographie Provençale du XIIIᵉ au XVIᵉ Siècle*, pp. 67, 75, 82, 87, 94-105, 120-21, etc.

27. Reincke, "Bevölkerungsverluste der Hansestädte durch den Schwarzentod," 88-90; Abel, *Geschichte der deutschen Landwirtschaft*, pp. 116, 117.

28. Our knowledge of the Black Death in Spain was limited for many years to Verlinden, "La Grande Peste de 1348 en Espagne," 103-46, but within the last decade new research has begun to give a fuller picture. See, for example, Gautier-Dalché, "La peste noire dans les Etats de la Couronne d'Aragon," pp. 65-80; Cabrillana, "Las crisis del siglo XIV en Castilla," 246-51, 255-56; and Valdeón Baraque, "Aspectos de la crisis castellana," 9-18.

29. Ziegler, *The Black Death*, pp. 117-71.

30. *Ibid.*, pp. 195-200; Rusell, "Effects of Pestilence and Plague, 1315-1385," 470.

31. Ziegler, *The Black Death*, p. 231. See also Chaunu, *L'Expansion Européenne*, p. 69.

32. Pollitzer, *Plague*, pp. 32-33, 115, 228-30, 350-35, 368, 401. See also Hirst, *The Conquest of Plague.*

33. Pollitzer, *Plague*, pp. 439-40, 450-51, 483-85, 505.

34. *Ibid.,* pp. 411-40, especially p. 418; Biraben and Le Goff, "La peste dans le Haut Moyen-Age," 1486-88. For modern death rates from plague see the many tables in *Plague in the Americas,* e.g., pp. 14, 42, 44-45.

35. Pollitzer, *Plague,* pp. 211, 418, 440-46, 483, 510; Biraben and Le Goff, "La peste dans le Haut Moyen-Age," 1487; Bennassar, *Recherches sur les Grandes Epidémies,* pp. 45-46, 64-65, 171-73.

36. Pollitzer, *Plague,* pp. 440-46; Biraben and Le Goff, "La peste dans le Haut Moyen-Age," 1487-88.

37. *Ibid.,* 1487; Emery, "The Black Death in Perpignan," 612-13.

38. E.g., Cousens, "Regional Death Rates," pp. 55-56. But of course when war, famine, and disease occur together the disaster is compounded. See, for example, Concannon, "The Third Enemy," 502, 511.

39. Slicher van Bath, *The Agrarian History of Western Europe,* pp. 88-89; Saltmarsh, "Plague and Economic Decline in England," pp. 25, 27, 30; Thrupp, "The Problem of Replacement-Rates in Late Medieval English Population," 107, 117-18; Bean, "Plague, Population and Economic Decline," 423-37. See also Dollinger, *The German Hansa,* pp. 59-61.

40. Postan, "Medieval Agrarian Society," p. 570. See the novel and stimulating article by Ladurie, "L'aménorrhée de famine (XVIIᵉ-XXᵉ siècles)," pp. 1589-1601, in which the author emphasizes the relationship between famine, shock, and sterility. On a similar theme, see the solid summary by Meuvret, "Demographic Crisis in France," pp. 520-21. See also Montari, ed., *Documenti su la popolazione di Bologna,* which shows a population which is not renewing itself, and which is burdened by a disproportionate number of dependents.

41. Saltmarsh, "Plague and Economic Decline in England," pp. 31-32; Pollitzer, *Plague,* pp. 500-502; Bean, "Plague, Population, and Economic Decline," pp. 423-37.

42. Two major works have noticed that the mortality of each plague was in inverse proportion to the proximity of the previous epidemic. See Goubert, "En Beauvaisis: Problèmes Démographiques du XVIIᵉ Siècle," 466; and Nadal and Giralt, *La population catalane de 1553 à 1717,* p. 39. See also, for the general picture, Rusell, *British Medieval Populations,* p. 280. It has also been argued that the disappearance of plague was related to a change in the rat populations of western Europe in the late seventeenth century. *Rattus rattus,* a house rat commensal with humans, gave way to the sewer rat (*rattus norvegicus*), which shuns humans (Saltmarsh, "Plague and Economic Decline in England," pp. 33-34). Others stress, however, that this change in rat populations was not absolute, and occurred in the eighteenth century, long after the last plague epidemic. See Pollitzer, *Plague,* p. 14. The two types of rat and their relationship to one another are discussed in Barnett, "Rats," 79-85.

43. Spengler, "Demographic Factors and Early Modern Development," 434; Chaunu, *L'Expansion Européenne,* pp. 69-72; Slicher van Bath, *Agricultural History of Western Europe,* p. 113. Contrast Lerner, *The Age of Adversity,* with Johnson and Percy, *The Age of Recovery.*

44. Hobsbawm, "The general crisis of the European economy in the 17th century," (5) 33-53; (6) 44-65; Helleiner, "The Population of Europe," 41-53; Chaunu, "Le XVIIᵉ siècle," vol. 1, pp. 337-55.

45. Slicher van Bath, *The Agrarian History of Western Europe,* pp. 109-11; Benassar, *Recherches, passim.*

46. For the plague of Justinian, the epidemics which followed it, and their consequences, see Biraben and Le Goff, "La peste dans le Haut Moyen-Age," pp. 1484-1510; and Rusell, "That Earlier Plague," 178-84.

47. E.g., Makower, "Biocenologic problems in Immunology," 780. See also Grmek, "Préliminaires d'une étude historique des maladies," 1473-83.

48. Slicher van Bath, *The Agrarian History of Western Europe,* p. 89; Genicot, "Crisis: From the Middle Ages to Modern Times," p. 675; Bean, "Plague, Popula-

tion, and Economic Decline," pp. 427-28; Cornwall, "English Population in the Early Sixteenth Century," 32-44.

49. Slicher van Bath, *The Agrarian History of Western Europe,* p. 106; Renouard, "Conséquences et interêt démographique," p. 465; Genicot, "Crisis: From the Middle Ages to Modern Times," pp. 677-94; Cabrillana, "La crisis del siglo XIV en Castilla," p. 258.

50. See "The Ordinance of Laborers of Edward III, 1349," ed. Herlihy, pp. 358-61. See also Farmer, "Some Livestock Price Movements in Thirteenth-Century England," 1-16; Genicot, "Crisis: From the Middle Ages to Modern Times," pp. 705-6; Verlinden, "La Grande Peste de 1348 en Espagne," pp. 104, 119-32.

51. See Abel, "Wandlungen des Fleischverbrauches," p. 411, and, to a lesser extent, Stouff, "La viande," 1431-48; Helleiner, "The Population of Europe," pp. 68-74.

52. Bowsky, "The Impact of the Black Death," pp. 18-20. For little or no municipal change, see Guilbert, "A Chalons-sur-Marne au XVe siècle," 1296.

53. E.g., Meiss, *Painting in Florence and Siena after the Black Death;* Tenenti, *Il Senso della Morte,* pp. 99, 154-65, 435-38; *The Dance of Death,* ed. Warren, pp. 2, 50, 70.

54. Wells, *The War of the Worlds.* Others have noticed this parallel. See, for example, Crosby, "Conquistador y Pestilencia," 321; Chaunu, *Conquête et Exploitation,* p. 136.

55. Makower, "Biocenologic Problems in Immunology," p. 780; Bates, "Man as an Agent in the Spread of Organisms," pp. 789-90; Borah, "¿América como modelo?" 179-81, 185.

56. For Hawaii, see Judd, IV, *Dr. Judd, Hawaii's friend,* pp. 57, 236, and the sources cited therein. For Tahiti and Australia, see the excellent survey by Moorehead, *The Fatal Impact,* Parts One and Two. For the Pacific in general, see Price, *The Western Invasions of the Pacific,* pp. 66, 149, 170-71, 215.

57. Thomson, *The Diversions of a Prime Minister,* p. 372. Also the remark credited to a German missionary in Spanish America in 1699: "The Indians die so easily that the bare look and smell of a Spaniard causes them to give up the ghost" (Stearn and Stearn, *The Effect of Smallpox,* p. 17.)

58. See, for example, *Indians of Brazil in the Twentieth Century,* ed. and trans. Hopper, pp. 81-92, 106, 113; and above all Lévi-Strauss's elegaic *Tristes Tropiques,* pp. 51, 137, 206, 298, 340-41, 392.

59. Bates, "Man as an Agent," pp. 789-90. For the absence of specific diseases in the Americas, see the following: Childs, *Malaria and Colonization,* pp. 24-27; Moodie, "Pott's Disease in Early Historic Peru," 356; Møller-Christensen, "Evidence of Tuberculosis, Leprosy, and Syphilis," pp. 233-36. See especially the articles of Dunn, e.g., "On the Antiquity of Malaria," 385-86, 391; and, with Watkins, "Parasitological Examinations of Prehistoric Human Coprolites," 180. Several accounts at the time of the conquest talk of the great epidemics of that time as being previously unknown in these areas, e.g., "Relación de las cirimonias y ritos," 68. A short but convincing article on syphilis is by Goff, "New Evidence of Pre-Colombian Bone Syphilis in Guatemala," vol. 1, pp. 312-19.

60. Cook, "The Incidence and Significance of Disease," 320-35; Gillmor, *The King Danced in the Marketplace,* pp. 107-20, and the same author's *Flute of the Smoking Mirror,* pp. 123-30.

61. Sanders and Price, *Mesoamerica.* The work of Borhegyi tends to support this argument of unilinear growth until a climax at the time of the conquest, e.g., his two articles in HMAI 2, pt. 1, 3-75.

62. E.g., Cowgill, "Soil Fertility, Population, and the Ancient Maya," 1009-11; Palerm, "Ecological potential and cultural development in Mesoamerica," pp. 1-37. See also the same author's "The Agricultural Basis of Urban Civilization in Mesoamerica," pp. 28-42. See also Sauer, *The Early Spanish Main,* pp. 51-59, 65-69, 239-44.

63. Examples of his work are, Cook, *Soil Erosion and Population in Central Mexico*, p. 86; his *Morphology and Occupation History*, pp. 281-334, especially pp. 332-33; and his *The Historical Demography and Ecology of the Teotlalpán*, pp. 16, 51-59. See also for Verapaz, Guatemala, the intriguing findings of Adams, "The Ceramic Chronology of the Southern Maya," pp. 5-8.

64. E.g., Cook, "Human Sacrifice and Warfare," 81-102. See also Cook, *The Historical Demography and Ecology of the Teotlalpán*, p. 54.

65. For the Mayan case see the tables in later chapters of this work. For the Incas see Cook, "La población indígena en el Perú colonial," p. 98. See also Gordon, *Human Geography and Ecology*, p. 69.

66. E.g., Cook and Borah, *The Indian Population of Central Mexico;* Cowgill, "Soil Fertility, Population, and the Ancient Maya"; Erasmus, "Monument Building," 277-301; Denevan, *The Aboriginal Cultural Geography of the Llanos de Mojos*. For a summation, see Cook and Borah, "On the Credibility of Contemporary Testimony," pp. 229-39.

67. Chaunu, *L'Expansion Europeénne*, p. 256; Chaunu, *Conquête et Exploitation*, pp. 382-83.

68. See the various methods examined in Dobyns, "Estimating Aboriginal American Populations," 395-416, 446-49.

69. This question will be examined in later chapters. Meanwhile see the classic, MacNutt, trans., "The Brevíssima Relación," pp. 340-56.

70. Recinos, Goetz, and Chonay, eds., *The Annals of the Cakchiquels*, pp. 115-16, 143, 149. For the unconvincing argument that the first outbreak was an epidemic of influenza, see McBryde, "Influenza in America," 296-97.

71. E.g., Recinos, Goetz, and Chonay, eds., *Annals of the Cakchiquels*, pp. 143, 149; *Cartas de Indias*, p. 331. For Europe, see Bennassar, *Recherches sur les Grandes Epidémies*, pp. 45-46, 64-65, 142-43, 171-73; Biraben and Le Goff, "La peste dans le Haut Moyen-Age," p. 1487.

72. Sauer, *Early Spanish Main*, pp. 200-204; Chaunu and Chaunu, *Séville et l'Atlantique*, 8¹: 494-517.

73. Sauer, *Early Spanish Main*, pp. 278-79, 283-89. See also Alba C., *Etnología y Población Histórica de Panamá*, pp. 5-11, 14-18; Anderson, *Old Panama and Castilla de Oro*, pp. 232, 281, 284; and Bennett, *Human Influences on the Zoogeography of Panama*, pp. 36-40, 51-55.

74. See the works of Simpson, Cook, and Borah in the Ibero-Americana series, especially the aforementioned *Indian Population of Central Mexico, 1531-1610*. See also, for a slightly different periodization, Spores, "Settlement, Farming Technology, and Environment in Nochixtlán Valley," 563-66.

75. For Peru see Cook, "La población indígena en el Perú colonial," pp. 83, 96, 98-100; and Dobyns, "An outline of Andean epidemic history to 1720," 493-515. For Chile, see Carmagnani, "Colonial Latin American Demography," 189-91; for Colombia, Colmenares, *Encomienda y Población*, and Friede, "Demographic Changes in the Mining Community of Muzo," 338-43. (Note that Friede blames the falling population in mining communities on overwork and exploitation rather than on disease.) The most complete general survey is Dobyns, "Estimating Aboriginal American Populations," pp. 416, 446-49.

76. Chaunu, *Conquête et Exploitation*, pp. 82-83, 365.

77. E.g., Gibson, *The Aztecs under Spanish Rule*, pp. 203-4, 246-47, 326, 387-90.

78. Simpson, *Exploitation of Land in Central Mexico;* Gibson, "The Aztec Aristocracy in Colonial Mexico," 169-96; Leonard, *Baroque Times in Old Mexico;* Borah, *New Spain's Century of Depression*.

Chapter 1

1. Today this area would include the Mexican state of Chiapas, most of the disputed colony of British Honduras, and the independent Central American nations of Guatemala, El Salvador, Honduras, Nicaragua, and Costa Rica.

2. To look for a correct descriptive title for this area is to enter an historical and semantic jungle. "Mesoamerica" would include much of Mexico, "Middle America" even more, while "the Audiencia of Guatemala" might give the false impression that this is to be an institutional or legal study, and would leave many believing that only the relatively small area which forms the present republic of Guatemala is under consideration. The use of expressions such as "The Kingdom of Guatemala" or "The Kingdoms of Guatemala" would present the same disadvantages. "Central America," however, was the name for an abortive but far-from-forgotten union of the area in the early nineteenth century, is used as a descriptive title for the area by people living there, and is the basis for an attempt at a common market and other enterprises. If the reader bears in mind that Chiapas has become part of Mexico, that the disputed colony of British Honduras may not become part of Central America, and that Panama may conceivably join one day, then "Central America" seems to be the most suitable descriptive title for the area under the Audiencia of Guatemala in the sixteenth, seventeenth, and eighteenth centuries.

3. West and Augelli, *Middle America,* pp. 35-52; Portig, "Central American Rainfall," 68-90; Sauer, "Geography of South America," 331, 334.

4. Petén centers grew up on areas of relatively good soils and along the rivers running into the Gulf of Honduras. See Stevens, "The Soils of Middle America," 265-315, especially the map, p. 308, which shows much of the Petén to consist of mildly leached and hydromorphic soils formed on limestone, but the Caribbean coast to be mostly intensely weathered soils subject to continuous leaching.

5. Cowgill, "Soil Fertility and the Ancient Maya," 1-56; Cowgill, "An Agricultural Study of the Southern Maya Lowlands," 273-86; Popenoe, "The Influence of the Shifting Cultivation Cycle," pp. 72-76.

6. Roys, *The Indian Background of Colonial Yucatán,* pp. 113, 117; Chamberlain, *Conquest and Colonization of Honduras,* p. 31; Chapman, "Port of Trade Enclaves in Aztec and Maya Civilizations," pp. 114-53.

7. See the body of evidence on this subject in the next chapter. For the moment, see Chamberlain, *Conquest and Colonization of Honduras,* pp. 101-2, 245.

8. This subject is discussed more fully in Chapter Nine. Meanwhile, see Dege, "Die Karibische Küste Guatemalas und ihre Häfen," 252, 255.

9. Vivó Escoto, "Weather and Climate of Mexico and Central America," 187-215, especially pp. 212-14, and Stevens, "The Soils of Middle America," map, p. 308.

10. West and Augelli, *Middle America,* p. 230 (map). There is some disagreement on the exact position of the Mesoamerican frontier. Some draw a fairly straight line from Trujillo directly to Lake Nicaragua and then continue it to the Gulf of Nicoya, which would put highland Honduras almost all within Mesoamerica. See HMAI, 1:4, 366. I prefer the first version. For today's population distribution see West and Augelli, *Middle America,* p. 2.

11. Vogt, "Chiapas Highlands," 139, 141-43; Adams, "Maya Archeology, 1958–1968," 31; Stone "Synthesis of Lower Central American Ethnohistory," 211-12; Arroyo S., "Nahuatismos y Nahuatlismos en Costa Rica," 13-17.

12. Longyear, "Archeological Survey of El Salvador," 152; Stone, "Synthesis," p. 230; Barberena, *Historia de El Salvador,* vol. 1, p. 101.

13. Mason, "The Languages of South American Indians," 174-75; Johnson, "The Linguistic Map of Mexico and Central America," pp. 88-114, especially the map facing p. 88; Kidder, "South American Populations," pp. 441-59.

14. Vázquez de Coronado, *Cartas de Relación* pp. 33-34, 49-51; Stone, "Synthesis," pp. 215-17.

15. The following should be read in conjunction. Sauer, *The Early Spanish Main,* pp. 51-59; Bronson, "Roots and the Subsistence of the Ancient Maya," 251-79; Vázquez de Coronado, *Cartas de Relación,* pp. 18, 19, 23, 25 *passim.*

16. Stone, "Synthesis," pp. 214-16, 228-29. See also Vázquez de Coronado, *Cartas de Relación,* and Sauer, *Early Spanish Main,* p. 239, for the simple nature of these societies.

17. The best general description of Mesoamerica and its unique traits as a culture area remains Kirchoff, "Mesoamerica," 92-107. For Central America see, for example, Milla ("Salomé Gil"), *Historia de la América Central,* pp. 108-21; Miles, "Summary of the Preconquest Ethnology," pp. 276-87; Fernández de Oviedo y Valdés, *Historia General y Natural,* vol. 11, pp. 65, 90, 109, 176-78, 194.

18. Miles, "Summary," pp. 280-82; Coe, "A Model of Ancient Community Structure," 97-114; Adams, "Maya Archeology," pp. 16-17, 25.

19. The material which follows is largely drawn from Palerm, "The Agricultural Basis of Urban Civilization," pp. 28-42. See also Willey, Ekholm, and Millon, "The Patterns of Farming Life and Civilization"; and Sauer, "Cultivated Plants of South and Central America," (6)519. For irrigation in Central America, see, for example, Thompson, *An Archeological Reconnaissance,* p. 38; Wauchope, *Excavations at Zacualpa, Guatemala,* p. 88; and Ricketson, "Maya Pottery Well," 103-5.

20. Slicher van Bath, *The Agrarian History of Western Europe,* tables II and III; Borah and Cook, *Price Trends of Some Basic Commodities,* p. 20, note 22; Chaunu, *L'Expansion Européenne,* pp. 335-38; and above all the same author's *Conquête et Exploitation,* pp. 377-79.

21. The information on settlement patterns which follows comes from several sources. E.g., Borhegyi, "Settlement Patterns in the Guatemalan Highlands, Past and Present," pp. 101-6, and "Settlement Patterns of the Guatemalan Highlands," HMAI, 2, pt. 1, pp. 59-75; Smith, *Archeological Reconnaissance,* pp. 78-80; AR, 2:177.

22. E.g., Díaz del Castillo, *Historia verdadera de la Conquista,* pp. 380-87, 395, 421; Fernández de Oviedo, *Historia General y Natural,* 11:64, 105-6, 166; Andagoya, *The Narrative of Pascual de Andagoya,* pp. 32-33; Alvarado, *An Account of the Conquest of Guatemala,* pp. 46, 51, 65, 88; Benzoni, *La Historia del Mondo Nuovo,* pp. 98-98v. See also Cook and Borah, "On the Credibility of Contemporary Testimony," pp. 229-39.

23. Lowe and Mason, "Archeological Survey," p. 197; Shook, "Archeological Survey of the Pacific Coast of Guatemala," pp. 193-94; Sanders and Price, *Mesoamerica,* pp. 168-69; Thompson, *Archeological Reconnaissance, passim.*

24. Scholes and Roys, *The Maya Chontal Indians,* pp. 3-4, 17, 30, 317-20; Roys, *Indian Background,* p. 113.

25. Lowe and Mason, "Archeological Survey," pp. 221, 234; Adams, "Maya Archeology," p. 31; Calnek, "Highland Chiapas before the Spanish Conquest," p. 101.

26. Sanders and Price, *Mesoamerica,* p. 169.

27. Extensive discussion of Central American cacao will follow in later chapters. For the moment, see Millon, "Trade, Tree Cultivation, and the Development of Private Property in Land," 698-712.

28. Tolstoy and Paradis, "Early and Middle Preclassic Culture," 350; see also Miles, "Summary," pp. 279-80.

29. Sanders and Price, *Mesoamerica,* pp. 168-69.

30. Alvarado Tezozomoc, *Crónica mexicana,* pp. 151-53; Chapman, "Port of Trade," pp. 141, 146; Glass, "Archeological Survey of Western Honduras," 161.

31. Castañeda Paganini, *La cultura tolteca-pipil de Guatemala;* Stone, "Los grupos mexicanos," 44-46; Chapman, *Los Nicarao y los Chorotega.*

32. Kidder, Jennings, and Shook, *Excavations at Kaminaljuyú, Guatemala,* pp.

252-55. See also the tentative conclusions in Sanders and Michels, *The Pennsylvania State University Kaminaljuyu Project—1968 Season*, pp. 166-67.

33. Coe, *The Maya*, pp. 87-90; Thompson, *Archeological Reconnaissance in the Cotzumalhuapa region, passim.*

34. Miles, "Summary," pp. 283-84; Borhegyi, "Archeological Synthesis," 46, 56; Thompson, *Archeological Reconnaissance*, pp. 13, 49.

35. Coe, *The Maya*, pp. 26, 78, 81. But, lest the balance swing too far towards a "Mexican" interpretation, see the argument for regional and multi-causal explanations in Sanders and Price, *Mesoamerica*, pp. 189-90.

36. Borhegyi, "Archeological Synthesis," pp. 43, 46, 53-56; Miles, "Summary," pp. 283-84.

37. McQuown, "The classification of the Maya languages," 191-95.

38. Coe, *The Maya*, pp. 42-45.

39. Coe, "The Olmec Style," 772-74. Olmec influence on Pacific Guatemala and El Salvador is questioned in Sanders and Price, *Mesoamerica*, pp. 117-20.

40. Borhegyi, "Archeological Synthesis," pp. 27-8; Coe, *The Maya*, pp. 69, 77-78.

41. Sanders and Price, *Mesoamerica*, pp. 31, 167-68; Coe, *The Maya*, p. 74.

42. Morley, *The Ancient Maya*, pp. 69-73; Sanders and Price, *Mesoamerica*, p. 32.

43. See the Introduction for evidence of cyclical population movements after the Formative period.

44. For population collapse or change in Central America at the end of the Classic, see, for the Petén, Morley, *Ancient Maya*, p. 68. This however, should be modified by Thompson, "The Maya Central Area at the Spanish Conquest and Later," pp. 23-37, which suggests relocation rather than population decline. For Pacific and highland Central America at the end of the Classic period, see Borhegyi, "Archeological Synthesis," pp. 31, 40-41; Borhegyi, "Settlement Patterns," p. 69; Rands and Smith, "Pottery of the Guatemalan Highlands," 134-35; Shook, "Archaeological Survey," p. 190. See also Kidder, Jennings, and Shook, *Excavations at Kaminaljuyú, Guatemala*, pp. 4, 241, 247.

45. The best summary of this history is by Recinos in his introduction to the *Popol Vuh*, pp. 3-7, 61-75. See also Carmack, *Toltec Influence*, pp. 69-92, especially pp. 72, 75-78, 82-83.

46. See the previously mentioned works by Cook, Borah, and Simpson on the demographic crisis. See also Durán, *The History of the Indians of New Spain*, pp. 216-17; Miles, "Summary," pp. 282-83; Alvarado Tezozomoc, *Crónica mexicana*, pp. 151-53; Díaz del Castillo, *Historia Verdadera*, p. 167.

47. Colón, *Vida del Almirante*, pp. 272-83.

48. Cortés' complaint is contained in his fifth letter to Charles V, in MacNutt, ed., *Letters of Cortés*, vol. 2, pp. 332-34. See also Milla, *Historia de la América Central*, vol. 1, pp. 156-60, and Chapter 2 of this book.

49. A summary of Nicuesa's career can be found in Fernández, *Historia de Costa Rica*, pp. 14-15. See also Sauer, *Early Spanish Main*, pp. 175-76. For the early reconnoiters on the Pacific coast, see Alvarez Rubiano, *Pedrarias Dávila*, pp. 319-27. See especially the documents on pp. 555-58. See also Milla, *Historia de la América Central*, vol. 1, pp. 161-95.

50. "Relación ... de Mechuacán," 75-77; Recinos, Goetz, and Chonay, eds., *The Annals of the Cakchiquels*, pp. 112-13; "Títulos de la Casa Ixquin-Nehaib," in *Crónicas Indígenas de Guatemala*, ed. Recinos, pp. 84-85.

51. "Relación ... de Mechuacán," pp. 77-78, 82-84.

52. MacNutt, *Letters of Cortés*, p. 178; Recinos, Goetz, and Chonay, *Annals of the Cakchiquels*, pp. 119-23; "Títulos de la Casa Ixquin-Nehaib," p. 85; Milla, *Historia de la América Central*, vol. 1, pp. 53-55, 60-62.

53. Recinos, Goetz, and Chonay, *Annals of the Cakchiquels*, pp. 119-22; Alvarado, *An Account of the Conquest of Guatemala in 1524*, pp. 60-65, 69-73.

54. "Relación . . . de Mechuacán," pp. 78, 83-85; Recinos, Goetz, and Chonay, *Annals of the Cakchiquels,* pp. 115-18; Seler, "Significance of the Maya Calendar," p. 334; Milla, *Historia de la América Central,* vol. 1, pp. 59-60; Boccaccio, *Il Decameron,* ed. Russo, pp. 5-15; Defoe, *A Journal of the Plague Year,* pp. 10-11, 122, 242.

55. Study of eighteenth-century bills of mortality in London led one observer to note that two out of every seventeen deaths before the advent of vaccination were caused by smallpox. Jurin, *An Account of the Success of Inoculating the Smallpox in Great Britain.* The standard modern work on smallpox, Dixon, *Smallpox,* says that in modern times unvaccinated populations have a case mortality of about 30 per cent; but, he adds, "a population that has experienced the disease for some generations, even if unvaccinated, appears to have a lower mortality than one that has never experienced it before." See pp. 317-18, 325-26. So it would seem safe to say that if smallpox were the epidemic in highland Guatemala in 1520, then one third of the population died. If the epidemic were pneumonic plague, or smallpox and pneumonic plague, or either with typhus, as seems likely from the descriptions (Recinos, Goetz, and Chonay, *Annals of the Cakchiquels,* p. 115), then mortality would have been still higher. (See the Introduction.) While recuperations from some benign varieties of smallpox may be surprisingly rapid, many are slow. Recoveries from plague are few and incomplete. Typhus leaves survivors extremely debilitated.

One author believes that the epidemic was cholera followed by smallpox and claims that half of the population of the Mam town of Zaculeu died. See Woodbury, "The History of Zaculeu," vol. 1, p. 10. See also "Papers from the Institute of Nutrition of Central America and Panama."

56. Fernández de Oviedo, *Historia General y Natural,* vol. 8, pp. 96-115; Chamberlain, *Conquest and Colonization of Honduras,* pp. 101, 123, 247-48; Bishop Pedraza to Crown, December 16, 1544, AGI/AG 164; Scholes and Roys, *The Maya Chontal Indians,* pp. 164-67; Lothrop, "Archeology of Lower Central America," p. 180.

57. Alvarado, *An Account of the Conquest of Guatemala,* pp. 55-65, 69-87; Woodbury, "The Ruins of Zaculeu," pp. 13-20; Recinos, *Pedro de Alvarado,* pp. 107-11; Milla, *Historia de la América Central,* vol. 1, pp. 338-47, 368-69; Smith and Kidder, *Excavations at Nebaj, Guatemala,* pp. 7-8.

58. Cortés to Emperor, fourth letter, and *ibid.* to *ibid.,* fifth letter in MacNutt, *Letters of Cortés,* vol. 2, pp. 194-96, 308-20, 328-30; Chamberlain, *Conquest and Colonization of Honduras,* pp. 36-39, 46, 98-99, 145.

59. Alvarez Rubiano, *Pedrarias Dávila,* pp. 319-37, 356-68. See also the documents in Peralta, *Costa-Rica, Nicaragua y Panamá en el siglo XVI,* pp. 3-33.

60. Alvarez Rubiano, *Pedrarias Dávila,* pp. 369-70; Milla, *Historia de la América Central,* vol. 1, pp. 377-79, 385-94; Juarros, *Compendio de la Historia de la Ciudad de Guatemala,* vol. 2, pp. 79-80; Fernández de Oviedo, *Historia General y Natural,* vol. 8, pp. 96-115, 148. Squabbling within each town was also common. E.g., "Información hecha por Pedrarias," (July 13, 1528) in Alvarez Rubiano, *Pedrarias Dávila,* p. 643; and Bishop Marroquín to Crown, January 20, 1539, AGI/AG 156.

61. Chamberlain, *The Governorship of the Adelantado Francisco de Montejo,* pp. 167-68. See the letter from Bishop Marroquín to the Crown in Sáenz de Santa María, *El Licenciado Don Francisco Marroquín,* p. 207, and Saint-Lu, *La Vera Paz,* pp. 52-53.

62. See the documents in Peralta, *Costa-Rica, Nicaragua y Panamá,* pp. 101-27, 175-99; and Vázquez de Coronado, *Cartas de Relación,* pp. 57-58.

63. Recinos, Goetz, and Chonay, *Annals of the Cakchiquels,* pp. 124-27; FX, 1:149-53; Arévalo, *Libro de actas del ayuntamiento de la ciudad de Guatemala,* pp. 114-19, 127-29, 138-47. The Vázquez chronicle suggests that it was the excessive labor exactions of Jorge de Alvarado for gold panning which caused the uprising. See FV, 1:73-4.

64. Alvarez Rubiano, *Pedrarias Dávila,* p. 360, 366; Chamberlain, *Conquest and Colonization of Honduras,* pp. 79-99; Fernández de Oviedo, *Historia General y*

Natural, vol. 8, pp. 118; vol. 11, pp. 190-91. For Indian revolts in south central El Salvador in the 1530s, see Barón Castro, *Reseña histórica de la Villa de San Salvador,* pp. 170-71.

65. E.g., Recinos, Goetz, and Chonay, *Annals of the Cakchiquels,* pp. 120, 127, 131-33; FV, 1:153-55; Chamberlain, *Conquest and Colonization of Honduras,* p. 101; Andagoya, *The Narrative,* pp. 7-8, 12.

66. AR, 1:203; 2:158-66; FV, 1:153-54; Kelly, *Pedro de Alvarado,* pp. 186-90, 209-11.

67. Bishop Marroquín to Crown, March 20, 1551, in Sáenz de Santa María, *El Licenciado Don Francisco Marroquín,* p. 266; Juan de Lerma to Crown, October 31, 1539, AGI/AG 49; CDI, 5:522-23; Fernández de Oviedo, *Historia General y Natural,* vol. 8, p. 148.

68. Recinos, Goetz, and Chonay, *Annals of the Cakchiquels,* pp. 134-35.

69. "Documentos relativos a la conversión de los indios jicaques," *Relaciones históricas y geográficas de América Central,* vol. 8, pp. 387-414; Fernández Guardia, *Reseña histórica de Talamanca,* pp. 47-124. A fair summation of the peculiar nature of this conquest is to be found in the early writings of the town council of Santiago. The conquest took place, the writer says, "in bits and pieces, revolts and reconquests." See Arévalo, *Libro de actas,* p. 170.

Chapter 2

1. Landa's *Relación de las Cosas de Yucatán,* ed. Tozzer, p. 9; Sauer, *The Early Spanish Main,* pp. 213, 292.

2. AGI, Patronato 170-1-23 (1525). See also Díaz del Castillo, *Historia Verdadera,* pp. 4, 450.

3. Chamberlain, *The Conquest and Colonization of Honduras,* pp. 120-22, 129; Fernández de Oviedo, *Historia General y Natural,* vol. 8, pp. 148; Benzoni, *La Historia del Mondo Nuovo,* 98-98v.; Díaz del Castillo, *Historia Verdadera,* p. 563; Veedor of Honduras to Crown, March 29, 1530, and Lerma to Crown, October 31, 1539, AGI/AG 49. For the more doubtful case in Yucatán see Tozzer's footnote in *Landa's Relación,* p. 61.

4. This comparison is made in the excellent study by Góngora, *Los grupos de conquistadores,* pp. 38, 103-5. Others have contrasted the conqueror of Mexico, Hernán Cortés, with island conquistadors in a similar way. E.g., Parry, *The Spanish Seaborne Empire,* p. 83.

5. Andagoya, *The Narrative,* p. 23; Porras Barrenechea, ed., *Cartas,* vol. 3, p. 24; CDI, 38:200. See also Alba C., *Etnología y población histórica de Panamá,* pp. 10-11, 14; Mercado Sousa, *El hombre y la tierra en Panamá (S. XVI),* pp. 215-19; Anderson, *Old Panama and Castilla de Oro,* pp. 232, 281.

6. CS, 1:453; Porras Barrenechea, *Cartas,* vol. 3, p. 24; Andagoya, *The Narrative,* pp. 7-8, 12.

7. CS, 2:16-25, 29, 32-8, 78-9; CS, 11:364; Alvarez Rubiano, *Pedrarias Dávila,* pp. 368, 681.

8. Fernández de Oviedo, *Historia General y Natural,* vol. 11, pp. 109. AR, 1:158 says, "The greatest trade of these times was the trade in slaves." (He was referring mainly to Peru.) See also Chaunu and Chaunu, *Séville et l'Atlantique,* 8¹:885-86. For the roles of Castañeda and Contreras, see for example, CS, 3:444, 459; 4:34-35, 52, 68, 202; 9:60; 10:168-69; 11:364. For others involved see CS, 2:85-88, 273, 501, 512; 4:203; 14:303. For mention of Nicaraguan slaves in Peru see Lockhart, *Spanish Peru, 1532-1560; A Colonial Society,* pp. 179, 199-205.

9. CS, 3:459-60; Borah, *Early Colonial Trade and Navigation,* p. 5. One ob-

server claimed that one third of all the Indians in Nicaragua had been enslaved; CS, 3:408-9. A list of some Indians shipped is in CS, 4:454-57. See also CS, 6:108. Treasurer Pedro de los Rios owned six ships, CS, 12:442. Las Casas put the number of exported slaves at 500,000. See his "Brevíssima Relación," in MacNutt, *Bartholomew De Las Casas*, p. 340. Of course many Spaniards left Central America to seek fortunes in Peru at this time, and some of these slaves may have been accompanying their masters. Alvarado, for example, was accused of taking 4,000 with him. See Porras Barrenechea, *Cartas*, pp. 70, 96, 113, 236; and Cabildo of Santiago de Guatemala to Crown, January 24, 1550, AGI/AG 41.

10. Alonso López de Cerrato to Crown, September 28, 1548, AGI/AG 9; CS, 14:339-40; Andagoya, *The Narrative*, p. 79; MacNutt, *Bartholomew De Las Casas*, p. 356.

11. CS, 3:408-9, 443, 459-60; 5:240-41; 6:108; 9:601. Las Casas put Indian mortality at about a third in his "Brevíssima Relación," MacNutt, *Bartholomew De Las Casas*, p. 380. To sail from Panama to Central America was difficult, CS, 12:419-20. The arduous sea journey between the isthmi and Peru is well described in Borah, *Early Trade*, pp. 29-35. Prevailing winds and weather between Guatemala and Peru are explained in Findley, *A Directory*, 1:141, 201, 226, 231, and 2:1192-99, 1307. He concludes, "the greatest difficulty at all times is getting either to the southward or westward of Panama."

12. CDI, 9:98; Carles, *220 años de período colonial*, pp. 35, 39.

13. Simpson, *Studies in the Administration of the Indians of New Spain*, *IV*, p. 37.

14. CS, 11:383; 14:300-305; Andagoya, *The Narrative*, pp. 35-36; García Peláez, *Memorias*, vol. 1, pp. 95-96.

15. E.g., CS, 11:364-75, 406-17.

16. Chamberlain, *Conquest and Colonization*, pp. 129, 237-38; Pedraza to Crown, May 1, 1547, AGI/AG 164; "Relación de la provincia de Honduras y Higueras," 384-434.

17. Alonso López de Cerrato to Crown, September 28, 1548, AGI/AG 9. The King's reply is in AGGG, A1.23, legajo 1511, f. 115 (June 1, 1549). The freeing of the slaves in San Salvador is in AGGG, A1.23, legajo 4575, f. 113 (1550), and RAH, Colección Muñoz, 85, ff. 148, 150v.

18. Guatemala's protests against abolition and López de Cerrato are summarized in Simpson, *The Emancipation*. pp. 5-7, 9, 13. There are several cédulas in CS demanding the return of exported slaves. E.g., CS, 7:118-20, 464-66, 535. As late as 1580 vecinos of Santiago were asking the Crown to repeal the laws against enslavement of Indians, AGGG, A1.2-5, 25235, 2833.

19. E.g., CDI, 9:98.

20. ANCR, Guatemala 092 (January 5, 1654); ANHH, paquete 2, legajo 78, document 17 (1672); ANHH, paquete 2, legajo 77, document 8 (1673).

21. Recinos, Goetz, and Chonay, *The Annals of the Cakchiquels*, pp. 129, 131.

22. For early mining and mining cuadrillas in Guatemala, see Arévalo, *Libro de Actas del Ayuntamiento de la Ciudad de Santiago de Guatemala*, pp. 115-16, 162-63; Batres Jáuregui, *La América Central*, vol. 2, pp. 408-9. One cronista claimed that the Cakchiquel uprising of 1524 was because of Gonzalo de Alvarado's exactions for cuadrillas. See FV, 1:73-74. For Chiapas, see Millares Carlo and Mantecón, *Indice y extractos*, vol. 1, p. 248 (the date is early 1528); Chamberlain, *The Governorship of Montejo*, p. 178, and Miranda, *La Función Económica del Encomendero*, p. 21.

23. For Alvarado's activities see Chapter Six. Meanwhile, for his Honduran invasions, see Chamberlain, *Conquest and Colonization*, pp. 55-61.

24. *Ibid.*, pp. 111-14.

25. Recinos, Goetz, and Chonay, *Annals of the Cakchiquels*, p. 129; CS, 10:464-66, 470-71; Fernández de Oviedo, *Historia General y Natural*, 8:154. ANCR, Complementario colonial 5004, January 24, 1564, shows similar methods of obtaining Indian labor for panning after the conquest of Costa Rica.

26. Chamberlain, *Conquest and Colonization,* pp. 111-16, 181-82; CDIU, 11: 426-27; Fernández de Oviedo, *Historia General y Natural,* vol. 8, p. 153.

27. Chamberlain, *Conquest and Colonization,* pp. 112, 115. For quantities mined before 1543 see pp. 233-34. See also the figures in AGI, Patronato 180, no. 74; Francisco Barrientos to Crown, February 25, 1534, AGI/AG 49; CDIU, 11:399.

28. Audiencia to Crown, December 30, 1545, AGI/AG 9; CS, 11:464, 470-71, 496; Andagoya, *The Narrative,* pp. 35-36; Peralta, *Costa-Rica, Nicaragua y Panamá,* p. 397 (Joan Dávila to the Crown, 1566).

29. Chamberlain, *Conquest and Colonization,* pp. 219-21, 224-25; Alonso de Maldonado to Crown, January 15, 1543, AGI/AG 9.

30. Chamberlain, *Conquest and Colonization,* p. 220; Alonso de Maldonado to Crown, January 15, 1543, AGI/AG 9; CDIU, 11:402, 426-27.

31. Chamberlain, *Conquest and Colonization,* p. 234; "Un libro de cartas a s.m. por varias personas seculares y eclesiasticas, 1549–1570," AGI/AG 8, f. 48.

32. Cabildo of San Pedro to Crown, November 1, 1539, AGI/AG 44 is an early complaint. See also President Landecho to Crown, July 16, 1560, AGI/AG 9; AGI, Patronato 182-1-17 (1565); CDIE, 107:349. For the same complaints about Nicaragua, see for example, President Villalobos to Crown, March 17, 1578, AGI/AG 10; CDIU, 17:212 (1604); see the comparison between mining and panning in Chaunu and Chaunu, *Séville et l'Atlantique,* 8¹:510-17, 547-49.

33. See, for example, Chamberlain, *Conquest and Colonization,* pp. 237, 247-49; Recinos, Goetz, and Chonay, *Annals of the Cakchiquels,* pp. 136-37.

34. Cerwin, *Bernal Díaz,* pp. 121, 124-31; Simpson, *The Emancipation,* pp. 5-9; CS, 13:486-87. Private individuals were shipping large sums of gold as late as 1550. See Archivo de Protocolos de Sevilla, Libro del año 1551—oficio XV: Libro II— Escribanía Alonzo de Cazalla—Folio 1894—Fecha: 6 de noviembre; and Libro del año 1551—oficio XV: Libro II—Escribanía Alonzo de Cazalla—Folio 1895 v.—Fecha: 7 de noviembre.

35. Simpson would agree. See his *The Emancipation,* pp. 7-8. See also Alonso de Maldonado to Crown, January 15, 1543, AGI/AG 9. Benzoni, *Historia,* 98v., noticed in the early 1540s that the gold around Trujillo had almost all been used up.

36. Chaunu and Chaunu, *Séville et l'Atlantique,* 8¹:850-51.

37. AGGG, A3.9, 39852, 2763 (1643); AGGG, A3.9, 27069, 1674 (1653); AGGG, A3.9, 39856, 2763 (1703); FG, 1:133. For Costa Rica, see ANCR, Cartago 064, April 10, 1681. For the hides trade, see Carlos Vázquez de Coronado to Crown, December 8, 1610, AGI/AG 7; Audiencia to Crown, May 8, 1607, AGI/AG 12; AGGG, A1.2-4, 15753, al98, f. 256 (1607).

38. AGI Patronato, 182-1-57. *Boletín del Archivo General del Gobierno* (Guatemala) 11, nos. 1 and 2 (March-June 1946): 6-8.

Chapter 3

1. García de Palacios, *Carta dirijida al rey de España,* pp. 52, 54, 111. See also the map facing the title page; Torquemada, *Monarquía,* vol. 1, p. 218. A little was also gathered around Comayagua, e.g., AGI, Patronato, 183-1-16, f. 9.

2. Acosta, *Historia natural y moral,* p. 190; López de Velasco, *Geografía y descripción universal,* p. 297; Torquemada, *Monarquía,* vol. 1, p. 328.

3. García de Palacios, *Carta,* pp. 52, 54; Vázquez de Espinosa, *Compendium,* pp. 228-29; CDIE, 57:399.

4. Vázquez de Espinosa, *Compendium,* pp. 228-29.

5. *Isagoge,* p. 339; BNM, 3178, f. 206, "Fructos mas Principales q.ª ay en las Provy.ᵃˢ sujetas a la Aud.ª Rl. de guatimala."
6. West and Augelli, *Middle America,* p. 51; López de Velasco, *Geografía,* p. 297; Gage, *The English-American,* pp. 224-25.
7. CDIU, 11:393; FG, 2:160; Gage, *The English-American,* pp. 224-25, 278.
8. Benzoni, *Historia,* 165v.; "Sobre las mantas y otras cosas de la Verapaz" (1582), AGI/AG 966; Herrera, *Historia,* vol. 1, pp. 127, 128; see also Manning and Moore, "Sassafras and Syphilis," 473-75.
9. Benzoni, *Historia,* 165 v.; Herrera, *Historia,* vol. 1, p. 127.
10. López de Velasco, *Geografía,* pp. 285, 305, 312-13; Vázquez de Espinosa, *Compendium,* pp. 235, 263; CDHCR, 5:361; BNM, 3000, f. 223; Gage, *The English-American,* pp. 224-25, 278.
11. Chaunu and Chaunu, *Séville et l'Atlantique,* 6²:1024. For a typical cargo, see Archivo de Protocolos de Sevilla, Libro del año 1580–oficio X: Libro 1–Escribanía: Diego Gabriel–Folio 63–Fecha: 11 January 1580. Drake took a ship in 1579 bound from Costa Rica to Panama loaded with sarsaparrilla and other goods. See Peralta, *Costa-Rica, Nicaragua y Panamá,* pp. 586-90.
12. AGI Patronato 183-1-6 (1590).
13. Audiencia to Crown (1584), AGI/AG 10; CDHCR, 7:415, 418, 420.
14. Chaunu and Chaunu, *Séville et l'Atlantique,* 6²:1024, 1042-43, 1050-51; Carlos Vázquez de Coronado to Crown, December 8, 1610, AGI/AG 7.
15. FX, 1:61. Small quantities were exported throughout the seventeenth and eighteenth centuries. E.g., *Isagoge,* p. 398.

Chapter 4

1. Urquhart, *Cocoa,* pp. 7, 15.
2. Heiser, "Cultivated Plants and Cultural Diffusion in Nuclear America," 933.
3. Cheesman, "Notes on the Nomenclature, Classification and Possible Relationships of Cacao Populations," 145.
4. *Popol Vuh,* ed. Recinos, Goetz, and Morley, pp. 134, 166; Recinos, Goetz and Chonay, *The Annals of the Cakchiquels,* pp. 48, 185; Torquemada, *Monarquía* vol. 2, pp. 49-50.
5. For the Tabasco, Yucatán, Honduras coastal areas, see for example, Herrera, *Historia,* vol. 2, pp. 426-27; *Landa's Relación,* ed. Tozzer, pp. 94-95, 234; Coe, *The Maya,* pp. 139-40; Sauer, *The Early Spanish Main,* pp. 128-30.
For Nicaragua, see Fernández de Oviedo, *Historia General,* vol. 2, p. 246; vol. 11, pp. 64, 90, 109, 167.
For New Spain, Soconusco, Guatemala, and the coast of present-day El Salvador, see Torquemada, *Monarquía,* vol. 2, pp. 560, 579; Díaz del Castillo, *Historia Verdadera,* p. 382; Motolinía, *Motolinía's History,* p. 218; Soustelle, *The Daily Life of the Aztecs,* pp. 81-82; Gibson, *The Aztecs under Spanish Rule,* p. 349; Coe, *The Maya,* p. 88. For the Mayan area in general see Coe, *The Maya,* pp. 18, 88; Rivet, *Maya Cities,* pp. 48, 65.
6. Cakchiquel mythology mentions cacao tribute payments during the tribe's legendary early wanderings; Recinos, Goetz, and Chonay, *Annals of the Cakchiquels,* p. 48. For pre-conquest tribute payments in cacao, see also Morley, *The Ancient Maya,* p. 175; Molins Fábrega, *El Códice Mendocino,* p. 34; and Fernández de Oviedo, *Historia General,* 2:247. See also Navarrete, "Cuentos del Soconusco, Chiapas," pp. 427-28.

For plantations on the Caribbean coast before the conquest see Coe, *The Maya*, p. 139; Chamberlain, *Conquest and Colonization*, p. 31; Díaz del Castillo, *Historia Verdadera*, p. 444.

For the amounts of cacao tribute from Tabasco and Soconusco mentioned by the Codex Mendoza see, Molins Fábrega, *El Códice Mendocino*, pp. 34-35. Alvarado reported to Cortés on his first invasion of Zapotitlán that the woods and the cacao groves were so thick that they provided good cover for the hostile Indians (Alvarado, *An Account of the Conquest*, pp. 44, 55). Other plantations further down the coast are mentioned in Coe, *The Maya*, pp. 20, 61, 88, 90. See also Molins Fábrega, *El Códice Mendocino*, p. 34. Fernández de Oviedo gives the impression that cacao had reached Nicaragua with late arrivals from other areas, and was not cultivated by the old inhabitants (Fernández de Oviedo, *Historia General*, vol. 11, p. 109). See also Chapman, *Los Nicarao y los Chorotega según las Fuentas Históricas*, pp. 26-28.

7. On the high cost of cacao before the conquest see Fernández de Oviedo, *Historia General*, vol. 2, pp. 246-47; Morley, *The Ancient Maya*, pp. 177-78. It was a luxury in some areas and thus used only by the nobility: Sahagún, *Historia General*, vol. 2, p. 307, vol. 3, p. 77; García de Palacios, *Carta dirijida al Rey de España*, pp. 33-40; Torquemada, *Monarquía*, vol. 2, p. 550; Soustelle, *Daily Life*, pp. 60, 149. In Nicaragua the common people did not relish eating their hard-earned coinage: Fernández de Oviedo, *Historia General*, vol. 2, pp. 247, 251-52; Andagoya, *The Narrative*, p. 33. Before the conquest ordinary people were forbidden the use of cacao in some areas. See Estrada and Niebla, "Descripción de la Provincia de Zapotitlán y Suchitepequez, Año de 1579," 73; Paso y Troncoso, *Papeles de Nueva España*, vol. 4, p. 186. For estimates on yield and consumption see the felicitously entitled work by Millon, "When Money Grew on Trees: A Study of Cacao in Ancient Mesoamerica," pp. 179-81, 198, 210-11, 219, 230-31.

8. García de Palacios, *Carta*, pp. 36-39. The same official repeated his warnings against pagan cacao rites in his "Relación y forma . . . de Bisitar," AGI/AG 128, f. 5. See also Fernández de Oviedo, *Historia General*, vol. 11, pp. 66-67, 167, and Rubio Sánchez, "El Cacao," 83-84. Rubio also suggests that Linneus may have known of cacao's ritualistic connections when he called it "theobroma cacao," the "food of the gods." In Yucatán, Hibueras, and Honduras it was also widely used in religious ceremonies: *Landa's Relación*, pp. 90, 106, 164-65. It was obviously of considerable religious significance. See also *The Book of the Jaguar Priest, a translation of the Book of Chilam Balam of Tizunin*, trans. Maud Worcester Makemson, p. 17. Its use as a medicine and in medical incantations can be seen in *Ritual of the Bacabs*, trans. Ralph L. Roys, pp. 6, 8, 37, 44. See also Roys, *The Ethno-Botany of the Maya*, pp. 33, 136, 222. The Nicaraos considered it a remedy for wounds and snake bite. See Fernández de Oviedo, *Historia General*, vol. 2, pp. 250, 252-54. Cacao contains theobromine.

9. Sahagún gives a list of recipes served to the upper classes of pre-conquest New Spain in his *Historia General*, vol. 2, p. 307. See also Thompson, "Notes on the Use of Cacao in Middle America," 107, and García Payón, *Amaxocoatl*, Fernández de Oviedo mentions the Indian preference for a red color in the drink in his *Historia General*, vol. 2, p. 249.

10. Benzoni, *Historia*, p. 103. Fernández de Oviedo describes it as looking like "filth" to Christians; see Fernández de Oviedo, *Historia General*, vol. 2, p. 250. Acosta claimed that only those who grew up drinking it learned to like it. Acosta, *Historia Natural y Moral*, pp. 180-81.

11. Gibson, *The Aztecs*, pp. 195-97.

12. Amazement at the increase in the use of cacao and the quantities consumed is expressed in Torquemada, *Monarquía*, vol. 2, p. 558. See also Estrada and Niebla, "Descripción," p. 73.

There are many sources which talk of the density of the Indian population on this coast at the time of the conquest. Others talk of the rapid disappearance of the Indians thereafter. See the table in this chapter. For Soconusco in particular, see

López de Velasco, *Geografía y descripción universal,* p. 302; CDIU, 17:167, which says (1561) that Soconusco "used to have more than forty villages." See especially AGI/AG 986B, Guatemala, no signature, no date. This important document states that the 30,000 vecinos of "40 years ago" now number 1,600. The document provides a clue by saying that Pedro Pacheco has just finished his term as governor. Pacheco became governor in 1567 (CDIU, 17:173), so this document probably dates from the early 1570s. The 30,000 vecinos, therefore, lived in Soconusco shortly after the conquest or before. John Chilton, who saw the province in the late summer of 1571, described it as "desolate." See Hakluyt, *The Principal Voyages,* p. 365; Governor Luis Ponce de León to the Crown, January 19, 1574, AGI/AG 40. For Zapotitlán, see Estrada and Niebla, "Descripción," p. 71, and Hakluyt, *The Principal Voyages,* p. 366.

13. Torquemada, *Monarquía,* vol. 2, p. 620; Vázquez de Espinosa, *Compendium and Description,* pp. 96-97, 225, 371; García de Palacios, *Carta,* p. 107. For modern comments, see Cheesman, "Notes," p. 148; Millon, "When Money Grew on Trees," pp. 11-12, 20-22.

14. For descriptions of cacao plantations and the work on them, see Torquemada, *Monarquía,* vol. 2, p. 620; Benzoni, *Historia,* pp. 101v.-2; Pineda, "Descripción de la provincia de Guatemala," 50-51, 55-56.

15. Central American cacao bushes were described in the sixteenth and seventeenth centuries as requiring lots of shade, care, and renewal. See Motolinía, *Motolinía's History,* pp. 217-18; Herrera, *Historia General,* vol. 1, p. 185; Torquemada, *Monarquía,* vol. 2, p. 620; FG, 2:96-97. Seventeenth-century writers found it to be more delicate than the bushes of Caracas and Guayaquil. E.g., Vázquez de Espinosa, *Compendium,* pp. 96-97. For perceptive comments on weaker varieties of cacao, cacao diseases and pests, the expense of rearing low-yield bushes, and erosion, see Urquhart, *Cocoa,* pp. 36-39, 67-68, 116-18, 125, 145-78, 230-31.

16. Pineda, "Descripción," pp. 50-51; Torquemada, *Monarquía,* vol. 2, p. 620; AGGG,A1.23, legajo 1524, f. 251; Millon, "When Money Grew on Trees," pp. 11-12.

17. Fernández de Oviedo, *Historia General,* vol. 2, pp. 247-48.

18. Torquemada, *Monarquía,* vol. 2, p. 620; FG, 2:97.

19. López de Velasco, *Geografía,* p. 302.

20. Bishop Zandoval to Crown, April 20, 1616, AGI/AG 161; Audiencia to Crown, 1584, AGI/AG 10; BNM 3047, f. 130 (1646); López de Velasco, *Geografía,* p. 302.

21. Torquemada, *Monarquía,* vol. 2, p. 620; Audiencia to Crown, June 2, 1612, AGI/AG 13; Governor to Crown, May 4, 1613, AGI/AG 40.

22. CDIU, 17:160, 164; Larrainzar, *Noticia Histórica,* p. 23; Diego Garcés to Crown, 1570, AGI/AG 968B; Governor to Crown, June 19, 1574, AGI/AG 40; "Razón de las tasaciones," AGI/AG 166.

23. There are at least two letters from priests in Soconusco to the King complaining about fraudulent governors, in AGI/AG 965. See also Lic. Arteaga Mendiola to Crown, March 30, 1571, AGI/AG 9; AGGG, A1.2, 16190, 2245, f. 168v. (August 12, 1636); Pineda, "Descripción," p. 56. For accusations against the clergy, see CDI, 4: 132-34.

24. Lic. Arteaga Mendiola to Crown, March 30, 1571, AGI/AG 9; AGGG, A1.24, 10211, 1567, f. 112 (June 15, 1676); Pineda, "Descripción," p. 56.

25. E.g., AGGG, A1.23, legajo 1513, f. 77 (December 22, 1605). For an excellent discussion of the failure of these royal efforts in Guatemala, see, Mörner, "La Política de Segregación," 137-51. See also AGGG, 16190, 2245, ff. 4, 172.

26. AGGG, A1.2-4, legajo 2196, f. 190 (February 4, 1560).

27. Governor to Crown, January 16, 1576, AGI/AG 40; cédula real to the Viceroy of New Spain, May 21, 1576, BNP, Fonds Mexicains, 119-48; cédula real to the President of the Audiencia, 1576, AGGG, A1.23, legajo 1513, f. 494.

28. For the two kinds of tribute see, Governor of Soconusco to Crown, May 4, 1613, AGI/AG 40. On Huehuetlán see Pineda, "Descripción," p. 56; López de

Velasco, *Geografía,* pp. 302-303; Governor Luis Ponce de León to Crown, January 19, 1574, AGI/AG 40.

29. For porters, see Gibson, *The Aztecs,* p. 348. For recuas and the origins of the merchants see Vázquez de Espinosa, *Compendium,* p. 206; AGGG, A1.23, legajo 1573, f. 494 (1576); Pineda, "Descripción," p. 56; Miranda, *España y Nueva España,* p. 92.

30. AGGG, A1.23, legajo 1522, f. 92.

31. Borah and Cook, *Price Trends of Some Basic Commodities,* p. 36.

32. Vecinos of Huehuetlán to Crown, January 1565, AGI/AG 44; Paso y Troncoso, *Epistolario de la Nueva España,* vol. 9, p. 155.

33. Audiencia to Crown, June 2, 1612, AGI/AG 13; Bishop Zandoval to Crown, May 12, 1619, AGI/AG 161; Audiencia to Crown, November 26, 1630, AGI/AG 15; Conde de Santiago to Crown, May 31, 1655, AGI/AG 19.

34. AGI/AG 40, January 19, 1574 and February 15, 1590; Diego Garcés to Crown, 1570, AGI/AG 968 B.

35. Diego Garcés to Crown, November 30, 1570, AGI/AG 9, and Lic. Arteaga Mendiola to Crown, March 30, 1571.

36. Alvarado, *An Account of the Conquest,* p. 44; Vázquez de Espinosa, *Compendium,* pp. 370-71; Urquhart, *Cocoa,* pp. 38-40, 67-68; Millon, "When Money Grew on Trees," p. 22.

37. Governor Luis Ponce de León to Crown, January 19, 1574, AGI/AG 40; Valverde, "Razón y parecer," 312-13.

38. Diego Garcés to Crown (1570?), AGI/AG 968 B; Frs. Viana, Gallego, and Cadena, "Relación de la Provincia: tierra de la Vera Paz," 147; AGGG, A1.23, legajo 1513, f. 520 (April 22, 1577); Pineda, "Descripción," pp. 50-51, 54, 57.

39. Viana et al., "Relación," p. 147; Pineda, "Descripción," p. 60, "of 500 who go, less than 400 return, and they spend all they took with them to return with 2 tostones." For a modern comparison see Oakes, *The Two Crosses,* p. 33.

40. Viana et al., "Relación," p. 147; Pineda, "Descripción," p. 60.

41. Pineda, "Descripción," p. 60. Oakes, *The Two Crosses,* p. 37, says "In 1946, for work on a finca, under contract, an Indian was paid one dollar a week plus corn for food and a hut in which to sleep. He usually came home with malaria, tropical ulcers, dysentery, or venereal disease." See also pp. 209, 241-42.

42. Otherwise the friars and other tribute collectors of the highland area would not have allowed the system to continue for so many years. See chapters Five to Seven.

43. Lic. Arteaga Mendiola to Crown, 30 March 1571, AGI/AG 9, f. 2.

44. See Chapter Two; AGI/AG 968 B, Guatemala, no signature, 1573?; López de Velasco, *Geografía,* p. 302; Governor to Crown, May 4, 1613, AGI/AG 40; AGI/AG 966, "Razón de las tasaciones" reflects this small but rapid population rise caused by immigration.

45. Francisco de Morales to Crown, in Paso y Troncoso, *Epistolario,* vol. 9, p. 155; Governor Luis Ponce de León to the Crown, January 19, 1574, AGI/AG 40; BNP, Fonds Mexicains, 119-48, May 21, 1576; AGGG, A1.23, legajo 1513, f. 494 (May 21, 1576).

Chapter 5

1. The best summation of cacao tribute in Central America between 1500 and 1548 is Bergmann, "The Distribution of Cacao Cultivation," 85-96. See especially the tribute map, p. 90, which is derived from "Tasaciones de los naturales" (1548–1551), AGI/AG 128.

2. Sherman, "A Conqueror's Wealth," 200, 202-203.
3. AGGG, A1.2-4, legajo 2196, f. 119 (11 March 1537).
4. Nicolás López to Crown, April 26, 1556, AGI/AG 52; CDI, 13:271; Benzoni, *Historia,* p. 108; Herrera, *Historia,* vol. 1, pp. 80-85.
5. Herrera, *Historia,* pp. 80-85, 87; Borah, *Early Colonial Trade and Navigation,* p. 24; Pardo, *Efemérides,* pp. 13, 16.
6. More than 20 ships were involved in 1535 (CS, 3:459; Borah, *Early Trade,* pp. 4-7.)
7. Borah, *Early Trade,* p. 5; FG, 3:293-98.
8. Borah, *Early Trade,* p. 71; García de Palacios, *Carta,* p. 41; BNM, 2468, ff. 104-5 (a derrotero of June 24, 1632). Several attempts were made to improve the port at Iztapa. Both López de Cerrato and Valverde tried to deepen it by diverting a river into the estuary there (1548–49 and 1579–80). CDI, 24:497; CS, 15:85; Valverde to Crown, September 4, 1579, AGI/AG 10. At the end of the century there was frequent talk of improving it. See, for example, the various letters in AGI/AG 11, and *Isagoge,* p. 354. Iztapa was often proposed as a possible terminus for trans-isthmian trade between Spain and Peru. For descriptions of Acajutla and Iztapa, see Findley, *A Directory for the Navigation of the Pacific Ocean,* vol. 1, pp. 247-49.
9. Borah, *Early Trade,* pp. 24-29, map, p. 27.
10. Benzoni, *Historia,* p. 108; Nicolás López to Crown, April 26, 1556, AGI/AG 52.
11. CDI, 13:271-72; Lardé y Larín, "Fundación de Sonsonate," 3-8; Landecho to Crown, March 2, 1563, AGI/AG 9. Landecho kept a jealous eye on the merchants' activities and obviously considered them rivals. See Pardo, *Efemérides,* p. 16.
12. Mörner, "La Política de Segregación," 139; Manuel Ungría Girón to Crown, 1605, AGI/AG 12; Konetzke, *Colección de documentos,* vol. 2, pp. 118-20; Pineda, "Descripción," 52, 56, 62.
13. López de Velasco, *Geografía y descripción,* p. 296; Audiencia to Crown (1558), AGI/AG 9.
14. For further information, see notes 15, 21-32, of this chapter. Morales had left Guatemala poverty-stricken and fleeing from his enemies, the cacao group, in 1553. Valverde and his oidores were fighting a clique composed of the Izalcos encomenderos allied to the ayuntamiento of Santiago. See Paso y Troncoso, *Epistolario,* vol. 9, pp. 146-56; Audiencia to Crown, April 23, 1582, and Audiencia to Crown, April 1, 1585, AGI/AG 10.
15. Paso y Troncoso, *Epistolario,* vol. 9, pp. 146-56, 224-26. From the Mexican end of the trade, oidor Zorita complained that much of the silver mined in Mexico "is sent to Guatemala to pay for the cacao that merchants bring from there." Zorita, *The Lords of New Spain,* p. 242. One example of the graft allegations against López de Cerrato will suffice here. His activities will be studied later. See RAH, Colección Muñoz, 85, ff. 336-42, in which several vecinos complained to the Emperor (1550).
16. Pardo, *Efemérides,* p. 13.
17. AGGG, A1.2-4, legajo 2196, ff. 140, 190; *Isagoge,* pp. 335-37, 343.
18. Pardo, *Efemérides,* p. 17.
19. Pardo, *Efemérides,* pp. 17-18; Paso y Troncoso, *Epistolario,* 9:224-26; FG, 3:214-17.
20. Pardo, *Efemérides,* 18-19; López de Velasco, *Geografía,* p. 283.
21. Valverde to Crown (1584), AGI/AG 10; Frs. Viana, Gallego, and Cadena, "Relación de la Provincia," 147.
22. Nicolás López to Crown, April 26, 1556, AGI/AG 55; Diego Robledo to Crown, April 10, 1556, AGI/AG 9; AGGG, A1.23, legajo 1513, f. 520, (April 22, 1577); Viana et al., "Relación," p. 147.
23. Viana et al., "Relación," p. 147; AR, 2:433-34.
24. Audiencia to Crown, April 23, 1582, AGI/AG 10, ff. 13-13v.; Valverde to Crown (1584), AGI/AG 10, f. 5. These two different tributes, levied in the cacao

areas, were still in existence in the early seventeenth century. See Bishop Juan Ramírez to Crown, February 3, 1603, and March 10, 1603, both in AGI/AG 156. For persistence of some of the patterns mentioned herein, see Oakes, *Beyond the Windy Place,* pp. 78-82. Indians were lured into debt by highland merchants, then sent to the coast to work off the debt on fincas. "When they have worked off their contract they will have to walk home five days, bringing no money, and probably sickness. Everyone brings back sickness from the fincas." (p. 80).

25. Valverde to Crown (1584), AGI/AG 10, f. 6v.

26. *Ibid.*

27. *Ibid.,* f. 6v.; Fiscal Thomas Spínola de la Plaza to Crown, March 30, 1585, AGI/AG 10. This practice was also noticed by Bishop Juan Ramírez in 1603. See his two letters cited above in note 24 from AGI/AG 156.

28. Valverde to Crown (1584), AGI/AG 10, ff. 4 v., 6.

29. *Ibid.,* f. 7.

30. *Ibid.,* f. 8.

31. *Ibid.;* Mila *Historia de la América Central,* p. 234; Valverde to Crown (1584), AGI/AG 10, ff. 4 v., 6.

32. Valverde to Crown (1584), AGI/AG 10, ff. 11-11v.; Audiencia to Crown, April 23, 1582, AGI/AG 10; a priest to Crown (1580), AGI/AG 170, ff. 22-24.

33. AGGG, A1.23, legajo 1513, f. 568 (November 23, 1579); AGGG, A1.23, legajo 4588, f. 38v. (May 22, 1565); Juan de Torres to Crown (1578), AGI/AG 55.

34. Juan de Torres to Crown (1578), AGI/AG 55; Audiencia to Crown, April 1, 1585, AGI/AG 10. Belatedly, the Crown recognized the problem. The salary of the oficial real of Sonsonate was raised from 400 to 500 pesos, May 19, 1587 (CDIU, 17:186).

35. For García de Palacios' long and varied martial career and constant ambitions, see Squier's introduction to García de Palacios, *Carta.* See also Schurz, *The Manila Galleon,* p. 68. His attitudes towards Indians can be found in the *Carta,* and in his "Relación y forma . . . de Bisitar," AGI/AG 128.

36. Audiencia to Crown, April 23, 1582, and Valverde to Crown (1584), ff. 9, 11-12, both in AGI/AG 10. The Creoles found him to their liking as an oidor, e.g., *Isagoge,* pp. 338-39.

37. Valverde to Crown (1584), AGI/AG 10, ff. 4-4v.; CDI, 24:474-93.

38. López de Velasco, *Geografía,* p. 296; Nicolás López to Crown, April 26, 1556, AGI/AG 52. Chaunu and Chaunu, *Séville et l'Atlantique,* 8¹:857, would go so far as to say, "One is in the presence of a quasi-monoculture. And it is precisely this monocultural nature which explains the relative fragility of Guatemalan cacao."

39. See Chapters Seven and Eleven for other cattle invasions of Indian crops.

40. AGI, Patronato 182-1-43 (1574), shows Acajutla collecting 8,757 pesos in almojarifazgo, while the Golfo Dulce collected only 520 pesos in the same year. López de Velasco, *Geografía,* p. 296, says 300,000 ducats worth of cacao left Acajutla yearly. For export totals from the various producing areas during the boom, see Paso y Troncoso, *Epistolario,* vol. 9, pp. 148-49, 155, and the three documents dated January 19, 1574, February 15, 1575, and January 16, 1576, all in AGI/AG 10.

41. AGGG, A1.23, legajo 1513, f. 494 (May 21, 1576).

42. AGGG, A1.23, legajo 1512, f. 407 (May 18, 1572); AGGG, A1.23, legajo 1512, f. 443 (March 23, 1574); Bancroft, *History of Central America,* vol. 2, p. 384.

43. Valverde to Crown (1584), AGI/AG 10, ff. 6, 7v.-8.

44. *Ibid.,* f. 7v.; Audiencia to Crown, April 23, 1582, AGI/AG 10.

45. Valverde to Crown (1584), AGI/AG 10, f. 9v.

46. *Ibid.,* f. 7v.; Fiscal Eugenio Salazar to Crown, March 13, 1577; and President Villalobos to Crown, March 17, 1578, f. 3v., both in AGI/AG 10.

47. Valverde to Crown (1584), AGI/AG 10, ff. 10-12; Audiencia to Crown, April 23, 1582, AGI/AG 10, ff. 12-14; Milla, *Historia de la América Central,* vol. 2, pp. 233-35.

48. Valverde to Crown (1584), AGI/AG 10, ff. 4v., 10, 12v.-13v. For a similar case in nearby Aguachapa, see Pineda, "Descripción," 62. This was not the end of

Guzmán's career. The ayuntamiento of Santiago was still giving him posts of honor in 1598, and the Audiencia was still frowning on the granting of favors to such a man, a clear case of early Creole-gachupín rivalry. See Milla, *Historia de la América Central,* vol. 2, p. 269. For Nicaragua, see AGGG, A1.15, 660, 81 (1587). (The village mentioned is Niquinohomo.)

49. Konetzke, *Colección de documentos,* vol. 2, pp. 118-20; AGI, Patronato 82-1-6, shows the decay of Naolingo. Other points are in Pineda, "Descripción," p. 51; Manuel Ungría Girón to Crown (1605), AGI/AG 12; Audiencia to Crown, November 11, 1606, AGI/AG 12; "Autos de hacienda real," (1606-7), AGI/AG 12.

50. García de Palacios, *Carta,* p. 63; AGGG, A1.24, 10201, 1557, f. 75 (January 31, 1609); AGGG, A3.30, 41706, 2864 (1609); AGGG, A1.24, 10202, 1558, f. 265 (February 27, 1638); Pineda, "Descripción," pp. 62–63; Peralta, *Costa-Rica y Colombia,* p. 33.

51. RAH, Colección Muñoz, 42, ff. 115-18; Torquemada, *Monarquía,* vol. 2, p. 609.

52. For destructive harvesting, see AGGG, A1.23, legajo 3671, f. 288 (1615). For floods see FX, 2:28. For the difficulty in restoring eroded cacao plantations, see Urquhart, *Cocoa,* pp. 67-68; Millon, "When Money Grew on Trees," pp. 21-22.

Chapter 6

1. E.g., Haring, *The Spanish Empire in America,* p. 258; Diffie, *Latin-American Civilization,* pp. 58-61, 66-74.

2. Simpson, *Exploitation of Land in Central Mexico;* Arévalo, *Libro de actas;* Konetzke, *Colección de documentos,* vol. 1, pp. 179, 258, 261-62.

3. Chaunu and Chaunu, *Séville et l'Atlantique,* 8¹:885-86. Central American archives and the AGI contain many petitions for slaves or encomiendas, hardly any for land at this early stage. See also Gibson, *The Aztecs,* p. 272.

4. E.g., López de Velasco, *Geografía,* pp. 285, 297, 300, 307-9, 311.

5. A comparison in the AGGG of the number of titles granted in this period and the numbers in later years, especially the 1570s to 1635, shows that formal land ownership was not a great preoccupation among many Spaniards. The ease with which the individual could gain title to land, however, may have been greater than in Mexico. See the revealing document comparing the two areas in Cuevas, *Documentos inéditos,* p. 181. For flight to Peru, see the references in earlier chapters, such as CDI, 24:192-93, 200. The attraction exerted by the cacao industry is shown in Chapter Five.

6. E.g., Recinos, Goetz, and Chonay, *The Annals of the Cakchiquels,* pp. 129-34.

7. *Ibid.,* pp. 129-30, 132-34; Milla, *Historia de la América Central,* p. 360. This matter will be discussed more fully in Chapter Seven.

8. AR, 1:201-5; Kelly, *Pedro de Alvarado,* pp. 186-201. Both accounts say that Alvarado took some 2,000 Indian slaves with him to Peru, and that none returned. (Other reports talk of 4,000). See Alvarado's explanations in Kelly, *Pedro de Alvarado,* pp. 249-65, and the contract between him and Diego de Almagro, *Ibid.,* pp. 266-67.

9. Chamberlain, *Conquest and Colonization,* pp. 55, 112, 123-24. See also "Requête de Plusieurs Chefs Indiens," Ternaux-Compans, *Voyages, Relations et Mémoires,* vol. 10, pp. 419-20, where the local caciques claim that they and hundreds of their subjects were taken to Honduras, Verapaz, and Nicaragua, by Alvarado, with the result that many died.

10. Pedraza, "Relación de varios sucesos ocurridos en Honduras," pp. 164-66. The Achíes whom Alvarado took to Honduras, and who caused such devastation,

were probably Tzutuhils. See BNP, Fonds Américains, 69. "Sermones en lengua Achi ó Tzutuhil."

11. Alvarez Rubiano, *Pedrarias Dávila,* pp. 334-36, 348, 369; Rodrigo del Castillo and Andrés de Cereceda to Crown, January 20, 1529, *Ibid.,* p. 658; Rodrigo del Castillo to Emperor, [n.d., 1529?], *Ibid.,* pp. 661-65; Andrés Cereceda to Crown, January 20, 1529, M-M 302, Bancroft Library, University of California, Berkeley. A list of some of these Indian slaves is in RAH, Colección Muñoz, 60, f. 137, February 28, 1529.

12. Fernández Guardia, *Historia de Costa Rica,* pp. 62-209; Dominicans of Cobán to Crown, April 18, 1582, AGI/AG 170; Stone, *Some Spanish Entradas,* pp. 209-96.

13. It is quite clear from Chamberlain's previously cited work on Montejo in Chiapas and Honduras that he considers Montejo to have been a superior and exceptional figure when compared to the other conquistadors of Central America.

14. Even Alvarado's friend Bishop Marroquín complained about his constant restlessness. See his letter to the Emperor, November 20, 1539, AGI/AG 156. See also FX, 1:173-74, 178-80, 184, 267; Keniston, *Francisco de los Cobos,* pp. 105-7; Milla, *Historia de la América Central,* vol. 1, pp. 441-43, 530-52, 539-47.

15. Sherman, "A Conqueror's Wealth," 199-213; FX, 1:235-236.

16. Alvarez Rubiano, *Pedrarias Dávila,* pp. 345, 350. (Remember that Alvarez seems at times somewhat of an apologist for Pedrarias). See also FX, 1:500, 504; CS, 11:285-305.

17. Milla, *Historia de la América Central,* vol. 1, pp. 348, 409; Bancroft, *History of Central America,* vol. 2, pp. 98, 209-11; FX, 1:161-62, 186, 500; Arévalo, *Libro de actas,* p. 150.

18. Arévalo, *Libro de actas,* pp. 105-6; Milla, *Historia de la América Central,* vol. 1, pp. 426-27; Sherman, "A Conqueror's Wealth," p. 203; FX, 1:163, 172-74, 207, 223; Recinos, *Pedro de Alvarado,* pp. 135, 137, 178-81, 205, 209.

19. AR, 1:278-92; FX, 1:235; Recinos, *Pedro de Alvarado,* pp. 229-38.

20. CDI, 24:174-75.

21. Antonio de Cereceda to Crown, "Carta al Rey," June 14, 1533, M-M 318, Bancroft Library, University of California, Berkeley; CS, 11:356, 369, 383; CDI, 24:174-75, 383-84. 398-99; Cabildo of León to Crown, (1544), AGI/AG 43; Ayón, *Historia de Nicaragua,* vol. 1, pp. 267-68; ANCR, Complementario colonial 6502 (1545).

22. E.g., FG, 1:338; 3:425; CS, 1:456; CDI, 24:182-83; *Isagoge,* p. 290; Recinos, Goetz, and Chonay, *Annals of the Cakchiquels,* pp. 115-17, 143-45.

23. Ayón, *Historia de Nicaragua,* vol. 1, p. 312; Lic. Castañeda to Crown, May 1, 1533, AGI/AG 9; Bishop Marroquín to Crown, January 15, 1543, and *ibid.* to *ibid.,* January 26, 1560, both in AGI/AG 156. For Soconusco, see Chapter Four, especially the table.

24. López de Velasco, *Geografía,* p. 297. See also Bishop Marroquín to Prince Philip, September 20, 1547, *Cartas de Indias,* pp. 449-50.

25. E.g., A royal cédula of 1549 which tried to stop entradas of this kind, in AGGG, Al.23, legajo 511, f. 128 (October 9, 1549).

26. ANCR, Cartago 1131 (December 10, 1615); ANCR, Complementario colonial 5204 (February 25, 1620); ANCR, Guatemala 058 (January 23, 1626); ANHH, paquete 5, legajo 66 (1698). Obviously such violent and illegal methods of recruiting labor will tend to be a feature of periods of manpower shortage. Thus we find far more cases in the seventeenth century than in the sixteenth.

27. CDI, 24:349, 360; Audiencia to Crown, December 30, 1545; Lic. Maldonado to Crown, January 15, 1543, both in AGI/AG 9; AGGG, Al.23, legajo 4575, f. 103 (1548); López de Cerrato to Crown, April 8, 1549, RAH, Colección Muñoz, 85, f. 157v.

28. Arévalo, *Libro de actas,* pp. 144-45; Andrés de Cereceda to Crown, January 20, 1529, M-M 320, Bancroft Library, University of California, Berkeley. That Spanish colonizers sought people even more than gold, and certainly before land, is

brought out succinctly by Chaunu, *L'Amérique et les Amériques,* p. 69. See also Friede, "Proceso de formación de la propiedad territorial," pp. 76-80.

29. The definitive work on Marroquín is the previously cited work by Sáenz de Santa María, *El Licenciado Don Francisco Marroquín.* For his disputes with the more vigorous Las Casas, see pp. 198, 435. See also Zavala, "Los esclavos indios en Guatemala," 460-62; Ricard, *La "Conquête Spirituelle" du Mexique,* p. 292; AR, 1:441-42.

30. Recinos, Goetz, and Chonay, *Annals of the Cakchiquels,* pp. 134-36; FV, 1:69. The clash between the new evangelical friars and the older, compliant priests can be seen clearly in the undated letter of a vecino of Ciudad Real de Chiapas to the Crown, in Ternaux-Compans, *Voyages, Relations et Mémoires,* vol. 16, pp. 279-83. See also FX, 1:485-86.

31. Fuentes y Guzmán, a Creole who detested reformist clerics, described the immediate antagonisms which their arrival created, in FG, 2:265-67. See also FX, 1:345, 415-18.

32. E.g., Bishops Las Casas and Valdivieso to Prince Philip (1545), *Cartas de Indias,* pp. 14-20; AR, 2:22-8; Pedraza, "Relación de varios sucesos," pp. 136-80.

33. This rebellion has not yet received the scholarly attention which it requires. For a summary description, see Ayón, *Historia de Nicaragua,* vol. 1, pp. 273-301; Juarros, *Compendio de la Historia de la Ciudad de Guatemala,* vol. 2, pp. 140-41.

34. AR, 1:461-69, 474-91; 2:104-5, 106-8; FX, 1:411-21; 3:342-47. Las Casas also made an attempt to free the Indian slaves in Chiapas. See CDI, 7:156.

35. FX, 1:415-18, 421, 448-49, 459-67; 3:350-51; AR, 2:176. Calpisques were already abusing caciques over tribute collection in 1529. (Arévalo, *Libro de actas,* pp. 140-41). See also AR, 2:176-77.

36. Ayuntamiento of Santiago to Crown, in Simpson, *The Encomienda in New Spain,* p. 230, or FX, 1:388-94. See also Arévalo, *Colección de documentos,* p. 72.

37. Bishop Marroquín to the Emperor (1545), and Bishop Marroquín to Prince Philip (1547), in Sáenz de Santa María, *El Licenciado Don Francisco Marroquín,* pp. 198, 216-24. See also p. 205. Another moderate reformer's analysis and denunciation of Las Casas' activities is contained in Motolinía's lengthy letter to the Crown (1555) in FV, 2:ix-xxviii.

38. Zavala, *Contribución a la historia de las instituciones coloniales de Guatemala,* p. 30. (This document is also to be found in Milla, *Historia de la América Central,* vol. 1, pp. 26-31.) The royal cédula permitting enslavement of recalcitrant Indians in Central America is in Konetzke, *Colección de documentos,* vol. 1, pp. 143-44.

39. The most coherent work on López de Cerrato has been by William L. Sherman. See, for example, his "Indian Slavery and the Cerrato Reforms," 25-50. (My thanks to Professor Sherman for permitting me to see an advance copy of this well-argued article. I have relied heavily on its factual basis, but the conclusions to which I have come about the motivations and effectiveness of President López de Cerrato differ somewhat from his own.) For further material, see López de Cerrato to Emperor, four letters, April 8, 1549, RAH, Colección Muñoz 85; AGGG, Al.23, legajo 4575, f. 113 (1550).

40. There are several appeals from the cabildo of Santiago to the Crown in AGI/AG 41. Long before the arrival of López de Cerrato the Cabildo of Santiago had defended Indian slavery to the King. E.g., AGGG, Al.25, 25235, 2833 (n.d., 1530s).

41. Sherman, "Indian Slavery," *passim;* López de Cerrato to the Crown, September 28, 1548, AGI/AG 9.

42. The effects of these kinds of movements have been noted in previous chapters. In this context, see Bishop Marroquín to the Crown, May 10, 1537, *Cartas de Indias,* p. 418; Chamberlain, *Conquest and Colonization,* pp. 113-14.

43. Zavala, "Los esclavos indios," pp. 462-64. See also Bishop Marroquín's letter to the Crown, May 4, 1549, in Sáenz de Santa María, *El Licenciado Don*

Francisco Marroquín, p. 224; and Simpson, "The Emancipation of the Indian Slaves," pp. 6-8.

44. Marroquín was one of the first to identify the cacao clique. See his letter to Prince Philip, September 20, 1547, *Cartas de Indias,* p. 448. Years later Marroquín objected to President López de Cerrato's unwillingness or inability to dislodge the most flagrantly exploitive cacao encomendero, Juan de Guzmán. (Whose son, see Chapter Five, followed closely in his father's footsteps). See Marroquín's letter to the Emperor, May 23, 1556, in Sáenz de Santa María, *El Licenciado Don Francisco Marroquín,* pp. 307-8. See also Oidor Mexía to the Crown, July 30, 1557, AGI/AG 9.

45. FX, 1:479.

46. Zavala, "Los esclavos indios," pp. 463-64; Bishop Marroquín to the Emperor, May 8, 1549, and *ibid.* to *ibid.,* February 3, 1550, Sáenz de Santa María, *El Licenciado Don Francisco Marroquín,* pp. 247, 257-58.

47. AR, 2:182; Zavala, *Contribución,* pp. 69-70; "Cuenta de los tributos," (1548-51), AGI/AG 128.

48. FX, 1:480; 3:350-52, 357, 361.

49. *Ibid.,* 1:402, 411-21, 479, 481-82.

50. *Ibid.,* 1:482.

51. CDI, 24:561-63; Bataillon, "Las Casas et Le Licencié Cerrato," 83-84. The document which is the basis of this article is AGI Indiferente General 1093 (1552?). After President López de Cerrato had died Crown policy continued to be to erode the power of the encomienda as an institution. E.g., AGGG, Al.12, legajo 1511, f. 22 (July 12, 1554). (López de Cerrato died in 1555).

52. Bataillon, "Las Casas et Le Licencié Cerrato," p. 86; Sherman, "Indian Slavery," p. 36.

53. Bataillon, "Las Casas et Le Licencié Cerrato," p. 86.

54. *Ibid.,* pp. 81-82.

55. *Ibid.,* p. 82.

56. *Ibid.,* pp. 82-84; Sherman, "Indian Slavery," pp. 40-42; *Isagoge,* p. 312; Larreinaga, *Prontuario de todas las reales cédulas,* p. 22. (This document has been left out of some copies).

57. Some of the royal cédulas ordering the building of roads so that Indian tamemes would be less burdened, are AGGG, Al.23, legajo 4575, f. 49 (1538); AGGG, Al.23, legajo 4575, f. 36v. (1546). Then the Crown tried to impose a minimum wage for the tamemes, AGGG, Al.23, Legajo 4575, f. 94v. (February 22, 1549). Seemingly the same abuses still existed to some extent in the early seventeenth century because the Crown was still recommending new roads to alleviate them, AGGG, Al.23, legajo 5576, f. 46v. (1601). Ximénez praised López de Cerrato for his road-building program (FX, 1:474), but the astute Marroquín saw quite early that the growth of the pack animal population would help to solve some of the tamemes' problems. See his letter to the Emperor, June 4, 1545, *Cartas de Indias,* p. 438.

58. Bishop Ramírez' early letters of complaint to Spain have been well analyzed and summarized in two articles. Biermann, "Don Fray Juan Ramírez de Arellano," 318-47; Sherman, "Abusos contra los indios," 5-28. See also FX, 2:36-45.

59. MacLeod, "Las Casas, Guatemala," 53-64. By the mid-50s the Central Americans had gotten rid of the last of the reformers. See Bancroft, *History of Central America,* vol. 2, p. 367; Zorita, *The Lords of New Spain,* pp. 35-6.

60. AR, 2:182. The connection between decline of Indian populations and the careful counting and rationing of Indians was suggested by Batres Jáuregui, *La América Central,* vol. 2, pp. 153-54.

Chapter 7

1. FX, 1:223, 335-46; FV, 1:69; Recinos, Goetz, and Chonay, *The Annals of the Cakchiquels,* pp. 134-35.
2. See, for example, the section known as "Fonds Americains" in the BNP. There are similar collections in the ACNL. (Nos. 1493, 1504, 1506, 1510, 1511, 1518, 1521, 1536-38, 1562, 1574-86, all have to do with Central America). See also *A Guide to Manuscripts Relating to the American Indian in the Library of the American Philosophical Society,* comp. John E. Freeman, Memoirs of the American Philosophical Society, vol. 65, pp. 86-7, 111-12.
3. FX, 1:130, 482; AR, 2:177-78. See also Vázquez de Coronado, *Cartas de Relación,* pp. 33-35, 46-49, 51; and Villa Rojas, "Notas sobre la tenencia de la tierra," 21-22, 30-31, 33, 37.
4. FX, 1:130. See the many site descriptions in Smith, *Archeological Reconnaissance.* See also FG, 2:445-47.
5. Talk of congregación begins in 1537. See Konetzke, *Colección de documentos,* vol. 1, pp. 182-83. See Bishop Marroquín's letter to the Crown in *Cartas de Indias,* pp. 413-25. The reasons for it are outlined in the same letter. An Indian account of congregación is in Recinos, Goetz, and Chonay, *Annals of the Cakchiquels,* p. 136. The possible connection between congregación and the vacating of good land is noted in, Milla, *Historia de la América Central,* p. 121; Batres Jáuregui, *La América Central,* vol. 2, p. 151. See also FV, 1:108; FG, 2:447-49.
6. See the many documents on and letters by Bishop Marroquín, some previously unpublished, which touch on this subject, in Sáenz de Santa María, *El Licenciado Don Francisco Marroquín,* pp. 227, 234, 257-58, 281. See also AR, 2:177-78; FV, 1:69, 107-9, 111; and for Verapaz, Villacorta C., *Prehistoria e Historia Antigua,* p. 424.
7. AR, 2:178-79; FX, 1:482-85; Termer, *Etnología y etnografía,* vol. 5, pp. 55-56.
8. FX, 1:483-84; AR, 2:179-80; FV, 1:108.
9. Fray Bernardo de Albuquerque to Council of the Indies, February 2, 1554, in Cuevas, *Documentos,* pp. 180-81. See also AR, 2:180, and FX, 1:484.
10. FX, 1:482; AR, 2:177-78, 180; FG, 2:446-49.
11. AR, 2:176-77; Milla, *Historia de la América Central,* vol. 2, pp. 120-21.
12. Cuevas, *Documentos,* pp. 180-81. Seemingly not all Central American congregación was so legally and tidily carried out. In 1565 the King warned that Indian villages should not be moved to new sites unless royal permission had been obtained. AGGG, A1.2, legajo 2196, f. 140 (June 30, 1565).
13. For the various meanings and interpretations which can be given to the term calpulli (and therefore, to some extent, to chinamit), see Nutini, "Clan Organization in a Nahuatl-Speaking Village," 62-78.
14. Miles, "Summary of Preconquest Ethnology," pp. 276-87; Beals, "Acculturation," pp. 451-52.
15. E.g., Bergman, "The Distribution of Cacao Cultivation," 85-96; Fernández de Oviedo, *Historia General y Natural,* vol. 2, pp. 57, 270; vol. 9, p. 192; Herrera, *Historia,* vol. 1, pp. 94-95; Andagoya, *The Narrative,* p. 36.
16. Elliott, *Imperial Spain,* pp. 107-9, 292; Lynch, *Spain under the Hapsburgs,* vol. 1, pp. 13-14, 103-4, 111, 114-15.
17. Bishko, "The Peninsular Background of Latin American Cattle Ranching," 494-95, 500-503, 512; Góngora, "Régimen Señorial y Rural," 23-24.
18. E.g., FX, 1:130; ANHH, Tierras (Yoro), 42 (1640); ACNL, 1106, G, 1, ff. 15v.-16.
19. For Santiago, see FX, 1:235; Arévalo, *Libro de actas,* pp. 45-46, 50-53, *passim;* AGGG, A1. 4-5, 17669, 2367, f. 1v. (September 14, 1552). For Puerto

Caballos, see CDI, 15:20; Chamberlain, "The founding of the City of Gracias a Dios," 2-18. For the seventeenth century, see "Fundación de la ciudad de Santiago de Talamanca," in Peralta, *Costa-Rica, Nicaragua y Panamá,* pp. 682-91.

20. Arévalo, *Libro de actas,* pp. 156-65; Zavala, *Contribución,* p. 11. In another context a recent book has noted that early Spanish observers, as a group, were little interested in describing landscape, but gave "detailed and acute descriptions of native inhabitants." Elliott, *The Old World and the New,* p. 20.

21. Arévalo, *Libro de actas,* pp. 144-45, 212-13. For Nicaragua see Andrés de Cereceda to Crown, January 20, 1529, M-M 302, Bancroft Library, University of California, Berkeley. For the origins of the encomienda system, see Chamberlain, "Castillian Background of the Repartimiento-Encomienda," 23-66.

22. Licenciado Carrasco [Bishop of Nicaragua] to the King, May 7, 1562; "Repartimiento de encomiendas," January 11, 1569; Gerónimo de Villegas to the King, June 10, 1569, all in Peralta, *Costa-Rica, Nicaragua y Panamá,* pp. 210-12, 419-31, 433-35. See also pp. 500-501, and CDHCR, 5:3-19.

23. FV, 1:107, 159; Bishop Marroquín to Emperor, November 20, 1559, AGI/ AG 156; Johannessen, *Savannas of Interior Honduras,* p. 42. By 1535 cattle and horses were already being exported from Nicaraguá to Peru in small quantities. CS, 4:488, 518-79. Another unique and prophetic event occurred in 1558. A shipment of honey and cheeses was sent from Honduras to Spain. The shipment was seized for the King's service and paid off in long-term juros. See Archivo de Protocolos de Sevilla, Libro del año 1577–Oficio: XV–Libro 1. Escribanía: Francisco Díaz–Folio 118–Fecha: 28 de enero.

24. The first mention of cattle destroying crops comes in 1527, only three years after the conquest, in Arévalo, *Libro de actas,* pp. 40, 150. Bishop Pedraza's complaint about cattle invasions in the Naco Valley is in CDIU, 11:423. See also Zorita, *The Lords of New Spain,* pp. 270-71. By 1553 the Crown was already disturbed at the number of Indians who were abandoning their lands and ordered that they be forced to cultivate them. See Juarros, *Compendio,* vol. 2, p. 219.

25. By 1536 the Crown was already warning that Spaniards should not buy land or waters from Indians because of the many frauds involved. See the real cédula of November 3, 1536, in Konetzke, *Colección de documentos,* vol. 1, p. 179. See also *Ibid.,* vol. 1, pp. 258, 261-62.

26. AR, 1:259, 279-88. Bishop Marroquín also had some interest in land, *Isagoge,* pp. 323-24. See also AGGG, A1.23, legajo 1512, f. 270 (18 July 1560).

27. Some examples of land acquisition between 1550 and 1575, are, AGGG, A3.30, 41701, 2683 (1560); AGGG, A1. Tierras, 51891, 5934, f. 39 (1566); AGGG, A1.20, legajo 1111, f. 521 (1567); AGGG, A1.1, 51935, 5937, f. 9 (1571). More usual were complaints that good land was being left empty by depopulation. E.g., CS, 11:356; Governor Luis Ponce de León (of Soconusco) to Crown, January 19, 1574, AGI/AG 40; García de Palacios, *Carta,* pp. 27, 63.

28. López de Velasco, *Geografía y descripción universal,* pp. 285, 306-12; Nicholás López to Crown, April 26, 1556, AGI/AG 52. When Perafán de Rivera left Honduras for his entrada into Costa Rica he took more than 400 head of cattle with him from La Choluteca. See Fernández Guardia, *Historia de Costa Rica,* pp. 213-14.

29. Chevalier, *La formation des grands domaines,* pp. 102-4, 114-15.

30. *Ibid.,* pp. 115-17; Simpson, *Exploitation of Land in Central Mexico,* pp. 1-6, *passim;* Arévalo, *Libro de actas,* pp. 154-56.

31. AR, 1:259, 279-88; Cabildo of Granada to Emperor, November 28, 1544, in Alvarez Rubiano, *Pedrarias Dávila,* pp. 693-702. See also *Ibid.,* pp. 368, 374-75. Contreras and his wife and sons held 22 Indian villages, his servants 17, and his tenientes 15. They were all forfeited after the revolt. See Cabildo of León to Crown (1544), AGI/AG 43; ANCR, Complementario colonial, 6502 (1545); CDI, 24:383-84 (1545).

32. Arévalo, *Libro de actas,* pp. 81, 212. A careful reading of the following book shows that the "conquistadores modestos," those of the second rank, failed to

benefit from their early encomiendas. Trejos, ed., *Los Conquistadores progenitores,* pp. 133, 143, 167-69, *passim.*

33. "Relación y forma . . . de Bisitar," f. 3, AGI/AG 128; AR, 2:433-34; Frs. Viana, Gallego, and Cadena, "Relación de la Provincia," 147. For the revival of trade, see Recinos, Goetz, and Chonay, *Annals of the Cakchiquels,* p. 131.

34. Some idea of the large number of encomiendas distributed by Maldonado and the first Audiencia can be gained from CDI, 24:358-59, 361-63, 378-80. Maldonado married his daughter to Montejo. The twenty most powerful encomenderos, nearly all in the cacao trade, were recent arrivals (i.e., with Maldonado). See the letters of Francisco Morales, in Paso y Troncoso, *Epistolario de la Nueva España,* vol. 9, pp. 151-52, 224-26; Bishops Valdivieso and Las Casas to Prince Philip, October 25, 1545, *Cartas de Indias,* pp. 14-15. Here the two reformers claim that Maldonado, his relatives, and his friends have more than 60,000 Indians in encomienda. Later, when Las Casas became disillusioned with President López de Cerrato he noted that the Salamanca encomenderos in the cacao areas were still the most powerful. See Bataillon, "Las Casas et le Licencié Cerrato," 81-84.

35. The wealth which this family derived from Santiago Atitlán alone can be gathered from "Requête de Plusieurs Chefs Indiens d'Atitlán à Philippe II," vol. 10, pp. 415-28. For Sancho de Barahona *père's* long battle with Pedro de Alvarado in which Barahona, after some setbacks, finally more than held his own, see AGI Justicia 295, "Sancho de Barahona con . . . Pedro de Alvarado" (1537).

36. Alonso García to Crown, February 1, 1546, CDI, 24:352-81. The evolution of this family, later known as León Cardona, is typical of that kind of region. Obviously the encomienda was transformed into land holdings, which were later subdivided within the family. The León Cardona clan became a locally powerful group of Creoles, but it was of little political significance or wealth compared to the vecinos of Santiago. See Gall, *Título del Ajpop,* pp. 29, 63-64, 68, 74-78. For the change from encomienda to hacienda by the heirs of Bernal Díaz del Castillo, see Chevalier, *La formation des grands domaines,* p. 156. For a more general statement of this situation in this part of Central America, see Zavala, *Contribución,* pp. 71-72. The pattern here, although not in other parts of Central America, follows that suggested by Lockhart, "Encomienda and Hacienda," 411-29.

37. CDI, 24:375-77.

38. Complaints about shrinking encomiendas and tributes are many. E.g., AGI Patronato 82-1-4, and AGI Patronato 82-1-6. See also the small annual tribute amounts mentioned by Las Casas, 80 or 100 pesos per annum, in Bataillon, "Las Casas et le Licencié Cerrato," p. 83. The best examination of the decline of one encomienda, although the emphasis is on the late sixteenth and seventeenth centuries, is in Simpson, "A Seventeenth-Century Encomienda," 393-402.

39. "Razón de las tasaciones" (1582), AGI/AG 966. On this same revision of the tribute, see Simpson, *The Encomienda in New Spain,* pp. 154-55. Yet, in 1563, the ayuntamiento of Santiago petitioned the King to change tribute counts less frequently. (Bernal Díaz was a signatory). Larreinaga, *Prontuario de todas las reales cédulas,* pp. 34-36. Similar attempts are mentioned in Audiencia to Crown, April 23, 1582, AGI/AG 10, ff. 13-13v.

40. An early example of an auction of tribute produce, is AGGG, A3.6, 36516, 2501 (1544). Much of the substance of this description of the entrepreneurial, diversified encomienda is drawn from two excellent studies: Miranda, *La Función Económica del Encomendero,* and Sherman, "A Conqueror's Wealth," 199-213.

41. López de Velasco, *Geografía,* pp. 60, 296.

42. See the encomendero table in this chapter, and Chapter Five. See also Alonso García to Crown, February 1, 1546, CDI, 24:357-59.

43. See Morales' letters again, in Paso y Troncoso, *Epistolario,* vol. 9, pp. 152, 224-26. Also Chapter Five. Remesal, writing early in the seventeenth century, was surprised at the importance of the encomiendas for the Spaniards. People resigned royal offices to obtain better encomiendas, something which nobody would have

done in Remesal's day, "and held the title of encomendero as better than that of Corregidor, Alcalde Mayor, Treasurer, or Royal Accountant." AR, 2:92. For the compadrazgo system among the oidores of the Audiencia, see Alonso García to Crown, February 1, 1546, CDI, 24:352-81.

44. E.g., López de Velasco, *Geografía,* 327. For the Genoese in Realejo in 1560, see Salvatierra, *Contribución a la historia de Centro-américa,* 1:302. (Most lived by trading with Peru.) For Genoese and other foreign clerics in San Salvador, see FX,1:494-96.

45. See the documents cited in note 38 above. For a similar "merits and services" petition from Nicaragua and Costa Rica, see "Información de servicios de Matias de Palacios," Peralta, *Costa-Rica, Nicaragua y Panamá,* pp. 660-78, especially pp. 671 and 678.

46. The Crown began to worry about the rapidly growing class of castas quite early, and expressed the hope that they would become an intermediate artisan group. See Konetzke, *Colección de documentos,* 1:333-34 (1555). Many of the Indians near Santiago were former slaves freed by President López de Cerrato. They were very hispanized. See López de Velasco, *Geografía,* p. 287. Others were Mexicans who had arrived with the conquistadors; "Conbentos de franciscanos en la Prov^a de Guat ^a, 1575" AGI/AG 169.

47. E.g., López de Velasco, *Geografía,* pp. 297, 300; AR, 2:107-8.

48. A note of nostalgia for the great days of the sixteenth century runs through the seventeenth century chronicles of FX, and particularly FG, who constantly harks back to the "good old days."

49. Much of this discussion will be based on the following two sources: Wagley, "The Effects of Depopulation upon Social Organization as Illustrated by the Tapirape Indians," 12-16; Lévi-Strauss, *Tristes Tropiques,* pp. 159, 206-8, 330.

50. The decline of clans in Quetzaltenango can be deduced from a careful reading of Gall, *Título del Ajpop,* pp. 7, 21, 30-31. See also AR, 2:179, and Dumond, "Population Growth and Cultural Change," 319, 332.

51. Fernández de Oviedo, *Historia General y Natural,* vol. 11, pp. 65, 195.

52. Zorita, *The Lords of New Spain,* pp. 92, 104, 272; FX, 1:91; Fernández de Oviedo, *Historia General y Natural,* vol. 11, p. 195.

53. See the complaint in the letter from Bernal Díaz del Castillo to Bartolomé de las Casas, February 20, 1558 (Madariaga, *Bernal Díaz y Simón Ruiz, de Medina del Campo,* pp. 398-401), in which some caciques sell land belonging to the community. See also Konetzke, *Colección de documentos,* vol. 1, p. 258.

54. FX, 1:123, 125, 150-53; Recinos, Goetz, and Chonay, *Annals of the Cakchiquels,* pp. 120, 133-34. For a similar disappearance of the "royal" families in Mexico, see Gibson, "The Aztec Aristocracy in Colonial Mexico," 171-72.

55. AGGG, A1.1, 052042, 5946 (1563).

56. Chamberlain, "The Concept of the *Señor Natural,*" 130-37.

57. FX, 1:421, 448-49, 459, 466-67; 3:350; "Testamento de los xpantzay," ed. Recinos, pp. 165, 167. (The document is dated November 21, 1554). See also López de Cerrato's letter, in CDI, 24:562-3. Franciscans attempted to restore "legitimate" caciques in some cases. E.g., Francisco de Zapata to Crown, February 19, 1547, M-M 320, Bancroft Library, University of California, Berkeley.

58. Arévalo, *Libro de actas,* pp. 140-41; Carrasco, "Don Juan Cortés," 254, 261; "Requête de Plusieurs Chefs Indiens," pp. 415-28.

59. "Requête de Plusieurs Chefs Indiens," pp. 415-28; Carrasco, "Don Juan Cortés," pp. 254, 261. Carrasco feels that the situation of caciques improved somewhat after 1555. His examples seem exceptions to the general rule to this observer.

60. Saint-Lu, *La Vera Paz,* pp. 145-50, 166; FX, 1:245-48; 2:502.

61. E.g., AR, 2:181; "Requête de Plusieurs Chefs Indiens," p. 425.

62. The caciques and principales of Sololá lost their reservado status in 1557, and were required to stop retaining some of the tribute. (Recinos, Goetz, and Chonay, *Annals of the Cakchiquels,* p. 141.) After 1560, because of population loss,

the number of reservados was severely curtailed. See Carrasco, "The Mesoamerican Indian," p. 76. For a comparison with Peru, see Spaulding, "Social Climbers," 645-64.

63. ACNL, 1106, G, 1, ff. 12v., 15v., 16. This document is an attack on "heads of calpuls," and supports the new Indian cabildos in the jurisdiction of the valle of Guatemala against the attacks of the traditional caciques. See also Ayuntamiento of Santiago to Crown, February 12, 1563, *Isagoge,* pp. 322-23; Carrasco, "The Mesoamerican Indian," pp. 78-79. García Peláez, following Juarros, believes that President Alonso López de Cerrato was the first to encourage Indian cabildos, in García Peláez, *Memorias,* vol. 1, p. 212. In Nicaragua it seems to have been the work of Caballón. Licenciado Caballón to the Emperor, February 27, 1555, M-M 320, Bancroft Library, University of California, Berkeley.

64. "Relación y forma . . . de Bisitar," AGI/AG 128; AR, 2:433-34; Recinos, Goetz, and Chonay, *Annals of the Cakchiquels,* pp. 130-31. See also note 33 above.

65. E.g., Pineda, "Descripción," 52-62; Sáenz de Santa María, *El Licenciado Don Francisco Marroquín,* p. 301.

66. The activities of some of these men have been previously noted. See also ACNL, 1106, G, 1, f. 10. The best summary of this subject is in Mörner, "La Política de Segregación," 137-51.

67. E.g., Saint-Lu, *La Vera Paz,* pp. 229-32.

68. The best example of this is the previously cited "Razón de las tasaciones" (1582), AGI/AG 966.

69. Calpisques were "free" Indians or naborias used by the caciques and the Spaniards for collecting tribute. AGGG, A1.2-4, 15769, 2195, f. 99 (April 17, 1553). For the jailing of caciques, see, for example, "Testimonio de las sentencias del pleyto de los yndios de la Verapaz," (1574-78), AGI/AG 966, and Carrasco, "Mesoamerican Indian," p. 83.

70. "Relación y forma . . . de Bisitar," ff. 1v., 4, 8, AGI/AG 128 contains warnings to caciques not to abuse their subjects. As early as 1552 López de Cerrato was criticizing their harshness. He felt that as a consequence many caciques were no longer respected by the people and should have their powers reduced. (CDI, 24: 561-63). Bishop Marroquín felt the same; Sáenz de Santa María, *El Licenciado Don Francisco Marroquín,* p. 301. A typical cacique complaint is "Requête de Plusieurs Chefs Indiens."

71. Zorita, *The Lords of New Spain,* pp. 272-73. The three caciques of Utatlán did not even have reservado status when Zorita saw them. See also the complaints of the caciques of Santiago Atitlán, in "Relación de los caciques y principales," 436-37. They complain that President Alonso López de Cerrato freed *their* slaves too! For similar events in Mexico, see Gibson, "The Aztec Aristocracy," pp. 193-96.

72. Pineda, "Descripción." However, this writer finds Pineda's report politically inspired, too optimistic, and therefore suspect.

73. A good summation of this process in Mesoamerica is in Nash, *Primitive and Peasant Economic Systems,* pp. 58-60, 80.

Chapter 8

1. Lcdo. Arteaga Mendiola to the Crown, March 20, 1571, AGI/AG 9; President Villalobos to the Crown, May 15, 1573, AGI/AG 9; Governor of Soconusco to the Crown, May 6, 1613, AGI/AG 60.

2. E.g., Konetzke, *Colección de documentos,* vol. 1, pp. 574-75.

3. Governor of Soconusco to the Crown, January 16, 1576, AGI/AG 40.

4. Governor of Soconusco to the Crown (1575), and *ibid.* to *ibid.* (1603), both in AGI/AG 40.

5. AGGG, A1.23, legajo 1513, f. 649 (November 15, 1585).

6. *Ibid.*

7. AGGG, A1.23, legajo 4576, f. 26 (November 19, 1618); Governor of Soconusco to the Crown (1613), and Governor of Soconusco to the Crown (1617), both in AGI/AG 40. For modern use of Indian labor from Chiapas in Soconusco plantations, see, Pozas, *Chamula,* pp. 25, 102-3, 115, 122-30.

8. AGGG, A1.23, legajo 4576, f. 26 (November 19, 1618); Bishop Zapata y Zandoval to the Crown, April 20, 1616, AGI/AG 161. Governor of Soconusco to the Crown, April 30, 1622, AGI/AG 40 contains the first Soconusco reference to a price collapse caused by "large" exports of cacao from Guayaquil to New Spain. See also Pardo, *Efemérides,* p. 51.

9. See the petitions already cited from AGI/AG 40.

10. Governor of Soconusco to the Crown, 4 May 1613, AGI/AG 40.

11. Governor of Soconusco to the Crown (1603), AGI/AG 40.

12. Governor of Soconusco to the Crown (1617), AGI/AG 40.

13. *Ibid.*

14. Audiencia to the Crown, June 2, 1612, AGI/AG 13, mentions a fall in the number of cacao trees in Zapotitlán of 30,000. See also AGGG, A1.23, legajo 1514, f. 225 (August 17, 1614), and AGGG, A1.23, legajo 1515, f. 17 (November 19, 1618).

15. West, "The Mining Economy of Honduras," 769-70.

16. *Ibid.*

17. *Ibid.*, p. 770. New strikes around Tegucigalpa in the 1640s, and in an area known as San Miguel in 1661 caused brief improvements, but lack of labor was blamed for the failure to fully develop them. AGGG, A1.23, legajo 1517, f. 84; ANHH, paquete 1, legajo 31 (1645–1647).

18. West, "The Mining Economy of Honduras," p. 770. An early complaint about the hardness of the local rocks is BPR, Miscelanea de Ayala, 10, 176v.

19. Juan Cisneros de Reynoso to the Crown, February 17, 1581, AGI/AG 55.

20. *Ibid.*; "Testimonio de los ensayos de las minas de Tegucigalpa y guacuran [sic] de Honduras en 1581," AGI/AG 55; West, "The Mining Economy of Honduras," p. 771.

21. Juan Cisneros de Reynoso to the Crown, February 17, 1581, AGI/AG 55. Obviously mercury was also brought in from Peru in both the sixteenth and the seventeenth centuries. See AGGG, A1.23, legajo 4575, f. 342v. (April 21, 1574); UT, G19, f. 259v.

22. See the various cédulas in AGI/AG 798. Nor could miners be jailed for debts; see Konetzke, *Colección de documentos,* 2^1:239-41. Mention of 100 quintals per year is in Miners of Honduras to the Crown (1639), AGI/AG 7, and in AGGG, A1.23, legajo 1519, f. 270 (December 9, 1670), one of the King's unkept promises to send 100 quintals per annum. See also Veitia Linaje, *Norte de la contratación de las Indias,* p. 94.

23. Chaunu and Chaunu, *Séville et l'Atlantique,* 4:119, 121, 215, 400, 442 *passim*; 5:15, 35, 43, 55, 81, 106 *passim* details mercury supply up to 1630. In 1639 the miners complained that no mercury had arrived for eight years. The King asked the viceroy in Mexico to send help. Miners of Honduras to the Crown, December 13, 1639, AGI/AG 5. A total of 2,103 quintals of mercury was sent to Honduras before 1650, which is only 7 per cent of all mercury sent to the New World by that time. Chaunu and Chaunu, *Séville et l'Atlantique,* 8^1:852-53. Between 1650 and 1700 Honduras' share sank still lower. Chaunu, *L'Amérique et les Amériques,* p. 95.

24. The Crown's attempt to fix the price of mercury and miners' complaints about its price can be found in, oficiales reales to the Crown, April 29, 1586, AGI/AG 49, and in the three letters dated June 14, 1635, June 25, 1638, and August 4, 1643, all in AGI/AG 798. See also ANHH, paquete 2, legajo 77 (1673).

25. The way in which mercury was used as a check on the quantity of silver mined is clearly apparent in the real cédula of September 1, 1610, in AGGG, A1.24, legajo 1514, f. 181. See also AGI Patronato 181-1-16, and several of the documents in AGI/AG 18. In the late seventeenth century the Crown was still expressing the same complaints. In a whole year the mines of Tegucigalpa had used only one quintal. What was the explanation? (AGGG, A1.23, legajo 1520, f. 6.) The Audiencia replied lamely that probably the miners could not afford to buy it, AGGG, A1.23, legajo 1520, f. 79 (1672). Fire was still the common smelting method in the early eighteenth century according to ANHH, paquete 6, legajo 44 (1718).

26. "Relación de los delictos [sic] que se le probaron en la visita al Thesorero Sanctiago y a su hermano Fernando de Chaves," AGI/AG 39. (The document is undated but is from the mid 1590s.)

Chapter 9

1. CDIU, 17:220-21; Alonso Criado de Castilla to Crown, 24 May 1609, AGI-/AG 129, ff. 3v., 10v.; Chaunu and Chaunu, *Séville et l'Atlantique,* 4:498; 6²:576-79.

2. See his two letters to the Crown dated May 22, 1605 and May 24, 1609, in AGI/AG 129. Milla claims that Criado stood by while the ayuntamiento of Santiago took the initiative. Milla, *Historia de la América Central,* vol. 2, pp. 286-87. The ayuntamiento itself, however, felt that President Criado was over-assertive. AGGG, A3.2, 39063, 2725 (1610).

3. Audiencia to the Crown, June 2, 1612, AGI/AG 13.

4. CDI, 16:530-38; CDIU, 17:158, 167, 176-77, 210-11, 226; "Descripción del Puerto de Caballos . . . hecha por Juan Bautista Antonelli," AGI Patronato 183-1-16, f. 2; Criado de Castilla to Crown, May 24, 1609, AGI/AG 129; Chaunu and Chaunu, *Séville et l'Atlantique,* 8¹:863-65.

5. CDIU, 17:210; AGI Patronato 183-1-16; Chaunu and Chaunu, *Séville et l'Atlantique,* 8¹:863-65; Milla, *Historia de la América Central,* vol. 2, 287-88. Typical materials exported to Guatemala from Spain are mentioned in AGGG, A3.6, 41789, 2871 (1660).

6. CDIU, 17:210; AGGG, A1.2, 15749 (11 June 1599), f. 104; AGI, Patronato 183-1-16.

7. CDIU, 17:167, 207, 209-10, 236-38.

8. See three expedientes (1605 and 1606) in AGI/AG 129; AR, 2:582; Pérez Valenzuela, *Santo Tomás de Castilla,* pp. 17-19.

9. Veitia Linaje, *Norte de la contratación de las Indias,* pp. 96-97. See the two letters from Alonso Criado de Castilla to the Crown, May 22, 1605, and May 24, 1609, in AGI/AG 129. Honduran objections are in Cabildo of Valladolid (Comayagua) to the Crown, April 19, 1583, AGI/AG 43. In 1627 Honduras was still objecting, CDIU, 17:215-6. See also AGGG, A1.23, legajo 1515, f. 180; CDIU, 17:214; Chaunu and Chaunu, *Séville et l'Atlantique,* 8¹:881-83.

10. AR, 2:582; Milla, *Historia de la América Central,* vol. 2, p. 237; Pardo, *Efemérides,* pp. 37, 43; Audiencia to the Crown, June 2, 1612, AGI/AG 13. For a full description of this coast see Dege, "Die Karibische Küste Guatemalas und ihre Häfen," 252, 255.

11. See the expedientes (1605 and 1606) in AGI/AG 129; Pardo, *Efemérides,* p. 37; *Isagoge,* p. 381.

12. Conde de la Gómera to the Crown, January 14, 1611, AGI/AG 13, f. 2; AGGG, A1.3, legajo 4576, f. 32v. (1619); AGGG, A1.23, legajo 4577, f. 63v. (December 8, 1632); Pérez Valenzuela, *Santo Tomás,* p. 21; Milla, *La América Central,* vol. 2, pp. 287-88.

13. Conde de la Gómera to the Crown, January 14, 1611, AGI/AG 13. For the uses made of the Golfo Dulice, see AGGG, A3.6, 39556, 2748 (1647); AGGG, A3.6, 39601, 2751 (1715). By 1643 these ports were all in use to some extent. See Vecinos of Guatemala and Honduras to the Crown, August 18, 1643, AGI/AG 7.

14. CDI, 9:81-119; 21:41-43; RAH, 11-4-4-85 (Relaciones Geográficas de América), p. 17; Borah, *Early Trade*, p. 4.

15. Moorhead, "Hernán Cortés and the Tehuantepec Passage," 370-73, 379; Borah, *Early Trade*, p. 29; ANCR, Complementario colonial, 5203, f. 6v.

16. Saint-Lu, *La Vera Paz*, p. 37; McAlister, "The Discovery and Exploration of the Nicaraguan Trans-isthmian Route," 259-76; Peralta, *Costa-Rica, Nicaragua y Panamá*, pp. 115-16; Chamberlain, "Plan del siglo XVI para abrir un camino de Puerto Caballos a la Bahía de Fonseca," 61-65; Bishop Marroquín to the Audiencia of Mexico, September 20, 1536, AGI/AG 156.

17. CS, 4:488, 506-7, 518-19; Licenciado Castañeda to the Crown, May 1, 1533, AGI/AG 9; Chaunu and Chaunu, *Séville et l'Atlantique*, 8¹:822, 861; Borah, *Early Trade*, p. 7; Salvatierra, *Contribución a la historia de Centro-américa*, vol. 1, p. 291.

18. CDIU, 17:164; *Isagoge*, p. 318; Chaunu and Chaunu, *Séville et l'Atlantique*, 8¹:869-70, 874-75, 879-81.

19. "Razón y Parecer de don Francisco de Valverde," 160-66, 209-16, 306-16, 384-93. (This document is no. 40 in the legajo known as "Relaciones Geográficas de América," in RAH. Its number is 11-4-4-854.) See also *Isagoge*, p. 354.

20. AGI Patronato, 183-1-16 (October 7, 1590); Herrera, *Historia*, vol. 1, p. 92.

21. Manuel Ungría Girón to the Crown (1605), AGI/AG 12.

22. Chaunu and Chaunu, *Séville et l'Atlantique*, 4:187, 194, 215.

23. Pardo, *Efemérides*, p. 38; *Isagoge*, p. 377; Milla, *Historia de la América Central*, vol. 2, pp. 298-302; Criado de Castilla to Crown, May 24, 1609, AGI/AG 129; Veitia Linaje, *Norte de la contratación*, p. 99.

24. This long and interesting document is in AGI, Indiferente General in a legajo described as "Descripciones, poblaciones y Derroteros de viajes: años de mil quinientos veinte y uno a mil ocho cientos diez y ocho: legajo primero." A copy in ANCR was used by the present author. It is numbered ANCR, Complementario colonial 5203 (January 23, 1620). See also Chaunu and Chaunu, *Séville et l'Atlantique*, 8¹:885, 890; Salvatierra, *Contribución*, vol. 1, pp. 552-60. The circuitous sea route described from Panama to Peru and the plentiful ships stores in Nicaragua are confirmed in Borah, *Early Trade*, pp. 5, 29-31, 34.

25. Borah, *Early Trade*, pp. 117-27. The cédulas of 1609 and 1620 were also sent to Guatemala. They are AGGG, A1.23, legajo 1515 (June 20, 1609, and March 28, 1620), f. 66.

26. "Nicaragua Avisos: Sobre lo que toca a la navegación a la China y otras cosas" (n.d., 1576?), AGI/AG 10.

27. García Peláez, *Memorias*, vol. 1, p. 184; Milla, *Historia de la América Central*, vol. 2, pp. 216-17.

28. CDIU, 17:184; Schurz, *The Manila Galleon*, p. 366.

29. Pardo, *Efemérides*, p. 34; Milla, *Historia de la América Central*, vol. 2, p. 255, suggests that trade with China may have taken place.

30. Rubio Sánchez, "Apuntes para el estudio del comercio marítimo," 72; AGGG, A3.6, 39717, 258 (1704); AGI, Patronato, 183-1-16; *Isagoge*, p. 354; Chaunu and Chaunu, *Séville et l'Atlantique*, 8¹:895; Borah, *Early Trade*, pp. 117-18; Ayón, *Historia de Nicaragua*, vol. 3, p. 52.

31. For the 1590s, see AGI Patronato 183-1-16. For the late 1630s, see ANCR, Guatemala 078, April 27, 1636; AGGG, A3.6, 39551, 2748 (1637); ANCR, Complementario colonial 0014, May 3, 1637; García Peláez, *Memorias*, vol. 2, p. 37; Pardo, *Efemérides*, pp. 53-54.

32. Prohibition of trans-shipment of Chinese goods via Guatemala is in Pardo, *Efemérides*, pp. 53-54. For Castilla y Guzmán, see ANCR, Guatemala 058, January 30, 1626.

33. For information on President Sandé as governor of the Philippines, see Schurz, *Manila Galleon,* pp. 64, 144, 366. It was under Sandé's administration in Manila that the trade with Acapulco was first established on a systematic basis. See, Trechuelo Spinola, "La conexión entre el Atlántico y el Pacífico," p. 528. Obviously he was deeply involved in the trade and carried his interest in it to Central America and then New Granada. The King's reproof to Sandé and his gang is in AGGG, A1.23, legajo 1513 (June 18, 1597), f. 757. The 1647 accusations are in UT, G 19 139, ff. 351v.-352, which is a communication from Alonso Moratella y Tebar to the Viceroy of New Spain.

34. Francisco Romero Valtodano to Crown. "Seen in Council," October 20, 1642, AGI/AG 7; AGGG, A1.23, 39221, legajo 4568 (April 22, 1643), f. 5.

35. The story of the Manila ship is told in the following documents. AGGG, A3.6, 39560, 2749; FX, 2:320-21; AGGG, A1.23, legajo 1519, f. 8 (July 31, 1659). See also Molina, *Antigua Guatemala,* pp. 96-98; Guijo, *Diario,* vol. 2, pp. 76, 80.

36. Milla, *Historia de la América Central,* vol. 2, pp. 386-87, 408. There is no mention of Guatemalan participation in the trade between the arribada galleon in 1656, and a royal cedula of 1685, in García Peláez, *Memorias,* vol. 2, p. 46.

37. AGGG, A3.1, 38942, 2716 (1652).

38. For the sailing directions off the northern coast of Peru, see Findley, *A Directory for the Navigation of the Pacific Ocean,* vol. 1, pp. 139-41, 181-82. For a description of the trade, see BM, Add. Mss. 139745, f. 229 (n.d., seventeenth century). A royal cédula of 1621 ordered a careful watch on the trade in asphalt from the pitch lake near Ancón in present-day Ecuador. Vessels from New Spain and Guatemala were ostensibly arriving to load pitch, but were really unloading Chinese merchandise picked up at Acapulco. See Borah, *Early Trade,* p. 127. Central Americans had no need for Guayaquil pitch; there was a good supply at Realejo. So it can be concluded that some Central American vessels were involved in carrying illegal Oriental goods from Acapulco to Peru. For activities at Acapulco and Puerto Marqués, see, for example, Schurz, *Manilla Galleon,* p. 370.

39. For royal trade permits, see AGGG, A1.23, legajo 4584 (March 29, 1678), f. 209v.; García Peláez, *Memorias,* vol. 2, p. 46. The revival of smuggling via Central America is most noticeable after 1700. E.g., UT, G19, ff. 177-7v., 219, 220, which mentions the use of monasteries. See also AGGG, A3.5, 39252, 2732 (1701); AGGG, A3.5, 39255, 3732 (1703).

40. Lee, "Cochineal Production," 449-53; Molins Fábrega, *El Códice Mendocino,* p. 50; Sahagún, *Historia General,* vol. 3, pp. 287-88.

41. Roys, *The Indian Background of Colonial Yucatan,* p. 107.

42. Lee, "Cochineal Production," 454-58, 467. For the role of cochineal in Europe, see Lee, "American Cochineal," 205-24.

43. Lee, "Cochineal Production," 460; Gage, *The English-American,* pp. 341-43; Vázquez de Espinosa, *Compendium,* pp. 249, 260; Chaunu and Chaunu, *Séville et l'Atlantique,* 6²: 980-81, 986-89; Hakluyt, *The Principal Voyages,* vol. 9, p. 367.

44. Gage, *The English-American,* pp. 152, 159, 167; Vázquez de Espinosa, *Compendium,* p. 207.

45. Juan Moreno Alvarez de Toledo to the Crown, January 8, 1576, AGI/AG 55; AGGG, A1.23, legajo 4588, f. 252v. (1595); Estrada and Niebla, "Descripción de le Provincia de Zapotitlán y Suchitepequez," 77.

46. AGGG, A1.23, legajo 4577, f. 4v. (May 12, 1619); AGGG, A1.23, legajo 4588, f. 252v. (1595).

47. "Autos hechos en razón de la planta de la grana cochinilla," June 15, 1618, AGI/AG 14; Conde de la Gómera to the Crown, June 20, 1618, AGI/AG 14. For Gómera's acquisitiveness, see "Seen in Council," May 9, 1626, AGI/AG 9; Gage, *The English-American,* p. 199. Both report that Gómera accumulated a fortune during his 15 years in office.

48. "Informe sobre el cultivo y benefico [sic] de la grana cochinilla," April 29, 1620, AGI/AG 14; "Sobre el beneficio de la grana, cochinilla y añil de Chiapa, y

Guatemala y Yucatan," May 8, 1620, AGI/AG 14; Juan Muñoz Descobar to the Crown, March 24, 1620, AGI/AG 14; Conde de la Gómera to the Crown, May 20, 1620, AGI/AG 14.

49. "Relación del beneficio . . . planta de los nopales de grana cochinilla" (1620), AGI/AG 14; "Sobre la plantación y cultivo de la cochinilla," May 21, 1620, AGI/AG 14.

50. Pardo, *Efemérides,* p. 43 (April 30, 1616); AGGG, A1.23, legajo 1515, f. 15 (November 19, 1618).

51. FG, 3:66, 198; BNM, 3047, f. 133v.; BNM, 12022, f. 9v. (1663); Gage, *The English-American,* pp. 204, 252, 341-43; BM, Add. Mss., 17583, f. 228; BM, Add. Mss., 13977, ff. 78-78v.; Chaunu and Chaunu, *Séville et l'Atlantique,* 6¹: 101; Veitia Linaje, *Norte de la contratación,* p. 120.

52. AGGG, A1.24, 10204, 1560, f. 63; Gage, *The English-American,* pp. 159, 205. For Nicaragua, see Vázquez de Espinosa, *Compendium,* pp. 237, 260.

Chapter 10

1. Heiser, "Cultivated Plants and Cultural Diffusion," 933; Morley, *The Ancient Maya,* 408-9; Sahagún, *Historia General,* vol. 3, p. 289; *Landa's Relación,* pp. 117-19; Roys, *The Ethno-Botany of the Maya,* p. 238.

2. AGGG, A1.23-18, legajo 1511, f. 237 (June 14, 1558). According to one source a detailed report was sent to the King. See Rubio, "El Añil o xiquilite," 317. Leggett, *Ancient and Medieval Dyes,* pp. 18, 20, 22-25, discusses European imports and use of indigo before American supplies began. See also Hakluyt, *The Principal Voyages,* p. 358.

3. Helmer, "Documentos Americanistas en el Archivo de Barbastro," 11. Document no. 33 is entitled "Método sobre la cría del añil en Nueva España, cuya semilla mandó S.M. por sus Reales Cédulas de 3 de febrero de 1573 se sembrare en los términos de Almería y Murcia." See also Rubio, "El Añil," p. 316.

4. Juan Moreno Alvarez de Toledo to the Crown, January 8, 1576, AGI/AG 55; Governor of Nicaragua to the Crown, November 12, 1579, AGI/AG 40, no. 2; Pedro Vanegas to the Crown (n.d., 1576?); President Villalobos to the Crown, March 17, 1578, both in AGI/AG 10. (Villalobos mentions that Spaniards had been involved in the making of indigo for more than ten years.)

5. Archivo de Protocolos de Sevilla, Libro del año 1580—Oficio X. Libro 1— Escribanía: Diego Gabriel—Folio 63—11 Enero 1580, mentions the import of 43 arrobas of indigo in 1579 at 7 ducats per quintal. The Chilton account is in Hakluyt, *The Principal Voyages,* pp. 366-67. For other exports of indigo from the New World in the sixteenth century, see Chaunu and Chaunu, *Séville et l'Atlantique* 6:988-93; Acosta, *Historia Natural y Moral,* p. 290.

6. President Villalobos to the Crown, March 17, 1578, f. 5v., AGI/AG 10; Fernández de Oviedo talks vaguely of a tree which made ink; see his *Historia General y Natural,* vol. 3, p. 5. The treasurer of Nicaragua gave an equally brief description about 1576, talking of a "grass" called "gigilite" which produced a fine blue dye with the aid of an unspecified coagulant ("quajo"). See Pedro de Vanegas to the Crown (n.d., 1576?), AGI/AG 10. Sahagún's description is similar, *Historia General,* vol. 3, p. 289.

7. The Spaniards who were obtaining title to land for growing indigo were unusually concerned with obtaining clear titles approved by the authorities. This contrasts with earlier attitudes during the cacao phase. Reasons will be examined in the next chapter. Examples of new indigo plantations in the jurisdiction of San Salvador are, AGGG, A1.23, legajo 4588, f. 131v. (1589); AGGG, A1.23, legajo 4588,

f. 261v. (1596); AGGG, A1.23, legajo 4588, f. 266v. (1599). For Nicaragua, see for example, AGGG, A1.23, legajo 4588, f. 106 (1588); AGGG, A1.23, legajo 4588, f. 115v. (1589); AGGG, A1.23, legajo 4888, f. 127v. (1589). A few were started in Chiapas and Guatemala. See AGGG, A1.23, legajo 4588, f. 135v. (1589); AGGG, Tierras, 51878, 1592 (1592); AGGG, A1.23, legajo 4575, f. 398v. (1581). As early as 1590 cacao and indigo were being called the only large exports of Central America, and cacao, it was pointed out, was in decline; AGI Patronato 183-1-16, f. 22. Indigo was identified as the largest enterprise in Nicaragua as early as 1583; see pieza no. 80, February 17, 1583, AGI/AG 40. The speed of its growth can be judged from observers. The encyclopedic Juan López de Velasco noted no indigo in the 1560s *(Geografía y descripción universal de las Indias)*, but a decade or so later Ponce's account mentions it as being important in San Salvador. (CDIE, 57:399.)

8. One authority felt that the Central American industry was hampered by its technological inflexibility. Rossignon, *Manual del cultivo del añil y del nopal.*

9. Heiser, "Cultivated Plants," p. 933, and West and Augelli *(Middle America*, p. 284), identify it as *indigofera suffructiosa.* Rubio, "El Añil," p. 315, Smith ("Indigo Production and Trade," 181, and Leggett *(Ancient and Medieval Dyes,* p. 18), say it was *indigofera tinctoria.*

10. Among the many descriptions of indigo cultivation and processing one of the most entertaining is "Relación de como se beneficia la tinta añir," sent to the King by Juan de Maldonado y Paz in 1611, and now in AGI/AG 13. Other details are in Smith, "Indigo Production," pp. 181-84; Rubio, "El Añil," pp. 317-18; Leggett, *Ancient and Medieval Dyes,* p. 20; Vázquez de Espinosa, *Compendium,* pp. 236-37.

11. For indigo in Chiapas, see note 7 above. For typical plantations in Honduras, see ANHH, paquete 3, legajo 40 (1676); ANHH, paquete 3, legajo 51 (1677); AGGG, A1.53, 51489, 5923 (1672).

12. Rubio notes that indigo never flourished in Soconusco or Zapotitlán. In terms of size he places San Salvador first, the León-Granada area second, and coastal Guatemala third. Rubio, "El Añil," pp. 316-17.

13. Vázquez de Espinosa, *Compendium,* pp. 223-25, 230-32, 254-60.

14. *Ibid.,* pp. 229-31, 233.

15. AGGG, A1.23, legajo 1514, f. 193 (Guatemala), f. 194 (Nicaragua), (1610); AGGG, A1.2-7, 11810, 1804, f. 16 (1604).

16. FG, 2:221; *Isagoge,* pp. 343, 400; FX, 1:61. For the decline in exports, see Chaunu and Chaunu, *Séville et l'Atlantique,* 6²:990; 8¹:851.

17. Typical complaints about the laws, and pleas to the King, can be found in Cabildo of San Salvador to the Crown, January 24, 1648, AGI/AG 43; Villa of San Vicente de Austria to the Crown, March 20, 1709, AGI/AG 279. A widespread fraudulent practice was the inclusion of earth in the indigo. E.g., ANHH, paquete 3, legajo 2 (1675), which talks of "more earth than dye" in one batch. See also Baltasar Pinto to the Crown, January 13, 1669, AGI/AG 19, and Smith, "Indigo Production," p. 185.

18. AGGG, 5493, 601 (1630); CDIU, 17:224 (1631); AGGG, A1.1, 18:1 (1667).

19. The following mention some 200 obrajes. CDIU, 17:223 (1631); Francisco Romero Valtodano to the Crown (1642), AGI/AG 7; FV, 1:238 (1695–1714 approx.).

20. Bibliothèque de l'Arsénal, Paris, Ms. 4788, f. 75. See also FV, 1:238; Smith, "Indigo Production," p. 186.

21. FV, 1:238; Vázquez de Espinosa, *Compendium,* pp. 221-22, 229; Rubio, "El Añil," p. 325.

22. Pardo, *Efemérides,* p. 26; CDIE, 57:319. (Both mention locust attacks in the sixteenth century.) Pardo, *Efémérides,* p. 43, describes the attack of 1616-19. Further seventeenth-century descriptions are in Conde de la Gómera to the Crown, June 14, 1617, and *ibid.* to *ibid.,* December 31, 1617, AGI/AG 13; AGGG, A1.23, legajo 1515, f. 15 (1617); AGGG, A1.23, legajo 4577, f. 4v. (1619); Gage, *The English-American,* pp. 289-90. There was a severe locust plague as late as 1847. Woodward, *Class Privilege and Economic Development,* p. 48.

23. Cattle replaced the disappearing Indians in many parts of Middle America. Here cattle replaced the Indians as a work force to some extent. The combination of cattle and indigo was frequently noticed. E.g., CDIE, 57:399; Vázquez de Espinosa, *Compendium,* pp. 230-31, 259; Gage, *The English-American,* pp. 204-5.

24. Gage, *The English-American,* pp. 204-5.

25. "Relación de como se beneficia la tinta añir" (1611), AGI/AG 13, describes the various types of work on an obraje and on a xiquilite plantation. Another document in the same legajo describes some of the abuses, Audiencia to the Crown, April 27, 1611, AGI/AG 13.

26. *Ibid.* Fuentes y Guzmán mentions that Indian caciques near San Miguel rented out their Indian subjects to the obrajes for the harvest season, FG, 3:427.

27. FG, 3:427, and especially "Razón de las tasaciones," (1582), AGI/AG 966. In 1583 Nicaraguans were already protesting that obraje owners were too poor to buy negro slaves, and were thus reduced to using Indians even though it was illegal to do so. See Vecinos of Nicaragua to the Crown, February 17, 1583, pieza 80, AGI/AG 40. (They asked that 200 negroes be sent.)

28. "Relacion de como se beneficia la tinta añir" (1611), AGI/AG 13; AGGG, A1.23, legajo 4575, f. 398v. (1581). Rubio claims that Indians were brought from tierra caliente to tierra fría to work on añil, and that this killed large numbers. Rubio, "El Añil," p. 321. Conversely, there is some evidence that Indians from Chiquimula and other highland areas were used on añil works on the coast at La Choluteca during the first decades of the seventeenth century. See Audiencia to the Crown, April 23, 1611, AGI/AG 13. For similar allegations and a description of unhealthy obrajes, see FG, 3:426.

29. AGGG, A1.23, legajo 4575, f. 398v. (1581); Alonso Maldonado to the Crown, May 31, 1612, AGI/AG 13; "Relación de como se beneficia la tinta añir," (1611), AGI/AG 13. Claims that obraje work was no longer harmful were frequent. E.g., FV, 2:334; AGGG, A1.23, legajo 4577, ff. 60v.-61 (1631). See also Smith, "Indigo Production," p. 190.

30. "Relación de como se beneficia la tinta añir" (1611), AGI/AG 13; Rubio, "El Añil," pp. 318, 320; Smith, "Indigo Production," pp. 185-86; García Peláez, *Memorias,* vol. 1, p. 240.

31. AGGG, A1.23, legajo 1513, f. 594 (1581). The following document reiterates decrees of 1609 and 1627 forbidding the use of Indians in añil obrajes: AGGG, A1.23, legajo 4577, f. 45 (1631).

32. AGGG, A1.23, legajo 4576, f. 46 (1601).

33. Smith, "Indigo Production," p. 187; García Peláez, *Memorias,* vol. 1, p. 240. See especially, Audiencia to the Crown, April 27, 1611, AGI/AG 13.

34. AGGG, A1.24, 10203, 1559, f. 360 (1642); AGGG, A1.24, 10222, 1578, f. 187 (1711).

35. AGGG, A1.23, legajo 1516, f. 6 (1631); Pedro Vázquez de Velasco to the Crown, March 17, 1648, AGI/AG 17. The use of canoas had been banned at the beginning of the seventeenth century (CDIU, 17:224), but some were still in use on small dye-works late in the century. See AGGG, A1.2-4, 15753, 2198, f. 245 (1689).

36. Smith, "Indigo Production," p. 187; Rubio, "El Añil," p. 322; Audiencia to Crown, April 27, 1611, AGI/AG 13. In Honduras it was decided to start the system in 1676, after debate; ANHH, paquete 3, legajo 40 (1676). Thereafter small fines were levied regularly; ANHH, paquete 3, legajo 51 (1677); ANHH, paquete 3, legajo 70 (1677); ANHH, paquete 3, legajos 79-80, and so on.

37. In Audiencia to the Crown, April 27, 1611, AGI/AG 13, fines of 200 *tostones* are mentioned for 1607-10. For the exclusion of obraje owners from offices, see Pardo, *Efemérides,* p. 38; AGGG, A1.24, legajo 4588, f. 243 (1609); and AGGG, A1.24, 10201, 1557, f. 196 (1633).

38. One of the frankest reports is the aforementioned by Juan Maldonado y Paz, "Relación de como se beneficia la tinta añir," (1611), AGI/AG 13. In 1621 the Cabildo and justices of San Salvador complained that the alcalde mayor was exacting

1, 2, or more quintals from each obraje owner in return for low fines. He collected more than 12,000 pesos worth of indigo in this fashion; Cabildo of San Salvador to the Crown, March 20, 1621, AGI/AG 43.

39. The documentation on these practices is vast. Typical examples are: AGGG, A1.24, 10206, 1562, f. 310 (1609); AGGG, A1.53, 40304, 4680 (1650); AGGG, A1.24, 10206, 1562, f. 298 (1692); AGGG, A1.53, 45118, 5349 (1708). Note that one alcalde mayor, as already mentioned, used this system to accumulate 12,000 pesos in two years. For the same kind of activities in Nicaragua, see AGGG, A1.24, 10225, 1581, f. 383 (1714).

40. A good report on the conduct of visitas to indigo obrajes is Francisco Romero Valtodano to the Crown, "Seen in Council," October 20, 1642, AGI/AG 7. See also AGGG, A1.23, legajo 1517, f. 35 (1643), and CDIU, 17:224. The higher fines seem to have been about 60 pesos around mid-century, in AGGG, A1.24, 10206, 1562, ff. 293-320, and AGGG, A1.24, 10207, 1563, f. 207 (1667). These two documents mention over 100 different cases. At the beginning of the eighteenth century the rate increased with returning prosperity. See *Isagoge,* p. 401; AGGG, A1.24, 10214, 1570, ff. 108-108v. (1697). In poorer areas such as Honduras the fines were 25 pesos or lower, e.g., ANHH, paquete 3, legajo 51 (1677); ANHH, paquete 3, legajo 134 (1681); ANHH, paquete 4, legajo 125 (1688).

41. The struggle between the Audiencia and the alcaldes mayores of San Salvador can be seen in AGGG, A1.24, 10201, 1557, f. 4 (1603); AGGG, A1.23, legajo 1516, ff. 179v., 150 (1632 and 1638); AGGG. A1.23, legajo 1517, f. 3 (1641); AGGG, A1.23, 39221, 4568, f. 29v. (1644); BNM, 3023, f. 303. Sometimes the Crown would support the Audiencia and give it authority to stop the "excesses" of the visitadores. See Larreinaga, *Prontuario de todas las reales cédulas,* p. 18. In other indigo growing zones the Audiencia sometimes appointed the visitadores itself. E.g., Francisco Romero Valtodano to the Crown, "Seen in Council," October 20, 1642, AGI/AG 7; AGGG, A1.53, 45111, 5348 (1671).

42. BNM, 3048, ff. 225-26v.

43. *Ibid.* The Justiniani Chavarri family is widely mentioned in Guatemalan documents. There are several letters about the clan in AGI/AG 2. See also FX, 2:248-49. The fall and ruin of some members of the family is described in Molina, *Antigua Guatemala,* pp. 39-40.

44. E.g., AGGG, A1.23, legajo 4577, f. 45 (1631); AGGG, A1.23, legajo 1517, f. 3 (1641). This second cédula was sent at the urging of the alcalde mayor of San Salvador, who may well have wished the obraje owners to have a reminder of their dependence upon his understanding and cooperation.

45. AGGG, A1.23, legajo 1517, f. 35 (1643). See also the King's marginal note in Francisco Romero Valtodano to the Crown, "Seen in Council," October 20, 1642, f. 1v., AGI/AG 7.

46. CDIU, 17:223-24. A similar offer is mentioned in AGGG, A1.23, legajo 1517, f. 35 (1643). The mention of a separate ramo for these fines (1659) is in García Peláez, *Memorias,* vol. 3, p. 149.

47. AGGG, A1.23, legajo 1519, f. 220 (1670). A similar, earlier inquiry by the King, which showed his full knowledge of the workings of the system, is AGGG, A1.23, legajo 4577, f. 61 (1631).

48. Smith, "Indigo Production," p. 191; García Peláez, *Memorias,* vol. 2, p. 26.

49. Barberena, *Historia de El Salvador,* vol. 2, pp. 308-10; Cabildo of León to the Crown, December 10, 1582, AGI/AG 43; Fiscal to the Crown, March 30, 1585, AGI/AG 10; Governor of Nicaragua to the Crown, February 17, 1683, AGI/AG 40.

50. According to AGGG, A1.2-4, 15755, 2199, f. 50 (1671), no slaves had been sent to Central America since 1638. Large shipments had arrived from time to time in the sixteenth and early seventeenth centuries. E.g., Pardo, *Efemérides,* p. 8. Several more seem to have arrived in the late seventeenth century. See Smith, "Indigo Production," p. 189. A typical appeal for more negro slaves in the sixteenth

century is, Fiscal to Crown, March 30, 1585, AGI/AG 10; and in the seventeenth, AGGG, A1.2-4, 15751, 2197, f. 97 (1660).

51. Audiencia to the Crown, January 14, 1630, AGI/AG 15; AGGG, A1.1, 25, 1, f. 5 (1630). Fears of Dutch contact with the runaways are expressed in AGGG, A1.23, legajo 4577, f. 63v. (1632); AGGG, A1.23, legajo 1516, f. 57 (1632). For cimarrones in Nicaragua, see AGGG, A1.23, legajo 1518, f. 21 (1657); García Peláez, *Memorias,* vol. 2, p. 27. A cimarrón uprising was put down in 1630, AGGG, A1.1, 25, 1, f. 1 (June 4, 1630).

52. The President reported cimarrones in an area called Guayaval. A vecino captured some of them. Conde de la Gómera to the Crown, November 14, 1611, AGI/AG 13; "Sobre la reducción y prisión de negros cimarrones," July 20, 1618, AGI/AG 14.

53. AGGG, A1.23, legajo 4575, f. 103 (1548). Gómera suspected the castas of having contacts with the cimarrones, Conde de la Gómera to the Crown, November 14, 1611, AGI/AG 13. See also Scelle, *La Traite Negrière,* p. 167. An attempted uprising of 2,000 negroes in San Salvador during Holy Week is mentioned in CDIU, 17:215; Smith, "Indigo Production," p. 189, and Larreinaga, *Prontuario,* p.111. See also García Peláez, *Memorias,* vol. 2, p. 26.

54. By 1617, agitation to prohibit importation of slaves had begun; Pardo, *Efemérides,* p. 43. But more probably arrived in 1620; *ibid.,* p. 45. In response to a royal question in 1671, the Audiencia replied that it did not want more slaves; Rubio, "El Añil," p. 324.

55. BNM, 3048, f. 213; López de Velasco, *Geografía,* p. 43; McAlister, "Social Structure and Social Change," 355.

56. Gómera complained that numerous free negroes and mulattoes were living with no masters, far from authority, and among the Indians. He proposed reducing them to towns and forcing them to work; Conde de la Gómera to the Crown, November 14, 1611, AGI/AG 13. Seemingly he did set up one such town, La Gómera (Vázquez de Espinosa, *Compendium,* p. 209). See also ANHH, paquete 5, legajo 41 (1695) for similar problems.

57. The best example of this kind of thinking is President Quiñones Osorio to the Crown, May 16, 1637, AGI Indiferente General 186. With few exceptions, castas and negroes were prohibited from bearing arms throughout the seventeenth century. See AGGG, A1.23, legajo 4588, f. 96 (1605), and AGGG, A1.23, 39223, 4568, f. 21 (1646).

58. AGGG, A1.23, legajo 4576, f. 7v. (1609); AGGG, A1.23, legajo 4577, ff. 60v.-61 (1631); AGGG, A1.2, 16190, 2245, f. 4 (1634). Andrés de Arrieto to the Crown, December 13, 1653, AGI/AG 43, mentions the establishment of six villages of vagabonds, some of whom were Indians. Most, however, were free negroes, mulattoes, and mestizos.

59. FG, 1:240; Gage, *The English-American,* p. 205. Smith mentions castas hiring Indians to do the work in the obrajes, in his "Indigo Production," p. 187. See also Audiencia to the Crown, April 27, 1611, AGI/AG 13.

60. Fiscal to the Crown, March 30, 1585, AGI/AG 10; AGGG, A1.2, 16190, 2245, f. 172 (1636). Typical criminal trials accusing castas of rustling are AGGG, A1.15, 32655, 4122 (1683); AGGG, A1.15, 32696, 4126 (1692). In AGGG, A1.23, legajo 4577, ff. 60v.-61 (1631), there is mention that the King has heard that there are some 6,000 negroes, mulattoes and Indian naborias who do not work and live by thieving. The King says they must be put to work in the obrajes. See also ANHH, paquete 5, legajo 84 (1698); FG, 1:240; 2:285; 3:44, 398.

61. Vázquez de Espinosa, *Compendium,* p. 224; Gage, *The English-American,* p. 205; FG, 2:287; ANHH, paquete 5, legajo 41 (1695); Manuel Ungría Girón to Crown, March 20, 1605, AGI/AG 12.

62. Fiscal to the Crown, March 30, 1585, AGI/AG 10; AGGG, A1.2, 16190, 2245, ff. 5v., 13v., 161 (1627); AGGG, A1.24, 10222, 1578, f. 208 (1711).

63. "Relación de como se beneficia la tinta añir" (1611), AGI/AG 13 describes how castas were paid per load of xiquilite, plus their daily food. Most of the workers,

however, inside the obrajes themselves, seem to have been Indian. See also ANHH, paquete 6, legajo 90 (1725); Gage, *The English-American,* p. 205.

64. Chaunu and Chaunu, *Séville et l'Atlantique,* 6²:988-89; Gray, *A History of Agriculture,* vol. 1, pp. 273-77; Alden, "The Growth and Decline of Indigo Production in Colonial Brazil," 35-60.

65. President Villalobos to the Crown, March 17, 1578, AGI/AG 10; CDIU, 17:224. For a traditional view of the role of taxation in Central America's seventeenth-century decline, see Batres Jáuregui, *La América Central,* vol. 1, p. 380.

66. Pardo, *Efemérides,* pp. 49, 80; García Peláez, *Memorias,* vol. 2, pp. 98-99. Batres, *La América Central,* vol. 1, pp. 397-98; AGGG, A1.23, legajo 1514, f. 92 (1608). A list of añileros who had evaded taxes is in UT, G19-129, ff. 292-292v. (n.d., early 1690s?). When Oidor Pedro Enríquez de Selva tried to collect alcabala on all goods entering or leaving Santiago an attempt was made to murder him (May 28, 1688). Soon thereafter a riot occurred. The King complained that the President and the Audiencia were not investigating these matters with any enthusiasm. Enríquez de la Selva was quietly moved to the Audiencia of Guadalajara and the matter was forgotten. AGGG, A1.23, legajo 4586, f. 161; AGGG, A1.23, legajo 1523, ff. 1, 129; AGGG, A1.2-4, 15755, 2199, f. 55.

67. AGGG, A1.1, 5741, 260, f.1 (1681); Pardo, *Efemérides,* p. 38.

68. Vázquez de Espinosa, *Compendium,* p. 237; CDIU, 17:223-24; President Villalobos to the Crown, March 17, 1578, AGI/AG 10; AGGG, A1.23, legajo 1518, f. 717 (1592); AGGG, A1.23, legajo 4579, f. 119v. (1638).

69. President Villalobos to the Crown, March 17, 1578, AGI/AG 10.

70. Batres Jáuregui, *La América Central,* vol. 2, pp. 396-400, is an incomplete listing of these exactions. See also Pardo, *Efemérides,* pp. 49, 73; AGGG, A1.24, 10223, 1579, f. 163 (1712); AGGG, A1.23, 14035, 2025, f. 5 (1692); President Jacinto de Barrios Leal to the Crown, April 15, 1690, AGI/AG 32.

71. AGGG, Tierras, 51878, 1592 (1592) in which a local dyer (tintero) starts an obraje of his own over an Indian landowner's opposition; Villa de San Vicente de Austria to the Crown, March 20, 1709, AGI/AG 279 mentions that the shipment to Havana was "formerly" considerable.

72. "Memoria al rey" from an official of Honduras (n.d., 1582?), AGI/AG 56 contains a list of the obrajes of Quito. Ships full of "Quito cloth" were taken by the pirates who visited the Pacific in the 1680s. E.g., Ringrose, "The Dangerous Voyages," pp. 65-66. See also Vázquez de Espinosa, *Compendium,* p. 363; González Suárez, *Historia General de la República del Ecuador,* vol. 4, pp. 472-77. A modern discussion of the textile obrajes of the mountain basins around Quito in the early seventeenth century is Phelan, *The Kingdom of Quito,* pp. 68, 71-72, 161.

73. E.g., Hernando de Salcedo to the Crown, May 25, 1614, AGI/AG 7; AGGG, A1.23, legajo 4577, ff. 60v.-61 (1631); Villa of San Vicente de Austria to Crown, March 20, 1709, AGI/AG 279. A typical cargo for Peru is ANCR, Cartago 049 (January 8, 1677). This was a ship bound from Realejo to Callao and "intermediate parts." Indigo was still being shipped regularly to Guayaquil in the mid-eighteenth century. See Flores y Caamaño, *Relación,* vol. 2, p. 2.

74. AGGG, A1.23, legajo 4577, ff. 60v.-61 (1631); AGGG, A3.5, 6568, 306 (1690); AGGG, A3.5, 37417, 2544 (1708); Chaunu and Chaunu, *Séville et l'Atlantique,* 5:988-89; 7:142-43.

75. Ayón, *Historia de Nicaragua,* vol. 1, pp. 332-36; Ringrose, "The Dangerous Voyages," pp. 69-70; Dampier, *Dampier's Voyages,* vol. 1, pp. 247-67; Audiencia to the Crown, May 15, 1607, AGI/AG 12.

76. Ayón, *Historia de Nicaragua,* vol. 1, p. 101; Robles, *Diario de sucesos notables,* vol. 1, p. 267; Pérez Valenzuela, *Santo Tomás de Castilla,* pp. 33-34; AGGG, A1.23, legajo 1519, f. 209 (1668). Foreign shipping in the Indies and trading with foreigners were both banned in the early sixteenth century. This ban was reiterated frequently during the seventeenth century; e.g., CDI, 18:423-25, and the several royal cédulas mentioned in Larreinaga, *Prontuario,* pp. 63, 120-21. See also

Haring, *Trade and Navigation,* pp. 101, 108. Typical cédulas which accuse Central Americans of violations are, AGGG, A1.23, legajo 1514, f. 228 (1614), and AGGG, A1.23, legajo 1521, f. 84v. (1661).

77. Gold and silver caused massive strains in the Spanish economy also; Hamilton, *American Treasure,* p. 212. See the observations of seventeenth-century foreign travelers in Spain in *Viajes de extranjeros,* vol. 2, pp. 404, 407, 414, 881, 885. See also Vicens Vives, *Historia Social y Económica,* vol. 3, 322, 338, 344-45.

78. Hamilton, *American Treasure,* p. 26; *Viajes de extranjeros,* vol. 2, pp. 114, 422, 424-25, 445, 685, 737, 916, 1063, 1348; Hamilton, *War and Prices in Spain,* pp. 4, 9, 129-30, 218-19; Domínguez Ortiz, *Política y Hacienda,* pp. 97-99, 285-90; Elliott, *The Revolt of the Catalans,* pp. 524-25.

79. For a confiscation of indigo belonging to a prominent vecino of Santiago, see Nicolás Justiniano to Crown, June 14, 1653, AGI/AG 2. For a general confiscation, see AGGG, A1.23, legajo 1515, f. 239 (December 31, 1630). For juros and their uses, see especially AGGG, A3.2, 32406, 2163 (1652), entitled "Bosquejo de los juros impuestos sobre la renta de la Tesorería de Guatemala." President Alonso Criado de Castilla complained to the Council of the Indies as early as 1599 that there were so many charges on the royal treasury, what with ayudas de costo, salaries, and juros, that all the royal income was gone, and thus for several years there had been none left to send to Spain. Criado to the Crown, May 20, 1599, AGI/AG 11. For seventeenth-century royal reassurances that confiscations would stop, see CDI, 17: 249-51; 21:85-8.

80. Chaunu and Chaunu, *Séville et l'Atlantique,* 6:76; 7:92-9.

81. *Ibid.,* 6:76. A first-hand description of the loading and unloading of one of these ships is in *Relaciones histórico-descriptivas de la Verapaz,* pp. 46-54.

82. Chaunu and Chaunu, *Séville et l'Atlantique,* 4:123, 143, 276-77, 498; 5:421, 988-89; 7:92-9, 142-43; 8¹:865-67. Audiencia to the Crown, April 20, 1647, AGI/AG 16, states that indigo is the principal product leaving Honduras ports.

83. Chaunu and Chaunu, *Séville et l'Atlantique,* 5:168-69, 180-81, 183. Both ships were also captured in 1602, with 250 quintals on board, *ibid.,* 4:137, 142-43. For 1656 and 1657, see Haring, *Trade and Navigation,* p. 237.

84. Chaunu and Chaunu, *Séville et l'Atlantique,* 6:101; 6²:988-89; 8¹:865-67.

85. *Ibid.,* 4:393; *Viajes de extranjeros,* pp. 603, 685, 1064; Haring, *Trade and Navigation,* pp. 113, 215; Elliott, *Imperial Spain,* pp. 339, 354.

86. The argument here is borrowed from Chaunu, *Conquête et Exploitation,* pp. 277-97. Chaunu's argument is itself an elaboration of the examination of the determinants of space, weight, speed, time, and profitability in Denoix, "Caractéristiques des navires de l'époque des grandes découvertes."

87. Pardo, *Efemérides,* p. 136. In AGI/AG 279, a long unsigned expediente mentions the two visits in 20 years. (The visits were in 1688 and 1695).

88. Larreinaga, *Prontuario,* p. 331.

89. Audiencia to the Crown, June 21, 1612, AGI/AG 13; Gage, *The English-American,* pp. 341-43; Pérez Valenzuela, *Santo Tomás de Castilla,* p. 32; *The Voyages of Captain William Jackson,* pp. vi, 22-25, 33.

90. Larreinaga, *Prontuario,* p. 244, contains the anxious royal cédula.

91. For the 1640s see Milla, *Historia de la América Central,* pp. 386-87. AGGG, A3.5, 6568, 306 (1690), covers legal añil shipments from 1675 to 1685. Most of it was sent via Veracruz. Small quantities left via the Golfo Dulce. By the early eighteenth century almost all legal indigo exports were passing through Veracruz. C.f., Bibliothèque de l'Arsénal, Paris, Ms. 4788, ff. 76-76v., 156. Typical of the few shipments via the Honduras ports in the second half of the seventeenth century are AGGG, A3.6, 29058, 1834 (1666); AGGG, A3.6, 39581, 2750 (1697). Occasionally the King would try to restore the former frequent use of the Honduran ports, and to try to halt the reliance on Veracruz. E.g., AGGG, A1.23, legajo 1522, f. 109 (1685); AGGG, A1.23, legajo 1523, f. 76 (1692).

92. Ayón, *Historia de Nicaragua,* vol. 1, pp. 183-84; García Peláez, *Memorias,* vol. 2, p. 98.
93. Pardo, *Efemérides,* pp. 98, 100. The King's concern at the cost of conveying silver overland to Veracruz is found in Larreinaga, *Prontuario,* p. 244. The fall in prices is mentioned in Chaunu and Chaunu, *Séville et l'Atlantique,* 6^2:1042-43, and in Cabildo of San Salvador to the Crown, January 24, 1648, AGI/AG 43.
94. AGGG, A3.5, 37417, 2544 (1708).

Chapter 11

1. E.g., Lcdo. Salazar to Crown, March 15, 1578, AGI/AG 10; *Isagoge,* p. 290.
2. Various letters from Juan Vázquez de Coronado to Crown in his *Cartas de Relación,* pp. 25, 27, 38-9, 56 *passim.*
3. *Ibid.,* and Joan Dávila to Felipe II (1566), Peralta, *Costa-Rica, Nicaragua y Panamá,* pp. 395-400.
4. E.g., Fernández León, *Historia de Costa Rica,* pp. 136-40; Governor Juan Francisco Sáenz to the Crown, May 20, 1675, AGI/AG 139.
5. Bishop of Honduras to the Crown, May 12, 1582, AGI/AG 165; Reina Valenzuela, "Comayagua Antañana," 21-34, 39-60, 21-32.
6. In 1607 the Crown began to seize the vacant encomiendas more vigorously (a step taken in Mexico several years before), and suspended the right of the President of the Audiencia of Guatemala to award these vacos to new tenants. See Konetzke, *Colección de documentos,* 2^1: 128-34. See also the confiscations of 1611, in *Isagoge,* p. 385. Taxes were constantly added to the shrinking encomienda, e.g., the mesada (one twelfth of income) on June 15, 1625, AGGG, A1.23, legajo 4578, f. 77v. See the two complaints (1605, 1606) about the subdividing of encomiendas into ever smaller pieces, in *Isagoge,* pp. 357, 364, 372, 374. See also the very small encomienda grants which were being distributed in the 1620s. Some were of "40 Indians," or of "20 pesos a year." AGGG, A1.1, 5034, 212 (1620); AGGG, A1.1, 5037, 212 (1622); AGI Patronato 82-1-4 ("Secreta").
7. AGGG, A1.2-4, 15749, 2195, f. 37 (April 21, 1574). One of the earliest repartimientos for a wheat farm was in 1565; see, AGGG, A1. 2-4, 2196, 134 (June 28, 1565). Extraordinary repartimientos were also levied in times of emergency. A typical one, raised for earthquake repairs, is AGGG, A1.1, 1, 1 (October 9, 1607).
8. Gage, *The English-American,* pp. 231-34; FG, 3: 306. For the King's secret enquiry about the question of using Indian labor in mines, see AGGG, A1.23, legajo 1514, f. 33v. (November 24, 1602). The monarch had shown the same ambivalence the year before about pearling, another dangerous occupation. See AGGG, A1.23, legajo 4576, f. 48 (November 24, 1601). See also Larreinaga, *Prontuario de todas las reales cédulas,* p. 287.
9. Jones, "Indian Labor in Guatemala," pp. 309-10; Zavala, *Contribución,* pp. 95-108. (Zavala sees repartimiento as more important and durable in Central America than in Mexico). Indians, especially caciques and principales, were punished for not supplying enough labor for the repartimientos; see AGGG, A1.1, 1, 1 (1607). Others were punished for using the system as a means of extortion; Larreinaga, *Prontuario,* p. 287. The annual amount turned over by jueces de repartimiento in Santiago was between 5,000 and 6,000 pesos (at 1/2 real per Indian per week). This must mean at least 2,000 Indians per week were drafted in the jurisdiction of the valle alone—a large industry. See Larreinaga, *Prontuario,* pp. 340-41.
10. Audiencia to the Crown, April 23, 1582, AGI/AG 10. (The village here is Comitán); AGGG, A1.23-1, 10189, 1553 (1600–1609), especially the document dated May 26, 1603; AGGG, A3.12, 40031, 2774 (1631); ACNL, 1106, G, I, ff.

10v.-11v.; Gage, *The English-American,* pp. 231-34, 273; FG, 1: 350; 3: 317-19; Larreinaga, *Prontuario,* p. 287.

11. ACNL, 1106, G, I, ff. 11-12; Gage, *The English-American,* pp. 231-34; Juarros, *Compendio,* vol. 2, p. 219; Bishop Juan Ramírez to the Crown, February 3, 1603; Bierman, "Don Fray Juan Ramírez de Arellano," 326-27. The year before the Crown had tried to explain to him that the repartimiento system really was legal, if the Indians were treated fairly, in AGGG, A1.23, legajo 1514, f. 35 (November 24, 1602). The Crown obviously detested the repartimiento system, but tried to tolerate it against the day when "free" labor would evolve. In 1609 the Crown reluctantly agreed to continue the system, "while waiting for the day when the nature of the Indians improves, and the lazy are put to work, and Indians exist that voluntarily hire themselves out as day laborers, and there are (more) Negro slaves—and meanwhile obligatory repartimientos should be very slowly abolished." (So much for an early seventeenth-century millennium!) AGGG, A1.23, legajo 4576, f. 7 (May 26, 1609). For heavy repartimientos in Costa Rica, see ANCR Cartago 1131 (December 10, 1615).

12. AGGG, A1.2.11.2, 48242, 5762 (1606); *Isagoge,* p. 383 (1611); AGGG, A1.23 legajo 1516, f. 179 (May 28, 1630); AGGG, A1.2, 16190, 2245, f. 8v. (January 24, 1634). See also, Bishop Juan Ramírez to Crown, March 10, 1603; Bierman, "Don Fray Juan Ramírez," pp. 340-41; Pardo, *Efemérides,* pp. 36, 38-39, 50, 53-54, 56; Milla, *Historia de la América Central,* vol. 2, pp. 218-19.

13. Fuentes y Guzmán claimed that this institution began as early as 1539, FG, 3: 307. The jueces were banned repeatedly. See the arguments in the following reales cédulas. AGGG, A1.23, legajo 1513, f. 646 (June 8, 1585); AGGG, A1.23, legajo 4576, f. 47v. (November 24, 1601); AGGG, A1.23, legajo 1516, f. 179 (May 28, 1630); Pardo, *Prontuario,* p. 35; Larreinaga, *Prontuario,* p. 267. See also Gage, *The English-American,* p. 264. As late as 1632 the ayuntamiento of Santiago was blaming the scarcity of maize and beans on the "laziness of the Indians," and consequently asking the Audiencia to restore the jueces de milpas in the valle. (Pardo, *Efemérides,* p. 50). At the end of the seventeenth century Fuentes y Guzmán was still hoping the office would be restored. See also the expedientes of 1651 in AGI/AG 131.

14. See the complaint from Bishop Juan de Sandoval y Zapata [sic], May 12, 1619, AGI/AG 161. See also FG, 3: 307-9. The letter-writing juez de milpas is mentioned in AGGG, A1. 30-13, 40644, 4699, ff. 18, 19v.

15. López de Velasco, *Geografía y descripción universal,* pp. 285, 306-9; Milla, *Historia de la América Central,* vol. 2, p. 310; Batres Jáuregui, *La América Central,* vol. 1, p. 379; Johannessen, *Savannas of Interior Honduras,* pp. 38-42. See also AGI Patronato 183-1-16, f. 22 (1590); AGGG, A1.2-7, 11810, 1804, ff. 18-19v. (1604); Gage, *The English-American,* pp. 183, 211, 214-18, 221-22.

16. Oidor Manuel de Ungría Girón to the Crown, March 20, 1605, AGI/AG 12; AGGG, A1.2-4, 15753, 2198, f. 256 (1607); "Relación de la visita hecha por don Juan de Guerra y Ayala a la gobernación de Honduras," p. 49. See also Graham, "The Recreative Power of Plant Communities," pp. 685-88.

17. AGGG, A1.23, legajo 1514, f. 77 (December 22, 1605). (The quantity of meat to be bought with a real fell from 40 to 17 lbs.) See also, Milla, *Historia de la América Central* vol. 2, p. 303; *Isagoge,* p. 383 (1611); Pardo, *Efemérides,* pp. 29, 40, 57. (Contrast the permission to export meat in 1587, p. 29, with the restrictions on meat exports in 1611, p. 40). To add to the difficulties Central America's money supply, and its quality, began to deteriorate in the early decades of the seventeenth century. See Chapter Fifteen, and in this context Zelaya, "Apuntes para la historia de la moneda en Honduras," 54-102.

18. AGGG, A1.23, legajo 1514, f. 77 (December 22, 1605); Oidor Manuel de Ungría Girón to the Crown, March 20, 1605, AGI/AG 12; AGGG, A1.2-4, 15753, 2198, f. 256 (1607); AGGG, A1.23, legajo 4588, f. 236 (May 19, 1609). See also Pardo, *Efemérides,* p. 40; Vázquez de Espinosa, *Compendium,* p. 244; *Relaciones histórico-descriptivas de la Verapaz,* p. 203.

19. Oidor Manuel de Ungría Girón to the Crown, March 20, 1605, AGI/AG 12; AGGG, A1.23, legajo 1514, f. 77 (December 22, 1605); Gage, *The English-American,* p. 205.

20. AGGG, A1.23, legajo 4588, f. 94v. (May 8, 1599); Oidor Manuel de Ungría Girón to the Crown, March 20, 1605, AGI/AG 12; AGGG, A1.23, legajo 4588, f. 96 (October 7, 1605); AGGG, A1.23, legajo 4588, f. 236 (May 19, 1609).

21. BNM, 3047, "Papeles varios, 1646," ff. 137-141v. See also Konetzke, *Colección de documentos,* vol. 1, pp. 584-85 (1587); Fiscal Thomas Spínola de la Plaça to the Crown, March 30, 1585, AGI/AG 10; Conde de la Gómera to the Crown, November 14, 1611, AGI/AG 13; Pardo, *Efemérides,* p. 48; Gage, *The English-American,* p. 205; García Peláez, *Memorias,* vol. 2, p. 28.

22. Pardo, *Efemérides,* pp. 37, 53; Johannessen, *Savannas of Interior Honduras,* p. 39; AGGG, A1.23, legajo 4588, f. 93 (April 16, 1603); AGGG, A1.2-4, 15753, 2198, ff. 256, 259v.-261 (1607). Typical cases of rustling are AGGG, A1.15, 32462, 4092 (1607); AGGG, A1.15, 32467, 4092 (1609).

23. Pardo, *Efemérides,* pp. 31, 40, 56. AGGG, A1.2-4, 15753, 2198, f. 256 (1607). A later attempt at enforcing strict warehousing of scarce goods is, AGGG, A1.23, legajo 1518, f. 17 (February 28, 1652). See also AGGG, A1.2. 11. 2, 48242, 5762 (1606).

24. Vázquez de Espinosa, *Compendium,* p. 242; García Peláez, *Memorias,* vol. 2, pp. 183-86, 200-16, 223-33; Gage, *The English-American,* pp. 196, 279. (Yet, to Gage, fresh from Europe, the cattle population was still abundant and meat was cheap.)

25. Pardo, *Efemérides,* p. 54; AGGG, A1.24, 10210, 1566, f. 119 (May 17, 1681); AGGG, A1.24, 10211, 1567, f. 284 (May 8, 1683). See also ANHH, paquete 2, legajo 60 (1672); ANHH, paquete 5, legajo 43 (1695); ANHH, paquete 5, legajo 43 (1695) for sporadic continuations of the bans on exporting foodstuffs from Honduras.

26. The rapid growth of the Spanish population cannot be explained by the rate of immigration. See the totals in Castro y Tosi, *Pasajeros a Indias.* Differential fertility will be discussed later. Meanwhile see Chaunu, *L'Amérique et les Amériques,* pp. 105-6.

27. AGGG, A1. Tierras, 51832, 5929 (1579) in which Indians from Masagua (Escuintla) explain that the seemingly empty monte is used by them for hunting deer, turtles, and iguanas. They find wild cacao and other produce there too. Similar arguments, mentioning needs for wood and thatch are in AGGG, A1. Tierras, 51961, 5939 (1627). The Indians lost both cases. See also Simpson, "Bernal Díaz del Castillo, Encomendero," 100-106, in which Indians explained that they had to move their plots every two years because the land "got tired." So land was empty because of the fallowing rotation.

28. Gage, *The English-American,* pp. 239-40. (Gage points out that those in Spanish towns ate more meat than rural Indians.) This gradual process has been well explained in West and Augelli, *Middle America,* pp. 286-88. In one of the cases above, however, AGGG, A1. Tierras, 51961, 5939 (1627), the Indians' spokesman objects to the monte being turned into an estancia because the Indians whom he represents "are deathly afraid of bulls" (ff. 9v.-10).

29. AGGG, A1. 22-41, 16190, 2245 (1634); AGGG, A1. 2, 16190, 2245 (1634). These are elaborations of legislation first started by Criado. Compare them with "The Ordinance of Laborers of Edward III, 1349," pp. 358-61; Cheyney, *The Dawn of a New Era,* pp. 328-29. See also Pardo, *Efemérides,* p. 53. On putting vagabonds and the unemployed to work, see AGGG, A1.23, legajo 4576, f. 47v. (November 24, 1601); AGGG, A1.23, legajo 1514, f. 130 (May 26, 1609); AGGG, 16190, 2245, f. 4 (July 20, 1634).

30. Pardo, *Efemérides,* pp. 48, 51. Typical vagabondage prosecutions are, AGGG, A1.15, 32414, 4086 (1596); AGGG, A1.15, 32536, 4105 (1622); AGGG, A2.2, 2473, 137 (1670).

31. López de Velasco, *Geografía,* p. 300; Díaz del Castillo, *Historia Verdadera,* p. 538; Herrera, Historia, vol. 1, pp. 87-88; Vázquez de Espinosa, *Compendium,* p. 205; BNM, 2468, f. 96; FG, 3: 44, 187; Alonso de Castilla y Guzmán to the Crown, 1620, CDHCR, 7: 156-57.

32. *Isagoge,* p. 365; Vázquez de Espinosa, *Compendium,* pp. 229-31; Gage, *The English-American,* pp. 155-86; CDHCR, 5: 133. "Relación de la visita hecha por don Juan de Guerra y Ayala," 48, talks of the exodus to the countryside as a new phenomenon, and of abandoned towns. There is a vast number of requests for land titles from vecinos of Santiago between 1576 and 1610. Typical of the many requests for tierras baldías or realengas, are AGGG, A3.15, 40276, 2786 (1579); A3.15, 51854, 5931 (1587); AGGG, A3.15, 51946, 5938, f. 14 (1614). See also Juan Moreno Alvarez de Toledo to the Crown, January 8, 1578, AGI/AG 55. There were at least ten large grants, mostly for wheat farms, near Mixco between 1590 and 1603. For Chiapas and the exodus there, see for example AGGG, A1.23 (Chiapas), legajo 4588, ff. 157 (May 22, 1591), 159 (July 18, 1591), 214v. (July 27, 1592), 276v. (November 18, 1599).

33. E.g. AGGG, A1.23, legajo 4588, f. 106 (1588) (Nicaragua), ff. 135v. (July 17, 1589), 175v. (December 10, 1591) (both Chiapas); AGGG, 57842, 5930 (1585); A1. Tierras, 53953, 6061 (1589); AGGG, A1. Tierras, 51942, 5938 (1600) (all Guatemala). Medida and composición was particularly heavy in San Salvador, center of the indigo industry. See the many requests in A1.23, legajo 4588.

34. FX, 2: 202; Molina, *Antigua Guatemala,* p. 24; AGGG, A1.23, legajo 4576, f. 27 (May 18, 1619); AGGG, A1.23, legajo 1515, f. 92 (June 28, 1621); *Relaciones histórico-descriptivas de la Verapaz,* pp. 154-55. Gage, *The English-American,* p. 198, describes the five wealthiest families: Siliezer (a Basque peninsular), Justiniano (a Genoese), Lira (a peninsular), Fernández (a Portuguese), and Nunnez [sic] (also Portuguese). There was no Creole among the top five.

35. The wealthiest family of all, the Justiniani Chavarris, whose ties with indigo were noted in Chapter Ten, hung on until the 1640s. Then they began to transfer themselves and their capital to Spain. See FX, 2: 248-49. See also Gage, *The English-American,* pp. 198, 212-13, which mentions another departure, and the case of a wealthy man who took to the countryside to escape supervision and the luxury costs of city living. In Central American industries the average production unit was small, and compared to today none of the industries—cacao, hides, or indigo—demanded much fixed capital. Thus an entrepreneur's capital was more in circulation and it was relatively easy to move out of an activity in bad times. This point has been well explained for England's seventeenth-century depression in Supple, *Commercial Crisis and Change in England,* pp. 3, 8-9, 11, 15.

36. AGGG, A1. Tierras, 51907, 5935 (1600) (wherein the former site of Comapa, moved because of congregación, is taken over); AGGG, A1. Tierras, 51881, 5933 (1593); ANHH, Tierras 40, La Paz (1599); AGGG, A1.24, 10201, 1557, f. 82 (July 31, 1610); AGGG, A1.45-7, 51957, 5939 (1626). See the two related cases in Santiago Patzicia, AGGG, A1.45-4, 44801, 5322 (1623), and AGGG, A1.45-8, 44802, 5322 (1631). Royal attempts to stop usurpations include Konetzke, *Colección de documentos,* 2^1: 287-88; AGGG, A1.2, 16190, 2245, f. 31 (September 11, 1616); AGGG, A1.2, 16190, 2245, f. 12v. (January 11, 1626). Some increased their lands by purchase from the Indians in their encomiendas, such as Francisco Díaz del Castillo, the chronicler's son. See AGGG, A1. Tierras, 52612, 5984, f. 7v. (1589); AGGG, A1. Tierras, 51930, 5937 (1606) (another case). A favorite device was to obtain a legitimate title and then to occupy more land than the quantity mentioned in the document. President Pedro de Villalobos' complaint against this practice is in AGGG, A1.1, 5672, 256, ff. 85v.-86 (1575).

37. The general outline given in the text here is a composite picture drawn from many documents. Most of the points mentioned, however, can be found in AGGG, A1. Tierras, 51832, 5929, f. 7 (1579); AGGG, A1. Tierras, 51859, 5931 (1588); AGGG, A1. Tierras, 51867, 5932 (1590); AGGG, A1. Tierras, 51952, 5939, ff. 1-17v. (1623); AGGG, A1. Tierras, 51961, 5939, ff. 9-11v. (1627).

38. An early royal cédula (1536) can be found in Konetzke, *Colección de documentos*, vol. 1, p. 179. See also *ibid.*, 2¹: 287-88; AGGG, A1.2, 16190, 2245, f. 31 (September 11, 1616).

39. The first composición de tierras followed a royal cédula of November 1, 1591 (AGGG, A1.23, legajo 4610, f. 293), but it seems to have had little immediate impact, and heavy composición began at the end of the decade. This composición demanded payment in return for a grant of land. The authorities also auctioned off vacant lands from time to time, e.g., AGGG, A3.15, 40286, 2786 (1612). The composición of 1631 demanded payment to quiet titles or secure title to unauthorized holdings. Composición in Nicaragua may not have started at all until 1631. See Pérez Estrada, "Breve historia de la tenencia de la tierra en Nicaragua," 17-18.

40. Vallejo, *Guía de Agrimensores*, pp. 45-46, 57-61; AGGG, A3.15, 40283, 2786 (1602); AGGG, A1. Tierras, 53957, 6062, f. 163v. (May 14, 1652); AGGG, A1.23, legajo 4586, f. 290v. (1696).

41. See, for example, the case of the village of Rabinal, in AGGG, A1. Tierras, 51898, 5935 (May 11, 1588); AGGG, A1. Tierras, 51983, 5941 (1634); AGGG, A1. Tierras, 51988, 5941 (1600) (this last is another case).

42. See the various complaints on these subjects by Bishop Juan Ramírez in the first decade of the seventeenth century, in Biermann, "Don Fray Juan Ramírez de Arellano," 318-47. See also the discussion on the double tribute in Central America, which in this respect is held to be like Peru but unlike Mexico, in Audiencia to the Crown, 1584, ff. 2-5v., AGI/AG 10.

43. AGGG, A1.23, legajo 1521, f. 176 (September 5, 1620); AGGG, A1.2, 16190, 2245, ff. 5v., 13v., 161 (June 12, 1627); AGGG, A1.23, legajo 1516, f. 20 (July 3, 1627 and October 8, 1631). See also AGGG, A1.23, legajo 1521, f. 176 for mention of a cédula as late as 1679. The Crown tried to stop adelantos in 1631 by informing Indians that if Spaniards offered them advances in pay, they would be entitled to accept the money, and then keep it as a gift! (Larreinaga, *Prontuario*, p. 305; Pardo, *Efemérides*, p. 48).

44. Bishop Marroquín noticed priests manipulating loans to Indians in the cacao fields of Soconusco as early as 1558. He ordered them to desist; CDI, 17: 133. An inventory taken at the death of a wealthy man in 1598 shows long lists of villagers who each owed petty sums, AGGG, A1.43, 41513, 4817, ff. 181v.-189, 197v.-205. A similar albacea is AGGG, A1.43, 41517, 4818, ff. 100-117v., 367-9 (1598); this man had 240 Indian debtors. See also AGGG, A1.43, 41553, 4827 (1604); García Peláez, *Memorias*, vol. 1, 227-28. (Even the upper classes were sometimes jailed for debts, but they could obtain their freedom if they could prove that they were hijosdalgo. AGGG, A1.15, 32554, 4108 [1628]).

45. Evidence for this arrangement tends to be covert, but see for example AGGG, A1.15, 57812, 6943, ff. 26-29v. (October 10, 1596).

46. Sherman, "Abusos contra los indios," 14. In 1601 the Crown was already trying to stop the widespread sale of Indians with the haciendas where they worked. They were, the Crown insisted, free laborers. See AGGG, A1.23, legajo 4576, f. 47 (November 24, 1601); AGGG, A1.22-41, 16190, 2245, f. 35v. (1634). The practice was, of course, widespread in the late seventeenth century, AGGG, A1.23, legajo 1519, f. 162 (August 25, 1667).

47. This preference is more noticeable after 1635, as we shall see, but there are cases in the half century before then. FV, 1: 109; Fiscal of the Audiencia to the Crown, March 30, 1585, AGI/AG 10. The pressure on a village can be clearly seen in the following documents, AGGG, A1.23, legajo 1514, f. 43 (1609); AGGG, A1.15, 961, 126 (1631); ANCR Guatemala 019 (August 29, 1609). The following document talks of groups of Indians fleeing and dispersing because of these pressures. CDHCR, 7: 415, 418, 420.

48. For petitions from encomenderos that Indians be brought back to their native villages, see, for example, AGGG, A3.6, 40531, 2803 (1626). For an encomendero defense of Indians' land against Spanish intrusion, see Simpson, "Bernal Díaz del Castillo," p. 106. The complaint about the encomendero's manipulation of

tribute arrears is in Audiencia to the Crown, f. 3v. (1584), AGI/AG 10. In Honduras, later in the century, the drift of Indians from villages to Spanish farms hurt the repartimientos for the mines. ANHH, paquete 5, legajo 68 (1698). See also AGGG, A1.15, 50029, 5905 (1599).

49. Milla, *Historia de la América Central,* vol. 2, 357-58; Gage, *The English-American,* pp. 212-18. For poor rural holdings, see ACNL, 1106 H, ff. 2v.-3 (1630), which claims that most Spaniards on the estancias suffered poverty, and even hunger in this period.

50. E.g., Sherman, "Abusos," pp. 15-16.

51. See the remark on the ex-slave Indians near Santiago. They were "muy españolados y ladinos." (López de Velasco, *Geografía,* p. 287.) On Chimaltenango in the 1620s see Konetzke, *Colección de documentos,* 2^1: 287-88. For other points, see Gage, *The English-American,* pp. 185-88; West and Augelli, *Middle America,* p. 292. Bishop Ramírez noted that the further an Indian village was from a Spanish settlement the more it was left in peace; Sherman, "Abusos," p. 18. See also Higbee, "The Agricultural Regions of Guatemala," 180, 188-89, 194; Reina, "Eastern Guatemalan Highlands," 104, 120.

52. BNM, 3023, ff. 291, 325 (1657-1659); Juan Moreno Alvarez de Toledo to the Crown, January 8, 1578, AGI/AG 55. See also Sherman, "Abusos," pp. 15-16.

53. West and Angelli, *Middle America,* p. 292; Mörner, "La Política de Segregación," 150; García Peláez, *Memorias,* vol. 3, 152-55; Gage, *The English-American,* pp. 214-16.

54. E.g., Vogt, "Chiapas Highlands," 133-51. (As in Guatemala, the proof of this matter lies in the overwhelming number of land titles granted to Spaniards in the lower areas.)

55. See note 54. See also Lic. Maldonado to the Crown, January 15, 1643, AGI/AG 9; Durón, *Bosquejo histórico de Honduras,* p. 94.

56. Audiencia to the Crown, April 23, 1582, ff. 9v.-10, AGI/AG 10; Miranda, *España y Nueva España,* p. 119; Chaunu, *L'Amérique et les Amériques,* pp. 105-6.

57. Audiencia to the Crown, April 1, 1585, f. 3v., AGI/AG 10; FV, 2: 32; Gage, *The English-American,* pp. 298-308, 317-25; Chinchilla Aguilar, "La Danza de Tum —Teleche o Loj—Tum," 17-20; Feria, "Relación que hace el Obispo de Chiapa," 479-87; AGGG, A1. 68-3, legajo 1751, f. 46 (1593).

Chapter 12

1. Except to urge the restoration of the notorious jueces de milpas. AGGG, A1.23, legajo 1515, f. 231 (May 28, 1630); AGGG, A1.2-4, 15751, 2197, f. 13 (September 4, 1640).

2. AGGG, A1.23, legajo 1520, f. 194 (July 20, 1675).

3. Gobernador to the Crown, Gueguetlan [sic], December 15, 1684, AGI Contaduría 815; AGGG, A1.23, legajo 1520, f. 194 (July 20, 1675).

4. Audiencia to the Crown, April 23, 1582, AGI/AG 10; Orozco y Jiménez, *Colección de documentos,* vol. 1, p. 1; AGGG, A1.23, legajo 1520, f. 98 (June 14, 1673); Bishop of Chiapas to the Crown, November 16, 1688, AGI/AG 44; AGGG, A1.57, 2079, 306 (1656).

5. See the table in Arcila Farias, *Comercio entre Venezuela y México,* p. 79. See also UT, G19, no. 139, f. 351v. (1647).

6. BNM, 3023, f. 291. Even in 1827 Soconusco's cacao was considered the best to be had in Europe. See Gallais, *Monographie du Cacao,* p. 103.

7. BNM, 3178, f. 206; BM, Additional Mss., 13,974, ff. 502v.-503.

8. E.g., AGGG, A1.24, 10203, 1559, f. 1 (January 3, 1642).

9. AGGG, A1.24, 10217, 1573, f. 239 (April 27, 1703).

10. AGGG, A1.24, 10220, 1576, f. 27 (1707); AGGG, A1.57, 44829, 5323 (1705); BNP, Mélanges de Colbert, 31, f. 398; FX, 1:353-54.

11. Cortés y Larraz, *Descripción Geográfico-Moral*, vol. 20, tome 1, 257 and especially 262.

12. So much land was planted to cacao in Guazacapán that none was left for maize. See FG, 2:160; FX, 1:60-61, 343-34; López de Velasco, *Geografía y descripción universal*, pp. 296, 317; Gage, *The English-American*, pp. 159, 167, 210, 224-25; Vázquez de Espinosa, *Compendium*, pp. 223-25, 232-33; AGGG, A1.26, 10220, 1576, f. 27 (1707).

13. FV, 1:171; FG, 2:260; Audiencia to the Crown, November 26, 1630, AGI /AG 15; Conde de Santiago to Crown, May 31, 1655, AGI/AG 15; AGGG, A1.2-4, 15757, 2197, f. 13 (1640); AGGG, A1.24, 10205, 1561 (n.d.); AGGG, A1.12, 7023, 333 (1707); AGGG, A1.1, 62,3 (1712). Rubio claims that cacao production in Guatemala was about 150,000 cargas in 1600, and fell to about 25,000 cargas in 1700. Rubio Sánchez, "El Cacao," 88-90, 102-3.

14. AGGG, A1.2, 16190, 2245, f. 168v. (1636); AGGG, A1.24, 10206, 1562, f. 247 (1658); AGGG, A1.24, 10211, 1567, f. 113 (1676); Bishop Juan Ramírez to the Crown, February 3, 1603, AGI/AG 156.

15. Batres Jáuregui, *La América Central*, vol. 1, 397-98; Pardo, *Efemérides*, p. 49; *Isagoge*, pp. 335, 343; Bancroft, *History of Central America*, vol. 2, p. 384.

16. FV, 2:51-52, 55; Vázquez de Espinosa, *Compendium*, pp. 215-16; Gage, *The English-American*, p. 239, and especially the various occupations in AGGG, A1.27, 11810, 1804. See also Bishop Juan Ramírez to the Crown, March 10, 1603, f. 4, AGI/AG 156.

17. Francisco de Sarassa to the Crown, January 6, 1683, AGI/AG 28; *Isagoge*, p. 398; FV, 1:171. A blight or "blast" struck the small fields of Jamaica, Cuba, and Hispaniola about 1669 or 1670. The governor of Jamaica could not explain it. "Neither wee nor our Neighbors of Spaniola, or Cuba, know what to attribute this last blast of the Cocoa to, some fancy its age, others worms, some think it want of Shade, or an ill quality of the winds. But most judge it some constellation, or ill disposition of the climate. We formerly might have made here 2 or 300,000de pound but these last yeares hardly 5,000. Yett are not people att all discouraged, but Plant it faster than ever." BM, Sloane, 11410, f. 241v. (1657). See also Bennett, "Cary Helyar, Merchant and Planter of Seventeenth-Century Jamaica," 60, 64-65, and Bennett, "William Whaley, Planter of Seventeenth-Century Jamaica," 114.

18. "Criollo" and "forastero" classification is somewhat arbitrary, and is not related to the Spanish meanings of these terms. Small quantities of Guatemalan "Criollo" cacao were sent even to Peru, which certainly did not lack cacao in the late seventeenth century. Guatemalan cacao was probably considered a luxury item there. See, ANCR, Cartago 049, January 8, 1677. Soconusco cacao was sent to the Philippines with that of Guayaquil: BNM, 3178, f. 206; Dampier, *Dampier's Voyages*, vol. 1, p. 175; Schurz, *The Manila Galleon*, pp. 275, 370.

According to one source the Venezuelan cacao plantations were created by transplanting wild cacao; see Vázquez de Espinosa, *Compendium*, p. 97. Those of Guayaquil were also new and somewhat untended; see *ibid.*, pp. 370-73. A Mexican source says that the Guayaquil groves consisted of wild cacao and were grown in swamps. See *Actas de cabildo de México*, 26:343-44.

For descriptions of the noxious nature and poor taste of Guayaquil "forastero" cacao, see for example pieza 23, ff. 1-2 (1629), AGI/AG 43; García Peláez, *Memorias*, vol. 2, p. 45. Milla thought these assertions were simply slanders by Guatemalan merchants who wished to prevent the importation of Guayaquil cacao, in Milla, *Historia de la América Central*, vol. 2, p. 351. The Nicaraguans, who badly needed Guayaquil cacao, held the same opinion. See pieza 23, f. 33 (1629), AGI/AG 43. But Mexicans held similar views to the Guatemalans; Gibson, *The Aztecs under Spanish Rule*, p. 349.

On the consumption of wild cacao, patlaxtli, among Indians, and on the supposed harm which it caused among ladinos, see Torquemada, *Monarquía*, vol. 2, p. 620; FG, 2:97-98; Sahagún, *Historia*, vol. 3, p. 54. (FG noted that it was exported to Yucatan, where it was popular). In Verapaz it was sometimes paid to Spaniards as a tribute item. See RAH, 11-4-4-854, 42, f. 4. In some areas patlaxtli trees were used to shade domesticated cacao bushes; e.g., René Francis Millon, "When Money Grew on Trees," p. 20.

19. In the 1570s it was still identified as an Indian drink by Henry Hawks. See Hakluyt, *The Principal Voyages*, p. 384. By 1615 Spaniards had taken to drinking it hot both in Mexico and Spain; Torquemada, *Monarquía*, vol. 2, p. 620; Acosta, *Historia*, pp. 180-81. In Gage's day it was still scorned by the English, but Creoles and Spaniards were drinking chocolate in huge quantities (Gage, *The English-American*, pp. 124, 128, 164-65, 238, 241; Dorantes de Carranza, *Sumaria Relación*, p. 117). Gage also compares Indian and Spanish recipes. See also *Actas de cabildo de México*, vol. 30, pp. 201, 232.

One Englishman in Jamaica was amazed at the Spanish craving for chocolate drinks, and claimed that "they seeme not able to live without them," BM, Sloane 11410, f. 321v. The same Jamaican noticed wide differences between various types of cacao. See *ibid.*, f. 324. After the Dutch seizure of Curaçao in 1634 large shipments of cacao to Europe increased the popularity of hot chocolate in Northern Europe, Amsterdam became the great cacao mart of Europe and even the Spaniards had to buy there. See García Payon, *Amaxocoatl*, pp. 77-78, 89; Gallais, *Monographie du Cacao*, p. 102. Europeans continued to despise the Indian recipes containing chile, achiote, and corn; De Chélus, *Histoire Naturelle*, pp. 98-99. For cosmetic and medicinal use, see Acosta, *Historia*, p. 285; FG, 2:98; Gage, *The English-American*, p. 124; Hughes, *The American Physitian*. By the middle years of the seventeenth century hot chocolate was a popular social and "society" beverage in all the capitals of western Europe. See Knapp, *Cacao and Chocolate*, pp. 11-13; Hubbes, *The Indian Nectar*. Chocolate was first introduced to England in 1652, probably by French merchants. We have notice of Samuel Pepys taking some for a "hangover" on April 24, 1661. A few years later he was drinking it for lunch, and pronounced it "very good." See Pepys, *Diary*, vol. 2, p. 24; vol. 4, p. 275. In France one recalls the famous remark about Louis XIV's Spanish queen: "Le roi et le chocolat furent les deux seules passions de Marie Therèse." By the eighteenth century its use had spread to all classes.

20. Soconusco cacao was often called the best in the Indies. See BNM, 3023, f. 328. Soconusco cacao was preferred in Spain but Guatemalans preferred that of Zapotitlán (Batres Jáuregui, *La América Central*, vol. 1, p. 280). The cheap, abundant, bitter-tasting Guayaquil cacao was drunk by the lower classes in the seventeenth century. See Arcila Farias, *Comercio*, pp. 42-43. Guayaquil cacao was not liked in Mexico. See, *Actas de Cabildo de México*, vol. 26, p. 343. In 1636, for example, the cabildo ranked Guatemalan cacao higher than that of Venezuela, with the Guayaquil product a poor third. See *Actas de Cabildo de México*, vol. 30, p. 201. An 1827 rating of cacao from the Indies, was (1) Soconusco, Maracaibo, Magdalena; (2) Caracas, Occana [sic], Trinidad; (3) Guayaquil; (4) Surinam; (5) Marañon, Pará; (6) Antilles; (7) Bourbon, Martinique, Cuba, and Bahia. (Gallais, *Monographie du Cacao*, p. 103.) The Central American "Criollo" variety is still considered superior, but is disappearing before hardier, more commercial types. See Cheesman, "Notes on Nomenclature," 145; Bergman, "Cacao," 43, 49.

21. One of the few references to Venezuelan cacao as a competitor is vecinos of Santiago to the Crown, May 1, 1709, AGI/AG 279. There was little or no cacao in Venezuela in the 1570s. See Cortés, *Antología*, especially pp. 50-68. Small exports were leaving La Guaira for Spain as early as 1607. See Arcila Farias, *Economía Colonial*, pp. 88-90. Cacao opened the trade between La Guaira and Veracruz, which flourished from about 1622. (Arcila Farias, *Comercio*, pp. 51-52). See also Robles, *Diario*, vol. 1, pp. 3, 213; vol. 2, pp. 121, 180, 229, 246; vol. 3, pp. 11, 34. For the

Curaçao trade with Venezuela, see García Payón, *Amaxocoatl,* pp. 77-78, 89; Gallais, *Monographie du Cacao,* p. 100. By mid-seventeenth century a wealthy class known as the grandes cacaos dominated the Creole aristocracy of Venezuela. See Morón, *A History of Venezuela,* p. 59.

22. There was no cacao there in the 1580s. (Acosta, *Historia,* p. 286.) But by 1590 heavy planting had started, and by the second decade of the seventeenth century the groves were flourishing. See Vázquez de Espinosa, *Compendium,* pp. 371-73; González Suárez, *Historia General,* vol. 4, pp. 101-3; León Borja and Szaszdi Nagy, "El Comercio del Cacao," 5-6.

23. González Suárez, *Historia General,* vol. 4, p. 101; *Actas de Cabildo de México,* vol. 26, p. 423. For Guayaquil in the late seventeenth century, see Raveneau de Lussan, *Journal of a Voyage,* pp. 206-11; Dampier, *Dampier's Voyages,* vol. 2, pp. 174-75; León Borja and Szaszdi Nagy, "El Comercio del Cacao," 11-14, 24.

24. Governor to the Crown, April 30, 1622, AGI/AG 40; *Actas de Cabildo de México,* vol. 26, p. 343. Cacao began to figure in Acapulco's import figures in 1617, although some probably arrived as early as the last years of the sixteenth century. After 1622 the trade to Acapulco became important, driving out imports from Sonsonate-Acajutla. See Chaunu, *Les Philippines,* pp. 64, 229, 239.

25. Rubio, "El Cacao," pp. 99-102; Pardo, *Efemérides,* pp. 51, 95, 96, 136; Borah, *Early Colonial Trade,* p. 127; AGGG, A3.6, 39548, 2748 (1629); AGGG, A1.23, legajo 4593, ff. 125-26 (July 28, 1695). Venezuelan interests also fought to have Guayaquil cacao banned because it flooded the Mexican market and thus lowered prices. See Arcila Farias, *Economía Colonial,* pp. 92-94.

26. Chart from Arcila Farias, *Comercio,* p. 78. For routes, methods, and supplies, see AGGG, A3.6, 39548, 2748 (1629); AGGG, A3.6, 10209, 1565, f. 222 (1677); AGGG, A1.23, legajo 1522, f. 6 (March 3, 1681); Francisco Sarassa to the Crown, January 6, 1683, AGI/AG 28; AGGG, A1.23, legajo 1522, f. 229 (December 16, 1687); Robles, *Diario,* vol. 2, pp. 114, 228, 229, 240, 284, 289, 295, 300, 311; vol. 3, pp. 9, 13; *Isagoge,* p. 394; Dampier, *Dampier's Voyages,* vol. 2, pp. 174-75; León Borja and Szaszdi Nagy, "El Comercio del Cacao," pp. 10, 13-14.

27. The monopolistic attempt in Guatemala is in AGGG, A3.6, 39548, 2748 (1627-29). The size of the Guayaquil shipments can be judged from the claims of Venezuelan merchants that they sometimes found as much as 100,000 fanegas from Guayaquil in Mexico when their yearly shipments were only about one quarter as large. (Arcila Farias, *Economía Colonial,* p. 93.) For royal officials' involvements, fines, bribes, confiscations, etc., see AGGG, A3.34, 41771, 2869 (1646); AGGG, A1.23, legajo 1522, ff. 229, 231 (December 16, 1687); Francisco Sarassa to Crown, January 6, 1683, AGI/AG 28. Above all, see the various piezas on this subject, in AGI/AG 279.

28. Fernández de Oviedo, *Historia,* vol. 2, p. 247; Sahagún, *Historia General,* vol. 3, p. 54; Millon, "When Money Grew on Trees," pp. 159, 203-12, 218; pieza 23, ff. 1-2, August 5, 1629, AGI/AG 43, which says, "the greatest harm which it does [i.e., Guayaquil cacao] is that those who bring it or buy it, mix it with the local [cacao] to defraud and harm the vecinos and their health." For similar fraud in Mexico, see *Actas de Cabildo de México,* vol. 26, p. 346.

29. Pieza 23, August 5, 1629, AGI/AG 43.

30. Clero of Nicaragua to the Crown, June 15, 1579; Cabildo of León to the Crown, July 12, 1579, both in AGI/AG 43. See also Villa of Realejo to Crown, July 11, 1579, ff. 1-1v., AGI/AG 44.

31. For the characteristics of the smuggling port of Realejo see Radell and Parsons, "Realejo—A Forgotten Colonial Port." (This article had not yet been published when these notes were revised. The author saw a manuscript copy of the article). See also Findley, *A Directory for Navigation,* vol. 1, pp. 236-44, vol. 2, pp. 1198-99. The lengthy proceedings outlined in the text are all contained in pieza 23, AGI/AG 43. See also CDIU, 17:224-25; UT, G19, f. 154 (January 23, 1644).

32. For internal problems in Nicaragua see Bishop of Nicaragua to the Crown, July 14, 1647, f. 2v., AGI/AG 162; AGGG, A1.23, legajo 1517, f. 162 (August 20, 1648); Salvatierra, *Contribución,* vol. 1, p. 323.

33. Heiser, "Cultivated Plants and Cultural Diffusion," 933; Gage, *The English-American,* pp. 168, 238, 241. For medicinal uses before and after the conquest see *Ritual of the Bacabs,* p. 10, and Sahagún, *Historia General,* vol. 3, p. 228.

34. Vázquez de Espinosa, *Compendium,* p. 238; De Chélus, *Histoire Naturelle,* p. 98. It had been used in the East for centuries as an orange-red dye for silk in spite of its fugitive nature, but this use was declining by the seventeenth century. See Leggett, *Ancient and Medieval Dyes,* p. 60.

35. BNM, 3047, f. 132 (1646); BNM, 12022, f. 9v. (1665); AGGG, A3.6, 24415, 1471 (1716); FG, 2:101; Vázquez de Espinosa, *Compendium,* pp. 227, 238; Gage, *The English-American,* pp. 168, 210, 224-25. Brazil also produced this dye (Leggett, *Ancient and Medieval Dyes,* p. 61). For some incomprehensible reason this inferior dye remained popular in England well into the eighteenth century. Small quantities found their way there for many years. See Fairlie, "Dyestuffs in the Eighteenth Century," 492, 499.

36. Bruman, "Culture History of Vanilla," 360-76; Heiser, "Cultivated Plants," p. 933.

37. BNM, 3047, f. 130; FX, 1:61; Bruman, "Culture History of Vanilla," pp. 366-67; Peralta, *Costa-Rica y Colombia,* pp. 68-69; Gage, *The English-American,* pp. 204-5.

38. A good description of vanilla planting in cacao plantations, is FG, 2:100, 260.

39. Bruman, "Culture History of Vanilla," pp. 367-68.

Chapter 13

1. ANHH, paquete 1, legajo 68 (1652). Other cases of trickery and fraud against Indians are numerous in the ANHH. As late as the middle of the eighteenth century there were complaints that Indians who discovered mines were persecuted and tricked. See BPR, Miscelanea de Ayala X, f. 176v.

2. ANHH, paquete 2, legajo 78 (1673), no. 22; ANHH, paquete 3, legajo 139 (1681); ANHH, paquete 1, legajo 30 (1647); "Memoria al rey del visitador de Honduras, [n.d., 1582?], AGI/AG 56; AGGG, A1.23, legajo 4581, f. 187 (1652). In the adjacent jurisdiction of Nueva Segovia in Nicaragua offenses were similar. E.g., AGGG, A1.24, 10115, 1581, f. 210 (May 18, 1716). For Costa Rican offenses see, ANCR, Cartago 027, f. 28 (July 6, 1583).

3. ANHH, paquete 6, legajo 52 (1722).

4. AGGG, A1.23, legajo 4586, f. 217 (August 19, 1695). At least twice the Crown ordered unused mercury surpluses to be sent to Mexico. See AGGG, A1.23, legajo 1520, f. 115 (February 8, 1674); García Peláez, *Memorias,* vol. 2, p. 139. On one occasion, before the mining industry had declined so greatly, 30 quintals of mercury were brought from New Spain to Tegucigalpa to help the flagging industry. Conde de la Gómera to Crown, December 31, 1617, AGI/AG 13.

5. The real cédula can be found in ANCR, Cartago 1074 (December 23, 1633). The cédula itself is dated May 28, 1632.

6. See Chapter Fifteen on the currency crisis. In a more local context, see AGGG, A1.23, legajo 4581, f. 187 (1652).

7. Examples of these astonished visitadores are BNM, 3025, ff. 46-47v., (1646); ANHH, paquete 1, legajo 80 (1655); ANHH, paquete 4, legajo 110 (1687). See also the two general visitas cited below.

8. ANHH, paquete 2, legajo 77 (1673). Accusations resulting from this visita dragged on for several years. E.g., "El Sn. Fiscal con D^n. Fernando Alfonso de Salvatierra, Alcalde Mayor del R^1 y Minas de Teguzipalpa [sic] sře fraudes y ocultaz ^{nes} en los R^1 Quintos," 4 piezas, "Corte," 1677, AGI Escribanía de Cámara 336. (This case was still unresolved in 1682).

9. ANHH, paquete 2, legajo 77 (1673). Another brief reform movement of the same kind took place in 1683 as a result of pressure on the alcalde mayor by higher authorities. See ANHH, paquete 4, legajo 62 (1683).

10. The visita to the Corpus settlements is contained in a lengthy legajo, AGI /AG 283. See also, on this series of events, AGGG, A1.27, 10422, 1711 (1695), and García Peláez, *Memorias*, vol. 3, p. 25. The prohibitions seemed to worry nobody. In 1692 José Coello Negrón, a priest, sued José Araujo for the recovery of a smelter; he intended to work it and said so quite openly. ANHH, paquete 5, legajo 10 (1692). Theft of gold at the Corpus mine and fraud over Peruvian mercury landed at the port of Realejo were two of the main issues in the uproar caused by the visita to Santiago de Guatemala by Francisco Gómez de la Madrid in 1700. See FX, 3:171-3, 197; UT, G19, f. 259v.

11. West, "The Mining Economy of Honduras," 772. Repeated requests for 300 to 500 negro slaves brought no response. E.g., Bishop of Honduras to the Crown, April 20, 1584, AGI/AG 164; Juan Cisneros de Reynoso to the Crown, February 17, 1581, AGI/AG 55; Cabildo of Valladolid (Comayagua), April 4, 1576, AGI/AG 43.

12. AGGG, A1.23, legajo 1514, f. 130 (May 26, 1609).

13. West, "The Mining Economy of Honduras," p. 772; "Una Memoria" (1585?), AGI/AG 56, places the number at about 800 tributaries.

14. CS, 13: 486-87 (July 5, 1546); Pardo, *Efemérides,* p. 36 (November 27, 1602).

15. AGGG, A1.23-1, 10189, 1553 (November 27, 1602).

16. AGGG, A1.23, legajo 1514, f. 33v. (November 24, 1602).

17. West, "The Mining Economy of Honduras," p. 772.

18. ANHH, paquete 2, legajo 77, diligencia 1, "Providencia del Capitán General Don Francisco de Escobedo para que se obligase a los indios de Texiguat a vivir en poblado," (1673); ANHH, paquete 5, legajo 68 (1698); ANHH, paquete 6, legajo 40 (1712). Indian dislike of mine work can be judged from a petition from the village of Chiantla in 1689 asking the authorities not to permit the establishment of a smelter there because of the "great harm" which it would do to the inhabitants. AGGG, A1.21-8, 46972, 5470 (1689).

19. ANHH, paquete 6, legajo 21 (1708).

20. AGGG, A1.23, legajo 1518, f. 115 (1654). See also BNM, 3035, f. 47v. Miners were still requesting Indians from Gracias a Dios and San Miguel in the mid-eighteenth century. BPR, Miscelanea de Ayala X, f. 177.

21. ANHH, paquete 5, legajo 66 (1698); "Relación de las minas que ay en la provy^a de Onduras," ff. 17-17v. (August 24, 1590), RAH, 11-4-4-854. For repartimiento at the beginning of the eighteenth century, see FG, 2:364; ANHH, paquete 6, legajo 21 (1708). A new repartimiento was made to a Spaniard for gold panning in Costa Rica in 1681. See ANCR Cartago 064, (April 10, 1681).

22. For gold mining in the Nueva Segovia region after 1570, see CDIU, 17:212; President Villalobos to the Crown, May 15, 1573, AGI/AG 9; AGGG, A1.23, legajo 4588, f. 110 (January 18, 1589). For the squabbles between Tegucigalpa and Nueva Segovia over escaped debt peons, see ANHH, paquete 3, legajos 104 and 106 (both 1679).

23. A typical year is 1683. Among the new mines registered were, ANHH, paquete 4, legajos 64, 66-70, 75, 79 (all 1683). See also ANHH, paquete 6, legajo 8 (1702).

24. ANHH, paquete 18, legajo 1 (1700); ANHH, paquete 6, legajos 38-39, 44 (all 1712).

25. "Petición que no se den minas a los Guirises que arruinaban esas minas," ANHH, paquete 3, legajo 146 (1681); West, "The Mining Economy of Honduras," p. 774.

26. Fuentes y Guzmán accused the "gurguses" of defrauding the Crown of the quinto, and called them "adventurers," FG, 2:362, 364. See also West, "The Mining Economy of Honduras," p. 774; ANHH, paquete 4, legajo 67 (1684).

27. AGGG, A1.23, legajo 4625, f. 175 (1762); West, "The Mining Economy of Honduras," p. 772.

28. West, "The Mining Economy of Honduras," p. 774; "Relación de las minas que ay en la provyᵃ de Onduras," f. 15 (August 24, 1590), RAH, 11-4-4-854. See AGGG, A1.23, legajo 4588, f. 110 (January 18, 1589), which is about two ranches near Nueva Segovia started specifically to feed miners near the village of Mozontle.

29. García Peláez, *Memorias,* vol. 3, p. 25. Cases of lawlessness in the ANHH are numerous. E.g., ANHH, paquete 1, legajo 47 (1648); ANHH, paquete 1, legajo 46 (1649); ANHH, paquete 2, legajo 67 (1672); ANHH, paquete 5, legajo 2 (1681); ANHH, paquete 5, legajo 61 (1697).

Chapter 14

1. ANCR Complementario colonial 5316, f. 2 (July 25, 1534).

2. For early imports of Peruvian wine, see Oficial Real of Sonsonate to the Crown, January 7, 1580, AGI/AG 50. See also López de Velasco, *Geografía,* p. 490; Vázquez de Espinosa, *Compendium,* p. 226; Acosta, *Historia,* pp. 203, 313-14. Gómera's letter, (November 14, 1611), is in AGI/AG 13. The argument about the noxious nature of Peruvian wine is similar to the one about Guayaquil cacao, and probably contained a similar mixture of truth and prejudice. See CDI, 17:219-22; 21:53-56 for this argument in Panama, and García Peláez, *Memorias,* vol. 2, p. 41.

3. Peruvian wine was banned in Panama in 1614, a year before Guatemala. See García Peláez, *Memorias,* vol. 2, pp. 40-43 for both decrees, and for other prohibitions. Lists of these prohibitions are also to be found in AGGG, A1.23, legajo 4578, f. 110 (May 18, 1615 and June 19, 1626); AGGG, A1.24, 10216, 1572, f. 341 (October 29, 1671).

4. "La provincia de Nicaragua en solicitud de q. se permitan entrar en ella los Vinos y Cacao del Peru," August 5, 1629, AGI/AG 43, pieza no. 23; CDIU, 17: 224-25. Realejo's large harbor became famous for its smuggling. See UT, G19, f. 154 (January 23, 1644); AGGG, A3.6, 39592, 2750 (1709); AGGG, A3.6, 24409, 1470 (1714). Other discussions of these issues are in, ecclesiastical cabildos of Comayagua and León to the Crown, May 29, 1709; Cabildo of San Miguel to the Crown, May 29, 1709, both in AGI/AG 279. A little wine did arrive from Cartagena at times. See ANCR Complementario colonial 0017, (1637).

5. See especially ANCR Guatemala 112 (October 24, 1679); ANCR Complementario colonial 3930 and 3947 (1693 and 1697). Also ANCR Guatemala 078 (April 27, 1636); ANCR Complementario colonial 3586 (January 16, 1643); pieza no. 5 (1704), AGI/AG 359; ANCR Cartago 151 (February 3, 1707); AGGG, A3.5, 1299, 67 (1712).

6. AGGG, A1.23, 39221, 4568, f. 5 (April 22, 1643); AGGG, A1.20, legajo 1490, ff. 39, 64 (March 23, 1646); García Peláez, *Memorias,* vol. 2, p. 46; AGGG, A1.2-7, 30495, 4007 (1673); AGGG, A1.23, legajo 1521, f. 157 (1679); AGGG, A1.2-5, 16283, 2247 (1716); Pardo, *Efemérides,* pp. 60, 90, 96, 98, 100.

7. The Consulado's case is found in "Expediente sobre el transporte y tráfico de vinos y acietes del Peru a la ciudad de Santᵍᵒ de Guatᵃ (1669–1718)," AGI/AG 279. The king's order on wine in the Honduras ships' cargoes is in AGGG, A1.23,

legajo 1520, f. 95 (January 29, 1673). See also Pardo, *Efemérides,* p. 134; García Peláez, *Memorias,* vol. 2, pp. 42-43.

8. The results of trying to supply wine to the New World were not altogether happy in Spain either. See Elliott, *Imperial Spain,* p. 180. On frequency of fleet arrivals, see Pardo, *Efemérides,* pp. 67, 134; *Isagoge,* p. 396; AGGG, A1.20, legajo 1490, f. 64 (March 23, 1643).

9. "Expediente sobre el transporte y tráfico de vinos y acietes," AGI/AG 279; AGGG, A1.1, 5672, 256, f. 167 (May 21, 1685). A typical renewal is AGGG, A1.23, legajo 1524, f. 173 (November 23, 1704). See also *Isagoge,* p. 396; García Peláez, *Memorias,* vol. 2, pp. 46-47; Pardo, *Efemérides,* pp. 100, 119, 140-43; Larreinaga, *Prontuario,* p. 61. Resentment against Sevillian merchants is expressed in AGGG, A1.20, legajo 1490, f. 64 (March 23, 1646); various ecclesiastical authorities to the Crown, April 1, 1709, AGI/AG 279.

10. For wine taxes in 1685 see, AGGG, A1.24, 15753, 2198, f. 155 (May 21, 1685); *Isagoge,* p. 396. For smuggling, 1685-1713, see Chapter Twenty. See also, here, AGGG, A1.24, 10213, 1569, ff. 175, 226 (May 5-15, 1694); AGGG, A3.1, 32170, 2136 (1704); AGGG, A3.6, 8299, 403 (1709).

11. Arcila Farias, *Comercio entre Venezuela y México,* p. 253; Veitia Linaje, *Norte de la contratación,* pp. 99-100.

12. AGGG, A1.23, 39221, 4568, f. 5 (April 22, 1645); AGGG, A1.20, legajo 1490, f. 64 (March 23, 1646).

13. Peru's lack of interest in Central American products is explained in AGGG, A1.23, legajo 1521, f. 157 (1679). For wine confiscations and admissions, see AGGG, A1.23, legajo 1517, f. 59 (November 22, 1644); AGGG, A3.4, 41771, 2869 (1646); AGGG, A1.24, 10205, 1561, f. 128 (1655).

14. AGGG, A1.1, 5666, 256 (1643).

15. See Chapters Fifteen and Nineteen. Above all, see the perceptive remarks in Chaunu, *Les Philippines,* pp. 250-53, 256. (Chaunu sees seventeenth-century Spanish Pacific trade as going through much the same depression as the Spanish Atlantic trade. It begins about 1618-20, and reaches a low point probably between 1666 and 1670. The Pacific revival, however, was inexplicably earlier, and more rapid between 1680 and 1740).

16. Pardo, *Efemérides,* pp. 78-79; AGGG, A1.23, legajo 1519, f. 148 (January 12, 1667); AGGG, A1.23, legajo 1520, f. 8 (December 14, 1672); ANCR Cartago 1078, f. 195 (February 21, 1676).

17. AGGG, A1.23, legajo 4584, f. 269v. (March 29, 1678).

18. AGGG, A1.1, 18, 1 (1667); AGGG, A1.23, legajo 1520, f. 225 (February 29, 1676); AGGG, A1.24, 10209, 1565, f. 222 (1677); Oficial Real of Sonsonate to the Crown, January 7, 1680, AGI/AG 51. (There are several other similar reports in this legajo). AGGG, A1.24, 10213, 1569, f. 226 (May 15, 1694); AGGG, A3.6, 42074, 2885 (1705). In 1669 the president refused to grant a permit to land 500 botijas of "vinegar," and was praised for his action by the King, AGGG, A1.23, legajo 1579, f. 268 (November 10, 1670). See also AGGG, A3.6, 8299, 403 (1709). Officials petitioned to legalize the trade in 1678, AGGG, A1.23, legajo 1521, f. 157 (1679), but had to wait a few years for their request to be granted, AGGG, A1.2-4, 15753, 2198, f. 155 (May 21, 1685).

19. Robles, *Diario,* vol. 1, pp. 84, 199; vol. 2, pp. 153, 155, 288, 299, 304; vol. 3, pp. 11-14, 17; Ringrose, "The Dangerous Voyages," pp. 29-31, 139; Pardo, *Efemérides,* pp. 86, 102, 119, 134-36; AGGG, A1.23, legajo 4592, f. 172 (November 27, 1697); AGGG, A1.20, legajo 633, f. 213v. (October 30, 1682); AGGG, A3.9, 3026, 156, f. 24v. (1699).

20. For some price fluctuations, see especially the shopping lists in AGGG, A1.7-4, 12022, 1820 (1660). The price varied between 28 and 40 pesos in 1692 alone, AGGG, A1.11, 8539, 409 (1690-95).

21. Pardo, *Efemérides,* p. 88, is an attempt to regulate the price of Castillian wine. See also *ibid.,* p. 100.

22. AGGG, A3.39, 41715, 2874 (1682). For "hoarding" in Honduras see, ANHH, paquete 2, legajo 32 (1667).
23. FX, 2:265. See also Molina, *Antigua Guatemala,* p. 50.
24. Pardo, *Efemérides,* pp. 80-81.
25. See especially the long document numbered AGGG, A1.1, 21, 1 (1691–?). See also "Testimonio de los Autos que el ss^or Presidente D^n Lope de Sierra Osorio Fulmino....," ff. 317-335v., AGI/AG 279; Arcila Farias, *Comercio,* p. 254. The case against the three Basques is in AGGG, A3.39, 41715, 2874 (1682).
26. "Expediente sobre el transporte y tráfico de vinos y acietes," AGI/AG 279. (This expediente covers most of the years between 1669 and 1718). Some sarcastic remarks about smuggling can be found in pieza 5 (April 15, 1676), f. 1, in the same legajo, AGI/AG 279.
27. Larreinaga, *Prontuario,* p. 280.
28. AGGG, A3.2, 19451, 1074 (1644); AGGG, A1.11, 8533, 409 (1661); AGGG, A1.1, 5672, 256, ff. 13-14v., 20v., 23 (1683); AGGG, A1.11, 6756, 328 (1688); AGGG, A3.24, 32031, 2118 (1692); AGGG, A1.11, 72, 4 (1717), which last contains a full list of all the religious institutions in Santiago at that time, and their requirements in wine. The seizure of the Spanish cargo is in AGGG, A3.2, 19458, 1074. For a total lack of wine for mass, see for example Cabildo of San Vicente de Austria to the Crown, March 20, 1709, AGI/AG 279.
29. BNM, 200.054^15 (July 20, 1710).
30. E.g., AGGG, A1.1, 72, 4, f. 6 (1717).
31. "Expediente sobre el transporte y tráfico de vinos y aceites" (1669–1718), AGI/AG 279; Larreinaga, *Prontuario,* p. 283.
32. BNM, 3047, f. 133v.; BM, Additional Ms. 13977, f. 77; CDIE, 57:478.
33. Vázquez de Espinosa, *Compendium,* p. 242; BNM, 3023, f. 328.
34. FG, 2:134; ANCR Cartago 037 (January 13, 1653); ANCR Cartago 077 (January 13, 1653); ANCR Complementario colonial (January 4, 1656); Peralta, *Costa-Rica y Colombia,* pp. 62, 72; AGGG, A3.1, 14842, 803 (1706). Cockburn, *The Unfortunate Englishman,* p. 75, describes the route from Nicaragua to Costa Rica.
35. CDHCR, 5:154; ANCR Cartago 002 (February 14, 1630); Juan Francisco Sáenz to Crown, May 20, 1675, AGI/AG 39; ANCR Complementario colonial 3904 (February 19, 1680); ANCR Cartago 083 (March 26, 1691), ff. 6, 10-13v.; ANCR Complementario colonial 6023 (1-80-85), ff. 18, 29.
36. CDHCR, 5:163, 247-49, 293, 476-96; 8:254, 257, 462. As late as 1680 Spaniards were still fighting recalcitrant Indians in Chiriquí and driving them off the mule road, ANCR Complementario colonial 5225 (December 31, 1680).
37. Peralta, *Costa-Rica y Colombia,* pp. 642-43 (1591); CDHCR, 5:154; ANCR Cartago 014 (June 3, 1638); ANCR Guatemala 083 (July 15, 1638); ANCR Cartago 022 (November 25, 1638); Chaunu and Chaunu, *Séville et l'Atlantique,* 8^1:891-92; CDHCR, 5:247-49, 290-91, 337, 363, 479-81; 8:293-94, 495; 9:144, 148; García Peláez, *Memorias,* vol. 3, pp. 31-32. For Realejo exports, see Pardo, *Efemérides,* p. 114; AGGG, A3.6, 2187, 119 (1713). For Chiriquí and Nicoya exports, see Cockburn, *Unfortunate Englishman,* pp. 54, 107; BNM, 2468, ff. 88-97.
38. CDHCR, 5:350; 8:348, 382, 407, 441. See, for example, the cargoes of ships plying between Peru and Panama as noted by pirates who seized these ships in the 1680s. E.g., Burney, *History of the Buccaneers,* pp. 135, 167, 191, 201, 330; Dampier, *Dampier's Voyages,* vol. 1, pp. 125, 166, 216. For other details, see ANCR, Cartago 081 (January 26, 1691); ANCR Cartago 090 (January 23, 1694); ANCR Guatemala 129 (August 20, 1703), f. 1; ANCR Guatemala 142 (June 30, 1709).
39. Fernández de Oviedo, *Historia,* vol. 11, p. 189; FX, 1:60; 2:380; Molina, *Antigua Guatemala,* p. 134; Peralta, *Costa-Rica y Colombia,* p. 31; AGGG, A1.24, 10225, 1581, f. 285 (1714); Cockburn, *Unfortunate Englishman,* p. 51.
40. Fernández de Oviedo, *Historia,* vol. 11, p. 189; FX, 1:60; ANCR Guatemala 132 (April 24, 1704); Gerhard, "Shellfish Dye in America," 177-83; Peralta, *Costa-Rica y Colombia,* pp. 125-26; Jinesta, "Las industrias del añil," 302-5; Fernández

Guardia, "La sublevación de los indios de Nicoya en 1760," 363-66. (There was also unrest in 1721 and 1753.)

41. Fernández de Oviedo, *Historia,* vol. 2, pp. 57, 270; vol. 11, p. 192; CS, 1:130; AGI Patronato, 183-1-16, ff. 16-17; Dampier, *Dampier's Voyages,* vol. 1, p. 242. (See map of Realejo.)

42. Vázquez de Espinosa, *Compendium,* pp. 249-50; López de Velasco, *Geografía,* pp. 301, 327; *Relaciones históricas y geográficas de América Central,* p. 468; ANCR Complementario colonial 5305, f. 9 (1564); AGGG, A1.23, legajo 1513, f. 565 (1579); Peralta, *Costa-Rica, Nicaragua y Panamá,* pp. 525-26, 596, 618-19, 624-25; Villa of Realejo to the Crown, July 11, 1597, f. 1v., AGI/AG 44; ANCR Complementario colonial 5203, ff. 10v.-11 (January 23, 1620). Nicoya was also a shipbuilding center from time to time. E.g., AGGG, A1.23, legajo 1514, f. 62 (1604); Dampier, *Dampier's Voyages,* vol. 1, pp. 139-60; BM, Sloane 49, f. 41.

43. Reduced quantities of naval stores and other agricultural produce did continue to go to Peru throughout the seventeenth century. E.g., ANCR Cartago 049 (January 8, 1677). For Realejo's decline in mid-century, see the aforementioned expediente on wine smuggling in AGI/AG 279. The King's efforts to stimulate and revive these industries can be seen in AGGG, A1.23, legajo 1515, f. 145 (1626).

44. AGI Patronato 183-1-16, ff. 16-16v.; Vázquez de Espinosa, *Compendium,* pp. 244-46; BNM, 3178, f. 206; BNM, 2468, ff. 100-101v. (This document dates from the 1630s.) See also Denevan, *The Upland Pine Forests of Nicaragua,* 258, 275-77, 279, 298-300. See also the maps on pp. 252, 257. Some pitch also went to the Caribbean via Granada and the Desaguadero. E.g., ANCR, Complementario colonial 5203, f. 3v. (1620).

45. Vázquez de Espinosa, *Compendium,* pp. 244-46. He described the area as "over 50 leagues of thick pine forests." Another source mentions 100 leagues of pines (BM, Additional Mss., 13977, ff. 77-77v.). For additional information consult AGGG, A1.24, 10201, 1557, f. 196 (September 9, 1633). For Vázquez de Espinosa's comments on the vineyards of Peru see the *Compendium,* pp. 453, 483-84, 498-99. Huatulco also sent some pitch to Peru at this early stage, *ibid.,* p. 180.

46. Vázquez de Espinosa, *Compendium,* pp. 251, 484. Note, however, the different set of figures on p. 499, which, while giving lower prices, would arrive at even higher profit percentages.

47. Bishop of Nicaragua to the Crown, July 14, 1647, AGI/AG 162.

48. Fr. Abreu to the Conde de Castrillo (1648), AGI/AG 2. See also the Consejo's report to the Crown on this document in "Seen in Consejo," November 10, 1648, AGI/AG 2. See also AGGG, A1.23, legajo 1517, f. 171 (December 2, 1648).

49. ANCR, Complementario colonial 5307 (March 8, 1663 and November 25, 1663).

50. AGGG, A1.24, 10209, 1565, f. 232 (November 17, 1677). García Peláez, *Memorias,* vol. 2, p. 227, mentions the corregidor of Sebaco as involved in the trade.

51. ANHH, paquete 3, legajo 23 (1676); ANHH, paquete 3, legajo 104 (1679); ANHH, paquete 3, legajo 106 (1679).

52. Bishop of Nicaragua to the Crown, December 19, 1680, AGI/AG 2, mentions that ships had not called for two years. AGGG, A1.60, 45344, 5364 (1688) finds the ayuntamiento of León blaming the pirates for destroying the brea industry in Nueva Segovia, and thus tribute collection and royal income in Nueva Segovia. The ayuntamiento urges the Captain General to provide protection. Yet some brea and other shipstores were still being shipped from Realejo to Guayaquil in the mid-eighteenth century. See, Flores y Caamaño, *Relación,* p. 2.

53. A revival in shipbuilding took place at the close of the century. E.g., "Seen in Council," June 26, 1698, AGI/AG 4; AGGG, A3.6, 39578, 2750 (1692); AGGG, A3.6, 39588, 2750 (1705); AGGG, A1.24, 10222, 1578, f. 238 (1711).

54. For beginnings, see Alonso de Arteaga to the Crown, May 15, 1555, AGI/AG 50. The Desaguadero trade, mostly agricultural produce, was still flourishing in 1604 (AGGG, A1.23, legajo 1514, f. 62 (1604); Chaunu and Chaunu, *Séville et*

l'Atlantique, 7:110). For the eighteenth century revival, see AGGG, A3.6, 24401, 1470 (1713), which shows a heavy rate of contraband.

Chapter 15

1. Zelaya, "Apuntes para la historia de la moneda en Honduras," 55-58; Lazo, "Historia de la moneda," 37-38; Borah, *Early Colonial Trade;* Haring, *The Spanish Empire in America,* pp. 289-92; *Isagoge,* p. 372.

2. For a discussion of the problem in Mexico, see Borah, *Early Trade,* pp. 83-84; Batres Jáuregui, *La América Central,* vol. 1, pp. 405-6.

3. AGGG, A3.1, 38942, 2716 (1652); Pardo, *Efemérides,* p. 63; Chevalier, *La formation des grands domaines au Mexique,* p. 136; Batres, *La América Central,* vol. 1, pp. 405-6.

4. Borah, *Early Trade,* p. 93. See especially Audiencia to the Crown, "tocante a los diezmos," September 7, 1666, AGI/AG 22, in which it is stated that money which used to come from Peru was lacking. The ships that used to bring silver are bringing wine and cacao, and as a result there is little silver coinage left in the area.

5. On the disappearance of small coinage, and its replacement by cacao, see AGGG, A1.23, legajo 1517, f. 162 (August 20, 1648); Molina, *Antigua Guatemala,* p. 30.

6. Lazo, "Historia de la moneda," p. 37; AGGG, A1.23, legajo 4581, f. 187 (1652); ANHH, paquete 3, legajo 139 (1681); Vallejo, *Guía de agrimensores,* p. 33. For similar devaluation in Lima and Quito in 1652 and 1656-57, see Herrera, "Apuntamientos de algunos sucesos," pp. 61, 63. (Further proof of Central America's having closer economic ties to Peru than to Mexico).

7. Pardo, *Efemérides,* pp. 61-63; FX, 3:285; Molina, *Antigua Guatemala,* p. 78. At first the royal order declared that the peso of 8 reales from Peru was to be devalued to 5 reales, but this severity was soon relaxed and changed to 6. See AGGG, A3.1, 38942, 2716 (1652).

8. AGGG, A3.1, 38942, 2716, ff. 1-2 (1652).

9. *Ibid.*

10. *Ibid.,* especially f. 25.

11. *Ibid.,* ff. 25v.-26, 31v., 44, 49, 64, 105, 117-19; AGGG, A3.1, 10, 1 (1660). The seventeenth-century Guatemalans were not the first from that area to have suffered from false or debased Peruvian coinage. Pedro de Alvarado complained in 1536 that the payment which he received from Diego de Almagro contained more copper than silver, and that he lost over 50 per cent as a result. Thus adulteration of Peruvian silver may antedate the conquest. *Libro viejo de la Fundación de Guatemala,* p. 313.

12. FX, 2:285; Molina, *Antigua Guatemala,* pp. 78-79, 82.

13. Pardo, *Efemérides,* pp. 63-65, 70; FX, 2:285; AGGG, A1.23, 39235, 4569, ff. 2v., 8 (1661).

14. AGGG, A3.10, 39898, 2766 (October 12, 1665); AGGG, A1.23, 39235, 4569 (August 1, 1661); AGGG, A3.1, 11, 1 (1661); Molina, *Antigua Guatemala,* p. 79.

15. Molina, *Antigua Guatemala,* p. 79; Pardo, *Efemérides,* p. 93.

16. Cabildo of San Miguel to the Crown, March 12, 1709; Cabildo of Santiago to the Crown, March 9, 1709, both in AGI/AG 279; Pardo, *Efemérides,* pp. 134, 153, 156, 166; *Isagoge,* p. 397. For smuggling of silver into Realejo see, AGGG, A1.23, legajo 1524, f. 276 (October 26, 1707).

Chapter 16

1. See especially the "Libro de copias de cartas que el Cavildo y el regimiento desta Muy Noble y Leal Ciudad de Santiago de Guathemala Escrive," in AGGG, A1.2-5, 15768, 2208 (1650-73). Four of the ten petitions extant for 1650-60 were made by widows of beneméritos. See also *Boletín del Archivo General del Gobierno,* vol. 2, no. 1 (October 1936), 3-19.

2. These figures are from a rapid count of grants in the AGGG under the asignatura A3.16. (Most of the expedientes are numbered in the 40,700s, the legajos in the 2,800s.) As a pension system the encomienda was unreliable. In the following cases widows were unable to collect the tribute and appealed to the authorities to do so. AGGG, A3.16, 19125, 1050 (1652); AGGG, A3.16, 40711, 2811 (1691); AGGG, A3.16, 40728, 2811 (1698); AGGG, A3.2, 13097, 706 (1701).

3. E.g. AGGG, A3.16, 40541, 2804 (1630); AGGG, A3.16, 40662, 2809 (n.d., 1640?); AGGG, A1.1, 42, 2 (1706); García Peláez, *Memorias,* vol. 2, p. 6.

4. AGGG, A3.16, 26375, 1600 (1634); Pardo, *Efemérides,* pp. 69, 103. See the slow increase in this practice between 1630 and 1670, in AGGG, A3.16, 40581, 2805 (1640); ANCR Cartago 071 (April 27, 1683).

5. Simpson, "A Seventeenth-Century Encomienda," pp. 393-402. For another imprisonment of a cacique for arrears of tribute, see AGGG, A1.15, 50062, 5905 (1641). For other cases of severe arrears in tribute, see for example AGGG, A3.16, 40569, 2805 (1645); AGGG, A3.16, 19125, 1050 (1652); AGGG, A1.24, 10206, 1562, f. 15 (1658). See also ANCR Complementario colonial 2280 (January 30, 1641).

6. Simpson, "A Seventeenth-Century Encomienda," p. 402. For taxation and other exactions imposed on the encomiendas, see for example ANCR Cartago 071 (April 27, 1638); AGGG, A1.2-5, 15768, 2208, f. 1 (May 27, 1650); AGGG, A1.23, legajo 1518, f. 212 (March 17, 1657); AGGG, A1.23, legajo 4586, f. 126 (September 17, 1690); Konetzke, ed., *Colección de documentos,* 2²:75-76. There are over 100 cases in the AGGG in which Indian villages request and obtain remission of tribute so as to build a church, recover from an epidemic, etc. Of course, if an individual could accumulate a number of encomiendas it might be a fairly worthwhile proposition, in spite of the many encumbrances. E.g., AGGG, A1.1, 25, 2 (1688).

7. Crown to the Audiencia of Guatemala, February 4, 1630; "Seen in Council," September 3, 1653, both in AGI/AG 43; Cabildo of Ciudad Real de Chiapas to the Crown, "Seen in Council," December 12, 1630, AGI/AG 44; AGGG, A3.12, 40048, 2774 (1640); AGGG, A3.16, 40593, 2805 (1642). See also the complaint from the corregidor of Nicoya, in ANCR Complementario colonial 5381 (June 28, 1642).

8. See note 2 above. In the last two or three years of the century many encomiendas began to fall vacant, and there were few applicants to fill them; they had ceased to be of value to anyone. See AGGG, A1.1, 5040, 212, especially ff. 117-122v., 129-136v., 173-175v., 177-179v. Encomiendas were not abolished until 1787. See Larreinaga, *Prontuario,* p. 111.

9. AGGG, A3.12, 40031, 2774 (1631); Konetzke, *Colección de documentos,* 2²:500, 570; Pardo, *Efemérides,* pp. 51-54; AGGG, A1.24, 10209, 1565, f. 156 (May 8, 1677); AGGG, A3.12, 40093, 2775 (1683); AGGG, A1.23, legajo 1522, f. 233 (December 19, 1687); ANCR Complementario colonial 5227 (February 20, 1690); AGGG, A1. 22.20, 45405, 5368 (1705). For modern repartimiento see Oakes, *The Two Crosses,* p. 38.

10. AGGG, A1.24, 1557, 125 (April 30, 1655) (San Miguel); AGGG, A1.23, legajo 1519, f. 162 (October 25, 1667); AGGG, A3.16, 34243, 2319 (1685); AGGG, A1.23, legajo 1522, f. 236 (December 19, 1687); AGGG, A1.9, 31178, 4042 (1693); AGGG, A3.12, 3984, 223 (1703); Pardo, *Efemérides,* p. 129; García Peláez, *Memorias,* vol. 1, pp. 226-27. On a few occasions Indian macehuales were exempted from

the draft for other tasks such as repairing the village church. E.g. AGGG, A3.12, 42184, 2886 (1672); AGGG, A3.12; 223, 3982 (1701).

11. Gage, *The English-American*, p. 233.

12. AGGG, A1.23, legajo 1519, f. 162 (1667), shows that the King was aware of this subterfuge.

13. FG, 3:306. For the large sums of money which passed through the hands of such an individual, see Larreinaga, *Prontuario*, p. 340. The King was aware of the graft involved and tried to abolish the position several times. E.g., AGGG, A1.23, legajo 1516, f. 20 (October 8, 1631); AGGG, A1.23, legajo 1517, f. 3 (March 25, 1641). (In this document it appears that the job was so lucrative in San Salvador that the local alcalde mayor managed to persuade the Crown to assign it to him.)

14. Zavala, *Contribución*, pp. 103-8. See also the real cédula of September 29, 1662, in which the King complains that the rights to repartimiento Indians are sold as part of the "good will" of some haciendas. He goes on to say that the importance of repartimiento is unfortunately far greater in Guatemala than in New Spain or Peru. See, Konetzke, *Colección de documentos*, 2²:500.

15. Audiencia to the Crown, May 3, 1681, AGI/AG 27; AGGG, A3.12, 3986, 223, f. 21 (July 30, 1693); Pardo, *Efemérides*, p. 136. As late as 1703 much of the village population of Totonicapán was recruited to build a road to the Petén, AGGG, A1.22-23, 26645, 2891 (1703). For complaints against high drafts near Granada, see AGGG, A1.15, 32705, 4126 (1695). Apparent attempts to abolish parts of the repartimiento system took place in the 1660s. See AGGG, A1.23, legajo 1519, f. 162 (October 25, 1669); Pardo, *Efemérides*, p. 72; Cabildo of San Salvador to the Crown, January 12, 1669, and *ibid.* to *ibid.*, June 18, 1670, both in AGI/AG 43. See also AGGG, A1.23, 10216, 1572, f. 337 (October 29, 1671). For the repartimiento in Cartago, known locally as the alquilón, see CDHCR, 5:298-99.

16. AGGG, A1.20-11, 53847, 6059, ff. 20v.-23 (1656); AGGG, A1.24, 10207, 1563, f. 104 (July 9, 1667); ANHH, paquete 3, legajos 104 and 106 (both 1679); AGGG, A1.20, 9974, 1497, ff. 4v.-5 (1687). Even ladinos and castas became increasingly subject to assignment to a creditor's house or estate until their debt was worked off. E.g., ANHH, paquete 2, legajo 10 (1661). See also ANHH, paquete 2, legajo 2 (1664).

17. Some of the few are, AGGG, A1.24, 10219, 1575, f. 45 (August 18, 1706), and AGGG, A1.23, legajo 1517, f. 3 (March 25, 1641), which also repeats the prohibition against employing Indians in dye works. In 1647 the King showed annoyance at contrived jailings of Indians in Ciudad Real de Chiapas to get them into debt. See "Chiapas, Libro de acuerdos ordinarios, 1640-1649," ff. 194v.-197v., M -M 1888, Bancroft Library, University of California, Berkeley.

18. The determined and irascible bishop's character comes out well in BPR, Miscelanea de Ayala, 23, ff. 77-78v., 80-90v. (1687). See also AGGG, A1.23, legajo 1520, f. 71 (August 10, 1672); AGGG, A1.23, legajo 1521, f. 176 (August 2, 1679); AGGG, A1.1,23,2 (1687).

19. AGGG, A1.24, 54648, 6071 (1672); AGGG, A1.24, 10211, 1567, f. 167 (March 5, 1683). The insistance on the payment of tribute by peons could be quite strict, however. See ANCR Cartago 039 (March 2, 1653). Jailings for debts continued. See ANHH, paquete 5, legajo 81 (1698) where both a man and his servant were imprisoned for debt. Of course, in a few localities it was considered more important to have village labor than hacienda labor. The Tegucigalpa mines, for example, depended heavily on repartimiento workers, so Indians nearby were often forced to return to their villages, even from haciendas. See the various documents in ANHH, paquete 5, legajo 68 (1698). See also ANHH, paquete 4, legajo 138 (1689).

20. E.g., AGGG, A1.24, 10204, 1560, f. 72 (February 13, 1649); AGGG, A1.24, 10205, 1561, f. 104 (April 27, 1655); AGGG, A1.24, 54649, 6071 (1672); AGGG, A1.24, 54650, 6071 (1679).

21. E.g., AGGG, A3.6, 40531, 2803 (1626).

22. Gage, *The English-American,* pp. 172-74; AGGG, A1.23, legajo 4577, f. 37v. (August 19, 1631). See also AGGG, A1.24, legajo 1566, f. 233 (August 21, 1681).

23. AGGG, A1.24, 10208, 1564, f. 115 (January 8, 1672).

24. Pardo, *Efemérides,* p. 140.

25. *Ibid.,* pp. 70, 98.

26. ANCR Cartago 064 (April 10, 1681).

27. Larreinaga, *Prontuario,* pp. 268-69; AGGG, A1.23, legajo 1522, f. 153 (August 16, 1686).

28. AGGG, A1.2-5, 15768, 2208, f. 46 (March 18, 1671). See also the reference to the King's letter of enquiry in the same document.

29. Pardo, *Efemérides,* is a fairly reliable year-to-year account of major events in the seventeenth century. A careful reading clearly shows this mid-century gap.

30. ANCR Cartago 029 (December 29, 1639); ANCR Complementario colonial 3435 (November 9, 1682); Peralta, *Costa-Rica y Colombia,* p. 64; Thompson, "Sixteenth and Seventeenth Century Reports on the Chol Mayas," 593; FX, 2:405-7. The second expedition to the Petén made heavy demands on Guatemalan villagers for porters, mules, and foodstuffs. See AGGG, A1.11, 2033, 94, ff. 25-25v., 32-32v., 94-95 (1696). In the following document the village of Santa Olaya, near Huehuetenango, asked not to have to supply men for the entrada to the Lacandones. AGGG, A1.23, legajo 1523, f. 110 v. (June 12, 1679).

31. Peralta, *Costa-Rica y Colombia,* p. 122; CDHCR, 5:468-69, 474; AGGG, A1.23, legajo 1518, f. 115 (1654); AGGG, A1.23, legajo 1518, f. 186 (January 28, 1656); AGGG, A1.24, legajo 1566, f. 95 (May 16, 1681).

32. ANCR Complementario colonial 5204 (February 25, 1620) is the account by Governor Alonso de Guzmán of his alleged suppression of a rebellion among the Aoyaque Indians. ANCR Guatemala 058 (January 30, 1626) is the claim that there was no such rebellion and that the whole affair was a pretext to "bring out" and put Aoyaque Indians to work.

33. ANHH, paquete 2, legajo 52 (1671); AGGG, A1. Tierras, 53118, 6024, f. 10 (1678); AGGG, A1. Tierras, 53965, 6063 (1682); AGGG, A1. Tierras, 52238, 5959 (1704). See also AGGG, A1.57 (Chiapas), 2255, 315 (1701). Another way of estimating the size of the flight to the countryside is to check where people were dying. The Guatemalan mortuales (nearly all in the asignatura A1.43), show that many more rich and prominent people died in the countryside between 1660 and 1700 than formerly.

34. E.g., AGGG, A1. Tierras, 53957, 6062, f. 163v. (May 14, 1652); ANCR Cartago 1078, f. 139 (October 7, 1653); AGGG, A3.30, 41715, 2864 (1676).

35. ANHH, paquete 4, legajo 39 (1683). See also AGGG, A1.2, 16190, 2245, f. 178v. (January 13, 1639); AGGG, A1.24, 10210, 1566, f. 113 (May 16, 1681). For even greater violence used in usurping land, see AGGG, A1. Tierras, 52684, 5990, f. 59 (1686).

36. E.g., AGGG, A1.24, 10203, 1559, f. 129 (May 9, 1642). The following are typical Indian complaints. AGGG, A1.24, 10203, 1559, f. 166 (1642); ANHH, paquete 1, legajo 75 (1653); AGGG, A1.24, 10211, 1567, f. 19 (April 9, 1682).

37. E.g., Pardo, *Efemérides,* pp. 53-55, 68.

38. Compare Pardo, *Efemérides,* p. 55, with Bishop Navas y Quevedo to the Crown, April 12, 1679, in Salvatierra, *Contribución,* vol. 1, p. 328. See also Hardoy and Aranovich, "Urban Scales and Functions," 67, 69, 75.

39. Salvatierra, *Contribución,* vol. 1, p. 323; Cabildo of León to the Crown, January 24, 1648, AGI/AG 43; Cabildo of San Salvador to the Crown, January 12, 1669, and *ibid.* to *ibid.,* June 18, 1670, both in AGI/AG 43; BNM, 2468, f. 96; BNM, 3025, ff. 46-47v.; Juan de Ortega y Montañés to the Crown, September 10, 1680, AGI/AG 158. In Oidor Antonio de Navia Bolaños to the Crown, July 28, 1685, ff. 1-1v., AGI/AG 29, it is stated that most vecinos of all the cities of Nicaragua and its

neighboring provinces lived in the countryside, and as a result "the cities remain depopulated." See also García Peláez, *Memorias,* vol. 3, pp. 31-32.

40. E.g., AGGG, A1.10, 31190, 4043 (1715).

41. See the remarks of Bishop Garret Arloví in 1711, after his visita, in BNM, 20054[15], ff. 3v.-4. CDHCR contains many complaints of this type from Costa Rican clerics.

42. CDHCR, 5:133.

43. An inspection of land titles granted between 1635 and 1685 shows that few were over 4 caballerias. After about 1685 the grants grew much larger. E.g., AGGG, A1. Tierras, 52190, 5957 (1700); AGGG, 52238, 5959 (1704); AGGG, A3.1, 5245, 19 (1712). See especially AGGG, A3.5, 35271, 2389 (1740) an award of 200 caballerias to the Jesuits. A similar document is AGGG, A1.24, 10225, 1581, f. 479 (October 30, 1714).

44. Reports on rural poverty are numerous and repititious. See BNM, 20054[15], ff. 3v.-4; AGGG, A3.1, 5245, 19 (1712).

45. FG, 1:290; Francisco de Escobedo to Crown, April 6, 1695, AGI/AG 24; Gage, *The English-American,* pp. 211-21.

46. E.g., Raveneau de Lussan, *Journal of a Voyage,* p. 129.

47. ANHH, Tierras 140 (1607).

48. AGGG, A3.15, 52004, 5943, f. 13 (1632); AGGG, A1.17, 5871, 268 (1691); AGGG, A1. Tierras, 52307, 5963 (1712). See also ANHH, Tierras, 41 (Comayagua) (1682); 173 (San Isidro Comayagua) (1692).

49. "Cuentas de las haciendas," AGGG, A1.11-15, 48954, 5801 (1651).

50. FG, 1:224.

51. FX, 2:145.

52. AGGG, A1.23, legajo 4585, f. 214 (June 7, 1687).

53. *Relaciones histórico-descriptivas de la Verapaz,* pp. 45-46.

54. AGGG, A1.24, 10211, 1567, f. 196 (1683).

55. Gage, *The English-American,* p. 328; FV, 4:35, 40-42, 60; Chinchilla Aguilar, "Tecpan Guatemala," 11-13. See also West and Augelli, *Middle America,* p. 275.

56. Cortés y Larraz, *Descripción Geográfico-Moral,* tome 2, 172.

57. FV, 4:48-49. For the same practice in Honduras see Gage, *The English-American,* p. 334.

58. FX, 2:247, 280-81, 332; FV, 3:206; Molina, *Antigua Guatemala,* pp. 64-67, 69, 70-73.

59. Pardo, *Efemérides,* pp. 100, 106-7, 110, 114; FX, 2:479.

60. Pardo, *Efemérides,* p. 123.

61. *Ibid.,* p. 124. See also Gage, *The English-American,* p. 292.

62. AGGG, A1.23, legajo 1517, f. 207 (December 12, 1649); BNM, 3023, f. 291 (1657-9); Oidor Antonio de Navia Bolaños to the Crown, July 28, 1685, ff. 1-2v., AGI/AG 29. See also AGGG, A1.1, 62, 3 (n.d.).

63. FV, 1:63-4; AGGG, A3.1, 58, 4 (1714). See the report on the relative sizes of tributary and hacienda populations in Costa Rica in, CDHCR, 8:291-97 (1663). See also CDHCR, 8:397.

64. AGGG, A1.24, 10205, 1561, f. 26 (February 22, 1655); Cabildo of San Salvador to Crown, January 12, 1669, AGI/AG 43; AGGG, A3.1, 57, 4 (1712).

65. AGGG, A1.2, 13510, 1979, f. 4v. (March 28, 1680); FV, 1:347; FG, 1:281; Nash, "Guatemalan Highlands," pp. 30, 34-35, 40; Mörner, "La Política de Segregación," 150. See also Chapter Eleven, especially note 53.

66. See Chapter Eleven, especially note 54.

67. For Huehuetenango there are a few titles after 1670. E.g., AGGG, A1. Tierras, 52054, 5946 (1670); AGGG, A1.24, 55414, 6095, f. 29 (August 6, 1694). By 1712 there were only 11 haciendas there, most of them small and poor. See AGGG, A3.1, 5244, 19 (1712). For Verapaz, see AGGG, A3.1, 5239, 19 (1712), which mentions 28 poor haciendas in the whole province.

Chapter 17

1. "Expediente sobre controversias entre los oidores de dicha audiencia por la antiguedad y preferencia. año de 1682," AGI/AG 138, contains many of the points made here. See also Larreinaga, *Prontuario,* pp. 46-49.

2. See the table from García Peláez, *Memorias,* vol. 1, pp. 226-29, partly reproduced in Hussey, "Analysis of a document," 705-6. The decline in encomenderos, merchants, and even in those interested in intensive agriculture, is clear. See also the complaints in AGGG, A1.7, 5866, 268, f. 18 (1656), and in AGGG, A1.23, legajo 4580, f. 17v. (July 12, 1640). For a comparison with Europe, see Trevor-Roper, "Religion, the Reformation, and Social Change," pp. 34, 36-37; Deyon, *Amiens,* pp. 477-79, 481.

3. E.g. Pardo, *Efemérides,* pp. 92, 100-102, 113; AGGG, A1.23, legajo 1518, f. 17 (February 28, 1652); AGGG, A3.3, 34690, 2356, (1670); ANCR Cartago 074 (January 26, 1684).

4. ANHH, paquete 2, legajo 78, document 3 (1669); ANHH, paquete 2, legajo 60 (1672); AGGG, A1.24, 10210, 1566, f. 119 (May 17, 1681); ANHH, paquete 4, legajo 6 (1682); AGGG, A1.24, 10211, 1567, f. 284 (May 8, 1683).

5. This is well explained by FG, 3:301-4, 310-11. In the 1644 "voluntary donation" the largest contributors were officials, perhaps not surprisingly, but also 23 of the 96 who paid were officials. They were now the elite of the town. See Hussey, "Analysis of a document," pp. 702-3, 707.

6. Larreinaga, *Prontuario,* pp. 234, 264; FG, 3:306; Oidor visitador to the Crown, May 9, 1626, AGI/AG 1; AGGG, A3.1, 8, 1 (1655). See also UT, G 19-139, f. 351 (1647), and the genuine amazement at a President's unheard of honesty in FX, 2:265.

7. AGGG, A1.1, 8363, 398, ff. 22, 45-5, 57 (1649); AGGG, A1.23, legajo 1519, f. 9 (July 31, 1659); AGGG, A1.19, 7217, 345 (1665).

8. See the lengthy discussion on the indigo industry (Chapter Ten), and for present purposes the dozens of cases of the fine-bribe system in the asignatura A1.53 of the AGGG.

9. E.g. AGGG, A1.1, 5039, 212 (1647–49). Most of the posts herein are minor, and are granted for only one year. See also FG, 3:366.

10. AGGG, A1.1, 5039, 212 ff. 123v.-132v. (1647–49); FG, 3:306; Juarros, *Compendio,* p. 219. Minor officials sometimes had problems in collecting even these pittances from the overburdened treasury. E.g., AGGG, A3.2-5, 41970, 2883 (1641); AGGG, A3.2, 39111, 2726 (1678); AGGG, A3.2, 39118, 2726 (1682); and the Crown was constantly deducting parts of these meager salaries for its own expenses. E.g. ANCR Cartago 1081, f. 118 (August 21, 1706).

11. See the various sixteenth-century abuses mentioned in Part One. See also the royal cédulas in AGGG, A1.24, 10205, 1561, f. 26 (February 22, 1655), and AGGG, A1.15, 32441, 4089 (1604).

12. Gage, *The English-American,* pp. 172-74; Larreinaga, *Prontuario,* pp. 305-6; BPR, Miscelanea de Ayala 23, ff. 77-90v. (1687).

13. AGGG, A1.23, legajo 4590, f. 100v. (November 24, 1692); Larreinaga, *Prontuario,* p. 307. See also the comment on how shocked newly arrived priests from Spain were at the practices, in FX, 1:345.

14. AGGG, A1.23, legajo 1523, f. 95 (November 24, 1692).

15. FX, 3:255-57; AGGG, A1.23, legajo 4577, f. 32v. (December 12, 1619).

16. Larreinaga, *Prontuario,* pp. 306, 312; CDHCR, 7:414-28.

17. AGGG, A1.2, 16190, 2245, f. 168v. (August 12, 1636); AGGG, A1.14-16, 31664, 4064, (1641); AGGG, A1.24, 10211, 1567, f. 113 (June 15, 1676); AGGG, A3.12, 40167, 2775 (1696).

18. AGGG, A1.24, 10211, 156, f. 114 (1676), (Quetzaltenango); "Seen in Council," July 16, 1677, AGI/AG 5; AGGG, A3.2, 39113, 2726 (1679), (San Andrés

Joyabaj); Larreinaga, *Prontuario*, pp. 287, 306-7; AGGG, A3.16, 37650, 2566 (1686); AGGG, A1.24, 10213, 1569, f. 37 (March 5, 1694), (Escuintla); AGGG, A1.24, 10217, 1573, f. 77 (1703), (Santo Domingo Sacapulas).

19. Larreinaga, *Prontuario*, p. 287; AGGG, A3.1, 60, 4, f.36 (July 16, 1717). For other "voluntary donations," see for example AGGG, A3.1, 1, 1 (1636); Hussey, "Analysis of a document," pp. 699-708; AGGG, A3.1, 12, 1 (1660); AGGG, A3.1, 21, 2 (1679); AGGG, A3.1, 43, 3 (1701).

20. AGGG, A1.23, legajo 1514, f. 138 (July 25, 1609); AGGG, A1.23, legajo 1517, f. 99 (May 7, 1646); AGGG, A1.15, 32598, 4115 (1646); Pardo, *Efemérides*, p. 53; AGGG, A1.23, legajo 1515, f. 3 (June 17, 1677).

21. See the hundreds of juros, some of them large, in the treasury account book numbered AGGG, A3.2, 11783, 600 (1641). The situation seemed to have improved somewhat by the end of the century. See AGGG, A3.2, 32406, 2163 ("Detalle de los juros impuestos sobre las rentas de la Caja de Guatemala") (1700).

22. AGGG, A1.23, legajo 1514, f. 58 (August 3, 1604); AGGG, A1.41, 45380, 5367 (1642); AGGG, A1.23, legajo 1517, f. 99 (May 7, 1646); BNM, 3047, "Papeles varios, 1646"; Larreinaga, *Prontuario*, p. 316. The King was especially suspicious of successors to an office conducting the court of enquiry into the performance of the previous officeholder. There were too many opportunities for collusion. See Larreinaga, *Prontuario*, p. 89.

23. Pardo, *Efemérides*, pp. 55-6, 65-7, 83; Larreinaga, *Prontuario*, p. 202; AGGG, A1.2-4, 15751, 2197, f. 13 (September 4, 1640); ANHH, paquete 2, legajo 3 (1662); ANHH, paquete 2, legajo 40 (1669).

24. E.g. AGGG, A1.19, 7217, 345 (1665). In 1675 even standard prices for offices collapsed and the king instructed his officials to sell all vendible offices for what they would bring. AGGG, A3.10, 31888, 2104, f. 16 (February 25, 1675). There are two excellent theoretical and descriptive works on the evolution of the sale of offices: Parry, *The Sale of Public Office*, and Porshnev, "The Legend of the Seventeenth Century in French History," 15-27.

25. García Peláez, *Memorias*, vol. 1, pp. 243-44; AGGG, A1. 23, legajo 1517, f. 99 (May 7, 1646), (Costa Rica); FG, 2:27; Governor Andrés de Arrieto to the Crown, December 13, 1653, AGI/AG 43; ANCR Complementario colonial 6512 (November 23, 1663).

26. See Appendix. Of course Mexican Creoles were no better. When Fernando Altamirano y Velasco arrived as governor in 1654 he brought a large family and several newhews, who hunted ruthlessly for money. See the comments in Molina, *Antigua Guatemala*, p. 89.

27. Castro y Tosi, *Pasajeros a Indias*, pp. 16, 28, *passim*. A typical case of indigence is that of the Bishop-elect of Nicaragua, Fray Agustín de Inojossa, who was forced to borrow money from the Crown to pay his passage. See the expediente of April 17, 1631, AGI/AG 1. A list of some of the posts at the disposal of the President of the Audiencia is in FG, 3:312-15. See also his comments on the short terms of Presidents, in FG, 2:25. See also the remarks on the strengthening of family ties in times of depression in Stein and Stein, *The Colonial Heritage*, p. 19.

28. Specific cases include AGGG, A1.23, legajo 4587, f. 151 (1682), (Quetzaltenango); AGGG, A1.23, legajo 1518, f. 21 (1652), (Realejo); Konetzke, *Colección de documentos*, 2^2 : 484-85; García Peláez, *Memorias*, vol. 2, p. 9; AGGG, A1.23, legajo 1519, f. 213 (March 10, 1660).

29. See the various minor awards to the Mencos family (1671 and 1672), in AGI/AG 3. See also the letter from the Conde de la Gómera's two sons, October 23, 1629, AGI/AG 1. There are many other mentions of these and similar Creole families; for example, AGGG, A1.2-4, 15754, 2198, f. 267 (January 9, 1649); "Testamento del Cap[n]. D. Pedro Criado de Castilla y Solórzano vezino y Encomendero de la Ciudad de Santiago de Guathemala en Indias," (November 15, 1665), BNM, 12022; Batres Jáuregui, *La América Central*, 246. (I am grateful to Professor Woodrow Borah for first suggesting this interpretation of the material on mobility).

30. See the introduction to FG.

31. Molina, *Antigua Guatemala,* pp. 39-40. See also his comments on the fall of the merchant class, p. 24. There are various other sporadic references to the family.

32. ANCR Complementario colonial 5380, ff. 4-4v. (March 18, 1637); ANCR, Complementario colonial 5293 (July 8, 1659). See the cédula of June 21, 1682 in Larreinaga, *Prontuario,* p. 82, as a typical example of the kind of decree which turned provincial hostility towards Santiago.

33. ANCR Complementario colonial 5382 (May 5, 1649).

34. E.g. Larreinaga, *Prontuario,* p. 264; Pardo, *Efemérides,* p. 58.

35. E.g., BNM, 3048, "Papeles varios y de Indias," ff. 211-18 (1646).

36. FV, 3:103; 4:247, 257-62; García Peláez, *Memorias,* 2:9.

37. FV, 3:103. Creole Franciscans outnumbered others by more than three to one in 1690. See FV, 4:12-33, 263-69.

38. Molina, *Antigua Guatemala,* p. 81; FX, 2:254-55, 273; AGGG, A1.23, legajo 1517, f. 113 (May 11, 1647); BNM, 3048, "Papeles varios y de Indias," ff. 211-18 (1646); "Seen in Consejo," March 28, 1647, AGI/AG 2; AGGG, A1.23, legajo 1578, f. 174 (June 10, 1655).

39. AGGG, A1.23, legajo 4580, f. 76 (March 5, 1644); Molina, *Antigua Guatemala,* pp. 53, 126-28; AHN, 347 (one folio only); FX, 2:273; *Isagoge,* p. 387.

40. AGGG, A1.23, legajo 1518, ff. 174, 199 (February 12, 1656); Molina, *Antigua Guatemala,* pp. 118, 128, 137-38, 143-44, 147. See also FG, 1:396, 397, 400; 2:314-17, 365-67; FV, 4:341.

41. Larreinaga, *Prontuario,* p. 108; Pardo, *Efemérides,* p. 90; AGGG, A1.23, legajo 1520, f. 88 (December 14, 1672). The Presidents regularly tried to interfere in the ayuntamiento elections to try to impose some of their own people. See Larreinaga, *Prontuario,* p. 109.

42. FG, 1:112, 132, 396; 2:21, 99. See also his reference to Bishop Marroquín's prophecy about the fate of the Creoles, in FG, 2:230.

43. FG, 1:345-46; 2:66, 104; Konetzke, *Colección de documentos,* 2²:79-80; Nash, "Guatemalan Highlands," pp. 30-45; Stein and Stein, *The Colonial Heritage,* pp. 75-76. Some villages were exceptions. Chimaltenango Indians still went to the coast to work on the salt pans, where they were badly mistreated, FG, 1:345-46, 2:104.

44. See the charts on the epidemics. Of course, at the village level smallpox or other plagues could still mean disaster. See FG, 1:339, where the author saw cattle eating over-ripe crops in Indian villages while an epidemic was raging there. Failure to pay tribute was often linked to a local epidemic. E.g., ANCR Cartago 041 (December 23, 1654); AGGG, A3.16, 26390, 1600 (1670).

45. For the old Spanish abuses, see Pardo, *Efemérides,* p. 81; AGGG, A1.24, 10203, 1559, f. 261 (July 28, 1642); AGGG, A1.21-1, 2953, 151 (1696). For abuses by Indian authorities, see AGGG, A1. Tierras, 50539, 5910 (1672); FX, 2:381, 475. For the increase in idolatry, see ANHH, paquete 2, legajo 76 (1673); FV, 2:32; 3:265; 4:319; AGGG, A1.11, 10220, 1576, f. 112 (May 14, 1707); FG, 2:147; 3:400; FX, 2:381-82; Pérez Valenzuela, *Estampas del pasado,* pp. 9-12. For the reemergence of "Indian" culture, see for example Villa Rojas, "Kinship and Nagualism in a Tzeltal Community," 580-83; Lincoln, "The Maya Calendar," pp. 103-8; Termer, *Etnología,* pp. 154, 206-8.

46. For the origins and organization of the cajas see the regulations in AGGG, A1.1, 36, 2 (1704); AGGG, A1.73, 39284, 4570 (February 27, 1706). See also Beals, "Acculturation," 458.

47. AGGG, A1.23, legajo 1514, f. 92 (October 28, 1608); AGGG, A1.2, 16190, 2245, f. 169v. (March 20, 1637); AGGG, A1.24, 10206, 562, f. 39 (January 22, 1658); Andrés de Tobilla to the Crown, "Seen in Council," April 11, 1660, AGI/AG 5. See also *ibid.* to *ibid.,* "Seen in Council," April 29, 1660, AGI/AG 2. The local corregi-

dor in Chiquimula collected 200 pesos each year from the caja there (1605-19), and
it took at least three decrees from the' King to stop him. See AGGG, A1.23, legajo
1514, ff. 65, 204; AGGG, A1.23, legajo 4576, f. 35v. The Crown tried to control the
activities of some cajas. E.g., AGGG, A1.24, 55431, 6095, f. 10 (1779).

48. Between 1627 and 1634 the account books of the caja of Tecpanatitlán
(Sololá) were in favorable balance. See AGGG, A1.1, 51201, 5919 (1627-34). By the
early years of the eighteenth century this was seldom the case. In the following
document 30 villages were all in debt and only Chichicastenango came close to
balancing its books. Patulul was typical: in 1710 its Indians paid in 60 tostones; 50
went to the village priest for various services, 30 were spent on the village fiesta, and
a host of small outlays brought the cost to 164 tostones, or 104 over income. Whole
villages, such as Patulul, were forced to borrow and to work off the debt, a variant
of debt peonage. See AGGG, A1.73, 48424, 5766 (1710). Other reports are in
AGGG, A1.73, 48420, 5766 (1689), and AGGG, A1.24, 10226, 1582, f. 209 (August
7, 1717), in which, surprisingly, an Indian caja de comunidad is accused of lending
money at high interest and told to stop.

49. The early church sponsorship of the cofradías is mentioned in several of the
chronicles, and in AGGG, A1.2, 16190, 2245, f. 169v. (March 20, 1637).

50. Núñez de la Vega, *Constituciones Diocesanas del Obispado de Chiappa,* pp.
18v.-21, 23v.; Fray Cristóbal de Echave to the Crown, 1748, AGI/AG 370 cited in,
Saint-Lu, *La Vera Paz.*

51. AGGG, A1.2, 16190, 2245, f. 169v. (March 20, 1637). The village of San
Miguel Taxisco founded at least 12 cofradías between 1637 and 1695. All these
foundings are under the asignatura A1.11-2. Many are in legajo 5976. Cofradías
began to buy various forms of property. For land purchases, see AGGG, A1.11-2,
52193, 5957, f. 3 (1666); AGGG, A1.24, 10213, 1569, f. 127 (March 23, 1694). See
the report of very wealthy cofradías in Totonicapán in FG, 3:53.

52. AGGG, A1.2, 16190, 2245, f. 169v. (March 20, 1637).

53. E.g., *ibid.;* Larreinaga, *Prontuario,* pp. 56-57; Pardo, *Efemérides,* p. 113.

54. AGGG, A1.68-3, legajo 1751, f. 46 (1593); AGGG, A1.68-3, 48127, 5555,
(1676); Konetzke, *Colección de documentos,* 2²:643-64; Chinchilla Aguilar, "La
danza de Tum-Teleche o Loj-Tum," 17-20. See also Kurath, "Drama, Dance and
Music," 158-90, and Rodríguez Rouanet, "Sobre una representación actual del Rabinal Achí," 45-47, 56.

55. FX, 2:192-94; FV, 4:387-88. See also Siegel, "Religion in Western
Guatemala," 62-76.

56. There is no substantive proof that this process began in the seventeenth
century, but it seems likely. (For the present day, see Vogt, *Zinacantan,* 583.) See
also FG, 1:292. Spaniards, priests, and laymen often interfered in Indian elections,
which must have slowed the process. E.g. AGGG, A1.24, 10206, 1562, f. 412 (December 3, 1658); AGGG, A1.21-11, 47524, 5505 (1671); AGGG, A1.21-11, 47829, 5533
(1713).

57. AGGG, A1.1, 2139, 310 (1716).

58. ANHH, paquete 2, legajo 77, document 1 (1673); AGGG, A1.24, 10207,
1565 (1677); AGGG, A1.1, 23, 2 (1687); AGGG, A1.24, 10214, 1570 (1695-98). For
a summing up see, Borhegyi, "Settlement Patterns," pp. 101-6.

Chapter 18

1. The Botes, or Votos, were growing cacao at the time of the conquest of Costa
Rica, according to Vázquez de Coronado, *Cartas,* pp. 18, 25. Other early mentions
of cacao in Costa Rica include ANCR Complementario colonial 5203, ff. 14v.-15v.,

January 23, 1620; CDHCR, 5:221; Fray Agustín de Ceballos to the Crown, March 10, 1610, in Peralta, *Costa-Rica, Nicaragua y Panamá,* p. 699.

2. ANCR Guatemala 81 (1636); ANCR Complementario colonial 2280 (1641); ANCR Complementario colonial 5177 (1662); CDHCR, 8:495; Cockburn, *The Unfortunate Englishman,* pp. 62-63; Ringrose, "The Dangerous Voyages," pp. 65-70.

3. AGGG, A1.23, legajo 1517, f. 99 (April 15, 1640); ANCR Cartago 1081, f. 273 (October 12, 1711).

4. ANCR Cartago 085 (1691).

5. One of the most frequently mentioned anchorages, Suerre, was first opened in 1590. See Bishop of Nicaragua to Crown, February 19, 1591, AGI/AG 162. As the exports of agricultural produce declined it fell into disuse. In 1650, however, Governor Juan Fernández opened it at a new site to stimulate the flagging agriculture of the region. He settled Indians and Spaniards there. The commodities for export, however, did not yet include cacao (CDHCR, 5:334-38). By 1663 there were small productive groves in Matina (ANCR Complementario colonial 3896 [1663]); García Peláez, *Memorias,* vol. 3, p. 31. A later governor described Portete, Matina, and Punta Blanca as principal ports. Cacao groves were flourishing near these ports by then. See CDHCR, 5:361, 476; 8:348-89.

6. It is implied in the report of 1691 that the entradas were undertaken with the express purpose of recruiting new labor for the cacao plantations. (ANCR Cartago 085 [1691]). This seems to be an oversimplification. Rodrigo Arias Maldonado, at least, is frequently described as a professional soldier eager to find new areas to conquer. His later clerical career indicates that his expressed desire to bring Indians to his faith was probably genuine. At any rate his relations with the Talamancan Indians, notoriously suspicious of Spanish intentions, were extremely good, and he treated them well. See Fernández Guardia, *History,* pp. 347-57; CDHCR, 8:291-95. Above all, see his residencia (ANCR, Complementario colonial 3585, July 24, 1665). It is probable, then, that the exploitation in the cacao plantations of the Indians whom he had settled around Urinama, did not begin until after Arias Maldonado's departure from Costa Rica.

7. ANCR, Complementario colonial 5227, February 20, 1690. Macotela was receiving his information from another friar. See the two letters of 1689 and 1690 from Sebastían de las Alas to Fray Diego Macotela, CDHCR, 8:502-6. The Urinamas revolted in 1678 but were defeated by Spanish soldiery. (Fernández Guardia, *History,* p. 370).

8. ANCR Cartago 085, October 19, 1691; CDHCR, 9:14. (This is a letter from Fray Melchor López and Fray Antonio Margil to Don Antonio de Barrios, 1690).

9. ANCR Cartago 166, May 24, 1708. Indian owners appear in the inventory of 1678, CDHCR, 8:376-77.

10. For seasonal rain damage, see, CDHCR, 5:476, and ANCR Guatemala 808, f. 10. For the sickliness of the coastal area and absentee landlords, see CDHCR, 3:349; 8:443-44, and ANCR Cartago 083, March 26, 1691. In the eighteenth century a popular saying held that "Matina makes cowards out of men and idiots out of mules." (See CDHCR, 9:319.)

11. ANCR Guatemala 116, March 27, 1685; ANCR Cartago 083, March 26, 1691; CDHCR, 3:481.

12. ANCR Complementario colonial 5100, June 10, 1675, and August 6, 1675; ANCR Complementario colonial 4964, f. 9v., November 15, 1679; CDHCR, 3:351, 358, 364; Fernández Guardia, *Crónicas coloniales,* p. 211.

13. CDHCR, 8:350, 381-83, 393-95, 399-400, 428.

14. CDHCR, 3:349, 361-64, 476-77; 8:312-13, 349, 352, 389, 429; ANCR Cartago 097, August 17, 1698; ANCR Cartago 111, March 19, 1702; Fernández Guardia, *Crónicas coloniales,* pp. 110-14, 146-47, 210-11; Salvatierra, *Contribución,* vol. 1, p. 352. As early as 1676 it was suggested that the cacao beans be dried near the fort so that the pirates could not seize them. CDHCR, 8:352.

15. Peralta, *Costa-Rica, Nicaragua y Panamá,* p. 699; CDHCR, 3:476; 8:349; Gage, *The English-American,* p. 365.

16. See the inventory of 1678 for the owners and the numbers of bushes owned (CDHCR, 8:376). By 1682 his holdings were allegedly smaller, but his declaration smacks of fraud. By this time he was also renting plantations from others (CDHCR, 8:400-403). Valerino was a member of the small Cartago elite and held various offices in the ayuntamiento and the militia (ANCR Cartago 079, February 17, 1690; ANCR Cartago 085, October 19, 1691). Neither was among the wealthier vecinos of Cartago in 1667, before the cacao plantations began their rapid development (CDHCR, 8:345).

17. "Autos sobre la expulsión de Antonio de Acosta Arévalo, griego." February 10, 1672, ANCR Guatemala 111. Another royal explusion order against foreigners in 1697 affected only one Englishman recently arrived in Costa Rica. He was expelled for obvious reasons and was probably a shipwrecked pirate or smuggler. See ANCR Cartago 1078, f. 433, May 25, 1697. About that time there were several foreigners in Cartago, including Acosta's Greek son-in-law Juan Foto, an Irishman known as Juan Matias de Mores (ANCR Cartago 1133, November 13, 1698), and two Italians, Juan Angel Malatesta and Agustín Caneba (ANCR Complementario colonial 3953, March 28, 1699). There are numerous other examples of foreigners living unmolested in Central America throughout the sixteenth and seventeenth centuries. Some of the unheeded expulsion decrees are listed in ANCR Cartago 1078, f. 186, January 26, 1674.

18. ANCR Guatemala 111, ff. 2v., 11-13. There was long history of Greek bombardiers and artillery officers in Spanish and other Mediterranean navies. Acosta Arévalo seems to have been one of this group. For Greek artillery officers in sixteenth-century Peru, see Lockhart, *Spanish Peru,* pp. 125-26; Rodríguez Vicente, "Los extranjeros y el mar en Perú," pp. 659, 666. I am indebted to don Norberto Castro y Tosi for drawing my attention to some of the documents about the two Greek vecinos.

19. ANCR Guatemala 111.

20. ANCR, Mortuales coloniales, Cartago 428 (1692).

21. ANCR Complementario colonial 3940, July 20, 1695.

22. ANCR, Mortuales coloniales, Cartago 743 especially ff. 1, 3, 10, 29-29v. (1699).

23. Mortuales which show signs of smuggled goods include, ANCR, Mortuales coloniales 2174 (1672); ANCR, Mortuales coloniales 2473 (1682). After the turn of the century smuggling became widespread.

24. ANCR Complementario colonial 3941, November 5, 1695; ANCR Complementario colonial 3953, March 28, 1699; ANCR Complementario colonial 3989, May 24, 1707.

25. ANCR Cartago 079, February 17, 1690; ANCR Cartago 081, January 26, 1691; ANCR Cartago 090, January 23, 1694; ANCR Guatemala 129, ff. 1-3v., August 20, 1703; ANCR Cartago 208, January 10, 1717.

26. CDHCR, 3:481-82. In 1711 vecinos of Costa Rica tried to enter the New Spain cacao markets via La Caldera and the Pacific. See ANCR Cartago 1081, f. 293 (1711).

27. ANCR Guatemala 129, ff. 1-3, August 20, 1703; ANCR Guatemala 142, June 30, 1709; ANCR Cartago 225, June 19, 1717; CDHCR, 3:482.

28. For smuggling with the Grillo slave ships, other unregistered Spanish vessels, and foreigners, in the last years of the seventeenth century, see for example ANCR Cartago 1078, f. 181, June 14, 1673; ANCR Cartago 1078, f. 294, June 15, 1685; Fernández Guardia, *Crónicas coloniales,* pp. 211-13. Royal officials were involved too. See AGGG, A1.24, 10211, 1567, f. 290 (1683).

29. By 1704 smuggling was widespread and most people were involved. See ANCR Cartago 127, July 1, 1704. (It was also considerable on the Pacific coast, e.g., ANCR Cartago 151, February 3, 1702, sometimes with the help of local royal offi-

cials, ANCR Guatemala 138, July 22, 1707. Incidents on the Caribbean coast, however, were far more frequent and systematic, and foreigners were usually involved.) Typical smuggling cases from the Caribbean coast are ANCR Cartago 121, March 26, 1704; ANCR Complementario colonial 3996, January 17, 1709. In ANCR Guatemala 163, July 14, 1717, cacao was being traded for cloth, and all the people living in the Matina valley were engaged in the trade. By 1721 it is obvious that Matina was little more than an exchange and mart for smuggled goods, and that systematized fines had been established so that local royal officials and the royal treasury might partake of the profits. Often the Zambos Mosquitos acted as the intermediaries between the Creoles and the English in Jamaica. See for example ANCR Complementario colonial 5842, f. 8; ANCR Complementario colonial 5795, f. 12; ANCR Complementario colonial 5799, f. 10; ANCR Complementario colonial 5800, f. 9, all of which are from the one year, 1721, and which involve many people in small fines and other minor punishments.

Chapter 19

1. Salvatierra, *Contribución,* vol. 1, pp. 347-82.
2. See the following visitas to Honduran pueblos and the average household size in each. ANHH, paquete 4, legajo 44 (1683), Nacaome village, average household, 3.251; ANHH paquete 4, legajo 45 (1683), Texiguat, 2.569; ANHH, paquete 4, legajo 46 (1683), Yuzgira, 2.818; ANHH, paquete 4, legajo 48 (1683), Colanco, 2.286; ANHH, paquete 4, legajo 61 (1683), Orocuina, 3.180. All the other visitas of this year confirm these low reproduction rates and household sizes.
3. Simpson, "A Seventeenth-Century Encomienda," 401-2; AGGG, A3.16, 40667, 2809 (July 27, 1674) (Quetzaltenango); AGGG, A1. Tierras, 52137, 5952 (1692). See also, for the whole of Chiapas, AGGG, A1.23, legajo 1521, f. 217 (June 6, 1680). For the Indian population revival in Mexico, see Miranda, "La población indígena de México," 183-85.

Typical reports of still falling Indian populations at this same period include, AGGG, A1.14-7, 31723, 4064 (1689); AGGG, A1.24, 10225, 1581, f. 458 (October 2, 1714); AGGG, A3.16, 36545, 2502, f. 27 (1716).
4. See the Introduction for a similar analysis applied to late medieval Europe.
5. In the following two cases large grants (over 16 caballerías and 19 caballerías) were made to vecinos of Huehuetenango and Quetzaltenango over the opposition of several Indian villages. (Santa Ana Malacatán appeared to protest in both cases.) AGGG, A1. Tierras, 52241, 5959 (1704); AGGG, A1. Tierras, 52278, 5961 (1709). For litigation between Indian villages at this period, see for example AGGG, A1. Tierras, 52148, 5954 (1696); AGGG, A1.24, 10216, 1572, f. 131 (April 18, 1701); AGGG, A1. Tierras, 52318, 5964 (1713); AGGG, A1. 14-13, 31765, 4065 (1716). For the continuing heavy losses of Indian land to Spaniards and Creoles, especially on the indigo frontier of San Miguel, see AGGG, A1.24, 10226, 1582, f. 223 (August 24, 1717).
6. See the information in Chapter Seventeen. Also, AGGG, A1. 14-16, 31664, 4064, (1641); AGGG, A1.24, 51202, 5919 (1677).
7. FX, 2:408-9; García Peláez, *Memorias,* vol. 2, pp. 112-13, 130; AGGG, A1.23, legajo 1522, f. 243 (October 21, 1686); AGGG, A1.39, 11756, 1762, f. 42v. (September 17, 1688); AGGG, A1.15, 24855, 2817 (1693); AGGG, A1.24, 10213, 1569, f. 191 (May 6, 1694); AGGG, A1.1, 54708, 6071 (1696); AGGG, A1.15, 26647, 2891 (1703); ANCR Complementario colonial 5117 (October 14, 1709); AGGG, A1.9-7, 47170, 5481 (1715). See also, Pineda, *Historia de las sublevaciones,* pp. 36-37, *passim.* The Tzeltal revolt of 1712 will be discussed later. There was also a riot led

by mulattoes and blacks in San Salvador in 1720, mentioned in AGGG, A1.56, 5795, 626 (January 15, 1720), and the slaves on two large haciendas revolted in 1726. (Pardo, *Efemérides,* p. 162.)

8. AGGG, A1.15, 24855, 2817 (1693); García Peláez, *Memorias,* vol. 2, pp. 112-13; Pineda, *Historia de las sublevaciones,* p. 37; AGGG, A1.19-17, 47170, 5481 (1715).

9. (The revival was led by the Jesuits and the Recollects of the Franciscan order). Espinosa, *Crónica de los Colegios,* pp. 545-50; Floyd, *The Anglo-Spanish Struggle,* pp. 39-40; Salvatierra, *Contribución,* vol. 1, p. 334; AGGG, A1.11, 10220, 1576, f. 112 (May 14, 1707).

10. E.g. Espinosa, *Crónica,* pp. 550-52.

11. *Ibid.,* pp. 550, 569-70; AGGG, A1.1, 23, 2 (1687).

12. AGGG, A1.23, legajo 4590, f. 100v. (November 24, 1692); AGGG, A1.23, legajo 4593, ff. 166, 290v. (March 4, November 27, 1697). By 1703 repartimientos were exceeding one quarter of the population. See AGGG, A3.12, 3984, 223 (1703). See also ANCR Guatemala 132 (April 24, 1704); AGGG, A1.24, 10219, 1575, f. 45 (August 18, 1706). Highland Indians were also being sent to coastal estancias on repartimiento duty. See AGGG, A1.22-30, 45405, 5368 (1705). See also AGGG, A1.24, 10224, 1580, f. 292 (September 28, 1713); AGGG, A1.24, 10226, 1582, f. 32 (January 3, 1717); Peralta, *Costa-Rica y Colombia,* p. 126. The illegal employment of Indians on indigo works increased after 1690. See the rate of prosecutions in AGGG, A1.53. For examples of entrada y saca between 1685 and 1720, see ANHH, paquete 5, legajo 66 (1698); ANHH, paquete 6, legajo 2 (1700); FX, 2:200; 3:138-39; Peralta, *Costa-Rica y Colombia,* pp. 122, 130. Also of significance was a revival in slave importation. See ANCR Complementario colonial 649 (February 28, 1702) in which 4 vecinos of Cartago were accused of buying slaves from pirates. A similar case some years later is in ANCR Complementario colonial 5837, f. 118 (July 20, 1719).

13. The expedientes on this revolt are in AGI/AG 293-96. They have been used by Herbert S. Klein in his "Peasant Communities in Revolt," pp. 247-63. See also FX, 3:256-343; "Informe sobre la sublevación de los Zendales," (June 5, 1716), ACNL 1691. The following contains details on the villages involved not found in the above: "Succinta Relazione," Mss. 2675, ff. 131-38, Biblioteca Casanatense, Rome. (Professor Woodrow Borah kindly supplied a film of this document.) See also AGGG, A1.23, legajo 1525, f. 240 (July 22, 1713), and AGGG, A1.18, 5023, 211, f. 9v. (1713), for royal thanks to the president, Audiencia, and bishop for their parts in the suppression of the revolt. In 1730, the Indians of Cancuc, the leading rebel village, who had been moved to another site, asked to be allowed to return to the old village. See AGGG, A1.10, 646, 61 (1730). For exclusivist feelings in these same villages today see, Redfield and Villa Rojas, "Notes on the Ethnography of Tzeltal Communities of Chiapas," 109-10.

14. E.g., Pardo, *Efemérides,* pp. 92, 100-102.

15. ANCR Cartago 081 (January 26, 1691); ANCR Cartago 090 (January 23, 1694); AGGG, A3.3, 34706, 2357 (1694); ANHH, paquete 5, legajo 66 (1695); AGGG, A1.2-11, 30759, 4014 (1698); AGGG, A1.2-11, 30761, 4014 (1702); AGGG, A1.2-11, 48190, 5759 (1703); AGGG, A1.24, 55421, 6095 (February 15, 1710); Pardo, *Efemérides,* pp. 112-16, 119-21, 128, 131-33, 151-55. The harvest of 1697 was described as excellent, yet supply problems continued. See AGGG, A1.21, 10012, 1508 (1654-1759). The size of awards of land definitely grew after 1690. See above, note 5, and AGGG, A1. Tierras, 52190, 5957 (1700); AGGG, A1.24, 10225, 1581, f. 485 (October 27, 1714).

Chapter 20

1. Such prohibitions were frequent and well-known. See, for example, the decree in Larreinaga, *Prontuario,* pp. 63, 120-21; Haring, *Trade and Navigation,* pp. 101, 108; González, *Tratado Iurídico-político del Contra-bando,* pp. 15-40.

2. Perhaps the most striking composición was that of the death penalty in criminal prosecutions. In 1654 the Crown decreed that all penalties, including the capital one, could be lowered one degree on the payment of a specific sum. AGGG, A1.23, legajo 4580, f. 153 (June 1, 1654). Smuggling was seldom susceptible to official composición in the New World, although it happened unofficially in the form of bribes to royal representatives. In Spain composición of contraband was regular and became institutionalized as indultos or manifestaciones. See Haring, *Trade and Navigation,* pp. 65-66, 113-14.

3. The financial predicament of royal officials has already been discussed. For a general discussion see Parry, *The Sale of Public Office,* p. 73. For Central American cases of high sums paid in Spain for offices in Santiago and other towns see the case of President Mencos below, and "Titulo de Juez Offiz[1] de la Villa de ss.^ma Trinidad y Puerto de Acajutla en la Nueba España a Pedro de Artacho porhaver servido con quatro mill pessos," Madrid, August 29, 1650, AGI/AG 51. A sixteenth-century discussion of this situation is CS, 3:403.

4. Study of the notarial archives in Seville led one observer to conclude that Genoese merchants were important in the Seville-Indies trade as early as 1505-20. See Sayous, *Le rôle des Génois,* pp. 4-5, 10. See also Pike, *Enterprise and Adventure,* pp. 67-8, 129-31, 144. Some of the devices used in Seville to circumvent regulation are described in Haring, *Trade and Navigation,* pp. 111-13. Foreigners dominated the entire Spanish economy after 1600, and even the provisioning of the fleet depended on imports. See Vicens Vives, *Historia social,* vol. 3, pp. 332, 338, 556, and especially the two charts, vol. 3, p. 346, which show foreigners in control of some 95 per cent of the declining American trade through Seville.

5. Central American indigo and Mexican cochineal were on sale in Amsterdam on a large scale as early as 1624. See Posthumus, *Inquiry into the History of Prices in Holland,* vol. 1, pp. 415-16, 420-21. (Gaps for 1655–59 and 1695–99 are noted on, 1:lxxxiv). See also the gross amounts of indigo at Amsterdam for the period 1620–99 on 1:xxviii. The English, to their annoyance, had to send much of their cloth to Holland for dyeing for most of the first half of the seventeenth century; Antwerp was the center of this industry for northern Europe. See Lucas, *The Beginnings of English Overseas Enterprise,* pp. 94-99, 170-73. See also the chart in Vicens Vives, *Historia social,* vol. 3, p. 346, for the provenance of goods sent to America.

6. AGGG, A1.1, 5666, 256 (1643). The Honduras case is in ANHH, paquete 3, legajo 75 (1677). Usually, and especially when the culprits were from the lower class, it was impossible to find out who they were or where they were from, far less apprehend them. See the strenuous but unsuccessful efforts made by the Audiencia and the Honduran authorities, in AGGG, A3.6, 39559, 2749 (1659).

7. Sluiter, "Dutch-Spanish Rivalry in the Caribbean," 165-96. Complaints about the dangerous coast and poor anchorages were frequent. See, for example, Chaunu and Chaunu, *Séville et l'Atlantique,* 4:143; 6²:578, 579; CDIU, 17:210. An early case of attempted smuggling was in Trujillo on March 26, 1572. An English ship came in and attempted to trade. Apparently it had some success, because the King, after hearing about the incident, felt obliged to warn the authorities in Santiago de Guatemala that trade with "non-Spanish subjects" was forbidden. See the real cédula of May 26, 1573 in AGGG, A1.23, legajo 1512, f. 431.

8. E.g., AGGG, A3.6, 39541, 2747 (1604).

9. AGGG, A3.6, 39540, 2747 (1604).

10. E.g., AGGG, A3.1, 53902, 6060 (1585).

11. For the large quantities of indigo seized by Dutch pirates in the 1620s, see Newton, *The European Nations,* pp. 152-53; Wright, *Nederlandsche Zeevarders,* pp. 101-9, which describes the seizure of the Honduras ships in 1624, 1627, and 1628. Even the Crown was confiscating Guatemalan indigo at Seville and sending it to the Low Countries when prices were good. See, "Seen in Consejo," June 14, 1653, AGI/AG 2.

12. Consejo de Indias, November 26, 1663, f. 1, AGI/AG 2; Pérez Valenzuela, *Estampas del pasado,* p. 56.

13. The confiscation of Justiniano Chavarri's indigo and his subsequent payment in juros is in Consejo de Indias, June 14, 1653, AGI/AG 2. His principal denunciation of Mencos is in the same legajo, Consejo de Indias, November 26, 1663.

14. Consejo de Indias, November 26, 1663, ff. 2-3, AGI/AG 2.

15. Bernardo del Valle to Consejo, November 26, 1663, AGI/AG 2.

16. President Mencos to Consejo, January 16, 1665, AGI/AG 21.

17. President Mencos to Consejo, February 27, 1668, AGI/AG 3.

18. "Seen in Council," December 17, 1668, AGI/AG 3.

19. "Seen in Council," April 29, 1671?, AGI/AG 3; "Seen in Council," 1672, AGI/AG 3.

20. See the two piezas on this case, 500 and 252 ffs. respectively, both "unproven," 1661?, AGI, Escribanía de Cámara 335.

21. AGGG, A1.15, 32613, 4117 (1660).

22. See for example, "Fraudes que se hacen en los puertos de Onduras y Yucatan," July 16, 1655, AGI/AG 5; AGGG, A3.39, 41715, 2874 (1682); AGGG, A1.15, 53905, 6060 (June 5, 1648). (This last involves many of the vecinos of Trujillo.) AGGG, A3.6, 42067, 2885 (1638) accuses yet another royal official, this time the royal treasurer in Comayagua. At times smuggling was the cause of deep dissension in the Audiencia. See FX, 2:354. For Central American produce on Dutch islands, see Davis, *A Primer of Dutch Seventeenth Century Trade,* p. 119; Newton, *The European Nations,* p. 282; Thornton, *West-India Policy,* pp. 23, 80, 83, 85.

23. There were royal decrees on arribadas throughout the century. See the several mentioned in ANCR Cartago 1078, f. 203 (April 8, 1677), or those sent to Guatemala in AGGG, A1.23, legajo 1514, f. 228 (November 19, 1644) and AGGG, A1.23, legajo 1521, f. 84v. (1661). AGGG, A1.23, legajo 1519, f. 47 (September 13, 1660) warns specifically against English arribadas maliciosas. See also "Titulos e Informes de jueces de arribadas," AGI Indiferente General 2273; Veitia Linaje, *Norte de la contratación,* pp. 216-17. An early example of arribada maliciosa in Central America was the small English ship which put into Trujillo with a cargo of raisins and wine in 1606. See Martín de Celaya to the Crown, June 8, 1606, AGI/AG 39.

24. Vecinos of Guatemala and Honduras to the Crown, August 18, 1643, AGI-/AG 7.

25. AGGG, A1.23, legajo 1519, f. 47 (September 13, 1660). Obviously there was an earlier decree on this matter but I have not found it.

26. The legal basis for the expulsion of Acosta Arévalo, the Greek cacao entrepreneur, has already been discussed. A typical royal cédula to the President of the Audiencia in Santiago ordered him to expel all Flemings who had not been naturalized, to forbid all foreigners to reside in the area, and to be especially wary of the Dutch, who always traded with their compatriots whenever the chance presented itself. See AGGG, A1.23, legajo 1514, f. 93 (1606). See also Larreinaga, *Prontuario,* pp. 120-21; ANCR Cartago 1078, f. 186 (January 26, 1674). Locally resident aliens did participate in smuggling of course. See "Fiscal con Lorenzo Andres Granajo, Alvacea y testamentario de Adan Diaz de Nacion Portugues," Corte, AGI, Escribanía de Cámara 335.

27. AGI/AG 282 is a lengthy expediente on this matter. More details can be found in UT, G 19-129, ff. 290-94. His son, like so many sons of officials, soon

occupied a secure but lesser place in Creole society, and soon lost his ties with the court in Spain. In 1717 he was Dean of the Cathedral in Santiago. See Pérez Valenzuela, *Estampas del pasado,* p. 142.

28. "Proposiciones del Marqués de Variñas, sobre los Abusos de Yndias, Fraudes en su Comercio y Fortificación de sus Puertos," CDI, 19:239-304, especially pp. 239, 241. See also Larreinaga, *Prontuario,* p. 63.

29. Haring, *The Spanish Empire in America,* p. 331; Newton, *The European Nations,* pp. 166-67.

30. One of the few examples is in AGI Escribanía de Cámara, 2 piezas, 34 ff., and 133 ff., the latter "visto en el año 1662," which concerns dealings between a vecino of Santiago and a Dutch pingue in Santo Tomás de Castilla in that year.

31. Nettels, "England and the Spanish-American Trade," 1-32; Pares, *War and Trade in the West Indies, 1739-1763,* pp. 6-7. Many English commentators at the time pointed out that England needed no more land in the Indies and should follow the example of the Dutch, "who have gott infinitely more by serving and corresponding fairly . . . than ever they did by Warr and Privateers," BM, Edgerton 2395, f. 575 (April 7, 1678). It was one thing to decide in favor of trade, however, and another to stop the pirates and their depredations. On this point see Haring, *The Buccaneers,* pp. 121-22, 232-72.

32. Newton, *The European Nations,* pp. 181-82. Note especially the early breach of faith, p. 257. See also Haring, *The Buccaneers,* pp. 121-22. An amusing account of Providence Island is in Means, *The Spanish Main,* pp. 174-86. For the quantities of indigo, sarsaparilla, and hides seized by Jackson at Trujillo and at the Desaguadero, see *The Voyages of Captain William Jackson* ed. Harlow, pp. vi, 23-25.

33. There are many accounts of the activities of Morgan and others between 1660 and 1680. See Roberts, *Sir Henry Morgan,* especially pp. 58-63; Newton, *The European Nations,* pp. 258-75, 321-22; Haring, *The Buccaneers,* pp. 138-39, 162. (The raid of 1679 caused a glut of indigo in Jamaica. See *ibid.,* p. 223.) An interesting document concerning the lesser-known sacking of Nueva Segovia is AGGG, A1.24, 10210, 1566, f. 412. The alcaldes were accused of cowardice and flight when the English attacked on May 12, 1676.

34. Newton, *The European Nations,* p. 182. Early settlement in the area now known as Belize or British Honduras is documented in Burdon, *Archives of British Honduras,* vol. 1, pp. 3, 42, 49-57. On the same topic see also Humphreys, *Diplomatic History,* p. 2. The information on Captain Blewfield and his ship at Cape Gracias a Dios is in BM, Sloane, 11410, f. 10. ("An Account of the Private Ships of Warr belonging to Jamaica and Turtudos in 1663.") Extensive trading between Providence Island and Cape Gracias a Dios is mentioned in the Public Records Office (London), Calendar of State Papers (Colonial), Colonial Entry Book IV, f. 79. For the gradual development of settlement on the so-called Mosquito Shore after about 1633, see the excellent description in Floyd, *The Anglo-Spanish Struggle,* pp. 18-19, 21-22, 29, 56-57.

35. As usual, the perceptive Governor Lynch saw the problem most clearly. Privateering stopped trade and local growth, "for privateering and planting are two things absolutely incompatible." See Public Records Office (London), Calendar of State Papers (Colonial), 1669-1674, f. 310. See also Thornton, "Spanish slave-ships in the English West Indies, 1660-1685," 378, 381; and especially Floyd, *The Anglo-Spanish Struggle,* pp. 22, 28-29, 56, 64-66.

36. Haring, *The Buccaneers,* pp. 201-202, 208, 269; Audiencia to the Crown, May 8, 1607, AGI/AG 12; Wilson, "The Logwood Trade."

37. A classic on the slave trade to the Spanish colonies is Scelle, *La Traite Negrière.* Scelle divides the asiento before 1700 into three phases: (1) the Spanish license period, 1518-1580; (2) the Portuguese period, 1580-1640; and (3) the period of transition or the Dutch period, 1640-1695. Dutch smugglers did visit Honduran ports frequently, of course, throughout the seventeenth century, but their visits were

not regular before 1660 as far as is known, and Central America was not one of their preferred areas. For specific Dutch visits, see notes 20, 30, and 49 of this chapter.

38. The enquiry into the Grillo asiento is a veritable mountain of paper (AGI Indiferente General 2830–2833). They were accused of widespread smuggling, fraud, and aiding foreigners to draw maps and plan attacks against Spanish forts. (It was also noted that they did not even build the ten ships which they had promised to the Crown, in AGI Indiferente General 2703). The Grillo's defense is to be found in the rare publication, Grillo, *Satisfacción* [sic] *a unos papeles que sin autor, y sin verdad se han publicado contra los assientos, y transacción que se han ajustado con Domingo Grillo.*

39. Thornton, "Spanish slave-ships," p. 384; Thornton, *West-India Policy,* pp. 80-85; Wright, "The Coymans Asiento," 25.

40. Grillo smuggling in Costa Rica was evidently large enough for the Queen Regent to issue a warning to the governor of Costa Rica forbidding further incidents. See ANCR Cartago 1078, f. 181 (January 26, 1674).

41. "Though the Truth is there is no possibility of doing anything. The Governors [i.e., of the Spanish colonies] are so fearful and the Grillos ffactors so carefull." BM, Sloane 11410, ff. 223-26v. See also *ibid.,* f. 99, which laments that "they want nothing else in the Indies for the Grillos Shipps fill all places underhand with dry goods."

42. Wright, "The Coymans Asiento." Wright notices persistent pressure from England against the holders of the asiento, and decides that it was ascendant England which really forced the Coymans, and by extension the Dutch, from their asiento position. See p. 62. Nevertheless, a few Spanish slave ships were calling at Jamaica before the Coymans asiento. See Thornton, *West-India Policy,* p. 80.

43. Thornton, "Spanish slave-ships," p. 384.

44. The history of this ship which sailed to Holland is in CDIE, 84:197-98, and in Chaunu and Chaunu, *Séville et l'Atlantique,* 5:506-7, 523. The Count of Peñaranda's letter is in CDIE, 84:361-62. A similar incident, the seizure of a Spanish ship by its foreign crew, took place in the New Spain fleet in the 1590s. The foreigners were mostly French and Flemish. See CDI, 17:426.

45. The enquiry into this affair is to be found in a very long expediente, AGI/AG 281, entitled "Expediente sobre la ida a Vera cruz de el Governador D^n Juan Tomas Milut con navios de registro para Honduras: años de 1688 a 1690." A Mexican diarist duly noted the unexpected arrival of the ships: "September 18, 1688. This day there was news of the arrival in port at Veracruz of two Honduras ships, with wine." See Robles, *Diario,* vol. 2, p. 163.

46. Spanish shippers frequently complained that the fleets were unable to sell their cargoes in Honduras and the Golfo Dulce because the prices were so low and the market was saturated. See, for example, Haring, *Trade and Navigation,* p. 150, and the many repetitions of this complaint in the expediente cited above in note 45.

47. Nettels, "England and the Spanish-American Trade," pp. 8-10.

48. Floyd, *The Anglo-Spanish Struggle,* pp. 58-59, 61; Nettels, "England and the Spanish-American Trade," pp. 3, 28; Christelow, "Contraband Trade," 310-13. See also Chaunu, *Conquête et Exploitation,* pp. 279-82.

49. Usher, "The growth of English shipping," 467; Davis, "English Foreign Trade," 150, 162-64.

50. Davis, "English Foreign Trade," 150, 162-66; Minchington, *The Growth of English Overseas Trade,* pp. 30-31; Farnie, "The Commercial Empire of the Atlantic," 206; Davis, "English Foreign Trade," 105.

51. Davis, "English Foreign Trade," 164-66. Campeche and logwood dyes are generally more expensive than and inferior to Central American indigo, which further encouraged smuggling. See Fairlie, "Dyestuffs in the Eighteenth Century," 490-91. For the increase in English demand and Central American sales see Alden, "The Growth and Decline of Indigo Production in Colonial Brazil," 40-41, 44-45.

52. BM, Sloane, 2902, f. 153; Ramsey, "The Smugglers' Trade," 131-57.

53. "Causa contra Presidente Barrios Leal y otros," AGI/AG 34; AGGG, A1.23, legajo 4590, f. 37 (1690).
54. See, for example, the royal cédula of December 30, 1698, in Larreinaga, *Prontuario,* p. 121. "Customs racketeering" seems to have been one of the bases of the colonial commercial system both in North and South America. See Bailyn, "Communications and Trade," 387.
55. See the very large number of documents on contraband in AGI/AG 33 ("Cartas y expedientes del Presidente y Oidores de la Audiencia, 1691").
56. On July 21, 1707, the governor of Costa Rica, Francisco Serrano de Reina, was heavily fined and perpetually excluded from all offices under the Crown for trading with the English in Moín and Matina in 1702 and before. (AGGG, A1.24, 10216, 1572, f. 239.)
57. Scelle, *La Traite Negrière,* vol. 2, pp. 45-46, 49, 54, 59. For the close relations between Portugal and both England and Holland in the second half of the seventeenth century, see Mauro, *Le Portugal et l'Atlantique,* pp. 459-60, 463. See also Means, *The Spanish Main,* pp. 204, 208.
58. In 1710 the governor of Honduras was accused of trading with Jamaica (AGGG, A1.23, legajo 1525, f. 99, June 21, 1710). In 1714 the governor of Nicaragua was accused of the same thing, in AGGG, A1.23, legajo 1525, f. 315 (April 26, 1714). See also AGGG, A1.23, legajo 1525, f. 19 (n.d.); AGGG, A1.15, 50106, 5906 (1703); AGGG, A1.15, 50111, 5906 (1713) for other cases. English trading difficulties during the War of Spanish Succession are described in Nettels, "England and the Spanish-American Trade," p. 32.
59. See the evidence presented in Chapter Eighteen. Also, ANCR Cartago 188 (December 7, 1711); ANCR Complementario colonial 3996 (January 17, 1709).
60. Vignols, "L'Asiento français (1701-1713) et anglais (1713-1750)," 403-36. Pares, *War and Trade,* p. 8. For English concern at the growth of this French trade, see BM Additional Mss., 34, 335 (Southwell Papers), f. 111.
61. For legal asiento slaving to the Golfo Dulce by a French ship, see for example AGGG, A3.1, 22037, 1273 (1708); AGGG, A1.56, 45270, 5357 (1709). For illegal smuggling of negroes and goods for sale into Costa Rica in 1703 and 1704, see AGI/AG 359 (piezas 1, 2, and 6). Other cases are ANCR Complementario colonial 6491 (February 28, 1702); ANCR Complementario colonial 5837, f. 118 (July 20, 1719).
62. Haring, *Spanish Empire,* p. 336; Villalobos R., "Contrabando francés en el Pacífico," 49-52.
63. Haring, *Spanish Empire,* p. 336; Villalobos R., "Contrabando francés," p. 55. Extensive discussions of French smuggling between 1702 and 1712 are in AGI Indiferente General 2720. See also AGGG, A1.1, 58, 3 (1711), in which a smuggler from Bayonne caught distributing his wares in the jurisdiction of Comayagua (Honduras) tried to maintain that he was a legal trader by reason of his French nationality.
64. Haring, *Spanish Empire,* p. 335. The King was still warning the Audiencia in Santiago against traders from St. Malo as late as 1715. AGGG, A1.23, legajo 1526, f. 29 (November 25, 1715). AGI Escribanía de Cámara 339 has one case, in five piezas, in which three French officers were prosecuted for an arribada maliciosa at Acajutla in the ship "La Confianza" after trading in the South Sea. The case was still unresolved in 1708. The offenses took place between 1700 and 1705.
65. A royal decree sent to Central America between 1706 and 1708 refers to "the contraband trade which French and English ships are wont to make" ("suelen hacer"). AGGG, A1.22, legajo 1524, f. 19. See also ANCR Cartago 1081, f. 248 (August 1, 1711), which concerns semi-legal trade in the Golfo Dulce. For the Dutch in Curaçao and the low prices there, see Nettels, "England and the Spanish-American Trade," pp. 20, 25.
66. For English activities after 1713, see Brown, "The South Sea Company and Contraband Trade," 662-78; Nelson, "Contraband Trade under the Asiento," pp. 55-67. The decline of French trade and further rise of that of England is described

in Vignols, "L'Asiento français," pp. 403-36. The English grasp of the situation at the time is reflected in the attitudes of Allen, *Essay.* (The book was subsidized by the South Sea Company.)

67. "Expediente sobre comiso de la fragata nombrada La Anunciacion apresada en el puerto del Golfo Dulce: años de 1706 a 1708," AGI/AG 291. See also AGGG, A3.2, 28558, 1792 (1706) which may be about the same case. It refers to smuggling in Chiquimula and Zacapa. A similar scandal in 1711 implicated the governor and contador of Comayagua. The contraband involved was English. See, AGGG, A1.1, 57, 3 (1711).

68. This letter from President Pedro de Rivera to his King is used by Brown in her "Contraband Trade," 185. See also Edwards, *History,* vol. 1, pp. 292-93; Pares, *War and Trade,* pp. 18, 21, 115-20, 417; Floyd, *The Anglo-Spanish Struggle,* pp. 113-14.

69. Szaszdi Nagy, "El Comercio Ilícito," 271-83.

Conclusion

1. Gage, *The English-American,* pp. 161-64, 238, 241. We have already seen the comments from the governor of Jamaica in BM, Sloane 11410, f. 321v. For a typical seventeenth-century cacao tribute summary, see AGGG, A3.24, 36765 (1634). While the use of cacao as a beverage increased in Mexico its use as coinage probably declined. (Gibson, *The Aztecs under Spanish Rule,* p. 349.) Not so in Central America; see, for example, García de Palacios, *Carta,* p. 77; FX, 2:234; pieza 23, ff. 13v., 33, AGI/AG 43; FV, 1:171, where cacao is called "the copper coinage" of the province. Exchange difficulties caused by a shortage of cacao are mentioned in Bishop of Nicaragua to the Crown, July 16, 1647, AGI/AG 162. In 1703 Costa Rican authorities established an official rate of 100 beans to a real of silver. (ANCR Guatemala 129, f. 1 [1703]; CDHCR, 3:476.) Cockburn found the rate to be 70 beans to the real in Granada in the 1730s. See Cockburn, *The Unfortunate Enlishman,* p. 56.

2. Wisdom, *The Chorti,* pp. 34, 36, 61; Redfield, "Primitive Merchants," 49.

3. E.g., Wisdom, *The Chorti,* pp. 60-61, 95, 292, 336; Oakes, *The Two Crosses,* pp. 39, 42, 63.

4. CDHCR, 5:412-14; 9:151-60; ANCR Cartago 298 (1722). Information on Governor Haya Fernández was given to me by Señorita Luz Alba de Umaña, whose book on the governor has recently appeared in Costa Rica. (I have not yet seen it.) See also Parsons, *San Andrés y Providencia,* 12.

5. See the postscript to Hobsbawm, "The Crisis of the Seventeenth Century," pp. 57-62; Chaunu, "Le renversement de la tendance majeure des prix," pp. 219-55; and the same author's "Le XVIIᵉ siècle," vol. 1, pp. 337-55.

6. These views have been expressed vehemently by André Gunder Frank in various writings, e.g., his *Latin America,* pp. 236-38. A similar case is argued by John Lynch in his *Spain under the Hapsburgs, Volume Two, Spain and America, 1598-1700,* pp. 195-212. (See also the review of this book by Phelan, in *Journal of Latin American Studies* 2, part 2 (November 1970), 211-13.

7. See the previous chapter on smuggling, Chapter Twenty. For a reevaluation of expansion during depressions, see the stimulating article by Malowist, "Un essai d'histoire comparée," 923-29.

8. See the *Relaciones Geográficas* of the 1740s in AGGG, A1.17-1, 5003, 210. Some of these have been published in *Boletín del Archivo General del Gobierno* (Guatemala) 1, no. 1 (October 1935), 7-48.

9. Hamilton, "American Treasure," 338-57; Elliott, *The Old World and the New,* pp. 66-68, 73, 102.

Glossary

Achiote. Arnatto, a fugitive red or yellow vegetable dye.

Adelantado. Governor of a frontier province, leader of a military or exploring expedition.

Adscrito. A laborer bound to a farm or hacienda, a serf.

Alcabala. A sales tax, a license.

Alcalde mayor. Spanish official in charge of a district.

Alcalde ordinario. Member of a cabildo.

Alcaldía mayor. District governed by an alcalde mayor.

Alguacil. Constable, police officer.

Alguacil mayor. Chief police officer, usually attached to a cabildo.

Almiranta. Second ship of a fleet.

Almojarifazgo. Import or export tax.

Alternativa. Rotation of offices between members of two groups.

Ambiente. Milieu, atmosphere of a place or time.

Anexo. Dependent church, and by extension a dependent village.

Añil. Indigo.

Añilero. Indigo grower.

Arribada maliciosa. The fraudulent docking of a ship with false papers, usually a smuggler; sometimes used of smugglers who claimed to be storm-driven to port.

Arroba. Measure, 25 lbs.

Asiento. A contract, herein the slave contracts entered into by the Spanish Crown.

Audiencia. Court or governing body of a region; by extension the region itself.

Auto acordado. Decree and proclamation from a body of government.

Ayuda de costo. Supplementary expense account; a pension granted for past favors.

Ayuntamiento. Town council or cabildo.

Balandra. One masted, small ship.

Barbecho. Fallowing, rotation.

Barlovento. Windward.

Barrio. Town subdivision or quarter.

Benemérito. An employee worthy of reward.

Boca costa. Pacific foothills in Guatemala.

Bohío. Rural cabin, made of wood and straw.
Botija. A flagon.
Brea. Pitch.
Buen oro. Refined gold.

Caballería. Unit of land, about 105 acres.
Cabecera. Head village, usually with several villages under its jurisdiction.
Cabildo. Municipal council.
Cacaotal. Grove of cacao trees.
Cacaotero. Cacao grove owner.
Cacicazgo. A hereditary position covering a definite territory and the people in it. Hereditary rights held by a cacique.
Cacique. Indian chief.
Caja de comunidad. Community chest or treasury.
Calpisque. Indian tax collector or administrative agent.
Calpulli. Indian territorial or clan unit.
Canoa. Trough, vat, canoe.
Carga. Load. Also a measure of 2 fanegas.
Casta. Caste. A person of mixed blood.
Castellaño. A Castilian. Lord of a castle.
Cédula. Decree, paper on which an order is written.
Chacra. Small farm.
Chinamit. See Calpulli.
Chinampa. Aquatic garden.
Cimarrón. Runaway (used of cattle or slaves).
Ciudad. City.
Cocoliztli. A plague of undetermined type.
Cofradía. Sodality or religious fraternity.
Compadrazgo. Ritual parenthood.
Composición. Legalization of an irregular situation by payment of a fee; purchases of a license or permit.
Composición de tierra. Legalization of an irregular land title by payment of a fee; purchase of a royal grant of land.
Congregación. Concentration of scattered people into centralized villages.
Consejo. Council.
Consulado de comercio. Guild of merchants.
Corregidor. Spanish officer in charge of a district.
Corregidor de Indios. Official in charge of an Indian district.
Corregimiento. Region governed by a corregidor.
Cuadrilla. Work gang.
Cuartillo. One fourth of a real.

Defensor. Defender.
Dejarretar. To cut the leg tendons of cattle with a lance or knife (in Spain, desjarretar).
Derechos de entrada. Entry fees or taxes.
Derramas. Additional illegal burdens or taxes.
Despoblado. Depopulated zone.

Encomendero. The holder of an encomienda grant.

Encomienda. Grant of Indians, originally for labor and tribute, later mainly for tribute.

Encomiendas vacas. Unassigned encomiendas, a source of pensions.

Entrada. Military expedition to an unconquered or unknown province.

Entrada y saca. Entry to unconquered areas to bring out captured Indians to settle them in conquered areas.

Estancia. A cattle farm, a lesser Indian village or hamlet.

Fanega. A measure of 116 lbs.

Flota. Fleet, the Spanish system of convoys.

Fiscal. Crown attorney, the oidor charged with financial matters.

Fueros. Special rights or privileges.

Grana. Cochineal.

Grana silvestre. Wild cochineal.

Gucumatz. See Cocoliztli.

Guïrises. The poor, folk miners of the Tegucigalpa region.

Hacendado. Owner of an hacienda.

Hato. Small cattle farm, a country cabin.

Indios bravos. Unconquered Indians.

Indios vacos. Indians in an unassigned encomienda.

Ingenio. A sugar mill.

Juez de arribadas. Judge charged with investigating smuggling and fraud in ports.

Juez de milpas. Spanish official charged with supervising Indian agriculture.

Juez repartidor. Spanish official charged with the recruiting and assignment of repartimiento labor.

Juro. A pension from public funds; repayment over time of a forced royal loan or "voluntary" donation.

Justiciador. A man who brings and imposes stern or bloody justice; title given to Pedrarias Dávila.

Juzgado. Tribunal.

Labrador. Spanish farmer.

Ladino. A non-Indian, Spanish-speaking inhabitant of Guatemala or Chiapas.

Latifundia. The system of latifundios; large, underutilized rural estates.

Limeño. A person from Lima.

Macehual. An Indian commoner.

Madre de Cacao. Large tree planted to shade cacao bushes.

Maravedí. 34th part of a real.

Marco. A coin.
Matlazáhuatl. A plague of disputed origin.
Mayorazgo. An entailed property.
Mayordomo. Overseer, foreman, manager.
Mestizo. Person of mixed white and Indian ancestry.
Milpa. Plot worked by an Indian.
Milpero. Worker on or owner of a milpa.
Moclón. Peruvian coin used in Central America.
Monte. Scrub, uncultivated land, abandoned land.
Mortual. An inventory of goods made upon the death of a person.

Naboría. Hacienda worker, "free" Indian laborer.
Nopal. Cochineal bearing cactus plant.
Nopalería. Cochineal plantation.

Obraje. Dye works, any workshop.
Obraje de Paños. Textile mill.
Oficial Real. Royal official.
Oidor. Judge of an Audiencia.

Palenque. A long house or communal dwelling, sometimes fortified.
Paniaguado. A dependent, a "hanger-on."
Parcialidad. Section of a town, an adjacent village.
Patronato Real. Royal patronage and rights in ecclesiastical matters.
Peninsular. A person from Spain
Peón. A foot soldier, later a hacienda worker or common laborer.
Perulero. From Peru, money of Peruvian origin.
Peso de oro. Gold peso.
Pesquisador. Inspector, investigator.
Pila. Large vat.
Pochteca. Indian merchant.
Policía. Order and government.
Primeros pobladores. First settlers.
Principal. Indian aristocrat.
Procurador. Representative sent from one agency to another.
Provincianos. People from the provinces (in Central America, those not
      from Guatemala).
Pueblo. Indian village.
Puntero. Man skilled in knowing the moment when indigo dye coagulates.

Quinto. The royal fifth (a tax).

Ranchería. A small rural settlement, also a rural cabin.
Real. Spanish coin.
Real caja. Royal treasury.
Realengas. Lands belonging to the Crown.
Recua. Mule-train.
Regidor. Council member of a cabildo.
Registro. A license; sometimes short for navío de registro, a licensed ship.

Relator. Clerk to the Audiencia; his duties included the taking of testimony and the condensation of documents for the judges.

Repartimiento. A system of Indian draft labor on a rotating, quota basis; also forced sales or purchases imposed on Indians or others of the poorer classes.

Reservado. An Indian exempt from tribute.

Salutación. An illegal tax which Indians were forced to pay priests or officials passing through their village.

Tameme. Indian porter.

Tanda. See Repartimiento.

Teniente de gobernador. Minor Spanish official, usually in the rural areas or smaller Spanish cities.

Tercio. Infantry regiment.

Ternativa. Rotation of offices among individuals representing three groups.

Tierras baldías. Vacant lands owned by the Crown; public lands.

Tierras realengas. See Realengas.

Tinta añil. Indigo dye.

Tostón. Half a peso.

Trajín. The transportation of goods or merchandise from one place to another; often refers to the crossing of the isthmus of Panama.

Tuna. See Nopal.

Urca. Cargo ship, broad-beamed.

Valle. Valley; by extension an unincorporated settlement of Spaniards in the countryside.

Vecino. Citizen freeholder of a Spanish city.

Villa. Small Spanish town.

Visita. Tour of inspection, or an investigation of an official's conduct while in office.

Visitador. Inspector, judge in a court of enquiry.

Xiquilite. Indigo plant.

Xiquilitero. Worker on an indigo plantation.

Zacate. Brush, hay, reeds.

Zopilote. Vulture.

Zurrón. Large leather sack for storing goods.

Bibliography

Archival research on colonial Central America presents certain difficulties. The main one is the appallingly scattered nature of the materials. Another is the paucity of the documentary collections for certain areas. Political and geological turbulence has destroyed most of the colonial holdings of El Salvador and Nicaragua, while those of Honduras tend to emphasize Tegucigalpa and have little on regions such as Comayagua, Gracias a Dios, or San Pedro Sula. As a consequence of these difficulties the researcher has an abundance of materials for some regions, epochs, or topics, and little for others of undoubted importance.

The two archives which have been most used in preparing this book are the Archivo General de Gobierno de Guatemala (AGGG) in Guatemala City, and the Archivo General de Indias (AGI), Seville. In the Archivo General de Gobierno de Guatemala, work was done in every section which held sixteenth- or seventeenth-century materials. In the Archivo General de Indias research was concentrated in the section Audiencia de Guatemala (AGI/AG). Some work was also done in Patronato, Escribanía de Cámara, Indiferente General, Justicia, and Contaduría, in about that order of intensity.

Two other archives in Central America provided useful material. The Archivo Nacional de Costa Rica (ANCR), San José, provided rich sources for that subregion, and was managed and cataloged so well that research was greatly facilitated. The Archivo Nacional de Historia de Honduras (ANHH), Tegucigalpa, had useful material on mining and on the Tegucigalpa area in general. The collections are spotty, however, before 1700, and research in them is difficult.

In Europe beyond the AGI several major archives were of some help. In the British Museum (BM), the Edgerton, Sloane, and Additional Mss. sections provided materials on Jamaica, piracy, and navigation. In Paris the Bibliothèque Nationale (BNP) held several different kinds of pertinent materials. The two special collections entitled Fonds Américains and Fonds Mexicains (the latter stored in "Oriental Languages") provided material on the Indians and on early missionary efforts. In the French materials proper, several sections (e.g., Fonds Colbert, Cinq Cents Colbert) held useful documents on contraband, piracy, the asiento, and the Franco-Spanish alliance of the early eighteenth century. Other archives in Paris provided useful items, especially the Bibliothèque de l'Arsénal, and the Bibliothèque de la Chambre de Députés.

In Madrid the two most useful archives were the Biblioteca Nacional (BNM) and the Biblioteca del Palacio Real (BPR). In the latter the *Miscelanea de Ayala* were particularly rich. The Real Academia de la Historia (RAH), also in Madrid, holds some important *Relaciones Geográficas* in the Muñoz collection, and the Archivo Histórico Nacional (AHN) has a few items of value from the late seventeenth and early eighteenth centuries.

In the United States several archives and libraries contain colonial documents from Central America. Brief visits were made to the Ayer Collection, Newberry Library, Chicago (ACNL), to the Library of the American Philosophical Society, and to the Bancroft Library of the University of California, Berkeley. The University Library, University of Texas (UT), kindly provided microfilmed material.

The published guides to Central American materials in the two archives most used in this study are of only general help. Tudela de la Orden, *Los manuscritos de América,* is a broad survey of materials in all of Spain, while the "Indice de documentos existentes en el Archivo de Indias de Sevilla que tienen interés para Guatemala" is far from complete and covers only the area of modern Guatemala. Torre Revello, *El Archivo General de Indias,* is of help in orientation. José Joaquín Pardo's *Indice* to the AGGG was not completed and may confuse those unfamiliar with the system of classification. For Honduras the Guide published by the Instituto Panamericano de Geografía e Historia is fairly complete. There is little in the way of a guide for Costa Rican sources.

Guides to the other European archives used here are more helpful. Mention should be made of the works of Boban, and of Calderón Quijano and Navarro García, of the *Catalogue de Manuscrits Mexicains de la Bibliothèque Nationale,* and of Gayangos. Volume 1 of Waldo G. Leland's *Guide* is helpful for Paris, while Morel-Fatio is somewhat out of date. Julián Paz's *Catálogo* is of use in the Biblioteca Nacional.

In the United States several guides are of help. Those by Brinton, Butler, Castañeda and Dabbs, and Pardo are especially notable. Published material on Central America is extensive, and considerable amounts are to be found in collections primarily devoted to other areas. The volumes so far published of the *Handbook of Middle American Indians* contain excellent bibliographies, as does Bancroft's still useful *History of Central America*.

The chroniclers of the conquest, such as Alvarado, Andagoya, and Díaz del Castillo, describe the events of the first contacts. Particularly useful for the sixteenth and seventeenth centuries are the great Central American chroniclers: Antonio de Remesal (AR), Francisco Antonio de Fuentes y Guzmán (FG), Francisco Vázquez (FV), and Francisco Ximénez (FX). Even more important are the large documentary publications. The CDI, CDIE, and others contain useful items. The CS and CDHCR are indispensable. Collections devoted mainly to Mexico, such as the two compiled by Francisco del Paso y Troncoso, contain Central American items of value.

Travelers' accounts are useful and entertaining. Among the more notable are those by Cockburn, Dampier, Gage, and Vázquez de Espinosa. Many of the large standard histories, for example those by Acosta, Benzoni, Fernández de Oviedo, Herrera, and López de Velasco, devote considerable attention to Central America. Scholars can find useful material by reading the appropriate sections in general works on Central American history, general works on the individual modern nations, or some books on specific topics which span both the colonial and the national periods. Equally important are the various revistas, boletines, and anales published by the national archives, and the several societies of geography, history, and anthropology in the five nations and Chiapas. These journals also publish colonial documents from time to time, and some have included partial catalogs to various local documentary deposits.

Central America has not drawn its proportionate share of modern scholars. The most outstanding ones for the purposes of this study are mentioned in the Preface or become apparent in the notes.

Abel, W. *Geschichte der deutschen Landwirtschaft vom frühen Mittelalter bis zum 19. Jahrhundert.* Deutsche Agrargeschichte, vol. 2, 2d ed. Stuttgart: Verlag Eugen Ulmer, 1967.
_____. "Wandlungen des Fleischverbrauches und Fleischversorgung im Deutschland seit dem ausgehenden Mittelalter." *Berichte über Landwirtschaft.* New ser. 12 (1937): 411-14.

Acosta, José de. *Historia natural y moral de las Indias.* Mexico: Fondo de Cultura Económica, 1940.
Actas de cabildo de la ciudad de México. Title varies. 54 vols. Mexico: Imprenta de "El Correo Español," 1889–1916.
Adams, Eleanor B. "A Bio-Bibliography of Franciscan Authors in Colonial Central America." *The Americas* 8 (1952), 431-71; 9 (1952), 37-86.
Adams, Richard E. W. "Maya Archeology 1958–1968, A Review." *Latin American Research Review* 4 (1969), 3-45.
_____. "The Ceramic Chronology of the Southern Maya, Second Preliminary Report: 1966." Mimeographed. Minneapolis: University of Minnesota, 1966.
A Guide to Manuscripts Relating to the American Indian in the Library of the American Philosophical Society. Compiled by John E. Freeman. Memoirs of the American Philosophical Society, vol. 65. Philadelphia: The American Philosophical Society, 1966.
Aguirre Beltrán, Gonzalo. *La población negra de México, 1519–1810.* Mexico, D.F.: Ediciones Fuente Cultural, 1946.
Alba C., M. M. *Etnología y población histórica de Panamá.* Panama: Imprenta Nacional, 1928.
Albores G., Eduardo J. *Chiapas pre-hispánico.* Tuxtla Gutiérrez: Instituto de Ciencias y Artes de Chiapas, 1959.
Alcedo, Antonio de. *Diccionario geográfico-histórico de las Indias occidentales ó América.* 5 vols. Madrid: Imprenta de Manuel González, 1786-89.
Alden, Dauril. "The Growth and Decline of Indigo Production in Colonial Brazil: A Study in Comparative Economic History." *The Journal of Economic History* 25 (1965), 35-60.
Allen, Robert. *An Essay on the Nature and Methods of Carrying on a Trade to the South Sea, by Robert Allen, Who Resided some Years in the Kingdom of Peru.* London: Richard Mount, 1712.
Alvarado, Pedro de. *An Account of the Conquest of Guatemala, in 1524.* Edited by Sedley J. Mackie. New York: The Cortes Society, 1924.
Alvarado García, Ernesto. *Los forjadores de la Honduras colonial; la conquista pacífica de Honduras, héroes y mártires.* Tegucigalpa: Talleres Tipográficos Nacionales, 1938.
Alvarado Tezozomoc, Hernando. *Crónica Mexicana.* Mexico: Imprenta Universitaria, 1943.
Alvarez Rubiano, Pablo. *Pedrarias Dávila.* Madrid: Consejo Superior de Investigaciones Científicas, Instituto Gonzalo Fernández de Oviedo, 1954.
A Nautical Description of the Gulf of Mexico and Bay of Honduras. 7th ed. London: J. Imray and Son, 1956.
Andagoya, Pascual de. *The Narrative of Pascual de Andagoya.* Edited and translated by Clements R. Markham. London: The Hakluyt Society, 1865.
Anderson, C. L. G. *Old Panama and Castilla del Oro.* New York: North River Press, 1911.
Andrade, Vicente de P. *Ensayo bibliográfico mexicano del siglo XVII.* 2d ed. Mexico: Imprenta del Museo Nacional, 1899.
_____. *Noticias biográficas de los Ilmos. Sres. Obispos de Chiapas.* 2d ed. Mexico: Imprenta Guadalupana, 1907.

Annis, Verne L. *La arquitectura de la Antigua Guatemala, 1543-1773.* Bilingual Edition. Guatemala: Universidad de San Carlos, Editorial Universitaria, 1968.

Araña, Tomás de. "Relación de los estragos y ruinas que ha padecido la ciudad de Santiago de Guatemala, por los terremotos y fuego de sus volcanes, en este año de 1717." *Anales de la Sociedad de Geografía e Historia* (Guatemala) 17 (1941), 148-60, 232-43.

Archivos nacionales de Costa Rica. *Indice de los protocolos de Cartago.* 6 vols. San José: Tipografía Nacional, 1909-30.

Arcila Farias, Eduardo. *Comercio entre Venezuela y México en los siglos XVI y XVII.* Mexico: El Colegio de México, 1950.

―――. *Economía colonial de Venezuela.* Mexico: Fondo de cultura económica, 1946.

Arévalo, Rafael de, ed. *Colección de documentos antiguos del Archivo del Ayuntamiento de la ciudad de Guatemala.* Guatemala: Imprenta "La Luna," Edición del Museo Guatemalteco, 1857.

―――. *Libro de actas del ayuntamiento de la ciudad de Santiago de Guatemala, desde la fundación de la misma ciudad en 1524 hasta 1530.* Guatemala: Tipografía Nacional, 1932.

Arroyo S., Victor Manuel. "Nauatismos y Nahuatlismos en Costa Rica." *Tlatoani* (Mexico) 2d ser. 7 (1953), 13-17.

Artiñano y de Galdácano, Gervasio de. *Historia del comercio con las Indias durante el dominio de los Austrias.* Barcelona: Talleres de Oliva de Vilanova, 1917.

Asturias, Francisco. *Historia de la medicina en Guatemala.* Guatemala: Editorial Universitaria, 1958.

Ayón, Tomás. *Historia de Nicaragua.* 2d ed. 3 vols. Madrid: Escuela Profesional de Artes Gráficas, 1956.

Baehrel, R. "La haine de classe en temps d'épidémie." *Annales, E. S. C.* 7 (1952), 351-60.

Bagú, Sergio. *Estructura social de la colonia. Ensayo de historia comparada de América Latina.* Buenos Aires: Librería "El Ateneo" Editorial, 1952.

Bailyn, Bernard. "Communications and Trade: The Atlantic in the Seventeenth Century." *The Journal of Economic History* 13 (1953), 378-87.

Baldwin, Robert E. "Export Technology and Development from a Subsistence Level." *Economic Journal* 73 (1963), 80-92.

―――. "Patterns of Development in Newly Settled Regions." *Manchester School of Economics and Social Studies* 24 (1956), 266-84.

Bancroft, Hubert Howe. *History of Central America.* 3 vols. San Francisco: The History Company, 1882-87.

Baratier, Edouard. *La Démographie Provençale du XIIIᵉ au XVIᵉ Siècle: Avec chiffres de comparaison pour le XVIIIᵉ siècle.* Ecole Pratique des Hautes Etudes—VIᵉ Section, Centre de Recherches Historiques, Démographie et Sociétés, 5. Paris: S.E.V.P.E.N., 1961.

Barberena, Santiago I. *Historia de El Salvador.* 2d ed. 2 vols. San Salvador: Imprenta Nacional, 1914-17.

Barlow, Robert H. *The Extent of the Empire of the Culhua Mexica.* Ibero-Americana, vol. 28. Berkeley and Los Angeles: University of California Press, 1949.

Barnett, S. A. "Rats." *Scientific American* 116, no. 1 (1967), 79-85.

Barón Castro, Rodolfo, *La población de El Salvador.* Madrid: Consejo

Superior de Investigaciones Científicas, Instituto Gonzalo Fernández de Oviedo, 1942.

_____. *Reseña histórica de la Villa de San Salvador.* Madrid: Ediciones Cultura Hispánica, Colección historia y geografia, 1950.

Bataillon, Marcel. "Las Casas et Le Licencié Cerrato." *Bulletin Hispanique* 55 (1953), 79-87.

_____. "La Vera Paz, Roman et histoire." *Bulletin Hispanique* 53 (1951), 235-300.

Bates, Marston. "Man as an Agent in the Spread of Organisms." In *Man's Role in Changing the Face of the Earth.* Edited by William L. Thomas, Jr., et al. Chicago: University of Chicago Press, 1956.

Batres Jáuregui, Antonio. *La América Central ante la historia.* 3 vols. Guatemala: Tip. Sánchez y De Guise, 1920.

Beals, Ralph L. "Acculturation." *Handbook of Middle American Indians.* vol. 6. Austin: University of Texas Press, 1967.

Bean, J. M. W. "Plague, Population and Economic Decline in England in the Later Middle Ages." *The Economic History Review* 2d ser. 15 (1963), 423-37.

Bennassar, Bartolomé. *Recherches sur les Grandes Epidémies dans le Nord de l'Espagne a la fin du XVIe siècle: Problèmes de documentation et de méthode.* Ecole Pratique des Hautes Etudes—VIe Section, Centre de Recherches Historiques, Démographie et Sociétés, 12. Paris: S.E.V.P.E.N., 1969.

Bennett, Charles F. *Human Influences on the Zoogeography of Panama.* Ibero-Americana, vol. 51. Berkeley and Los Angeles: University of California Press, 1968.

Bennett, J. Harry. "Cary Helyar, Merchant and Planter of Seventeenth-Century Jamaica." *The William and Mary Quarterly.* 3d ser. 21 (1964), 40-76.

_____. "William Whaley, Planter of Seventeenth-Century Jamaica." *Agricultural History* 40 (1966), 113-23.

Benzoni, Girolamo. *La Historia del Mondo Nuovo.* Venice: Appresso Francesco Rampazetto, 1565.

Bergmann, J. F. "Cacao and its Production in Central America." *Tijdschrift voor economische en sociale Geografie* 48 (1957), 43-49.

_____. "The Distribution of Cacao Cultivation in Pre-Columbian America." *Annals of the Association of American Geographers* 59 (1969), 85-96.

Biermann, Benno. "Der Zweite Missionversuch bei den Choles in der Verapaz (1672–1676)." *Jahrbuch für Geschichte von Staat, Wirtschaft und Gesellschaft Lateinamerikas* 2 (1965), 245-56.

_____. "Don Fray Juan Ramírez de Arellano, O. P. und sein Kampf gegen die Unterdrückung der Indianer." *Jahrbuch für Geschichte von Staat, Wirtschaft und Gesellschaft Lateinamerikas* 4 (1967), 318-47.

_____. "Missiongeschichte der Verapaz in Guatemala." *Jahrbuch für Geschichte von Staat, Wirtschaft und Gesellschaft Lateinamerikas* 1 (1964), 117-56.

Biraben, Jean-Noël. "Certain Demographic Characteristics of the Plague Epidemic in France, 1720–22." *Daedalus* 97 (1968), 536-45.

_____, and J. Le Goff. "La peste dans le haut moyen-age." *Annales, E.S.C.* 24 (1969), 1485-1510.

Bishko, Charles Julian. "The Peninsular Background of Latin American

Cattle Ranching." *Hispanic American Historical Review* 32 (1952), 491-515.

Blanco-Fombona, Rufino. *El conquistador español del siglo XVI: ensayo de interpretación.* Madrid: Editorial Mundo Latino, 1921.

Blom, Frans. "Commerce, trade and monetary units of the Maya." *Middle American Research Series* 4 (1932), 531-56.

Boban, Eugene. *Documents pour servir a l'histoire du Mexique: Catalogue Raisonné de la Collection de M.E. Eugene Goupil.* 2 vols. Paris: Ernest Leroux, editeur, 1891.

Boccaccio, Giovanni. *Il Decameron.* Edited by Luigi Russo. Firenze: Sansoni, 1939.

Boletín del Archivo General del Gobierno (Guatemala). 11 vols. (1935-46).

Bonet de Sotillo, Dolores. *El tráfico ilegal en las colonias españolas.* Instituto de Estudios Hispanoamericanos de la Facultad de Humanidades y Educación. Caracas: Editorial Sucre, 1955.

Bonnassieux, Pierre. *Les Grandes Compagnies de Commerce.* Paris: E. Plon, Nourrit et Cie., Imprimeurs-Editeurs, 1892.

Borah, Woodrow. "¿América como modelo? El Impacto Demográfico de la Espansión Europea sobre el mundo no Europeo." *Cuadernos Americanos* 125, no. 6 (1962), 176-85.

————. *Early Colonial Trade and Navigation between Mexico and Peru.* Ibero-Americana, vol. 38. Berkeley and Los Angeles: University of California Press, 1954.

————. *New Spain's Century of Depression.* Ibero-Americana, vol. 35. Berkeley and Los Angeles: University of California Press, 1951.

————. "Race and Class in Mexico." *Pacific Historical Review* 23 (1954), 331-42.

————, and Sherburne F. Cook. "Conquest and Population: A Demographic Approach to Mexican History." *Proceedings of the American Philosophical Society* 113, no. 2 (1969), 177-83.

————. "La despoblación del México Central en el siglo XVI." *Historia Mexicana* 12 (1962), 1-12.

————. *Price Trends of Some Basic Commodities in Central Mexico, 1531-1570.* Ibero-Americana, vol. 40. Berkeley and Los Angeles: University of California Press, 1958.

————. *The Aboriginal Population of Central Mexico on the Eve of the Spanish Conquest.* Ibero-Americana, vol. 45. Berkeley and Los Angeles: University of California Press, 1963.

————. *The Indian Population of Central Mexico, 1531-1610.* Ibero-Americana, vol. 44. Berkeley and Los Angeles: University of California Press, 1960.

————. *The Population of Mexico in 1548.* Ibero-Americana, vol. 43. Berkeley and Los Angeles: University of California Press, 1960.

Borhegyi, Stephan F. de. "Archeological Synthesis of the Guatemalan Highlands." *Handbook of Middle American Indians,* vol. 2. Austin: University of Texas Press, 1965.

————. "Settlement Patterns in the Guatemalan Highlands: Past and Present." In *Prehistoric Settlement Patterns in the New World.* Edited by Gordon R. Willey. Viking Fund Publications in Anthropology, no. 23. New York: Wenner-Gren Foundation for Anthropological Research, Inc., 1956.

———. "Settlement Patterns of the Guatemalan Highlands." *Handbook of Middle American Indians,* vol. 2, *Archeology of Southern Mesoamerica,* part 1. Austin: University of Texas Press, 1965.

———. "The Development of Folk and Complex Cultures in the Southern Maya Area." *American Antiquity* 21 (1956), 343-56.

Boserup, Ester. *The Conditions of Agricultural Growth.* Chicago: Aldine Publishing Company, 1965.

Bowsky, W. M. "The Impact of the Black Death upon Sienese Government and Society." *Speculum* 34 (1964), 16-20.

Brasseur de Bourbourg, Charles Etienne. *Bibliothèque mexico-guatémalienne.* Paris: Maisonneuve et cie., 1871.

———. *Histoire des nations civilisées du Mexique et de l'Amérique-Centrale.* 4 vols. Paris: A. Bertrand, 1857-59.

Braudel, Fernand. *La Mediterranée et le Monde mediterranéen à l'époque de Philippe II.* Paris: Librairie Armand Colin, 1949.

Bravo de la Serna y Manrique, Marcos. *Carta pastoral, en silvas de un prelado, a los ministros de su rebaño.* Guatemala: Joseph de Pineda Ibarra, 1678.

Brinton, Daniel G. "A notice of some manuscripts in Central American languages." *American Journal of Science and Arts.* 2d ser. 47 (1869), 222-30.

———. "Catalogue of the Berendt Linguistic Collection." *Bulletin of the Free Museum of Science and Arts* (University of Pennsylvania) 2 (1900), 1-32.

———. *Nagualism: a Study in Native American Folklore and History.* Philadelphia: MaCCalla and Company, 1894.

Bronstad, Johannes. *The Vikings.* Baltimore: Penguin Books, 1965.

Bronson, Bennet. "Roots and the Subsistence of the Ancient Maya." *Southwestern Journal of Anthropology* 22 (1966), 251-79.

Brown, Vera Lee. "Contraband Trade: A Factor in the Decline of Spain's Empire in America." *Hispanic American Historical Review* 8 (1928), 178-78.

———. "The South Sea Company and Contraband Trade." *The American Historical Review* 31 (1926), 662-78.

Bruman, Henry. "The Culture History of Mexican Vanilla." *Hispanic American Historical Review* 28 (1948), 360-76.

Bunzel, Ruth. "The Role of Alcoholism in Two Central American Cultures." *Psychiatry* 3 (1940), 361-87.

Burckhardt, J. *The Civilization of the Renaissance in Italy.* 2 vols. New York: Harper and Row, Publishers, Inc., 1958.

Burdon, Sir John Alder. *Archives of British Honduras.* 2 vols. London: Sifton Praed and Co., Ltd., 1931.

Burney, James. *History of the Bùccaneers of America.* London: George Allen and Unwin, Ltd., 1949.

Burns, Sir Alan. *History of the British West Indies.* 2d ed., rev. London: George Allen and Unwin, Ltd., 1965.

Butler, Ruth Lapham. *A Check List of Manuscripts in the Edward E. Ayer Collection.* Chicago: The Newberry Library, 1937.

Cabrillana, Nicolás. "Las crisis del siglo XIV en Castilla: La Peste Negra en el Obispado de Palencia." *Hispania: Revista Española de Historia* 28, no. 109 (1968), 245-58.

Calderón Quijano, José Antonio. "El fuerte de San Fernando de Omoa: su historia e importancia que tuvo en la defensa del golfo de Honduras." *Revista de Indias* 3 (1942), 515-48.

———, and Luis Navarro García. *Guía de los documentos, mapas, y planos sobre historia de América y España moderna en la Biblioteca Nacional de París, Museo Británico y Public Record Office de Londres.* Seville: Escuela de Estudios Hispano-Americanos, 1962.

Callendar, Guy Stevens, ed. *Selections from the Economic History of the United States, 1765-1860.* Boston: Ginn, 1909.

Calnek, Edward E. "Highland Chiapas before the Spanish Conquest." Ph.D. dissertation, University of Chicago, 1962.

Cancian, Frank. "Political and Religious Organizations." *Handbook of Middle American Indians,* vol. 6. Austin: University of Texas Press, 1967.

Cánovas del Castillo, Antonio. *Historia de la decadencia de España desde el advenimiento de Felipe III al trono hasta la muerte de Carlos II.* 2d ed. Madrid: J. Ruiz, 1910.

Carles, Rubén Darío. *220 años del período colonial en Panamá.* Panama: Talleres de The Star and Herald Co., 1949.

Carmack, Robert M. *Toltec Influence on the Postclassic Culture History of Highland Guatemala.* Middle American Research Institute, Publication 26. New Orleans: Tulane University Press, 1968.

Carmagnani, Marcello. "Colonial Latin American Demography: Growth of Chilean Population, 1700-1830." *Journal of Social History* 1 (1967), 179-91.

Carpentier, Elisabeth. "La peste noire: Famines et épidémies au XIVᵉ siècle." *Annales, E.S.C.* 17 (1962), 1074-85.

———. *Une ville devant la peste: Orvieto et la Peste Noire de 1348.* Ecole Pratique des Hautes Etudes—VIᵉ Section, Centre de Recherches Historiques, Démographie et Sociétés, 7. Paris: S.E.V.P.E.N., 1962.

Carrasco, Pedro. "Don Juan Cortés, cacique de Santa Cruz Quiché." *Estudios de cultura Maya* 6 (1967), 251-66.

———. "The Mesoamerican Indian during the Colonial Period." *Indian Mexico, Past and Present.* Edited by Betty Bell. Los Angeles: University of California at Los Angeles, Latin American Center, 1967.

Cartas de Indias. Madrid: Imprenta de Manuel G. Hernández, 1877.

Casarrubias, Vicente. *Rebeliones indígenas en la Nueva España: con una introducción sobre las rebeliones indígenas de Guatemala.* Biblioteca de Cultura Popular, no. 18. Guatemala: Editorial del Ministerio de Educación Pública, 1951.

Castañeda, Carlos E., and Jack Autrey Dabbs. *Guide to the Latin American Manuscripts in the University of Texas Library.* Committee on Latin American Studies, American Council of Learned Societies. Cambridge, Mass.: Harvard University Press, 1939.

Castañeda Paganini, Roberto. *La cultura tolteca—pipil de Guatemala.* Guatemala: Editorial del Ministerio de Educación Pública "José de Pineda Ibarra," 1959.

Castro y Tosi, Norberto de. "La población de la ciudad de Cartago en los siglos XVII y XVIII," *Revista de los Archivos Nacionales* (Costa Rica) 28 (1964), 3-28.

_____. *Pasajeros a Indias para Centro-américa.* San José: Supremo Tribunal y Colegio de Armas, 1961.

Catalogue des manuscrits mexicains de la Bibliothèque Nationale. Paris: Librairie Emile Bouillon, Editeur, 1899.

Cerwin, Herbert. *Bernal Díaz, Historian of the Conquest.* Norman: University of Oklahoma Press, 1963.

Céspedes del Castillo, Guillermo. *La Avería en el comercio de Indias.* Seville: Publicaciones de la Escuela de Estudios Hispano-Americanos de la Universidad de Sevilla, 15, 1945.

Chamberlain, Robert S. "Castillian Backgrounds of the Repartimiento-Encomienda." *Contributions to American Anthropology and History* 5, no. 25 (1939), 23-66.

_____. "Ensayo Sobre el Adelantado don Francisco de Montejo y sus proyectos para el desarrollo económico de la Provincia de Honduras e Higueras." *Anales de la Sociedad de Geografía e Historia.* (Guatemala) 20 (1946), 209-17.

_____. "Plan del siglo XVI para abrir un camino de Puerto Caballos a la Bahía de Fonseca en sustitución de la ruta de Panamá." *Anales de la Sociedad de Geografía e Historia* (Guatemala) 21 (1946), 61-65.

_____. "The Concept of the Señor Natural as Revealed by Castillian Law and Administrative Documents." *Hispanic American Historical Review* 19 (1939), 130-37.

_____. *The Conquest and Colonization of Honduras, 1502–1550.* Washington, D.C.: Carnegie Institution of Washington, Publication 598, 1953.

_____. *The Conquest and Colonization of Yucatan, 1527–1550.* Washington, D.C.: Carnegie Institution of Washington, Publication 582, 1948.

_____. "The founding of the City of Gracias a Dios, first seat of the Audiencia de los Confines." *Hispanic American Historical Review* 26 (1946), 2-18.

_____. *The Governorship of the Adelantado Francisco de Montejo in Chiapas, 1539–1544.* Washington, D.C.: Carnegie Institution of Washington, Publication 574, Contribution 46, 1947.

Chapman, Anne M. *Los Nicarao y los Chorotega Según las Fuentes Históricas.* Serie Historia y Geografía, no. 4. San José: Universidad de Costa Rica, 1960.

_____. "Port of Trade Enclaves in Aztec and Maya Civilization." *Trade and Market in the Early Empires.* Edited by Karl Polanyi et al. Glencoe: The Free Press, 1957.

Chaunu, Pierre. *Conquête et Exploitation des Nouveaux Mondes (XVIᵉ Siècle).* Nouvelle Clio, L'Histoire et ses problèmes, 26 bis. Paris: Presses Universitaires de France, 1969.

_____. *L'Amérique et les Amériques.* Paris: Librairie Armand Colin, 1964.

_____. "Le renversement de la tendance majeure des prix et des activités au XVIIᵉ siècle. Problèmes de fait et de méthode." In *Studi in onore di Amintore Fanfani, IV, (Evo Moderno).* Milan: Dott. A. Guiffrè-Editore, 1962.

_____. *Les Philippines et le Pacifique des Iberiques (XVIᵉ, XVIIᵉ, XVIIIᵉ siècles).* Paris: S.E.V.P.E.N., 1960.

_____. *L'Expansion Européenne du XIIᵉ au XVᵉ Siècle.* Nouvelle Clio,

L'Histoire et ses problèmes, 26. Paris: Presses Universitaires de France, 1969.

————. "Le XVIIe siècle: Problèmes de conjoncture, conjoncture globale et conjonctures rurales françaises." In *Mélanges d'Histoire économique et sociale en hommage au professeur Antony Babel,* vol. 1. Geneva: Imprimerie de la Tribune de Genève, 1963.

————. "Une histoire hispano-américaniste pilote; en marge de l'oeuvre de l'Ecole de Berkeley." *Revue Historique* 224 (1960), 339-68.

————, and Huguette Chaunu. "Le climat des rapports franco-espagnols à Cadiz dans la seconde moitié du XVIIe siècle." *Mélanges offerts à Marcel Bataillon.* Bordeaux: Féret et Fils, Editeurs, 1962.

————. *Séville et l'Atlantique.* 8 vols. in 13. Paris: Colin, 1955–59.

Cheesman, E. E. "Notes on the Nomenclature, Classification and Possible Relationship of Cacao Populations." *Tropical Agriculture* 21 (1944): 144-59.

Chevalier, François. *La formation des grands domaines au Mexique. Terre et société aux XVIe-XVIIe siècles.* Institut d'Ethnologie, Travaux et Mémoires. Paris: Université de Paris, 1952.

Cheyney, Edward P. *The Dawn of a New Era, 1250–1453.* The Rise of Modern Europe Series. New York: Harper and Row, Publishers, Inc., 1936.

Childs, St. Julien Ravenel. *Malaria and Colonization in the Carolina Low Country, 1526–1696.* The Johns Hopkins Studies in Historical and Political Science, Series 58, no. 1. Baltimore: The Johns Hopkins Press, 1940.

Chinchilla Aguilar, Ernesto. *El ayuntamiento colonial de la ciudad de Guatemala.* Guatemala: Editorial Universitaria, vol. 37, 1961.

————. "El Ramo de Aguas de la ciudad de Guatemala en la Epoca Colonial." *Antropología e Historia de Guatemala* 5 (1953), 19-31.

————. *Historia del arte en Guatemala, 1524–1962. Arquitectura, pintura, y escultura.* Guatemala: Ministerio de Educación Pública, Centro Editorial "José de Pineda Ibarra," 1963.

————. "La danza de Tum-teleche o Loj-tum." *Antropología e Historia de Guatemala* 7 (1951), 17-20.

————. *La inquisición en Guatemala.* Publicaciones del Instituto de Antropología e Historia. Guatemala: Editorial del Ministerio de Educación Pública, 1953.

————. "Tecpan Guatemala." *Antropología e Historia de Guatemala* 13 (1961), 9-14.

Christelow, Allan. "Contraband Trade between Jamaica and the Spanish Main, and the Free Port Act of 1766." *Hispanic American Historical Review* 22 (1942), 309-43.

Cid Fernández, Enrique del. *Don Gabino de Gainza y otros estudios.* Colección de autores guatemaltecos, vol. 4. Guatemala: Editorial Universitaria, 1959.

Cockburn, John. *The Unfortunate Englishman . . . A Journey over Land from the Gulph of Honduras to the Great South Sea.* "A new edition." London: W. Cavell, 1794.

Coe, Michael D. "A Model of Ancient Community Structure in the Maya Lowlands." *Southwestern Journal of Anthropology* 21 (1965), 97-114.

_____. *The Maya.* New York: Frederick A. Praeger, Publishers, 1966.

_____. "The Olmec Style and its Distributions." *Handbook of Middle American Indians,* vol. 3. Austin: University of Texas Press, 1965.

Colby, Benjamin N., and Pierre L. van de Berghe. *Ixil Country.* Berkeley and Los Angeles: University of California Press, 1969.

Cole, W. A. "Trends in Eighteenth-Century Smuggling." *The Economic History Review.* 2d ser. 10 (1958), 395-410.

Colección de documentos inéditos para la historia de España. Edited by Martín Fernández Naverrete et al. 112 vols. Madrid, 1842-95.

Colección de documentos inéditos para la historia de Ibero-América. Title varies. 14 vols. Madrid, 1927-32.

Colección de documentos inéditos relativos al descubrimiento, conquista y organización de las antiguas posesiones españolas de América y Oceanía, sacados de los archivos del reino, y muy especialmente del de Indias. Title varies. 42 vols. Madrid, 1864-84.

Colección de documentos inéditos relativos al descubrimiento, conquista y organización de las antiguas posesiones españolas de ultramar. 25 vols. Madrid, 1885-1932.

Colección de documentos para la historia de Costa Rica. Compiled by León Fernández. 10 vols. San José, Paris, Barcelona, 1881-1907.

Colección Somoza: Documentos para la historia de Nicaragua. Edited by Andrés Vega Bolaños. 17 vols. Madrid, 1954-57.

Colmenares, G. *Encomienda y Población en la Provincia de Pamplona, 1549-1650.* Bogota: Universidad de los Andes, Facultad de Artes y Ciencias, 1969.

Colón, Hernando. *Vida del Almirante Don Cristóbal Colón.* Biblioteca Americana, Cronistas de Indias. Mexico: Fondo de Cultura Económica, 1947.

Concannon, R. J. G. "The Third Enemy: The Role of Epidemics in the Thirty Years War." *Journal of World History* 10 (1967), 500-511.

Contreras R., J. Daniel. *Breve historia de Guatemala.* Guatemala: Editorial del Ministerio de Educación Pública, 1951.

Cook, David Noble. "La población indígena en el Perú colonial." *América colonial: población y economía.* Anuario del Instituto de Investigaciones Históricas, 8 (1965), 73-111.

Cook, Sherburne F. *Erosion Morphology and Occupation History in Western Mexico.* Anthropological Records, vol. 17, no. 3. Berkeley and Los Angeles: University of California Press, 1963.

_____. "Human Sacrifice and Warfare as Factors in the Demography of Pre-Colonial Mexico." *Human Biology* 18 (1949), 81-102.

_____. "Reconstruction of Extinct Populations." *Revista Mexicana de Estudios Antropológicos* 16 (1960), 173-82.

_____. *Soil Erosion and Population in Central Mexico.* Ibero-Americana, vol. 34. Berkeley and Los Angeles: University of California Press, 1949.

_____. *The Historical Demography and Ecology of the Teotlalpán.* Ibero-Americana, vol. 33. Berkeley and Los Angeles: University of California Press, 1949.

_____. "The Incidence and Significance of Disease Among the Aztecs and Related Tribes." *Hispanic American Historical Review* 26 (1946), 320-35.

————, and Woodrow Borah. "On the Credibility of Contemporary Testimony on the Population on [sic] Mexico in the Sixteenth Century." In *Summa Anthropologica en homenaje a Roberto J. Weitlaner.* Mexico: Instituto Nacional de Antropología e Historia, 1966.

————. *The Indian Population of Central Mexico, 1531–1610.* Ibero-Americana, vol. 44. Berkeley and Los Angeles: University of California Press, 1960.

————, and Lesley Byrd Simpson. *The Population of Central Mexico in the Sixteenth Century.* Ibero-Americana, vol. 31. Berkeley and Los Angeles: University of California Press, 1948.

Cooper, Donald B. *Epidemic Disease in Mexico City, 1761–1813: An Administrative, Social and Medical Study.* Institute of Latin American Studies, Latin American Monographs, no. 3. Austin: University of Texas Press, 1965.

Cornwall, Julian. "English Population in the Early Sixteenth Century." *The Economic History Review.* 2d ser. 23 (1970), 32-44.

Cortés y Larraz, Pedro. *Descripción geográfico-moral de la diócesis de Goathemala.* Biblioteca "Goathemala," vol. 20, tomes 1 and 2. 2 vols. Guatemala: Sociedad de Geografía e Historia, 1958.

Cortés, Santos Rodulfo. *Antología Documental de Venezuela, 1492–1900.* Caracas: Impresos Tipográficos Santa Rosa, 1960.

Cousens, S. H. "Regional Death Rates in Ireland during the Great Famine, from 1846 to 1857." *Population Studies* 14 (1960), 55-74.

Covarrubias, Miguel. *Indian Art of Mexico and Central America.* New York: Alfred A. Knopf, 1957.

Cowgill, Ursula M. "An Agricultural Study of the Southern Maya Lowlands." *American Anthropologist* 64 (1962), 273-86.

————. "Soil Fertility and the Ancient Maya." *Transactions of the Connecticut Academy of Arts and Sciences* 42 (1961), 1-56.

————. "Soil Fertility, Population, and the Ancient Maya." *Proceedings of the National Academy of Sciences* 46 (1960), 1007-11.

Cowie, Leonard W. *Plague and Fire: London 1665–66.* The Putnam Documentary History Series. New York: G. P. Putnam's Sons, 1970.

Crosby, Alfred W. "Conquistador y Pestilencia: The First New World Pandemic and the Fall of the Great Indian Empires." *Hispanic American Historical Review* 47 (1967), 321-37.

Cuevas, Mariano, ed. *Documentos inéditos para la historia de México.* Mexico: Talleres del Museo Nacional de Arqueología, Historia y Etnología, 1914.

Dampier, William. *Dampier's Voyages.* 2 vols. London: E. Grant Richards, 1906.

Davies, R. Trevor. *Spain in Decline: 1621–1700.* London: Macmillan and Company Ltd., 1957.

Davis, David William. *A Primer of Dutch Seventeenth Century Trade.* The Hague: Martinus Nijhoff, 1961.

Davis, Ralph. "English Foreign Trade, 1660–1700." *Economic History Review* 2d ser. 7 (1954), 150-66.

————. "English Foreign Trade, 1700–1714." *Economic History Review* 2d ser. 15 (1962), 99-106.

De Chélus, A. *Histoire Naturelle du cacao et du sucre.* 2d ed. Amsterdam: Henri Strik, 1720.

Deffontaines, Pierre. "L'introduction du bétail en Amérique Latine." *Les Cahiers d'Outre Mer* 10 (1957), 3-22.
Defoe, Daniel. *A Journal of the Plague Year.* Stratford on Avon: Shakespeare Head Press, 1928.
Dege, Wilhelm. "Die Karibische Küste Guatemalas und ihre Häfen." *Geographische Rundschau* 10 (1958), 59-77.
Delatouche, R. "Agriculture médiévale et population." *Les Etudes Sociales.* No. 28 (1955), 13-23.
Denevan, William M. *The Aboriginal Cultural Geography of the Llanos de Mojos of Bolivia.* Ibero-Americana, vol. 48. Berkeley and Los Angeles: University of California Press, 1966.
_____. *The Upland Pine Forests of Nicaragua: A Study in Cultural Plant Geography.* University of California Publications in Geography, vol. 12, no. 4. Berkeley and Los Angeles: University of California Press, 1961.
Denoix, L. "Caractéristiques des navires de l'époque des grandes découvertes." *Ve Colloque d'Histoire Maritime.* Paris: S.E.V.P.E.N., 1966.
Deyon, Pierre. *Amiens, capitale provinciale: étude sur la société urbaine au 17e siècle.* Civilisations et Sociétés, 2. Paris: Ecole Pratique des Hautes Etudes, Sixième Section: Sciences Economiques et Sociales, Centre de Recherches Historiques, 1967.
Díaz del Castillo, Bernal. *Historia verdadera de la Conquista de la Nueva España.* 2d ed. Mexico: Editorial Porrua, S. A., 1962.
Díaz Vasconcelos, Luis Antonio. *Apuntes para la historia de la literatura gualtemalteca.* Guatemala: Tipografia Nacional, 1942.
Diez de la Calle, Juan. *Memorial y Noticias Sacras y Reales de las Indias Occidentales.* 2d ed. Mexico: Bibliófilos Mexicanos, 1932.
Diffie, Bailey W. *Latin-American Civilization, Colonial Period.* Harrisburg, Pa.: Stackpole Sons, 1945.
D'Irsay, Stephen. "Defense Reactions During the Black Death, 1348-1349." *Annals of Medical History* 2 (1927), 169-79.
Dixon, C. W. *Smallpox.* London: J. and A. Churchill, 1962.
Dobyns, Henry F. "An outline of Andean epidemic history to 1720." *Bulletin of the History of Medicine* 37 (1963), 493-515.
_____. "Estimating Aboriginal American Populations, An Appraisal of Techniques with a new Hemispheric Estimate." *Current Anthropology* 7 (1966), 395-416, 425-35.
Dockstader, Frederick J. *Indian Art in Middle America.* Greenwich, Conn.: New York Graphic Society Publishers, Ltd., 1964.
Dollinger, Phillippe. *The German Hansa.* Translated and edited by D. S. Ault and S. H. Steinberg. Stanford, Calif.: Stanford University Press, 1970.
Domínguez Bordoña, Jesús, ed. *Manuscritos de América.* Catálogo de la Biblioteca del Palacio, tome 9. Madrid: Talleres de Blass, S. A. 1935.
Domínguez Ortiz, Antonio. *Política y Hacienda de Felipe IV.* Editorial de Derecho Financiero, Serie III, Historia Financiera, vol. 1. Madrid: Editorial de Derecho Financiero, 1960.
Dorantes de Carranza, Baltasar. *Sumaria Relación de las cosas de la Nueva España.* Mexico: Imprenta del Museo Nacional, 1902.
Duby, Georges. *L'économie rurale et la vie des campagnes dans l'Occident médiéval.* 2 vols. Paris: Aubier, 1962.

Dumond, D. E. "Population Growth and Cultural Change." *Southwestern Journal of Anthropology* 21 (1965), 302-24.
————. "Swidden Agriculture and the Rise of Maya Civilization." *Southwestern Journal of Anthropology* 17 (1961), 301-16.
Dunn, Frederick L. "On the Antiquity of Malaria in the Western Hemisphere." *Human Biology* 37 (1965), 386-93.
————, and R. Watkins. "Parasitological Examinations of Prehistoric Human Coprolites from Lovelock Cave, Nevada." *Contributions of the University of California Archeological Research Facility*. No. 10 (July 1970), 176-85.
Durán, Fray Diego. *The History of the Indians of New Spain*. Translated by Doris Hayden and Fernando Horcasitas. New York: Orion Press, 1964.
Durón, Rómulo E. *Bosquejo histórico de Honduras*. 2d ed. Tegucigalpa: Publicaciones del Ministerio de Educación Pública, 1956.
Edwards, Bryan. *The History, Civil and Commercial of the British West Indies*. 5th ed. 5 vols. London: T. Miller, 1819.
Elliott, J. H. *Imperial Spain, 1469-1716*. New York: St. Martin's Press, 1964.
————. "The Decline of Spain." In *Crisis in Europe, 1560-1660*. Edited by Trevor Aston. Garden City, New York: Doubleday and Company, Inc., Anchor Books, 1967.
————. *The Old World and the New, 1492-1650*. Cambridge Studies in Early Modern History. Cambridge: Cambridge University Press, 1970.
————. *The Revolt of the Catalans*. Cambridge: At the University Press, 1963.
Emery, Richard W. "The Black Death in Perpignan." *Speculum* 42 (1967), 611-23.
Encinas, Diego de. *Cedulari◆indiano*. 4 vols. Madrid: Ediciones Cultura Hispánica, 1945.
Erasmus, Charles J. "Monument Building: some field experiments." *Southwestern Journal of Anthropology* 21 (1965), 277-301.
Espinosa, Fray Isidro Félix de. *Crónica de los Colegios de Propaganda Fide de la Nueva España*. Franciscan Historical Classics, 2. Washington, D.C.: American Academy of Franciscan History, 1964.
Estrada, Juan de, and Fernando de Niebla. "Descripción de la Provincia de Zapotitlán y Suchitepequez. *Anales de la Sociedad de Geografía e Historia* (Guatemala) 28 (1955), 68-84.
Estrada Molina, Ligia. *La Costa Rica de don Tomás de Acosta*. Biblioteca de Autores Costarricenses. San José: Editorial Costa Rica, 1965.
Exquemeling, John. *Bucaniers of America Or, a True Account of the Most Remarkable Assaults Committed of late Years upon the Coasts of the West-Indies by the Bucaniers of Jamaica and Tortuga, both English and French*. London: Printed for William Crooke, at the Green Dragon without Temple-bar, 1684.
Fairlie, Susan. "Dyestuffs in the Eighteenth Century." *The Economic History Review* 2d ser. 17 (1965), 488-510.
Farmer, D. L. "Some Livestock Price Movements in Thirteenth-Century England." *The Economic History Review* 2d ser. 22 (1969), 1-16.
Farnie, D. A. "The Commercial Empire of the Atlantic, 1607-1783." *Economic History Review* 2d ser. 15 (1962), 205-18.

Feria, Fray Pedro de. "Relación que hace el Obispo de Chiapa sobre la reincidencia en sus idolatrías de los indios de aquel país después de treinta años de cristianos." *Anales del Museo Nacional de México* 6 (1898), 479-87.

Fernández, León. *Historia de Costa Rica durante la dominación española, 1502-1821.* Madrid: Tip. de M. Ginés Hernández, 1889.

Fernández del Castillo, Francisco. *Don Pedro de Alvarado.* Mexico: Ediciones de la Soc. Mex. de Geografía y Estadística, 1945.

Fernández de Oviedo y Valdés, Gonzalo. *Historia General y Natural de las Indias, Islas, y Tierra Firme del Mar Océano.* 11 vols. Asuncion: Editorial Guarania, 1945.

Fernández Guardia, Ricardo. *Cosas y gentes de antaño.* San José: Trejos hermanos, 1939.

———. *Crónicas coloniales.* San José: Trejos hermanos, 1921.

———. *Historia de Costa Rica: el descubrimiento y la conquista.* San José: Imprenta de Avelino Alsina, 1905.

———. *History of the Discovery and Conquest of Costa Rica.* Translated by Harry Weston Van Dyke. New York: Thomas Y. Crowell Company, 1913.

———. "La sublevación de los indios de Nicoya en 1760." *Revista de los Archivos Nacionales* (San José) 2 (1938), 363-66.

———. *Reseña histórica de Talamanca.* San José: Alsina, 1918

Figueroa Marroquín, Horacio. *Enfermedades de los conquistadores.* El Salvador. Ministro de Cultura, Departamento de Educación, 1957.

Findley, Alexander G. *A Directory for the Navigation of the Pacific Ocean.* 2 vols. London: R. H. Laurie, 1851.

Flores M., Rosa. *Chiquimula en la Historia.* Chiquimula, Guatemala: Imprenta "La Cultura," 1952.

Flores y Caamaño, Alfredo, ed. *Relación inédita de la ciudad y provincia de Guayaquil.* Antiguallas históricas de la colonia, vol. 2. Quito: Universidad Central del Ecuador, 1924.

Floyd, Troy S. "Bourbon Palliatives and the Central American mining industry, 1765-1800." *The Americas* 18 (1961), 103-25.

———. *The Anglo-Spanish Struggle for Mosquitia.* Albuquerque: University of New Mexico Press, 1967.

———. "The Guatemalan merchants, the government, and the provincianos, 1750-1800." *Hispanic American Historical Review* 41 (1961), 90-110.

Foster, George M. *Culture and Conquest: America's Spanish Heritage.* New York: Viking Fund Publications in Anthropology, No. 27, 1960.

Frank, André Gunder. *Latin America: Underdevelopment or Revolution.* New York: Monthly Review Press, 1969.

Friede, Juan. "Demographic Changes in the Mining Community of Muzo after the Plague of 1629." *Hispanic American Historical Review* 47 (1967): 338-43.

———. "Proceso de formación de la propiedad territorial en la América intertropical." *Jahrbuch für Geschichte von Staat, Wirtschaft und Gesellschaft Lateinamerikas* 2 (1965), 75-87.

Fuentes y Guzmán, Francisco Antonio de. *Preceptos historiales.* Guatemala: Editorial del Ministerio de Educación Pública, 1957.

———. *Recordación Florida; discurso historial y demostración Natural, material, militar y política del Reyno de Guatemala.* 2d ed. 3 vols. Biblioteca "Goathemala," vols. 6-8. Guatemala: Sociedad de Geografía e Historia, 1932-33.

Gage, Thomas. *The English-American: A New Survey of the West Indies, 1648.* Edited by A. P. Newton. Guatemala: El Patio, 1946.

Gall, Francis, ed. *Título del Ajpop Huitzitzil Tzunún. Probanza de Méritos de los de León y Cardona.* Guatemala: Ministerio de Educación Pública, Editorial "José de Pineda Ibarra," Publication no. 11, 1963.

Gallais, A. *Monographie du Cacao, ou Manuel de l'Amateur du Chocolat.* Paris: Chez Debauve et Gallais, 1827.

Gámez, José Dolores. *Historia de la costa de Mosquitos hasta 1894.* Managua: Talleres Nacionales, 1939.

——. *Historia de Nicaragua desde los tiempos prehistóricos hasta 1860.* Managua: Tip. de "El Pais," 1889.

Ganshof, François Louis, and Adriaan Verhulst. "Medieval Agrarian Society at its Prime; France, The Low Countries and Western Germany." *The Cambridge Economic History of Europe, Volume I, The Agrarian Life of the Middle Ages.* Edited by M. M. Postan. 2d ed. Cambridge: At the University Press, 1966.

García de Palacios, Diego. *Carta dirijida al rey de España, año 1576.* Edited by Ephraim George Squier. Collection of rare and original documents, concerning the discovery and conquest of America, No. 1. Albany: J. Munsell, 1860.

García Payón, José. *Amaxocoatl, o Libro del chocolate.* Toluca: Tip. Escuela de Artes, 1936.

García Peláez, Francisco de Paula. *Memorias para la historia del antiguo reino de Guatemala.* 2d ed. 3 vols. Guatemala: Tipografía Nacional, Biblioteca "Payo de Rivera," 1943-44.

Gautier-Dalché, J. "La peste noire dans les Etats de la Couronne d'Aragon." *Mélanges offerts à Marcel Bataillon.* Bordeaux: Féret et Fils, Editeurs, 1962.

Gayangos, Pascual de. *Catalogue of the Manuscripts in the Spanish Language in the British Museum.* 4 vols. London: William Clowes and Sons, 1875-1893.

Genicot, Léopold. "Crisis: From the Middle Ages to Modern Times." In *The Cambridge Economic History of Europe.* 2d ed. Vol. 1. Cambridge: At the University Press, 1966.

Gerhard, Peter. *Pirates on the West Coast of New Spain, 1565-1742.* Glendale, Calif.: A. H. Clark, 1960.

——. "Shellfish Dye in America." *Actas del XXXV Congreso Internacional de Americanistas* 3 (1964), 177-91.

Gibson, Charles. "The Aztec Aristocracy in Colonial Mexico." *Comparative Studies in Society and History* 2 (1959-60), 169-96.

——. *The Aztecs Under Spanish Rule: A History of the Indians of the Valley of Mexico, 1519-1810.* Stanford: Stanford University Press, 1964.

Gillmor, Frances. *Flute of the Smoking Mirror.* Tucson: University of Arizona Press, 1968.

——. *The King Danced in the Marketplace.* Tucson: University of Arizona Press, 1964.

Giralt, E. and G. Nadal. *La population catalane de 1553 à 1717.* Paris: S.E.V.P.E.N., 1967.

Girard, Albert. *Le Commerce français à Seville et Cadix au temps des Hapsbourg: contribution à l'étude du commerce étranger en Espagne aux XVIe et XVIIe siècles.* Paris: E. de Boccard, 1932.

Glass, John B. "Archeological Survey of Western Honduras." *Handbook of Middle American Indians.* Vol. 4. Austin: University of Texas Press, 1966.

Goff, Charles Weer. "New Evidence of Pre-Colombian Bone Syphilis in Guatemala." *The Ruins of Zaculeu.* Edited by Richard B. Woodbury and Aubrey S. Trisk. vol. 1. Richmond, Va.: The United Fruit Company, 1953.

Góngora, Mario. *Los grupos de conquistadores en Tierra Firme (1509–1530).* Santiago de Chile: Universidad de Chile, Centro de Historia Colonial, 1962.

———. "Régimen Señorial y Rural en la Extremadura de la Orden de Santiago en el Momento de la Emigración a Indias." *Jahrbuch für Geschichte von Staat, Wirtschaft und Gesellschaft Lateinamerikas* 3 (1965), 1-29.

González, Luis Felipe. *El Gobierno Eclesiástico en Costa Rica durante el régimen colonial.* San José: Imprenta nacional, 1957.

González, Pedro. *Tratado Iuridico-político del Contra-bando.* Madrid: Diego Díaz de la Carrera, 1654.

González Suárez, Federico. *Historia general de la república del Ecuador.* 7 vols. Quito: Imprenta del Clero, 1890-1903.

Gordon, B. Le Roy. *Human Geography and Ecology in the Sinú Country of Colombia.* Ibero-Americana, vol. 39. Berkeley and Los Angeles: University of California Press, 1957.

Goubert, Pierre. "En Beauvasis: Problèmes Démographiques du XVIIe Siècle." *Annales, E. S. C.* 7 (1952), 453-68.

Graham, Edward H. "The Recreative Power of Plant Communities." In *Man's Role in Changing the Face of the Earth.* Edited by William L. Thomas, Jr., et al. Chicago: University of Chicago Press, 1956.

Gray, Lewis Cecil. *A History of Agriculture in the Southern United States to 1860.* 2 vols. Washington, D.C.: Carnegie Institution of Washington, Publication 430, 1932.

Grillo, Domingo. *Satisfacion* [sic] *a unos papeles que sin autor, y sin verdad se han publicado contra los assientos, y transaccion que se han ajustado con Domingo Grillo.* Madrid: ?, 1670.

Grmek, Mirko D. "Préliminaires d'une étude historique des maladies." *Annales, E. S. C.* 24 (1969), 1473-83.

Guijo, Gregorio M. de. *Diario, 1648–1664.* 2 vols. Mexico: Editorial Porrua, S. A., 1953.

Guilbert, S. "A Chalons-sur-Marne au XVe siècle: un conseil municipal face aux épidémies." *Annales, E. S. C.* 23 (1968): 1283–1300.

Guillot, Carlos Federico. *Negros rebeldes y negros cimarrones.* Buenos Aires: Fariña Editores, 1961.

Guiteras Holmes, Calixta. "Clanes y sistema de parentesco de Cancuc (México)." *Acta Americana* 5 (1947), 1-17.

Gutiérrez y Ulloa, Antonio. *Estado general de la provincia de San Salvador:*

Reyno de Guatemala, año de 1807. 2d ed. San Salvador: Ministerio de Educación, Dirección General de Publicaciones, Colección Historia, 9, 1962.

Habig, Marion A. "The Franciscan Provinces of Spanish North America." *The Americas* 1 (1944–1945), 330-33.

Hakluyt, Richard. *The Principal Voyages Traffiques and Discoveries of the English Nation.* 12 vols. Volume 9 used throughout. Glasgow: James MacLehose and Sons, 1904.

Hamilton, Earl J. *American Treasure and the Price Revolution in Spain, 1501–1650.* New York: Octagon Books, 1965.

_____. "American Treasure and the Rise of Capitalism, 1500–1700." *Economica.* No. 27, (1929): 338-57.

_____. *War and Prices in Spain, 1651–1800.* Harvard Economic Studies, 81. Cambridge, Mass.: Harvard University Press, 1947.

Hannay, David. *The Great Chartered Companies.* London: Williams and Norgate, Ltd., 1926.

Hardoy, Jorge E., and Carmen Aranovich. "Urban Scales and Functions in Spanish America Toward the Year 1600: First Conclusions." *Latin American Research Review* 5 (1970), 57-91.

Haring, Clarence Henry. *The Buccaneers in the West Indies in the XVII Century.* Hamden, Conn.: Archon Books, 1966.

_____. *The Spanish Empire in America.* New York: Oxford University Press, 1947.

_____. *Trade and Navigation between Spain and the Indies in the Time of the Hapsburgs.* Harvard Economic Studies, 19. Cambridge, Mass.: Harvard University Press, 1918.

Heiser, Charles B. Jr. "Cultivated Plants and Cultural Diffusion in Nuclear America." *American Anthropologist* 57 (1965), 930-49.

Helleiner, Karl F. "The Population of Europe from the Black Death to the Eve of the Vital Revolution." *The Cambridge Economic History of Europe, IV, The Economy of Expanding Europe in the Sixteenth and Seventeenth Centuries.* Edited by E. E. Rich and C. H. Wilson. Cambridge: At the University Press, 1967.

Helmer, Marie. "Documentos Americanistas en el Archivo de Barbastro." *Anuario de Estudios hispanoamericanos* 8 (1941), 543-67.

Herlihy, D. "Population, Plague and Social Change in Rural Pistoia." *Economic History Review.* 2d ser. 18 (1965), 225-44.

Herrera, Antonio de. *Historia general de los hechos de los castellanos en las islas y tierra firme del mar océano.* 5 vols. Madrid: Real Academia de la Historia, 1934.

Herrera, Pablo. "Apuntamientos de algunos sucesos que puedan servir para la Historia de Quito, sacados de las actas del Consejo Municipal y del Cedulario de la Corte Suprema." *Quito a través de los siglos.* Edited by Eliecer Enríquez B. Vol. 2, part 2. Quito: Editorial Artes Gráficas, 1942.

Hester, Joseph A. "Natural and Cultural Bases of Ancient Maya Subsistence Economy." Ph.D. diss. University of California, Los Angeles, 1954.

Hewett, Edgar L. *Ancient Life in Mexico and Central America.* Indianapolis and New York: The Bobbs-Merrill Company, 1936.

Higbee, E. C. "The Agricultural Regions of Guatemala." *The Geographical Review* 37 (1947), 177-201.

Hirst, L. Fabian. *The Conquest of Plague; a Study of the Evolution of Epidemiology.* Oxford: Clarendon Press, 1953.

Hobsbawm, E. J. "The Crisis of the Seventeenth Century." In *Crisis in Europe, 1560–1660.* Edited by Trevor Aston. New York: Anchor Books, 1970.

————. "The Crisis of the Seventeenth Century." *Past and Present* 5 (1954), 33-53; 6 (1954), 44-65.

Holleran, Mary P. *Church and State in Guatemala.* New York: Columbia University Press, 1949.

Houdaille, Jacques. "Les français et les afrancesados en Amérique Centrale, 1700–1810." *Revista de Historia de América,* no. 44 (1957), 305-30.

Hubbes, Henry. *The Indian Nectar, or a Discourse Concerning Chocolate.* London: ?, n. d.

Hughes, William. *The American Physitian, whereunto is added a Discourse on the Cacao-Nut-Tree.* London: Printed by J. C. for W. Crook, 1672.

Hume, Martin A. S. *The Court of Philip IV; Spain in Decadence.* "A new Edition." New York: Brentano's Publishers, 1930.

Humphreys, R. A. *The Diplomatic History of British Honduras, 1638–1901.* London: Oxford University Press, Royal Institute of International Affairs, 1961.

Hussey, Roland D. "Analysis of a document concerning a 'Voluntary Donation' in Guatemala in 1644." *Hispanic American Historical Review* 24 (1944), 699-708.

Indians of Brazil in the Twentieth Century. Edited and translated by Janice H. Hopper. Washington, D.C.: Institute for Cross-Cultural Research, 1967.

"Indice de los documentos existentes en el Archivo de Indias que tienen interés para Guatemela," *Anales de la Sociedad de Geografía e Historia* (Guatemala) 16 (1940), 401-24.

Instituto Panamericano de Geografía e Historia: Comisión de Historia. *Honduras. Guía de los documentos.* Mexico: Instituto Panamericano de Geografía e Historia, 1967.

Isagoge Histórica apologética de las Indias Occidentales y especial de la provincia de San Vicente de Chiapa y Guatemala de la Orden de Predicadores. Biblioteca "Goathemala," vol. 13, Guatemala: Sociedad de Geografía e Historia, 1935.

Jinesta, Ricardo. "Las industrias del añil y de caracol de púrpura." *Revista de los Archivos Nacionales* (San José) 4 (1940), 302-5.

Johannessen, Carl L. *Savannas of Interior Honduras.* Ibero-Americana, vol. 46. Berkeley and Los Angeles: University of California Press, 1963.

Johnson, Frederick. "The Linguistic Map of Mexico and Central America." In *The Maya and Their Neighbors,* 2d ed. New York: D. Appleton-Century Company, Inc., 1960.

Johnson, Jerah, and William A. Percy, Jr. *The Age of Recovery; The Fifteenth Century.* Ithaca: Cornell University Press, 1970.

Jones, Chester Lloyd. *Guatemala: Past and Present.* Minneapolis: University of Minnesota Press, 1940.

_____. "Indian Labor in Guatemala." In *Hispanic American Essays: a memorial to James Alexander Robertson.* Chapel Hill, N.C.: University of North Carolina Press, 1942.

Juarros, Domingo. *Compendio de la historia de la ciudad de Guatemala.* 3d ed. 2 vols. Guatemala: Tipografía Nacional, 1936.

Judd, Gerrit P., IV. *Dr. Judd, Hawaii's friend; a biography of Gerrit Parmele Judd (1803–1873).* Honolulu: University of Hawaii Press, 1960.

Jurin, James. *An Account of the Success of Inoculating the Smallpox in Great Britain.* London: J. Peele, 1724.

Kamen, Henry. "The Decline of Castille: the last Crisis." *Economic History Review.* 2d ser. 17 (1964), 63-76.

_____. *The War of Succession in Spain, 1700–1715.* Bloomington: Indiana University Press, 1969.

Kelly, John Eoghan. *Pedro de Alvarado, Conquistador.* Princeton: Princeton University Press, 1932.

Keith, Robert Gordon. "The Origins of the Hacienda System on the Central Peruvian Coast." Ph.D. diss. Harvard University, 1969.

Keniston, Hayward. *Francisco de los Cobos, Secretary of the Emperor Charles V.* Pittsburgh: University of Pittsburgh Press, 1959.

Kidder, Alfred, II. "South American Populations in Middle America." In *The Maya and Their Neighbors.* 2d ed. New York: D. Appleton-Century Company, 1960.

Kidder, Alfred V., and Jesse D. Jennings and Edwin M. Shook. *Excavations at Kaminaljuyú, Guatemala.* Washington, D.C.: Carnegie Institution of Washington, Publication 561, 1946.

Kirchoff, Paul. "Mesoamerica." *Acta Americana* 1 (1943), 92-107.

Klein, Herbert S. "Peasant Communities in Revolt: The Tzeltal Republic of 1712." *Pacific Historical Review* 35 (1966), 247-63.

Knapp, A. W. *Cacao and Chocolate: Their History from Plantation to Consumer.* London: Chapman and Hall, Ltd., 1920.

Konetzke, Richard, ed. *Colección de documentos para la historia de la formación social de Hispanoamérica, 1493–1810.* 4 vols. Madrid: Consejo Superior de Investigaciones Científicas, 1958–62.

Kurath, Gertrude Prokosch. "Drama, Dance and Music." *Handbook of Middle American Indians.* vol. 7. Austin: University of Texas Press, 1967.

La Farge, Oliver. "Maya Ethnology: The Sequence of Cultures." In *The Maya and Their Neighbors.* 2d ed. New York: D. Appleton-Century Company, Inc., 1940.

Lamadrid, Lázaro. "Bishop Marroquín—Zumárraga's Gift to Central America." *The Americas* 5 (1949), 331-41.

_____. "Estudios franciscanos en la Antigua Guatemala." *Anales de la Sociedad de Geografía e Historia.* (Guatemala) 18 (1942), 279-305.

Landa's Relación de las Cosas de Yucatán. Edited by Alfred A. Tozzer. Papers of the Peabody Museum of American Archeology and Ethnology, vol. 18. Cambridge, Mass.: Harvard University Press, 1941.

Lanning, John Tate. "The Church and the Enlightenment in the Universities." *The Americas* 15 (1959), 33-49.

_____. *The Eighteenth-Century Enlightenment in the University of San Carlos de Guatemala.* Ithaca, New York: Cornell University Press, 1956.

――――. *The University in the Kingdom of Guatemala.* Ithaca, New York: Cornell University Press, 1955.

Lardé y Larín, Jorge. *El Salvador, historia de sus pueblos, villas y ciudades.* Colección Historia, vol. 3. San Salvador: Ministerio de Cultura, Departmento Cultural, 1957.

――――. "Fundación de Sonsonate." *Anales del Museo Nacional "David J. Guzmán"* 4 (1953), 3-8.

――――. "Historia Erupcio-Sísmica de la América Central Durante el Siglo XVI." *Anales del Museo Nacional "David J. Guzmán"* 1 (1950), 29-41.

――――. "Orígenes de la Villa de Choluteca." *Revista del Archivo y de la Biblioteca Nacional de Honduras.* 24 (1946), 482-89.

――――. "Orígenes de la Villa de la Santísima Trinidad de Sonsonate." *Anales del Museo Nacional "David J. Guzmán"* 1 (1950), 46-59.

Larrainzar, Manuel. *Noticia histórica de Soconusco y su incorporación a la República Mexicana.* Mexico: Imprenta de J. M. Lara, 1843.

Larraz, José. *La época del mercantilismo en Castilla (1500–1700).* 2d ed. Madrid: Ediciones Atlas, 1943.

Larreinaga, Miguel. *Prontuario de todas las reales cédulas, cartas acordadas y órdenes comunicadas a la Audiencia del Antiguo Reino de Guatemala desde el año de 1600 hasta 1818.* Guatemala: Imprenta La Luna, 1857.

Lazo, José Esteban. "Historia de la moneda en Honduras." *La Academia* (Tegucigalpa), 1 (1888), 37-38.

Leal, Ramón. *Guatemalensis Ecclesiae Monumenta.* Madrid: ?, 1744.

Lee, Raymond L. "American Cochineal in European Commerce, 1526–1625." *The Journal of Modern History* 23 (1951), 205-24.

――――. "Cochineal Production and Trade in New Spain to 1600." *The Americas* 4 (1948), 449-73.

Leggett, William F. *Ancient and Medieval Dyes.* Brooklyn, New York: Chemical Publishing Co., Inc., 1944.

Leland, Waldo G. *Guide to materials for American History in the Libraries and Archives of Paris.* 2 vols. Washington, D.C.: Carnegie Institution, 1932.

León Borja, Dora, and Adam Szaszdi Nagy. "El Comercio del Cacao de Guayaquil." *Revista de Historia de América* nos 57-58 (1964), 1-50.

Leonard, Irving A. *Baroque Times in Old Mexico.* Ann Arbor: University of Michigan Press, 1959.

Lerner, Robert E. *The Age of Adversity: The Fourteenth Century.* Ithaca, New York: Cornell University Press, 1969.

Le Roy Ladurie, Emmanuel. *Histoire du climat depuis l'an mil.* Paris: Flammarion, Editeur, 1967.

――――. "L'aménorrhée de famine (XVIIᵉ-XXᵉ siècles)." *Annales, E. S. C.* 24 (1969), 1589-1601.

Lévi-Strauss, Claude. *Tristes Tropiques.* Translated by John Russell. New York: Atheneum, 1964.

Lewis, Archibald R. "The Closing of the Medieval Frontier, 1250–1350." *Speculum* 33 (1958), 475-83.

Libro Viejo de la fundación de Guatemala, y papeles relativos a D. Pedro de Alvarado. Biblioteca "Goathemala," vol. 12. Guatemala: Sociedad de Geografía e Historia, 1934.

Lincoln, J. Steward. "The Maya Calendar of the Ixil of Guatemala." *Contributions to American Anthropology and History* 7 (1942), 99-128.

Lines, Jorge A., ed. *Anthropological bibliography of aboriginal Costa Rica.* Provisional edition. Occasional paper no. 7. San José: Tropical Science Center, 1967.

_____. *Anthropological bibliography of aboriginal Guatemala, British Honduras.* Provisional edition. Occasional paper no. 6. San José: Tropical Science Center, 1967.

Lines, Jorge A., Edwin M. Shook, and Michael D. Olien, eds. *Anthropological Bibliography of Aboriginal El Salvador.* Provisional Edition. San José: Tropical Science Center, 1965.

_____. *Anthropological Bibliography of Aboriginal Honduras.* Provisional Edition. San José: Tropical Science Center, 1966.

_____. *Anthropological Bibliography of Aboriginal Nicaragua.* Provisional Edition. San José: Tropical Science Center, 1965.

Lipschutz, Alejandro. "La despoblación de las Indias después de la Conquista." *América Indígena* 26 (1966), 229-47.

Lockhart, James. "Encomienda and Hacienda: The Evolution of the Great Estate in the Spanish Indies." *Hispanic American Historical Review* 49 (1969), 411-29.

_____. *Spanish Peru, 1532–1560; A Colonial Society.* Madison, Wisconsin: University of Wisconsin Press, 1968.

Longyear, John M., III. "Archeological Survey of El Salvador." *Handbook of Middle American Indians.* vol. 4. Austin: University of Texas Press, 1966.

Lopez, R. S., and H. A. Miskimin. "The Economic Depression of the Renaissance." *Economic History Review.* 2d ser. 14 (1962), 408-26.

López de Velasco, Juan. *Geografía y descripción universal de las Indias.* Madrid: Establecimiento Tipográfico de Fortanet, 1894.

López Gutiérrez, Gustavo. *Chiapas y sus epopeyas libertarias.* Tuxtla de Gutiérrez: Talleres Tipográficos del Gobierno del Estado, 1932.

López Mayorical, Mariano. *Investigaciones históricas.* Guatemala: Ministerio de Educación Pública, 1958.

Lothrop, S. K. "Archeology of Lower Central America." *Handbook of Middle American Indians.* vol. 4. Austin: University of Texas Press, 1966.

_____. "The Southeastern Frontier of the Maya." *American Anthropologist.* New ser. 41 (1939), 42-54.

Lowe, Gareth W., and J. Alden Mason. "Archeological Survey of the Chiapas Coast, Highlands, and Upper Grijalva Basin." *Handbook of Middle American Indians.* vol. 2, part 1. Austin: University of Texas Press, 1965.

Lucas, Sir C. P. *The Beginnings of English Overseas Enterprise: A Prelude to the Empire.* Oxford: Clarendon Press, 1917.

Lucas, H. S. "The Great European Famine of 1315, 1316, and 1317." *Speculum* 5 (1930), 343-77.

Lynch, John. *Spain under the Habsburgs.* 2 vols. New York: Oxford University Press, 1964-69.

Mackie, J. D. *A History of Scotland.* Baltimore: Penguin Books, 1964.

MacLeod, Murdo J. "Colonial Central America." In *The Caribbean: The Central American Area.* Edited by A. Curtis Wilgus. Series 1, vol. 11. Gainesville, Fla.: University of Florida Press, 1961.

————. "Las Casas, Guatemala, and the Sad but Inevitable Case of Antonio de Remesal." *Topic: A Journal of the Liberal Arts.* No. 20 (Fall 1970), 53-64.

MacNutt, Francis Augustus, ed. *Bartholomew De Las Casas.* New York and London: G. P. Putnam's Sons, 1909.

————. *Letters of Cortes.* 2 vols. New York and London: G. P. Putnam's Sons, The Knickerbocker Press, 1908.

Madariaga, Juan José de. *Bernal Díaz y Simón Ruiz, de Medina del Campo.* Madrid: Ediciones Cultura Hispánica, 1966.

Makower, Henryk. "Biocenologic problems in Immunology." *Transactions of the New York Academy of Sciences.* 2d ser. 20 (1958), 765-84.

Malowist, Marian. "Un essai d'histoire comparée: Les mouvements d'expansion en Europe au XVe et XVIe siècles." *Annales, E.S.C.* 17 (1962), 923-29.

Manning, Charles, and Merrill Moore. "Sassafras and Syphilis." *The New England Quarterly* 9 (1936), 473-75.

Maravall, José Antonio, *La teoría española del estado en el siglo xvii.* Madrid: Instituto de Estudios Políticos, 1944.

Marcus, G. J. "The Greenland Trade Route." *Economic History Review* 2d ser. 7 (1954), 71-80.

Markman, Sidney David. *Colonial Architecture of Antigua Guatemala.* Philadelphia: American Philosophical Society, Memoirs, vol. 64, 1966.

————. "San Cristóbal Las Casas." *Anuario de Estudios Americanos* 19 (1962), 307-421.

Mason, J. Alden. "The Languages of South American Indians." *Handbook of South American Indians,* vol. 6. New York: Cooper Square Publishers, Inc., 1963.

————. "The Native Languages of Middle America." In *The Maya and Their Neighbors.* 2d ed. New York: D. Appleton-Century Company, Inc., 1960.

Mata Gavidia, José. *Fundación de la Universidad en Guatemala, 1548–1688.* Guatemala: Editorial Universitaria, 1954.

Martínez Durán, Carlos. *Las Ciencias médicas en Guatemala. Origen y evolución.* 3d ed. Guatemala: Editorial Universitaria, 1964.

Mauro, Frédéric. *Le Portugal et l'Atlantique au XVIIe Siècle (1570–1670); Etude économique.* Paris: S.E.V.P.E.N., 1960.

McAlister, L. N. "Social Structure and Social Change in New Spain." *Hispanic American Historical Review* 43 (1963), 349-70.

————. "The Discovery and Exploration of the Nicaraguan Trans-isthmian Route, 1519–1545." *The Americas* 10 (1954), 259-76.

McBryde, Felix Webster. *Cultural and Historical Geography of Southwest Guatemala.* Washington, D.C.: Smithsonian Institution, Institute of Social Anthropology, Publication 4, 1947.

————. "Influenza in America During the Sixteenth Century (Guatemala, 1523, 1559–1562, 1576)." *Bulletin of the History of Medicine* 8 (1946), 296-302.

McLachlan, Jean O. *Trade and Peace with Old Spain, 1667–1750.* Cambridge: The University Press, 1940.

McQuown, Norman A. "The classification of the Mayan Languages." *International Journal of American Linguistics* 22 (1956), 191-95.

Means, Philip Ainsworth. *The Spanish Main: Focus of Envy, 1492–1700.* New York: Charles Scribner's Sons, 1935.

Medina, Alberto. *Efemérides nicaragüenses, 1502–1941.* Managua: Editorial La Nueva Prensa, S. A., 1945.

Medina, José Toribio. *La imprenta en Guatemala, (1660–1821).* 2d ed. 2 vols. Colección bibliográfica del tercer centenario de la fundación de la primera imprenta en Centro América, vol. 2. Guatemala: Tipografía Nacional, 1960.

Meek, Wilbur T. *The Exchange Media of Colonial Mexico.* New York: King's Crown Press, 1948.

Meiss, Millard. *Painting in Florence and Siena after the Black Death.* Princeton: Princeton University Press, 1951.

Meléndez Ch., Carlos. "Tipos de población en Costa Rica a mediados del siglo XVI." *Actas del XXXIII Congreso Internacional de Americanistas.* Vol. 2. San José: Lehman, 1959.

Menkman, W. R. *De Nederlanders in het Caraibische Zeegebied.* Amsterdam: P. N. Van Kampen and Zoon, N. V., 1942.

Mercado Sousa, Elsa. *El hombre y la tierra en Panamá (s.XVI), según las primeras fuentes.* Madrid: Seminario de Estudios Americanistas, 1959.

Merriman, Roger Bigelow. *The Rise of the Spanish Empire in the Old World and in the New.* 4 vols. New York: Cooper Square Publishers, 1962.

Meuvret, J. "Demographic Crisis in France from the Sixteenth to the Eighteenth Century." In D. V. Glass and D. E. C. Eversley, eds. *Population in History.* London: Edward Arnold (Publishers) Ltd., 1965.

Miles, Sarah W. "The Sixteenth-Century Pokom-Maya: a Documentary Analysis of Social Structure and Archeological Setting. *Transactions of the American Philosophical Society.* New ser. 47, part 4 (1957), 735-81.

————. "Summary of the Preconquest Ethnology of the Guatemalan Chiapas Highlands and Pacific Slopes." *Handbook of Middle American Indians.* vol. 2, part 1. Austin: University of Texas Press, 1965.

Milla, José. *Historia de la América Central.* 2d ed. 2 vols. Colección "Juan Chapín," Obras completas de Salome Jil (José Milla), vol. 11, tomes 1 and 2. Guatemala: Tipografía Nacional, 1937.

————. *Libro sin nombre.* 4th ed. Colección "Juan Chapín," Obras completas de Salome Jil (José Milla), vol. 3. Guatemala: Tipografía Nacional, 1935.

Millares Carlo, Agustín, and J. I. Mantecón. *Indice y extractos de los Protocolos del Archivo de Notarias de México.* 2 vols. Mexico: El Colegio de México, 1945.

Millon, René F. "Trade, Tree Cultivation and the Development of Private Property in Land." *American Anthropologist* 52 (1955), 698-712.

————. "When money grew on trees. A study of cacao in ancient Mesoamerica." Ph. D. diss. Columbia University, 1955.

Minchington, W. E., ed. *The Growth of English Overseas Trade in the Seventeenth and Eighteenth Centuries.* London: Methuen and Co., Ltd., 1969.

Miranda, José. *El Tributo Indígena en la Nueva España durante el Siglo XVI.* Mexico: Fondo de cultura económica, El Colegio de México, 1952.

_____. *España y Nueva España en la Epoca de Felipe II.* Mexico: Universidad Nacional Autónoma de México, 1962.

_____. *La Función Económica del Encomendero en los Orígenes del Régimen Colonial (Nueva España, 1525–1531).* Cuadernos del Instituto de Investigaciones Históricas, no. 12. Mexico: Universidad Nacional Autónoma de México, 1965.

_____. "La población indígena de México en el siglo XVII." *Historia Mexicana* no. 2 (1962), 182-89.

Mitchison, Rosalind. *A History of Scotland.* London: Methuen, 1970.

Molina, Antonio de. *Antigua Guatemala, memorias de Fray Antonio de Molina.* Guatemala: Unión Tipográfica, 1943.

Molina Argüello, Carlos. *El Gobernador de Nicaragua en el siglo XVI.* Seville: Escuela de Estudios Hispano-Americanos, publicación 47, serie 2, no. 12, 1949.

_____. "Gobernaciones, Alcaldías Mayores y Corregimientos en el Reino de Guatemala." *Anuario de Estudios Americanos* 17 (1960), 105-32.

Molins Fábrega, N. *El Códice Mendocino y la economía de Tenochtitlán.* Biblioteca Mínima Mexicana, 30. Mexico: Libro-Mex. Editores, 1956.

Moller-Christensen, V. "Evidence of Tuberculosis, Leprosy and Syphilis in Antiquity and the Middle Ages." *Current Problems in the History of Medicine.* Proceedings of the 19th International Congress for the History of Medicine. Basel: S. Karger, 1966.

Montari, Paolo, ed. *Documenti su la popolazione di Bologna alla fine del Trecento.* Fonti per la Storia de Bologna, Testi 1. Bologna: Instituto per la Storià de Bologna, 1966.

Montero de Miranda, Francisco. "Descripción de la Provincia de la Verapaz, año de 1574." *Anales de la Sociedad de Geografía e Historia* (Guatemala) 27 (1953), 342-58.

Montgomery, G. W. *Narrative of a Journey to Guatemala in Central America in 1838.* New York: Wiley and Putnam, 1839.

Montúfar, Lorenzo, *Reseña histórica de Centro América.* 7 vols. Guatemala: Tip. de "El Progreso" 1878–1888.

Moodie, Roy L. "Pott's Disease in Early Historic Peru." *Annals of Medical History* 9 (1927), 355-58.

Moorehead, Alan. *The Fatal Impact, An Account of the Invasion of the South Pacific, 1767–1840.* New York: Harper and Row, Publishers, 1966.

Moorhead, Max L. "Hernán Cortés and the Tehuantepec Passage." *Hispanic American Historical Review* 29 (1949): 370-79.

Morán, Fr. Pedro. *Arte y Diccionario en lengua Choltí.* Baltimore: The Maya Society, Publication no. 9, 1935.

Morel-Fatio, A. P. V. *Catalogue des manuscrits espagnols et des manuscrits portugais de la Bibliothèque Nationale.* Paris: Bibliothèque Royale, 1892.

Morley, Sylvanus Griswold. *The Ancient Maya.* 3d ed. Stanford: Stanford University Press, 1967.

Mörner, Magnus. "La Política de Segregación y el Mestizaje en la Audiencia de Guatemala." *Revista de Indias* 24, nos. 95-96 (1964): 137-51.

Morón, Guillermo. *A History of Venezuela.* Translated by John Street. New York: Roy, 1964.

Motolinia, Fray Toribio. *Motolinia's History of the Indians of New Spain.*

Edited and Translated by Elizabeth Andros Foster. Berkeley: The Cortes Society, New Series, No. 4, 1950.

Mowat, Farley. *Westviking, The Ancient Norse in Greenland and North America.* New York: Minerva Press, 1965.

Nadal, J., and E. Giralt. *La population catalane de 1553 à 1717: L'immigration française et les autres facteurs de son développement.* Ecole pratique des hautes études - VIe Section, Centre de Recherches Historiques, Démographie et Sociétés, 3. Paris: S.E.V.P.E.N., 1960.

Nash, Manning. "Guatemalan Highlands." *Handbook of Middle American Indians.* vol. 7, part 1. Austin: University of Texas Press, 1969.

———. *Primitive and Peasant Economic Systems.* San Francisco: Chandler Publishing Company, 1966.

Navarrete, Carlos. "Cuentos del Soconusco, Chiapas." *Summa Anthropologica en homenaje a Roberto Weitlaner.* Mexico: Instituto Nacional de Antropología e Historia, 1966.

Nelson, George H. "Contraband Trade under the Asiento, 1730–1739" *American Historical Review* 51 (1945), 55-67.

Nettels, Curtis. "England and the Spanish-American Trade, 1680–1715." *The Journal of Modern History* 3 (1931), 1-32.

Newton, Arthur Percival. *The European Nations in the West Indies, 1493–1688.* 2d ed. New York: Barnes and Noble, 1967.

Núñez de la Vega, Fray Francisco. *Constituciones Diocesanas del Obispado de Chiappa.* Guatemala: ?, n. d.

Nutini, Hugo G. "Clan Organization in a Nahuatl-Speaking Village of the State of Tlaxcala, Mexico." *American Anthropologist* 63 (1961), 62-78.

Oakes, Maud. *Beyond the Windy Place: Life in the Guatemalan Highlands.* New York: Farrar, Straus and Youngs, 1951.

———. *The Two Crosses of Todos Santos.* Bollingen Series, 27. Princeton: Princeton University Press, 1951.

Orozco y Jiménez, Francisco, ed. *Colección de documentos inéditos relativos a la iglesia de Chiapas.* 2 vols. in 1. San Cristóbal de las Casas: Impr. de la "Sociedad católica," 1906.

Ots Capdequi, José María. *El Estado Español en las Indias.* 2d ed. Mexico: Fondo de Cultura Económica, 1946.

———. *Instituciones sociales de la América española en el período colonial.* La Plata: Imprenta López, 1934.

Palerm, Angel. "Ecological potential and cultural development in Mesoamerica." In *Studies in Human Ecology.* Social Science Monographs, no. 3. Washington, D. C.: Pan American Union, 1957.

———. "The Agricultural Basis of Urban Civilization in Mesoamerica." In *Irrigation Civilizations: A Comparative Study.* Edited by Julian Steward et al. Social Science Monographs, no. 1. Washington, D. C.: Pan American Union, 1955.

Paniagua, Flavio Antonio. *Catecismo elemental de historia y estadística de Chiapas.* San Cristóbal Las Casas: Imprenta del "Porvenir," 1876.

"Papers from the Institute of Nutrition of Central America and Panama." *The American Journal of Clinical Nutrition,* 9 (1961).

Pardo, José Joaquín. *Catálogo de los manuscritos existentes en la colección Latino Americana de la Biblioteca de la Universidad de Texas relativos a la historia de Centro América.* Guatemala: Publicaciones de la sección de divulgación del departamento de historia de la facultad de humanidades, 1958.

————. *Efemérides para escribir la historia de la muy noble y muy leal ciudad de Santiago de los Caballeros del Reino de Guatemala.* Guatemala: Tipografía Nacional, Publicaciones de la Sociedad de Geografía e Historia, 1944.

————. *Indice de los documentos existentes en el Archivo General de Gobierno.* vol. 1. Guatemala: Archivo General de Gobierno, 1947.

————. *Prontuario de reales cédulas, 1529–1599.* Guatemala: Unión tipográfica, 1941.

Pares, Richard. *War and Trade in the West Indies, 1739–1763.* Oxford: Clarendon Press, 1936.

Paret-Limardo de Vela, Lise. *La Danza del venado en Guatemala.* Colección Contemporáneos, 75. Guatemala: Ministerio de Educación Pública, Editorial "José de Pineda Ibarra," 1963.

Parry, J. H. *The Sale of Public Office in the Spanish Indies under the Hapsburgs.* Ibero-Americana, vol. 37. Berkeley and Los Angeles: University of California Press, 1953.

————. *The Spanish Seaborne Empire.* London: Hutchinson, 1966.

Parsons, James J. *San Andrés y Providencia: English Speaking Islands in the Western Caribbean.* University of California Publications in Geography, 12, no. 1 (1956). Berkeley and Los Angeles: University of California Press, 1956.

Paso y Troncoso, Francisco del, ed. *Epistolario de Nueva España.* 16 vols. Biblioteca Histórica Mexicana de Obras Inéditas, Segunda Serie. Mexico: Antigua Librería Robredo de José Porrua e Hijos, 1940.

————. *Papeles de Nueva España.* 7 vols. Madrid: Establecimiento tip. "Sucesores de Rivadeneyra," 1905–10.

Paz, Julián. *Catálogo de manuscritos de América existentes en la Biblioteca Nacional.* Madrid: Tipografía de Archivos, Patronato de la Biblioteca Nacional, 1933.

Pedraza, Cristóbal. "Relación de varios sucesos ocurridos en Honduras, y del estado en que se hallaba esta provincia." *Relaciones históricas de América, Primera Mitad del Siglo XVI.* Edited by Manuel Serrano y Sanz. Sociedad de bibliófilos españoles. Madrid: "Imprenta ibérica" de E. Maestro, 1916.

Pepys, Samuel. *The Diary of Samuel Pepys.* 8 vols. Edited by Henry B. Wheatley. London: G. Bell and Sons, Ltd., 1952.

Peralta, Manuel M. de, ed. *Costa Rica, Nicaragua y Panamá en el siglo XVI.* Madrid: M. Murillo, 1883.

————. *Costa-Rica y Colombia 1573 a 1881.* Madrid: M. Murillo, 1886.

Pérez Estrada, Francisco. "Breve historia de la tenencia de la tierra en Nicaragua." *Revista Conservadora del pensamiento centroamericano* (Managua) 10, no. 51 (1964), 15-22.

Pérez Valenzuela, Pedro. *Estampas del pasado: Crónicas de la época colonial.* Guatemala: Tipografía Nacional, 1934.

————. *Historias de pirates.* Guatemala: Tipografía Nacional, 1936.

————. *Santo Tomás de Castilla: Apuntes para la historia de las colonizaciones en la costa atlántica.* Guatemala: Tipografía Nacional, 1956.

Pescador del Hoyo, María del Carmen. *Documentos de Indias, siglos XV-XIX: Archivo Histórico Nacional.* Madrid: Dirección General de Archivos y Bibliotecas, 1954.

Phelan, John Leddy. Book Review, *Journal of Latin American Studies* 2 (1970), 211-13.

―――. *The Kingdom of Quito in the Seventeenth Century: Bureaucratic Politics in the Spanish Empire.* Madison: The University of Wisconsin Press, 1967.

Pike, Ruth. *Enterprise and Adventure: The Genoese in Seville and the Opening of the New World.* Ithaca: Cornell University Press, 1966.

Pineda, Emeterio. "Descripción Geográfica del Departamento de Chiapas y Soconusco." *Boletín de la Sociedad Mexicana de Geografía y Estadística* 3 (1852), 341-431.

Pineda, Juan de. "Descripción de la Provincia de Guatemala, Año de 1594." *Anales del Museo Nacional "David J. Guzmán."* 4 (1952), 46-69.

Pineda, Vicente. *Historia de las sublevaciones indígenas habidas en el estado de Chiapas.* Chiapas: Tip. del gobierno, 1888.

Plague in the Americas. Washington, D. C.: Pan American Health Organization, 1965.

Pollitzer, R. *Plague.* Geneva: World Health Organization, 1954.

Popenoe, Hugh. "The Influence of the Shifting Cultivation Cycle on Soil Properties in Central America." *Proceedings, Ninth Pacific Science Congress* 7 (1957), 72-7.

Popenoe, Wilson. "Batido and Other Indian beverages prepared from cacao." *American Anthropologist* 21 (1919), 403-9.

Popol Vuh: The Sacred Book of the Ancient Quiché Maya. Edited by Adrián Recinos, Delia Goetz, and Sylvanus G. Morley. Norman: University of Oklahoma Press, 1950.

Porras Barrenechea, Raúl, ed. *Cartas del Perú (1524-1543).* Colección de documentos inéditos para la historia del Perú, vol. 3. Lima: Edición de la Sociedad de Bibliófilos Peruanos, 1959.

Porshnev, B. F. "The Legend of the Seventeenth Century in French History." *Past and Present* no. 8 (1955), 15-27.

Portig, W. H. "Central American Rainfall." *Geographical Review* 55 (1965), 68-90.

Postan, M. M. "Medieval Agrarian Society at its Prime, England." In *The Cambridge Economic History of Europe.* 2d ed., vol. 1. Cambridge: At the University Press, 1966.

―――. "Some Evidence of Declining Population in the Later Middle Ages." *Economic History Review* 2d ser. 2 (1950), 221-46.

―――. "Village Livestock in the Thirteenth Century." *Economic History Review* 2d ser. 15 (1962), 219-49.

Posthumus, N. W. *Inquiry into the History of Prices in Holland.* Leiden. 2 vols. E. J. Brill, Publications of the International Scientific Committee on Price History, 1946, 1964.

Pozas, Ricardo. *Chamula: un pueblo indio de los altos de Chiapas.* Memorial del Instituto Nacional Indigenista, 8. Mexico: Ediciones del Instituto Nacional Indigenista, 1959.

Price, Archibald Grenfell. *The Western Invasions of the Pacific and its Continents.* Oxford: Clarendon Press, 1963.

Radell, David R., and James J. Parsons. "Realejo—A Forgotten Colonial Port and Shipbuilding Center in Nicaragua." *Hispanic American Historical Review* 51 (1971), 295-312.

Ramírez, José Fernández, ed. *Proceso de residencia contra Pedro de Alvarado.* Mexico, D. F.: Valdés y Redondas, 1947.

Ramsey, G. D. "The Smugglers' Trade: A Neglected Aspect of English Commercial Development." *Transactions of the Royal Historical Society.* 5th ser. 2 (1952), 131-57.

Rands, Robert L., and Robert E. Smith. "Pottery of the Guatemalan Highlands." *Handbook of Middle American Indians.* vol. 2. Austin: University of Texas Press, 1965.

Raveneau de Lussan, Sieur de. *Journal of a Voyage into the South Sea in 1684 and the following years with the Filibusters.* Translated by Marguerite E. Wilbur. Cleveland: The Arthur H. Clark Company, 1930.

Recinos, Adrián, ed. *Crónicas Indígenas de Guatemala.* Guatemala: Editorial Universitaria, 1957.

Recinos, Adrián. *Doña Leonor de Alvarado y otros estudios.* Guatemala: Editorial Universitaria, Publicación no. 25, 1958.

———. *Monografía del departamento de Huehuetenango.* 2d ed. "aumentada". Guatemala: Editorial del Ministerio de Educación Pública, Colección Monografías, no. 2, 1954.

———. *Pedro de Alvarado: conquistador de México y Guatemala.* Mexico: Fondo de cultura económica, 1952.

———, Delia Goetz, and Dionisio José Chonay, eds. *The Annals of the Cakchiquels: Title of the Lords of Totonicapán.* Norman: University of Oklahoma Press, 1953.

Redfield, Robert. "Primitive Merchants of Guatemala." *The Quarterly Journal of Inter-American Relations,* 1 (1939), 42-56.

———. *The Primitive World and its Transformations.* Ithaca: Cornell University Press, 1953.

———, and Alfonso Villa Rojas. "Notes on the Ethnography of Tzeltal Communities of Chiapas." *Contributions to American Anthropology and History* 5 (1939), 107-19.

Reina, Rubén E. "Eastern Guatemalan Highlands. The Pokomames and Chorti." *Handbook of Middle American Indians.* vol. 7. Austin: University of Texas Press, 1969.

Reina Valenzuela, José. "Comayagua Antañana." *Revista de la Sociedad de Geografía e Historia* (Honduras) nos. 45-7 (1967–1968), 21-34, 39-60, 21-32.

———. "La Viruela durante la colonia." *Actas del XXXIII Congreso Internacional de Americanistas,* vol. 2. San José: Lehman, 1959.

Reincke, H. "Bevölkerungsverluste der Hansestadte durch den Schwartzentod." *Hansische Geschichtsblätter.* 72 (1954), 88-98.

"Relación de las cirimonias y ritos, población y gobierno de los indios de la provincia de Mechuacán." *Colección de documentos inéditos para la historia de España.* vol. 53. Edited by Martín Fernández Navarrete et al. Madrid, 1842–95.

"Relación de la visita hecha por don Juan de Guerra y Ayala a la gobernación de Honduras - Año 1608." *Boletín del Archivo General del Gobierno.* (Guatemala) 11 (1946), 44-54.

"Relación de los caciques y principales del pueblo de Atitlán, 1 Febrero del Año 1571." *Anales de la Sociedad de Geografía e Historia* (Guatemala) 26 (1952), 435-38.

Relaciones histórico-descriptivas de la Verapaz, el Manché y Lacandón, en Guatemala. Edited by France V. Scholes and Eleanor B. Adams. Guatemala: Editorial Universitaria, vol. 35. 1960.

Relaciones históricas y geográficas de América Central. Edited by Manuel Serrano y Sanz. Colección de libros y documentos referentes a la historia de América, vol. 8. Madrid: Victoriano Suárez, 1908.

Remesal, Antonio de. *Historia general de las Indias Occidentales y particular de la gobernación de Chiapa y Guatemala.* Edited by Carmelo Sáenz de Santa María. Biblioteca de Autores Españoles, vols. 175 and 179. 3d ed. Madrid: Ediciones Atlas, 1964–66.

Renouard, Y. "Conséquences et intêret démographique de la Peste noire de 1348." *Population* 3 (1948), 459-66.

"Requête de plusieurs Chefs Indiens d'Atitlán à Philippe II." In Henri Ternaux-Compans, ed. *Voyages, Relations et Mémoires originaux pour servir à l'histoire de la Découverte de l'Amérique.* 20 vols. Paris: Bertrand, 1837, vol. 10, 415-28.

Reyes M., José Luis. *Acotaciones para la historia de un libro. (El puntero apuntado con apuntes breves.)* Guatemala: Ediciones del Ministerio de Educación Pública, "José de Pineda Ibarra," 1960.

Ricard, Robert. *La "conquête spirituelle" du Mexique.* Travaux et Mémoires de l'Institut d'Ethnologie, 20. Paris: Université de Paris, 1933.

Richetson, Oliver G., Jr. "Maya Pottery Well from Quirigua Farm, Guatemala." *Maya Research* 2 (1935): 103-5.

Ringrose, Basil. "The Dangerous Voyages and Bold Attempts of Capt. Barth. Sharp, Watlin, Sawkins, Coxon, and others in the South Sea, Written by Basil Ringrose, Gent. who was a companion therein, and Examined with the Original Journal." *Buccaneers of the Americas.* London: Thomas Newsborough, 1699.

Ritual of the Bacabs. Translated by Ralph L. Roys. Norman: University of Oklahoma Press, 1965.

Rivet, Paul. *Maya Cities.* Translated by Miriam and Lionel Kochan. New York: G. P. Putnam's Sons, 1960.

Roberts, W. Adolphe. *Sir Henry Morgan.* New York: Covici, Friede, 1933.

Robles, Antonio de. *Diario de sucesos notables.* 2 vols. Colección de escritores mexicanos. Mexico: Editorial Porrua, S. A., 1946.

Rodríguez Cabal, Fr. Juan, O. P. *Apuntes para la vida del M. R. P. Presentado y Predicador General Fr. Francisco Ximénez, O. P.* Guatemala: Tipografía Nacional, 1935.

———. "Catálogo de escritos domínicos en la Capitanía General de Guatemala." *Anales de la Sociedad de Geografía e Historia.* (Guatemala) 34 (1961), 106-67.

Rodríguez del Valle, Mariana. *Castillo de San Felipe del Golfo Dulce. Historia de las fortificaciones de Guatemala en la edad moderna.* Seville: Escuela de Estudios Hispano-Americanos de Sevilla, 1962.

Rodríguez Rouanet, Francisco. "Sobre una representación actual del Rabinal Achi o baile del tun." *Guatemala Indígena* 2 (1962), 45-56.

Rodríguez Vicente, María Encarnación. "Los extranjeros y el mar en Perú." *Les Routes de l'Atlantique, travaux du neuvième Colloque International d'Histoire Maritime.* Collection Bibliothèque Generale. Paris: Ecole Pratique des Hautes Etudes, Centre Historique, 1969.

Rosenblat, Angel. *La población indígena de América desde 1492 hasta la actualidad.* Buenos Aires: Institución Cultural Española, 1945.

―――. *La población de América en 1492: viejos y nuevos cálculos.* Publicaciones del Centro de Estudios históricos, 1. Mexico: El Colegio de México, 1967.

Rossignon, Julio. *Manual del cultivo del añil y del nopal o sea extracción del indigo, educación y cosecha de la cochinilla.* Paris: Librería de Rosa y Bouret, 1859.

Roupel, G. *La ville et la campagne au XVIIᵉ siècle.* Paris: S.E.V.P.E.N., 1967.

Roys, Ralph L. "Lowland Maya Native Society at Spanish Contact." *Handbook of Middle American Indians.* vol. 3, part 2. Austin: University of Texas Press, 1965.

Roys, Ralph L., ed. *The Book of Chilam Balam of Chumayel.* Norman: University of Oklahoma Press, 1967.

Roys, Ralph L. *The Ethno-Botany of the Maya.* Middle American Research Series, Publication No. 2. New Orleans: The Tulane University of Louisiana, 1931.

―――. *The Indian Background of Colonial Yucatán.* Washington, D. C.: Carnegie Institution of Washington, Publication 548, 1943.

Rubio Sánchez, Manuel. "Apuntes para el estudio del comercio marítimo en la Capitanía General de Guatemala, durante el Siglo XVI." *Antropología e Historia de Guatemala* 5 (1953), 63-74.

―――. "El añil o xiquilite." *Anales de la Sociedad de Geografía e Historia.* (Guatemala) 26 (1952), 313-49.

―――. "El Cacao." *Anales de la Sociedad de Geografía e Historia (Guatemala) 31 (1958), 81-129.*

Rusell, Josiah C. *British Medieval Populations.* Albuquerque: University of New Mexico Press, 1949.

―――. "Effects of Pestilence and Plague." *Comparative Studies in Society and History* 8 (1965–66), 464-73.

―――. *Late Ancient and Medieval Populations.* Transactions of the American Philosophical Society, New Series, vol. 48, part 3. Philadelphia: American Philosophical Society, 1958.

―――. "That Earlier Plague." *Demography* 5 (1968), 178-84.

Sáenz de Santamaría, Carmelo. *El licenciado Don Francisco Marroquín, Primer Obispo de Guatemala (1499–1563); su vida—sus escritos.* Madrid: Ediciones Cultura Hispánica, 1965.

―――. "La tradición lascasiana y los cronistas guatemaltecos. El caso del cronista Fray Antonio Remesal, O. P." *Revista de Indias* 16 (1956), 267-85.

―――. "Remesal, La Verapaz y Fray Bartolomé de las Casas." *Estudios Lascasianos: IV Centenario de la muerte de Fray Bartolomé de las Casas (1566–1966).* Seville: Facultad de Filosofía y Letras de la Universidad de Sevilla, Escuela de Estudios Hispano-Americanos, 1966.

Sahagún, Fr. Bernardino de. *Historia general de las cosas de Nueva España.* 5 vols. Mexico: Editorial Pedro Robredo, 1938.

Saint-Lu, André. *La Vera Paz: Esprit Evangélique et Colonisation.* Paris: Institut d'Etudes Hispaniques, Centre de Recherches Hispaniques, 1968.

Salazar, Ramón A. *Historia del desenvolvimiento intelectual de Guatemala.* 3 vols. Guatemala: Editorial del Ministerio de Educación Pública, 1958.

Saltmarsh, John, "Plague and Economic Decline in England in the Later Middle Ages." *The Cambridge Historical Journal* 7 (1941), 23-41.

Salvatierra, Sofonías. *Contribución a la historia de Centroamérica: monografías documentales.* 2 vols. Managua: Tip. Progreso, 1939.

Samayoa Guevara, Héctor Humberto. *Los gremios de artesanos en la ciudad de Guatemala.* Guatemala: Editorial Universitaria, Publicación no. 39, 1962.

Sanabria, Victor. *Bernardo Augusto Thiel, segundo obispo de Costa Rica.* San José: ?, 1941.

Sánchez de Aguilar, Pedro. "Informe contra Idolorum Cultores." *Anales del Museo Nacional de México.* 6 (1898), 13-122.

Sanders, William T. "Settlement Patterns." *Handbook of Middle American Indians.* vol. 6. Austin: University of Texas Press, 1967.

_____, and Barbara J. Price. *Mesoamerica: The Evolution of a Civilization.* Random House Studies in Anthropology. New York: Random House, 1968.

Sanders, William T., and Joseph W. Michels. *The Pennsylvania State University Kaminaljuyu Project—1968 Season. Part 1—The Excavations.* Department of Anthropology, Occasional Papers in Anthropology, No. 2. College Park, Pa.: Pennsylvania State University, 1969.

Sauer, Carl O. *Colima of New Spain in the Sixteenth Century.* Ibero-Americana, vol. 29. Berkeley and Los Angeles: University of California Press, 1948.

_____. "Cultivated Plants of South and Central America." *Handbook of South American Indians.* vol. 6. New York: Cooper Square Publishers, 1963.

_____. "Geography of South America." *Handbook of South American Indians.* vol. 6. New York: Cooper Square Publishers, 1963.

_____. *The Early Spanish Main.* Berkeley and Los Angeles: University of California Press, 1966.

Sayous, André E. *Le rôle des Gênois lors des premiers mouvements reguliers entre l'Espagne et le Nouveau-Monde (1505-1520) d'après des actes inédites des Archives notariales de Séville.* Sociedad Geográfica Nacional, Serie B. no. 12, 1932.

Scelle, Georges. *La Traite Negrière aux Indes de Castille.* 2 vols. Paris: De la Société du Recueil, J-B. Sirey et du Journal du Palais, 1906.

Scholes, France V. "Franciscan Missionary Scholars in Colonial Central America." *The Americas* 8 (1952), 391-416.

_____, and Ralph L. Roys. *The Maya Chontal Indians of Acalan-Tixchel.* 2d ed. Norman: University of Oklahoma Press, 1968.

Schurz, William Lytle. *The Manila Galleon.* New York: Dutton, 1959.

Seler, Eduard. "Significance of the Maya Calendar in Historic Chronology." *Mexican and Central American Antiquities, Calendar Systems, and History.* Bureau of American Ethnology, Bulletin 28. Washington, D.C.: Smithsonian Institution, 1904.

Sherman, William L. "Abusos contra los Indios de Guatemala (1602–1605). Relaciones del Obispo." *Cahiers du Monde Hispanique et Luso-Brési-lien. Caravelle* 11 (1968), 5-28.

––––––. "A Conqueror's Wealth: Notes on the Estate of Don Pedro de Alvarado." *The Americas* 26 (1969), 199-213.

––––––. "Indian Slavery and the Cerrato Reforms." *Hispanic American Historical Review* 51 (1971), 25-50.

Shook, Edwin M. "Archeological Survey of the Pacific Coast of Guatemala." *Handbook of Middle American Indians.* vol. 2, part 1. Austin: University of Texas Press, 1965.

––––––, Jorge A. Lines, and Michael D. Olien, eds. *Anthropological Bibliography of Aboriginal Panama.* Provisional Edition. San José: Tropical Science Center, 1965.

Shumpeter, Elizabeth Boody. *English Overseas Trade Statistics, 1697–1808.* Oxford: Clarendon Press, 1960.

Siegel, Morris. "Religion in Western Guatemala: A Product of Acculturation." *American Anthropologist* 43 (1941), 62-76.

Simpson, Lesley Byrd. "A Seventeenth-Century Encomienda: Chimaltenango, Guatemala." *The Americas* 15 (1959), 393-402.

––––––. "Bernal Díaz del Castillo, Encomendero." *Hispanic American Historical Review* 17 (1937), 100-106.

––––––. *Exploitation of Land in Central Mexico in the Sixteenth Century.* Ibero-Americana, vol. 36. Berkeley and Los Angeles: University of California Press, 1952.

––––––. "Mexico's Forgotten Century." *Pacific Historical Review* 22 (1953), 113-21.

––––––. *Studies in the Administration of the Indians of New Spain, IV, The Emancipation of the Indian Slaves and the Resettlement of the Freedmen, 1548–1553.* Ibero-Americana, vol. 16. Berkeley and Los Angeles: University of California Press, 1940.

––––––. *Studies in the Administration of the Indians of New Spain, III, The Repartimiento System of Native Labor in New Spain and Guatemala.* Ibero-Americana, vol. 13. Berkeley and Los Angeles: University of California Press, 1938.

––––––. *The Encomienda in New Spain. The Beginning of Spanish Mexico.* Berkeley and Los Angeles: University of California Press, 1950.

––––––. "The Medicine of the Conquistadores, an American Pharmacopoea of 1536." *Osiris* 3 (1938), 143-64.

Skelton, R. A. "The Vinland Map." In *The Vinland Map and the Tartar Relation.* New Haven: Yale University Press, 1965.

––––––, Thomas E. Marston, and George D. Painter. *The Vinland Map and the Tartar Relation.* New Haven: Yale University Press, 1965.

Slicher van Bath, B. H. *The Agrarian History of Western Europe, A.D. 500–1850.* Translated by Olive Ordish. New York: St. Martin's Press, 1964.

Sluiter, Engel. "Dutch-Spanish Rivalry in the Caribbean Area, 1594–1609." *Hispanic American Historical Review* 27 (1948), 165-96.

Smith, E. Ledyard. *Archeological Reconnaissance in Central Guatemala.*

Washington, D.C.: Carnegie Institution of Washington, Publication 608, 1955.

———, and Alfred V. Kidder. *Excavations at Nebaj, Guatemala.* Washington, D.C.: Carnegie Institution of Washington, Publication 594, 1951.

Smith, Robert S. "Documents. Statutes of the Guatemalan Indigo Growers' Society." *Hispanic American Historical Review* 30 (1950), 337-45.

———. "Indigo Production and Trade in Colonial Guatemala." *Hispanic American Historical Review* 39 (1959), 181-211.

———. "Origins of the Consulado of Guatemala." *Hispanic American Historical Review* 26 (1946), 150-61.

Soley Güell, Tomás. *Historia económica y hacendaria de Costa Rica.* San José: Imprenta Nacional, 1947.

Solórzano Fernández, Valentín. *Historia de la evolución económica de Guatemala.* Mexico: Universidad Nacional Autónoma de México, 1947.

Soustelle, Jacques. *The Daily Life of the Aztecs on the Eve of the Spanish Conquest.* Translated by Patrick O'Brian. London: Weidenfeld and Nicolson, 1961.

Spaulding, Karen. "Social Climbers: Changing Patterns of Mobility among the Indians of Colonial Peru." *Hispanic American Historical Review* 50 (1970): 645-64.

Spengler, Joseph J. "Demographic Factors and Early Modern Development." *Daedalus* 97 (1968), 433-46.

Spores, Ronald. "Settlement, Farming Technology and Environment in Nochixtlán Valley." *Science* 167, no. 3905 (1969), 563-66.

Stearn, E. Wagner, and Allen E. Stearn. *The Effect of Smallpox on the Destiny of the Amerindian.* Boston: Bruce Humphries, Inc., Publishers, 1945.

Stein, Stanley J., and Barbara H. Stein. *The Colonial Heritage of Latin America: Essays on Economic Dependence in Perspective.* New York: Oxford University Press, 1970.

Stevens, Rayfred L. "The Soils of Middle America." *Handbook of Middle American Indians.* vol. 1. Austin: University of Texas Press, 1964.

Stoll, Otto. *Etnografía de Guatemala.* 2d ed. Guatemala: Editorial del Ministerio de Educación Pública, 1958.

Stone, Doris Z. "Los grupos mexicanos en la América Central y su importancia." *Antropología e Historia de Guatemala* 1 (1949), 43-47.

———. "Some Spanish Entradas." *Middle American Research Series,* no. 4 (1932), 213-96.

———. "Synthesis of Lower Central American Ethnohistory." *Handbook of Middle American Indians.* vol. 4. Austin: University of Texas Press, 1966.

Stouff, L. "La viande. Ravitaillement et consommation à Carpentras au XVᵉ siècle." *Annales, E. S. C.* 24 (1969), 1431-48.

Stoye, John. *Europe Unfolding, 1648–1688.* New York: Harper and Row, Publishers, 1969.

Sturluson, Snorri. *Heimskringla, (Part Two), Sagas of the Norse Kings.* Rev. ed. London: Dent, Everyman's Library, 847, 1961.

Supple, B. E. *Commercial Crisis and Change in England, 1600–1642: A Study in the Instability of a Mercantile Economy.* Cambridge: Cambridge University Press, 1959.

Szaszdi Nagy, Adam. "El Comercio Ilícito en la Provincia de Honduras." *Revista de Indias* 17 (1967): 271-83.

Tax, Sol. "Culture and Civilization in Guatemalan Societies." *Scientific Monthly* 48 (1939), 463-67.

Tenenti, Alberto. *Il Senso della Morte e L'Amore della Vita nel Rinascimento (Francia e Italia)* Studi e ricerche, 5. Turin: G. Einaudi, 1957.

Termer, Franz. *Etnología y Etnografía de Guatemala.* Seminario de Integración Social Guatemalteca, 5. Guatemala: Editorial del Ministerio de Educación Pública, 1957.

_____. "The Density of Population in the Southern and Northern Maya Empires as an Archeological and Geographical Problem." *The Civilizations of Ancient America.* Edited by Sol Tax. Chicago: University of Chicago Press, 1951.

Ternaux-Compans, Henri, ed. *Voyages, Relations et Mémoires originaux pour servir à l'histoire de la Découverte de l'Amérique.* 20 vols. Paris: Bertrand, 1837.

"Testamento de los xpantzay." *Crónicas Indígenas de Guatemala.* Edited by Adrián Recinos. Guatemala: Editorial Universitaria, 1957.

The Book of the Jaguar Priest, a translation of the Book of Chilam Balam of Tizunin. Translated by Maud Worcester Makemson. New York: Henry Schuman, 1951.

The Dance of Death. Edited by Florence Warren. London: Early English Text Society, 1931.

"The Ordinance of Laborers of Edward III, 1349." In *Medieval Culture and Society.* Edited by David Herlihy. New York: Harper and Row, Publishers, 1968.

The Vinland Sagas (Graenlendinga Saga and Eirik's Saga.) Edited and translated by Magnus Magnusson and Hermann Pálsson. Baltimore, Md.: Penguin Books, 1965.

The Voyages of Captain William Jackson (1642–1654). Edited by Vincent T. Harlow. Camden Miscellany, 3d ser., vol. 34. London: Offices of the Society, 1923.

Thiel, Bernardo Augusto. "Datos Cronológicos para la historia eclesiástica de Costa-Rica." *El Mensajero del Clero* (1897–8), 27-315.

_____. "Monografía de la población de Costa Rica en el siglo XIX." *Revista de Costa Rica en el Siglo XIX.* San José: Tipografía Nacional, 1902.

Thompson, Donald E. *Maya Paganism and Christianity. A History of the Fusion of Two Religions.* Middle American Research Institute, Publication 19. New Orleans: The Tulane University of Louisiana, 1954.

Thompson, J. Eric S. *An Archeological Reconnaissance in the Cotzumalhuapa Region, Escuintla, Guatemala.* Washington, D.C.: Carnegie Institution of Washington, Publication 574, Contribution 44, 1948.

_____. "Notes on the Use of Cacao in Middle America." *Notes on Middle American Archeology and Ethnology* 5, no. 128 (1956), 95-116.

_____. "Sixteenth and Seventeenth Century Reports on the Chol Mayas." *American Anthropologist* 40 (1938), 584-604.

_____. "The Maya Central Area at the Spanish Conquest and Later: A Problem in Demography." *Proceedings of the Royal Anthropological Institute of Great Britain and Ireland for 1966.* London: Royal Anthropological Institute of Great Britain and Ireland, 1967.

———. *The Rise and Fall of Maya Civilization.* London: Victor Gollancz, Ltd. 1956.

Thomson, Sir Basil Home. *The Diversions of a Prime Minister.* Edinburgh and London: W. Blackwood and Sons, 1894.

Thornton, A. P. "Spanish slave-ships in the English West Indies." *Hispanic American Historical Review* 35 (1955), 374-85.

———. *West-India Policy under the Restoration.* Oxford: At the Clarendon Press, 1956.

Thrupp, Sylvia L. "The Problem of Replacement-Rates in Late Medieval English Population." *Economic History Review* 2d ser. 18 (1965), 107-18.

Tibesar, Antonine. "The Alternativa: A Study in Spanish-Creole Relations in Seventeenth Century Peru." *The Americas* 11 (1955), 229-83.

Titow, J. Z. "Some Evidence of the 13th Century Population Increase." *Economic History Review* 2d ser. 14 (1962), 218-24.

"Títulos de la Casa Ixquin-Nehaib." *Crónicas Indígenas de Guatemala.* Edited by Adrián Recinos. Guatemala: Editorial Universitaria, 1957.

Tolstoy, Paul and Louise I. Paradis. "Early and Middle Preclassic Culture in the Basin of Mexico." *Science* 167 (1970), 344-51.

Torquemada, Juan de. *Monarquía Indiana.* 3 vols. Madrid: Nicolas Rodríguez Franco, 1723.

Torre Revello, José. *El Archivo General de Indias de Sevilla: Historia y clasificación de sus fondos.* Buenos Aires: Talleres s.a. Casa Jacobo Peuser, ltda., 1929.

Torres Lanzas, Pedro. *Relación descriptiva de los mapas, planos, etc. de la Audiencia y Capitanía general de Guatemala . . . existentes en el Archivo de Indias.* Madrid: Tip. de la Revista de Archivos, 1903.

Tozzer, Alfred M. "A Spanish manuscript letter on the Lacandones in the Archives of the Indies at Seville." *Proceedings of the 18th International Congress of Americanists.* 2 vols. London: Harrison and sons, 1913.

Trechuelo Spinola, María Lourdes Díaz. "La conexión entre el Atlántico y el Pacífico hasta Fray Andrés de Urdañeta." *Les Routes de l'Atlantique, Travaux du neuvième Colloque International d'Histoire Maritime.* Collection Bibliothèque Generale. Paris: Ecole Pratique des Hautes Etudes, Centre Historique, 1969.

Trejos, José Francisco, ed. *Los Conquistadores progenitores de los Costarricenses.* Biblioteca Patria, vol. 4. San José: Imprenta Lehmann, 1940.

Trens, Manuel B. *Bosquejos históricos de San Cristóbal Las Casas.* Mexico: Imprenta de la H. Cámara de Diputados, 1957.

———. *Historia de Chiapas.* 2d ed. vol. 1. Mexico, D.F.: Talleres Gráficos de la Nación, 1957.

Trevor-Roper, H. R. "Religion, the Reformation, and Social Change." In *Historical Studies, IV.* Edited by G. A. Hayes McCoy. London: Bowes and Bowes, 1963.

———. "The General Crisis of the Seventeenth Century." In, *Crisis in Europe, 1560–1660.* Edited by Trevor Aston. Garden City, New York: Doubleday and Company, Inc., Anchor Books, 1967.

Trigueros, Roberto. "Las defensas estratégicas del Río de San Juan de Nicaragua." *Anuario de Estudios Americanos* 11 (1954), 413-513.

Tudela de la Orden, José. *Los manuscritos de América en las Bibliotecas de España.* Madrid: Ediciones Cultura Hispánica, 1954.

Urquhart, D. H. *Cocoa.* 2d ed. London: Longmans, Green and Co., 1955.

Usher, A. P. "The growth of English shipping, 1572–1922." *Quarterly Journal of Economics* 42 (1927–8), 465-78.

Utterström, Gustaf. "Climatic Fluctuations and Population Problems in Early Modern History." *The Scandinavian Economic History Review* 3 (1955), 3-47.

Valdeón Baraque, Julio. "Aspectos de la crisis castellana en la primera mitad del siglo XIV." *Hispania: Revista Española de Historia* 29 (1969), 9-18.

Valenzuela, Gilberto. *La imprenta en Guatemala.* Guatemala: Folletín del Diario de Centro América, 1933.

Vallejo, Antonio R. *Compendio de la historia social y política de Honduras.* 2d ed. Tegucigalpa: Tipografía Nacional, 1926.

————. *Guía de Agrimensores o sea Recopilación de leyes agrarias.* Tegucigalpa: Tipografía Nacional, 1914.

————. "Minas de Honduras, Noticia Histórica." *Revista de la Sociedad de Geografía e Historia* (Honduras) nos. 10-12 (1956), 32-40.

Valverde, Francisco de. "Razón y Parecer de don Francisco de Valverde, acerca de la mudanza de la navegación de Puerto de Nombre de Dios al de Caballos." *Revista de la Universidad* (Tegucigalpa) 2 (1910), 160-66, 209-16, 306-16, 384-93.

Van Hoboken, W. J. "The Dutch West India Company: The Political Background of its Rise and Decline." In *Britain and the Netherlands,* vol. 1. Edited by J. S. Bromley and E. H. Kossmann. London: Chatto and Windus, 1960.

Vázquez, Francisco. *Crónica de la provincia del Santísimo Nombre de Jesús de Guatemala.* Biblioteca "Goathemala," vols. 14-17. Guatemala: Sociedad de Geografía e Historia, 1937-44.

Vázquez de Coronado, Juan. *Cartas de relación sobre la conquista de Costa Rica.* 2d rev. ed. San José: Academia de Geografía e Historia de Costa Rica, 1964.

Vázquez de Espinosa, Antonio. *Compendium and Description of the West Indies.* Translated by Charles Upson Clark. Miscellaneous Collections, vol. 102. Washington D.C.: Smithsonian Institution, 1942.

Veitia Linaje, Joseph de. *Norte de la contratación de las Indias.* Seville: I. F. de Blas, 1672.

Verlinden, Charles. "La Grande Peste de 1348 en Espagne. Contribution à l'Etude de ses Conséquences Economiques et Sociales." *Revue Belge de Philologie et d'Histoire* 17 (1938), 103-46.

Viajes de extranjeros por España y Portugal. Edited by J. García Mercadel. 2 vols. Madrid: Aguilar, S. A. de Ediciones, 1952.

Viana, Fr. Francisco, Prior de, Fr. Lucas Gallego and Fr. Guillermo Cadena. "Relación de la Provincia: tierra de la Vera Paz . . . desde el año de 1544 hasta éste de 1574." *Guatemala Indígena* 2 (1962), 141-60.

Vicens Vives, Jaime. *Approaches to the History of Spain.* Translated by Joan Connelly Ullman. 2d Ed. Revised. Berkeley and Los Angeles: University of California Press, 1970.

————, ed. *Historia Social y Económica de España y América.* 5 vols. Barcelona: Editorial Teide, 1957-59.

Vignols, Léon. "L'Asiento français (1701–1713) et anglais (1713–1750) et le commerce franco-espagnol vers 1700–1730." *Revue d'histoire économique et sociale* 17 (1929): 403-36.

Villa Rojas, Alfonso. "Kinship and Nagualism in a Tzeltal Community, Southeastern Mexico." *American Anthropologist* 49 (1947), 578-87.

———. "Notas sobre la tenencia de 'la tierra entre los Mayas de la Antiguedad." *Estudios de Cultura Maya* 1 (1961), 21-37.

Villacorta Calderón, J. Antonio. *Bibliografía guatemalteca.* Guatemala: Tipografía Nacional, 1944.

———. *Historia de la Capitanía General de Guatemala.* Guatemala: Tipografía Nacional, 1942.

———. *Prehistoria e historia antigua de Guatemala.* Guatemala: Tipografía Nacional, 1938.

Villagutierre Soto-mayor, Juan de. *Historia de la conquista de la provincia de el Itza, reducción, y indios bárbaros de la mediación de el reyno de Guatimala a las provincias de Yucatán en América Septentrional. (Primera Parte).* Madrid: Impr. de L. A. de Bedmar, y Narváez, 1701.

Villalobos R., Sergio. *Comercio y contrabando en el Río de la Plata y Chile, 1700–1811.* Buenos Aires: Editorial Universitaria de Buenos Aires, 1965.

———. "Contrabando francés en el Pacífico, 1700–1724." *Revista de Historia de América.* no. 51 (1961), 49-80.

Vivó Escoto, Jorge A. "Weather and Climate of Mexico and Central America." *Handbook of Middle American Indians.* vol. 1. Austin: University of Texas Press, 1964.

Vogt, Evon Z. "Chiapas Highlands." *Handbook of Middle American Indians.* vol. 7. Austin: University of Texas Press, 1969.

———. *Zinacantan: A Maya Community in the Highlands of Chiapas.* Cambridge, Mass.: Belknap Press of Harvard University Press, 1969.

Wafer, Lionel. *A New Voyage and Description of the Isthmus of America.* New Series, no. 73. Oxford: Hakluyt Society, 1934.

Wagley, Charles. "The Effects of Depopulation upon Social Organization as Illustrated by the Tapirape Indians." *Transactions of the New York Academy of Sciences.* 2d ser. 3 (1940), 12-16.

———. "The Maya of Northwest Guatemala." *Handbook of Middle American Indians.* vol. 7. Austin: University of Texas Press, 1969.

Wagner, Philip L. *Nicoya: a Cultural Geography.* University of California Publications in Geography, vol. 12, no. 3. Berkeley and Los Angeles: University of California Press, 1958.

Wauchope, Robert. *Excavations at Zacualpa, Guatemala.* Middle American Research Institute, Publication 14. New Orleans: Tulane University Press, 1948.

Wells, Herbert George. *The War of the Worlds.* Racine, Wis.: Whitman, 1964.

Wells, William V. *Explorations and Adventures in Honduras, Comprising Sketches of Travels in the Gold Regions of Olancho, and a Review of the History and General Resources of Central America.* New York: Harper and Brothers, Publishers, 1857.

West, Robert C. "The Mining Economy of Honduras during the Colonial Period." *Actas del XXXIII Congreso Internacional de Americanistas* 2 (1959), 767-77.

———, and John P. Augelli. *Middle America: Its Lands and Peoples.* Englewood Cliffs, N.J.: Prentice-Hall Inc., 1966.

Willey, Gordon R., Gordon F. Ekholm and René F. Millon. "The Patterns of Farming Life and Civilization." *Handbook of Middle American Indians.* vol. 1. Austin: University of Texas Press, 1964.

Wilson, A. M. "The Logwood Trade in the 17th and 18th Centuries." In *Essays in the History of Modern Europe.* Edited by D. C. Mackay. Freeport, N.Y.: Books for Libraries Press, 1968.

Winston, Alexander P. *No Purchase, No Pay: Sir Henry Morgan, Captain William Kidd, Captain Woodes Rogers in the Great Age of the Privateers and Pirates, 1665–1715.* London: Eyre and Spottiswoode, 1970.

Wisdom, Charles. *The Chorti Indians of Guatemala.* Chicago: University of Chicago Press, 1940.

Wolff, Philippe. "Trois Etudes de Démographie Médiévale en France Meridionale." *Studi in Onore di Armando Sapori.* vol. 1. Milan: Instituto Editoriale Cisalpino, 1957.

Woodbury, Nathalie F. S. "The History of Zaculeu." *The Ruins of Zaculeu Guatemala.* Edited by Richard B. Woodbury and Aubrey S. Trik. 2 vols. Richmond, Va.: The United Fruit Company, 1953.

Woodward, Ralph Lee, Jr. *Class Privilege and Economic Development. The Consulado de Comercio of Guatemala, 1793–1871.* The James Sprunt Studies in History and Political Science, 48. Chapel Hill: University of North Carolina Press, 1966.

Wright, Irene Aloha. *Nederlandsche Zeevarders op de eilanden in de Caraïbische Zee en aan de Kust van Columbia en Venezuela gedurende de Jaren 1621–1648 (9).* Vol. 1. Utrecht: Kemink en Zoon, N. V., 1934.

_____. "The Coymans Asiento (1685–1689)." *Overdruk Uit Bijdragen voor Vaderlandsche Geschiedenis en Oudheidkunde* 6 (1924), 23-62.

_____, ed. *Further English Voyages to Spanish America, 1583–1594: Documents from the Archives of the Indies at Seville illustrating English Voyages to the Caribbean, the Spanish Main, Florida, and Virginia.* New Series, no. 99. London: Hakluyt Society, 1934.

Ximénez, Francisco. *Historia de la provincia de San Vicente de Chiapa y Guatemala de la órden de predicadores.* Biblioteca "Goathemala," vols. 1-3. Guatemala: Sociedad de Geografía e Historia, 1929-31.

Yeo, Cedric A. "The Economics of Roman and American Slavery." *Finanzarchiv* N.F.13(1952),445-85.

Zavala, Silvio. *Contribución a la historia de las instituciones coloniales en Guatemala.* Biblioteca de Cultura Popular, vol. 42. Guatemala: Ministerio de Educación Pública, 1953.

_____. *De Encomiendas y Propiedad Territorial en algunas regiones de la América Española.* Mexico: Antigua Librería Robredo, de José Porrua e Hijos, 1940.

_____. "Los esclavos indios en Guatemala." *Historia Mexicana* 19 (1970), 459-65.

_____. "Relaciones históricas entre indios y negros en Iberoamérica." *Revista de las Indias* (Bogotá) 28 (1946), 53-65.

Zelaya, Manuel A. "Apuntes para la historia de la moneda en Honduras." *Cultura* (Tegucigalpa) 11 (n. d.), 54-102.

Ziegler, Philip. *The Black Death.* London: Collins, 1969.

Zorita, Alonso de. *The Lords of New Spain.* Translated by Benjamin Keen. London: Phoenix House, 1965.

Index